S0-AYS-778

gilbert

LAW SUMMARIES

TORTS

Twenty-First Edition

Marc A. Franklin
Professor of Law
Stanford University

THE **barbri** GROUP

HARCOURT BRACE LEGAL AND PROFESSIONAL PUBLICATIONS, INC.

EDITORIAL OFFICES: 111 W. Jackson Blvd., 7th Floor, Chicago, IL 60604

gilbert
LAW SUMMARIES

REGIONAL OFFICES: Chicago, Dallas, Los Angeles, New York, Washington, D.C.

Distributed by: **Harcourt Brace & Company** 6277 Sea Harbor Drive, Orlando, FL 32887 (800)787-8717

PROJECT EDITOR
Steven J. Levin, B.A., J.D.
Attorney At Law

SERIES EDITOR
Elizabeth L. Snyder, B.A., J.D.
Attorney At Law

QUALITY CONTROL EDITOR
Blythe C. Smith, B.A.

gilbert
LAW SUMMARIES

Titles Available

Administrative Law
Agency & Partnership
Antitrust
Bankruptcy
Basic Accounting for Lawyers
Business Law
California Bar Performance
Test Skills
Civil Procedure
Commercial Paper & Payment Law
Community Property
Conflict of Laws
Constitutional Law
Contracts
Corporations
Criminal Law
Criminal Procedure
Dictionary of Legal Terms
Estate & Gift Tax
Evidence

Family Law
Federal Courts
First Year Questions & Answers
Future Interests
Income Tax I (Individual)
Income Tax II (Partnership Corporate)
Labor Law
Legal Ethics (Prof. Responsibility)
Legal Research, Writing,
   & Analysis
Multistate Bar Exam
Personal Property
Property
Remedies
Sale & Lease of Goods
Secured Transactions
Securities Regulation
Torts
Trusts
Wills

Also Available:
First Year Program
Pocket Size Law Dictionary
The Eight Secrets of Top Exam Performance In Law School

All Titles Available at Your Law School Bookstore,
or Call to Order: 1-800-787-8717

Harcourt Brace Legal and Professional Publications, Inc.
111 W. Jackson Boulevard, 7th Floor
Chicago, IL 60604

SUMMARY OF CONTENTS

gilbert

capsule summary

torts

INTRODUCTION
Tortious harms are generally divided into personal injury, property damage, and invasion of interests such as reputation. There are three main bases of liability—***intent, negligence,*** and ***strict liability***.

I.   INTENTIONAL TORTS

A.   TORTS TO THE PERSON

1.   **Battery:** A ***prima facie case*** involves an act by D, with intent to inflict harmful or offensive touching, a harmful or offensive touching, and causation . . . .   [1]

   a.   **Act by D:** Refers to ***volitional*** movement of D's body . . . .   [2]

     (1)   **Unconscious acts:** Unconscious acts are not "volitional" (*e.g.,* epileptic seizures, persons asleep) . . . .   [3]

     (2)   **Reflex action:** Muscular reaction by a person in command of his senses is "volitional" unless it is a purely reflex action . . . .   [4]

     (3)   **Acts by incompetents:** Persons not legally competent are capable of volitional acts . . . .   [5]

   b.   **Intent:** D must act with the intent to inflict a harmful or offensive touching .   [6]

     (1)   **Test:** Intent is determined by whether D acted with the ***desire*** to cause the result or with the ***belief*** that the result was ***substantially certain*** to occur. This is a subjective test . . . .   [7]

     (2)   **Motives:** Motives are immaterial, but if malice is present, D may be liable for punitive damages . . . .   [9]

     (3)   **Transferred Intent:** Under transferred intent doctrine, if D acts intending to cause battery, assault, false imprisonment, trespass to land, or trespass to chattels, he will be liable even if the particular harm or plaintiff is unexpected . . . .   [10]

   c.   **Harmful or offensive touching:** This must involve contact with P's person or something closely associated with P (*e.g.,* knocking P's hat off her head) . . . .   [11]

     (1)   **"Harmful" or "offensive":** Touching is "harmful" if it inflicts pain, injury, or impairment of the body; it is "offensive" if it would offend a reasonable person's sense of dignity . . . .   [12]

     (2)   **Note:** P need ***not*** have knowledge of the touching at the time thereof .   [16]

   d.   **Causation:** D's conduct must ***directly or indirectly*** bring about the injury. Setting in motion the force that actually causes the touching suffices .   [17]

   e.   **Damages:** Actual damages are not required. Compensatory (*e.g.,* pain and suffering, medical bills, etc.) and punitive damages (if D acted maliciously) are recoverable. However, some states do not award punitive damages . . . .   [19]

2.   **Assault:** A ***prima facie case*** involves an act by D, with intent to cause apprehension of immediate harmful or offensive touching, apprehension, and causation . . . .   [24]

   a.   **Act by D:** Requires a volitional movement of the body. ***Words alone*** are ordinarily ***insufficient*** except where surrounding circumstances force P to rely on mere words (*e.g.,* threat to a blind person) . . . .   [25]

    (1) **D knows the danger is terminated;**

    (2) **D uses excessive force**—this may give P the right to use force in self-defense;

    (3) **P's conduct is privileged;** or

    (4) **D intentionally injures a third person** (unintentional injuries create liability only if D is negligent).

  e. **Reasonableness:** This is tested objectively (reasonable person standard) . [116]

3. **Defense of Third Persons:** An actor is privileged to use reasonable force to protect **any** third person from immediate harm . . . . [117]

  a. **Effect of mistake:** The majority protects D only if the person protected is **actually privileged** to defend herself. The minority protects the actor's reasonable mistake . . . . [119]

4. **Defense of Land or Chattels**

  a. **Nondeadly force:** D is privileged to defend land or chattels with nondeadly force, if: . . . . [122]

    (1) **Intrusion by P is not privileged** (or P led D to believe same); **and**

    (2) **D reasonably believes force is necessary** to prevent or terminate the intrusion; **and**

    (3) **D, prior to the use of force, makes a demand** that the intruder desist (unless the demand appears futile).

  b. **Mechanical devices:** Such devices may be used only where: (i) **reasonable and necessary, or customary** in the locale; **and** (ii) **adequate warning** is given or posted. If the devices threaten **death or serious bodily harm**, intrusion must **in fact** constitute a threat of death or serious bodily harm to D or D's family . . . . [123]

  c. **Threats:** The Restatement permits D to threaten greater force than he is actually privileged to use, as long as threats only cause apprehension . . [125]

5. **Force to Recover Possession of Land Wrongfully Withheld:** The majority view in such a case recognizes **no privilege.** The minority view permits prompt and reasonable nondeadly force when dispossession is achieved by fraud, force, duress, or without claim of right . . . . [126]

6. **Force to Effect Recapture of Chattels Wrongfully Withheld**

  a. **Tortious dispossessions:** D is privileged to use **reasonable nondeadly force** to recapture chattels of which he was tortiously dispossessed under the following conditions: . . . . [130]

    (1) **Immediate right to possession:** D is **in fact** entitled to immediate possession . . . . [131]

    (2) **Demand:** Demand for return has been made by D and ignored, or the demand appears futile . . . . [132]

    (3) **Fresh pursuit:** D is in "fresh pursuit" . . . . [133]

    (4) **Holder at fault:** Recapture is effected from the dispossessor or a third party having knowledge that the property was stolen, etc. . . . . . [134]

  b. **Other dispossessions:** In cases of nontortious dispossession, there is no privilege to use force. But in conditional sales contract situations where the buyer defaults, the seller may repossess **peacefully** . . . . [135]

  c. **"Shopkeeper's privilege":** In most states, a storekeeper is privileged to **detain temporarily** for investigation if: . . . . [137]

    (1) There are **reasonable grounds to suspect the person detained**;

    (2) Detention is on the **store premises or in the immediate vicinity**;

    (3) **Only reasonable, nondeadly force** is used; and

    (4) An **investigation is conducted in a reasonable manner** and only for a **reasonable period of time**.

7. **Privilege of Arrest**

  a. **Arrests for felonies without warrant:** A **police officer** is privileged if there are **reasonable grounds to believe** that a **felony** has been committed and this particular person committed it. A **private citizen** is privileged

II. NEGLIGENCE

A. INTRODUCTION
Negligence, the second broad category of tort liability, imposes liability for results that were not intended by D. D is at fault for failing to perform some legal duty ....

B. NEGLIGENCE ("DUTY OF DUE CARE")

III. STRICT LIABILITY

A. IN GENERAL

B. ANIMALS

C. ABNORMALLY DANGEROUS ACTIVITIES

feasible. Otherwise she must warn consumers or discontinue distribution. There is a duty to take reasonable steps to warn those who bought before the risk was discovered . . . .

    (3) **Inadequate warnings:** Defects may arise from packaging and inadequate instructions, warnings, or labels. Inadequate warnings may make a product defective when the dangers are not apparent to consumers or users . . . .

        (a) **Unexpected dangers:** The danger must be something that a reasonable user would have no reason to expect or anticipate in the product. If the danger is also unexpected by D because it could not be anticipated, most courts will analyze it as a negligence question . . . .

        (b) **Unavoidably unsafe products:** Many useful products are unavoidably unsafe (*e.g.,* knives), but this does not render them defective, because there is no safer way to make them. To create liability for failure to warn of such danger, the danger must be not reasonably apparent (*e.g.,* danger from short-burning dynamite fuse) . . . .

        (c) **Testing who must receive warning:** Usually the warning must reach the person at risk from the danger (*e.g.,* supplier of glue to bookbinding plant must warn workers who come in contact with glue of its dangers) . . . .

            1) **Learned intermediary exception:** Most courts hold that as to pharmaceuticals, an adequate warning need reach only the prescribing physician . . . .

4. Scope of Liability

    a. **Parties liable—commercial suppliers:** All participants in the marketing of the product may be held liable . . . .

        (1) **Sellers:** Liability applies to manufacturers, retailers, and distributors .

        (2) **Lessors:** Liability applies to commercial bailor or lessor . . . .

        (3) **Assemblers of components:** Liability applies to manufacturer of component and to assembler of finished product . . . .

        (4) **Contractors:** A contractor who provides a defective product may be liable. . . . .

        (5) **Successors in interest to manufacturers of defective products:** Such persons are generally *not* liable *unless* assumption agreement or goodwill is purchased and product line is continued . .

        (6) **Sellers of used products:** Some courts hold used product sellers liable for safety defects attributable to the design or manufacture if product fails to meet purchaser's reasonable expectations; other courts bar strict liability unless the seller makes representations of quality . . . .

        (7) **Franchisors:** Franchisors may be liable if they retain some control over franchisees . . . .

        (8) **Trademark licensors:** Trademark licensors may be liable if they participate in product design and marketing . . . .

        (9) **Mass-produced house builder:** Builders of mass-produced houses, but not the occasional builder, may be liable . . . .

    b. **Compare—noncommercial supplier:** Only those regularly engaged in the business of manufacturing, selling, or leasing can be held strictly liable . . . .

    c. **Parties who may invoke liability**

        (1) **Ultimate user or consumer:** The ultimate user of a product as well as purchaser may invoke doctrine . . . .

        (2) **Bystanders:** Most states permit suit by bystanders . . . .

        (3) **Rescuers:** Some case authority permits suit by rescuers . . . .

E. LIABILITY BASED ON BREACH OF WARRANTY

1. **Express Warranty:** Purchaser may recover for breach of express promise . . [885]
2. **Implied Warranties**
   a. **Fitness for particular purpose:** Where seller should know buyer is purchasing for a particular purpose and that buyer is relying on seller's expertise, the product is warranted to be fit for that particular use . . . . [888]
   b. **Merchantability:** Seller who deals in goods of that kind warrants that goods are generally *fit for normal use* . . . . [889]
   c. **Transactions covered:** The U.C.C. applies only to *sales of goods* . . . . [891]
      (1) **Bailments:** Bailments are covered by analogy to U.C.C. . . . . [892]
      (2) **Sale of real property:** Some courts extend warranties to construction and sale of a new home . . . . [893]
      (3) **"Goods" vs. "services":** Warranties are *not* implied in contracts for services, although sometimes it is difficult to distinguish goods from services (*e.g.,* sale of food in restaurant is "sale of goods," but most states treat blood transfusions as "services") . . . . [894]
      (4) **Dealers:** Generally, only those who "deal" regularly in the product are subject to warranty liability . . . . [897]
3. **Effect of Breach of Warranty:** Warrantors are liable regardless of fault or negligence . . . . [898]
4. **Requirement of "Privity of Contract"**
   a. **Former rule:** Initially, implied warranties ran only to the immediate buyer. But express warranties were extended to the ultimate purchaser who relied on them in acquiring the product . . . . [900]
   b. **Modern law:** The modern view is a modified interpretation of privity under U.C.C. alternatives; privity extends to: . . . . [904]
      (1) *Members of family and guests;* or
      (2) *Any natural person reasonably expected to use or be affected by goods who is injured;* or
      (3) *Any person reasonably expected to use or be affected by goods who is injured.*
   c. **Abandonment of "privity" as to dangerous products:** Historically, certain products, such as foodstuffs and firearms, were excluded from the "privity" requirement. Today, due to public policy considerations, this concept has been expanded by many courts to encompass *any dangerous product* and extends to all persons within the *foreseeable scope of use* . . . . [907]
   d. **Consumer protection statutes:** Some states have abolished the privity requirement between the manufacturer and the purchaser of *non-dangerous* consumer goods . . . . [910]
   e. **Impact—"warranty" as a device justifying strict liability:** By the abolition of the privity requirement, the supplier is made the *insurer* of its products . . . . [911]
   f. **Causation:** D is not liable where, because of an independent superseding event, its breach is not the proximate cause of the damage . . . . [912]
   g. **Damages:** Damages are generally the same as in a strict liability tort action, although a few states bar damages for wrongful death on a warranty theory . . . . [914]
5. **Defenses to Warranty Actions:** Although contributory negligence is not formally a defense to a breach of warranty action, most courts have developed an analogous defense to parallel the tort developments; *i.e.,* comparative fault defense. If P discovers a defect and unreasonably uses the product in such condition, *assumption of the risk* is a complete defense in warranty actions. Under limited conditions, disclaimers may limit liability . . . . [915]

V. NUISANCE

A. IN GENERAL
A *prima facie case* consists of an act by D that constitutes a nontrespassory invasion of P's interest in the use and enjoyment of P's land and that causes substantial and unreasonable harm . . . . [924]

B. PRIVATE NUISANCE VS. PUBLIC NUISANCE
1. **Private Nuisance Defined:** Nuisance is an unreasonable interference with the possessory interest of an individual in the use or enjoyment of her land. Distinguish trespass, which requires *entry* of a person or thing onto P's property. For example, the casting of invisible chemical particles onto P's land may be a trespass; an intrusion by means of noise, odor, or light can only be nuisance. (*But note:* Some acts may be *both* trespass and nuisance; *e.g.,* blasting that causes rocks to fall on P's land) . . . . [925]
2. **Public Nuisance Defined:** A public nuisance inconveniences the public at large. A private individual may maintain the action only if she suffered an injury "peculiar in kind"—*i.e.,* apart from that suffered by the public . . . . [926]

C. PLAINTIFF'S INTEREST
P must be in actual *possession* or have the right to immediate possession. Some courts extend nuisance to interference with business interests as well as land . . . . [929]

D. DEFENDANT'S CONDUCT
D's act can be intentional, negligent, or actionable under strict liability rules; the distinction is necessary to ascertain available defenses . . . . [933]

E. SUBSTANTIAL AND UNREASONABLE HARM TO PLAINTIFF
1. **"Substantial":** This refers to something that would offend a reasonable person . . . . [938]
2. **"Unreasonable":** This means the harm outweighs justification for D's conduct . . . . [939]
   a. **Factors:** Factors to consider are neighborhood, values of respective properties, cost to cure, social benefits, etc. . . . . [940]
   b. **Aesthetic considerations:** Most courts have held that aesthetic considerations may not ordinarily create a nuisance . . . . [941]
   c. **Prior occupation:** "Coming to the nuisance" (*i.e.,* D was there first) is relevant but not conclusive . . . . [942]
   d. **Effect of zoning:** Zoning ordinances permitting D's activity are not conclusive (presumptive defense in some states) . . . . [944]
3. **Minority Rule—Substantial Interference Enough:** Substantial interference suffices regardless of reasonableness if D acted intentionally . . . . [945]

F. CAUSATION
Same as battery if D acted intentionally; same as negligence if conduct is inadvertent . . . . [946]

G. REMEDIES
Compensatory damages are available. Injunction may lie if nuisance is continuing in nature, and self-help remedy of abatement may be available . . . . [947]

H. DEFENSES
1. **Contributory or Comparative Negligence:** D may reduce or escape liability for inadvertent conduct by proving P was negligent . . . . [950]
2. **Assumption of the Risk:** This may also be available to relieve D of liability . . [954]
   a. **"Coming to" the nuisance:** The fact that the activity existed before P came is *not* necessarily a defense . . . . [956]

VI. MISCELLANEOUS FACTORS AFFECTING RIGHT TO SUE

VII. STATUTORY CHANGES IN PERSONAL INJURY LAW

A. CHANGES TARGETING SPECIFIC KINDS OF TORT CLAIMS

1. **Workers' Compensation:** Before passage of workers' compensation laws, workers were generally barred from recovering for work-related injuries under tort principles because of the doctrines of contributory negligence and assumption of the risk, in addition to the fellow-servant doctrine. Today, well over 80% of workers are covered by comprehensive, mandatory workers' compensation laws that allow them to recover for all claims for personal injuries arising out of and in the course of their employment, ***regardless of fault*** . . . . [1066]

   a. **Impact:** These statutes provide the ***exclusive remedy*** for an employee against the employer. However, the worker can usually still sue a third party in tort . . . . [1072]

2. **"No-Fault" Auto Insurance:** No-fault insurance is designed to alleviate problems arising from a "fault" basis—*e.g.,* uncompensated victims, high premium rates, etc. It eliminates "fault" as the basis for liability in auto accident cases in about half of the states. The essential provisions of the various plans include: (i) insurance for all car owners is ***mandatory;*** (ii) coverage includes ***all claims*** arising from ***use or operation of any motor vehicle;*** (iii) injured car occupants make claims against the policy covering the cars they were riding in; and (iv) damages are limited to ***economic losses*** (no pain and suffering) . . . . [1079]

   a. **Impact of "no-fault" plans:** The plans limit some of the traditional negligence actions. Also, there is automatic subrogation for payments by other insurers (no double recovery) . . . . [1086]

3. **Medical Malpractice:** Rapidly escalating malpractice insurance rates have resulted in controlling legislation. These laws include provisions that shorten the applicable statute of limitations, limit pain and suffering awards, require periodic rather than lump sum payments if an award exceeds some minimum figure, limit legal fees, allow deduction of collateral sources from awards, and establish malpractice panels . . . . [1090]

4. **Products Liability:** Manufacturers and retailers have encouraged legislation to lessen their financial burden created by common law rules. About half of the states have enacted more moderate laws regarding strict liability, the most common change being the enactment of ***statutes of repose,*** which limit the time during which an action on a defective product may be brought. Also, Congress has enacted a limited no-fault compensation scheme for injuries caused by certain vaccines . . . . [1099]

5. **Miscellaneous Statutory Changes to Personal Injury Law:** A few states have a broad statutory ***duty to rescue*** others exposed to grave physical harm, and many states have enacted ***dram shop laws*** concerning liability of tavern owners and social hosts for actions of intoxicated people. Most states have laws compensating ***victims of violent crimes.*** Many nations, including the United States, have joined the ***Warsaw Convention,*** which provides victims of international air mishaps with strict liability recovery of a ***limited*** amount. Federal legislation provides limited no-fault compensation to ***nuclear accident victims*** and to miners afflicted with ***black lung disease*** . . . . [1108]

B. CHANGES AFFECTING TORT CLAIMS GENERALLY

1. **Motivation:** In the mid-1980s, some perceived the tort system to be in a state of crisis, *e.g.,* excessive damage awards, disproportionate payments by joint tortfeasors, high insurance premiums . . . . [1116]

2. **Response:** A large majority of the states have adopted legislation to reduce these problems . . . . [1117]

   a. **Joint and several liability:** About 10 states have abolished this. A number of other states have limited damages based on a defendant's degree of fault. Other limitations are based on the nature of the tort (*e.g.,* no joint

3. **Strict Liability:** Although "publication" requires intent or negligence, "harm to reputation" at common law is based on strict liability; *e.g.,* it is irrelevant whether

D anticipated that some readers would understand an article as it is now claimed they did. Constitutional law restricts strict liability (*see infra*, §§1277 *et seq.*) . . . [1194]

D. FALSE FACTS

1. **Falsity:** At common law, the burden was on D to prove the statement was true . . . . [1195]
   a. **Truth is complete defense:** General view is that truth of the defamatory matter is a *complete* defense . . . . [1196]
2. **Plaintiff's Burden to Prove Falsity:** At least where the statement involves a *matter of public concern,* the First Amendment requires P to bear the burden of proving the statement is false . . . . [1199]
3. **Statement Cannot Be False Unless it Contains Assertions of Fact:** To meet the burden of proving falsity, P must show that alleged defamation contained statements of fact or implied unstated facts that were false . . . . [1201]
   a. **No automatic protection for "opinion":** An opinion may be defamatory if it can be reasonably interpreted by the recipient as being based on underlying defamatory facts . . . . [1202]
   b. **Specificity of language:** The more specific the language, the more likely it is to be reasonably interpreted as either a statement of fact or a statement based on underlying facts . . . . [1204]

E. CAUSATION

Same as for negligence, except recovery of special damages is limited to *foreseeable* damages . . . . [1205]

F. DAMAGES AND OTHER REMEDIES

The kind of damages under common law depends on the form of the publication—libel or slander—as well as on the motives with which it was uttered. Also, there may be constitutional limitations for Ds protected by the First Amendment . . . . [1206]

1. **"Libel" and "Slander" Distinguished**
   a. **"Libel":** Libel is a defamation reduced to some *permanent physical embodiment*—usually written or printed (representation to the eye) . . . . [1207]
   b. **"Slander":** *Oral* defamation—less permanent (representation to the ear)—is slander . . . . [1208]
   c. **Borderline cases:** Consider permanence of form, area of dissemination, and deliberate or premeditated character of publication . . . . [1209]
      (1) **Broadcasting:** Under the newer view, all radio and TV publications are libel, but state statutes are split . . . . [1210]
2. **Damages Rule for Slander:** Slander is not actionable without a showing of *special damages,* unless deemed "actionable per se" . . . . [1211]
   a. **"Special damages":** These are pecuniary damages actually suffered and not presumed by law. Once some special damages are proved, P may recover general damages . . . . [1212]
      (1) **"General damages":** These compensate for harm to P's reputation. Even if not provable, their existence can be presumed based on the likely effect of the defamation considering the number of persons likely to hear it, the nature of the charge, and the identity of the speaker and the plaintiff . . . . [1214]
   b. **"Slander per se"—special damages not required:** Proof of special damages is *not* required in four situations: . . . . [1215]
      (1) Where D charges that P committed a serious, *morally reprehensible crime,* or that P has been *incarcerated* for such a crime;
      (2) Where D imputes to P a presently existing *loathsome communicable disease* (*e.g.,* venereal disease or leprosy);
      (3) Where D imputes to P conduct, associations, or characteristics *incompatible with proper performance of P's business, trade, office, or profession;* and

H. CONSTITUTIONAL PRIVILEGES

D. UNJUSTIFIABLE LITIGATION

TEXT CORRELATION CHART

Gilbert Law Summary Torts	Wade, Schwartz, Kelly, Partlett Prosser, Wade, and Schwartz's Torts Cases and Materials 1994 (9th ed.)	Keeton, Keeton, Sargentich, Steiner Tort and Accident Law Cases and Materials 1989 (2nd ed.)	Henderson, Pearson, Siliciano The Torts Process 1994 (4th ed.)	Franklin, Rabin Tort Law and Alternatives Cases and Materials 1996 (6th ed.)	Epstein Cases and Materials on Torts 1995 (6th ed.)	Dobbs Torts and Compensation 1993 (2nd ed.)	Christie, Meeks Cases and Materials on the Law of Torts 1990 (2nd ed.)
I. INTENTIONAL TORTS							
A. Torts to the Person	17-62	3-7, 25-47, 81-99, 123-129	9-34, 817-873	801-835	3-31, 64-91	21-61	35-51, 935-965, 1149-1158
B. Defenses and Privileged Invasions of Personal Interests	91-117, 124-129	47-80, 99	34-109	818-820, 835-846	4-53	73-91	58-88, 1149-1158
C. Torts to Property	62-89, 840-841	100-106, 120-123, 138-142	497-499, 506-513	588-594, 1077-1078	9-12, 120-123, 642-651	62-67	20-32, 51-57
D. Defenses and Privileged Invasions of Land and Chattels	118-124, 486-489, 633	112-119	93-99, 499	838, 846-852	50-66	78-82, 91-101	80-96
II. NEGLIGENCE							
A. Introduction	130-131	7-10	185-201	22-30	93-163, 165-167	104-107	97-98
B. Negligence (Based on the "Duty of Due Care")	132-198, 200-205, 227-343, 403-407, 416-421, 436-460, 507-545	144-201, 219-238, 331-356, 371-408, 423-440	111-164, 201-227, 241-288, 340-463, 675-755	31-62, 75-115, 269-381, 613-672, 680-693	167-250, 275-319, 467-542, 863-897, 907-914	107-126, 146-254, 779-816	98-146, 167-322, 464-472, 686-697, 701-736
C. Special Duty Questions	198-199, 205-227, 386-403, 407-416, 436-448, 461-506, 638-659	10-15, 201-218, 239-264, 415-422, 504-523	165-184, 227-241, 288-340, 393-463	17-21, 62-75, 116-257	250-275, 450-466, 542-640	127-145, 315-398, 438-448, 473-537, 540-571	47-48, 121-122, 146-167, 319-320, 322, 384-388, 438-524
D. Defenses to Negligence	566-604, 661-663	280-330, 523-527	463-486	382-430	319-398	255-314	323-382
E. Effect of Liability Insurance	292	459-503	757-775	672-717	979-1012	714-718, 942-954	801-842
III. STRICT LIABILITY							
A. In General	664	134-135, 528-533, 570	535	454-460	93-163, 641	572-580	525-528
B. Animals	664-669, 690-692		535-538		651-659	580-581, 594	528-572
C. Abnormally Dangerous Activities	669-685	15-20, 132-138, 537-571	538-560	431-453	659-681	588-603	528-572
D. Extent of Liability	686-690		549-560	460-472	97-98, 730-749	601-603	549-551, 555-561, 565-572
E. Defenses	692-693, 776, 780	530-532, 564-568		452	319, 324-325, 394, 669	603-608	561-563, 565
IV. PRODUCTS LIABILITY							
A. In General	694-700		561	473-479	727-730, 732-733	609-612	573-585
B. Liability Based on Intentional Acts	725						
C. Liability Based on Negligence	535-536, 695-700, 720, 724-725, 767-769, 801-807	635-642, 659-662	562-565, 595-603, 611-626	473-492, 550-559	474-475, 730-741, 752-769, 820-837, 851-862	609-615, 618, 634-651, 680-683, 693-698, 703-708	573-585
D. Strict Liability in Tort	535-536, 713-719, 720-807	662-755	575-668	454-472, 485-550, 555-578	741-749, 755-768, 771-862	612-712	596-684
E. Liability Based on Breach of Warranty	701-713, 769-775, 792-801	642-659, 663	565-575, 632-640	478-479, 515-516, 578-587	741-755, 761-771	611-624	585-596, 673-684

TEXT CORRELATION CHART—continued

Gilbert Law Summary Torts	Christie, Meeks Cases and Materials on the Law of Torts 1990 (2nd ed.)	Dobbs Torts and Compensation 1993 (2nd ed.)	Epstein Cases and Materials on Torts 1995 (6th ed.)	Franklin, Rabin Tort Law and Alternatives Cases and Materials 1996 (6th ed.)	Henderson, Pearson, Siliciano The Torts Process 1994 (4th ed.)	Keeton, Keeton, Sargentich, Steiner Tort and Accident Law Cases and Materials 1989 (2nd ed.)	Wade, Schwartz, Kelly, Partlett Prosser, Wade, and Schwartz's Torts Cases and Materials 1994 (9th ed.)
V. NUISANCE							
A. In General		581-588		594			810-811
B. Private Nuisance vs. Public Nuisance	871-874, 882-893	581-587	122, 128, 682-687, 717-725	594-597	499-505	596-597, 603-608	
C. Plaintiff's Interest	874-875, 880-882	583-584	682-687, 689	596	501-502	107, 109, 608-623	813-814
D. Defendant's Conduct	875	585-586	686	596-598	502-503	106-111, 572-576, 584-597, 618-625	819-820
E. Substantial and Unreasonable Harm to Plaintiff	876, 880-882		686-700	597-605	503-533	109-111, 576, 584-603, 608-617, 626-634	820-827
F. Causation				610-611			
G. Remedies	877-893	586-587	706-717	598-612	520-533		839-840
H. Defenses		586	585, 700-706	607	520-523, 533	629-634	827-838
VI. MISCELLANEOUS FACTORS AFFECTING RIGHT TO SUE							
A. Survival of Tort Actions	737-747	460-473	919-920	16	742-743	443-450	550, 556, 558-565
B. Wrongful Death	737-751	460-473	914-920	16, 640-645	427-433, 742-743	429, 438-440, 443-451	546-565
C. Injuries to Members of the Family	751-800	433-438, 448-460, 989-900		16, 247-251, 257-268, 397-398	417-447	440-443, 451-458, 822-823, 1288-1291, 1305-1306	421-436, 1123-1126
D. Tort Immunity	1202-1243	67-72, 398-431, 481-492, 552-553	939-977	188-225, 852-875	104-105, 486-495	265-279	368-369, 604-637
E. Release and Contribution Among Joint Tortfeasors	426-437	200-203, 730-740	400-427, 435-450	322-341, 391, 399, 717	476-482	352-358, 361-364, 369-370, 819	353-369
F. Indemnity	380, 428-429	200-203, 733-740	427-434	17-18, 399-400, 692-693, 717		362-368, 819-822	368-373
VII. STATUTORY CHANGES IN PERSONAL INJURY LAW							
A. Changes Targeting Specific Kinds of Tort Claims	186-187, 319-320, 685, 697-698, 700-701, 708-709, 718-719, 731, 843-870	387-398, 695-712, 868-926, 943-954	229-233, 254-255, 265, 270-275, 571, 892-894, 1014-1079	726-795	311-312, 668-673, 777-816	754, 806-895	198-199, 226, 326-328, 405, 411, 517-525, 535-536, 541-543, 711-712, 1191-1214
B. Changes Affecting Tort Claims Generally	687-698, 700-701, 728-730	535, 730, 736-738, 760-767, 792-810, 813-814, 825-866	489-490, 870-874, 880-886, 889-894, 897-905, 907-914	718-725, 795-800	143-145, 678-683, 719, 744-755	369-370, 481-497, 781-805, 895-909	196-198, 351-353, 514-525, 542-543, 1127-1174
VIII. DEFAMATION							
A. In General	966-976	961-964	1083-1085, 1093-1097		875-880	1159-1162	842-844
B. Publication to a Third Party	989-995	961	1085-1092	880-881, 927-928, 999-1001, 1010-1017	889-891	1159-1163, 1180-1186	844-847, 869, 872-877, 901-903

TEXT CORRELATION CHART—continued

Gilbert Law Summary Torts	Christie, Meeks Cases and Materials on the Law of Torts 1990 (2nd ed.)	Dobbs Torts and Compensation 1993 (2nd ed.)	Epstein Cases and Materials on Torts 1995 (6th ed.)	Franklin, Rabin Tort Law and Alternatives Cases and Materials 1996 (6th ed.)	Henderson, Pearson, Siliciano The Torts Process 1994 (4th ed.)	Keeton, Keeton, Sargentich, Steiner Tort and Accident Law Cases and Materials 1989 (2nd ed.)	Wade, Schwartz, Kelly, Partlett Prosser, Wade, and Schwartz's Torts Cases and Materials 1994 (9th ed.)
C. Harm to Reputation	966-1007, 1052-1053, 1063-1065	961-963	1093-1101, 1125-1127, 1181-1182	876-895, 927, 999-1001	876-882, 891-892	1163-1185	844-851, 855-864, 889-901
D. False Facts	976, 1007-1011, 1063-1065, 1086	963-964, 968, 975	1101-1121	969-971, 994-999	898-899	1095-1119, 1187-1200, 1222-1223	851-856, 889-900, 919-933
E. Causation				967-969		1177-1179	908-912
F. Damages and Other Remedies	966-970, 1000-1007, 1031-1032, 1056-1057, 1070, 1073, 1086-1087	962-964, 974-975	1121-1143	895-902, 923-927	882-889	1120-1158, 1170-1186	856, 864-871, 901-903, 907-911, 913, 933-942, 942-946
G. Defenses	999-1032	963-964, 968	1144-1169	902-928, 972-976	892-902	1187-1246	901-903, 933-942
H. Constitutional Privileges	1032-1087	964-976	1169-1214	928-1010, 1017-1027	903-923	1053-1158	872-932
I. Related Torts						1089-1095, 1179	947-948, 973-978, 980-995
IX. WRONGFUL INVASION OF PRIVACY							
A. Intrusions into Plaintiff's Private Life or Affairs	1090, 1097-1111	984	1268-1284	1069-1092	930, 933-940	1134-1135, 1276-1278, 1291-1297	954-968
B. Public Disclosure of Private Facts	1111-1133	984-988	1241-1260	1028-1059	930-931, 940-960	1280-1286	958-968
C. Appropriation of Plaintiff's Name or Likeness	8-16, 1088-1090, 1111, 1133-1148	985, 1000-1002, 1006	1223-1241	1092-1117	932-933, 967-973	1278-1280	948-958
D. Publicity Placing Plaintiff in a "False Light"	1090-1096	985-988	1260-1268	1059-1069	931-932, 961-966	1065-1069	968-973
E. Claims Involving Privacy of Third Persons	1147-1148		1237-1241				952
F. Important—Related Torts						1085-1095	973-979
X. OTHER TORTS							
A. Misrepresentation	894-934	1018-1037	1285-1330	1118-1140	975-1018	1023-1084, 1210	1013-1072
B. Injurious Falsehood		991-994	1101-1102, 1380-1381	1156-1157, 1159		1085-1100, 1145-1158	1073-1085
C. Interference with Economic Relations		1007-1017	1330-1387	1140-1165	1018-1036	1101-1153	1085-1122
D. Unjustifiable Litigation	1159-1175	976-984				1002-1022	996-1012

approach to exams

A course in Torts deals with a number of distinct and separate legal problems that are to a large extent governed by dissimilar principles and doctrines. For example, the rules governing liability in a battery case are entirely different from those governing liability in a case involving the sale of contaminated foodstuffs; yet both are "torts" problems. In the battery case, the applicable rules reflect a policy judgment to deter the defendant's wrongful conduct, even though the plaintiff may not have been physically injured. In the foodstuffs case, the principles governing liability seem to reflect a policy judgment to provide compensation to an injured consumer, with less attention to whether the defendant was at fault.

This interplay between the policies of _providing adequate compensation_ to an injured plaintiff, and of _deterring wrongdoers_ underlies much of the law of Torts. In effect, when the reasons for taking money from the defendant and giving it to the plaintiff coincide, tort liability will follow. When either reason is missing, the question of liability is likely to be difficult. In determining the relative strength and applicability of these policies, you need to consider certain factors.

Use the following analytical approach to focus on these factors and determine the key issues for you to analyze in answering your exam question. (Also review the chapter approach sections found at the beginning of each chapter.)

1. **Identify the Tort:** The nature and scope of liability that may be imposed, as well as the matters that may be considered by way of defense, vary significantly depending upon which particular tort is involved. Consequently, the first thing you need to do is to determine from the facts which particular tort (or torts) may be a possible basis for liability.

   Keep in mind that there is no fixed, rigid classification of recognized torts. While there are a number of "classic" tort situations (_e.g.,_ battery, false imprisonment, defamation, etc.), there are also many cases that do not fit into the "classic torts" but may still be actionable (_see infra,_ §§1386 _et seq._). In such cases, and indeed with all tort problems, the nature and scope of liability that may be imposed rest upon a determination of two factors:

   a. **The nature of plaintiff's interest that has been injured:** There are many different types of protectable interests—one's person, property, reputation, emotional well-being, advantageous business relationships, etc. You must determine exactly which interests have been injured, because the scope of liability may vary radically (_e.g.,_ the scope of liability that will be imposed upon a defendant for a negligent injury to plaintiff's body is greater than that imposed for negligent injury to plaintiff's economic well-being).

   b. **The nature of defendant's conduct:** The second crucial factor in identifying the tort is the concept of fault: Did the defendant act intentionally to cause the result that occurred? Or was the conduct negligent? Or was the defendant's conduct blameless under the circumstances? As you might expect, the greater defendant's "fault" in causing the plaintiff's injuries, the greater the extent to which liability will usually be imposed on the defendant for his acts and the fewer the matters that may be permitted by way of defense. For example, if defendant _intentionally_ injures the plaintiff's person, the defendant will almost certainly be held liable for all harm ensuing, whether or not foreseeable; whereas if the defendant's conduct was merely _negligent_, liability may be limited to foreseeable injuries (_infra,_ §§348 _et seq._).

2. **Apply the Prima Facie Case:** By identifying each interest of the plaintiff that has been invaded, and evaluating the defendant's conduct with regard to that interest, you can establish the particular area of tort liability—*e.g.,* an intentional invasion of the plaintiff's real property ("trespass to land"), negligent injury to plaintiff's person ("negligence"), etc. It is neither necessary nor advisable to go into any more elaborate "definition" of the particular tort involved. Rather, focus your attention on the prima facie case of that tort—*i.e.,* the **essential elements** that the plaintiff must establish as a basis for liability. These essential elements "define" the tort.

   In answering your question, analyze the facts given to make sure that **each element** of the prima facie case is present. Remember, in some situations, a single wrongful act by defendant (*e.g.,* false publication regarding plaintiff's private life) may conceivably be the basis for **several entirely different tort theories** (*e.g.,* defamation, invasion of privacy, infliction of emotional distress). Hence, consider the **prima facie case of each tort** that could conceivably be in issue. In close cases, weigh the policy factors of compensating the plaintiff and deterring the defendant in the particular tort involved.

3. **Consider Defenses or Limitations on Liability:** After you have found the elements of the prima facie case, look for any defenses that might be available to the defendant. Remember that the matters that may be asserted by way of defense, or to mitigate or limit liability, will vary with the two factors that "identify" the tort—the **nature of plaintiff's interest** and the **nature of the defendant's conduct.** For example, where the defendant negligently causes physical injury to the plaintiff's person, the defendant may prove by way of complete or partial defense that the plaintiff was also negligent; whereas, if the defendant had intentionally caused the same injuries, this would not be a permissible defense.

4. **Note—Evaluate the Facts:** Often, the rules of law in Torts are easier to state than they are to apply. This is because Torts problems invariably involve difficult **factual** issues that must be resolved before the applicable rules of law can be determined. For example, the prima facie case of certain torts requires a finding of "unreasonable" conduct by defendant; the rules of causation may be based on determinations of "foreseeability" of harm; various privileges and defenses are lost by "excessive" or "unreasonable" acts; etc. However, these are all ultimate **conclusions** that can be reached only after careful evaluation of facts given in the particular problem. For a good answer, avoid discussing these matters in the abstract, or making snap judgments as to the outcome. Rather, consider all operative facts in the problem, together with the logical inferences to be drawn therefrom, and remember, a conclusion concerning "reasonableness," "foreseeability," etc., will be only as good as the factual analysis upon which it is based.

5. **Other Considerations**

   a. **Parties:** Be sure of the parties. Be certain you know who is the plaintiff and who is the defendant. In fact situations involving multiple parties, consider the rights and liabilities of **each** party. As to each party-plaintiff, consider and analyze separately each **interest** that has been invaded; and, as to each party-defendant, analyze separately the **nature of that person's conduct** and responsibility for the plaintiff's injuries.

   b. **Relationship:** Check the relationship, if any, between the parties. This may be important for these reasons:

      (1) There may be a basis for **imputing liability** from one to another (*e.g.,* master-servant cases, *see infra,* §494);

(2) If there is a marital or family relationship between the plaintiff and the defendant, there may be possible *immunity* from suit (*see infra,* §§1011 *et seq.*);

(3) The relationship may *increase the amount of care* owed by one party to the other (*e.g.,* a common carrier's higher standard of care owed to a passenger; *see infra,* §478); or

(4) The relationship may *decrease the standard of care* owed (*e.g.,* a landowner's limited duty to social guests; *see infra,* §§531 *et seq.*).

c. **Effect of death of party:** Whenever any party—plaintiff or defendant—has died subsequent to commission of the tort, consider problems of *survival* of causes of action and the applicability of *wrongful death* (*see infra,* §§959 *et seq.*).

d. **Statutes:** Although the law of Torts is primarily judge-made, in certain areas (*e.g.,* "guest" statutes, wrongful death statutes, survival statutes, comparative negligence statutes), legislative enactments are found so frequently that any analysis of a problem in such areas must include a discussion of the effect of the relevant statutes.

6. **Caution—One Fact May Raise (and Influence) Several Issues:** Perhaps the greatest danger in Torts problems lies in treating the various issues and elements as separate, when they are usually interrelated. For example, if P decides to cross a street in the face of oncoming traffic, this single fact bears significantly on a number of legal doctrines that may be applicable—*e.g.,* D's duty under the circumstances, P's own negligence, P's assumption of the risk. A correct analysis will emphasize that these various issues are related and dependent on each other: Whether P assumed the risk or was negligent is related to and dependent on what duty, if any, D is held to owe to P under the circumstances. Keep in mind, then, that a single fact may influence more than one issue in the case, and that each issue should be treated as interrelated with others in the problem.

INTRODUCTION

This Summary is organized around two main themes. First, it considers the basic clusters of tortious *harms*—personal injury, property damage, and invasion of other interests such as reputation. Second, it treats the three main *bases of liability*—intentional harm, negligent harm, and torts based on strict liability. Thus, the progression is from intentional infliction of personal injury and property damage, to negligent infliction of such harm, and then to situations in which strict liability will lie. The Summary then considers protection of plaintiff's other interests: reputation, privacy, protection from unjustified litigation, and the protection of economic interests such as freedom from interference with contract relationships.

Remember that tort law is always concerned with both subjects at once—*i.e., what interests of plaintiff* should be protected from what kinds of *interferences by defendant.*

I. INTENTIONAL TORTS

chapter approach

Intentional torts, which are among the most basic instances of the imposition of tort liability, should be approached by the following basic framework:

1. *First identify all the possible torts.* Oftentimes, a fact situation creates the possibility of several different torts. You may immediately see one tort (*e.g.,* a battery), but don't stop there. Consider what other torts are suggested by the facts. In other words, sort the facts out into the various cubbyholes of intentional torts.

2. *Then consider the prima facie case* of each tort and see whether you have all the elements. The prima facie case is usually quite simple—the only common problem may be the element of *intent.* Remember to apply the term "intent" to the *result* that occurred, *not* to the act the defendant engaged in; *i.e.,* the defendant must have desired that a particular result occur or have been substantially certain that such a result would occur.

3. *After you have found that the defendant has committed a particular tort,* think about whether the defendant had a *privilege or defense* to his action. (Note that if there is no plausible privilege or defense, the defendant has behaved very badly indeed, and the conduct borders on the criminal.) Issues in this area may present analytical difficulties by overlapping in a particular fact situation. For example, if you are attacked on the street, you are privileged to engage in appropriate self-defense, but what kind of force can you use without losing the privilege? If you disarm your assailant, is the privilege ended? Before the attack, did the assailant challenge you to a fight and did you "consent" to the fracas? The facts may slide back and forth among the various privileges. Be sure to remain flexible in your thinking about which privilege or privileges apply to the facts.

A. TORTS TO THE PERSON

1. **Battery:** [§1] Prima facie case:

    Act by Defendant
    Intent
    Harmful or Offensive Touching
    Causation
    (*Lack of Consent*—discussed as a defense, *see infra,* §§80 *et seq.*)

    a. **Act by defendant:** [§2] The word "act" as used in intentional torts means an external manifestation of the actor's will; it refers to some *volitional movement* by the actor of some part of his body. Thus, if D intentionally drove his automobile into P, the "act" complained of would not be the driving of the automobile, but rather the movement by D of his *arms and legs* in setting the automobile into motion and directing it at P. [Restatement (Second) of Torts ("Rest. 2d") §2 (1965)]

        (1) **Unconscious acts:** [§3] Because of the requirement of a "volitional" movement, the movements of persons having an epileptic seizure or of persons asleep or under the influence of drugs are not generally sufficient "acts" for the purpose of establishing liability for intentional torts. [Lobert v. Pack, 9 A.2d 365 (Pa. 1939)]

        (2) **Reflex actions:** [§4] On the other hand, a muscular reaction by a person in command of his senses is always an "act" unless it is purely a reflex action in which the mind and will have no share. Thus, the blinking of eyelids in defense against an approaching missile is not an "act" because it is purely reflexive. But if someone, finding himself about to fall, stretches his hand out to save himself, the stretching out of his hand *is* an "act"; his mind has grasped the situation and dictated a muscular contraction in an effort to prevent the fall.

        (3) **Acts by incompetents:** [§5] Persons who are not legally competent are still capable of volitional conduct; *i.e.,* insane persons or minors may be held liable for their acts. [McGuire v. Almy, 8 N.E.2d 760 (Mass. 1937); Goff v. Taylor, 708 S.W.2d 113 (Ky. 1986)]

    b. **Intent:** [§6] The defendant must have done the "act" with the intent *to inflict a harmful or offensive touching* on the plaintiff or a third person. [Rest. 2d §13(a)]

        (1) **Test—desire or belief in substantial certainty:** [§7] Whether the defendant had the requisite intent is measured by whether he acted with the *desire* to cause the result *or believed that the result was substantially certain* to occur; *i.e.,* the defendant must have desired a harmful or offensive touching *or* believed that such a touching was substantially certain to result from his act. [Garratt v. Dailey, 279 P.2d 1091 (Wash. 1955); Frey v. Kouf, 484 N.W.2d 864 (S.D. 1992)]

            (a) **Example:** D shoved P, a young child, to get her out of the area in which some boys were playing. P fell and broke her elbow; D has committed a battery. Even if D did not desire the result, he believed that an offensive (if not harmful) touching was substantially certain to occur. [Baldinger v. Banks, 26 Misc. 2d 1086 (1960)]

(b) **Test is subjective:** [§8]   The issues of "desire" and what the defendant "believed" to be substantially certain to occur turn on the subjective consideration of what was in the defendant's mind when he acted. Although juries may make inferences about the defendant's state of mind from objective facts, the basic question is **not** what a reasonable person would have desired or believed, but what the defendant **in fact** desired or believed.

(2) **Motives immaterial:** [§9]   The same distinction must be made between "malice" and "intent" in tort law as is drawn in criminal law. (*See* Criminal Law Summary.) "Malice" refers to the defendant's **motives** (**why** the defendant acted as he did), and motives are generally immaterial. Tort law is concerned only with whether the defendant had the requisite **intent** under the "desire or belief in substantial certainty" test, above.

(a) **But note:** If "malice" (intent to injure) exists, the defendant may be held liable for **punitive** damages (*see* below).

(3) **Transferred intent doctrine:** [§10]   The old common law form of action called "trespass" gave rise to five modern actions: battery, assault, false imprisonment, trespass to land, and trespass to chattels. Under the doctrine of transferred intent, if the defendant acts intending to cause one of these harms to a person, the defendant will be liable on an intentional tort theory if **any** of the five harms occurs to that person or to **another person** (the plaintiff)—even though the other person is unexpected and the harm is unexpected.

(a) **Example:** D attempted to strike X, who ducked. The blow hit P, who had unexpectedly appeared. *Held:* D committed a battery on P. [Carnes v. Thompson, 48 S.W.2d 903 (Mo. 1932)]

(b) **Example:** D unlawfully shot at X's dog and hit P. Even though D had no reason to know that anyone might be in the area, D committed a battery on P. [Corn v. Shepard, 229 N.W. 869 (Minn. 1930); Altieri v. Colasso, 362 A.2d 798 (Conn. 1975)—attempted assault on X led to battery on P]

(c) **Comment:** Although phrased as involving "intent," the better explanation for the doctrine is that the courts are imposing strict liability on D because of his serious misbehavior in directing the initial act against X.

c. **Harmful or offensive touching:** [§11]   The defendant's intentional act must have resulted in the infliction of a harmful or offensive touching of the plaintiff's person, or something so closely associated with the plaintiff as to make the touching tantamount to a physical invasion of the plaintiff's person. Things "closely associated" with the plaintiff's person would cover situations where the defendant knocks the plaintiff's hat off his head, grabs a plate out of his hand, etc. [Fisher v. Carrousel Motor Hotel, Inc., 424 S.W.2d 627 (Tex. 1967); Rest. 2d §18] *Note:* There must be **actual physical contact**—"coming close" is not enough to constitute a battery.

(1) **"Harmful" touching:** [§12] A touching is "harmful" if it inflicts any pain, injury, disfigurement, or impairment of any bodily organ or function.

(2) **"Offensive" touching:** [§13] Any touching of the plaintiff, or something "closely associated with his person," that would offend a *reasonable person's sense of personal dignity* is regarded as an "offensive" touching.

   (a) **Plaintiff's hypersensitive reaction insufficient:** [§14] A touching that would not cause a reasonable person to take offense, but at which the plaintiff does take offense, is not sufficient to impose liability. [Rest. 2d §19]

      1) **Example:** P, a mortician who embalmed the deceased, sued Hospital for battery because Hospital did not tell P that the deceased had died of AIDS. P had worn protective gear during the embalming process and therefore had not been exposed to the AIDS virus. *Held:* P's claim was based on fear that was unreasonable and thus insufficient to impose liability. [Funeral Services by Gregory, Inc. v. Bluefield Community Hospital, 413 S.E.2d 79 (W. Va. 1991)]

      2) **Exception—knowledge of hypersensitivity:** [§15] This rule may *not* apply in a situation in which the defendant knows of the plaintiff's hypersensitivity but proceeds anyway. Thus, under circumstances where it might generally be acceptable to gain someone's attention by tapping him lightly on the back, the defendant may be liable for a battery if he lightly taps the plaintiff on the back knowing that the plaintiff does not wish such contact. [Rest. 2d §27]

(3) **Plaintiff unaware of touching:** [§16] The plaintiff need not have knowledge of the touching at the time thereof. Thus, if the defendant kisses the plaintiff while the plaintiff is asleep, but does not waken or harm her, the kiss may be a sufficiently "offensive" touching to establish liability—even though the plaintiff does not learn of the contact until a later time. [Rest. 2d §19, comment d]

d. **Causation—direct or indirect results:** [§17] The harmful or offensive touching must be legally caused by the defendant's act or some force that act sets in motion. This causation element is satisfied if the defendant's conduct "directly or indirectly" results in the injury. [Rest. 2d §13]

   (1) **Example:** D throws a piece of timber at P, intending to injure her. The wood misses the mark but strikes a pile of rocks, setting loose an avalanche of rocks that kills P. D's act directly or indirectly brought about the injuries that led to P's death by setting loose the rocks. D is therefore liable for battery.

(2) **Example:** D chases P with the intent to strike her. As P is fleeing, she is struck by a cornice falling from a building. D is *not* liable for P's injuries because D's act did not set the falling cornice in motion. D's act must do more than simply put P in a place in which some totally independent and unexpected force may injure her.

(3) **Compare—negligence liability:** [§18] The law holds an *intentional* wrongdoer liable for the direct and indirect consequences of his acts, *whether or not foreseeable.* [Rest. 2d §13] However, in *negligence* cases, causation rules may operate to terminate liability at an earlier point so that a negligent tortfeasor may be excused from liability for injuries for which an intentional tortfeasor would be held liable (*see infra,* §§348 *et seq.*).

e. **Damages:** [§19] The tort is complete upon commission of the harmful or offensive touching. Even if no actual harm is suffered—as in the case of some offensive touchings—the court will award *nominal* damages. This is often a symbolic amount of one dollar.

(1) **Compensatory damages:** [§20] In addition to nominal damages, the plaintiff may recover damages to *compensate* her for the harm suffered.

(a) **General damages:** [§21] "General damages" are unidentified damages deemed to result from the touching—such as embarrassment at being hit in the face with a pie, pain or suffering, disfigurement or disability, etc.

(b) **Special damages:** [§22] "Special damages" refers to specific, identifiable economic losses—such as medical bills or lost wages.

(2) **Punitive damages:** [§23] Wherever it appears that the defendant's act was motivated by an intention *to injure or harm the plaintiff,* most courts also permit juries to award *punitive* ("exemplary") damages against the defendant.

(a) **Jury discretion:** Even if the defendant's conduct would justify a punitive award, the jury is not required to make one. The jury must be charged as to the criteria to consider in deciding whether to make an award.

(b) **Review of jury award:** If the jury does make an award, state law usually requires careful post-trial review and appellate review of the amount of the award.

(c) **Constitutional law:** The Eighth Amendment prohibition on excessive fines does not apply to punitive damages awards in tort cases between private parties. [Browning-Ferris Industries of Vermont, Inc. v. Kelco Disposal, Inc., 492 U.S. 257 (1989)] Punitive damage awards can, however, violate the Due Process Clause where the defendant did not have adequate notice of the possible severity of the penalty. The Supreme Court has indicated it will look to the following factors in determining whether the defendant had adequate notice that a severe penalty might be imposed:

(i)   The **reprehensibility** of the conduct;

(ii)   The **disparity** between the **compensatory award** and the punitive award; and

(iii)   The **difference** between the punitive award and **possible criminal and administrative penalties for such conduct**.

[BMW of North America, Inc. v. Gore, 116 S. Ct. 1589 (1996)—striking $2 million punitive damage award where car manufacturer repainted new car and sold it without disclosing that fact, causing $4,000 in compensatory damages; Court emphasized: only harm was economic and no safety threat, great disparity in awards, and criminal penalties were minor]

2.   **Assault:** [§24]   Prima facie case:

> *Act by Defendant*
> *Intent*
> *Apprehension*
> *Causation*
> (***Lack of Consent***—discussed as a defense, *see infra*, §§80 *et seq.*)

a.   **Act by defendant:** [§25]   The requirement of some act by the defendant that causes apprehension in the plaintiff is satisfied by the same type of act as is required in battery: a **volitional** movement of some portion of the body.

(1)   **Words alone not sufficient:** [§26]   Because of the requirement that the act create in plaintiff an apprehension of an **immediate** touching (*see* below), words alone are generally not enough to constitute an assault. There must also be some volitional movement of the body, however slight. [Western Union Telegraph Co. v. Hill, 150 So. 709 (Ala. 1933); Rest. 2d §31; Cullison v. Medley, 570 N.E.2d 27 (Ind. 1991)—entry without permission plus reaching for pistol in holster sufficient]

(a)   **Example:** If D merely says to P, "You are about to die," there is no assault. But if D accompanies such statement by the slightest movement of his hand toward a pistol on the table, this act may be sufficient to constitute an assault.

(b)   **Exception for certain threats:** [§27]   Occasionally, the **impact** of the words alone may create a sufficient apprehension of immediate harm to constitute an assault. *Examples:* Verbal threats to a blind person may constitute an assault, or if D comes up behind P saying, "Don't turn around or I'll shoot you," this may be an assault (because the surrounding circumstances force P to rely on the words alone—*i.e.*, it is unsafe for P to turn around to see if D really has a gun). [Rest. 2d §31, comment d]

(c)   **Compare—emotional distress:** [§28]   Note that words alone, even if insufficient for an assault, may be sufficient to impose liability for intentional infliction of emotional distress (*see infra*, §63).

b. **Intent:** [§29]   The defendant must have intended *to inflict a harmful or offensive touching* on the plaintiff or a third person, *or to put* the plaintiff or a third person *in apprehension of an immediate harmful or offensive touching.*

   (1) **Test:** Again, the defendant's intent is measured by the *"desire or belief in substantial certainty"* test (*see supra,* §7). No malice need be shown. [Langford v. Shu, 128 S.E.2d 210 (N.C. 1962)]

   (2) **Transferred intent:** The transferred intent doctrine is likewise applicable (*see supra,* §10).

c. **Apprehension:** [§30]   The defendant's intentional act must have placed the plaintiff in apprehension of an *imminent* harmful or offensive touching of her person. [Proffitt v. Ricci, 463 A.2d 514 (R.I. 1983)]

   (1) **Plaintiff's awareness of threat:** [§31]   The apprehension requirement means that the plaintiff cannot complain of an assault unless she was aware of the threat *at the time thereof.* For example, there is no actionable assault if all the defendant did was silently point a gun at the plaintiff while her back was turned. [Rest. 2d §22]

      (a) **Compare—battery:** The rule is different in battery, where apprehension is not required, and where the plaintiff need not have knowledge of the touching at the time thereof (*see supra,* §16).

   (2) **Nature of harm threatened:** [§32]   Moreover, the plaintiff must be apprehensive of a touching *to her own person.* Threats to her home or property, or to the person or property of any third person (even members of her own family), are not enough. [Rest. 2d §26]

      (a) **Compare—emotional distress:** But such threats may be sufficient to impose liability for emotional distress (*see infra,* §63).

      (b) **Compare—false imprisonment:** Threats to a member of the plaintiff's family may create a false imprisonment (*see infra,* §51).

   (3) **Source of threatened harm:** [§33]   Although normally the threat is from the defendant himself, or from some force he sets in motion, this is not essential; the defendant may be liable for an assault where he arouses apprehension of harm *from someone else* (or even from an act of God). [Rest. 2d §25]

      (a) **Examples:** For the purpose of making P apprehensive, D falsely says, "Watch out! A snake is about to bite you!" or, "Duck! X just threw a rock at you!" D may be liable for assault. (These are also examples in which "words alone" are sufficient; *see supra,* §27.)

   (4) **Imminence of threatened harm:** [§34]   The plaintiff must be placed in apprehension of an imminent harmful or offensive touching. Thus, even where menacing gestures are involved, if the words used *negate* any immediate threat, there is no actionable assault. For example, if the defendant shakes his fist at plaintiff saying, "If you weren't such an old fool, I'd break your neck," the words negate the immediacy of the threat.

(a) **Threats of future harm insufficient:** [§35] Likewise, where the words used make it clear that some significant interval of time remains before the harm will be inflicted, there is no assault. [Rest. 2d §29(2)]

   1) **Example:** D points a gun at P saying, "The next time we meet, you're dead!" There is no assault.

   2) **Compare—emotional distress:** Again, however, threats of future harm may be sufficient for the tort of intentional infliction of emotional distress (*see infra,* §63).

(b) **Conditional threats may be sufficient:** [§36] A threat of immediate harm may constitute an assault even though the threat is conditional, provided the condition is one that the defendant is not privileged to assert. [Rest. 2d §30]

   1) **Example:** D points a gun at P saying, "Take back what you said about my sister, or I'll kill you!" D is liable for an assault, since no privilege exists for him to force a retraction in this manner.

   2) **What is privileged:** As to the circumstances under which one person is privileged to use or threaten harm against another, *see* self-defense (*infra,* §§99 *et seq.*) and privilege of arrest (*infra,* §§144 *et seq.*).

(5) **Nature of plaintiff's apprehension**

(a) **Fear not required:** [§37] The plaintiff need only be placed in apprehension of an actual touching; she need *not* be frightened. Thus, it is immaterial that the plaintiff may be able, and knows that she is able, to escape or prevent the threatened touching. For example, a midget may commit an assault on a giant by threatening to strike her, even though the giant knows that she can overpower the midget or can step away before the midget can possibly touch her. [Rest. 2d §24]

   1) **And note:** It is also immaterial that a reasonable person would not have been placed in apprehension by the defendant's act. Actual apprehension is the test. [Rest. 2d §27]

(b) **Apparent ability sufficient:** [§38] It is sufficient if the defendant had the actual *or apparent* ability to inflict the touching. [Allen v. Hannaford, 244 P. 700 (Wash. 1926); Rest. 2d §27]

   1) **Example:** If D intends to make P apprehensive by appearing to menace her with a loaded gun from 50 feet away, an assault has been committed even if the gun is in fact unloaded.

   2) **Compare—criminal assault:** The rule may be different for a criminal assault. (*See* Criminal Law Summary.)

d. **Causation:** [§39] The plaintiff's apprehension must have been legally caused by the defendant's act or something the defendant set in motion. As to what is sufficient causation, *see* discussion of this element in Battery, *supra,* §17.

e. **Damages:** [§40] The damage rules discussed in Battery (*supra,* §19) generally apply. The plaintiff need not have suffered any emotional distress, physical injuries, or other damages (although, again, these are recoverable if sustained).

3. **False Imprisonment:** [§41] Prima facie case:

> *Act by Defendant*
> *Intent*
> *Confinement*
> *Causation*
> (***Lack of Consent***—discussed as a defense, *see infra,* §§80 *et seq.*)

a. **Act by defendant:** [§42] There must be some act by the defendant that causes the confinement of the plaintiff. As in battery or assault, the act required is usually a volitional movement by the defendant of some part of his body.

(1) **Compare—words alone sufficient:** [§43] In false imprisonment, words alone *may be* a sufficient act. Thus, *threats* of physical force (*see* below), or words asserting legal authority ("I arrest you"), may result in false imprisonment without any accompanying physical movement. [Martin v. Houck, 54 S.E. 291 (N.C. 1906)]

b. **Intent:** [§44] The act must have been done by the defendant with the intent *to confine* the plaintiff or some third person.

(1) **Test:** Again, intent is measured by the *"desire or belief in substantial certainty"* test (*supra,* §7).

(2) **Transferred intent:** The transferred intent doctrine applies (*see supra,* §10).

c. **Confinement:** [§45] The defendant's intentional act must result in the confinement of the plaintiff within boundaries fixed by the defendant for some period of time, however short. "Confinement" requires that the plaintiff be restricted to a limited area without knowledge of a reasonable means of escape.

(1) **What constitutes "confinement"**

(a) **Area of confinement:** [§46] Normally, there must be some *specific area* in which the plaintiff is *completely* confined by the defendant's acts.

1) **Example:** Where P is prevented from going in a certain direction (*e.g.,* by D's blocking a highway), there is *not* a sufficient confinement to constitute false imprisonment. [Bird v. Jones, 115 Eng. Rep. 668 (1845)]

(b) **No means of escape available:** [§47]   There is no confinement if *reasonable* means of escape are available *and known* to plaintiff. [Davis & Allcott Co. v. Boozer, 110 So. 28 (Ala. 1926)]

   1) **But note:** The plaintiff is under no duty to search for a means of escape or to run any risk of harm to her person or property (*e.g.*, clothing) by attempting to escape. [Rest. 2d §36]

   2) **And note:** If the defendant asserts that he will free the plaintiff if the plaintiff complies with some unlawful condition (*e.g.*, payment of money which plaintiff is under no obligation to pay), compliance is *not* deemed a "reasonable" means of escape.

(c) **Plaintiff's awareness:** [§48]   There can be no confinement unless the plaintiff *knows* that she is confined *at the time* of the confinement *or* is *harmed* by the confinement. [Rest. 2d §42]

(2) **How confinement caused:** [§49]   Plaintiff's confinement may be effected by any of the following:

(a) **Physical force:** [§50]   The defendant's use of physical force against either the plaintiff or a member of the plaintiff's *immediate family* constitutes confinement.

   1) **Note:** Where physical force is used, the reasonableness of the plaintiff's submission thereto is immaterial (*e.g.*, a giant may be detained by a midget who grabs the giant's coat, intending to detain him). [Rest. 2d §39]

(b) **Threats or duress**

   1) **Threats to plaintiff or plaintiff's family:** [§51]   Confinement may be effected by submission to threats of *immediate* physical harm to the plaintiff or a member of her *immediate family*. *Example:* D may confine P by threatening to shoot P's child standing beside her if P tries to leave the room. [Rest. 2d §40A]

      a) **Compare—future harm:** [§52]   There is no actionable confinement where the plaintiff submits to threats of *future* harm (*e.g.*, "Unless you stay with me, I'll kill your husband when he gets off work"). [Rest. 2d §40, comment b]

   2) **Threats to plaintiff's property:** [§53]   Threats to inflict immediate harm upon the plaintiff's property may also be sufficient. *Example:* Without any privilege to do so, D removes a valuable stamp from P's stamp collection, and threatens to tear it in half unless P stays in the room. This is an effective confinement. [Rest. 2d §40A]

   3) **Threats to plaintiff's economic well-being:** [§54]   Submission to words of another usually does not constitute false imprisonment where the plaintiff stays to avoid losing her job.

[Faniel v. Chesapeake & Potomac Telephone Co., 404 A.2d 147 (D.C. 1979)]

(c) **Actual or apparent physical barriers to escape:** [§55]   Physical barriers may be in the form of an enclosure, fence, walls, etc. Similarly, acts that deprive the plaintiff of the ability to escape may cause confinement by physical barrier (*e.g.,* taking away the crutches or wheelchair from a crippled person; or, where P is down a well, taking away the ladder that is the only way up). [Rest. 2d §38]

   1) **Refusing to release:** [§56]   In addition, the barriers may consist of refusing to release the plaintiff or to assist her in leaving *when under a duty to do so.* [Rest. 2d §45]

      a) **Limitation:** Of course, absolute freedom of movement at all times cannot be expected. For example, when a passenger boards a commercial airliner or bus, she impliedly agrees to abide by the rules of entrance and exit at scheduled stops only. It follows that there is no actionable confinement if the passenger is denied permission to depart at a nonscheduled stop.

      b) **Compare—plaintiff in defendant's custody:** On the other hand, where the plaintiff submits herself to the defendant's care or custody (*e.g.,* by boarding defendant's pleasure yacht) with the implicit understanding that the defendant will assist her in leaving any time she wishes, if the defendant subsequently refuses to allow the plaintiff to leave, and it is actually or apparently impossible for the plaintiff otherwise to escape, there is a sufficient confinement to establish false imprisonment. [Whittaker v. Sanford, 85 A. 399 (Me. 1912)]

(d) **Arrest:** [§57]   A confinement may also be effected by *the defendant's assertion of legal authority* (*i.e.,* an arrest) *and submission thereto by the plaintiff.* [Martin v. Houck, *supra,* §43; Rest. 2d §41]

   1) **But compare—filing complaint:** [§58]   A private citizen who does no more than file a complaint with the police regarding another is *not* liable for false arrest because it is the police who assert legal authority and confine the person against whom the complaint is made. [Baker v. Coon, 166 N.W. 555 (Neb. 1918)] (*But note:* The citizen who files a false complaint may be liable for malicious prosecution; *see infra,* §1511.)

d. **Causation:** [§59]   The confinement must have been legally caused by the defendant's intentional act or some force set in motion thereby (*see* discussion of this element, *supra,* §17).

e. **Damages:** [§60]   The tort is complete upon the confinement, and recovery may be had even though the plaintiff suffers no special damages—*e.g.,* injuries, loss of earnings, etc. (However, if sustained, these damages are also recoverable.)

(1) **Injuries while attempting escape:** [§61]   "False imprisonment invites escape"; thus, a plaintiff can also recover for any injuries sustained in a *reasonable* attempt to escape. [*But see* Sindle v. New York City Transit Authority, 33 N.Y.2d 293 (1973)—no recovery for injuries suffered in *unreasonable* escape attempt]

4. **Intentional Infliction of Emotional Distress:** [§62]   Prima facie case:

> *Act by Defendant—"Extreme" and "Outrageous" Conduct*
> *Intent*
> *Causation*
> *Severe Emotional Distress*

a. **Act by defendant—extreme and outrageous conduct:** [§63]   Unlike the intentional tort of assault (*see supra,* §24), *words alone* may be a sufficient "act" here. Or liability may be predicated on any other gesture, conduct, or action by the defendant. However, courts generally require that the conduct be *"extreme" and "outrageous"—i.e.,* exceeding "all bounds of decent behavior." [Rest. 2d §46]

   (1) **Examples of extreme and outrageous conduct**

   (a) *Threatening language by bill collectors,* bullying tactics of landlords seeking their rent, insults hurled in public, and deliberately killing P's pet dog are typical cases of extreme and outrageous conduct. [Sherman v. Field Clinic, 392 N.E.2d 154 (Ill. 1979)] But leaving collection agency business cards on P's door and contacting P's neighbors, apartment manager, and former employer did *not* amount to "extreme and outrageous" conduct when debtor, P, would not respond to the agency. [Munley v. ISC Financial House, Inc., 584 P.2d 1336 (Okla. 1978)]

   (b) *An insurance company's refusal to pay benefits clearly owing* (for purpose of forcing a policyholder to settle a claim for less than due) has been held sufficiently "outrageous" that the policyholder could recover for emotional distress. [Fletcher v. Western National Life Insurance Co., 10 Cal. App. 3d 376 (1970)]

   (c) *A moving company's failure to deliver* P's household goods until several months after the date promised, coupled with its *knowingly false assurance* to her during the interim that delivery was imminent, and its *knowledge* that P's emotional state was at the breaking point over the delivery problem, has been held sufficiently "outrageous" conduct. [Hanke v. Global Van Lines, 533 F. 2d 396 (8th Cir. 1976)]

   (d) *A doctor's having sexual relations* with his nurse, knowing that he had an active case of herpes and was likely to infect her, was extreme and outrageous because the doctor was aware that the disease was painful and incurable. [B.N. v. K.K., 538 A.2d 1175 (Md. 1988)]

(e) *A psychologist's initiation of affair* with his patient's wife, knowing that his patient was emotionally unstable, was sufficiently outrageous that the patient could recover for emotional distress. [Figueiredo-Torres v. Nickel, 584 A.2d 69 (Md. 1991)]

(f) *However, a doctor's act in telling P, the mother of a deceased patient,* that he "had her son's brain in a jar" for autopsy purposes did *not* amount to extreme and outrageous conduct even though she had asked that a brain examination not be performed. [Burgess v. Perdue, 721 P.2d 239 (Kan. 1986)]

(g) *And making 340 "hang-up" phone calls* to P over a two month period after P refused to date D a second time was *not* sufficient for the tort. [Russo v. White, 400 S.E.2d 160 (Va. 1991)]

(2) **Note:** In determining whether conduct is extreme and outrageous, consider the *"totality of circumstances,"* not each isolated individual incident.

(3) **Compare—petty insults:** [§64]   There is no redress for simple insults, annoyances, or petty indignities (*e.g.,* where a frustrated telephone user curses at the operator). [Rest. 2d §46, comment d]

(4) **Exception—special carrier-utility rule:** [§65]   Common carriers and public utilities have been held liable for gross insults that would not otherwise be actionable under the common law requirement of extreme and outrageous conduct.

(5) **Exception—harassment:** [§66]   Cases involving insults or attacks based on race or gender may be actionable harassment claims even if not amounting to the traditional tort of intentional infliction of emotional distress. [Meritor Savings Bank v. Vinson, 477 U.S. 57, *on remand,* 801 F.2d 1436 (D.C. Cir. 1992)—unwelcome sexual advances that create hostile working environment violate Title VII of 1964 Civil Rights Act; Franklin v. Gwinnett County Public Schools, 503 U.S. 60 (1992)—sexual harassment of high school student by teacher may create private remedy under Title IX of Educational Amendments Act of 1972]

b. **Intent:** [§67]   The defendant must have intended *to cause severe emotional distress or mental anguish* to the plaintiff. *Reckless* conduct will also suffice (*i.e.,* where the defendant acts in deliberate disregard of a high probability that his actions will cause emotional distress). [*See* Womack v. Eldridge, 210 S.E.2d 145 (Va. 1974)]

(1) **Inference of intent:** [§68]   Such intent or recklessness may be inferred where *the defendant knows that the plaintiff is particularly sensitive* or susceptible to emotional distress, but acts in disregard of the probability that such harm is likely to occur (*e.g.,* abusive words used to persons who are ill or elderly, to pregnant women, or to children). [*See* Hanke v. Global Van Lines, *supra*]

(2) **No transferred intent among torts:** [§69]   If the defendant intended to cause bodily harm or property damage to the plaintiff but did not succeed, and *only* unintended emotional distress resulted, the defendant is

not liable for intentional infliction of the emotional distress (no intent). (Negligent infliction of emotional distress is discussed *infra, §§627 et seq.*)

(3) **Distinguish—assault:** [§70] Intentional infliction of emotional distress is to be distinguished from assault. In assault, the defendant must have intended to harmfully or offensively *touch* the plaintiff or a third person or to place the plaintiff or third person *in apprehension* of such a touching. Also, liability in assault is complete upon occurrence of the apprehension—whether or not any mental anguish, emotional distress, or physical injury results.

c. **Causation**

(1) **Early view—physical injuries required:** [§71] Early cases held that the defendant's intentional act had to be the cause in fact and proximate cause of a severe emotional disturbance in the plaintiff, which in turn caused *demonstrable physical injuries.* (This was to assure against fraudulent claims.) [Wilkinson v. Downton, 2 Q.B.D. 57 (1897); Clark v. Associated Retail Credit Men, 105 F.2d 62 (D.C. Cir. 1939)]

(2) **Modern approach—distress alone suffices:** [§72] However, the modern view is that where the defendant intentionally and successfully causes severe emotional distress to the plaintiff, recovery is allowed even though there are no demonstrable physical injuries resulting therefrom. *Rationale:* The *outrageous nature* of the defendant's conduct may be a more reliable indication of damage to the plaintiff than actual physical injury. [State Rubbish Collectors v. Siliznoff, 38 Cal. 2d 330 (1952); Rest. 2d §46]

(a) **Note:** Whether the defendant's conduct is sufficiently "outrageous" to cause mental anguish is a fact question in each case. Changing attitudes and social conditions are relevant to this issue. [Alcorn v. Anbro Engineering, 2 Cal. 3d 493 (1970)—racial slurs held actionable]

(3) **Liability to third persons:** [§73] When the defendant's conduct was aimed only at a particular person, the defendant is also liable for infliction of emotional distress to *members of that person's family* present at the time of the conduct—if the defendant knew of their presence. *Rationale:* Under the circumstances, the defendant must have known that his conduct toward the person was substantially certain to hurt the plaintiff (family member), or the conduct was at least reckless toward the plaintiff. [Grimsby v. Samson, 530 P.2d 291 (Wash. 1975)]

d. **Severe emotional distress:** [§74] Although much passes as emotional distress for purposes of recovery in other torts (*e.g.,* embarrassment, humiliation, shame, fright, and grief), the distress must be *severe* to allow recovery for this tort. It must be more than a reasonable person could be expected to endure. [Harris v. Jones, 380 A.2d 611 (Md. 1977)]

(1) **Example:** If D attempts to carry out a cruel practical joke, but P is aware of the joke and thus is only angered at D, rather than humiliated, P

has not suffered severe emotional distress—even though D's conduct may well have been extreme and outrageous.

(2) **Example:** Where P is a corporation, P could not have suffered severe emotional distress no matter how extreme and outrageous D's conduct. [Chamberlaine & Flowers v. Smith Contracting, 341 S.E.2d 414 (W. Va. 1986)]

e. **Defenses**

(1) **Common law defenses:** [§75] Although theoretically the common law defenses available to other intentional torts (*see* below) should apply here, in reality these defenses are not available because the prima facie case requires such an extreme level of misbehavior. Therefore, defenses based on good faith or reasonable mistake are not relevant to this tort.

(a) **Note:** Some courts will not allow a claim for emotional distress if the same facts would have supported a claim for criminal conversation, which has been abolished in most states (*see infra,* §§1007-1008). [Koestler v. Pollard, 471 N.W.2d 7 (Wis. 1991)]

(2) **Constitutional defenses:** [§76] The First Amendment may be a defense to this tort where allowing the suit would curb the freedom of speech and press or the free exercise of religion.

(a) **Freedom of speech:** [§77] Where the defendant's act is a *statement* that injures the plaintiff, the act may be protected speech (*see infra,* §§1267 *et seq.*) even though the act constitutes extreme and outrageous behavior. [Hustler Magazine v. Falwell, 485 U.S. 46 (1988)—gross insults aimed at public person not actionable unless defamatory or an invasion of privacy]

(b) **Free exercise of religion:** [§78] Where the defendant is a church or other religious organization, and the act is part of a religious activity, some courts have held that the Free Exercise Clause bars recognition of this tort. [Paul v. Watchtower Bible & Tract Society, 819 F.2d 875 (9th Cir. 1987)—Jehovah's Witnesses' practice of "shunning" a disassociated church member is protected from suit for outrageous conduct; Molko v. Holy Spirit Association for the Unification of World Christianity, 46 Cal. 3d 1092 (1991)—threats of divine retribution made by church members were protected religious speech and could not form the basis for emotional distress claim; Murphy v. I.S.K.CON of New England, 571 N.E.2d 340 (Mass. 1991)—no claim of emotional distress by mother of child who became involved with defendant group because claim could only be proved by testimony about the group's religious beliefs]

f. **Damages:** [§79] In addition to compensatory damages, punitive damages may be recoverable in all cases because of the nature of the defendant's act.

(1) **Exception:** Because of free speech concerns, some states that usually permit punitive damages may bar them where the tortious conduct is entirely speech. [Hall v. May Department Stores, 637 P.2d 126 (Or. 1981)]

B. DEFENSES AND PRIVILEGED INVASIONS OF PERSONAL INTERESTS

1. **Consent:** [§80]   The plaintiff's consent to the defendant's conduct may prevent the defendant from being liable for an intentional tort. Most courts require the *defendant* to affirmatively plead and prove that the plaintiff consented. A few hold *lack of consent* an element of the prima facie case that the plaintiff must plead and prove.

   a. **Types of consent:** [§81]   There are two basic types of consent: consent based on the plaintiff's behavior and consent implied by law.

      (1) **Consent based on plaintiff's behavior:** [§82]   The plaintiff may consent by:

         (i) *Actual express consent*—when the plaintiff actually communicates to the defendant a willingness to submit to the defendant's conduct; or

         (ii) *Apparent consent*—implied from the *plaintiff's conduct* in light of the circumstances, *i.e.,* plaintiff, by conduct, has led defendant reasonably to believe that plaintiff is willing to submit to defendant's act.

            (a) **Example:** P's failure to object to a vaccination D is preparing to give P conveys apparent consent to the injection. [O'Brien v. Cunard, 28 N.E. 266 (Mass. 1891)]

            (b) **Example:** One who enters into a sport impliedly consents to normal contacts.

            (c) **Example:** Similarly, one who walks on the streets or uses mass transportation impliedly consents to taps on the shoulder or brushings.

      (2) **Consent implied by law:** [§83]   The plaintiff's consent may be implied by law to a bodily contact (*e.g.,* surgery) that is necessary to save her life or some other cardinal interest in person or property *if*:

         (i) *The plaintiff is unconscious* or otherwise *unable* to consider the matter and grant or withhold consent;

         (ii) *An immediate decision* is necessary;

         (iii) *There is no reason to believe that the plaintiff would not consent* if able to do so; *and*

         (iv) *A reasonable person in the plaintiff's position would consent.*

         [Rest. 2d §62; Miller v. Rhode Island Hospital, 625 A.2d 778 (R.I. 1993)—emergency room personnel may dispense with consent where patient is unable to give it due to intoxication]

   b. **When consent is not a defense:** [§84]   Consent is *not* effective in the following circumstances:

(1) **Acts in excess of consent given:** [§85] There is no effective consent where the invasion goes beyond the limits of the consent given.

    (a) **Example:** P consents to an operation to remove her appendix. In the middle of the operation, doctor D decides also to remove P's kidney although there is no emergency requiring this. D's doing so is an unprivileged battery because it went beyond the limits of the consent given. [Mohr v. Williams, 104 N.W. 12 (Minn. 1905)]

(2) **Fraud:** [§86] The plaintiff's consent to the invasion is ineffective if procured by fraud. Thus, if P allows D to take blood from P's arm because D represents that this is necessary to save P's life, and D's representations were knowingly untrue, the consent is void. [*See* Bartell v. State, 82 N.W. 142 (Wis. 1900)—magnetic healer taking indecent liberties with young woman while purporting to treat her]

    (a) **Compare—fraud only collateral:** [§87] If the fraud is only with respect to a *collateral matter,* the consent is effective. For example, if P consented to D's taking blood from P's arm because D had given P a $20 bill, the consent remains effective even if the bill proves to be counterfeit. [Desnick v. American Broadcasting Cos., 44 F.3d 1345 (7th Cir. 1995)]

(3) **Duress:** [§88] The plaintiff's consent is ineffective if given under duress (physical force or threats thereof) against plaintiff or a member of plaintiff's family. [Neibuhr v. Gage, 108 N.W. 884 (Minn. 1906)]

(4) **Mistake:** [§89] The plaintiff's consent is also ineffective where given under mistake if the mistake was caused by the defendant or if the defendant was aware of it. [Rest. 2d §892]

    (a) **Mistake of law:** [§90] A mistake of law caused by the defendant may render the plaintiff's consent ineffective. For example, P is hurt while leaving a train, and the conductor tells P that P must file an accident report before he can get medical aid. Although P stays, his consent does not bar a subsequent suit for false imprisonment, because it was given under a mistake of law caused by the conductor. [Whitman v. Atchison, 116 P. 234 (Kan. 1911)]

    (b) **Mistake of fact:** [§91] The plaintiff's mistake as to the *essential nature or consequences* of the invasion of her person or property is treated as a mistake of fact and voids any consent to such invasion.

        1) **Lack of consent in medical treatment:** [§92] It is on this very basis that a patient's consent to surgery or other medical treatment is sometimes held ineffective, thereby exposing the doctor to liability for battery. [Gray v. Grunnagle, 223 A.2d 663 (Pa. 1966); *and see supra,* §85]

        2) **Lack of informed consent:** [§93] Where the plaintiff asserts that she consented to the surgical procedure performed, but that she had not been adequately informed of the risks and benefits of the procedure, the claim is generally treated as one

for negligence rather than an intentional tort. [Cobbs v. Grant, 8 Cal. 3d 229 (1972); *and see infra,* §275]

(5) **Incapacity to consent:** [§94]   There is no valid consent where the plaintiff is known to be a person *incapable* of giving consent (*e.g.,* is an infant, drunk, or mental incompetent). [Hollerud v. Malamis, 174 N.W.2d 626 (Mich. 1969)]

(6) **Criminal acts:** [§95]   There is a split of authority on whether the plaintiff's consent is effective if the act consented to is a *crime.*

   (a) **Majority view:** [§96]   Most cases distinguish between criminal acts that involve *breaches of the peace,* and those that do not: If no breach of the peace was involved (*e.g.,* an illegal abortion), the plaintiff's consent is effective. On the other hand, if the consented-to act involved a breach of the peace (*e.g.,* a fight in the streets), these courts hold the plaintiff's consent *not* effective, thus permitting the plaintiff to recover from the defendant for any injuries sustained. [Teeters v. Frost, 292 P. 356 (Okla. 1930)]

      1) **Rationale:** Where a breach of the peace is involved, there is a public interest in seeing the participants bear full liability—criminal and *civil*—for their acts.

   (b) **Minority view:** [§97]   Some courts hold the plaintiff's consent effective in any case, thus barring any later claims by the plaintiff based on the illegal act. [Hart v. Geysel, 294 P. 570 (Wash. 1930); Rest. 2d §60]

      1) **Rationale:** No reason is seen to invalidate the plaintiff's consent (and thus allow her a cause of action) merely because the act consented to was a crime. Moreover, participants in criminal acts should be left in the status quo; if they are allowed to recover from each other, one might "profit" from her own wrongdoing. [Sayadoff v. Warda, 125 Cal. App. 2d 626 (1954)]

      2) **Example:** Consent to an illegal abortion may bar a claim for malpractice against the doctor if the abortion is *negligently performed.* [*See* Reno v. D'Javid, 42 N.Y.2d 1040 (1977)]

      3) **Exception—plaintiff is a member of protected class:** [§98] Even under this view, however, the plaintiff's consent will be disregarded if the plaintiff is a member of the particular class of persons for whose benefit the statute was enacted. For example, if a statute forbids boxing matches unless licensed by the state boxing commission, and also demonstrates a concern for the safety of participants, a boxer who is hurt in an unlicensed match may sue the promoter. [Hudson v. Craft, 33 Cal. 2d 654 (1949)]

2. **Self-Defense**

a. **Using nondeadly force:** [§99]   When acting in self-defense, a defendant is privileged to use force *not* likely to cause death or serious bodily harm, subject to the following conditions [Rest. 2d §63]:

   (1) **Reasonable apprehension of any bodily contact:** [§100]   The plaintiff has acted so as to lead the defendant to *reasonably* believe (either correctly or by reasonable mistake) that the plaintiff is about to inflict an *immediate* harmful or offensive contact upon him; and

   (2) **Reasonable means used:** [§101]   The defendant uses only those means that appear reasonably necessary to avoid or prevent the contact threatened.

   (3) **No duty to retreat:** [§102]   There is generally no duty to retreat or comply with any demand made by the person threatening the force, *except that:*

      (a) *Where the defendant recognizes that the plaintiff is not intentionally creating the risk,* there is a duty to retreat if he can safely do so; and

      (b) *Where the defendant recognizes that the plaintiff has mistaken the defendant's identity,* the defendant must make reasonable efforts to resolve the matter instead of using force in self-defense.

b. **Using deadly force:** [§103]   The defendant is privileged to use force *likely to cause death* or serious bodily harm when acting in self-defense, subject to the following conditions [Rest. 2d §65]:

   (1) **Reasonable apprehension of serious harm:** [§104]   The plaintiff has acted so as to lead the defendant to reasonably believe that the plaintiff is about to inflict an immediate harmful or offensive contact upon him, *and* the defendant reasonably believes that such contact would inflict *death or serious bodily harm.*

   (2) **Duty to retreat:** [§105]   There is a split over whether, as an alternative to using deadly force in self-defense, the defendant must retreat if it is safe to do so.

      (a) **Majority view:** [§106]   Most courts hold that there is *no duty* to retreat as an alternative to using deadly force. [*See* People v. Bush, 111 N.E.2d 326 (Ill. 1953)]

         1) **Rationale:** When one is threatened with deadly force, the feasibility of retreat should not be second-guessed by courts after the event. And as between the actor and the person threatening him, the actor has the "right" to be where he is. [People v. Estrada, 60 Cal. App. 477 (1923)]

      (b) **Minority view:** [§107]   A minority of courts impose a duty to retreat before using deadly force where this can be done safely. [Rest. 2d §65]

1) **Rationale:** The social interest in preventing deadly affrays outweighs the actor's "right" to stand his ground when threatened. [16 Harv. L. Rev. 657]

   a) **But note:** Where *guns* are involved, there is rarely a means of safe retreat; thus, the minority view will not apply.

2) **Exceptions in certain situations:** [§108] Even under the minority view, there is *no duty* to retreat where: (i) the defendant *is in his own home* (or also, in some states, his *place of business*); (ii) retreating would endanger a third party; or (iii) the defendant is attempting a valid arrest. [Rest. 2d §65(2)]

c. **Threats of force:** [§109] The defendant is privileged to *threaten* more force than he would in fact be privileged to use in self-defense, provided he has no reason to believe his threats will do more than place the plaintiff in apprehension. (This protects the defendant from liability for assault based on such threats.) [Rest. 2d §70(2)]

d. **Limitations on right of self-defense:** [§110] The privilege to act in self-defense is not unlimited.

   (1) **Danger terminated:** [§111] There is no privilege of self-defense where the *defendant knows that the danger has terminated.* [Germolus v. Sausser, 85 N.W. 946 (Minn. 1901)—D continued to whip P after P was disarmed]

   (2) **Excessive force used:** [§112] Nor is there any privilege to use force *in excess of* that which the defendant is privileged to use to defend himself (*e.g.,* P slaps D across the face; D could easily prevent further harm by holding plaintiff's arms, but instead stabs P with a knife). When excessive force is used:

   (i) *The defendant is liable* for whatever amount of the force is excessive; *and*

   (ii) *The plaintiff then has a privilege of self-defense* to protect herself against the degree of force being inflicted by the defendant. (In the example above, P might become privileged to use deadly force to defend against D's knife attack.)

   [Rest. 2d §71]

   (3) **Plaintiff using privileged force:** [§113] There is no privilege of self-defense against *privileged* action by another (*e.g.,* a lawful arrest). [Rest. 2d §72; Ellis v. State, 596 N.E.2d 428 (Ohio 1992)—trespasser not entitled to assert self-defense to justify assault on another who had legitimately used nonlethal force to exclude trespasser from property]

   (4) **Third person intentionally injured:** [§114] Finally, the privilege of self-defense does not justify the defendant's *intentional* use of harmful

force *against a third person*. *Example:* X threatens D with serious bodily harm. If, in attempting to escape from X, D intentionally runs over P, causing her injury, D is liable to P for battery. [Rest. 2d §73]

(a) **Compare—unintentional harm:** [§115]   But if the defendant *unintentionally* injures a third person while reasonably attempting to defend himself, he will be liable only if he was *negligent* toward the third person. [Helms v. Harris, 281 S.W.2d 770 (Tex. 1955)]

e. **"Reasonableness":** [§116]   Self-defense rules are couched in terms of "reasonableness." This is an *objective test—i.e.,* how the situation would have looked to the reasonable person in the same or similar circumstances, *not* how the defendant actually perceived it *or* how it actually was.

3. **Defense of Third Persons:** [§117]   The defendant may also be privileged to use force to defend another person. However, the defendant is privileged to use force only under the same conditions as that person would be privileged to use force to defend himself. Use of force in this situation raises certain additional issues:

a. **Who may be defended:** [§118]   Under modern law, the policy is to encourage a person to go to the aid of *anyone* who is endangered—even where the person defended is a complete stranger to the defendant.

b. **Effect of defendant's mistake in intervening:** [§119]   Nevertheless, the courts are split on whether the defendant is privileged where the person defended was not actually entitled to defend himself. For example, undercover police officer P attempts to arrest X; D does not realize P is a police officer, thinks P is beating up X, and goes to X's aid, injuring P.

(1) **Older view:** [§120]   Most courts hold that if D intervenes, he must "stand in the shoes" of the person he is defending, so that *unless the person being helped was actually privileged* to defend himself, D is subject to tort liability (*e.g.,* battery). Thus, the privilege cannot be based on the defendant's mistake, no matter how reasonable.

(2) **Modern view:** [§121]   The Restatement and recent cases allow a reasonable mistake in exercise of the privilege. Hence, D is privileged to use force to defend a third person as long as it *reasonably appears* that:

(i) The *third person (X) was privileged* to defend himself and to use the *means* of defense (deadly vs. nondeadly) and *amount* of force that D used, and

(ii) D's intervention was *reasonably necessary* to protect such third person.

[Rest. 2d §76]

4. **Defense of Land or Chattels**

a. **Use of nondeadly force:** [§122]   A defendant is privileged to defend his land or chattels only through the use of force *not* likely to cause death or serious bodily harm *if*:

(i) ***The intrusion by plaintiff is not privileged,*** or is conducted so as to lead defendant to reasonably believe that it is not privileged; ***and***

(ii) ***Defendant reasonably believes that force is necessary*** to prevent or terminate plaintiff's intrusion; ***and***

(iii) ***Defendant, prior to the use of force, demands that plaintiff desist or leave,*** and the demand is ignored. (No demand need be made, however, where it would be futile or would further endanger defendant's property.)

[Rest. 2d §77]

b. **Use of mechanical devices:** [§123] The defendant is privileged to use mechanical devices (high-voltage fences, spring traps, etc.) in defense of his land or chattels ***only where:***

(i) ***The use of such means*** to protect property is ***reasonable and necessary*** under the circumstances, or ***customary*** in the locale; ***and***

(ii) ***Adequate warning*** of the use thereof is given or posted.

[Rest. 2d §84; Allison v. Fiscus, 100 N.E.2d 237 (Ohio 1951)]

(1) **Deadly mechanical devices:** [§124] If the devices employed threaten ***death or serious bodily harm,*** their use is privileged only if the intrusion ***in fact constitutes*** (not just reasonably appears to constitute) a threat of death or serious bodily harm to the defendant or his family. [Rest. 2d §85]

(a) **Rationale:** Simple trespass, vandalism, or theft is ***not*** sufficient justification for use of deadly devices. [Katko v. Briney, 183 N.W.2d 657 (Iowa 1971)—spring gun; *but see* Alaska Stat. §09.017.030 (Supp. 1987)—no recovery for personal injury or death sustained in the commission of a felony]

c. **Use of threats:** [§125] According to the Restatement, a defendant is privileged to ***threaten*** a ***greater*** amount of force than he would actually be privileged to use in defense of his property (*e.g.,* farmer pointing shotgun at trespasser crossing field)—provided that he has no reason to believe that such threats would cause anything more than fright or apprehension in the plaintiff. [Rest. 2d §81]

5. **Force to Recover Possession of Land Wrongfully Withheld**

a. **Majority view:** [§126] Under the present majority rule, there is ***no privilege*** to use force to recover possession of land wrongfully withheld even where the owner has been "tortiously dispossessed" (below). If the owner does use force to retake possession, he will be liable for the resulting harm (*e.g.,* battery or trespass to chattels). His title or right to possession of land is ***no defense*** to the tort. [Daluiso v. Boone, 71 Cal. 2d 484 (1969)]

(1) **Rationale:** In practically all states today, there are judicial procedures (*e.g.,* ejectment, unlawful detainer, etc.) that provide a quick and effective

remedy for the recovery of land wrongfully withheld. Such procedures are supported by public policy favoring resort to courts, rather than self-help, to settle land disputes.

b. **Minority view:** [§127]   A minority of jurisdictions follow the Restatement rule that a person who is entitled to possession of land, and who has been "tortiously dispossessed" therefrom, may use *reasonable, nondeadly force* to regain possession—provided he acts promptly upon discovering the dispossession. [Shorter v. Shelton, 33 S.E.2d 643 (Va. 1945); Rest. 2d §§89, 91]

(1) **"Tortious dispossession":** [§128]   This means that the plaintiff obtained possession *by fraud, force, or duress,* or without any claim of right (*e.g.,* is a trespasser).

(2) **Compare—other dispossessions:** [§129]   If there was *no tortious dispossession,* there is no privilege to use *any* force to recover possession of land, on the rationale that the owner's right to possession is less important than avoidance of the affrays and violence which the use of force might entail. [Rest. 2d §88]

(a) **Example:** P cannot use force against a tenant who overstays the lease, or a person who moves onto property in the honest but mistaken belief that he owns it.

6. **Force to Effect Recapture of Chattels Wrongfully Withheld**

a. **Tortious dispossession cases:** [§130]   A defendant who has been *tortiously dispossessed* of chattels (*e.g.,* by a pickpocket, shoplifter, or defrauder) is privileged to use *reasonable, nondeadly force* in recapture of those chattels. [Rogers v. Kabakoff, 81 Cal. App. 2d 487 (1947)] This privilege, however, is subject to the following conditions [Rest. 2d §§101-106]:

(1) **Immediate right to possession:** [§131]   The defendant is in fact *entitled to the immediate possession* of the chattel. (No mistake, however reasonable, is permitted.)

(2) **Demand:** [§132]   The defendant has *demanded return* of the chattel and the demand has been ignored, or no demand was made because it would have been futile or dangerous to do so.

(3) **Fresh pursuit:** [§133]   The recapture is effected promptly—*i.e.,* the defendant must be in *"fresh pursuit."* This encompasses two factors: (i) the defendant must have been reasonably diligent in *discovering* the loss; and (ii) following discovery, the defendant must have been reasonably diligent in his *efforts* to retake the chattel. Both concepts are measured by a "reasonable person" standard.

(4) **Holder at fault:** [§134]   The defendant has effected the recapture from the person who tortiously dispossessed him, or from a third party with notice that the chattels involved were stolen, etc.

(a) **Compare—transfer to innocent person:** If the thief has sold or given the chattels to an innocent party, this cuts off the defendant's privilege to use force to effect their recapture, even if he can show "fresh pursuit."

b. **Other dispossessions:** [§135] Where the defendant has *not* been tortiously dispossessed of chattels (*i.e.,* no fraud, force, etc.), the general rule is that he is *not privileged to use any force* to effect their recapture. Redress must be in the courts.

    (1) **Examples:** B borrows A's book and later decides not to return it; or, A parks his car in B's parking lot, and B later refuses to release the car. In either case, A has no privilege to use force to get back his property.

    (2) **Conditional sales contracts:** [§136] When a buyer defaults on a conditional sales contract, the seller is entitled to *peacefully* repossess; neither force nor fraud is permitted. [Stallworth v. Doss, 194 So. 2d 566 (Ala. 1967)] In fact, even if the sales contract purports to allow for a forceful recapture, most courts will find such a provision void as against public policy. [Girard v. Anderson, 257 N.W. 400 (Iowa 1934)]

c. **"Shopkeepers' privilege":** [§137] Most states today recognize a privilege, usually limited to storekeepers, to *detain temporarily* for investigation anyone whom they reasonably suspect of having tortiously taken their goods. [Bonkowski v. Arlan's Department Store, 162 N.W.2d 347 (Mich. 1968); Rest. 2d §120A]

    (1) **Rationale:** This privilege has been justified by the very practical need for some degree of protection for storekeepers in their dealings with suspected shoplifters. Absent such privilege, a storekeeper would be faced with the dilemma of either allowing suspects to leave without challenge or acting upon his suspicion and risking a false arrest if mistaken.

    (2) **Requirements:** [§138] Proper exercise of the privilege requires that *all* of the following conditions be satisfied:

        (a) **Reasonable suspicion:** [§139] The storekeeper has *reasonable grounds to suspect* the *particular person* detained.

        (b) **Investigation on or near premises:** [§140] The detention itself is effected either on the store premises or in the *immediate vicinity* thereof.

        (c) **Reasonable force:** [§141] Only *reasonable, nondeadly* force is used to effect the detention.

        (d) **Reasonable period and manner of detention:** [§142] The detention itself is only for the period of time necessary for reasonable investigation (usually very short) and is conducted in a reasonable manner. [Collyer v. Kress, 5 Cal. 2d 175 (1936)]

    (3) **Effect—reasonable mistake protected:** [§143] Where these conditions are established, the storekeeper is immune from liability for false arrest, battery, etc.—even though it turns out that the person detained was innocent of any wrongdoing. [Teel v. May Department Stores, 155 S.W.2d 74 (Mo. 1941)]

7. **Privilege of Arrest**

    a.   **Arrests for felonies without a warrant:** [§144]   There is a distinction between arrests made by the police and those made by private citizens.

        (1)   *A police officer* is privileged to arrest for a felony without a warrant if he has reasonable grounds for believing that a felony has been committed *and* that the person he arrests committed it. [Rest. 2d §121]

        (2)   *A private citizen* is privileged to arrest for a felony without a warrant only if a felony has *in fact* been committed, and he has reasonable grounds for believing that the person he arrests committed it. [Rest. 2d §119]

    b.   **Arrests for misdemeanors without a warrant:** [§145]   According to the general view, both police officers and private citizens are privileged to arrest for misdemeanors without a warrant if the misdemeanor involves a *breach of the peace* and has *in fact* been committed in the presence of the arresting party, who makes the arrest in *fresh pursuit.*

        (1)   **Minority view:** [§146]   Under a minority view, a *police officer* is privileged to arrest for a misdemeanor based on the *reasonable belief* that the misdemeanor was being committed *in his presence* and that the *party arrested is guilty*. [Coverstone v. Davies, 38 Cal. 2d 315 (1952)]

    c.   **Arrests under arrest warrant:** [§147]   An arrest made under a warrant "fair on its face" is privileged—even if it develops that the warrant was improperly issued and the person arrested is innocent of any crime.

        (1)   **"Fair on its face":** [§148]   A warrant is "fair on its face" as long as it is free of defects *on its face* that a reasonable police officer would discover. (*See* Criminal Procedure Summary for discussion of warrant requirements.)

        (2)   **Search warrant:** [§149]   An arrest made without an arrest warrant and without probable cause while the officer is executing a *search* warrant gives rise to an action for false arrest. [Barr v. County of Albany, 50 N.Y.2d 247 (1980)]

    d.   **Amount of force privileged**

        (1)   **Misdemeanors:** [§150]   When the arrest is for a misdemeanor, both the police officer and the private person are privileged to use that degree of force necessary to effect the arrest, but *never deadly force.* [Noback v. Town of Montclair, 110 A.2d 339 (N.J. 1954)]

        (2)   **Felonies:** [§151]   Where the arrest is for a *felony,* there is a split of authority as to the permissible use of deadly force:

            (a)   **Traditional view:** [§152]   The traditional common law rule (still followed in a number of states) provides that in a lawful arrest for *any* felony, *deadly* force may be used by police officers or private persons, if reasonably necessary to effect the arrest. [Rest. 2d §131]

    (b) **Some states—"serious" felonies:** [§153] Some states now limit the right to use deadly force to arrests for "serious" felonies (*e.g.,* murder, rape, robbery, etc.) and do *not* permit deadly force in arrests for other felonies, such as larceny. [Peterson v. Long Beach, 24 Cal. 3d 238 (1979)]

    (c) **Constitutional definition of "deadly force":** [§154] The Supreme Court has held that deadly force is reasonable under the Fourth Amendment only where necessary to prevent a felon's escape (or to capture a suspect) *and* where there is probable cause to believe that the felon or suspect poses a *significant threat of death or serious injury* to the officer or others. [Tennessee v. Garner, 471 U.S. 1 (1985); *and see* Model Penal Code §3.07]

        1) **Effect on state tort law:** States are free to define defenses to a state tort claim. Therefore, a state statute may privilege a defendant's use of force in the plaintiff's state tort claim, even if the same action is a violation of the plaintiff's constitutional rights under the *Garner* standards for deadly force. [Brown v. City of Clewiston, 848 F.2d 1534 (11th Cir. 1988)]

        2) **Effect on constitutional torts:** However, in a federal civil action where the plaintiff sues the defendant for violating the plaintiff's constitutional rights, the defendant's force is privileged only if it meets the *Garner* standards.

e. **Right to invade land:** [§155] The privilege of arrest carries with it the privilege of entering another's land for the purpose of effecting an arrest. [Rest. 2d §204]

f. **Effect of defendant's misconduct following arrest:** [§156] What happens if the initial arrest was privileged, but the defendant subsequently uses excessive force against the arrestee or unreasonably delays arraignment (so that the arrestee is held an unreasonably long time without being able to get out on bail)? The modern view is that the person making the arrest is liable only for such harm as is attributable to his misconduct following the arrest—*i.e.,* only for the force or detention exceeding the amount that was otherwise privileged. [Dragna v. White, 45 Cal. 2d 469 (1955); Rest. 2d §136]

g. **Resisting arrest:** [§157] Although the traditional view allowed a person unlawfully arrested to use reasonable force to resist, the modern trend has been to deny such a privilege. [State v. Koonce, 214 A.2d 428 (N.J. 1965)] Moreover, in some states, failure to submit to asserted legal authority is itself a crime [*see, e.g.,* Cal. Penal Code §834a] so that even though the original arrest was improper, the officer may use reasonable force to arrest for the *crime of resisting arrest.*

8. **Privilege of Discipline:** [§158] Parents and teachers are recognized as having the privilege to use such "reasonable" force or confinement as they believe "reasonably" necessary for the proper control, training, and education of children in their care. [Rest. 2d §147] A similar privilege is recognized in military service. [Rest. 2d §146]

a. **But note:** Some legislatures and courts have rejected the common law approach as applied to corporal punishment. [*See* Rodriguez v. Johnson, 132 Misc. 2d 555 (1986)—school bus matron who slapped rowdy child was liable for battery although the slap was not excessive use of force]

C. TORTS TO PROPERTY

1. **Trespass to Land:** [§159]   Prima facie case:

    Act by Defendant
    Intent
    Intrusion upon Land
    Plaintiff in Possession or Entitled to Immediate Possession
    Causation

    a. **Act by defendant:** [§160]   There must be a volitional movement by defendant of some part of his body that results in an intrusion onto another's land or that sets in motion a force resulting in such intrusion.

        (1) **Example:** If D pushes X onto P's land, there is an invasion of P's land—but D and not X is the trespasser (because there was no volitional movement by X).

    b. **Intent:** [§161]   The defendant must have intended *to do the act that causes the intrusion* onto the land. However, he need not realize that the land belongs to another; he is liable for an intentional entry even though he acts in good faith, believing himself to be the owner.

        (1) **Compare—negligence:** [§162]   When it appears that the defendant's invasion of the land was not intentional, he might still be liable on a negligence theory (*see infra,* §§244 *et seq.*). For example, if D drives his automobile down the highway with knowledge that his luggage rack is not fastened securely, and the rack flies off the car and onto P's land, D might very well be held liable for negligence—*if* P can show *damages.* (Damages are required where liability is based on negligence, but *not* where the trespass is intentional; *see infra,* §406.)

        (2) **Compare—strict liability:** [§163]   Alternatively, certain invasions may be actionable on the theory of strict liability (*see infra,* §§721 *et seq.*)—*e.g.,* rocks hurled onto P's land as the result of D's exploding dynamite on neighboring property.

        (3) **Transferred intent:** The transferred intent doctrine applies to trespass (*see supra,* §10).

    c. **Intrusion upon land:** [§164]   The defendant's intrusion may be by personal entry on the plaintiff's land or by causing some third person or thing to enter (*e.g.,* D obstructs a stream so that water flows onto P's land). Alternatively, it may consist of the defendant's failure to leave the land, or remove property therefrom, after permission to remain has expired. [Rogers v. Board of Road Commissioners, 30 N.W.2d 358 (Mich. 1948); Rest. 2d §158]

(1) **Note:** Where the intrusion is nonphysical in nature, courts usually treat it as a *nuisance* (*see infra*, §§924 *et seq.*) rather than a trespass (*e.g.*, D's factory emitting smoke, vibrations, and noise, which D knows will be carried over onto P's adjoining property).

d. **Plaintiff in possession or entitled to immediate possession:** [§165]   At the time of the trespass, the plaintiff's interest in land must be either actual possession or the right to immediate possession.

   (1) **"Actual possession":** [§166]   The person actually in possession may bring an action for trespass because any possession is a legal possession as against a trespasser. Thus, even a wrongful occupier (*e.g.*, adverse possessor) may maintain a trespass action against a wrongful intruder. [Rest. 2d §157]

   (2) **"Right to immediate possession":** [§167]   *If no one is in actual possession,* then the person who has the *right to immediate possession* may maintain the action. ("Immediate" means the holder of some present possessory estate, as contrasted with a future interest; *see* Property Summary.)

      (a) **Dispossessed owner cannot sue:** [§168]   Where an owner has been ousted from possession by another (*e.g.*, by an adverse possessor), the owner *cannot* maintain a suit for trespass because the *dispossessor* is in "actual possession." The owner must bring suit to *eject* the person who dispossessed her and make him account for any damage to the property during the time he held it. [Kelman v. Wilen, 283 App. Div. 1113 (1954)]

      (b) **Lease cases:** [§169]   During the term of a lease, the tenant has *both* actual possession and the right to immediate possession. The landlord has neither (*i.e.*, he has only a future interest—a reversion).

         1) **Modern rule:** [§170]   Under the modern rule, *either* the landlord or the tenant can maintain trespass. However, the *recovery* available depends on who sues:

            a) *If the tenant sues,* some courts allow her to recover only for interference with her interest (*i.e.*, the right to exclusive possession until the end of her term). Other courts allow her to also recover for any permanent injury to the property, but these latter damages must be held in trust for the landlord.

            b) *If the landlord sues,* most courts allow recovery *only* for the damages to the *landlord's* interest (*i.e.*, for permanent injury to the property).

   (3) **Extent of possession—airspace above land:** [§171]   There has never been much doubt that a certain amount of the airspace above land is deemed part of the occupant's "actual possession," so that an intrusion thereof (*e.g.*, by telephone lines or by an overhanging building) can constitute an actionable trespass. But the question is *how high* the right to exclusive possession extends. This issue is of particular importance where the intrusion is by aircraft.

    (a) **Above normal flight altitude:** [§172] Under modern authority, a landowner has no right to possession of that portion of the airspace that extends *above* the minimum altitudes for normal aircraft flights (excluding landing and takeoff). In effect, such upper airspace is a "public highway" in which no private possessory rights exist; hence, no trespass action will lie for its invasion. [United States v. Causby, 382 U.S. 256 (1946)]

    (b) **Beneath normal flight altitude:** [§173] On the other hand, the landowner may have a protectable right to the airspace below minimum flight altitude.

        1) **Modern view—"immediate reaches" standard:** [§174] Modern authority holds that a landowner's right to possession extends to the airspace within the *"immediate reaches"* of the land, but at the same time, invasions of such lower airspace are deemed *privileged* as long as they do not "interfere substantially with the landowner's use and enjoyment of his land." [Rest. 2d §159(2)—based on United States v. Causby, *supra*]

            a) **Note:** The term "immediate reaches" of the land has yet to be defined, but the Restatement suggests that any flight under 50 feet is clearly within the "immediate reaches," while any flight over 500 feet clearly is not.

    (c) **Compare—nuisance:** [§175] Even where the landowner has no right to possession of the airspace involved (*e.g.,* flights through upper airspace or in airspace not directly over landowner's premises), the landowner may be entitled to protection against unreasonable interference (through noise, fumes, vibrations, etc.) with the use and enjoyment of the land on a *nuisance* theory. [Nestle v. Santa Monica, 6 Cal. 3d 920 (1972); *and see infra,* §§924 *et seq.*]

  e. **Causation:** [§176] Finally, the invasion must be legally caused by the defendant's intentional act or some force set in motion thereby. (As to what is sufficient causation, *see* discussion of this element, *supra,* §17.)

    (1) **And note:** A trespasser is liable for harm to person or property caused to the owner even if the harm was not foreseeable. [Baker v. Shymkiv, 451 N.E.2d 811 (Ohio 1983); Rest. 2d §162] Such harm may include emotional distress and any resulting illness or physical harm. [Hammond v. County of Madera, 859 F.2d 797 (9th Cir. 1988)]

  f. **Damages:** [§177] It is immaterial whether any actual damages were caused. [Rest. 2d §163] The tort is complete upon the defendant's intentional intrusion, and the defendant will be liable for at least nominal damages. *Rationale:* The defendant's conduct if repeated might otherwise ripen into a *prescriptive right* (*see* Property Summary). (As to punitive damages, *see supra,* §23.)

    (1) **But note:** Where there is a continuing trespass by intrusion of chemical pollutants, the plaintiff may be required to plead actual and substantial damages. [Bradley v. American Smelting & Refining, 709 P.2d 782 (Wash. 1985)]

2. **Trespass to Chattels:** [§178]   Prima facie case:

> *Act by Defendant*
> *Intent*
> *Invasion of Chattel Interest*
> *Plaintiff in Possession or Entitled to Immediate Possession*
> *Causation*
> *Damages* (where only intermeddling involved)

a. **Act by defendant:** [§179]   There must be a volitional movement by the defendant of some part of his body that results in dispossession of or damage to the chattels of another. (Note that "chattel," as used herein, includes any tangible identifiable object, but does not include a purely monetary debt.)

b. **Intent:** [§180]   It is necessary only that the defendant intended *to deal with the chattel in the manner in which he did deal;* the fact that he may have been acting under a mistaken claim of right, thinking the chattel belonged to him all the time, is immaterial.

    (1) **Note:** If intent to deal with the chattel cannot be shown, *negligence* or *strict liability* may possibly be a basis for an alternative cause of action.

    (2) **Transferred intent:** The transferred intent doctrine applies (*see supra,* §10).

c. **Invasion of chattel interest:** [§181]   The defendant's volitional act (or some force set in motion thereby) must have resulted in either a *"dispossession" or* an *"intermeddling"* with the chattel of another. [Rest. 2d §217] (The principal reason for this distinction concerns the damages requirement, below.)

    (1) **"Dispossession":** [§182]   "Dispossession" refers to conduct amounting to the defendant's assertion of a proprietary interest in the chattel over the interests of the rightful owner. Examples include theft or destruction of the chattel, or even a barring of the rightful owner's access to it.

    (2) **"Intermeddling":** [§183]   "Intermeddling" embraces conduct by the defendant that does *not* challenge the rightful owner's interest in the chattel, although the defendant may have gone so far as to carry the chattel away. "Intermeddling" includes throwing a stone at another's automobile, beating another's animals, or stampeding another's herd of cattle.

d. **Plaintiff in possession or entitled to immediate possession:** [§184]   This is the same as in a trespass to land; the plaintiff must either be in actual possession or must have the right to immediate possession. (*See supra,* §§166-167.)

e. **Causation:** [§185]   As with a trespass to land, the invasion must have been legally caused by the defendant's intentional act or a force set in motion thereby. (Again, for further discussion of this element, *see supra,* §17.)

f. **Damages:** [§186]   When the defendant's conduct amounts to a *"dispossession,"* or the defendant otherwise deprives the plaintiff of the chattel's use, the plaintiff can recover for loss of possession (*e.g.,* rental value) even if the chattel itself has not been damaged. In cases of dispossession, the plaintiff may choose to sue for conversion of chattels (*see infra*). But if the defendant's act accomplishes only an *"intermeddling"* short of interfering with plaintiff's possession, a trespass action will not lie absent a showing of *actual damage* to the chattel. [Glidden v. Szybiak, 63 A.2d 233 (N.H. 1948)] (As to punitive damages, *see supra,* §23.)

3. **Conversion of Chattels:** [§187]   Prima facie case:

> *Act by Defendant*
> *Intent*
> *Invasion of Chattel Interest*
> *Plaintiff in Possession or Entitled to Immediate Possession*
> *Causation*

a. **Act by defendant:** [§188]   There must be a volitional movement by the defendant of some part of his body that results in an interference with another's possession of her chattels.

b. **Intent:** [§189]   The defendant need only have intended *to deal with the chattel in the manner in which he actually did deal with it.* Thus, if the defendant did to the chattel what he intended to do, it is no defense that he was *not* a conscious wrongdoer (as where he mistakenly thought he was the owner). [Rest. 2d §244]

    (1) **Example:** A towing company is liable for conversion when it refuses to deliver an impounded car until outstanding charges are paid—even though it mistakenly believes it has a lien on the car for such charges. [Murrell v. Trio Towing Service, Inc., 294 So. 2d 331 (Fla. 1974); *but see* Simonian v. Patterson, 27 Cal. App. 4th 773 (1994)—no conversion in helping daughter move belongings that appeared to be hers]

    (2) **Note:** Remember the possibility of invoking *negligence* or *strict liability* as bases for other actions where the requisite intent to establish a conversion cannot be shown.

c. **Invasion of chattel interest of another:** [§190]   The invasion required for a conversion claim is greater than that required for a trespass to chattels claim. The following invasions will suffice:

    (1) **Serious dispossession:** [§191]   Where the defendant takes a chattel from another without the other's consent, bars the possessor's access to her chattel, or obtains possession of a chattel by fraud, there is a conversion. [Russell-Vaughn Ford v. Rouse, 206 So. 2d 371 (Ala. 1968)]

        (a) **Compare—trespass to chattels:** [§192]   However, where the defendant merely intermeddles with the owner's rights in the chattel rather than dispossesses the owner of a substantial number of these rights, the owner has at most a trespass claim against the defendant. [Zaslow v. Kroenert, 29 Cal. 2d 541 (1946)]

(2) **Destroying or altering:** [§193]   Where the defendant destroys or materially alters a chattel, there is a conversion.

(3) **Unauthorized use by bailee:** [§194]   Where the defendant receives possession of the chattel as bailee and uses it in such a manner as to constitute a *material breach* of his authority, there is a conversion.

    (a) **Note:** An important factor is whether any harm to the chattel was caused by *or during* the improper use (*e.g.,* car rented for trip to Baltimore, driven instead to Miami, where it is seriously damaged in a collision). This is usually enough to constitute a conversion—even if the harm was entirely accidental and *not the fault of the bailee!* [Perham v. Coney, 117 Mass. 102 (1875)]

(4) **Buying or receiving stolen property:** [§195]   When the defendant buys or receives stolen property even though he acts in good faith, there is a conversion, because this still involves the requisite intent to assert ownership rights and to deal with the chattel in a manner inconsistent with the rights of the true owner. [Rest. 2d §229]

(5) **Selling or disposing of stolen property:** [§196]   If the defendant sells or otherwise disposes of the stolen property, even though acting in good faith, there is a conversion.

(6) **Misdelivering a chattel:** [§197]   If the defendant misdelivers a chattel, there is a conversion even though the defendant acts in good faith. This covers the situation where a bailee, acting under an innocent mistake, delivers the chattel to the wrong person; or where he violates some condition in delivering it, even though he did deliver to the right person. For example, if the bailor says, "Give this ring to X if he pays you $10," and bailee delivers the ring without receiving $10, there is a conversion. [Marshall & Michel Grain Co. v. Kansas City, Ft. Scott & Memphis Railroad, 75 S.W. 638 (Mo. 1903); Baer v. Slater, 158 N.E. 328 (Mass. 1927)]

(7) **Refusing to surrender a chattel on demand:** [§198]   Where the acquisition itself was not wrongful, there must be a demand for return of the chattel before there can be a conversion. [Rest. 2d §237; *and see* Sporting Goods Distributors, Inc. v. Whitney, 498 F. Supp. 1088 (N.D. Fla. 1980)]

    (a) **But note:** A carrier or bailee (*e.g.,* finder) in possession of the chattel is privileged to make a *qualified* refusal to deliver, for the purpose of investigating the claimant's right to the chattel.

(8) **Application—multiple acts of conversion:** [§199]   Note that a defendant's conduct may result in *several* distinct invasions of the plaintiff's interest—*i.e.,* several different acts of conversion. For example, if D steals the chattel, sells it to an innocent purchaser, later buys it back, and then refuses to give it to P upon demand, D has committed four separate acts of conversion.

d. **Plaintiff in possession or entitled to immediate possession:** [§200]   This is the same as in a trespass to land; the plaintiff must be in actual possession or have the right to immediate possession. (*See supra,* §§166-167.)

e. **Causation:** [§201]   This is also the same as in preceding sections (*see supra*, §§176, 185).

f. **Remedies:** [§202]   Where the defendant's conduct amounts to a "dispossession" (*i.e.,* an assertion of ownership rights in the chattel inconsistent with the rights of the true owner), the plaintiff will often have a choice of actions:

   (1) **Replevin, detinue, or claim and delivery:** [§203]   The plaintiff may obtain return of the chattel and collect damages for its detention.

   (2) **Forced-sale damages:** [§204]   The plaintiff may recover the *value* of the chattel *plus damages* for the dispossession. Hence, satisfaction (*i.e.,* payment) of the judgment operates as a *forced sale of the chattel to the defendant.* (*See* Remedies Summary.)

   (a) **Measure of value:** [§205]   The measure of recovery is ordinarily the market value of the goods at *the time of the conversion* (plus interest to date of suit). [Nephi Processing Plant, Inc. v. Talbott, 247 F.2d 771 (10th Cir. 1957)]

   1) *Where the property has a fluctuating value,* some courts allow the plaintiff to recover the highest value between the time of the conversion and the time of trial. [United States v. Merchants Mutual Bonding Co., 242 F. Supp. 465 (N.D. Iowa 1965)]

   2) *Where property has no market value,* resort may be had to replacement value or to the actual value of the property to the plaintiff. [Jensen v. Chicago & Western Indiana Railroad, 419 N.E.2d 578 (Ill. 1981)—spare rods for antique steam locomotives]

   (b) **Effect of offer to return:** [§206]   An offer by the defendant to return the chattel does not affect the defendant's basic liability, but it will *mitigate* damages recoverable if the defendant acquired the property innocently and in good faith—provided he made the offer to return promptly after learning that the plaintiff was the rightful owner, and provided the chattel was not impaired in value or condition since originally converted. [Rest. 2d §922]

   (3) **Compare—trespass to chattels:** [§207]   Under a trespass theory, the plaintiff can recover damages for the dispossession, but she does not concern herself with the location of the chattel (*i.e.,* plaintiff either has it back, or the chattel is completely destroyed, etc.).

D. DEFENSES AND PRIVILEGED INVASIONS OF LAND AND CHATTELS

1. **Consent:** [§208]   The plaintiff's consent (expressly or by conduct) to the invasion of her land or chattels operates as a defense, so that no action by her to impose such liability for such invasion will lie. (*See supra,* §§80-83.) However, consent may not be effective: as to trespasses that go beyond the scope of the consent; if consent was obtained through fraud, duress, or mistake; if the person giving consent

lacked capacity; etc. [*See supra,* §§84-98; *and see* Copeland v. Hubbard Broadcasting, Inc., 526 N.W.2d 402 (Minn. 1994)—fact question whether consent given for educational purposes extended to secret videotaping for later broadcast; *but see* Desnick v. American Broadcasting Cos., *supra,* §87—consent given to reporters posing as patients extended to their later reporting on what they observed]

2. **Privileged Invasion of Another's Land to Reclaim Chattels:** [§209]   The scope of this privilege depends on where the fault lies for the presence of the defendant's chattels on plaintiff's land:

a. **Landowner at fault:** [§210]   Where the presence of the chattels on plaintiff's land is due to the fact that the *plaintiff has tortiously dispossessed the defendant* of them (or has received the chattels from some third person who she *knows* has tortiously dispossessed the defendant), the defendant has a *complete* privilege to enter the land for the purpose of retaking possession.

(1) **Reasonable entry:** [§211]   The defendant must effect the entry at a reasonable time and in a reasonable manner. [Rest. 2d §198]

(2) **Demand generally required:** [§212]   Additionally, before entry, the defendant must make a demand for permission to enter the land for the purpose of reclaiming the chattel—*unless* it appears that such demand would be futile or that delay would subject the property to danger of harm.

(3) **Extent of privilege:** [§213]   The privilege is *"complete"*—meaning the defendant cannot be held liable for any harm done to the plaintiff's land in the reasonable exercise of the privilege.

(a) **Limitation—no mistake:** [§214]   The defendant is liable for trespass if he breaks and enters a building other than that in which his chattels are kept. An honest mistake will *not* justify a trespass.

(b) **Force to person of landowner:** [§215]   If the plaintiff resists the defendant's lawful attempts to come onto the plaintiff's land, the defendant is privileged to use *reasonable, nondeadly force* to the plaintiff's person, subject to the same conditions as in the exercise of the privilege of recapture of the chattel (*see supra,* §§130-134). In other words, it must appear not only that the defendant was tortiously dispossessed by the plaintiff or some third party in complicity with the plaintiff, and that a demand for return of the chattel was made or was unnecessary, but also that the recapture is effected promptly—*"fresh pursuit."* [Arlowski v. Foglio, 135 A. 397 (Conn. 1926)]

b. **Chattel owner at fault:** [§216]   Where the defendant's chattels are on the plaintiff's land through the *defendant's own fault* (*e.g.,* where the defendant negligently allows his cattle to wander), the defendant has *no privilege of any type* to go onto the plaintiff's property to recover possession. Rather, he must bring an action for replevin, detinue, claim and delivery, etc. [Rest. 2d §200]

c. **Act of God:** [§217]   Where the defendant's chattels are on the plaintiff's land through the fault of *neither the plaintiff nor the defendant,* but, rather, because of "an act of God" (*e.g.,* storm, wind, flood, etc.), the defendant has an *incomplete* privilege to enter the land to reclaim the chattel.

(1) **Extent of privilege:** [§218]   The privilege is *"incomplete"* in that the defendant is liable for actual damage done to the plaintiff's land in the process of recapturing the chattel, although the defendant is not liable for damage caused merely from the chattel being deposited there. [Rest. 2d §198, comment k]

    (a) **Example:** A freak windstorm causes D's tower to fall onto P's land, where it crashes into P's house. In removing the tower, D tramples P's flower beds. D is liable for the damage to the flower beds but not to the house.

(2) **Conditions of privilege:** [§219]   Other than the fact that the privilege is "incomplete," the conditions and scope of privilege are the same as where the landowner is at fault (above); *i.e.,* entry must be made at a reasonable time and in a reasonable manner, and ordinarily a request for permission to enter is required.

(3) **Caution—necessity to determine underlying causal factor:** [§220] Where the defendant's chattels are deposited on the plaintiff's land through flood, storm, etc., it is always a question of fact whether the causal factor is the storm or flood ("act of God") or the *defendant's negligence* in failing to secure his chattels, properly construct his property, etc. If the cause is the defendant's negligence, the defendant has *no* privilege (*see supra,* §216).

d. **Third party at fault:** [§221]   Where the defendant's chattels are on the plaintiff's land because of the tortious dispossession *by a third party,* but the plaintiff is not aware of the presence of the chattels on the land (or if she does know of their presence, is not aware that the third party tortiously dispossessed the defendant), the defendant again has an *incomplete* privilege to enter the land to reclaim the chattel. [Rest. 2d §198]

e. **Limitation—privilege cannot be based on mistake:** [§222]   In all of the above cases, the defendant must *in fact* be entitled to possession of the chattels, both at the time he was dispossessed and at the time he seeks to enter the plaintiff's land for the purpose of reclaiming the chattels. If the defendant is *not* in fact entitled to possession of the chattels, he can in no case claim the privilege—even though he reasonably and in good faith believes that he is the owner of the chattels. Here again, an honest mistake will not excuse a trespass.

3. Privilege to Exclude or Evict Trespassing Chattels of Another

a. **Conditions of privilege:** [§223]   A defendant is *completely* privileged to use reasonable force to evict or exclude the chattels of another, when such force is *reasonably believed to be necessary* to protect the defendant's interest in the exclusive possession of his land or chattels (*e.g.,* defendant's shooting a neighbor's dogs in defendant's chicken coop). [Rest. 2d §260]

b. **Determining reasonableness:** [§224]   The "reasonableness" of the force used should be judged by (i) the *necessity for immediate action* to prevent the injury or destruction threatened by the invading chattels; (ii) whether the *force used was excessive* or only that necessary to terminate or prevent the intrusion; and (iii) the *comparative values* of the property threatened and the chattels to which the force is applied—*i.e.,* in the above example, are the dogs worth more than the chickens?

4. **Privileged Invasion of Another's Land or Chattels as a Public Necessity**

    a. **Averting public disaster:** [§225]   A person—public official or private citizen—is *completely* privileged to enter land or interfere with chattels in the possession of another if necessary—or if it *reasonably appears* necessary—to avert a *public disaster.* [South Dakota Department of Health v. Heim, 357 N.W.2d 522 (S.D. 1984)—state's destruction of P's diseased elk herd was privileged where necessary to avert public health risk; Rest. 2d §196]

        (1) **Extent of privilege:** [§226]   This is a *complete* privilege; *i.e.,* the defendant is not liable for any damage or destruction to the land or chattels involved, as long as this was done in the proper exercise of the privilege.

            (a) **Damage to improvements:** The defendant is also completely privileged to break and enter fences and any buildings, *including dwellings.*

            (b) **Force to the person:** Moreover, if the property owner resists the defendant's attempt to enter the land or deal with the chattels, the defendant may use whatever force is reasonably necessary to effect the privilege, including *deadly* force if necessary.

    b. **Detouring around obstructed highway:** [§227]   A traveler on a public road that is, or *reasonably appears* to be, impassable has an *incomplete* privilege to enter neighboring lands in the possession of another, "as a matter of public right" in continuing the journey. [Rest. 2d §195]

        (1) **Conditions of privilege—reasonable need:** [§228]   The privilege exists only if the entry "reasonably appears" to be necessary. Courts consider: (i) the availability of alternate routes; (ii) the urgency of the traveler's business; and (iii) whether the obstruction of the road could have been removed by the traveler with reasonable efforts.

        (2) **Extent of privilege:** [§229]   This is an *incomplete* privilege—meaning the defendant is liable for any *actual* harm caused to the land during proper exercise of the privilege.

        (3) **Limitation—traveler at fault:** [§230]   There is no privilege at all if the obstruction on the road was caused by the *fault of the traveler.*

    c. **Media:** [§231]   The First Amendment does not give the media a privilege that allows reporters to enter land whenever they seek information—even important information. [Green Valley School, Inc. v. Cowles Florida Broadcasting, Inc., 237 So. 2d 810 (Fla. 1976); Le Mistral v. Columbia Broadcasting System, 61 App. Div. 2d 491 (1978)]

5. **Privileged Invasion of Another's Land or Chattels as a Private Necessity**

a. **Conditions of privilege:** [§232]   A person is privileged to enter land or interfere with chattels in the possession of another where such entry or interference is—or reasonably appears to be—necessary to protect *any person* (the actor, the owner of the land or chattels, or some third person) from *death or serious bodily harm;* or, where it is—or reasonably appears to be—necessary to protect *any land or chattels* from *destruction or injury.* [Rest. 2d §§197, 263]

   (1) **"Reasonableness" limitation:** The entry or interference must be reasonable considering the harm that it is intended to prevent, as compared with the harm to land or chattels that it is likely to cause.

b. **Extent of privilege**

   (1) **Force to person or property:** [§233]   The defendant may break and enter fences and buildings, *including dwellings.* Similarly, if the owner of the land or chattels resists the invasion, the defendant may use "reasonable" force to effect the privilege. (However, it is doubtful that deadly force would be privileged, since the policy factors in cases where the invasion is a *public* necessity would not be present here.)

   (2) **Privilege incomplete:** [§234]   The privilege is *incomplete;* the defendant is liable for all harm done to the land or chattels in exercise of this privilege. [Vincent v. Lake Erie Transportation Co., 124 N.W. 221 (Minn. 1910)—D liable for damages to P's dock resulting from D's tying his boat to P's dock to ride out a storm]

c. **Supersedes owner's privilege to exclude trespassers:** [§235]   The privilege to invade another's land or chattels as a private necessity *supersedes* the privilege of the possessor of land or chattels to use reasonable force to protect her property from invasion. Hence, any force used by the landowner to exclude the defendant is wrongful and subjects the landowner to liability. Moreover, the landowner is liable to the defendant for the harm the defendant suffers as a result of being denied entry (*e.g.,* loss of boat, etc.). [Ploof v. Putnam, 71 A. 188 (Vt. 1908)]

   (1) **Note:** This same principle applies to *all of the entry privileges* discussed in this section.

6. **Privileged Invasion of Land or Chattels to Abate a Nuisance**

a. **Conditions of privilege:** [§236]   A "nuisance" is any unreasonable interference with the use or enjoyment of another's property; *see infra,* §§924 *et seq.* A defendant is *completely* privileged to invade the land or chattels of another for the purpose of abating a private nuisance created or maintained on the land or chattels of the other, subject to the following conditions:

   (1) **Ownership or possessory interest:** [§237]   The defendant must be the owner or possessor (*e.g.,* tenant) of land or chattels injuriously affected by the nuisance.

   (2) **Demand:** [§238]   The defendant must first make a demand that the nuisance be abated, unless it reasonably appears that such demand is impractical or useless.

(3) **Reasonableness:** [§239]   The defendant must enter at a reasonable time and use only *reasonable force* to effect the abatement. [Rest. 2d §201]

b.   **Extent of privilege:** [§240]   Since this is a *complete* privilege, the defendant is not liable for any harm resulting to land or chattels in the proper exercise of the privilege. But the privilege does *not* extend to using force against a resisting property owner. *Rationale:* There is less urgency here than in the "public necessity" or "private necessity" privileges—so that if the owner resists, the actor should withdraw and seek judicial relief. [Rest. 2d §201, comment k]

c.   **Compare—public nuisance:** [§241]   The privilege discussed in this section applies only to the abatement of a *private nuisance*—i.e., one affecting the defendant's enjoyment of his own land. If the nuisance is a public one (affecting all persons or property in substantially the same manner), a private individual generally has *no* privilege of abatement unless the public nuisance is causing him some injury "peculiar in kind"—so that as to him it is a private nuisance as well. (*See infra,* §§926-928.)

7.   **Effect of Misconduct by Actor**

a.   **While exercising privilege:** [§242]   As noted above, many of these privileges are conditioned on "reasonableness"; *i.e.,* the defendant must enter at a reasonable time, in a reasonable manner, etc. If the defendant is unreasonable in coming onto the land (using excessive force, etc.), the required conditions do not exist and the defendant's entry is not privileged. [Rest. 2d §214(1)]

b.   **Subsequent to exercise of privilege:** [§243]   A related problem is the effect of misconduct by a defendant *subsequent* to an initially privileged intrusion. If, after properly entering through an open gate to reclaim his chattels, the defendant unnecessarily tears down the landowner's fences to leave, the modern view is that the defendant does *not* lose the privilege by virtue of his subsequent tortious conduct. Thus, the defendant is liable only for damages caused by his subsequent misconduct; and no damages can be recovered for the initially privileged intrusion. [Rest. 2d §214(2)] (The old view held the defendant liable for the entire episode under the doctrine of "trespass ab initio.")

II. NEGLIGENCE

chapter approach

Negligence is the most important area of tort law. It is also the most frequent subject of exam questions, both because of its importance and because it requires special care in applying the bare rules to the varied fact situations. Whereas intentional torts tend to be a series of cubby-holes and categories—both in the prima facie case and in the privileges—this is not true in negligence. Here, there are a few critically important standards and some rules. Your task is not so much remembering them as it is *applying* them to the facts.

Some general guidelines for you to follow:

1. The most important habit to acquire is to go through the *sequence of elements* methodically in every case. This means finding an appropriate act or actionable omission *before* turning to the issue of "duty," and concluding that there was a breach of duty *before* considering causation. Analyzing each element in turn allows you to determine whether the troublesome issue is duty or causation, and allows you to address each in the terms set out in this chapter.

2. Be sure to look at the relationship between the plaintiff and the defendant and identify the *appropriate duty* to impose on the defendant. You must *never assume* that the defendant owes a duty of care. Even though that is usually the case, you must explain why a duty exists in each case.

3. Remember that the plaintiff must show actual cause ("cause in fact") *and* proximate cause ("legal cause"), and you should discuss each of these elements.

4. Finally, determine whether the facts suggest any *defense* to the negligence (*e.g.*, contributory negligence, etc.). Defenses are usually less important in negligence cases; the focus is almost always on the prima facie case.

A. INTRODUCTION [§244]

The second broad basis for tort liability is negligence. Here, liability may be imposed for results that were not intended by the defendant. Still, this is *not* "liability without fault" (strict liability). It must be shown in every case that the defendant was *at fault*—*i.e.*, that the defendant failed to perform some *duty* that the law required of the defendant under the circumstances. Depending on the circumstances, there may be either (or both) of two types of duties owed: (i) the duty to conduct oneself as a reasonable person would under the same or similar circumstances—the so-called duty of due care; or (ii) some special duty, imposed by statute or case law, which may be *in addition to*, *or in place of*, the duty of due care (*see infra*, §§437 *et seq.*).

B. NEGLIGENCE (BASED ON THE "DUTY OF DUE CARE") [§245]

Prima facie case: *Act or Actionable Omission by Defendant*
Duty of Due Care
Breach of Duty (Lack of due care)

> *Actual Cause* ("Cause in fact")
> *Proximate Cause* ("Legal cause")
> *Damages*

1. **Act or Actionable Omission by Defendant:** [§246]   In addition to the type of "act" required for intentional torts (*i.e.*, a volitional movement by defendant of some part of his body), liability for negligence may be predicated on a willful omission to act *when under an affirmative duty to act*. Thus, as discussed in the "special duties" section, *infra*, the law imposes certain affirmative duties of care (*e.g.*, the duty of a person charged with the care of another to aid that person in an emergency). Failure to perform such a duty is ordinarily not a sufficient "act" for intentional tort purposes, but it may be sufficient for purposes of negligence. [L. S. Ayres & Co. v. Hicks, 40 N.E.2d 334 (Ind. 1942)]

2. **Duty of Due Care**

   a. **"Reasonable person" standard:** [§247]   Each person owes a duty to behave as a reasonable person would *under the same or similar circumstances*. [Brown v. Kendall, 60 Mass. 292 (1850); Rest. 2d §283]

      (1) **Objective test:** [§248]   This is an objective standard, and it is therefore immaterial that the defendant believed in good faith (subjectively) that he was being careful. The issue is *not* what the defendant believed, but how the *"reasonable person of ordinary prudence"* would have acted. [Vaughan v. Menlove, 132 Eng. Rep. 490 (1837)]

         (a) **Note:** The test for duty is not based on how any specific individual or group would have acted. For this reason, it is improper to instruct the jurors in a negligence trial to decide the case by asking themselves how *they* as individuals would have acted. The question is how the reasonable person would have acted (although jurors no doubt consider themselves "reasonable persons"). [The Germanic, 196 U.S. 589 (1905)]

      (2) **Standard remains same under all circumstances:** [§249]   Although the amount of care and the kind of conduct required will vary with the circumstances, the *standard itself never varies*. It is always whatever care the reasonable person would have exercised *under the circumstances*. [Triestram v. Way, 281 N.W. 420 (Mich. 1938)]

         (a) **Application—risk of harm:** The greater the foreseeable risk of harm involved, the greater the care required; *e.g.*, the reasonable person no doubt handles chemicals more carefully than less dangerous products. Whatever the situation, the amount of care required is determined by the reasonable person standard. [Stewart v. Motts, 654 A.2d 535 (Pa. 1995)—single standard of due care applies to handling of gasoline]

         (b) **Application—emergency:** Likewise, certain conduct may be acceptable in *emergency* but not in nonemergency situations because the need for immediate action justifies acts that otherwise could be considered unreasonable. However, the standard still remains the same—*i.e.*, how the reasonable person would have acted under the circumstances (*i.e.*, in the emergency). [Rest. 2d §296; Rivera v. New York City Transit Authority, 77 N.Y.2d 322 (1991)]

(c) **Exception for common carriers:** [§250]   A large number of courts hold that the duty of due care is inadequate when the defendant is a common carrier transporting passengers for hire; *i.e.*, a higher standard is required. [Widmyer v. Southeast Skyways, Inc., 584 P.2d 1 (Alaska 1978)—"the highest degree of care"; *and see infra*, §477]

b. **How standard established:** [§251]   The reasonable person standard depends in any particular case on how the trier of fact thinks a reasonable person would have acted. Thus, it is always *dependent upon proof of the circumstances* that existed at the time of the defendant's conduct—*e.g.*, the location of the parties, the conditions of traffic, etc. If that proof is open to differing interpretations, the trier of fact determines what a reasonable person would have done under the facts as found, and measures the defendant's conduct against this standard. Even if the facts are agreed upon, the trier of fact will decide how a reasonable person would have acted under those facts—if different conclusions could be drawn.

(1) **Effect of custom:** [§252]   Custom in the community is admissible as *evidence* of the standard of care owed, but it is *never conclusive* (indeed, some customs may be found to be negligent). The fact that the defendant has acted (or failed to act) as others in the community customarily do may provide a clue as to the reasonableness or unreasonableness of the conduct. The test remains whether the reasonable person would have so acted under the same or similar circumstances. [Texas & Pacific Railway v. Behymer, 189 U.S. 468 (1903); The T. J. Hooper, 60 F.2d 737 (2d Cir.), *cert. denied*, 287 U.S. 662 (1932); Rest. 2d §295A]

(a) **Proof of compliance with custom:** [§253]   Although not binding on courts, proof of a defendant's *compliance* with custom may indicate to the court that an adverse decision will affect many people (*i.e.*, an entire industry may have to alter its customs). It may also suggest that there is no better way to perform the task in question. [Williams v. New York Rapid Transit, 272 N.Y. 366 (1936); Low v. Park Price Co., 503 P.2d 291 (Idaho 1972)]

1) **Example:** P, a motel guest, claimed that D, the motel owner, had a duty to provide emergency lighting in each room in case of a power failure. Evidence that no motel or hotel provided such emergency lighting was properly admitted, since although industry custom is not conclusive as to what is reasonably prudent conduct in a given case, it may be a useful guide, unless it is apparent that under the circumstances of the case, no reasonable person would conform to industry-wide custom. [LaVallee v. Vermont Motor Inns, Inc., 569 A.2d 1073 (Vt. 1989)]

(b) **Proof of deviation from custom:** [§254]   Showing of the defendant's *deviation* from customary conduct in the community may aid the plaintiff because it shows the court that a determination of negligence in the case will *not* upset the practices of an entire industry. Moreover, the fact that others perform the task in a safer manner suggests that an alternative not only was feasible, but that the defendant knew or should have known of the custom. [Levine v. Russell Blaine Co., 273 N.Y. 386 (1937); 42 Colum. L. Rev. 1147]

(2) **Effect of compliance with statute:** [§255]   The fact that the defendant complied with applicable statutes governing the conduct is admissible on the question of whether the defendant's conduct was negligent, but again, it is *not conclusive*. The standard of "due care" is still the reasonable person test, and the statute may or may not have demanded such a level of conduct. [Clinkscales v. Carver, 22 Cal. 2d 72 (1943)]

  (a) **Example:** The fact that the defendant manufactured its drugs in accordance with government regulations did not absolve it of negligence, where the regulations were minimal and a reasonable person would have exercised greater care under the circumstances. [Stromsodt v. Parke-Davis & Co., 257 F. Supp. 991 (D.N.D. 1966)]

  (b) **Exception:** [§256]   If the facts closely resemble those contemplated in the statute and the court concludes that the statute's command is reasonable (rather than minimal), compliance may satisfy the duty of care. [Rest. 2d §288C; Josephson v. Meyers, 429 A.2d 877 (Conn. 1980); Espinoza v. Elgin, Joliet & Eastern Railway, 649 N.E.2d 1323 (Ill. 1995)—administrative approval of grade crossing is conclusive in tort action]

  (c) **Compare—conduct in violation of statute:** [§257]   However, if the defendant's conduct *violated* some applicable statute (the conduct fell below the statutory standard), the plaintiff may be able to establish negligence simply by proving the violation. (*See infra*, §§438-454.)

c. **To whom does the standard apply?** [§258]   The standard applies to all persons—the reasonable person standard is flexible enough to cover any individual or class of individuals:

(1) **Children:** [§259]   Minors are held to the reasonable person standard, with the age, intelligence, and experience of the individual being considered as *part of the circumstances*. Thus, the question is: What is to be expected of the reasonable person having this child's actual age, intelligence, and experience, with regard to such matters as judgment, memory, and risk perception? [Peterson v. Taylor, 316 N.W.2d 869 (Iowa 1982)]

  (a) **Minority view:** [§260]   A few courts disagree and attempt to set up separate standards for children—*e.g.*, those under age seven are conclusively presumed incapable of negligence, while those seven to fourteen are rebuttably presumed incapable, etc. [Price v. Kitsap Transit, 886 P.2d 556 (Wash. 1994)—four-year-old child conclusively presumed incapable of negligence]

(b) **Exception—adult activities:** [§261] Where children engage in dangerous activities normally undertaken only by adults (*e.g.*, operating cars, airplanes, motorboats, etc.), **no special allowance is made** for their immaturity or limited experience. They are held to the same standard as an adult. [Robinson v. Lindsay, 598 P.2d 392 (Wash. 1979)—driving a snowmobile]

(2) **Persons with physical disability:** [§262] Persons with physical disabilities (crippled, blind, deaf, etc.) are held to the reasonable person standard, with their disability as one of the circumstances. [*See, e.g.*, Hill v. Glenwood, 100 N.W. 522 (Iowa 1904); Rest. 2d §283C]

(a) **Knowledge of disability one of the "circumstances":** [§263] Thus, such persons are charged with knowledge that they have such disability, and may be found negligent for engaging in any activity that a **reasonable person with the same disability** would not have attempted.

1) **Example:** If D has poor vision, she is held only to the standard of care that a reasonable person with such vision would exercise. But if a reasonable person would realize that it was unreasonably unsafe for her to drive a car, D's driving under normal circumstances would be negligent. [Roberts v. Ring, 173 N.W. 437 (Minn. 1919)]

(b) **Compare—voluntary intoxication:** [§264] If the physical impairment results from voluntary intoxication, it is **disregarded** in determining liability; *i.e.*, a person who uses alcohol or drugs is held to the same standard as would be expected if she were not under their influence. [42 Iowa L. Rev. 38]

(3) **Adults with mental deficiency:** [§265] Adults are judged by the reasonable person standard **without any allowance** for their mental deficiency. Hence, although a **child's** intelligence is taken into account in determining whether he was negligent (*supra*), an adult's is not! This is true whether the defendant's limitation is subnormal intelligence or outright insanity. [Breunig v. American Family Insurance Co., 173 N.W.2d 619 (Wis. 1970); Rest. 2d §283B]

(a) **Rationale:** The difficulty of determining what kind of mental aberration will lessen the care owed, plus the fear of complicating tort law the way the insanity defense has complicated criminal trials, are some of the reasons for this rule. (*See* Criminal Law Summary.)

(b) **Compare—contributory negligence:** [§266] Note, however, that some cases have allowed evidence of the **plaintiff's** low intelligence in determining whether his conduct was **contributorily** negligent. [Lynch v. Rosenthal, 396 S.W.2d 272 (Mo. 1965); *and see infra*, §650]

(4) **Knowledge and skills:** [§267] All persons are held to certain **minimum** standards in their activities. [Delair v. McAdoo, 188 A. 181 (Pa.

1936)] If they have acquired special competence, they are held to a standard commensurate with their *superior* knowledge or skills. [Rest. 2d §289(b)]

(a) **Profession or trade:** [§268]   If the defendant undertakes to render any service in a recognized profession or trade (doctor, attorney, plumber, etc.), she is held, at a *minimum*, to the standard of care customarily exercised by members of that profession or trade—whether or not she personally possesses such skills. [Heath v. Swift Wings, Inc., 252 S.E.2d 256 (N.C. 1979); Rest. 2d §299A]

1) **General rule—"same or similar" community standard:** [§269]   Generally, persons engaged in a trade or profession are required to exercise the degree of care that would be exercised by members of their profession in "same or similar" communities. [Rest. 2d §299A]

a) **Rationale:** As the dissemination of knowledge and information increases, professionals and those in the trades in most localities are not only confronting the same problems, but have the same knowledge at their disposal to solve those problems. This means that the standard will be "national" (when there are no significant differences among communities).

2) **Medical profession**

a) **Older view—local standard:** [§270]   Some early cases limited the standard of care for physicians to that of other physicians in the *same* community or locality.

b) **Modern trend—"same or similar" community standard:** [§271]   However, this distinction is disappearing in modern cases so that, as with other professionals, courts are holding that physicians must meet the standard of care existing in the "same *or similar*" communities—and experts from such communities may testify as to the appropriate standards (*i.e.*, country doctors will be held to the same standard of care as other country doctors, but not necessarily to the same standard as big-city doctors). [Tallbull v. Whitney, 564 P.2d 162 (Mont. 1977)]

1/ **And note:** Some courts impose a *national* standard of care on *nationally certified* medical specialists. [Robbins v. Footer, 553 F.2d 123 (D.C. Cir. 1977)—board-certified obstetrician; Morrison v. MacNamara, 407 A.2d 555 (D.C. 1979)—certified laboratory and medical technician]

c) **Establishing a standard:** [§272]   To prevail, the plaintiff must establish the particular standard of medical care that is required. Since the standard is measured in relation to professional understandings, the plaintiff must generally present expert testimony to establish the standard.

1/ **Note:** The modern trend permits experts in one specialty to testify against those in another field of medicine if they have sufficient knowledge of the other field. [Melville v. Southward, 791 P.2d 383 (Colo. 1990)—orthopedic surgeon must be shown to be familiar with standards of podiatry or the standards of the two must be shown to be substantially identical]

2/ **Obvious-occurrence exception:** [§273] Where a physician's conduct is so egregious and obvious that a layperson could identify the breach of duty, no expert testimony is needed to establish a duty of care. [Heimer v. Privratsky, 434 N.W.2d 357 (N.D. 1989)—allowing toxic substance to come in contact with patient's eye obviously negligent to layperson]

d) **Controversial techniques:** [§274] When respectable medical opinions differ as to the best technique, courts will allow a doctor to follow either view [Furey v. Thomas Jefferson University Hospital, 472 A.2d 1083 (Pa. 1984)] or even one followed by a "respectable minority" of the medical profession [Head v. Phillips, 537 S.W.2d 291 (Tex. 1976)].

e) **Informed consent:** [§275] Doctors have a duty to disclose relevant information about benefits and risks inherent in proposed treatment, alternatives to that treatment, and the likely results if the patient remains untreated. [Canterbury v. Spence, 464 F.2d 772 (D.C. Cir. 1972); Moore v. Regents of the University of California, 51 Cal. 3d 120 (1990)—relevant information includes physician's research interest in body parts that patient is agreeing to have removed; *and see supra*, §93]

1/ **Standard of disclosure:** [§276] The courts are split between those that require only the level of disclosure customary in the medical profession [Woolley v. Henderson, 418 A.2d 1123 (Me. 1980)] and those that require disclosure of what the doctor should reasonably recognize would be material to the patient's decision [Korman v. Mallin, 858 P.2d 1145 (Alaska 1993)].

a/ **Applications:** Disclosure of a 1-3% chance of pregnancy has been required. [Hartke v. McKelway, 707 F.2d 1544 (D.C. Cir. 1983)] But a trier of fact could conclude that a chance of death of 8.6 in one million need not be disclosed. [Smith v. Shannon, 666 P.2d 351 (Wash. 1983)]

2/ **Exceptions:** [§277] Only two exceptions to the doctor's duty of disclosure are recognized:

a/ **Emergencies:** [§278] There is no duty of disclosure in an emergency situation (*e.g.*, where the patient is unconscious or unable to comprehend, and prompt medical treatment is required).

b/ **Therapeutic privilege:** [§279] Where the patient is so distraught or unstable that the physician *reasonably* concludes that full disclosure would be *detrimental* to the patient's well-being, there may be no duty to disclose. (But the burden of proving these facts is on the doctor.) [Canterbury v. Spence, *supra*]

3/ **Causation:** [§280] In informed consent cases, most courts hold that the patient must show that if properly informed *neither* the patient *nor a reasonable person* in similar circumstances would have undergone the procedure. [Largey v. Rothman, 540 A.2d 504 (N.J. 1988); Reikes v. Martin, 471 So. 2d 385 (Miss. 1985)]

a/ **Minority view:** Some jurisdictions adopt a subjective standard by which plaintiffs establish causation by persuading the trier of fact that the plaintiff personally would not have consented to the procedure. [Scott v. Bradford, 606 P.2d 554 (Okla. 1980); Arena v. Gingrich, 748 P.2d 547 (Or. 1988)—treating reasonableness of patient's conduct as issue of proximate cause]

(b) **Learners or beginners:** [§281] An inexperienced person who engages in activities involving a known risk of harm to others (*e.g.*, driving a car on a public street) is held to the same standard of care as an experienced reasonable person. *Rationale:* Those who engage in such activities—rather than the innocent victim—should bear the risk of loss. [Dellwo v. Pearson, 107 N.W.2d 859 (Minn. 1961)—operation of motorboat; Rest. 2d §299, comment d]

d. **To whom is the duty of care owed?** [§282] If a reasonable person would *not* have foreseen injury to *anyone* from the conduct, there is no duty owed to any person who is unexpectedly hurt by the defendant's actions. There is a split of authority, however, where the defendant could reasonably have foreseen danger to *someone*.

(1) **The unforeseeable plaintiff**

(a) **Broad view—if duty owed to anyone, duty owed to all:** [§283] The broad view is that the defendant's duty of due care is owed to *anyone* in the world who suffers injuries as a *proximate result* of the defendant's breach of duty. Where the plaintiff is injured by the defendant's negligent act, the defendant is responsible regardless of whether the reasonable person would have foreseen a risk of harm in the circumstances to this particular person, as long as the plaintiff's injuries were *proximately caused* by the defendant's negligence toward someone. (As to what constitutes "proximate cause," *see infra*, §§348 *et seq.*)

   1) **Note:** This is the *"Andrews view,"* referring to the dissenting opinion written by Judge Andrews in the famous *Palsgraf* case. [Palsgraf v. Long Island Railroad, 248 N.Y. 339 (1928)]

(b) **Narrow view—duty owed only to "foreseeable plaintiffs":** [§284] The contrasting view is the *"foreseeable plaintiff"* or *"zone of danger" doctrine* espoused by Judge Cardozo in his majority opinion in the *Palsgraf* case: Defendant owes a duty of care only to those persons as to whom the reasonable person would have foreseen a risk of harm under the circumstances. Therefore, before the defendant may be held liable under any duty of care to the plaintiff, it must appear that the reasonable person would have *foreseen a risk of harm to the plaintiff or a class of persons to which the plaintiff belongs—i.e.*, that plaintiff was a "foreseeable plaintiff," located in a foreseeable "zone of danger." [*See also* Rest. 2d §281(b)]

(c) **Application**

   1) *Palsgraf* **facts:** [§285] The circumstances of the *Palsgraf* case clearly illustrate the division of views noted above. X, a passenger, was running to catch one of D's trains that was beginning to move. In helping X aboard the train, one of D's employees dislodged an innocent-looking package from X's arms. The package contained fireworks which exploded so violently that the concussion knocked over some heavy scales, many feet away at the other end of the platform. The scales fell upon and injured P.

      a) **"Cardozo view":** Under the "Cardozo view," D was not liable. While a risk of harm to X or X's package might have been foreseeable (or even a risk to persons near X if he should trip while being helped or drop the package on someone's feet), a reasonable person would not have foreseen any risk to P (who was a considerable distance away). Hence P was not within the "zone of danger," and D owed her *no duty* of due care. (X, since he knew he was carrying explosives, would owe a duty of due care to a wider group.)

      b) **"Andrews view":** Under the "Andrews view," however, D owed P a duty of due care. In helping a passenger board the moving train, D's duty was owed not only to that passenger and those nearby, but to anyone else in the world who might be injured because of D's careless conduct. (Remember that finding a duty is only one element of the tort. Andrews still had to consider causation questions, among others.)

c) **Comment—limited role of *Palsgraf*:** Although many courts have purported to follow or distinguish *Palsgraf*, harm is rarely caused to an unforeseeable plaintiff. Indeed, there are so few comparable situations that it is hard to identify either view as being the majority or minority position.

2) **Rescuers:** [§286] If the defendant owes a duty to someone, it generally follows that such duty is also owed to any other person who goes to the rescue of the person imperiled. The theory is that "danger invites rescue."

a) **Rationale:** Even under the narrow "Cardozo view," the "zone of danger" includes any person who comes to the rescue of one imperiled by the defendant's conduct. The rescuer, therefore, is as much a foreseeable plaintiff as the person actually imperiled, and hence is within the scope of the defendant's duty. [Wagner v. International Railway, 232 N.Y. 176 (1928)]

b) **Harm caused by rescuer:** [§287] Likewise, the above result and reasoning apply where the rescuer *causes* injury to another in a reasonable rescue attempt. For example, if D negligently imperils X, and Y attempts to come to X's aid, and in so doing injures P, D's duty of due care extends to P. (Same result where the rescuer aggravates the injury to X.)

c) **Defendant as victim of own negligence:** [§288] The same result and reasoning also apply even though the person imperiled by the defendant's conduct is the ***defendant himself***. For example, where D (through his own negligence) has placed himself in a position of peril and P, seeing this, reasonably attempts to come to D's aid and is injured in so doing, D's duty of due care extends to P. [Lowrey v. Horvath, 689 S.W.2d 625 (Mo. 1985)]

d) **Reasonableness limitation:** [§289] Keep in mind, however, that in every case the rescue attempt must not be foolhardy under the circumstances (*see infra*, §647). If the attempt was foolhardy, the original defendant may not be liable for the resulting injuries (*see infra*, §387). In a comparative negligence state, the defendant's liability may be reduced by plaintiff's fault in acting rashly. [Bridges v. Bentley, 769 P.2d 635 (Kan. 1989)]

e) **Limitation—professional rescuers:** [§290] Where professionals undertake rescue operations, it is generally held that the person whose negligence occasioned the need for rescue is *not* liable for harm suffered by the rescuers. This situation is analogous to the case in which a person's carelessness requires the services of firefighters, who injure themselves putting out the fire (*see infra*, §687). [Maltman v. Sauer, 530 P.2d 254 (Wash. 1975)]

(2) **The foreseeable plaintiff:** [§291] The general rule is that a duty is owed to foreseeable plaintiffs.

(a) **Plaintiff injured by acts of third parties**

1) **Controllers of dangerous substances or instrumentalities:** [§292] Those who have dangerous substances or instrumentalities within their control owe a duty to exercise such control as to prevent foreseeable harm to others. Thus, a service station owner who sells gasoline to a six-year-old child owes a duty of care not only to the child but to her playmates as well, since it is foreseeable that one so young might misuse the substance. [Jones v. Robbins, 289 So. 2d 104 (La. 1974)]

2) **Encouraging dangerous acts:** [§293] A defendant has a duty not to create an unreasonable risk of harm from third parties. Thus, a radio station has been held liable for the death of a motorist whose car was forced off the road by a teenager racing to locate a "traveling disc jockey" to win a radio contest. [Weirum v. RKO General, Inc., 15 Cal. 3d 40 (1975)]

3) **Special relationship:** [§294] When a defendant has a special relationship with the victim or a third party, the defendant may have a duty to warn the victim of possible harm from another. Thus, where a doctor or psychotherapist has reason to know that a patient is likely to harm a *specific* third party, the doctor owes a duty to use care to warn the intended victim or the police of the danger. [Tarasoff v. Regents of the University of California, 17 Cal. 3d 425 (1976); Coath v. Jones, 419 A.2d 1249 (Pa. 1980)—employer who negligently hires a rapist for position requiring visits to private homes must advise customers when employment is terminated; Hamman v. County of Maricopa, 775 P.2d 1122 (Ariz. 1989)—psychiatrist who knew or should have known schizophrenic child posed serious danger of violence to others owed duty to child's parents even in absence of specific threat against them; *but see* Thompson v. County of Alameda, 27 Cal. 3d 741 (1980)—correctional authority had no duty to warn neighborhood when it released prisoner who had threatened *general* harm]

a) **Failure to warn patients:** [§295] Most courts emphasize foreseeability in imposing a duty on a physician to those who might be injured by the patient if the physician does not adequately warn the patient about a condition. [Pate v. Threlkel, 661 So. 2d 278 (Fla. 1995)—duty on surgeon who discovers a congenital condition to warn patient's children about the dangers they face; *but see* Tenuto v. Lederle Laboratories, 207 App. Div. 2d 541 (1994)—no duty to warn infant's father about dangers of getting polio from coming into contact with excrement of recently immunized infant; Clark v. Hoek, 174 Cal. App. 3d 208 (1985)—no duty on physician reviewing surgery team at behest of hospital to intervene when he observes malpractice occurring]

(b) **Possible limitations:** [§296] Just because a plaintiff is foreseeable does not mean that such a person is owed a duty. Courts look at each fact pattern to decide whether to extend a duty in that situation. [RK Construction Co. v. Fusco Corp., 650 A.2d 153 (Conn. 1994)—"many harms are quite literally 'foreseeable,' yet for pragmatic reasons, no recovery is allowed"]

1) **Factors:** [§297] The courts in California have been more explicit than most in identifying the considerations that go into deciding whether to impose a duty. These include *in addition to foreseeability*: the closeness of the connection between D's conduct and the injury; the moral blame attached to D's conduct; the policy of preventing future harm; the extent of the burden to D and the consequences to the community of imposing a duty of care. [Tarasoff v. Regents of the University of California, *supra*] Other courts impose similar limitations on duty but may do so by focusing on the relationship that exists between the parties.

2) **Examples**

   a) **Crushing liability:** [§298] Some courts fear crushing liability in situations that do not involve privity relationships even though the victims are foreseeable. [Strauss v. Belle Realty Co., 65 N.Y.2d 399 (1985)—fear of extended liability led court to deny duty for injuries incurred during blackout by a tenant who was not in privity with negligent utility; *and see infra*, §476]

   b) **Conflict with other duties:** [§299] If a doctor negligently performs an abortion, the physical injury to the mother might foreseeably cause birth defects in a child yet to be conceived. But because such a doctor's duty to a child not yet conceived would be difficult to define and might create a conflict with the duty owed the patient, and any such duty might last for generations, a court may hold that a duty to a future child does not exist. [*See* Albala v. City of New York, 54 N.Y.2d 269 (1981); Enright v. Eli Lilly & Co., 77 N.Y.2d 377, *cert. denied*, 502 U.S. 868 (1991)—no duty to third generation DES victim; *but see*

Renslow v. Mennonite Hospital, 367 N.E.2d 1250 (Ill. 1977)—duty to child born years after D negligently transfused blood to mother]

c) **Not every act:** [§300] The fact that an act happens to have an impact on the plaintiff does not, by itself, create an obligation on the defendant to do that act carefully. Thus, for example, where an employer's workers' compensation insurance carrier has reserved the right to inspect the employer's plant to reduce accidents, this does not give rise to a duty to the workers at that plant to do the inspection with due care. [Jansen v. Fidelity & Casualty Co., 79 N.Y.2d 867 (1992)]

3) **Comment:** Whatever the factors used, every court confronting the question of whether to impose a duty must decide how much weight to give to the factor of *foreseeability*. Any difference in result is much more likely to depend on the role the court gives to foreseeability in making its decision rather than any list of factors or considerations it may offer. The more the court stresses foreseeability, the more likely it is to impose a duty in favor of a foreseeable plaintiff.

3. **Breach of Duty:** [§301] Once it is shown that the defendant owed a duty of due care to the plaintiff, it must then be shown that the defendant breached this duty through an act or omission exposing others to an *unreasonable risk of harm*. These three elements—*i.e.*, an act or omission by the defendant, a duty of due care owed to the plaintiff, and a breach of duty by creation of an unreasonable risk of harm—together constitute a *"negligent act."* (However, the elements of *causation* and *damages*, *infra*, must also be satisfied in order to establish *liability* for the negligent act—*i.e.*, to establish "negligence.") *Note:* Whether the defendant has breached a duty of due care requires a two-step demonstration: (i) proof of what actually happened, and (ii) a showing that the defendant acted unreasonably under those circumstances.

a. **Proving what actually happened:** [§302] There are two basic methods of proof available for the plaintiff to establish what in fact occurred:

(1) **Direct evidence:** [§303] In some cases, direct evidence (*e.g.*, witnesses who can testify to the facts) may be available.

(a) **Example:** A broken ladder rung in a negligence case against the ladder's manufacturer.

(b) **Example:** N, a neighbor, observes D throw a brick from his second floor window and sees the brick strike P in the street below; N's testimony as to what occurred is direct evidence.

(2) **Circumstantial evidence:** [§304] In other situations, the plaintiff may rely on circumstantial evidence to create an inference of what occurred.

(a) **Example:** P is injured when she trips over something in D's darkened theater. If P can show that a pipe was lying near the place at which she tripped and that a scuff mark on her shoe was made by a pipe-like object when she fell, a jury could infer that P fell over the pipe.

(b) **Example:** If P, a customer who slips in the supermarket, must show that the slippery substance was on the floor long enough for a reasonable market to find it and remedy the condition, P may do this by showing that the product on the floor was "dirty and messy." [Negri v. Stop and Shop, Inc., 65 N.Y.2d 625 (1985)] (A few courts in supermarket cases allow the jury to find negligent operation from the market's mode of operation, rather than from how long the object was on the floor. [Chiara v. Fry's Food Stores, 733 P.2d 283 (Ariz. 1987); Dumont v. Shaw's Supermarkets, Inc., 664 A.2d 846 (Me. 1995)])

b. **Determining whether conduct proved is unreasonable ("balancing test"):** [§305]   The second step in determining whether there was a breach of duty by the defendant (*i.e.*, a negligent act) is whether the defendant's conduct was unreasonable. This requires a *balancing of the risks and benefits* of the conduct. [Rest. 2d §291]

(1) **Risk—"magnitude of the risk":** [§306]   The risk of the defendant's conduct is a combination of (i) the *severity* of damage that might occur, and (ii) the *probability* that the damage will occur. Thus, in each situation, consider the social value that the law attaches to the interests endangered by the defendant's conduct, the likelihood of an actual injury by the conduct, and the extent or degree of injury threatened (including the number of individual interests imperiled). [United States v. Carroll Towing, 159 F.2d 169 (2d Cir. 1947)]

(2) **Benefit—"utility of the conduct":** [§307]   The benefit of running the risk is usually the expense or inconvenience spared in not taking safety precautions. In determining whether the defendant's conduct is otherwise justified, consider the social value that the law attaches to the type of conduct involved, the likelihood that the conduct will achieve some desirable end, the availability of safer alternative methods; and the costs of such methods. [United States v. Carroll Towing, *supra*]

(3) **Application of balancing test—risks vs. benefits analysis:** [§308] The defendant's conduct will be considered unreasonable—and therefore negligent—if the magnitude of the risk perceived in advance by a reasonable person in the defendant's position *outweighs* its utility. Obviously, this determination will vary in each case, depending on the specific circumstances involved.

(a) **General rule:** Where the risk of injury is low and the cost of alternative methods is high, the defendant's conduct is more likely to be considered reasonable (*i.e.*, nonnegligent). [McCarty v. Pheasant Run, Inc., 826 F.2d 1554 (7th Cir. 1987)]

(b) **Compare:** Where the utility of the conduct is slight and where less dangerous alternatives are available at little cost or effort, it is more likely that negligence will be found—especially if the risk of injury is significant. [Pease v. Sinclair Refining Co., 104 F.2d 183 (2d Cir. 1939)—D provided demonstration kit with kerosene in bottles labeled "water"; a simple warning or an accurate label would have avoided the accident that occurred when P used the "water"]

(c) **Cost of safeguarding:** [§309] The costs of safeguarding against the risk must always be measured by the *likelihood* and *gravity* of damage. The more probable and more grievous the harm, the greater the effort and expense that must be undertaken to avoid that harm. And conversely, the less likely the harm, the less effort and expense that need be undertaken. (This explains why shooting a gun in a densely populated city is more likely to be negligent than engaging in the same activity in an unpopulated area.)

c. **Res ipsa loquitur ("the thing speaks for itself"):** [§310] In certain cases, *the very fact that a particular harm has occurred* may itself tend to establish *both* parts of the breach requirement: what happened and that it was through the defendant's unreasonable conduct. Then the law may permit an *inference or a presumption* that defendant was at fault.

(1) **Essential elements:** [§311] Three essential factors must be established to invoke res ipsa loquitur:

(i) The accident must be of a type that *normally does not occur* in the absence of someone's negligence;

(ii) The indicated source of negligence must be *within the scope of a duty* that the defendant owes the plaintiff; and

(iii) It must appear that neither the plaintiff nor any third person *contributed to or caused* the plaintiff's injuries.

[Anderson v. Service Merchandise Co., 485 N.W.2d 170 (Neb. 1992); Hull v. L. & A. Montagnard Social Club, Inc., 498 A.2d 597 (Me. 1985)]

(a) **Accident of a type that normally does not occur without negligence:** [§312] If the accident is one that normally does not occur in the absence of negligence, the courts hold that the *occurrence itself* will permit the conclusion that *someone* was negligent. [Brannon v. Wood, 444 P.2d 558 (Or. 1968)]

1) **Examples:** Injuries suffered from eating canned spinach containing large chunks of glass, or from the collapse of bleachers at a baseball game, or from a barrel falling from an upper floor of a building are all examples of events that normally do not occur unless someone is negligent. [Byrne v. Boadle, 159 Eng. Rep. 299 (1863)]

2) **Compare—accidents without fault:** [§313] However, many accidents can occur without anyone's fault: *e.g.*, a tire blowout, injuries resulting from a falling tree or from fires of unknown

origin. [Klein v. Beeten, 172 N.W. 736 (Wis. 1919)] In these cases, without further evidence, res ipsa loquitur *cannot* be applied.

3) **Necessity for expert testimony:** [§314] Sometimes, expert testimony is required to determine whether negligence can be inferred from the happening of the accident.

    a) **Example:** In medical malpractice cases involving *complex care* or treatment, expert testimony is usually required to establish the probability that the injuries resulted from someone's negligence, the rationale being that lay jurors are not competent to infer negligence merely from the occurrence of injury in the course of complicated medical treatment. [Connors v. University Associates, 4 F.3d 123 (2d Cir. 1993)]

    b) **But note:** Even in medical malpractice cases, expert testimony is *not* required where the *occurrence is so bizarre* that someone's negligence is obvious even to a lay juror (*e.g.*, surgical instrument left in the patient's abdomen following ordinary surgery), or where the medical *procedure itself* is so *routine* that common knowledge may be relied upon to determine whether the accident could occur in the absence of someone's negligence. [Bardessono v. Michels, 3 Cal. 3d 780 (1970)]

4) **Analysis—ultimate issue of probabilities:** [§315] Whether the accident is of a type that normally does not occur in the absence of someone's negligence is ultimately a matter of *probabilities*; it must appear that the trier of fact could reasonably conclude that, on the whole, it is more likely than not that negligence was associated with the harm.

(b) **Indicated source of negligence within scope of defendant's duty to plaintiff:** [§316] This element requires that it appear more likely than not that the inference of negligence arising from proof of the first factor (above) can be *focused on the defendant*.

1) **Defendant's control over source of harm:** [§317] Whether a showing of "control" by the defendant is essential for res ipsa loquitur purposes, and if so, what the nature of that control must be, is a subject of divergent views:

    a) **"Exclusive control" standard:** [§318] Some courts require that the instrumentality causing the plaintiff's injury be shown to have been under the defendant's *"exclusive control"* at the time of the injury.

        1/ **Example:** Pedestrian P is struck by a sign that falls from D's store building. D is deemed in "control" of the sign, and res ipsa loquitur is applied. [Both v. Harband, 164 Cal. App. 2d 743 (1958)]

2/ **Example:** Passenger P is injured when D's bus goes out of control and turns over; D is deemed to be in "control" of the instrumentality causing injury for purposes of res ipsa loquitur. [Whitney v. Northwest Greyhound, 242 P.2d 257 (Mont. 1952)]

3/ **Compare:** Hotel guest P is injured when water in D's hotel shower suddenly turns hot. There is evidence that P adjusted the faucets before the incident. P has not shown that D is in "control" of the water. [Malvicini v. Stratfield Motor Hotel, Inc., 538 A.2d 690 (Conn. 1988)]

4/ **Compare:** If D leaves his car parked on a hill, and it starts rolling and injures P, res ipsa applies—at least if there was only a short interval between the time D left his car and the time it started rolling. But after a *long* time interval has elapsed, other causes—for which D was *not* responsible—would appear to be more likely. [Hill v. Thompson, 484 P.2d 513 (Okla. 1971)—time lapse of four hours held not enough to prevent inference of D's negligence]

b) **"Control" only one factor to consider:** [§319] The better view is that showing the defendant's "control" over the instrumentality that caused the injury is only one way of proving the defendant's responsibility. The essential question is whether the injury to the plaintiff was one *that the defendant owed a duty to guard against.* [Corcoran v. Banner Super Market, 19 N.Y.2d 425 (1967)]

1/ **Example:** A tire manufacturer may be liable under res ipsa loquitur for injuries to a consumer who was mounting a tire for the first time when it exploded, even though the tire had been purchased over a year before. D was no longer realistically in "control" of the tire, but the type of injury was one that D owed a duty to guard against. [Baker v. B.F. Goodrich Co., 115 Cal. App. 2d 221 (1953)]

2/ **And note:** The same result and reasoning apply in the *"bursting bottle"* cases (*i.e.*, plaintiff injured by explosion of defendant's bottled beverage purchased from retailer), as long as it appears that the bottle was not subjected to unusual treatment by the plaintiff, retailer, or any other customer. [Zentz v. Coca-Cola Bottling Co., 39 Cal. 2d 436 (1952)]

c) **Compare—inability to identify specific source of harm (unconscious patient problem):** [§320] Some courts have purported to find "exclusive control" in a *group* of physicians and nurses when an unconscious patient, with whom each defendant had some contact, suffers harm of a type that might be found attributable to someone's negligence. Rather than nonsuit the plaintiff for failure to identify the specific person whose negligence caused the harm, the courts—sympathizing with the plaintiff's inability to obtain such proof—have treated the individual defendants as members of a joint enterprise and imposed responsibility for the harm upon each defendant who cannot exculpate himself. [Ybarra v. Spangard, 25 Cal. 2d 486 (1944); Kolakowski v. Voris, 415 N.E.2d 397 (Ill. 1981); *but see* Hoven v. Rice Memorial Hospital, 396 N.W.2d 569 (Minn. 1986)—questioning Ybarra]

1/ **Example:** In *Ybarra*, P sustained a shoulder injury while under an anesthetic during an appendectomy. Res ipsa loquitur was held applicable against all doctors and hospital employees connected with the operation, even though there was no proof when the injury occurred or which defendants were present at that time. *Rationale:* Each defendant was charged with a special responsibility for P's care under the circumstances—*i.e.*, each owed a duty to guard against the injury.

2/ **Limitation:** The doctrine will not be invoked where multiple defendants lack the cohesiveness of a unit. [Fireman's Fund American Insurance Companies v. Knobbe, 562 P.2d 825 (Nev. 1977)—res ipsa loquitur not invoked against four social friends for fire negligently started by one of them (who cannot be identified)]

3/ **Limitation:** Where P is unable to identify the tortfeasor, and it is not certain that the tortfeasor is among a large number of defendants sued, courts refuse to make defendants prove their nonculpability. [Cliff v. Nelson, 608 P.2d 647 (Wash. 1980)—when only one in crowd caused injury, and 10 of 30 members of crowd were sued, P had to identify the tortfeasor]

(c) **Plaintiff or any third party did not contribute to or cause plaintiff's injuries:** [§321]   There is no inference of negligence if it appears that the plaintiff's own conduct (or that of some third person for whom defendant is not responsible) was the likeliest cause of the accident. [169 A.L.R. 953]

1) **Distinguish contributory negligence:** This requirement must be distinguished from the issue of contributory negligence (*see infra*, §643). For example, res ipsa loquitur is inapplicable in the crash of a dual-control airplane where human error was the cause and the student pilot (whose family is seeking damages) was at one of the controls and could have been the party at fault. [Udseth v. United States, 530 F.2d 860 (10th Cir. 1975)]

(2) **Other factors affecting use of res ipsa loquitur**

    (a) **Accessibility of evidence:** [§322]   Most courts hold that if the above three elements are met, the doctrine will apply even if the defendant cannot add any evidence on the issue of what happened. [Judson v. Giant Powder Co., 107 Cal. 549 (1885)—explosion of nitroglycerine factory destroyed all evidence, but res ipsa loquitur was still applied]

        1) **Note:** Some courts rely on the defendant's special access to information in denying motions for nonsuits where the plaintiffs have done the best they can to identify the cause of the accident—*even if* the traditional elements of res ipsa are absent. This is probably the explanation for the unconscious patient cases (*see supra*, §320), though, as seen, courts often try to force such cases into the three-part test of the basic res ipsa doctrine.

    (b) **Effect of proving specific acts of negligence:** [§323]   When the plaintiff attempts to prove specific acts of negligence to explain what happened, she may still use res ipsa loquitur as long as the three-part test is met. (The jury may reject the plaintiff's specific proof but may accept the general inference of negligence from the happening of the accident.) [Ward v. Forrester Day Care, Inc., 547 So. 2d 410 (Ala. 1989)—P tried to prove D negligent in supervision of day care center; P could also use res ipsa, since introduction of evidence on how accident could have happened does not preclude its application if evidence does not clearly resolve culpability; Abbott v. Page Airways, 23 N.Y.2d 502 (1969)—P tried to prove that helicopter fell from sky because pilot flew too slowly and was not paying attention; P also allowed to use res ipsa because helicopters do not usually fall without some negligence; *but see* Malloy v. Commonwealth Highland Theatres, Inc., 375 N.W.2d 631 (S.D. 1985)—P presented too much direct evidence to be allowed to rely also on res ipsa loquitur]

(3) **Effect of establishing res ipsa loquitur**

    (a) **Majority view—inference:** [§324]   Most courts treat res ipsa loquitur as creating only a permissible *inference* of negligence—*i.e.*, a conclusion that the trier of fact *may* (or may not) choose to draw from the facts, the strength of the inference depending on, and varying with, the circumstances of each case. [Gardner v. Coca-Cola Bottling Co., 127 N.W.2d 557 (Minn. 1964)]

        1) **But note:** Even in inference states, facts may be so strong that an inference *must* be drawn if not rebutted. [Farina v. Pan American World Airways, 116 App. Div. 2d 618 (1986)—plane ran off runway while landing]

    (b) **Minority view—presumption:** [§325]   A few courts, however, give res ipsa loquitur the status of a *rebuttable presumption* of breach of duty owed; *i.e.*, it shifts the burden of going forward with the evidence to the defendant (to give a satisfactory explanation of how the injuries occurred, by a *preponderance* of evidence), and if the defendant fails to do so, the plaintiff would be entitled to a directed verdict on liability. [Weiss v. Axler, 328 P.2d 88 (Colo. 1958); *see* Evidence Summary for further discussion of inferences and presumptions]

(c) **Minority view—"disappearing" presumption:** [§326] In still other states, res ipsa is classified as a presumption, but one that is dispelled by counterevidence. [Cal. Evid. Code §646] Thus, if the defendant can simply produce evidence sufficient to sustain a finding of fact in his favor (*see* Evidence Summary), the presumption has no further evidentiary effect; the burden of proof is back on the *plaintiff* to produce a preponderance of evidence that the defendant breached his duty of care under the circumstances.

4. **Actual Cause ("Cause in Fact"):** [§327] The defendant's negligent act must be the cause of the plaintiff's injuries in order to impose liability. This involves two separate determinations: (i) whether the defendant's conduct was the *actual cause* (or cause in fact) of the injuries (as discussed in this section) *and* (ii) whether it was the *proximate* (or legal) *cause* thereof (discussed *infra*, §§348 *et seq.*).

   a. **"But for" rule:** [§328] The defendant's negligent act must have been the *cause in fact* of the plaintiff's injuries. If the plaintiff would *not* have been injured *but for* the defendant's act, that act is a cause in fact of the injury. [Chaney v. Smithkline Beckman Corp., 764 F.2d 527 (8th Cir. 1985)—Arkansas would not permit recovery when expert said "20 to 80% chance" that D caused P's injury]

      (1) **Note:** If the plaintiff would have sustained the same injury regardless of the defendant's act, the act is *not* the cause in fact of the injury and the defendant usually is not liable to the plaintiff. Thus, actual cause is missing where the plaintiff's land is flooded because of the defendant's failure to maintain its railroad embankment in proper condition if it appears that the storm was severe enough to have caused the collapse of even a reasonably maintained embankment.

   b. **Concurrent liability rule:** [§329] Where the separate negligent acts of the defendant and a third party concur to cause a single injury, and it appears that the plaintiff would *not* have been injured *but for the concurrence*, then *both* the defendant and the third party are actual causes. [47 Harv. L. Rev. 1127; Hill v. Edmonds, 26 App. Div. 2d 554 (1966)]

      (1) **Example:** Where a collision of two vehicles injures a pedestrian, and the collision was caused by the negligence of *both* drivers (*i.e.*, "but for" the negligence of both, the accident would not have occurred), the pedestrian can recover from both for any indivisible injuries suffered.

         (a) **But note:** Although the traditional common law rule was that of joint and several liability, many states have recently abolished that rule or limited its applicability. (*See infra*, §1118.)

(2) **Compare—jointly engaged tortfeasors:** [§330] Similar rules apply where the injury is inflicted by one of several defendants *jointly engaged* in a course of negligent conduct. In such a case, *each defendant* is liable even though only one of them actually inflicted the injury. [Rest. 2d §876; *and see infra*, §1053]

    (a) **Example:** All participants in an illegal "drag race" on a public highway are liable to bystanders who are consequently injured, even though the accident involved only one of the racing cars. [Bierczynski v. Rogers, 239 A.2d 218 (Del. 1968)]

(3) **Successive tortfeasors:** [§331] When successive acts of independent tortfeasors, unrelated in time or causation, produce a single harm, the tortfeasors must try to disprove their responsibility for the injury. For example, a woman suffering from arthritis is injured in an auto accident. The injuries are worsened by another accident several weeks later. Although each defendant is responsible only for the portion of the injury that he caused, the burden of allocating that causation is placed on the defendants. [Phennah v. Whalen, 621 P.2d 1304 (Wash. 1980)]

c. **"Substantial factor" rule:** [§332] If the plaintiff sustains injury as the result of the negligent conduct of both the defendant and a third party, and it appears that the conduct of *either one* alone would have been sufficient to cause the injury, *both* are nevertheless liable if each person's conduct was a "substantial factor" in causing the injury. [Anderson v. Minneapolis, St. Paul & Sault Ste. Marie Railroad, 179 N.W. 45 (Minn. 1920)]

    (1) **Example:** Where two motorcycles simultaneously pass P's horse, thereby frightening it and causing it to run away, and either motorcyclist alone would have caused the fright, the conduct of each of them is a "substantial factor." [Corey v. Havener, 65 N.E. 69 (Mass. 1902)]

    (2) **Analysis—distinguish "but for" and concurrent liability rules:** [§333] In this type of case, it is really *not* the concurrence that causes the damage, because either force by itself would have resulted in the same injuries. Moreover, if the "but for" rule (above) were strictly applied, both the defendant and the third party would escape liability, since in testing the defendant's liability one would find that the injuries would have occurred *despite* the defendant's acts; and the same would apply to the third party's liability. That is why courts have worked out the "substantial factor" rule to cover this type of case. [Rest. 2d §§431-433A]

d. **Problem of alternative liability:** [§334] Where a plaintiff has been injured through the negligence of one of several possible defendants, and it is not clear which one caused the injury—but it is clear that only one of them did—how can causation be established? For example, D and X are *both negligent* in firing their rifles near P. P is struck by a bullet from one of the rifles, but it is impossible to tell from which rifle the bullet came.

    (1) **"But for" rule would exclude liability:** [§335] Application of the "but for" rule will not work; since it cannot be shown which defendant's fault caused the harm, it is impossible to ascertain whether the injury would have occurred "but for" that defendant's acts.

(2) **Better view shifts burden to each defendant:** [§336]   Only a few courts have recently dealt with this problem. These decisions hold that where P cannot show whether D's or X's negligence was the actual cause of P's injuries, *the burden of going forward with the evidence shifts to each defendant* to show that his negligence was *not* the actual cause. [Summers v. Tice, 33 Cal. 2d 80 (1948); Rest. 2d §433B(3)]

(3) **Shifting burden where only one defendant negligent:** [§337]   The above view may be an eminently desirable result when there is some evidence that *both* the defendant and the third party were acting negligently, even if not acting jointly. However, where there is no evidence as to where culpability lies, and it appears as a matter of fact that *only one* of the two defendants *could* have been negligent—although the plaintiff does not know which one—application of the "shifting burden" rule may impose a hardship on the innocent defendant because he must assume the burden of proving his innocence, which he may be unable to do unless he can effectively prove the culpability of the other defendant. [Garcia v. Joseph Vince Co., 84 Cal. App. 3d 868 (1978)—P who cannot show which saber caused fencing accident cannot invoke any burden shifting]

(4) **Market share liability:** [§338]   Suits against manufacturers of the pregnancy drug diethylstilbestrol ("DES") have led to a theory of causation called market share liability. This theory is useful in situations where even if all the defendants are assumed negligent, it is uncertain which one of them actually caused the plaintiff's injury due to the passage of time and the fact that the defendants' drugs were generally indistinguishable. Several views have emerged that vary both as to scope of the doctrine and whether it involves joint or several liability.

   (a) **New York view:** [§339]   Under the New York view, all defendants are liable based on their culpability. Culpability is measured by the risk each defendant imposes on the public-at-large; *i.e.*, the risk each defendant causes is measured by its *national* market share of the product. Defendants cannot exculpate themselves from liability, even if they can show that they could not have caused the plaintiff's injury, unless they demonstrate that they did not produce the product for the use that injured the plaintiff (in this case, as a pregnancy drug). Liability is several. [Hymowitz v. Eli Lilly & Co., 73 N.Y.2d 487, *cert. denied*, 493 U.S. 944 (1989)]

   (b) **Washington view:** [§340]   Under the Washington view, after the plaintiff makes out a prima facie case against at least one defendant, all others may then exculpate themselves by showing that they could not have caused the injuries. The remaining defendants may then rebut the presumption of equal market shares by showing their true market shares. Plaintiffs may recover less than full damages if every defendant can prove its true market share and some absent possible causes exist. Liability is several. [Martin v. Abbott Laboratories, 689 P.2d 368 (Wash. 1984); George v. Parke-Davis, 733 P.2d 507 (Wash. 1987)]

   (c) **California view:** [§341]   Under the California view, if the defendants in the action represent a *substantial share* of the market for the product, they will be liable for a percentage of the plaintiff's injuries equal to their market share. Defendants can exculpate themselves if they can show that they could not have caused the plaintiff's injuries. Those liable are only severally liable for damages. [Brown v. Superior Court, 44 Cal. 3d 1049 (1988); Sindell v. Abbott Laboratories, 26 Cal. 3d 588, *cert. denied*, 449 U.S. 912 (1980)]

(d) **Rejection of market share liability:** [§342]   Some jurisdictions have rejected market share liability in any form and rely on traditional notions of causation. [Smith v. Eli Lilly & Co., 560 N.E.2d 324 (Ill. 1990)]

(e) **Extension beyond DES cases:** [§343]   Most states willing to use market share for DES cases have been reluctant to extend the doctrine to other products—sometimes because of fact differences. [Goldman v. Johns-Manville Sales Corp., 514 N.E.2d 691 (Ohio 1987)—since asbestos products can be distinguished from one another in terms of harmfulness, market share theory is rejected; *but see* Wheeler v. Raybestos-Manhattan, 8 Cal. App. 4th 1152 (1992)—market share theory applied to manufacturers of brake pads because they used asbestos fibers that were very similar in harmfulness; Santiago v. Sherwin Williams Co., 3 F.3d 546 (1st Cir. 1993)—proof inadequate to permit theory to apply against defendants who marketed lead paint over a 30-year period; *but see* Smith v. Cutter Biological, Inc., 823 P.2d 717 (Hawaii 1991)—applying theory to blood-coagulating factor used by hemophiliacs]

e. **Loss of a chance:** [§344]   Traditionally, a plaintiff could not recover for a loss unless she could prove that she had lost something that she was *more likely than not* to have acquired or retained but for the defendant's conduct.

(1) **Medical exception:** [§345]   In medical cases, courts have recently begun to allow suits for losses of recovery chances that are less than 50%. [Falcon v. Memorial Hospital, 462 N.W.2d 44 (Mich. 1990)—P could sue where D's negligence reduced P's chances of recovery with damages to be based on that lost percentage; Scafidi v. Seiler, 574 A.2d 398 (N.J. 1990)—D's negligence increased risk of adverse consequences; *but see* Kramer v. Lewisville Memorial Hospital, 858 S.W.2d 397 (Tex. 1993); Fennell v. Southern Maryland Hospital Center, Inc., 580 A.2d 206 (Md. 1990)—refusing to recognize action for loss of a 40% chance of survival]

(2) **Compare—emotional distress:** [§346]   When physical injury is present, courts allow recovery for fear of further harm, such as cancer. [Mauro v. Raymark Industries, Inc., 561 A.2d 257 (N.J. 1989)] But where there is no present physical injury, recovery for *fear* about future developments is much less likely. [Potter v. Firestone Tire & Rubber Co., 6 Cal. 4th 965 (1993)—prolonged exposure to toxic landfill does not permit recovery for emotional distress without a showing that it is "more likely than not that the plaintiff will develop cancer in the future due to the toxic exposure"]

    f. **Problem where defendant's negligence has deprived plaintiff of proof:** [§347] A similar approach may be taken in cases where the plaintiff finds herself unable to prove "but for" causation because the defendant's negligence has *deprived the plaintiff of evidence* of the actual cause. In such cases, the burden may be shifted to the defendant to prove that his negligence was *not* the cause in fact of the plaintiff's injuries.

        (1) **Example:** D, the owner of a hotel, negligently fails to provide a lifeguard at the swimming pool, as required by statute. P's husband drowns while using the pool, but P is unable to show how the drowning occurred *because* no lifeguard (or other witness) was present; *i.e.*, the absence of the required lifeguard not only was negligence as to P's husband, but deprived P of the means of establishing the cause of his death. Under such circumstances, the burden of proof may be shifted to D to show that its failure to provide lifeguard service was *not* the cause of death. [*See* Haft v. Lone Palm Hotel, 3 Cal. 3d 756 (1970)]

        (2) **Rationale:** This is an extension of *Summers v. Tice, supra,* §336; *i.e.,* unless the burden were shifted to the defendant, the defendant's negligence would go unredressed because the plaintiff *would otherwise have no way to prove causation*.

        (3) **Extension:** In a few cases, this rationale has been extended to include instances in which negligence by its nature does not become apparent until many years later. [*See* Sindell v. Abbott Laboratories, *supra*]

5. Proximate Cause (Legal Cause)

    a. **Introduction:** [§348] Besides showing that the defendant's conduct was the "cause in fact" of the plaintiff's injuries, the plaintiff must also establish that such conduct was the *"proximate cause"* of the injuries. Proximate cause deals with the defendant's liability for unforeseeable or unusual occurrences or consequences following the defendant's act.

        (1) **Policy judgment:** [§349] "Causation" is actually a misleading term here because all issues of cause and result have already been considered under "actual cause," above. Rather, proximate cause is a policy determination: Under some circumstances, it is deemed unfair to hold the defendant legally responsible for all consequences of his wrongful conduct, hence the question, *"How far does the defendant's liability extend for consequences caused by his negligent acts?"* (This accounts for the alternate term "legal cause.")

        (2) **Foreseeability approach:** [§350] Although proximate cause questions may be approached in several ways, the emphasis on *foreseeability* is the most prominent today. (Another approach, that of Judge Andrews, is discussed *infra*, §399.) Under the foreseeability approach, troublesome proximate cause questions fall into three basic patterns (and will be analyzed in this order):

            (a) **Unforeseeable manner:** A foreseeable result occurs but it has come about in an unforeseeable manner.

(b) **Unforeseeable result:** The foreseeable plaintiff has been injured, but an unexpected result or type of harm has occurred.

(c) **Unforeseeable plaintiff:** Although the defendant's act exposed a certain group of potential victims to a foreseeable risk, the person hurt was not a member of that group.

(3) **Cross-refer—duty:** [§351] Remember that the proximate cause discussion assumes that the *duty question* has already been resolved in the plaintiff's favor. Thus, under the Cardozo view of duty (*see supra*, §285), an unforeseeable plaintiff loses at the duty stage. Since the defendant owed no duty to such a plaintiff, there is no need to reach the issue of proximate cause at all.

(a) **But note:** If a duty is found owing to the plaintiff under the Cardozo view, two issues remain: was the manner of occurrence foreseeable, and was the result foreseeable? Under the Andrews approach (*see supra*, §285), foreseeability of manner, result, and plaintiff are among the factors considered in deciding whether the defendant proximately caused the plaintiff's injury (*see infra*, §399).

(4) **Terminology:** [§352] If the manner, result, or plaintiff was unforeseeable, this may be either because the defendant had no reason to know the nature of the situation on which his negligence would operate or because an unexpected new force has come into play.

(a) **Direct causation—no intervening forces:** [§353] "Direct causation" means that there was no intervening force or agency operating between the defendant's negligent act and the occurrence of the harm to the plaintiff. In other words, the defendant acts upon a "set stage"—*i.e.*, all of the contributing factors are already in place on the stage as the defendant acts. (Visualize knocking over a row of dominoes.)

(b) **Indirect causation—intervening factors present:** [§354] "Indirect causation" means that some force or agency *intervened* between the defendant's negligent act and the occurrence of the plaintiff's harm, and either *extended* the results of the defendant's negligence or *combined* with the defendant's act to produce the injury. Some intervening forces are foreseeable and some are unforeseeable. Note, however, that although sometimes the nature of the intervening force may be crucial, the existence of intervening forces does not necessarily terminate the defendant's liability. The determinative factor in each case is usually whether, at the time the defendant acted, it was *reasonably foreseeable that the result* that occurred would in fact occur.

1) **What is an "intervening act"?** [§355] An intervening act can consist of an "act of God" (storm, flood, etc.), an act of a third person, or an act of an animal.

a) **Caution—distinguish contributory negligence:** Acts of the *plaintiff* should *not* be analyzed as intervening forces.

The plaintiff's conduct may establish contributory negligence or assumption of the risk, but these are affirmative defenses to a negligence action (*see infra*) and do not affect the prima facie case of negligence.

2) Factors that are not "intervening acts"

a) **Preexisting conditions:** [§356]   Contributing factors that are already in operation when the defendant acts (*i.e.*, the "set stage," above) are not intervening acts. For example, the plaintiff's physical condition, which may combine with the defendant's negligence to cause an unexpected injury, is *not* an intervening act—"defendant takes his victim as he finds him." (*See infra*, §359.)

b) **Force set in motion:** [§357]   Similarly, a force set in motion by the defendant's conduct is not deemed an intervening act. Thus, where D (driving negligently) runs into a garbage truck, causing debris to fly through the air and injure P, the debris is a force set in motion by D.

c) **Omissions to act:** [§358]   And although a third person's failure to act may have contributed to the plaintiff's injury, such omission is not deemed to be an intervening act—even though the third person may have been under a legal duty to act; however, in extreme cases, this may nonetheless affect the defendant's liability (*see infra*, §§391-392).

(c) **Caution—ultimate issue is foreseeability:** [§359]   Although some courts still give important weight to the difference between direct and indirect causation when deciding proximate cause issues, this is generally an outmoded view. The causal sequence may help sort out the various fact patterns that present themselves, but the ultimate issue is *foreseeability*.

1) **Example:** P was injured when he fell on broken glass that D city negligently allowed to remain on a playground. Even though P's fall was caused by some boys pushing P, D's negligence was a proximate cause of the harm since falling in a playground—from whatever cause—was foreseeable. [Parness v. City of Tempe, 600 P.2d 764 (Ariz. 1979)]

b. **Direct causation:** [§360]   Where there are no intervening acts operating on the particular fact situation, the case is one of direct causation. Whether the defendant should be deemed the proximate cause of the plaintiff's injury turns on the "foreseeability" of the results.

(1) **What is the "result"?** [§361]   The definition of "result" is one developed on a case-by-case basis through judicial use of common sense. For example, where D carelessly drives her automobile through a crosswalk, she should reasonably expect to run down a pedestrian and break his leg. If the broken bones are wrapped around each other in a bizarre "figure

eight pattern," D may try to avoid liability by asserting that the extent to which the bones were broken was not foreseeable. However, it is clear that the *"result"* is the broken leg (due to impact from the car)—not the figure eight pattern. Results would seldom be foreseeable if so narrowly defined.

(2) **Foreseeable results lead to liability:** [§362] Where the defendant causes a foreseeable injury, this presents such a clear case of liability that proximate cause is rarely in issue. Thus, in the example above, had D negligently failed to keep her eyes on the road, thereby running over P and breaking his leg, this would be a clear case of a foreseeable result occurring to a foreseeable plaintiff in a foreseeable manner—and D would be liable for the damages resulting from the broken leg.

(a) **Exceptions—no liability for certain foreseeable results**

1) **Unusual manner:** [§363] Some courts, and the Second Restatement, refuse to impose liability on the negligent defendant where, from hindsight, the *result*—although foreseeable—has come about in a "highly extraordinary" *manner*. [Rest. 2d §435(2)]

a) **Example:** D takes her eyes off the road while driving her small car. She returns her eyes to the road just in time to see P carefully crossing the street in a marked crosswalk. D has no time to stop, so she swerves to the right. The car hits a parked truck and ricochets to the other side of the street, where it bounces off another truck and back into the street, knocking P down and breaking his leg. Because of the bizarre sequence of events, courts following the Restatement might protect D from liability to P because of the bizarre chain of events.

b) **Compare—contrary view:** [§364] Other courts think it fair that the defendant be held liable as long as the result was foreseeable—no matter how odd the sequence.

2) **"New York fire rule":** [§365] Suppose the defendant carelessly fails to control a flame or sparks in a populated area. Although it is foreseeable that such negligence can cause a fire that may spread to adjoining buildings, the New York courts have held that expansion of the fire beyond burning of the first building is not "foreseeable." [Ryan v. New York Central Railway, 35 N.Y. 210 (1866); Rose v. Pennsylvania Railway, 236 N.Y. 568 (1923)—limiting liability to owner of first structure burned] *Rationale:* Since potential liability for this type of carelessness could extend almost indefinitely, public policy requires an arbitrary cut-off point.

a) **Compare:** Most other states treat fire cases under a general foreseeability approach on a case-by-case basis. [Osborn v. City of Whittier, 103 Cal. App. 2d 609 (1951)]

(3) **Unforeseeable results:** [§366]   In some cases, the defendant's negligence, although occurring upon a "set stage," causes unexpected results. Here, two types of cases must be distinguished: unforeseeable type of injury cases and unforeseeable extent of injury cases.

    (a) **Unforeseeable type of injury:** [§367]   Where one type of injury to the plaintiff was foreseeable, but an entirely different injury occurred without any intervening force, there is no clear consensus; courts split over whether the defendant should be held liable.

        1) ***"Polemis"* view—liability for unforeseeable consequences:** [§368]   Some courts hold the defendant liable for ***all direct*** consequences of his wrongful conduct—despite the occurrence of an unforeseeable type of injury to plaintiff. *Rationale:* The plaintiff is an innocent victim and thus the defendant, having acted negligently, should bear the loss.

            a) **Example:** While unloading P's ship, worker D negligently knocked a plank into the hold. (This was negligent because of the unreasonable danger posed to cargo, to anyone working below, and to the ship's hull.) Unknown to D, gas fumes were present in the hold. When the plank hit the bottom, it created a spark that ignited an unforeseeable fire, which in turn destroyed the ship. D was held liable, primarily on the theory that a negligent defendant should be liable for all harm he has ***directly*** caused; the fact that the actual risk created by D (explosion) differed from that reasonably to be anticipated (minor impact damage or plank hitting person) was deemed immaterial. [*In re* Polemis, 3 K.B. 560 (1921)]

        2) ***"Wagon Mound"* view—no liability for unforeseeable consequences:** [§369]   Most courts reject the approach of the *Polemis* court and its rigid reliance on direct causation. The majority emphasizes ***foreseeability*** and assert that when an unforeseeable result occurs, it is unfair to hold the defendant liable—no matter what causation pattern has transpired. [Wagon Mound No. 1, 1961 A.C. 338 (1961)] (*See* further discussion, *infra*, §393.)

            a) **Example:** In *Wagon Mound*, D negligently discharged furnace oil into the bay. A fire resulted and P's dock was burned. D was held ***not*** liable because, under the circumstances, only minor cloggage damage to P's dock could have been foreseen; fire was not a foreseeable risk created by the negligence.

    (b) **Unforeseeable extent of injury—"thin-skulled plaintiffs":** [§370] The most common example of a defendant's negligent act directly causing an unforeseeable result involves cases in which the nature of plaintiff's injuries is unexpected. This is the so-called thin-skulled plaintiff (or preexisting condition) situation (*e.g.*, D's negligence causes P to fall and cut his hand slightly; P is a hemophiliac and bleeds to death before help can be summoned). In these cases, *all courts* hold D liable for the *full extent* of P's injuries (*i.e.*, even courts following the *Wagon Mound* approach). *Rationale: "A tortfeasor takes his victim as he finds him."* [McCahill v. New York Transportation Co., 201 N.Y. 221 (1912); Steinhauser v. Hertz Corp., 421 F.2d 1169 (2d Cir. 1970); Freyermuth v. Lufty, 382 N.E.2d 1059 (Mass. 1978)]

  1) **But note:** Such a latent condition would almost certainly have lowered the plaintiff's life expectancy, thus reducing the damages that the defendant must pay for future years, or, should plaintiff die, for wrongful death. [Steinhauser v. Hertz Corp., *supra*]

c. **Indirect causation—in general:** [§371] As noted, indirect causation exists when an intervening force has come into play after the defendant has acted and has either extended the plaintiff's injuries or combined with the defendant's act to produce the plaintiff's injuries. Among such situations, factors to consider are:

(i) Even though an unforeseeable force has intervened, the defendant will generally be liable for the harm where the negligent act produces a *foreseeable result*.

(ii) In a few exceptional cases, the defendant may be found to be the proximate cause of the plaintiff's harm even though *both* the intervening force and result are unforeseeable.

(1) **Caution:** It is crucial to keep in mind the interplay between the presence of intervening forces and the foreseeability of results; *i.e.*, both the nature of the intervening act and the nature of the result will affect the proximate cause determination, although the *result* is the more important factor.

d. **Indirect causation—rules focusing on nature of intervening act**

(1) **Dependent intervening forces:** [§372] A "dependent" intervening force is an act of a third person or an animal that is a *normal response* to the situation created by the defendant's negligent act. Since such forces are responses arising because of the defendant's negligence, they are deemed foreseeable and will *not* relieve the defendant of liability for the harm caused if they lead to foreseeable results.

(a) **Main types of cases involving dependent intervening forces**

  1) **"Checking forces":** [§373] D's negligence causes P serious harm, and P is taken to a hospital. The surgeon improperly diagnoses P's case and performs an unnecessary operation (or, after proper diagnosis, performs a necessary operation carelessly). It is reasonably foreseeable both that P would have to go to the hospital as a result of the injuries inflicted by D, and that P would receive unsuccessful medical treatment, whether or not

the result of negligence. (This is deemed a normal risk incurred in hospitalization.) Hence, D is liable for the additional harm sustained by P in the hospital. [Thompson v. Fox, 192 A. 107 (Pa. 1937); Atherton v. Devine, 602 P.2d 634 (Okla. 1979)—ambulance accident on way to hospital after initial injury]

    a) **Exception—recklessness:** [§374]   This analysis does *not* apply to reckless medical conduct or to deliberate efforts to maim the plaintiff—*e.g.*, operation by a drunk surgeon or performance of an operation completely unrelated to P's condition. [Upham's Case, 139 N.E. 433 (Mass. 1923); *see* further discussion below]

2) **"Rescue forces":** [§375]   D's negligence has imperiled P or P's property. X sees the situation and attempts to go to the aid of P or P's property. In doing so, X is acting reasonably, but nevertheless inadvertently aggravates P's injuries and also injures himself. Since "danger invites rescue" (*see supra*, §286), the reasonable person should have foreseen the rescuer's attempts and also that such attempts might cause further harm. Thus, D is liable for both the aggravated injuries to P and the injuries to X. [Rest. 2d §445; *but see* Snellenberger v. Rodriguez, 760 S.W.2d 237 (Tex. 1988)—no liability on original tortfeasor where police officer-rescuer's heart attack was not foreseeable result of automobile driver's negligence]

3) **"Escape forces":** [§376]   Because of D's negligence, an elevator crashes to the bottom of the shaft. The passengers panic and in rushing to the exit, push P to the ground and trample him. The attempts of individuals threatened with harm to escape are reasonably foreseeable, as is the possibility that such attempts may endanger others. Hence, D is liable for P's injury. [Crow v. Colson, 256 P. 971 (Kan. 1927); Griffin v. Hustis, 125 N.E. 387 (Mass. 1919)]

4) **Other "response" forces:** [§377]   Other reactions by animate forces may also be held foreseeable:

    a) **Example:** D negligently explodes a firecracker, frightening the horse P is riding. The horse throws P to the ground, injuring P and Y's dog, that was trotting alongside. D is liable for both injuries, since the horse's reaction is held a normal, and thus foreseeable, response. [Quinlan v. Philadelphia, 54 A. 1026 (Pa. 1903)]

    b) **Example:** D's negligence causes P such serious injury that P becomes insane and ***further injures or kills*** himself or a third party. P's reaction is held foreseeable (a "normal" response to the situation created by D), so that D's negligence is the proximate cause of such injuries. [Fuller v. Preis, 35 N.Y.2d 425 (1974)—suicide by P seven months after accident, caused by mental breakdown resulting from accident; *but see* District of Columbia v. Peters, 527 A.2d 1269 (D.C. 1987)—no causal link without showing that D's act produced an "irresistible or uncontrollable impulse to commit suicide"]

(b) **Caution—response must be normal:** [§378]   The crucial requirement in all of the above cases is that the response to the situation created by the defendant's negligent act be a *normal* one. If the response or reaction is *highly unusual*, it is held *not* to be a dependent intervening force (*see infra*, §382).

(2) **Independent intervening forces:** [§379]   An "independent" intervening force is one that operates upon the situation created by the defendant's negligent act but which is *not a response or reaction thereto*. (Such force may be the act of a third person or an animal, or an "act of God.") Where such is the case, the defendant will remain liable for the foreseeable results of his act unless the force is an unforeseeable intentionally tortious or criminal act. [Rest. 2d §442B] (However, unforeseeable intervening forces may also lead to liability; *see infra*, §382.)

(a) **Example:** D negligently causes an automobile collision in which a bystander, P, is injured. Surgery for P is required, and, in the course of surgery, bacteria from the air (foreseeable intervening force) enter the open wound and infect it, eventually causing P's death. D may be held liable for P's death. [Hastie v. Handeland, 274 Cal. App. 2d 599 (1969)]

(b) **Example:** D negligently causes a collision with a truck carrying noxious gas. The truck overturns, discharging the gas into the air, and a fresh wind carries the gas onto P's nearby land, damaging P's crops. Since wind is reasonably foreseeable, D is liable for the crop damage.

(c) **Problem—intervening tortious or criminal acts:** [§380]   Ordinarily, criminal acts on the part of others are not reasonably foreseeable. However, if the defendant's negligent conduct has created a situation in which a reasonable person would have foreseen that negligent, intentional, or even criminal acts might be committed by others (*i.e.*, if defendant has *increased the risk* that this type of act will occur), then the occurrence of such acts is held a *foreseeable intervening force* that does not terminate the defendant's liability.

1) **Example:** Because D negligently blocks the area alongside a road, P is forced to walk in a roadway, where he is struck by a truck. It is reasonably foreseeable that negligent motorists may strike persons forced into the street by D; thus, D is liable if P is run down. [Grainy v. Campbell, 425 A.2d 379 (Pa. 1981)—careless act by third party, if foreseeable, does not foreclose D's liability]

2) **Example:** D's train fails to stop at the station and the conductor negligently tells P to walk home. To get home, P must walk

back through a hobo encampment. The criminal rape of P by a hobo is foreseeable, and D would be civilly liable for the rape. [Hines v. Garrett, 108 S.E. 690 (Va. 1921)]

3) **Example:** A landlord who fails to install proper locks on entrances to the common areas of an apartment building in a high-crime neighborhood may be held liable to a tenant for injuries inflicted by a mugger in the hallway of the building. [Trentacost v. Brussel, 412 A.2d 436 (N.H. 1980); *see infra*, §578—lessor's general duty to safeguard premises against crime]

e. **Indirect causation—rules focusing on results of defendant's negligence:** [§381] As alluded to earlier, there remain three fact situations calling for special consideration: (i) what if a *foreseeable* result is caused by an *unforeseeable* intervening force; (ii) what if an *unforeseeable* result is caused by a *foreseeable* intervening force; and (iii) what if an *unforeseeable* result is caused by an intervening force that is itself *unforeseeable*?

(1) **Foreseeable results produced by unforeseeable intervening forces:** [§382] The fact that an intervening force was not reasonably foreseeable under the circumstances does *not* usually excuse the defendant from liability as long as the *result was foreseeable*.

(a) **General rule:** [§383] Where the ultimate result was reasonably foreseeable under the circumstances, liability is usually imposed even though the harm occurred in a totally unexpected manner.

1) **Example:** D negligently allowed gas vapors to accumulate in the hold of its ship. The resulting explosion and damage to nearby persons and property (the results) were foreseeable, and D was therefore held liable—even though the explosion was actually set off by an unprecedented stroke of lightning (the intervening force) that was *not* foreseeable. [Johnson v. Kosmos Portland Cement Co., 64 F.2d 193 (6th Cir. 1933)]

(b) **Compare—intentional or reckless intervening conduct:** [§384] However, despite the occurrence of foreseeable results, some courts will hold the defendant not liable where the intervening act involves intentional or reckless misconduct.

1) **Example:** In the example above, suppose an *arsonist* had sneaked aboard the ship and started the fire and explosion. Some courts would hold that the arsonist's deliberate misconduct *supersedes* D's negligence so that D should not be held liable. The resulting explosion is just as foreseeable, whether it be set off by a stroke of lightning or by an arsonist—both of which are unforeseeable intervening forces. Yet, in some jurisdictions, D would be held liable in the lightning case, but not in the arson case. In these courts, the arsonist's great moral culpability overwhelms D's moral responsibility for the injuries sustained. [McLaughlin v. Mine Safety Appliances Co., 11 N.Y.2d 62 (1962)]

(c) **Application:** [§385] The following examples illustrate how the courts have applied the foregoing principles:

1) **Acts of God:** [§386] Extraordinary and unprecedented floods, storms, or other weather conditions are usually held to be unforeseeable intervening forces. But they are *not* considered "superseding causes" where they lead to the *result threatened by the defendant's original negligence*.

2) **Abnormal rescue attempts by third persons:** [§387] An abnormal or foolhardy effort by a third person to avert a risk created by the defendant is deemed an *unforeseeable* intervening force, and *relieves the defendant from liability* for injuries—even if it leads to a foreseeable result. This would be a "moral responsibility" decision similar to that involving the arsonist, *supra*. [Robinson v. Butler, 33 N.W.2d 821 (Minn. 1948)]

3) **Unforeseeable tortious or criminal acts:** [§388] Where a third person's tortious or criminal conduct was not reasonably foreseeable (*i.e.*, defendant's conduct has *not* enhanced the risk that such acts will occur; *see supra*, §380), but the ultimate *result* was nonetheless foreseeable, the defendant's liability turns on the *culpability* of the intervening act.

   a) **Intentional or criminal acts:** [§389] If the defendant had no reason to expect intentionally tortious or criminal acts by a third person, some courts hold the defendant *not* liable for harm caused thereby, even though his negligence afforded an opportunity for such conduct, and foreseeable harm resulted. [Rest. 2d §448] (Recall the arsonist case, above.)

      1/ **Note:** At least one court has refused to rule as a matter of law that the requested "mercy killing" of an accident victim by his brother, after severe injuries sustained as a result of the defendant's negligence, is an unforeseeable result. [Zygmaniak v. Kawasaki Motors Corp., 330 A.2d 56 (N.J. 1974)] (Recall the suicide cases, *supra*, §377.)

   b) **Negligent acts:** [§390] On the other hand, a third person's negligent conduct does *not* relieve the defendant of liability—even though such conduct was unforeseeable—if it causes a *result* similar to that threatened by the defendant's conduct, unless the action was "highly extraordinary" under the circumstances (*i.e.*, *more than* unforeseeable). [Rest. 2d §447(b)]

      1/ **Example:** D negligently allows its telephone pole to become rotten with termites. The pole falls and injures P, but only after having been jarred by a careening automobile negligently driven by X. D would be held liable for P's injuries because the pole's toppling and injuring a passerby was the *foreseeable result* of D's original negligence. The fact that this result was brought about by X's negligent driving is *not* so highly extraordinary as to cut off causation. [Gibson v. Garcia, 96 Cal. App. 2d 681 (1950)]

c) **Third person's failure to prevent harm:** [§391] Although not actually deemed an "intervening act" (*see supra*, §358), proximate cause issues involving a third person's omission to act generally are treated in the same manner as affirmative negligence by a third person. Thus, the failure of a third person to act so as to prevent the harm threatened by the defendant's negligent conduct does *not* relieve the defendant of liability, even where the third person is under some legal duty to act (and is therefore negligent in failing to avert the harm). [Rest. 2d §452]

1/ **Example:** Where D negligently allows poisonous gas to escape from its pipeline, it is liable for injuries to workers in the vicinity (foreseeable result), even though the workers' employer, X, *knew* of the danger and was negligent in failing to protect them. X's negligence was foreseeable and did not supersede D's liability. [Ewart v. Southern California Gas Co., 237 Cal. App. 2d 163 (1965)]

2/ **Limitation—"neutralization of the risk":** [§392] In certain cases, the third person's failure to act may be deemed so culpable or extraordinary that it will be held to have "neutralized the risk" created by the defendant's original negligence, and the failure to act will be treated as the superseding cause of the harm suffered by P. [Rest. 2d §452]

a/ **Example:** D negligently leaves dynamite caps on the ground and a young child, P, picks one up and shows it to his father. If P's father recognizes what it is but fails to take it away, the father's negligence will be considered so "highly extraordinary" as to have "neutralized the risk" created by D's original negligence so that if the cap subsequently explodes and injures P or a third person, D is not liable. [Kingsland v. Erie County Agricultural Society, 298 N.Y. 409 (1949)]

(2) **Unforeseeable results produced by foreseeable intervening forces:** [§393] Even though an intervening force may be foreseeable, some courts will terminate the defendant's liability if the *result* was unforeseeable, while others would nevertheless impose liability. This presents a variation on the *"Polemis-Wagon Mound"* debate (*see supra*, §§368-369).

(a) **Example—"narrow" view:** P's father had heated a pot of water on the kitchen stove because D landlord negligently failed to provide hot water to the apartment. P collided with his father, who was carrying the water to the bathroom, and was burned when the water spilled on him. *Held:* No liability because the kind of injury was unlike that reasonably expected from D's original negligent act. [Martinez v. Lazaroff, 48 N.Y.2d 819 (1979); *but see* Enis v. Ba-Call Building Corp., 639 F.2d 359 (7th Cir. 1980)—contra (on almost identical facts)]

(b) **Example—"broad" view:** D negligently moored its ship in the river. The ship was set adrift by current (foreseeable intervening force) and was carried downstream, where it struck and collapsed a bridge. The collapse created an ice jam, which caused water to back up and flood P's factory on the riverbank (unforeseeable result). (The foreseeable damage to P's factory was being crashed into by the ship.) D was liable for the flooding. [Kinsman Transit Co. No. 1, 338 F.2d 708 (2d Cir. 1964)]

(3) **Unforeseeable results produced by unforeseeable intervening forces:** [§394] As a general rule, whether courts emphasize the foreseeability of the result or the foreseeability of the intervening force, where *both* are unforeseeable, all courts agree that defendant is *not liable*.

(a) **Example:** D negligently blocked a road, forcing P to take a detour along a more dangerous path. While P was on the detour, he was struck by a falling airplane. The court denied liability. [Doss v. Big Stone Gap, 134 S.E. 563 (Va. 1926)] *But note:* If the path were more dangerous because of the risk of falling rocks, and a rock fell on P, D would be liable (foreseeable result).

(b) **Common carrier exception:** [§395] Some courts—because of the high standard of care they impose on common carriers—will hold a defendant carrier liable for any loss or damage that occurs to goods delayed in transit, even though such damage (the result) was unforeseeable and caused by an unforeseeable flood or other "act of God" (the manner). [Green-Wheeler Shoe Co. v. Chicago, Rock Island & Pacific Railway, 106 N.W. 498 (Iowa 1906)]

(4) **Comment—ultimate result depends on degree of emphasis on foreseeability:** [§396] Note again that every case involving an unforeseeable result is by definition a bizarre situation involving some danger that the defendant could not reasonably expect. This factor favors the defendant; but on the other hand, the fact that the defendant has been negligent and the actual cause of the plaintiff's harm also enter into the court's determination. The choice depends ultimately on the importance the court gives to foreseeability.

f. **Unforeseeable plaintiff:** [§397] This situation recalls the *Palsgraf* case (*see supra*, §284) involving the falling scales. Courts following the *Cardozo* approach would reject an unforeseeable plaintiff at the duty stage. But those courts following the *Andrews* view must still face the proximate cause question and may consider the plaintiff's unforeseeability simply as a factor favoring the defendant in the proximate cause issue.

(1) **Rare situation:** [§398] Probably because of the unusual sequences involved, few courts have faced a true *Palsgraf* situation. However, where the case does arise, most courts *deny* liability—whether analyzed as a duty or proximate cause question.

    (a) **Example:** X is struck by bus and tossed in the air so as to hit P, who had been in what appeared to be a safe spot. The court found no liability. [Dahlstrom v. Shrum, 84 A.2d 289 (Pa. 1951)]

    (b) **Example:** D negligently ran down X. Seven years later, X, who had suffered brain damage from the accident, shot and wounded P. The court denied liability against D because the passage of time permitted the intervention of many other possible factors. [Firman v. Sacia, 7 App. Div. 2d 579 (1959)]

(2) **Andrews view:** [§399] Since Judge Andrews would permit a jury to find liability in *Palsgraf*, he must reject the majority's total reliance on foreseeability. After finding that the defendant was negligent, Judge Andrews stated that proximate cause was a matter of expedience and "practical politics" and was not primarily an issue of "fairness" to the defendant.

    (a) **"Andrews factors":** Judge Andrews set out several factors to be considered in deciding whether a jury could properly find that a defendant's negligence was the proximate cause of a plaintiff's harm. These included: directness of the connection between the act and the harm; whether there was a natural and continuous sequence between the two; whether the harm could have been reasonably foreseen; and remoteness in time and space. No one factor necessarily prevailed over the others.

g. **Summary of proximate cause**

(1) **Role of foreseeability:** [§400] Although the concept of foreseeability is playing a role at three points in proximate cause analysis, the term probably plays a different role at each point.

    (a) **Manner:** [§401] Generally, it is irrelevant whether a particular manner of occurrence was foreseeable as long as the result was. Rather the test is a negative one: *Manner of occurrence is irrelevant unless* the sequence was "highly extraordinary"—in which case courts split over the result. Some courts conclude that it is unfair to hold a defendant responsible for such sequences. Others conclude that if the defendant's negligence led to a foreseeable result, this is enough to create liability, and a highly extraordinary manner raises no moral argument to relieve the defendant from liability that would otherwise exist.

        1) **Intervening intentional or criminal acts:** [§402] If intervening intentional or criminal acts are foreseeable, liability will

follow. But if they are unforeseeable, the greater moral blame-worthiness of the third party's act leads some courts to hold that it supersedes the defendant's liability, even when a fore-seeable result occurs.

(b) **Result:** [§403]   Courts are split over how important it is that the result that befalls the plaintiff have been reasonably foreseeable. Although courts that follow *Wagon Mound* (*see supra*, §369) give foreseeability great weight (except in "thin-skull" cases), courts following *Polemis* (*see supra*, §368) reject it in "direct" cases, and courts following *Kinsman Transit Co. No. 1* (*see supra*, §393) de-emphasize it in "indirect" cases.

(c) **Plaintiff:** [§404]   Foreseeability of the plaintiff is absolutely central to the courts following the majority in *Palsgraf*, while other courts give it some weight when considering proximate cause.

(2) **Compare—duty:** [§405]   Remember that the duty element involves the question of who is owed a duty of due care. Foreseeability is used in that analysis under both the Cardozo view (foreseeability of plaintiff or group to which plaintiff belongs) and the Andrews view (foreseeability of harm to anyone).

6. **Damages:** [§406]   Once a negligent act and causation are established, the plaintiff must show damages resulting therefrom in order to impose liability on the defendant. Unlike intentional torts, in every case where liability is based on *negligence*, there must be a showing of *actual damages* to person or property.

a. **Accrual of action:** [§407]   Since damage is an essential element, there is no cause of action until damage has been sustained, and hence the statute of limitations commences to run only from that date. In some cases, it begins to run only from the discovery of the harm or the discovery of the negligence. [Flanagan v. Mt. Eden General Hospital, 24 N.Y.2d 427 (1969); *but see* Garrett v. Raytheon, 368 So. 2d 516 (Ala. 1979)]

b. **Types of damages recoverable:** [§408]   The basic purpose of awarding damages in negligence cases is compensatory, rather than punitive—*i.e.*, to restore the plaintiff insofar as possible to her condition before she was injured, rather than to punish the defendant.

(1) **"Special" damages:** [§409]   The plaintiff is entitled to recover *all economic losses and expenses* ("special" damages) she has suffered as a result of the injury—*e.g.*, medical bills, lost wages or business profits, cost of hiring household help, etc. This includes expenses already incurred, and expenses that the plaintiff proves she probably will incur in the *future* (as where she remains under medical care or is unable to return to work).

(a) **Computing lost wages—the tax question**

1) **Traditional rule:** [§410]   Until recently, the uniform practice was to measure wage loss by gross earnings before income tax deductions. [63 A.L.R.2d 1393]

2) **Federal rule:** [§411]   In cases under the Federal Employers Liability Act, and perhaps other federal actions, the wage loss must be calculated on an after-tax basis unless the difference between the two methods would be trivial. [Norfolk & Western Railway v. Liepelt, 444 U.S. 490 (1980)]

3) **State rule:** [§412]   Although many states have adhered to the traditional rule [Johnson v. Manhattan & Bronx Surface Transit Operating Authority, 71 N.Y.2d 198 (1988)], others have insisted that after-tax income is the only permissible basis for assessing the loss [Caldwell v. Haynes, 643 A.2d 564 (N.J. 1994)].

(b) **Future economic losses:** [§413]   The recovery for future loss of earnings and medical expenses, etc., can take into account whatever period of time the plaintiff's disability is expected to last.

1) **Child's loss of earning capacity:** [§414]   Where a child has suffered a severe injury with lasting or permanent effects that will likely impair the child's ability to earn, a number of jurisdictions now allow juries to consider the child's loss of income-earning capacity even without specific quantifying evidence. [Lesniak v. County of Bergen, 563 A.2d 795 (N.J. 1989)]

2) **Effect of inflation:** [§415]   If the plaintiff's disability is expected to continue over a period of years, modern courts allow the jury to take into consideration expert testimony as to probable future inflation rates in computing the plaintiff's loss of future earnings and future medical expenses. [*See* United States v. English, 521 F.2d 63 (9th Cir. 1975)]

3) **Award must be discounted to present value:** [§416]   However, after factoring in the inflation rate (if any), most courts require the award for future economic losses to be discounted to its *present* value, *i.e.*, the amount of money that if now invested at reasonable rates would defray the economic losses that the plaintiff is expected to sustain in the future. [Jones & Laughlin Steel Corp. v. Pfeifer, 462 U.S. 523 (1983)]

a) **Compare—pain and suffering:** Most courts do *not* discount awards for future pain and suffering (below) because such awards are not really mathematically computable. [Brant v. Bockholt, 532 N.W.2d 801 (Iowa 1995); *but see* Metz v. United Technologies Corp., 754 F.2d 63 (2d Cir. 1985)—contra]

4) **Minority rule—offsetting factors:** [§417]   Some courts have concluded that the discount factor and the inflation rate are likely to be about the same, so that there is no need to take account of either factor. The plaintiff should be awarded the full amount awarded by the jury without discount. [Beaulieu v. Elliott, 434 P.2d 665 (Alaska 1967)]

(2) **"General" damages:** [§418]   In addition to all special damages incurred, the plaintiff is entitled to recover those damages deemed *inherent in the injury itself*—*e.g.*, pain and suffering (past, present, and future), and any disfigurement (loss of limb, scars, etc.) or disability (loss of mobility, etc.) attributable to the injury. These are "general" damages.

    (a) **Pain and suffering before death:** [§419]   D is liable for the pain and suffering experienced by P before death from an accident D negligently caused, even when P lives only a very short time. Thus, an award of $30,000 for the two minutes a 14-month-old infant suffered while drowning was appropriate [Landreth v. Reed, 370 S.W.2d 486 (Tex. 1978)], and $70,000 was not excessive when P was conscious for 60 minutes after she was hit by a train [Juiditta v. Bethlehem Steel Corp., 75 App. Div. 2d 126 (1980); *but see* Cal. Prob. Code §573—contra].

        1) **Pre-impact fear and post-impact pain:** [§420]   Several courts award damages for fear caused by apprehension of impending death. [Haley v. Pan American World Airways, Inc., 746 F.2d 311 (5th Cir. 1984)—$15,000 for four to six seconds of fear felt by passenger who sensed impending fatal crash; Pregeant v. Pan American World Airways, Inc., 762 F.2d 1245 (5th Cir. 1985)—$20,000 for a few seconds of post-crash impact; *but see* St. Clair v. Denny, 781 P.2d 1043 (Kan. 1989)—no recovery for pre-impact distress where skid marks from P's car were only 60 feet long]

    (b) **Victim conscious:** [§421]   Courts require that the victim be sufficiently conscious to experience the pain and suffering. [McDougald v. Garber, 73 N.Y.2d 246 (1989)]

    (c) **Loss of enjoyment of life:** [§422]   Most courts have refused to recognize a separate item of damages called loss of enjoyment of life that would cover such matters as the inability to be active or to play the violin. These items are properly considered as a component of pain and suffering. [McDougald v. Garber, *supra*; Leiker v. Gafford, 778 P.2d 823 (Kan. 1989)—P must be conscious that such a loss occurred; *but see* Fantozzi v. Sandusky Cement Products Co., 597 N.E.2d 474 (Ohio 1992)—concluding that separate measurement of lost enjoyment would achieve greater precision in measurement as long as duplication of items was avoided]

    (d) **Unexpected damages included:** [§423]   Remember that "the tortfeasor takes his victim as he finds him" (*see supra*, §370) so that the defendant is liable for all injuries actually sustained by the plaintiff even if they are due to the plaintiff's abnormal sensitivities, to aggravation of some preexisting illness or condition (*e.g.*, a minor impact that causes a previously dormant condition to "flare up," resulting in permanent disability), or if they make the plaintiff susceptible to an illness or condition that she otherwise would not have suffered (*e.g.*, complications following surgery required by the original injury).

(3) **Damages for destruction of personal property:** [§424] When personal property has a *market value*, that value is the measure of damages for its destruction. If it has no market value but can be reproduced or replaced, the *cost of reproduction or replacement* is the measure. If the property has no market value and can be neither replaced nor reproduced, damages are measured by its *value to the owner*, but excluding "unusual sentimental value." [Mieske v. Bartell Drug Co., 593 P.2d 1308 (Wash. 1979)—loss of treasured family movie film]

(4) **Punitive damages not recoverable:** [§425] As indicated above, damages in a negligence case are intended to be compensatory only. Hence, punitive damages—sometimes allowed for intentional torts (*see supra*, §23)—are *not* recoverable for negligent conduct.

   (a) **Compare—"reckless conduct":** Some states do permit punitive damages when the defendant has engaged in conduct that courts consider "reckless"—*e.g.*, *drunk driving*. *Rationale:* The voluntary act of driving while intoxicated evinces a sufficiently reckless attitude to support an award of punitive damages. [Taylor v. Superior Court, 24 Cal. 3d 890 (1979); Johnson v. Rogers, 763 P.2d 771 (Utah 1988)]

c. **"Avoidable consequences" rule:** [§426] Some courts refer to the "avoidable consequences" rule as "plaintiff's duty to mitigate damages": An injured party must act reasonably to minimize her loss or injury, and where the damages are unnecessarily aggravated or increased through her failure to do so, the *additional* damages are *not recoverable*. [Zimmerman v. Ausland, 513 P.2d 1167 (Or. 1973)]

   (1) **Example:** P unreasonably refuses to submit to medical care following a personal injury caused by D's negligence. D is liable only for the damages originally inflicted and those likely to have occurred after reasonable treatment—not for any added pain, suffering, or disfigurement that could have been avoided had P sought medical attention. [Withrow v. Becker, 6 Cal. App. 2d 723 (1935)]

   (2) **Burden of proof:** [§427] While the plaintiff always has the burden of proving her damages, the burden is on the *defendant* to prove that the plaintiff unreasonably failed to mitigate those damages (as by refusing to submit to surgery or other medical treatment).

   (3) **What constitutes "unreasonableness":** [§428] Factors considered in determining the reasonableness of the plaintiff's failure to mitigate damages include: (i) the *risk* involved in the mitigating conduct; (ii) the *probability of success*; (iii) the *pain and effort* involved; and (iv) whether *the plaintiff could financially afford* the course of action (*e.g.*, medical treatment, etc.). [Hall v. Dumitru, 620 N.E.2d 668 (Ill. 1993)—no duty to undergo any surgery whether major or minor]

   (4) **"Anticipatory" avoidable consequences:** [§429] Although most avoidable consequences cases involve the plaintiff's unreasonable conduct after

an accident (*e.g.*, failure to get proper medical attention after injury), the issue also may arise where the plaintiff acted unreasonably *prior to* an accident.

(a) **Application—failure to wear safety belts:** [§430]   Thus, the refusal to wear a safety belt may be an unreasonable failure to minimize harm from a future automobile collision—on the theory that had the safety belt been used, the plaintiff's injuries might not have been as severe (or may have been avoided entirely).

   1) **Judicial opinion:** [§431]   However, only a few courts faced with the issue (*e.g.*, New York and California), applying the reasonable person standard (*i.e.*, whether a reasonable person would have worn the belts), have concluded that such neglect is to be considered in determining the plaintiff's damages. [Spier v. Barker, 35 N.Y.2d 444 (1974)]

   2) **Legislation:** [§432]   Although many states now have statutes requiring use of safety belts, most of these laws bar (or limit the effect of) evidence of failure to use the belts to establish the plaintiff's contributory negligence or to establish an unreasonable failure to mitigate damages.

(5) **Impact of comparative negligence:** [§433]   As to the effect of comparative negligence on the avoidable consequences rule, *see infra*, §679.

d. **"Collateral sources" rule:** [§434]   In most states, the plaintiff is entitled to recover the full amount of her damages from the defendant without any deduction for benefits that she may have received from sources "collateral" to the tortfeasor, such as insurance protection or benefits program that the victim has provided for herself, or that has been provided for her by her employer or by the government.

(1) **Rationale:** The defendant's liability should not be lessened by the fact that the plaintiff (or her employer or the government) was prudent enough to provide insurance against the kind of loss that the defendant caused. [Helfend v. Southern California Rapid Transit, 2 Cal. 3d 1 (1970); Bandel v. Friedrich, 584 A.2d 800 (N.J. 1991)]

(2) **Criticism—"double recovery":** [§435]   This result has been criticized as permitting the plaintiff to recover twice for the same losses, so that awarding those items of damages against the defendant is inefficient and is more punitive than compensatory in nature.

   (a) **Answer to criticism—subrogation:** However, insurance law and written policies increasingly provide for *subrogation* (below) or otherwise require the injured party to *refund* to the insurer any benefits paid upon ultimate recovery from the tortfeasor and so, in practice, there is often no "double recovery."

(3) **Subrogation rights of plaintiff's insurer:** [§436]   To whatever extent the plaintiff's own insurance company has paid any benefits to the plaintiff (*e.g.*, for medical expenses or property damage to her car), legal rules

and most policies today provide that the insurance company is "subrogated" to the claims the plaintiff may have against the person who caused those losses—*i.e.*, an automatic *assignment*.

(a) **Note:** Usually, insurance policies give the insurance company the right to sue the defendant in the name of the insured (plaintiff). In practice, however, the plaintiff more frequently maintains her own action against the defendant (for pain and suffering and whatever other damages or losses she has sustained), and her insurance company then asserts a right to *reimbursement* out of any settlement or judgment plaintiff obtains.

(b) **And note:** The insurance company, as subrogee (assignee), "stands in the plaintiff's shoes" with respect to its right to recover from the defendant. Thus, whatever defenses could be asserted against the plaintiff—*e.g.*, contributory negligence—can likewise be asserted against her insurance company.

C. SPECIAL DUTY QUESTIONS

1. **Introduction:** [§437]   This section deals with the circumstances under which the defendant may owe some special duty of care to the plaintiff. Usually, this will be a duty owed *in addition to* the general duty of due care the defendant owes under the "reasonable person" standard, *supra*. However, in a few instances (*e.g.*, when dealing with land occupiers, *see infra*), the special duty of due care is *in place of* the general duty of due care. As a matter of analysis, where the circumstances indicate that some special duty of care may be in point, consider first whether there is a breach of such special duty.

2. **Duties and Breach Measured by Statute—"Negligence Per Se"**

   a. **Nature of statute**

   (1) **Civil statutes:** [§438]   Some statutes regulating conduct provide a *civil* remedy for their violation. In such cases, the plaintiff can *sue directly under the statute* and usually need not be concerned with common law negligence.

   (2) **Criminal statutes:** [§439]   The concern here is with statutes that provide only *criminal penalties* for their violation (*e.g.*, the usual traffic code). Under appropriate circumstances, violation of such statutes may subject a defendant to civil as well as criminal liability; *i.e.*, courts may refer to the terms of the statute to create a *specific duty of care*, so that violation of the criminal statute operates to establish both *duty and breach* in a civil negligence action. [Osborne v. McMasters, 41 N.W. 543 (Minn. 1889)]

   (a) **Note—not children:** Under the majority rule, the doctrine of "negligence per se" is not invoked against children engaged in children's activities. [Bauman v. Crawford, 704 P.2d 1181 (Wash. 1985)] The children's standard is discussed, *supra*, §259.

b. **Requirements:** [§440]   For a criminal statute to establish a specific duty of care for civil negligence purposes the following must appear:

(1) **Statutory duty clear:** [§441]   The statute itself must be clear and unambiguous. It must specify exactly what conduct or duty is required, of whom it is required, and what constitutes a breach of that duty.

(2) **Violation within statutory purpose:** [§442]   It must also appear that in enacting the statute, the legislature was seeking to accomplish two separate objectives: (i) to prevent the particular type of injury, and (ii) to protect the particular class of plaintiff.

(a) **To prevent type of injury:** [§443]   The legislative purpose must have been to prevent the type of injury actually suffered by the plaintiff. [Matamco Oil Co. v. Arctic Mechanical, Inc., 796 P.2d 1336 (Alaska 1990); Darmento v. Pacific Molasses Co., 81 N.Y.2d 985 (1993)]

1) **Example:** A statute makes it unlawful for auto owners to leave their vehicles parked with the keys in the ignition. Auto owner D violates this statute and thief X steals D's car, drives it negligently, and injures P. Is D liable for P's injuries? Probably not. It is doubtful that the legislature intended to prevent *this type* of injury. More likely, the legislative intent was to make auto theft more difficult or to protect innocent purchasers of stolen cars. [Anderson v. Theisen, 43 N.W.2d 272 (Minn. 1950); Pendrey v. Barnes, 479 N.E.2d 283 (Ohio 1985); *but see, e.g.,* Ney v. Yellow Cab Co., 117 N.E.2d 74 (Ill. 1954)—contra]

2) **Example:** D practices medicine without a license in violation of statute. However, D's violation does not make him liable for a patient's injuries, because *licensing statutes* seek only to protect the public against incompetents; lack of due care in treatment must be shown for D to be liable for the injuries. [Hardy v. Dahl, 187 S.E. 788 (N.C. 1936)]

3) **Example:** Defendant gas station sells gas to arsonists in violation of a statute forbidding the sale of gas in plastic containers. Arsonists use the gas to accelerate a fire that kills and injures plaintiffs. Defendant is not liable to plaintiffs under statutory-violation analysis because the statute was designed to make the transport and storage of gas safer, not to make it harder to buy untanked gas. [Morales v. City of New York, 70 N.Y.2d 981 (1988)]

(b) **To protect class of persons:** [§444]   The legislature must also have intended to protect a class of persons of which plaintiff is a member. [Kelly v. Henry Muhs Co., 59 A. 23 (N.J. 1904)]

1) **Example:** D makes an illegal left-hand turn in violation of the Vehicle Code, collides with an oncoming car, and crashes into P's building on the side of the road. D's violation is probably

irrelevant because P was not among the *class of persons* sought to be protected by the statute; *i.e.*, its apparent objective is to protect other motorists on the highway, not owners of property along the roadside. [Erickson v. Kongsli, 240 P.2d 1209 (Wash. 1952)]

(3) **No excuse:** [§445]   Often a violation of statute is reasonable. The statute can be invoked to set a specific duty of care only where the defendant has no legally acceptable excuse for its violation.

(a) **Application:** If the defendant had no good reason for the infraction, this presents the clearest case for a finding of negligence. [Robinson v. District of Columbia, 580 A.2d 1255 (D.C. 1990)—proof of custom of crossing street outside crosswalk cannot excuse violation of traffic regulation] On the other hand, even though a person failed to comply with the statute's technical language, it is still possible that she acted reasonably under the particular circumstances. In such cases, she has not been negligent and should not be held liable for violating the statute. [Tedla v. Ellman, 280 N.Y. 124 (1939)]

1) **Example:** It has been held not to be negligence where D disobeys the letter of a statute because of physical circumstances beyond his control, as where his lights unexpectedly fail on the highway at night or where he is forced to drive on the left because the right is blocked. [Brotherton v. Day & Night Fuel Co., 73 P.2d 788 (Wash. 1937)]

2) **Rationale:** Violations of statute permit the court to use a *specific* duty of care to replace the more general duty of care already discussed. However, this can be justified only as long as the basic assumption that it is reasonable to obey the criminal law holds; *i.e.*, when a reasonable person would violate the law, the theory fails.

(b) **Excuses must be heard:** [§446]   Moreover, unless the legislature intended to foreclose consideration of excused violations (which is rarely the case), the court is bound to hear excuses offered by defendant; to do otherwise would be tantamount to imposing strict liability.

c. **Effect of violation of statutory duty**

(1) **Unexcused violations:** [§447]   If the defendant makes no effort to justify or excuse his prima facie violation of a criminal statute, and that statute was enacted to protect a class of persons of which the plaintiff is a member from the type of injury the plaintiff actually suffered, liability will be analyzed under one of three views:

(a) **Majority view—"negligence per se":** [§448]   Under the widely followed majority view, such a showing will lead the trial judge to conclude that the defendant was negligent *as a matter of law*; there will be no question for the jury on the questions of duty or breach of duty. [Martin v. Herzog, 228 N.Y. 164 (1920); Rest. 2d §288B]

(b) **Minority view—rebuttable presumption:** [§449] One minority view holds that the violation creates only a rebuttable presumption of negligence and does not establish negligence per se. But, as indicated below, this view significantly differs from that of the majority *only* when the defendant offers an *excuse* for his behavior. Absent such a showing, the presumption of negligence cannot be rebutted, and negligence will be found as a matter of law, just as under the majority view. [Satterlee v. Orange Glenn School District, 29 Cal. 2d 581 (1947)]

(c) **Minority view—evidence only:** [§450] A second minority view holds that violation of a statute or ordinance is never more than *evidence* of breach of duty and is not binding on the trier of fact. Thus, subject to the usual limits on the jury's role, a jury might find even an unexcused violation to be nonnegligent behavior. [French v. Willman, 599 A.2d 1151 (Me. 1991)—car crossing center line on road is "evidence of negligence"]

(2) **Where excuse offered for violation**

(a) **Majority view:** [§451] Where the defendant attempts to justify his behavior, in the majority of jurisdictions the trial judge will decide the validity of the offered excuse. If the excuse is found valid (and supported by the facts), the judge will rule for the defendant. (If crucial facts are disputed, the jury will determine these.)

1) **But note:** If the excuse is *unacceptable*, even if supported by the facts, the excuse will not justify the violation.

(b) **Minority view—rebuttable presumption:** [§452] Under this view, the apparent violator has the burden of persuading the trier of fact that the behavior was reasonable even though it may have violated a statute. If the defendant does not meet this burden, the plaintiff will prevail.

(c) **Minority view—evidence only:** [§453] Here the jury is instructed that the burden is on the plaintiff to establish negligence as in the usual common law case. The asserted statutory violation is treated as one of the circumstances of the case and will have whatever effect the jury decides to give it (operating within the usual limits on jury power).

d. **Caution—causation and damage must still be shown:** [§454] Remember that violation of a statutory duty establishes only the duty and breach elements. To recover, the plaintiff must also prove that the defendant's violation of the statute was the *cause* of the plaintiff's injury and must prove damages.

(1) **Note:** Proximate cause will rarely be a problem because the statutory violation will not be used in the first place unless the person hurt was in the group to be protected and the resulting harm was the type the statute sought to prevent. Since these factors are also critical in proximate cause analysis, once the statute is relied on to establish duty and breach, a finding of proximate cause is virtually assured.

3. **Duty to Aid Others in Emergency**

a. **General rule—no duty:** [§455]   Under the general common law rule, a defendant owes *no* duty to go to the aid of a stranger in an emergency—at least where the defendant was in no way responsible for that person's injury or predicament. *Rationale:* Tort law is not concerned with purely moral obligations. [Bishop v. Chicago, 257 N.E.2d 152 (Ill. 1970)]

b. **Exceptions—duty owed where special factors present:** [§456]   However, where certain factors are present, the law does impose upon a defendant a duty to act:

   (1) **Special relationship to plaintiff:** [§457]   Courts recognize that a defendant owes a duty to go to the aid of another in an emergency where some *special relationship* exists between them—*e.g.*, family, employer-employee, host-guest, carrier-passenger, jailer-prisoner, etc. [Carey v. Davis, 180 N.W. 889 (Iowa 1921); *and see* Farwell v. Keaton, 240 N.W.2d 217 (Mich. 1976)—extending duty to social friends]

   (2) **Responsibility for plaintiff's peril:** [§458]   Likewise, a defendant who is responsible for the plaintiff's injury or peril is under a duty to go to the plaintiff's aid *and* to exercise reasonable care in so doing.

      (a) **What if defendant not at fault?** [§459]   Although earlier decisions found such a duty only where the defendant's responsibility was tortious, current decisions recognize a duty to aid a person in peril even where the defendant's original conduct was *innocent* but has nevertheless created a perilous situation (*e.g.*, where D's golf ball strikes P on the head and no risk to P had been foreseeable, D still owes a duty to render assistance). [Rest. 2d §321]

   (3) **Statutory exceptions:** [§460]   The no-duty rule has also been limited in several states by statutes requiring persons to assist others in certain emergency situations:

      (a) **Example:** Several states have statutes making it a criminal offense for the driver of an automobile to fail to go to the aid of any person involved in an accident with his car, even though the driver was in no way at fault in causing the accident. [*See* Cal. Veh. Code §20003] Civil liability may also be imposed.

      (b) **And note:** By statute, a few states impose criminal liability for failure to go to the aid of anyone whom the defendant recognizes to be in serious peril, provided this would not greatly endanger defendant. [12 Vt. Stat. Ann. §519]

   (4) **Special relationship to harmer:** [§461]   If defendant has some relationship with the person who does the harm, courts may use that to recognize a duty to use due care to avoid the harm. (*See supra*, §294, *and see infra*, §§483-530.)

c. **Compare—duty owed where defendant undertakes to aid plaintiff ("Good Samaritan obligation"):** [§462] Note that where the defendant clearly owed no duty to aid the plaintiff initially (*i.e.*, where the defendant was not responsible for the plaintiff's predicament and no special relationship existed between them), if the defendant *voluntarily undertakes* to aid the plaintiff, he must do so carefully. That is, the defendant need not act at all, *but if he does, he owes a duty of reasonable care*. [Zelenko v. Gimbel, 158 Misc. 904 (1935)]

(1) **Example:** D finds a stranger (P) Lying unconscious in the street and decides to take her to a hospital. In doing so, D owes a duty to exercise reasonable care in moving P and driving to the hospital. If D acts unreasonably, he will be liable for any injuries attributable to his lack of care.

(2) **Effect of abandonment:** [§463] However, the fact that the defendant has undertaken to aid the plaintiff does not necessarily require him to continue his efforts. In some states, he may terminate his services at any time without liability *provided* the subsequent abandonment leaves the plaintiff in *no worse condition* than that in which the defendant found her. Thus, suppose in the above example that on the way to the hospital D decides he does not want to become involved and abandons P by the side of the road. D will not be liable as long as he has not thereby placed P in greater peril or deprived P of the chance of aid by others. [Miller v. Arnal Corp., 632 P.2d 987 (Ariz. 1981)] In some states, however, D must exercise due care at least to the extent of not shifting P to a position of peril comparable to that from which she was rescued. [Parvi v. City of Kingston, 41 N.Y.2d 553 (1977); Rest. 2d §324, comment g]

(3) **Statutory exception for physicians:** [§464] So as not to discourage physicians (who may be concerned about malpractice liability should the due care standard apply) from assisting others in emergencies, so-called Good Samaritan statutes have been adopted in virtually all states, *exempting physicians* who render aid in an emergency from liability for negligence. [21 S. Tex. L.J. 327 (1981)]

4. **Affirmative Duty to Prevent Harm:** [§465] In addition to the special duties imposed under the specific categories below, courts increasingly are finding a duty of care owed by defendants who share a special relationship with the plaintiff to prevent harm, whether or not inflicted by another person. Such a duty builds on situations in which the defendant may be liable even though an intervening negligent or intentional act by a third party separates the defendant's act or omission from the injury to the plaintiff. (Examples of such relationships are carrier and passenger, innkeeper and guest, school district and pupil, etc.) But not every relationship suffices. [*See* Harper v. Herman, 499 N.W.2d 472 (Minn. 1993)—captain owes no duty to warn guest of danger in diving off side of pleasure boat]

a. **Voluntary assumption of care:** [§466] Defendant may assume such a special duty voluntarily by certain acts that cause plaintiff to be more vulnerable to injury from a third person than had defendant not acted at all. Thus, where D, the owner of a building in a high-crime neighborhood, hires an attendant to watch the lobby, a visitor might reasonably be lulled into a false sense of security and neglect normal safety precautions. If P is attacked by a third person while the attendant is inexcusably absent, D may be liable. [Nallan v. Helmsley-Spear, Inc., 50 N.Y.2d 507 (1980); Cross v. Wells Fargo Alarm Services, 412 N.E.2d 472 (Ill. 1980)—municipal housing authority that provided part-time security guard service increased danger to tenants during hours when guards not present]

b. **Governmental entities' duty to protect:** [§467] The general rule is that in such protective capacities, absent special circumstances, the government's duty is owed to the public generally, not to any particular members of the public, and so recovery is barred. [*See* Riss v. City of New York, 22 N.Y.2d 579 (1968); City of Jordan v. Rome, 426 S.E.2d 861 (Ga. 1993)—no duty to protect P, who had sought police aid because she feared harm from disappointed suitor who had threatened her; Davidson v. City of Westminster, 32 Cal. 3d 197 (1982)—police in stakeout owed no duty to victim hurt before police closed in]

c. **Compare—"special circumstances":** [§468] "Special circumstances," under which a duty may lie, include a separate legal basis for arrest of a third person who had threatened harm [Sorichetti v. City of New York, 65 N.Y.2d 461 (1985)]; or a statute that is construed to create a duty to particular plaintiffs [Busby v. Municipality of Anchorage, 741 P.2d 230 (Alaska 1987)—statutory obligation on police to assist persons apparently incapacitated by alcohol].

5. **Duty to Perform Promises—Nonfeasance vs. Misfeasance**

a. **Gratuitous promises:** [§469] In general, a defendant's *failure to perform a gratuitous promise* to render service or assistance does not give rise to a basis for tort liability—even where the defendant knew that the plaintiff would suffer damage as a result of nonperformance. [Thorne v. Deas, 4 Johns. 84 (1809)]

   (1) **Example:** D voluntarily promises to obtain insurance on P's building but fails to do so, and the building is then destroyed by fire. D is not liable in tort to P. [Brawn v. Lyford, 69 A. 544 (Me. 1907)]

   (2) **Rationale—distinction between misfeasance and nonfeasance:** It is a deep-rooted principle that, absent some legal duty to act, tort liability is predicated only on *misfeasance—not on nonfeasance*. Thus, a promisor's failure to perform his promise is not by itself a sufficient basis for tort liability. (*But see infra*, §1390, imposing liability where defendant makes a promise with no intention of fulfilling it.)

   (3) **Compare—duty owed where defendant enters upon performance:** [§470] However, even where the promise is gratuitous, a defendant-promisor who "enters upon its performance" in any manner must perform with reasonable care. Failure to do so is "misfeasance," and is a sufficient basis for tort liability. Thus, although the Federal Aviation Authority need not publish air charts, it will be held liable for any injuries caused by inaccuracies in charts it does publish. [Reminga v. United States, 631 F.2d 449 (6th Cir. 1980)]

(4) **Minority view—duty owed based on foreseeable reliance:** [§471]   A number of cases have held the defendant liable for failing to perform his promise where he knew or should have known that plaintiff was *refraining from obtaining other necessary assistance in reliance* on the promise. *Example:* Sheriff D, under no legal obligation to do so, promised to warn P before X was released from jail, because X had threatened to kill P. D failed to do so; X killed P, and D was held liable to P's heirs. [Morgan v. Yuba, 230 Cal. App. 2d 938 (1964); Hartley v. Floyd, 512 So. 2d 1022 (Fla. 1987)]

b.   **Contractual promises:** [§472]   Generally, the rules for gratuitous promises apply to contractual promises.

(1) **Nonfeasance:** [§473]   Thus, tort liability normally *cannot* be predicated solely on the defendant's failure to perform a contract. Where the defendant simply fails or refuses to begin *any* performance under the contract, the plaintiff's remedy is strictly in contract. [Louisville & Nashville Railroad v. Spinks, 30 S.E. 968 (Ga. 1898)—carrier failed to furnish transportation for goods as agreed]

(2) **Misfeasance:** [§474]   On the other hand, a defendant who undertakes performance of a contract owes a duty of reasonable care; improper performance may constitute *both* a breach of contract and an actionable tort, allowing the plaintiff to bring either action.

(a) **Example:** P hires D to erect a windmill on P's property. If D never shows up on the job, he may be liable for breach of contract, but not in tort. However, once he starts the construction, he must exercise due care; and if, as the result of improper design or construction, P's property is damaged or some other loss ensues, D may be liable either in contract or in tort. [Flint & Walling v. Beckett, 79 N.E. 503 (Ind. 1906)]

1) **Proof in medical cases:** A plaintiff who alleges that a medical doctor breached a contract to achieve a certain medical result may find it hard to establish the existence of a contract promising a particular result. *Rationale:* Doctors rarely can, in good faith, promise specific results, and patients have a tendency to transform their doctor's optimistic statements into firm promises. [Clevenger v. Haling, 394 N.E.2d 1119 (Mass. 1979)]

(b) **Application to other contractual relationships:** Similarly, other relationships, contractual in the first instance, impose a tort obligation once performance is undertaken—*i.e., carrier-passenger; innkeeper-guest; bailor-bailee.*

(3) **Liability to third parties:** [§475]   A defendant's *misfeasance* in the performance of a contract with one person may involve a foreseeable risk of harm to others (*e.g.*, a railroad worker who throws the wrong switch may cause harm to passengers). In such cases, the defendant's liability to any third persons injured thereby is judged on straight negligence standards—foreseeability of harm—and no privity or contractual relationship

need be established. But, again, no tort liability can be predicated solely on *nonfeasance*.

   (a) **Exception—water company cases:** [§476]   However, most courts have held that a private company that contracts with the city to furnish water is *not liable* to a private citizen when the service fails at a critical moment—*e.g.*, when water pressure drops and a house is destroyed by fire. [H.R. Moch Co. v. Rensselaer Water Co., 247 N.Y. 160 (1928); *but see* Weinberg v. Dinger, 524 A.2d 366 (N.J. 1987)—contra where the loss is uninsured]

      1) **Judicial rationale:** The failure of water service is deemed only "nonfeasance," on the theory that the private utility had not undertaken any direct performance to the private citizen; hence, there is no tort liability.

         a) **And note:** Private citizens cannot recover on a contract theory, because these courts hold the citizens to be only "incidental beneficiaries" of the utility's contract with the city. (*See* Contracts Summary.)

      2) **Underlying rationale?** Although the above rationale has been criticized for years, the rule is still generally followed. The explanation may be that virtually all improved property is insured against loss by fire, so that this suit is really one by a subrogated fire insurer against a liability insurer. This is thought to be an administratively wasteful suit, especially since one result might be to raise the price of water. [Libbey v. Hampton Water Works Co., 389 A.2d 434 (N.H. 1978)]

6. **Duty Owed by Common Carrier:** [§477]   Modern authorities treat the duty owed by one legally charged with the care of others as simply a duty of due care, with the obligation being one of the "circumstances." However, older courts treated this duty as imposing a *separate, affirmative standard of care*, demanding the "highest caution consistent with the undertaking." [Gardner v. Boston Elevated Railway, 90 N.E. 534 (Mass. 1910)] But wherever the defendant is legally charged with the safety of another (*e.g.*, carrier transporting passengers) or protecting the property of another (*e.g.*, bailee in possession of bailor's chattels), a high *amount* of care—if not a different standard of care—is clearly called for. [Acosta v. Southern California Rapid Transit, 2 Cal. 3d 19 (1970)]

a. **"Highest degree of care":** [§478]   Thus, a common carrier must *always* choose the course of action *least likely to expose its passengers to harm*. [Spelt v. Eaton, 192 A. 576 (N.J. 1937)—bus driver's use of force to eject boisterous passenger negligent because it endangered other passengers, even though driver was otherwise privileged to use such force; *see supra*, §250]

   (1) **Note:** Carrier employees have an affirmative duty to use due care to aid passengers when they become ill or are attacked by robbers. [Lopez v. Southern California Rapid Transit District, 40 Cal. 3d 780 (1985)]

   (2) **And note:** Courts sometimes impose liability on common carriers notwithstanding *intervening forces* that would excuse other defendants (*see supra*, §395).

b. **Compare—liability of auto driver to "guest" or "passenger": [§479]** The high degree of care owed by a common carrier to its passengers (above) has not been imposed on the driver of a private automobile with respect to riders therein.

(1) **Common law rule: [§480]** The driver of an automobile owes any rider therein a duty to exercise reasonable care to warn of any known dangers or defective conditions that are not reasonably apparent, and to exercise reasonable care in operating the car. [Higgins v. Mason, 255 N.Y. 104 (1930)]

(a) **Rationale:** This common law duty developed by analogy to the duty owed by a *land occupier* to guests or licensees (*see infra*, §564).

(2) **"Guest statutes": [§481]** A few jurisdictions still have statutes that eliminate ordinary negligence liability of the driver of an automobile to some riders therein. Such statutes provide that the driver is liable to a "guest" rider only for *"wanton" or "gross" negligence*, or for accidents due to intoxication or willful misconduct.

(a) **"Guest" vs. "passenger": [§482]** The most frequent problem in applying these statutes is to determine whether the injured rider is a "guest" or is a "passenger," as to whom the general common law duty of due care applies (by analogy to an invitee on land, *see infra*, §568). [Davis v. Davis, 622 So. 2d 901 (Ala. 1993)] Generally, if there has been some payment made (money, services, or property) that operates as a motivating influence for the driver's furnishing the ride, the rider is a passenger and may recover for *ordinary negligence*. [Bozanich v. Kenney, 3 Cal. 3d 567 (1970)] Note that sharing expenses *may* be sufficient by itself to qualify the rider for "passenger" status.

7. **Duty to Control Third Persons: [§483]** This section considers situations in which the defendant may be held liable for *nonfeasance*—failure to control the conduct of third persons over whom the defendant had the power of control.

a. **Distinguish direct liability from vicarious liability: [§484]** Where the defendant is *present* at the time of the third person's wrongful conduct, his failure to exercise control to stop such conduct may be an act of negligence on his own part. However, where the defendant is *not* present, he may be charged with liability for the acts of third persons only in limited situations. These latter cases include *imputing* the third person's acts to the defendant, who is said to be *vicariously liable* therefor (master-servant cases, etc.; *see* below).

b. **Bailment cases**

(1) **Liability based on bailor's negligence: [§485]** If the bailor of chattels permits the bailee to use them, the bailor has a right to control such use and will be liable in two situations for failure to exercise due care to prevent the intentional or negligent acts of the bailee while using the bailed chattel:

(a) **Committed in bailor's presence:** [§486]   The bailor will be held directly liable when the bailee's wrongful conduct is committed in the bailor's presence (*e.g.*, D permits X to drive D's car at an excessive speed while D rides beside him).

    1)   **Exception:** In some jurisdictions, the presence of the owner in the car as a passenger does not necessarily impose a duty to control the driver, but it may be a factor to consider. [Bauer v. Johnson, 403 N.E.2d 237 (Ill. 1980)]

    2)   **Compare—nonowner passenger:** Generally, automobile passengers owe no duty to the driver or to third parties to advise the driver in the operation of the vehicle. [Hale v. Allstate Insurance Co., 639 P.2d 203 (Utah 1981)]

(b) **"Negligent entrustment doctrine":** [§487]   Even if the tortious act has not been committed in the bailor's presence, he will be liable if he has failed to exercise reasonable care in *selecting* the bailee; *i.e.*, he knows or should know that the bailee is likely to cause harm to others. [Rest. 2d §390]

    1)   **Example:** Entrusting his car to an inexperienced driver, or to a driver known to be irresponsible or likely to become intoxicated, may make the bailor liable. [Mitchell v. Churches, 206 P. 6 (Wash. 1922)]

    2)   **Example:** Parents have been held liable for negligently entrusting a vehicle to a child with known reckless propensities [Allen v. Toledo, 109 Cal. App. 3d 415 (1980)], even where title to the car is in the child [Kahlenberg v. Goldstein, 431 A.2d 76 (Md. 1981)—parents helped child buy car].

    3)   **Compare—no liability where no right to control:** [§488] But a service station operator who sells gasoline to a recognizably intoxicated motorist is not liable for harm caused by the motorist. *Rationale:* The service station operator is a *seller*, not a bailor; *i.e.*, he has no right to control the use of the gasoline he sells. [Fuller v. Standard Stations, 250 Cal. App. 2d 687 (1967); *but see* Vince v. Wilson, 561 A.2d 103 (Vt. 1989)—auto seller may be liable for selling car to driver with known poor driving record, and person providing money for purchase may also be liable]

(2) **Liability where bailor not negligent:** [§489]   The general rule is that if the bailor has exercised reasonable care in the selection of the bailee (thus avoiding the "negligent entrustment doctrine"), he is *not liable* for negligent or intentional harm inflicted by the bailee outside the bailor's presence.

(a) **Exceptions—vicarious liability in automobile cases:** [§490]   However, there are two exceptions, both involving automobiles, in which the owner may be held liable for harm inflicted by the bailee *without any showing of negligence* on the part of the owner (*i.e.*, even though the owner was *careful* in selecting the bailee and was *not present* at the time of the bailee's tortious conduct). In these two cases, for public policy purposes, the owner is held *vicariously liable* for the torts committed by the bailee:

1) **"Family purpose doctrine":** [§491] Many jurisdictions by statute or case law hold an automobile owner liable for injuries resulting from the bailee's negligent operation of the vehicle, even outside the owner's presence, if the bailee is a member of the owner's immediate *family or household and* is driving with the *express or implied permission* of the owner. [Leonard v. Wilson, 468 N.W.2d 604 (Neb. 1991)]

2) **"Permissive use statutes":** [§492] Legislation in other states goes even further. So-called permissive use statutes render the owner of an automobile liable for damages (sometimes in a limited amount) caused by the negligence of *anyone* (not just family members) driving the automobile with the owner's express or implied consent. [*See, e.g.*, Cal. Veh. Code §17150]

(3) **Compare—duties with respect to condition of bailed chattel:** [§493] In addition to whatever liability a bailor may have for wrongful conduct by the bailee in use of the bailed chattel, a bailor also owes certain duties as to the safety of the bailed chattel itself. Thus, where the bailee was using the chattel properly, but the chattel itself was defective, the bailor may be liable to third persons injured thereby (as well as to the bailee). (*See* detailed discussion, *infra*, §§763 *et seq.*)

c. **Master-servant cases**

(1) **Liability based on employer's own negligence:** [§494] Where the employee's torts cannot be imputed to the employer under respondeat superior (*e.g.*, because outside scope of employment; *see* below), consider whether the employer can be held liable therefor on the basis of the *employer's own negligence*. (This, of course, is not vicarious liability.) There are two possible theories:

(a) **Failure to control acts in employer's presence:** [§495] An employer owes an affirmative duty to use due care to control the conduct of his servants in his presence. Therefore, if the employee's tortious acts were committed in the presence of the employer, the employer may be held *directly* liable for negligence. [Hogle v. Franklin Manufacturing Co., 199 N.Y. 388 (1910)]

(b) **Negligent hiring of employee:** [§496] An employer may be held liable for willful or criminal actions of an employee if the employer should reasonably have foreseen such tortious action by employee, even if those actions were outside the scope of the employee's job duties. [J. v. Victory Tabernacle Baptist Church, 372 S.E.2d 391 (Va. 1988)] This liability may also extend to negligence in training or supervising the employee.

(2) **Doctrine of respondeat superior—vicarious liability:** [§497] An employer is *vicariously* liable for any tortious acts committed by his employee *within the scope of the employment*. This fundamental rule of agency law applies whether the acts were committed in the presence of the employer or otherwise; *i.e.*, whether or not the employer had the actual ability to control the employee's conduct. (*See* Agency and Partnership Summary.)

  (a) **Crucial requirement—"scope of employment":** [§498] The doctrine of respondeat superior does not apply where the tort is committed by the employee *outside* the scope of employment. Thus, if D's employee leaves the place of employment and while pursuing some private objective injures P, D cannot be held liable under respondeat superior.

   1) **Application—intentional torts:** Batteries and other intentional torts committed by an employee *may* be within the scope of employment where the employee's duties involve the use of physical force on others (*e.g.*, bodyguards, bouncers) or force to further the employer's interests (*e.g.*, to collect debt due employer).

  (b) **Employee's immunity from tort liability immaterial:** [§499] Note that the employer may be held liable for torts committed by his employee within the scope of employment *even where the employee is immune*! For example, where a husband negligently injures his wife while acting in the scope of his employment, the wife may hold the employer liable for the husband's negligence, even if she cannot maintain an action directly against the husband because of interspousal tort immunity (*see infra*, §§1011-1015). [Fields v. Synthetic Ropes, 215 A.2d 427 (Del. 1965)]

  (c) **Caution—employee's tortious conduct must be established:** [§500] However, keep in mind that the employer's liability under respondeat superior is strictly vicarious; *i.e.*, it must always be shown first that the employee *was acting tortiously* before the employer can be held liable. [Louie Queriolo Trucking v. Superior Court, 252 Cal. App. 2d 194 (1967)—if employee is exonerated, no judgment can be returned against employer]

d. **Independent contractor cases**

  (1) **Liability based on employer's own negligence:** [§501] An employer may be held directly liable for the torts of an independent contractor where the employer has failed to exercise due care in selecting a competent contractor. This is liability imposed for the employer's *own* negligence, and it is immaterial whether there is also a basis for imposing vicarious liability (*see* below).

  (2) **Vicarious liability:** [§502] As a general rule, one who employs an independent contractor will *not* be held vicariously liable for the negligent

conduct of the independent contractor—even while the independent contractor is acting within the scope of the contract. *Rationale:* The employer has **no right to control the manner** in which an independent contractor performs the contract. (*See* Agency and Partnership Summary.)

(a) **Exceptions:** [§503]   But an increasing number of "exceptions" to this no-liability rule are recognized:

1) **Nondelegable duties:** [§504]   For example, if the employer's duty is *nondelegable* as a matter of law, the employer cannot avoid liability by hiring an independent contractor to perform. [Rest. 2d §424]

   a) **Duty to maintain automobile:** [§505]   It is generally recognized that an automobile owner is under a duty to maintain the car in a safe condition. (Frequently this is required by statute. [*See, e.g.,* Cal. Veh. Code §26453]) Because of the substantial risk of harm inherent in the operation of automobiles, some courts hold this duty to be *nondelegable*. Thus, for example, the owner is liable if his brakes prove defective—even though he had employed a reputable garage to service his car, and had no independent ability to do the work himself or to inspect to see that it was done properly! [Maloney v. Rath, 60 Cal. 2d 442 (1968); *but see* Hackett v. Perron, 402 A.2d 193 (N.H. 1979)—contra]

   b) **Duty to maintain public premises:** [§506]   The duty to keep premises safe for business visitors has also been held nondelegable. Hence, D, a shopping center landlord, is vicariously liable where his independent contractor negligently repairs leased premises resulting in injuries to the business invitee of D's tenant. [Misiulis v. Milbrand Maintenance Corp., 218 N.W.2d 68 (Mich. 1974)]

   c) **Health care providers:** [§507]   A health care provider may be held vicariously liable to a client or patient for negligence by an independent contractor. *Rationale:* A patient has no choice in provider's selection of a subcontractor, and the subcontractor may be judgment-proof or underinsured. [Marek v. Professional Health Services, 432 A.2d 538 (N.J. 1981)—x-ray film negligently read]

      1/ **Example:** Under the "captain-of-the-ship" doctrine, most states impute the negligence of nonemployees to surgeons [Rudeck v. Wright, 709 P.2d 621 (Mont. 1985); Ravi v. Coates, 662 So. 2d 218 (Ala. 1995)], although a minority require a showing that the surgeon was personally negligent [Anglin v. Kleeman, 665 A.2d 747 (N.H. 1995)].

      2/ **Note:** A patient who goes to a hospital seeking medical services and is forced to rely on the hospital's choice of physician to render those services may hold the hospital vicariously liable for physician's negligence. [Thomas v. Raleigh General Hospital, 358 S.E.2d 222 (W. Va. 1987)]

3/ **And note:** Even a state that rejects vicarious liability on a hospital for the negligence of an independent contractor is likely in appropriate cases to hold the hospital liable for its own negligence in granting staff privileges to unqualified persons. [Strubhart v. Perry Memorial Hospital Trust Authority, 903 P.2d 263 (Okla. 1995)—hospital's obligation includes checking before granting privilege in first place, and also checking after reports of complaints or problems]

d) **Other nondelegable duties:** [§508]   Other duties deemed to be nondelegable include the duty to provide employees with a safe place to work, to refrain from obstructing a public highway, and to afford lateral support to adjacent land, as well as the duty of a carrier to transport its passengers carefully and that of a landlord to maintain common passageways. Thus, the employer will be vicariously liable for the negligence of an independent contractor in connection with the performance of any of these obligations.

2) **Dangerous activities—"peculiar risk" doctrine:** [§509]   If the activity involved is so intrinsically *dangerous* that the employer should realize it involves a peculiar risk of physical harm, the employer cannot avoid liability by hiring an independent contractor to perform. Examples of such dangerous activities include blasting, use of fire to clear land, etc. [Rest. 2d §416]

3) **Contractor's assumption of liability does not overcome exception:** [§510]   Where the case comes within the nondelegable duty or dangerous activity exceptions, the fact that the independent contractor has (by contract) "assumed all risks" in connection with performance does *not* insulate the employer from liability *to third persons* injured by the contractor's negligence. But it does give express recognition to the employer's cause of action against the contractor for *indemnification*. [Van Arsdale v. Hollinger, 68 Cal. 2d 245 (1968); *and see infra*, §1062]

(b) **Collateral negligence—exception to exception:** [§511]   An employer who would otherwise be liable under the nondelegable duty or dangerous activity exceptions may nevertheless escape liability if the independent contractor's negligence is considered "collateral" to the special risk that gives rise to vicarious liability in the first place. For example, carelessly dropping a paint bucket from a window while painting inside a private room with poisonous paint would be collateral negligence (collateral to the poison hazard); but dropping the bucket while painting a sign over a sidewalk would not be collateral since the very risk that made the duty nondelegable (danger to the public below) is what occurred.

e. **Partners and joint venturers:** [§512] Persons who engage in a joint enterprise are vicariously liable for the conduct of the other members within the scope of the enterprise. *Rationale:* Those engaged in such an enterprise have an *equal right to control* its operation, and whether or not all members in fact exercise such control is immaterial.

(1) **Requirements:** [§513] A joint enterprise requires: (i) a *mutual right to control* the management or operation of the enterprise; and (ii) in some jurisdictions, a common *business purpose* in which all persons involved have a mutual interest.

(2) **Application—automobile trips:** [§514] A frequent issue is whether there is a joint enterprise between the owner of an automobile and a rider when they have embarked on a "share the expenses" trip, having reached some sort of agreement that they will take turns driving, will mutually agree on an itinerary, and will split all costs.

(a) **Note:** Some courts hold this to be a joint enterprise; if there is an accident, an injured third person can hold liable either of the persons in the car, no matter who was driving at the time of the accident.

(b) **Compare:** Other states refuse to find a joint enterprise unless a *business purpose* is involved (*see* above). In such jurisdictions, sharing the expenses on vacation or pleasure trips does *not* amount to a joint enterprise. [Winslow v. Hammer, 527 N.W.2d 631 (Neb. 1995)—no joint enterprise without pecuniary interest and thus husband and wife in van were not in joint enterprise]

f. **Liability of parent for torts of child**

(1) **Common law rule—no vicarious liability:** [§515] Under the general common law rule, a parent is *not* vicariously responsible for torts committed by her child. The rationale is that the parent simply does not have sufficient control to justify imputing liability where the parent was not otherwise negligent.

(a) **Statutory changes:** [§516] However, the common law rule has been modified by statute in many states today, so that vicarious liability will be imposed under certain circumstances. [*See, e.g.*, Cal. Civ. Code §1714.1—making parent liable up to $25,000 for any "willful misconduct" of child; Cal. Veh. Code §17708—making parents liable for damages caused by negligence of child driving a car on public highways with parents' express or implied permission]

(2) **Liability based on parent's own negligence:** [§517] Even if not vicariously liable for a child's torts (above), a parent—or anyone else having care or custody of a child—can be held liable for injuries caused by the child *where the parent himself was negligent*. In other words, these

are cases based on the parent's *own liability*—and not any imputed or vicarious liability. Thus, the parent may be liable for:

(a) *Failing to control the acts of the child committed in the parent's presence.* [Rest. 2d §316; Richards v. Soucy, 610 A.2d 268 (Me. 1992)—negligent supervision]

(b) *Failing to exercise reasonable care* to protect against *the child's known dangerous tendencies* (*e.g.*, allowing child who had previously caused fires to have access to matches). [Linder v. Bidner, 50 Misc. 2d 320 (1966)]

(c) *Failing to warn* others with whom the child is likely to come into contact about child's known dangerous tendencies. [Ellis v. D'Angelo, 116 Cal. App. 2d 310 (1953)—babysitter injured by violent four-year-old]

(d) *Failing to prevent child's foreseeable use of inherently dangerous instrumentalities* (*e.g.*, leaving dynamite caps or loaded firearms in child's presence). [Kuhns v. Brugger, 135 A.2d 395 (Pa. 1957)]

(e) *Negligent entrustment*; *see supra*, §487.

g. **Liability of tavernkeeper**

(1) **Common law rule—no liability:** [§518]   At common law, the seller of intoxicating beverages was not liable for injuries resulting from the purchaser's intoxication—whether the injuries were sustained by the purchaser or by another as the result of the purchaser's subsequent conduct. [Quinnett v. Newman, 568 A.2d 786 (Conn. 1990)]

(2) **Statutory undermining of common law rule—"Dram Shop Acts":** [§519]   To alter the common law rule, many states have passed "Dram Shop Acts." [*See, e.g.*, Minn. Stat. Ann. §340A.801] These statutes create a cause of action against the tavernkeeper in favor of *third parties* injured by an intoxicated patron.

(a) **Nature of tavernkeeper's fault:** [§520]   Some of these statutes allow recovery only if the tavernkeeper had *prior notice* of a danger in selling to such a patron.

(b) **Recovery limited to injured third person:** [§521]   Only a few statutes allow the intoxicated patron to recover for his *own* injuries, but many allow the patron's *spouse* to recover for *loss of support* resulting from injuries or death to the intemperate patron. [Kiriluk v. Cohn, 148 N.E.2d 607 (Ill. 1958)—allowing patron's widow to recover for the loss of his support, even where she had killed him, the killing being in self-defense against his drunken rage]

(c) **Who can be held liable?** [§522]   Most statutes are restricted to *commercial establishments*—*i.e.*, those in the business of furnishing liquor (taverns or liquor stores).

(d) **Defenses:** [§523]   Some jurisdictions do not recognize contributory negligence, comparative negligence, or assumption of risk defenses in a dram shop action. [Feuerherm v. Ertelt, 286 N.W.2d 509 (N.D. 1979)]

(3) **Judicial rejection of common law rule:** [§524]   A growing number of courts have reevaluated the common law rule and have imposed liability on tavernkeepers for injuries inflicted by their intoxicated patrons on others, even *without* a "Dram Shop Act." [Nazareno v. Urie, 638 P.2d 671 (Alaska 1981); Vesely v. Sager, 5 Cal. 3d 153 (1971)] *But note:* California's legislature rejected *Vesely* and declared that the act of the drunk was the proximate cause of harm except in situations involving minors. [Cal. Bus. & Prof. Code §25602]

(a) **Rationale—common law negligence:** From a *duty* standpoint, the question is whether the risk to third persons was reasonably foreseeable and, if so, whether any policy factors suggest rejecting a duty. Foreseeability depends, of course, on what knowledge the bartender had or should have had as to the patron's propensities, how intoxicated the patron appeared to be, etc. From a *proximate cause* standpoint, the intoxicated patron's negligent acts must be held *foreseeable*, and thus do *not* bar the tavernkeeper's liability. Indeed, the likelihood that the patron may inflict such injuries is the very hazard that makes the tavernkeeper negligent in the first place! [Rappaport v. Nichols, 156 A.2d 1 (N.J. 1959); Rest. 2d §449]

(b) **Possible "negligence per se":** [§525]   If it appears that the patron was *already intoxicated*, the furnishing of the liquor is generally made a crime by statute—and negligence per se may exist (*see supra*, §§438 *et seq.*)—because such statutes are designed to protect the public from this kind of harm.

(c) **Scope of liability**

1) **Recovery by drunk patron for his own injury?** [§526]   So far, most courts following this view have allowed recovery only for injuries sustained by *third parties*. [Kindt v. Kaufman, 57 Cal. App. 3d 845 (1976)] A few courts permit recovery by the intoxicated patron for *his own* injuries. [Soronen v. Olde Milford Inn, 218 A.2d 630 (N.J. 1966); *but see* Wright v. Moffitt, 437 A.2d 554 (Del. 1981)—contra]

2) **Recovery against social host?** [§527]   Also, virtually all courts have allowed recovery only against *commercial* dispensers of alcoholic beverages, rejecting liability on a private individual who serves liquor to an obviously intoxicated guest. [Klein v. Raysinger, 448 A.2d 620 (Pa. 1982)]

a) **Exception—intoxicated minors:** [§528]   However, several courts have imposed liability against a social host for furnishing liquor to a *minor* who became intoxicated and later caused injury to another in a traffic accident—at least where it is shown that the host *knew* that the minor would be driving a car after consuming the liquor. [Brockett v. Kitchen Boyd Motor Co., 24 Cal. App. 3d 87 (1972); *and see* Cal. Bus. & Prof. Code §25602.1; *but see* Slicer v. Quigley, 429 A.2d 855 (Conn. 1980)—passenger in car not liable for giving beer to 19-year-old driver, in violation of statute, because driver's voluntary consumption of the beer was proximate and superseding cause of accident; Charles v. Seigfried, 651 N.E.2d 154 (Ill. 1995)—denying action against social host who served alcohol to minor who then hurt herself]

b) **New exception—adults:** [§529] A few courts have extended liability to social hosts whose intoxicated adult guests have injured the plaintiff. [Kelly v. Gwinnell, 476 A.2d 1219 (N.J. 1984); *but see* Ferreira v. Strack, 652 A.2d 965 (R.I. 1995)—contra] *But note:* A New Jersey statute has substantially limited the *Kelly* case. [2A N.J.S.A. §§15-5 *et seq.*]

(4) **Compare—liability of tavernkeeper as land occupier:** [§530] Even in states that have retained the common law rule of no liability, a tavernkeeper may be held liable if she fails to exercise the duties required of her as a *land occupier* to *business visitors* on the premises (*see infra*, §576). Thus, if the tavernkeeper knows that one patron may become belligerent and dangerous if drunk, she must exercise due care to prevent that person from injuring the person or property of *other patrons on the premises*, or at least warn them of the danger. [Priewe v. Bartz, 83 N.W.2d 116 (Minn. 1957)]

8. **Duties Owed by Land Occupiers:** [§531] The common law rule, and still the great weight of authority, is that the general duty of due care under the circumstances does *not* apply to occupiers of land. Rather, land occupiers are accorded a special status that *limits* their liability for injuries to others arising from conditions or activities on their land. In short, land occupiers in most states do *not* have to conduct themselves as "reasonable persons under the circumstances"; it is sufficient that they comply with the limited duties and standards of care discussed below. (*But see* the minority view *infra*, §585.)

a. **"Land occupier" defined:** [§532] "Land occupier" refers to the person *in possession of the land*, whether the owner, tenant, adverse possessor, or any other type of possessor. [Merritt v. Nickelson, 287 N.W.2d 178 (Mich. 1980)]

b. **"Foreseeable risk" defined:** [§533] The "foreseeability" element in all the cases below is a risk of harm to either person or property interests, with the same proximate cause complexities as discussed previously where the risk foreseeable was to one type of interest (person or property) and the actual harm sustained was to the other type.

c. **Duties owed to persons outside the land**

(1) **Natural conditions:** [§534] *No duty* of care is owed with respect to natural conditions, such as native trees or boulders in place, in rural areas. [Rest. 2d §363]

(a) **Exception:** A land occupier in an *urban* area owes a duty of due care to prevent *native trees* growing on her land from creating an unreasonable risk of harm to travelers on adjacent public streets. [Meyers v. Delaney, 529 N.W.2d 288 (Iowa 1995)—no liability to neighbor for fall of decayed tree without actual or constructive notice of danger]

(b) **Minority:** A large minority of states hold that in both rural and urban areas, the occupier owes a duty of care to protect those outside the land from natural conditions on the land. [Sprecher v. Adamson Cos., 30 Cal. 3d 358 (1981)]

(2) **Artificial conditions:** [§535]   *No duty* is owed as to artificial conditions (buildings, excavations, fences erected, etc.) beyond what is owed for natural conditions.

(a) **Exception:** If portions of any building, fence, etc., protrude onto or abut adjacent land, there is a duty to exercise due care to *inspect and maintain* such structures. [Rest. 2d §368]

(b) **Exception:** If the conditions "substantially adjoin" a *public road*, there is a duty to exercise due care to protect users of the road from harm; this may involve a duty to erect and maintain fences, prune plantings, etc.

(3) **Activities:** [§536]   Defendant owes a duty not to engage in any activities (business or any other use to which land is put) that a reasonable person would foresee as involving an unreasonable risk of harm to persons or property outside the land. Hence, the land occupier owes the same duty of due care as if she were conducting her activities in some *neutral place*. [Salevan v. Wilmington Park, Inc., 72 A.2d 239 (Del. 1950)]

d. **Duties owed to persons coming onto the land**

(1) **Ordinary trespassers**

(a) **"Ordinary trespassers" defined:** [§537]   An "ordinary trespasser" is anyone coming onto the land without the express or implied permission of the land occupier or without a legal privilege. [Blakely v. Camp Ondessonk, 38 F.3d 325 (7th Cir. 1994)] (*But note:* "Child trespassers" are given greater protection; *see* below.)

(b) **Duties owed to ordinary trespassers**

1) **Presence unknown:** [§538]   There is *no duty* owed to a trespasser whose presence on the land is unknown, nor is there a duty to discover the presence of trespassers. This is true with respect to both natural and artificial conditions, and all activities on the land. [Amblo's Administratrix v. Vermont Associated Petroleum Corp., 144 A. 460 (Vt. 1929); Micromanolis v. The Woods School, Inc., 989 F.2d 696 (3d Cir. 1993)—only duty is to refrain from willful and wanton misconduct]

2) **Presence known:** [§539] However, if the land occupier *knows*—or from known facts should reasonably realize—that there is a trespasser on the land, the land occupier is under a duty to exercise due care to warn the trespasser of, or make safe, *artificial conditions* that involve *a risk of death or serious bodily harm* (*e.g.*, a concealed pit) *and all activities that involve any risk of harm* that the trespasser is unlikely to discover. [Rest. 2d §§333, 336-337]

(2) Constant trespassers upon a limited area ("CTULA")

(a) **"CTULA" defined:** [§540] This refers to persons habitually intruding upon the land or a certain portion thereof—*e.g.*, those who cut across a portion of the land occupier's fields as a shortcut to town. [Louisville & Nashville Railway v. Spoonamore's Administrator, 129 S.W.2d 175 (Ky. 1939)]

1) **Knowledge of land occupier:** [§541] The land occupier must be shown to know (or have reason to know) that persons are in the habit of cutting across her fields, etc. Physical evidence on the land ("the beaten path") will usually be sufficient to charge the land occupier with such knowledge.

2) **Prevention of CTULAs:** [§542] The land occupier may prevent intruders from obtaining CTULA status by acts showing that she objects to the intrusion. Thus, if the land occupier posts "No Trespassing" signs on the area in which the intrusion occurs, this may be sufficient to *convert* persons who would otherwise qualify as CTULAs into ordinary trespassers (to whom a lower standard of care applies; *see* above), *unless* the intrusions still continue, and the land occupier knows this but fails to do anything further about it.

(b) **Duties owed to CTULAs:** [§543] A CTULA is afforded a higher duty of care than an "ordinary trespasser" on the theory that if the land occupier knows that persons are in the habit of trespassing on a section of her land and does nothing about it, their presence is at least tolerated; *i.e.*, the land occupier has given a *type of implied consent* to their presence.

1) **Duty to discover:** [§544] The land occupier owes a duty *to discover* whether or not CTULAs as a class are intruding.

2) **Activities and artificial conditions within scope of duty:** [§545] If charged with knowledge that CTULAs are intruding, the land occupier owes a duty to exercise due care to warn them of, or make safe, *artificial conditions and activities* that involve *a risk of death or serious bodily harm* and that they are unlikely to discover. [Rest. 2d §335]

3) **No duty regarding other conditions and activities:** [§546] With respect to *natural conditions* involving any risk of harm,

and artificial conditions and activities threatening less than death or serious bodily injury, there is *no duty* owed.

(3) **Child trespassers—"attractive nuisance doctrine":** [§547] The "attractive nuisance doctrine" imposes a special duty of care on the land occupier with respect to conditions on the land that involve a risk of harm to *children* unable to recognize the danger involved. [McKiddy v. Des Moines Electric Co., 206 N.W. 815 (Iowa 1926); Rest. 2d §339]

   (a) **Rationale:** Society has a greater interest in the safety of children than in a land occupier's right to do as she pleases with her land.

   (b) **Minority view:** [§548] A few courts still reject the attractive nuisance doctrine. A few others apply the doctrine only to a hazard that has attracted the child onto the land. [Johnson v. Bathey, 376 So. 2d 848 (Fla. 1979); Logan v. Old Enterprise Farms, Ltd., 564 N.E.2d 778 (Ill. 1990)]

   (c) **"Child trespasser" defined:** [§549] To be a "child trespasser," the child must be *so immature as to be unable to recognize the danger involved*. In practice, children over the age of 14 years seldom qualify (*see* below). [Pierce v. United Gas & Electric Co., 161 Cal. 176 (1911)]

   (d) **Duties owed to child trespassers**

      1) **No obligation to discover:** [§550] The land occupier owes no duty to exercise due care to discover trespassing children on her property.

      2) **Artificial conditions within scope of duty:** [§551] But if the land occupier discovers children trespassing, or is charged with such knowledge, she then owes a duty to exercise due care to *warn or protect* them from artificial conditions involving a risk of *death or serious bodily harm* to children, *provided*:

         (i) **Foreseeability of trespass:** [§552] The place where the condition is maintained is one where children are *known or likely* to trespass; *and*

         (ii) **Foreseeability of harm:** [§553] The possessor knows, or has reason to know, of the existence of the artificial condition on the land, and realizes (or should realize) that it involves an *unreasonable risk* of death or serious bodily harm to such children; *and*

         (iii) **Risk outweighs utility of condition:** [§554] The *utility to the possessor* of maintaining the condition and the *burden of eliminating* the danger are *less* than the risk to children; *and*

         (iv) **Child unaware of danger:** [§555] The condition is such that children, because of their youth, do not discover it or *do not realize the danger involved*. In other words, the condition or device that causes the injury must be unfamiliar to children of similar age—*i.e.*, "in the nature of a trap" for such children. [Reynolds v. Wilson, 51 Cal. 2d 94 (1985)] This is usually the central dispute in litigation. [Merrill v. Central Maine Power Co., 628 A.2d 1062 (Me. 1993)—nine-year-old trying to cook eel on D's live wire understood the risk]

[Rest. 2d §339]

a) **Application:** [§556]   Using the foregoing yardstick, unattended vehicles, machinery, explosives, etc., have been held to qualify as "attractive nuisances."

   1/ **Compare—"ordinary risks":** [§557]   On the other hand, ordinary risks involved in fire, bodies of water, or falling from a height or onto an excavation or sandpile are known to young children and therefore ordinarily do *not* qualify. [Holland v. Baltimore & Ohio Railroad, 431 A.2d 597 (D.C. 1981)—moving train is a known risk to a nine-year-old child]

      a/ **But note:** Even a body of water may become an attractive nuisance if some other dangerous condition is involved therein—*e.g.*, concealed high-suction drain at bottom of pond, or swimming pool maintained at deceptively low water level. [Reynolds v. Wilson, *supra*]

   2/ **Note—fact question:** [§558]   In any event, the question of whether a child is capable of realizing the danger is ultimately one of *fact*. The younger the child, the more likely a condition will be held to be an "attractive nuisance." Thus, if a child is actually too young to realize the danger, even a swimming pool may be an attractive nuisance. [King v. Lennen, 53 Cal. 2d 340 (1959)—18-month-old child drowned in neighbor's pool] However, beyond age 14, there are fewer conditions for which there can be recovery; and at some point (probably beyond age 16) the "child trespasser" doctrine no longer applies. [O'Keefe v. South End Rowing Club, 64 Cal. 2d 729 (1966)]

   3/ **Removal of hazardous object:** [§559]   Some states extend the doctrine to any harm that results when the trespassing child carries a hazardous object from defendant's property. [Christians v. Homestake Enterprises, Ltd., 303 N.W.2d 608 (Wis. 1981)—blasting cap taken by child from defendant's premises later explodes]

3) **Compare—no similar duty regarding activities or natural conditions:** [§560] The land occupier owes the above duty with respect to highly dangerous *artificial* conditions. No such duty is owed with respect to *natural* conditions or *activities*. [Loney v. McPhillips, 521 P.2d 340 (Or. 1974)—no duty to 13-year-old drowned in dangerous ocean cove; *but see* Rest. 2d §339—questions this limitation]

(e) **Child trespasser doctrine as defense to trespass:** [§561] The child trespasser doctrine has also been extended by a few courts to bar any action by the land occupier *against the children* (or their parents, where they would otherwise be liable) for damages the children cause to the property. [Aetna Insurance Co. v. Stringham, 440 F.2d 103 (6th Cir. 1971)—children attracted onto P's land to play in empty barn toyed with matches and burned down barn] (Compare the extraordinary liability of adult trespassers, *supra*, §176, for harm done during the trespass.)

(4) Licensees

(a) **"Licensee" defined:** [§562] A "licensee" is a person coming onto the land, with the express or implied *permission* of the land occupier, for the *entrant's own purposes*, conferring no particular benefit on the land occupier or on any use to which the occupier is putting the land. [Barmore v. Elmore, 403 N.E.2d 1355 (Ill. 1980); Carter v. Kinney, 896 S.W.2d 926 (Mo. 1995); Rest. 2d §330]

1) **Examples—persons held to be "licensees":** This category generally covers *social guests* and *visiting relatives*. [Hall v. Duke, 513 S.W.2d 776 (Tenn. 1974)] It also covers business visitors (*infra*) or privileged entrants (*infra*) who have strayed from that part of the premises to which they were invited or authorized to enter, door-to-door salespersons (unless the property is posted otherwise), and process servers. [Prentiss v. Evergreen Presbyterian Church, 644 So. 2d 475 (Ala. 1994)—member of local chorus allowed to use church for its rehearsals is licensee of church; Young v. Paxton, 873 S.W.2d 546 (Ark. 1994)—son-in-law hurt trimming trees during social visit is licensee]

2) **"Permission to enter" broadly interpreted:** [§563] The courts construe "implied permission" broadly and thus accord licensee status to many who would otherwise be outright trespassers. For example, persons who solicit money for charity, who come to borrow tools, or who come on personal business dealings with employees of the land occupier (*e.g.*, child bringing lunch to his father) are all held to enter with at least the implied permission of the land occupier.

(b) **Duties owed to licensees:** [§564] The land occupier owes a duty to exercise due care to warn licensees of, or make safe, *natural or artificial conditions or activities* involving *any risk of harm known* to the land occupier and not obvious to a reasonable person coming onto the land—including threats of harm by *third persons* already on the land. [Indianapolis Street Railway v. Dawson, 98 N.E. 909 (Ind. 1903)—where D invited P onto his premises, *knowing* that X was already there and that X intended to attack P, D owed duty to warn P of danger]

1) **No duty to discover danger:** [§565]   Note that the land occupier is under no duty with respect to dangerous conditions or activities of which she is not actually aware. *Nor is the land occupier under a duty to inspect* the land to discover such dangers. [Rest. 2d §342]

2) **Warning usually sufficient:** [§566]   The land occupier may effectively discharge the duty to licensees by posting signs, etc., warning of the danger, unless she knows such signs to be ineffective.

3) **Knowledge of licensee's presence:** [§567]   Although the land occupier owes no duty to discover licensees generally, she must conduct her activities as though some licensees *may have accepted the occupier's permission* and entered the premises; *i.e.,* the defendant's lack of knowledge that a particular licensee was actually present is no defense, as the defendant must use reasonable care in the exercise of all activities.

(5) **Invitees**

(a) **"Invitee" defined:** [§568]   This refers to a person who enters by the express or implied invitation of the land occupier for some purpose *related to the activities or interests of the land occupier*. An invitee may be either a "public invitee" or a "business visitor," and sometimes is both. [Rest. 2d §332]

1) **"Public invitee":** [§569]   A "public invitee" is a person who is invited to enter or remain upon land as a member of the public for a purpose for which the land is held open to the public. [Dowd v. Portsmouth Hospital, 193 A.2d 788 (N.H. 1963)]

a) **Compare—premises need not be public:** [§570]   Note that the premises involved may be either public or private: A person entering a public library (public premises) to borrow a book is an invitee; as is a person entering a drugstore (private premises) to use the public telephone. [Clark v. Moore Memorial United Methodist Church, 538 So. 2d 760 (Miss. 1989)—parishioner who slips and falls while leaving Sunday School class is a public invitee]

b) **Being public is not enough:** [§571]   The fact that the premises in question are public does not by itself make users public invitees. [Provencher v. State of Ohio, 551 N.E.2d 1257 (Ohio 1990)—person hurt on steps of a public roadside rest stop is not a public invitee because element of invitation is lacking]

2) **"Business visitor":** [§572] A "business visitor" is a person coming onto the land for the primary purpose of business dealings with the land occupier or some purpose connected with the use to which the land occupier is putting the land.

    a) **Examples—persons held to be "business visitors":** [§573] This generally covers store customers, as well as any person entering premises held open for admission (free or paid) to the general public—*i.e.*, theatres, hotels, airports, etc. [Dickau v. Rafala, 104 A.2d 214 (Cnn. 1954)] It also covers workers, garbage collectors, etc., who come onto the land to further the use to which the land occupier is putting the premises—as well as building inspectors, etc., who are concerned with regulating such use. [Holzheimer v. Johannesen, 871 P.2d 814 (Idaho 1994)—fact question whether farmer borrowing boxes or buying them at cost was business visitor or licensee obtaining a favor from neighbor]

    b) **Immaterial that business dealings fail to materialize:** [§574] The entrant need only have a *reasonable belief* that he is going on the land for the purpose of business dealings with the land occupier. Even if it turns out that no such business dealings are possible, he will still qualify as an invitee. [Chatkin v. Talarski, 193 A. 611 (Conn. 1937)—P came into D's mortuary to inquire about engaging D's services for a friend; it later turned out the friend was alive, but P still qualified as a business visitor in the mortuary]

3) **Caution—change of status:** [§575] An invitee retains such status *only when on that part of the premises that he was invited to enter*. If he wanders elsewhere, he becomes a licensee or perhaps even a trespasser (*e.g.*, when a store customer enters area marked "employees only").

    a) **Example:** When P exceeded the scope of a limited invitation by not complying with D's request that he notify her as to when he was coming to her home, P became a trespasser when he came onto her land without notice. [Buzzell v. Jones, 556 A.2d 106 (Vt. 1989)]

(b) **Duties owed to invitees:** [§576] The land occupier owes invitees a duty to use due care to *inspect and discover* the presence of any dangerous *natural or artificial* conditions or activities and to exercise due care to warn the invitees of such dangers *or make the conditions or activities safe*. [Rest. 2d §343; Flemington v. Arrington, 610 So. 2d 1160 (Ala. 1992)—no need to warn where invitee saw ants four hours before they attacked her]

1) **Warning enough?** [§577] Traditionally, a warning will satisfy the duty owed. However, a modern trend requires the land occupier to actually make the premises safe where, under the particular facts, a warning would *not* render the condition or activity reasonably free from danger; *i.e.*, in some cases a mere warning will not suffice. [Wilk v. Georges, 514 P.2d 877 (Or. 1973); Tharp v. Bunge Corp., 641 So. 2d 20 (Miss. 1994)]

   a) **Note:** No warning at all is needed if the condition is not one that presents sufficient danger. [Howe v. Stubbs, 570 A.2d 1203 (Me. 1990)—no need to warn invitee of danger that car might crash into shop located on a "T" intersection at the foot of the hill where this had happened only three times in 25 years]

2) **Safeguarding activities of third persons:** [§578] In addition, the land occupier may be required to exercise reasonable care to warn or protect invitees from *foreseeable tortious or criminal acts of third persons*.

   a) **Example:** Those holding their premises open to the public for commercial purposes are charged with a duty to use due care to protect their customers—as well as licensees (*see supra*)—from foreseeable injuries at the hands of third persons. [Taco Bell, Inc. v. Lannon, 744 P.2d 43 (Colo. 1987)—restaurant in high crime area has duty to take *reasonable measures* to protect patrons from consequences of armed robbery by third parties; *but see* Williams v. Cunningham Drug Stores, Inc., 418 N.W.2d 381 (Mich. 1988)—merchant in high crime area has no duty to provide armed, visible security guards to protect customers from armed robbery by third parties]

3) **Safeguarding chattels:** [§579] A land occupier who undertakes *to supply equipment, tools, or other chattels* to persons coming onto the premises for business purposes owes a duty to exercise due care to inspect and discover any defective condition in the chattels that she supplies. [The Student, 243 F. 807 (4th Cir. 1917)—D liable for furnishing unsafe scaffolding to workers on the premises]

(6) **Public entrants**

(a) **"Public entrants" defined:** [§580] "Public entrants" refers to any public employee entering the land under a privilege recognized by law and irrespective of any express or implied consent from the land occupier—*i.e.*, someone whose entry the land occupier has *no right to prevent*.

   1) **Examples:** Firefighters, police officers, sanitation inspectors, postal workers, meter readers, tax assessors, etc., are all public entrants—as long as they are acting in the scope of their official duties.

2) **Compare—private entrants:** Any "private person" entering under one of the recognized entry privileges—*e.g.*, to recapture chattels, etc. (*supra*, §209)—is treated as a *licensee*. [Rest. 2d §345(1)]

(b) **Duties owed to public entrants:** [§581] The duty owed to public entrants depends on the *purpose* of their entry.

1) **Business purpose:** [§582] If they enter for some purpose involving business dealings with the land occupier (*e.g.*, postal workers, garbage collectors, meter readers, sanitation inspectors, tax assessors, etc.), they are owed the same duties as *invitees*.

2) **Nonbusiness purpose but privileged entry:** [§583] If the entry is not for a business visit with the land occupier, but under some other privilege afforded by law (*e.g.*, entry by police to chase a burglar), most courts hold that the public entrant is entitled only to the status of a *licensee*. [Rest. 2d §345] A few consider the entrant an invitee. [Dint v. Naiditch, 170 N.E.2d 881 (Ill. 1960)]

a) **Distinguish—entry on business premises:** Keep in mind, however, that if the entry is on *business premises* (held open to the public) during normal business hours, the entrant would be treated as an *invitee*—the same as any other member of the public. [Meiers v. Koch, 229 N.Y. 10 (1920)—police officer entering store during business hours to make routine investigation]

(7) **Recreational land users:** [§584] Virtually every state has enacted legislation that protects owners of land against lawsuits brought by persons who have been using the land for recreational purposes, unless the owner has engaged in willful or wanton conduct. [Ornelas v. Randolph, 4 Cal. 4th 1095 (1993); Cal. Civ. Code §846]

e. **Minority view—duty of land occupiers determined by reasonable person standard:** [§585] About 15 jurisdictions today reject the common law rules above and hold that a land occupier's duty does not depend entirely upon the entrant's status (trespasser, licensee, invitee, etc.). Rather, the test is whether the occupier has acted as a *reasonable person in the management of her property in view of the likelihood of injury to others* (*i.e.*, the general duty of due care under the circumstances). [Rowland v. Christian, 69 Cal. 2d 108 (1968); Jones v. Hansen, 867 P.2d 303 (Kan. 1994); *but see* Carter v. Kinney, *supra*, §562—adhering to traditional categories]

(1) **Split over trespassers:** [§586] Some states that apply the general duty of due care under the circumstances when the entrant is an invitee or a licensee continue to apply a separate standard when the entrant is a trespasser. [O'Leary v. Coenen, 251 N.W.2d 746 (N.D. 1977); *but see* Rowland v. Christian, *supra*—contra]

      (2) **Rationale:** Under modern law, human safety is at least as important as a land occupier's right to act as she chooses on her land. Consequently, there is no longer any reason to immunize landowners from general negligence liability. [Smith v. Arbaugh's Restaurant, 469 F.2d 97 (D.C. Cir. 1972); *but see* Musch v. H-D Electric Cooperative, Inc., 460 N.W.2d 149 (S.D. 1990); Younce v. Ferguson, 724 P.2d 991 (Wash. 1986)—adhering to traditional analysis]

      (3) **Analysis—plaintiff's status only one of the "circumstances":** [§587] Under this view, the status of the plaintiff (as trespasser, licensee, invitee, etc.) may be considered, but it is no longer conclusive on the scope of duty owed by the defendant land occupier. Rather, the defendant's duty depends on all the pertinent circumstances, including—in addition to the plaintiff's status—the foreseeability of harm, the relation between the defendant's conduct and the plaintiff's injury, the moral blameworthiness attached to the defendant's conduct, the availability of insurance, and the like. [Pagelsdorf v. Safeco Insurance, 284 N.W.2d 55 (Wis. 1979)]

9. **Duties Owed by Entrants on Another's Land:** [§588] The problem here is whether an invitee or licensee can "stand in the shoes of the land occupier" with respect to duties owed to other persons coming onto the land. For example, suppose D, a postal worker who is delivering a parcel to O (the land occupier) on O's premises (D thus being an invitee), negligently backs up his truck while on the land and injures P, a trespasser whose presence is not known to anyone. Is D held to the general standard of due care under the circumstances, or can he claim the restricted duty that O might assert if the trespasser were injured through O's negligence?

    a. **Prevailing view—general duty of due care applies:** [§589] Although there is authority to the contrary, most courts hold that those not in possession of the land are *not* entitled to the advantage of the occupier's limited duty—even if such persons have entered with the occupier's consent. The rationale is that the special policy considerations given to possessors of land do not extend to persons on the land of others. [Musch v. H-D Electric Cooperative, Inc., *supra*; *but see* Robbins v. Minute Tapioca Co., 128 N.E. 417 (Mass. 1920)—contra]

    b. **Restatement view—middle position:** [§590] The Restatement provides that those on the land working for the occupier, or acting under the occupier's orders, need only meet whatever limited duty the occupier has; but others, although legally on the land, are not entitled to such protection (*i.e.*, they are subject to the general standard of due care). [Rest. 2d §§383 *et seq.*]

10. **Duties Owed by Lessors of Land:** [§591] One who has leased possession of land to another may owe certain duties with respect to dangerous conditions on the property. And such duties may be owed not only to the lessee but also to persons who come onto the property or pass outside it. In either case, however, the lessor's liability is *generally limited*. This reflects the fundamental rationale that tort liability for hazardous conditions on land is based on *control* thereof—so that where control has been transferred to another (by lease or conveyance), special circumstances must exist to justify imposing tort liability. [Borders v. Roseberry, 532 P.2d 1366 (Kan. 1975)]

a. **Duties owed to persons outside the land:** [§592]   Suppose the lessor leases a building to a tenant. One month later, a passerby on the street is struck by an awning falling off the side of the building. Who is liable to the passerby?

(1) **Dangerous conditions existing at time of transfer:** [§593]   Those duties that the lessor would have owed as a land occupier to persons outside the land had she retained possession *continue* for a reasonable length of time after she leases it. (*See supra*, §§534 *et seq.*)

(a) **Duty to repair or warn lessee:** [§594]   Thus, the lessor of land owes a duty to exercise due care to discover and repair *existing* dangerous conditions on the land of which she has reason to know, *or at least warn the lessee thereof*, prior to transferring possession. [Both v. Harband, *supra*, §318]

1) **"Dangerous conditions":** [§595]   "Dangerous conditions" refers to *artificial* conditions on the land involving *any* risk of harm. Most courts impose no duty with respect to natural conditions (except as to trees in urban areas adjoining public roads).

2) **"Existing" dangerous conditions:** [§596]   "Existing" dangerous conditions include conditions that may be only *potentially dangerous* at the time of transfer, if they are likely to develop into actual dangers later on (*e.g.*, awning support badly rusted but not yet broken at time of transfer).

(b) **Duration of duty limited:** [§597]   The lessor's duty to persons outside the land continues only until the lessee has had a *reasonable opportunity* to discover the condition and remedy it (*e.g.*, if the transferor warned the transferee at time of transfer, the duty continues only through that period of time required to repair). After such period, the lessee's own negligence—as a land occupier—is regarded as a *superseding cause* of any injury suffered by persons outside the land from that condition.

1) **Compare—deliberate concealment:** However, if the lessor actively concealed the danger, her liability continues until the lessee *actually discovers* the danger and has a reasonable time to remedy it.

b. **Duties owed to lessee**

(1) **Dangerous conditions existing at time of transfer:** [§598]   Whether the lessor owes any duty to the lessee depends on whether the dangerous condition is apparent (patent) or concealed (latent).

(a) **Patent dangers—no duty:** [§599]   With regard to dangerous conditions (artificial or natural) that are reasonably apparent, there is *no duty* owed; *i.e.*, the lessor has no obligation to repair the condition or even warn the lessee of its existence. And if the condition is such that a reasonable person would have been aware of it (*e.g.*, excavation in backyard, missing banister on stairway, etc.), the lessee will be charged with such knowledge. [Kearns v. Smith, 55 Cal. App. 2d 532 (1942)]

(b) **Latent dangers—duty to repair or warn:** [§600]   However, as to concealed or hidden dangerous conditions (artificial or natural) that involve *any* risk of harm and that are *known to the lessor*, there is a *duty to repair* the same *or warn* the lessee. [Smith v. Green, 260 N.E.2d 656 (Mass. 1970)]

   1) **No duty to investigate:** [§601]   Note that the duty here is limited to conditions of which the lessor was aware at the time of transfer. The lessor is under no duty to inspect or investigate for defects in the absence of some reason to believe that there is a danger. [Newman v. Golden, 144 A. 467 (Conn. 1929)]

(2) **Dangerous conditions arising after transfer:** [§602]   Having transferred possession of the premises to the lessee, the lessor owes *no duty* with respect to dangerous conditions arising thereafter—subject to the exceptions noted below.

   (a) **Exception—lessor negligent in making repairs:** [§603]   To the extent that the lessor has undertaken to repair such conditions on the premises, and has done so negligently, she is liable for any injuries attributable to that negligence (*e.g.*, where landlord attempts to repair water heater, but does so negligently, causing scalding water to injure tenant). Note that such liability will be imposed whether the lessor undertook the repairs gratuitously, pursuant to an obligation under the lease, or because of a statutory duty to repair.

   (b) **Exception—lessor fails to make repairs as covenanted in lease**

   1) **Traditional view—no tort liability:** [§604]   Until recently, most courts in this situation followed the *"nonfeasance vs. misfeasance"* distinction (discussed *supra*, §§469, 473-474)—so that where the landlord had covenanted in the lease to make certain repairs, her total failure to do so was considered *"nonfeasance"* (which would not support tort liability). [Jacobson v. Leventhal, 148 A. 281 (Me. 1930)]

   2) **Modern trend—tort liability applies:** [§605]   Today, many courts do allow recovery in tort against a landlord who has failed to undertake repairs required by the lease. [Faber v. Creswick, 156 A.2d 252 (N.J. 1959); Rest. 2d §357]

      a) **Rationale:** The lessor's covenant to repair is the kind of promise upon which the lessee had a *right to rely* in refraining from making the needed repairs himself.

      b) **Statutory developments:** [§606]   Moreover, statutes increasingly require the landlord to maintain rented premises in a safe condition, and some courts hold that the landlord's failure to make repairs is a violation of her statutory duty (*i.e.*, "negligence per se"). [Daniels v. Brunton, 80 A.2d 547 (N.J. 1951)]

c) **Compare—gratuitous promises:** [§607]   However, if the landlord's promise to repair was *gratuitous* (not required by lease or statute), most courts will *not* impose tort liability, on the ground that the tenant's reliance here is not as justifiable as where the landlord was legally obligated to make the repairs. [Rest. 2d §357, comment b]

d) **Caution—knowledge and opportunity to repair required:** [§608]   Remember that even if there is a basis for allowing recovery in tort, any landlord's liability is always contingent on showing that she *knew or should have known* of the defective condition (*e.g.*, as by tenant complaints), *and* that she had a *reasonable opportunity* prior to the injury to make the repairs.

(c) **Exception—general duty of care (minority):** [§609]   A few states hold that a lessor owes a lessee a duty of ordinary care in all cases. Issues of notice of a defect, its obviousness, and control of the premises are considered in these states only in defining the care that is owed. [Pagelsdorf v. Safeco Insurance Co., *supra*, §587]

c. **Duties owed to third persons coming onto land with lessee's express or implied consent:** [§610]   Suppose the lessor leases land to the tenant, who invites the plaintiff onto the premises, and the plaintiff is injured by a dangerous condition thereon.

(1) **Traditional view—no tort liability for lessor:** [§611]   The early view held that with the exception of leases contemplating the entry of many people, the lessor owed *no duty* to third persons coming onto the premises on the theory that there was no "privity" between the lessor and the injured party. [McKenzie v. Cheetam, 22 A. 469 (Me. 1891)]

(2) **Modern trend—same duty as owed to lessee:** [§612]   Today, many courts treat third persons who enter the premises with the express or implied consent of the lessee as falling within the scope of the lessor's general tort liability. Thus, to the extent the lessor owes a duty of care to the lessee (*supra*), she also owes a similar duty to persons entering the premises with the lessee's express or implied consent.

(a) **Example—latent dangers:** [§613]   Hence, a landlord's liability with respect to *known, latent defects* (*see supra*, §600) would extend to both the tenant and the tenant's guests or visitors, if injured thereby. [Scholey v. Steele, 59 Cal. App. 2d 402 (1943); Rest. 2d §358]

1) **Duration of liability:** [§614]   However, the lessor's liability terminates when the tenant has had sufficient opportunity to discover and remedy the dangerous condition. At that point, the tenant's own breach of duty (as land occupier) to visitors is regarded as a *superseding cause* of injuries suffered by such

visitors. [Rest. 2d §353(2); *and see* Borders v. Roseberry, *supra*, §591—lessor not liable to tenant's social guest who fell on icy steps, since tenant knew of condition and should have warned guest]

(b) **Example—failure to make promised repairs:** [§615] Moreover, jurisdictions that hold the lessor liable in tort for failing to make repairs as required by the lease or statute (above) generally hold the lessor liable to third persons coming onto the leased premises with the tenant's consent. [Krieger v. Ownership Co., 270 F.2d 265 (3d Cir. 1959)]

d. **Duties owed where lessor has retained control of common areas:** [§616] Where the leased premises consist of multiple units (*e.g.*, office building, apartment house, etc.), the lessor normally retains control of common areas (*e.g.*, elevators, stairways, restrooms, etc.). As to such areas, the lessor is regarded as the *land occupier* and owes whatever duties of care a land occupier would owe—both to tenants in the building *and* to persons entering the premises as guests or business visitors of such tenants. [Taneian v. Meghrigian, 104 A.2d 689 (N.J. 1954)]

(1) **Duty to safeguard against crime?** [§617] Several courts have enlarged this duty to include taking *reasonable precautions against foreseeable criminal acts of third parties*—e.g., installing a security guard service to protect against muggings and robberies in hallways of an apartment house where criminal acts had occurred frequently, or replacing faulty deadbolt locks. [Kline v. 1500 Massachusetts Avenue, 439 F.2d 477 (D.C. Cir. 1970); *but see* Rowe v. State Bank of Lombard, 531 N.E.2d 1358 (Ill. 1988)—no duty unless landlord voluntarily assumes it]

e. **Duty owed where lessor has right to control dangerous activity or condition created by tenant:** [§618] If the landlord has *actual knowledge* that a tenant has created a dangerous condition or activity on the premises, *plus* the right to terminate the same, the landlord is under a duty to exercise due care so as to prevent such condition (or activity) from injuring third persons.

(1) **Example:** A landlord has been held liable for failure to remove tenant's vicious dog, which attacked a young child playing with the tenant's children. The court found that the landlord knew of previous attacks by the dog. Landlord's right to terminate tenant's lease on two weeks' notice was deemed sufficient right to remove the dog. [Uccello v. Laudenslayer, 44 Cal. App. 3d 504 (1975); Gallick v. Barto, 828 F. Supp. 1168 (M.D. Pa. 1993)—landlord had duty to begin eviction proceedings against tenant whose ferret later bit plaintiff; *but see* Frobig v. Gordon, 881 P.2d 226 (Wash. 1994)—no duty on landlord to protect third person from tenant's dangerous tiger]

11. **Duties Owed by Vendors of Land:** [§619] Under the same rationale that justifies limiting a lessor's liability—*i.e.*, that control has been transferred to another (*see supra*, §591)—the general rule is that after possession has been transferred, vendors are *not* liable for harm suffered by those on or outside the premises. [Preston v. Goldman, 42 Cal. 3d 108 (1986)]

a. **Exception—failure to disclose latent dangerous conditions:** [§620]   However, a vendor who fails to disclose *known* dangerous conditions is liable to those harmed thereby—including the vendee, vendee's family, and third persons entering the land with the vendee's consent. [Rest. 2d §353] *Rationale:* Failure to warn is tantamount to a type of fraud.

b. **Exception—persons outside the premises:** [§621]   And if the property sold contained an unreasonable risk of harm to persons outside the premises, the vendor will remain liable for a reasonable period after the transfer of possession. [Derby v. Public Service Co., 119 A.2d 335 (N.H. 1955)]

c. **Duration of liability under exceptions:** [§622]   Generally, the vendor's liability lasts only until the vendee has had a reasonable time to discover and remedy the condition. But if the vendor *actively concealed* the hazardous situation, liability continues until the vendee *actually discovers* the danger and has a reasonable opportunity to remedy it. [Narsh v. Zirbser Bros., 268 A.2d 46 (N.J. 1970)]

d. **Compare—strict liability of vendor:** [§623]   In some states, a vendor who has *built* a defective home may be held liable to vendees for breach of an implied warranty of habitability. [House v. Thornton, 457 P.2d 199 (Wash. 1969)] Indeed, liability in such situations may even be extended to a form of strict liability in tort (*see infra*, §833).

12. **Duties Owed by Bailors of Chattels:** [§624]   This is really part of "Products Liability," discussed *infra*, §§763 *et seq.* However, it is worth noting at this point that the bailor of a chattel owes a certain duty of care (negligence liability) with respect to the condition of the chattel, which duty is owed both to the bailee and to all other persons within the foreseeable scope of use of the chattel (*e.g.*, pedestrians on the streets where a bailed auto may be driven). The *scope* of the bailor's duty depends on the *nature* of the bailment, and in this regard, it is analogous to that owed by a land occupier (*supra*).

a. **Gratuitous bailment:** [§625]   Where the bailment is gratuitous, the bailor owes a duty only to *warn of known*, *concealed* defects (analogous to the duty owed by a land occupier to a licensee). [Hills v. Lyons, 457 S.W.2d 503 (Ky. 1970)]

b. **Bailments for hire:** [§626]   A greater duty is owed in the case of bailments for hire. Here, the bailor must exercise due care not only to warn of known, concealed defects, but also to make a *reasonable inspection* of the chattel before bailing it in order to determine its safety (analogous to the duty owed by a land occupier to an invitee). [Collette v. Page, 114 A. 136 (R.I. 1921)]

(1) **Note:** Unlike gratuitous bailment cases, the bailor's warning to the bailee may *not* be enough to discharge this duty to third persons injured by the bailee's use of a defective chattel. Indeed, a number of modern courts impose *strict liability* in tort against commercial bailors. [Price v. Shell Oil, 2 Cal. 3d 245 (1970); *and see infra*, §813]

13. **Duties Relating to Emotional Distress**

a. **Traditional view—nature of duty owed:** [§627]   The traditional view rejects a duty of due care to prevent infliction of emotional distress on others as such. Rather, the duty owed is to exercise due care not to subject others to a foreseeable risk of physical injury, through physical impact or threat thereof, that might foreseeably result in emotional distress *and* consequent physical injuries to them. [Battalla v. State, 10 N.Y.2d 237 (1961)] In most jurisdictions, however, the duty has been broadened (*see infra*).

    (1) **Compare—recovery as parasitic damages:** Remember that where physical injury (*e.g.*, battery) causes emotional distress, damages for the distress are recoverable as part of the action for personal injury. In the usual negligence case, pain and "suffering" may include emotional distress related to the physical injury.

b. **Actual or threatened physical injury or impact:** [§628]   The early view required the plaintiff to show that the defendant, by failing to exercise the due care required above, subjected the plaintiff to *actual* physical impact. Today, however, the virtually universal view is that a *threat* of impact to the plaintiff (*i.e.*, plaintiff is within the "zone of danger" from defendant's negligent conduct) will suffice. [Battalla v. State, *supra*]

    (1) **Compare:** *Intentional* infliction of emotional distress does not require physical injury, or even threat of physical injury, to plaintiff.

    (2) **Limitation in AIDS cases:** [§629]   The threat in cases in which the plaintiff has been in contact with someone who had AIDS and who now fears having acquired the disease must be an *actual* threat in the sense of actual exposure to the virus. It is not enough that the plaintiff fear that the contact resulted in the transmission. [K.A.C. v. Benson, 527 N.W.2d 553 (Minn. 1995); Brzoska v. Olson, 668 A.2d 1355 (Del. 1995)—treatment of plaintiff patient by an AIDS-infected physician or dentist is not enough; *but see* Faya v. Almaraz, 620 A.2d 327 (Md. 1993)—permitting recovery for emotional distress during the window of uncertainty before negative test results received]

c. **Injury or threat of injury to another (bystander recovery)**

    (1) **Older view rejects duty:** [§630]   The older view requires a showing that the defendant's negligence endangered the plaintiff personally. The plaintiff must be in the "zone of danger" to recover for physical manifestations resulting from emotional distress. [Bovsun v. Sunperi, 61 N.Y.2d 219 (1984)—requiring zone of danger but not physical manifestation] This rule prevents plaintiffs from recovering in cases in which they were not personally at risk. [Williams v. Baker, 572 A.2d 1062 (D.C. 1990)—mother could not recover for harm she sustained after witnessing malpractice D committed on her young son]

    (2) **Broader view:** [§631]   But a growing and substantial number of states permit the plaintiff to recover for severe emotional distress—with or without physical manifestations—where the defendant's negligence injures or threatens a member of the plaintiff's family, but not the plaintiff. [Dillon v. Legg, 68 Cal. 2d 728 (1968)—mother may recover for

emotional distress and consequent physical injury resulting from seeing her child run over in a traffic accident]

(3) **Determinative factors:** [§632] Under this view, the plaintiff must meet three requirements [Thing v. LaChusa, 48 Cal. 3d 644 (1989)—these are requirements, not just guidelines]:

   (a) **Close relationship:** [§633] The plaintiff and the victim must have been closely related. [Elden v. Sheldon, 46 Cal. 3d 267 (1988)—no recovery for seeing injury to long-term live-in lover; *but see* Dunphy v. Gregor, 642 A.2d 372 (N.J. 1994)—contra; Leong v. Takasaki, 520 P.2d 758 (Hawaii 1974)—recognizing family relationship between child and stepfather's mother]

   (b) **Physical proximity and contemporaneous observance:** [§634] The plaintiff must be at the scene of the accident that injures the victim and must be aware at that time that the victim is suffering from injuries. [Thing v. LaChusa, *supra*—no recovery to mother who was not present at scene when accident occurred]

      1) **"Contemporaneous":** In some states, this does not mean simultaneous. [Corso v. Merrill, 406 A.2d 300 (N.H. 1979)—father viewed injured daughter after wife's screams summoned him to scene]

      2) **Note:** In some states, the other person need not in fact have been seriously hurt. It is enough if the plaintiff reasonably believes that the type of accident observed would seriously harm those involved. [Barnhill v. Davis, 300 N.W.2d 104 (Iowa 1981)]

   (c) **Suffer extraordinary emotional distress:** [§635] The plaintiff must suffer distress beyond that likely to be suffered by an unrelated bystander who sees the accident. [Thing v. LaChusa, *supra*]

(4) **Foreseeability (minority):** [§636] A few jurisdictions analyze specific circumstances for foreseeability in a traditional negligence review rather than requiring the three determinative elements set out above. [Ferriter v. Daniel O'Connell's Sons, Inc., 413 N.E.2d 690 (Mass. 1980)—allowing recovery to children who first viewed father's injuries at hospital where he was taken following industrial accident; *but see* Stockdale v. Bird & Son, Inc., 503 N.E.2d 951 (Mass. 1987)—denying recovery to mother who did not learn of accident for several hours and did not see body for 24 hours]

(5) **Limitation:** [§637] The plaintiff's rights may be derivative only. Even where recovery by a third person (parent) is permitted, the right of action is apparently *derivative*; *i.e.*, it is dependent upon the imperiled person's (child's) right to recover. Thus, if the defendant was found not liable for the harm to the child (*e.g.*, because of the child's contributory negligence), the parent would not be permitted to recover for emotional distress in witnessing the child's injury. [Dillon v. Legg, *supra*]

d. **Damage to property:** [§638]   A few cases permit the plaintiff to recover for emotional distress **and** consequential injuries when property interests are negligently damaged or threatened. [Rasmussen v. Benson, 280 N.W. 890 (Neb. 1938)—P's cattle were fed poisoned bran through D's negligence; P suffered emotional distress **and** subsequent heart trouble from fear that he had sold poisoned milk to customers and that it would ruin his dairy business]

e. **Resulting physical injury required:** [§639]   The general view requires that the emotional distress be manifested by **tangible physical injuries** to plaintiff (*e.g.*, miscarriage, nervous breakdown, paralysis, etc.). [Reilly v. United States, 547 A.2d 984 (R.I. 1988)—identifying as majority rule; Muchow v. Lindblad, 435 N.W.2d 918 (N.D. 1989); Nancy P. v. D'Amato, 517 N.E.2d 824 (Mass. 1988); Rest. 2d §463A; *but see infra*]

    (1) **Rationale:** Proof of demonstrable physical injuries is insisted upon by most courts to preclude the likelihood of fraudulent claims (*i.e.*, simulated emotional distress) and unlimited liability.

    (2) **Exception—false death reports and corpse cases:** [§640]   Some states following the general view allow recovery for emotional distress without physical manifestations under two circumstances: erroneously reporting a relative's death or mishandling the corpse of a relative. *Rationale:* These cases involve a special likelihood of genuine and serious mental distress, which guarantees that the plaintiff's claim is not fictitious.

        (a) **Example—false death report:** D hospital negligently notifies P, a close relative of a living patient, that the patient has died. P may recover for emotional distress without physical injury. [Johnson v. State, 37 N.Y.2d 378 (1975); *but see* O'Brien v. Western Union, 113 F.2d 539 (1st Cir. 1940)—most states following the general rule do not recognize this exception]

        (b) **Example—corpse mishandling:** Where D's lack of due care caused the corpse of P's deceased husband to be mutilated or injured in public, some courts that usually follow the general rule nonetheless permit recovery without proof of physical injury. [Cohen v. Groman Mortuary, 231 Cal. App. 2d 1 (1964); *but see* Dunahoo v. Bess, 200 So. 541 (Fla. 1941)—most states following general rule do not recognize this exception]

    (3) **Minority—no resulting physical injury:** [§641]   A growing minority view allows recovery for severe emotional distress **without** physical manifestation or threat of injury to the plaintiff. [Gammon v. Osteopathic Hospital of Maine, Inc., 534 A.2d 1282 (Me. 1987)—duty based on reasonable foreseeability applied to case in which mortuary sends stranger's leg to plaintiff in package supposed to contain personal effects of plaintiff's deceased father; Bowen v. Lumberman's Mutual Casualty Co., 517 N.W.2d 432 (Wis. 1994)—no requirement of physical manifestations where mother sues for distress when child was killed; Johnson v. Ruark Obstetrics & Gynecology Associates, 395 S.E.2d 85 (N.C. 1990)—negligence producing foreseeable and actual "severe" emotional distress suffices

without proof of physical manifestation in suit against physician by parents of stillborn fetus]

  (a) **But note:** Even courts that are willing to eliminate rigid requirements in direct victim cases retain such requirements in bystander cases. [Cameron v. Pepin, 610 A.2d 279 (Me. 1992)—because of fear of unlimited liability, refusing to apply its foreseeability approach in direct victim cases like *Gammon, supra,* in a bystander case in which the parents first saw their son in the hospital shortly after the accident.

  (4) **Minority—property damage:** [§642] A small minority permits recovery of emotional distress without physical manifestations for negligent destruction of a plaintiff's property. [Rodrigues v. State, 472 P.2d 509 (Hawaii 1970)—recovery permitted for emotional distress alone where D's negligence permitted six inches of water to enter house that P had just finished building with his own hands; *but see* Day v. Montana Power Co., 789 P.2d 1224 (Mont. 1990)—emotional distress alone insufficient in suit by restaurant owner for negligent destruction of his restaurant]

D. DEFENSES TO NEGLIGENCE

1. Contributory Negligence

  a. **"Contributory negligence" defined:** [§643] Contributory negligence is conduct on the part of a plaintiff that is a *contributing cause to her own injuries,* and that falls below the standard to which she is required to conform for her own protection. [Rest. 2d §463]

    (1) **Compare—"avoidable consequences":** [§644] As previously discussed (*see supra,* §426), a plaintiff is required to exercise reasonable care to mitigate damages and cannot recover for "avoidable consequences"—*e.g.,* aggravated or increased injuries that could have been avoided by seeking reasonable medical care. But this is a *rule of damages;* it has nothing to do with contributory negligence because the plaintiff's failure to mitigate damages *in no way caused or contributed to the original accident.* Avoidable consequences operates only to reduce the *amount* of damages that plaintiff can recover, whereas contributory negligence may be a *complete defense* to the plaintiff's claim (*see* below).

  b. **Prima facie case:** [§645] The prima facie case for contributory negligence is similar to the prima facie case for negligence, except that the duty here is not owed to any other person; rather, it is a duty to exercise due care in the circumstances to avoid *one's own* injury at the hands of another. Also, there is *no* requirement of an "act"; the duty of self-protection always exists and is often violated by *unreasonable inaction* in the face of danger.

    (1) **General standard of care:** [§646] The plaintiff's conduct is always measured by what the reasonable person would have done *under the same or similar circumstances.* [Solgaard v. Guy F. Atkinson Co., 6 Cal. 3d 361 (1971)]

(a) **Application—emergency cases:** [§647] Thus, if the plaintiff is confronted with an emergency not of her own making, she is judged as would a reasonable person in such an emergency. For example, where the plaintiff is faced with *imminent peril* to herself (or to a third person), she may assume extraordinary risks or perform dangerous acts in attempting to avoid the peril (or to rescue the third person) without being held contributorily negligent. [Eckert v. Long Island Railroad, 43 N.Y. 502 (1871)]

(b) **Application—children:** [§648] Courts differ over whether acts of children may be examined for contributory negligence. Most modern courts instruct the jury to consider the behavior of plaintiff in light of her age and other circumstances [Lester v. Sayles, 850 S.W.2d 858 (Mo. 1993)—child age 4.75 years may be found contributorily negligent], while others follow the rule that assigns presumptions, varying with age, that a child is incapable of negligence [Price v. Kitsap Transit, *supra*, §260; Glorioso v. Young Men's Christian Association, 556 So. 2d 293 (Miss. 1989)—nine-year-old child incapable of contributory negligence].

(c) **Application—forgetfulness:** [§649] Momentary forgetfulness is not contributory negligence as a matter of law but is a question for the jury. [Cohen v. St. Regis Paper Co., 65 N.Y.2d 752 (1984)]

(d) **Exception:** [§650] In some states, an adult plaintiff who is unstable need only act reasonably within her limits. [Tobia v. Cooper Hospital University Medical Center, 643 A.2d 1 (N.J. 1994)—where duty includes exercise of care to prevent elderly patient from engaging in self-damaging conduct, patient's engaging in such conduct cannot be raised as contributory negligence]

(2) **Statutory standards of care:** [§651] Another significant factor is whether the plaintiff has complied with statutes enacted for her own protection, and if not, whether the violation of such statutes will necessarily affect her claim.

(a) **"Contributory negligence per se":** [§652] Where the plaintiff has violated a statute designed for her own protection as well as the protection of others (*e.g.*, speed or traffic laws), the violation by itself may establish duty and breach. [Rest. 2d §469]

(b) **Violation must be contributing cause:** [§653] In any case, however, the violation must be a contributing cause to the accident; *e.g.*, driving without a valid driver's license is *not* contributory negligence. [Moore v. Hart, 188 S.W. 861 (Ky. 1916); Crawford v. Halkovics, 438 N.E.2d 890 (Ohio 1982)]

(c) **Exception—plaintiff member of class needing special protection:** [§654] Where it is shown that the plaintiff is a member of a special class sought to be protected by the statute—so that the statutory objective would be defeated if the plaintiff's fault were held to be a defense—the plaintiff's violation of the statute may be *disregarded*. [Chainani v. Board of Education, 87 N.Y.2d 370 (1995)—school bus driver violating statute requiring use of lights and waiting until passenger has crossed the street may not use child's contributory negligence as defense]

c. **Common law effect of contributory negligence:** [§655]   At traditional common law, a plaintiff's contributory negligence was an *absolute and complete bar* to any recovery for the negligence of the defendant. And this was true *no matter how slight the negligence* of plaintiff as compared to the negligence of defendant. [Rest. 2d §467]

   (1) **Note:** Contributory negligence was a defense *only to negligence*. It was no defense at all to intentional torts [Trachtel v. Essex Group, Inc., 452 N.W.2d 171 (Iowa 1990)] or to recklessness. (As to its role in strict liability, *see infra*, §758.)

   (2) **And note:** By judicial or legislative action, virtually all states have adopted comparative negligence. (*See infra*, §665.)

d. **Exception—last clear chance doctrine:** [§656]   To soften the "complete defense" rule for contributory negligence, courts held that a plaintiff's contributory negligence would not bar or reduce recovery if the defendant, immediately prior to the accident, had the "last clear chance" to avoid the accident and failed to do so. [Davies v. Mann, 152 Eng. Rep. 588 (1842); *but see infra*, §674]

   (1) **Rationale:** In these cases, the plaintiff was contributorily negligent and thereby placed herself in a position of either *"helpless"* or *"inattentive"* peril.

   (2) **"Helpless peril" cases:** [§657]   In this situation, the plaintiff—through her contributory negligence—had placed herself in a position of danger from which she was *powerless to extricate* herself by the exercise of reasonable care. In other words, even though the plaintiff was aware of the danger, the only remaining opportunity to avert the peril rested with the defendant (*e.g.*, while plaintiff was carelessly running across a busy street she fell and sprained her ankle). Most courts allowed recovery if the defendant had actual knowledge of the plaintiff's peril or should have had such knowledge.

   (3) **"Inattentive peril" cases:** [§658]   Here the plaintiff, through contributory negligence, placed herself in a situation of peril, but from which she *could* have extricated herself by the exercise of reasonable care practically up to the moment of injury. In other words, the only reason the plaintiff did not avoid the harm was that she was unaware that it was about to occur (*e.g.*, she crossed the street without looking for oncoming cars; had she been paying attention, she would have discovered defendant motorist's approach and could have averted the imminent peril). In these situations, the overwhelming weight of authority required that the defendant have had *actual knowledge* of the plaintiff's presence in time to have avoided the accident by due care before last clear chance applied.

e. **Imputed contributory negligence:** [§659]   Although contributory negligence was frequently imputed in older cases to bar the plaintiff's recovery, today it is imputed in only three major situations: (i) *master-servant*, (ii) *joint enterprise*; and (iii) cases in which the plaintiff is suing because of an *injury to someone else*. [Rest. 2d §485; LaBier v. Pelletier, 665 A.2d 1013 (Me. 1995)—mother's negligence not imputed to child]

(1) **Master-servant:** [§660]   A servant's negligence may be imputed to the master. For example, Chauffeur is driving Employer to work in Employer's car. A collision occurs between the cars driven by Chauffeur and D, due to the negligence of both Chauffeur and D. Employer is injured. Chauffeur's negligence will be imputed to Employer in any suit that she brings against D. [Smalich v. Westfall, 269 A.2d 476 (Pa. 1970)]

(2) **Joint enterprise:** [§661]   Similarly, if P and X are engaged in a joint enterprise (*see supra*, §512) and due to the combined negligence of both X and a third person (D) P is injured, X's negligence will be imputed to P to bar her recovery against D. *But note:* This rule applies only where one joint enterpriser sues a person *other than* the negligent joint enterpriser. Thus, should P sue *X*, P will *not* be barred from recovery by X's negligence. [Rest. 2d §491, comment k]

(3) **Suit based on injury to third persons:** [§662]   In actions brought for *wrongful death* (*see infra*, §§964 *et seq.*), for *loss of consortium* (*see infra*, §§979 *et seq.*), or for *bystander emotional distress* (*see supra*, §637), most courts will impute to the plaintiff the negligence of the person killed or injured. [Rest. 2d §494; Lee v. Colorado Department of Health, 718 P.2d 221 (Colo. 1986)]

(4) **Compare—bailees:** [§663]   Most courts do *not* impute the negligence of a bailee in suits brought by the bailor against a third party (D) for negligence. For example, the bailor may sue D for damages to the bailor's car caused by the joint negligence of the bailee and D, and the bailee's negligence will *not* be imputed to the bailor in that action. But the negligence *will be* imputed if D sues the bailor. [York v. Day's, Inc., 140 A.2d 730 (Me. 1958)]

(a) **Note:** The same refusal to impute contributory negligence appears in family purpose cases (*see supra*, §491). [Bartz v. Wheat, 285 S.E.2d 894 (W. Va. 1982)]

(5) **Compare—spouses:** [§664]   Ordinarily, negligence or assumption of the risk (below) by one spouse is *not* imputed to the other so as to bar recovery for injuries received in an accident in which both the first spouse and third party (D) were negligent. [Rest. 2d §487]

(a) **Note:** This is important because one spouse may not be able to sue the other for injuries due to intrafamily tort immunity (*see infra*, §§1011-1015), but may still be able to recover by suing the third party.

(b) **But note:** In some community property states (but not California), one spouse's negligence *is* imputed to the other to bar recovery against the defendant. *Rationale:* Such states view the recovery as community property in which the negligent spouse would have an interest, and thus, to prevent the negligent spouse from profiting by his own wrong, the negligence is imputed to the innocent spouse. (*See* Community Property Summary.)

2. **Comparative Negligence:** [§665]   This doctrine—*now adopted by virtually all states* by statute or judicially—*rejects* the notion that contributory negligence is always a complete bar to recovery by the plaintiff. Instead, the comparative negligence approach attempts to individualize accident recoveries by placing the economic "sting" on the parties in proportion to their fault. In every case where contributory negligence is shown, the trier of fact must make a special finding on each party's negligence and plaintiff's damages are reduced accordingly or sometimes barred. [Li v. Yellow Cab Co., 13 Cal. 3d 804 (1975)]

   a. **Example:** If P suffered $50,000 worth of injuries and the jury finds that D was 80% at fault in causing the accident and P was 20% at fault, P would recover 80% of her damages, or $40,000.

   b. **"Pure" vs. "partial" comparative negligence:** [§666]   There are two basic types of comparative negligence formulae for assessing liability:

      (1) **"Pure":** [§667]   A number of jurisdictions (*e.g.*, California and New York) have "pure" comparative negligence, which allows the plaintiff to recover a percentage of her damages even where her own negligence *exceeds* that of the defendant (*e.g.*, if a jury determines that the plaintiff was 90% at fault, she can still recover 10% of her damages).

      (2) **"Partial":** [§668]   Most states, however, recognize only "partial" comparative negligence, in that they *deny any recovery* to a plaintiff whose own negligence passes some threshold level.

         (a) **"49% limit" plans:** [§669]   Some states deny recovery to the plaintiff if her negligence *equals or exceeds* that of defendant. Thus, if the plaintiff is 49% to blame, she can recover 51% of her damages, but if the breakdown is 50-50, she gets nothing. [Bevan v. Vassar Farms, Inc., 793 P.2d 711 (Idaho 1990)]

         (b) **"50% limit" plans:** [§670]   Some jurisdictions turn this around and allow the plaintiff to recover where *defendant's* negligence equals or exceeds that of the plaintiff's (the so-called "equal to or less than" or "50% limit" plans). Under this approach, if the jury finds that the plaintiff was 50% at fault, she can still recover half her damages.

         (c) **Multiple defendants:** [§671]   Where *several* defendants are negligent, but are not *jointly liable*, some states following the "partial" approach hold that the plaintiff's negligence must be less (or no greater) than that of *any* defendant. Thus, where the jury determines that two defendants acting independently were each 30% at fault, and the plaintiff was 40% at fault, no recovery would be possible. [Delvaux v. Langenberg, 387 N.W.2d 751 (Wis. 1986)] But *most* states allow aggregation of defendant's percentages. Therefore, in the example above, the plaintiff could recover despite being 40% at fault. [Elder v. Orluck, 515 A.2d 517 (Pa. 1986)]

1) **Absent parties:** [§672]   In apportioning fault, the jury is to be told to consider the behavior of all persons, whether or not they happen to be parties to the case before the court. [Bowman v. Barnes, 282 S.E.2d 613 (W. Va. 1981); American Motorcycle Association v. Superior Court, 20 Cal. 3d 578 (1978); *but see* Baldwin v. City of Waterloo, 372 N.W.2d 486 (Iowa 1985)—contra]

c. **Impact of comparative negligence doctrine on other rules:** [§673]   A comparative negligence standard (of whatever type) affects certain other rules:

(1) **Last clear chance:** [§674]   Under any comparative negligence system, the defendant's negligence *as a whole* is compared to that of the plaintiff. It should make no difference, therefore, whether the defendant's negligence occurred before or after discovering the plaintiff's predicament. Consequently, almost all courts hold that the doctrine of last clear chance is *abolished* under comparative negligence. [Bokhoven v. Klinker, 474 N.W.2d 553 (Iowa 1991)]

(2) **Wanton or reckless conduct by defendant:** [§675]   Most comparative negligence states that have ruled on the issue have held that a negligent plaintiff's damages can be reduced even where the defendant's conduct was "reckless," "wanton," or "grossly negligent." [Sorenson v. Allred, 112 Cal. App. 3d 717 (1980)]

(a) **Compare—intentional tort by defendant:** [§676]   However, the plaintiff's negligence will *not* be considered where the defendant has committed an intentional wrong. [Billingsley v. Westrac Co., 365 F.2d 619 (8th Cir. 1966)]

(b) **Compare—intentional act by one party combined with negligence by other party:** [§677]   In the very common situation in which one defendant's negligence has facilitated an intentional tort or crime by a third party, the courts are split. This issue has become very important since states have begun altering the rule of joint and several liability, *supra*, §329.]

1) **Better view—noncomparison:** Where a negligent landlord facilitates attacks on his tenants, the landlord should *not* be permitted to reduce his share of liability by arguing that the attacker deserves the overwhelming percentage of fault. [Veazey v. Elmwood Plantation Associates, Ltd., 650 So. 2d 712 (La. 1994)] *Rationale:* The defendant's negligence encompassed the very risk of attack and should not be reduced when the foreseeable risk comes to pass.

2) **Other view—comparison:** Some states think it unfair to compare only negligent conduct while leaving the intentional acts

out of consideration. [Reichert v. Atler, 875 P.2d 379 (1994)—allocating liability 1/3 to bartender, who failed to protect patron from foreseeable killing by another patron, and 2/3 to the killer]

(c) **Compare—reckless plaintiff:** [§678]   In a "pure" comparative negligence state, a reckless plaintiff may recover some damages from a negligent defendant. [Zavala v. Regents of the University of California, 125 Cal. App. 3d 646 (1981); *but see* Barker v. Kallash, 63 N.Y.2d 19 (1984)—totally barring claim by 15-year-old who was hurt while making pipe bomb]

(3) **Avoidable consequences:** [§679]   The plaintiff's unreasonable failure to mitigate damages caused by the defendant's negligence will serve to decrease the plaintiff's damages, rather than bar recovery. [Ostrowski v. Azzara, 545 A.2d 148 (N.J. 1988)—plaintiff's unreasonable postoperative conduct in malpractice case merely decreased her damages; Foley v. City of West Allis, 335 N.W.2d 824 (Wis. 1983)—failure to wear safety belt reduces recovery]

(a) **Failure to wear safety belt:** [§680]   Where the legislature has refused to pass a law mandating use of safety belts, the courts may hold evidence of failure to wear a safety belt inadmissible on the issue of comparative negligence or avoidable consequences. [Swajian v. General Motors Corp., 559 A.2d 1041 (R.I. 1989)] In states with statutes mandating the use of safety belts, evidence of failure to wear one can be admitted (unless the statute bars use in civil proceedings). [Dahl v. Bayerische Motoren Werke, 748 P.2d 77 (Or. 1987)]

(4) **Jury instructions:** [§681]   Courts are split over whether the jury in a comparative negligence case should be told about how the law works (so that the jurors will know the consequences of their apportionment). [Roman v. Mitchell, 413 A.2d 322 (N.J. 1980)—should tell the jury; *but see* Delvaux v. Langenberg, *supra*, §671—reversible error to tell jury]

(5) **Imputation of comparative negligence:** [§682]   The availability of comparative negligence has led some courts to alter rules to permit imputation of negligence. [Mist v. Westin Hotels, Inc., 738 P.2d 85 (Hawaii 1987)—victim's negligence imputed to spouse for loss of consortium]

(6) **Rescuers:** [§683]   Although some states have concluded that rescuers no longer need any special protection, in light of comparative negligence, most courts have retained the earlier rule. [Ouellette v. Carde, 612 A.2d 687 (R.I. 1992)—comparative negligence rule does not fully protect underlying policy of rescuer doctrine; rescuer's conduct that is negligent at most should not permit reduction in award]

(7) **Drunk plaintiffs:** [§684]   Some states have concluded that allowing partial recovery to a drunk plaintiff against a negligent tavernkeeper or liquor vendor will serve to discourage defendants' negligence in these cases. [Estate of Kelly v. Moguls, Inc., 632 A.2d 360 (Vt. 1993)—since

neither party will be made whole, both will be deterred; *but see* Estate of Kelly v. Falin, 896 P.2d 1245 (Wash. 1995)—contra, because allowing suit would encourage drunk driving]

(8) **Res ipsa loquitur:** [§685]   Most states have concluded that after the introduction of comparative' negligence, the plaintiff need no longer show freedom from contributory negligence as part of the res ipsa case. [Giles v. City of New Haven, 636 A.2d 1335 (Conn. 1994)]

(9) **Punitive damages:** [§686]   A plaintiff may not recover punitive damages where the jury has attributed more fault to the plaintiff than to the defendant. Permitting punitive damages in this situation would undermine the purpose of comparative negligence. [Tucker v. Marcus, 418 N.W.2d 818 (Wis. 1988)]

3. Assumption of the Risk

a. **General rule:** [§687]   If the plaintiff expressly or impliedly consents to confront the harm from a particular risk created by the defendant, the plaintiff is held to have assumed that risk and thus is barred from any recovery for negligence (or strict liability, *infra*). In every case, however, it must be shown that plaintiff (i) *recognized and understood* the particular risk or danger involved; and (ii) *voluntarily chose* to encounter it.

(1) **Note—consent to risk of harm essential:** Mere heedlessness of or indifference to the risk is insufficient to establish assumption of the risk; plaintiff must actually consent for the defense to succeed. [Thomas v. Holliday, 764 P.2d 165 (Okla. 1988)—security guard thrown from fleeing suspect's car had not consented to risk of injury]

(2) **Application—firefighter's rule:** When police or firefighters are hurt while responding to some emergency or when in some dangerous situation, they are almost universally barred from suing the persons whose acts brought about the emergency. One rationale is that the very nature of their jobs exposes police and firefighters to these risks of harm. [England v. Tasker, 529 A.2d 938 (N.H. 1987)—police officer hurt while attempting to pull person from auto wreck cannot sue allegedly negligent driver who caused accident; Zanghi v. Niagara Frontier Transportation Commission, 85 N.Y.2d 423 (1995)—suits by police officers and firefighters barred in several fact situations]

b. **Assumption of risk by agreement—"exculpatory clauses":** [§688]   Where the relationship between the plaintiff and defendant arises out of a contract, the defendant may attempt to limit or exclude liability in advance by the use of so-called exculpatory provisions—*e.g.*, a notice printed on a railroad ticket stating that "carrier shall not be liable for injury to person or property" (or limiting liability to a specified dollar amount). Whether the plaintiff is barred or limited by assumption of risk in this situation depends on the enforceability of such provisions, as a matter of *contract law*. [Barnes v. New Hampshire Karting Association, 509 A.2d 151 (N.H. 1986)—race participant barred by release]

(1) **Offer and acceptance problem:** [§689]   First of all, it must be determined that the provision *is* part of the contract—*i.e.*, that a prudent person would have been aware of it at the time the agreement was entered into, so that it would be part of the offer and acceptance. This usually requires a showing that the provision was printed in large type, or that there were large signs posted calling attention to the limitation on liability. Therefore, "fine print provisions" on the backs of tickets or receipts may be totally unenforceable because not deemed part of the parties' contract. (*See* Contracts Summary.)

   (a) **Note:** Explicit use of the terms "negligence" and "breach of warranty" is *not* necessary for an exculpatory agreement to shield a party from claims based on negligence and breach of warranty; the intent of parties guides interpretation of the agreement. [Heil Valley Ranch, Inc. v. Simkin, 784 P.2d 781 (Colo. 1989)]

(2) **Limitation—adhesion contract:** [§690]   Assuming the provision is deemed part of the contract, its enforceability may depend on the *bargaining position of the parties*:

   (a) **Equal bargaining positions:** [§691]   Where the parties are in an equal bargaining position (*e.g.*, a merchant ordering goods from a manufacturer), exculpatory provisions are usually upheld. There is no public policy that prevents the parties from limiting liability for *negligence*; and indeed, the limitation of liability may very well have been one of the factors relied upon in fixing the contract price.

   (b) **Unequal bargaining positions—public policy limitations:** [§692]   However, where it appears that one party set all terms to the contract and the other had no opportunity to negotiate—so-called *adhesion contracts*, such as exculpatory clauses in employment agreements, contracts for public utility services or public transportation—provisions that would exclude or limit liability may be held *invalid* as a violation of *public policy*. [Restatement (Second) of Contracts §575]

      1) **Example:** A release of liability contained in a *hospital admission form* purporting to "waive" any claim the patient might have for medical malpractice against the hospital or attending physicians is contrary to public policy. [Tunkl v. Regents of University of California, 60 Cal. 2d 92 (1963)]

      2) **Example:** A provision in a *form lease* whereby an apartment house tenant purported to waive any claim he might ever have against landlord for injuries arising out of landlord's failure to maintain common areas for which landlord was responsible (*e.g.*, elevators, stairways, etc.) is contrary to public policy. [McCutcheon v. United Homes Corp., 486 P.2d 1093 (Wash. 1971)]

      3) **Example:** A release relieving a school district from liability for students' injuries, signed as a condition of participation in interscholastic athletics, is contrary to public policy. [Wagenblast v. Odessa School District, 758 P.2d 968 (Wash. 1988)]

(3) **Limitation—intentional torts:** [§693]   Even where valid, exculpatory provisions are enforceable only with respect to **negligence** claims. They can never be used to excuse a tortfeasor from liability for **intentional** or wanton or reckless torts. [Restatement (Second) of Contracts §574; Thomas v. Atlantic Coast Line Railroad, 201 F.2d 167 (5th Cir. 1953); Sommer v. Federal Signal Corp., 79 N.Y.2d 540 (1992)]

c.   **Implied assumption of the risk by conduct:** [§694]   In the absence of any contract, the issue is whether the plaintiff, by conduct, can be held to have **voluntarily** assumed the **particular** risk involved. This is the more common (and more difficult) issue in negligence cases. [Dillard v. Little League Baseball, 55 App. Div. 2d 477 (1977)—umpire hit in groin by pitch]

(1) **Subjective test:** [§695]   The plaintiff's knowledge of the danger and voluntary exposure to it are measured **subjectively**—i.e., by what the plaintiff personally was aware of and intended, and **not** by what a reasonable person would know and do. However, the plaintiff's subjective state of mind may be determined from **external manifestations**—words, conduct, etc. [Hildebrand v. Minyard, 494 P.2d 1328 (Ariz. 1972)]

(a) **Example:** If P attends a baseball or hockey game, most courts hold that in seeking admission, P must be regarded as having chosen to encounter the well-known risk of flying baseballs or hockey pucks, which attend such sports. [Kennedy v. Providence Hockey Club, 376 A.2d 329 (R.I. 1977); *and see* Maddox v. City of New York, 66 N.Y.2d 270 (1986)—professional baseball player assumed risk of muddy field]

(b) **Limitation—plaintiff must fully appreciate risk:** [§696]   On the other hand, there is no assumption of the risk where, due to **age or inexperience**, the plaintiff does not in fact comprehend the danger—even though a reasonable person might have.

(c) **Compare—extraordinary risks:** [§697]   Moreover, one who participates in sporting events does not impliedly assume the risk of an opponent's flagrant violations of the rules that result in serious injuries. [Nabozny v. Barnhill, 334 N.E.2d 258 (Ill. 1975)—soccer goalie kicked in head]

(2) **Knowledge of specific danger:** [§698]   It must also be shown that the plaintiff was aware of the **particular risk** by which she was injured, not merely of danger generally. For example, the fact that the plaintiff was aware that the car in which she was riding was being driven at an excessive speed does not mean that she assumed the risk that another car would rear-end it when the driver stopped short.

(3) **Voluntary assumption:** [§699]   The plaintiff's conduct must likewise manifest a **voluntary choice** to encounter the risk involved (and implicitly relieve the defendant from the duty of due care); i.e., the risk is not assumed where the plaintiff has no reasonable alternative.

(a) **Application:** Where it appears that the plaintiff's decision was dictated by **necessity, force, or fraud**, there is no assumption of the risk. For example, those who dash into a dangerous situation to save their own property or the lives or property of another do not "voluntarily" assume the risk unless the risk is out of all proportion to the value of the interest sought to be protected. [Cote v. Palmer, 16 A.2d 595 (Conn. 1940)]

(b) **And note:** Generally, the plaintiff is not required to surrender a valuable legal right (such as the use of her own property as she sees fit) simply because defendant's conduct has threatened her with harm if the right is exercised. Hence, P does not "assume the risk" where—to get to work—she attempts to drive her car out of a driveway that D has negligently excavated, even though P knows of the danger. (But P's conduct may be contributory negligence; *see* below.) [Conroy v. Briley, 191 So. 2d 601 (Fla. 1966)]

d. **Exception—no assumption of risk where plaintiff is member of statutorily protected class:** [§700]   Where the defendant's negligence consists of violation of a statute designed for the *protection* of a certain class of persons, a plaintiff who is a member of that class is deemed legally incapable of assuming the risk—either expressly or by implication. Thus, a factory's violation of safety regulations instituted for protection of employees is not excused by an employee's continuing to work there, even though the employee knowingly and "voluntarily" chooses to subject herself to the risk. [Suess v. Arrowhead Steel Products Co., 230 N.W. 125 (Minn. 1930); Rest. 2d §496F]

(1) **Rationale:** The fundamental purpose of such statutes is to protect specific persons against their own inability to protect themselves (*e.g.*, because of lack of judgment or unequal bargaining power) and if the plaintiff were held to assume the risk, this purpose would be defeated.

e. **Compare—contributory negligence:** [§701]   There may be *both* contributory negligence and assumption of the risk by plaintiff in the same case. Thus if P, a rider in an automobile negligently driven by D, fails to object, this failure may be construed as contributory negligence or assumption of the risk, or both. [Koster v. Matson, 30 P.2d 107 (Kan. 1934)]

(1) **Example:** Jaywalkers who cross against a traffic light do not voluntarily assume the risk that drivers will run them down. (Quite the contrary, it is probably assumed that the drivers will slow down and let them through.) However, jaywalking may be enough to establish contributory negligence. [Rest. 2d §496C, comment h]

(2) **Example:** Accepting a ride with a driver known to be drunk might be unreasonable depending on the circumstances, but it is not assumption of risk. [Gonzalez v. Garcia, 75 Cal. App. 3d 874 (1977)—comparative negligence applies to this situation]

f. **Minority view—abolition of implied assumption of risk:** [§702]   In recent years, a growing number of states have concluded that implied assumption of risk is *not* a useful doctrine and have therefore *abolished* it. [Meistrich v. Casino Arena, 155 A.2d 90 (N.J. 1959); Rutter v. Northeastern Beaver County School District, 437 A.2d 1198 (Pa. 1981)] Instead, what most states analyze as assumption of risk, the minority handles as a question of duty or contributory negligence.

(1) **Example:** Where P is hurt by a foul ball at a baseball game, the minority view denies recovery on the theory that D has met its limited duty (*e.g.*, to provide some seats behind a screen). Note that under this view, D would win regardless of the extent of P's knowledge about the dangers of baseball. [Brown v. San Francisco Baseball Club, 99 Cal. App. 2d 484 (1950)]

(2) **Effect—defenses limited:** [§703]   In these states, once the prima facie case of negligence is established against the defendant, the only defense available is that the plaintiff behaved ***unreasonably*** (was contributorily negligent). There is no longer room for discussion about voluntarily encountering a known risk.

g. **Minority view—primary and secondary assumption of risk**

(1) **"Primary" and "secondary" assumption of risk:** [§704]   A few states tend to follow the minority approach just stated but instead of speaking directly of "duty" and "contributory negligence," they speak instead of "primary" and "secondary" assumption of risk. The issues are ***exactly the same*** despite the different language.

(a) **Primary assumption of risk:** [§705]   This involves a determination that the defendant has met whatever duty the court thinks appropriate to impose—and thus there is no basis for any liability.

1) **Example:** In a friendly touch football game, D, trying to defend against a pass, accidentally knocked P over and stepped on her hand. Recovery was denied. [Knight v. Jewett, 3 Cal. 4th 296 (1992)—person hurt by an inherent risk of a sport loses because of "primary" assumption of the risk; the defender did not owe a duty of due care in this case but only a duty not to recklessly or intentionally hurt P]

a) **Note:** Since P would lose in this case even if totally ignorant of the risks, the court's real basis must be no breach of duty and ***not*** "knowing" and "voluntary" assumption of risk.

b) **Rationale:** In participant sports cases, a duty of due care would chill the fervor of athletic competitions. [Crawn v. Campo, 643 A.2d 600 (N.J. 1994); Knight v. Jewett, *supra*; *but see* Lestina v. West Bend Mutual Insurance Co., 501 N.W.2d 28 (Wis. 1993)—adopting negligence as the governing principle in sports injury cases]

(b) **Secondary assumption of risk:** [§706]   Here the court has found a duty of due care and breach. If the defendant asserts that the plaintiff has also acted unreasonably in the accident, the issue is one of contributory negligence. Although some courts refer to this issue as "secondary" assumption of the risk, it operates *exactly* as does comparative negligence in that state—either to reduce or possibly bar recovery. [*See* Knight v. Jewett, *supra*]

(2) **Comment—application uncertain:** In *Knight v. Jewett, supra*, the court split several ways in selecting the proper standard, and some justices disagreed in how the standard should be applied. Three justices use "primary assumption of risk" and concluded that using negligence in this case would chill the vigor of amateur sports competition; a fourth judge agreed in the result but preferred to abolish "assumption of risk" language and use only "duty" language—saying that the defendant owed no duty of due care in this type of case. Three justices used traditional assumption of risk terminology. Two of these justices found that the plaintiff had voluntarily and knowingly assumed the risk of being hurt in the game, so they concurred in the result; the third justice, using the traditional approach, did not find knowing acceptance of the risk and dissented.

E. EFFECT OF LIABILITY INSURANCE

1. **Present "Third Party" Liability Insurance System:** [§707] At present, most car owners carry insurance against whatever liability (up to the policy's maximum coverage) they may incur to third parties in connection with the operation of their vehicles (hence, known as "third party" or "liability" insurance). Such insurance is also carried for homeowner's liability, products liability (*infra*), and malpractice; and the same principles apply.

   a. **General operation of "third party" insurance system:** [§708] When an accident covered by third party insurance occurs, the defendant's insurance carrier investigates the claims of the injured party and defends any lawsuit that is filed. The insurer has a duty to defend any lawsuit that might be covered by the policy, regardless of the claim's actual merit. Note that the duty exists even if there may be doubts as to whether the claim is covered by the policy; *i.e.*, the duty to defend is broader than the duty to pay any judgment. [Voorhees v. Preferred Mutual Insurance Co., 607 A.2d 1255 (N.J. 1992)]

      (1) **Insurance carrier's role in lawsuit:** [§709] In most states, the suit is defended in the name of the insured defendant (rather than in the name of the insurance company), and the jury generally is not told whether the defendant is, or is not, insured. (*See* Evidence Summary.)

         (a) **Direct action against insurer?** [§710] Most liability insurance policies insure the defendant only against liability established by a *judgment* against her in a legal action (or a settlement agreed to by insurer). Therefore, until a judgment is returned, most states provide that the injured party (the plaintiff) has *no direct action* against the defendant's insurance company. (A very few states are contra by statute.)

            1) **Compare:** Once a judgment is returned, however, the plaintiff is treated as a *third party beneficiary* of the defendant's insurance company's promise to pay any judgments against the

defendant, and hence the plaintiff can sue the defendant's insurer directly if it fails to discharge the judgment against defendant.

(2) **Effect of intentional or "wanton and reckless" conduct:** [§711] Most liability insurance policies cover only *negligent* conduct by a defendant or strict liability. Hence, in cases where the plaintiff alleges that the defendant was acting "wantonly and recklessly" (usually in an attempt to claim punitive damages), the defendant's insurance carrier may be liable for the compensatory part of any award but not for the punitive part. If the act was intentional, the insurer may not be liable for any part of the award.

    (a) **Note:** If the policy terms cover punitive damages, most courts require the insurer to pay them. [Harrell v. Travelers Indemnity Co., 567 P.2d 1013 (Or. 1977)] However, some states statutorily prohibit insurance company payment of punitive damages by forbidding coverage of losses caused by the insured's willful acts. [Cal. Ins. Code §533; J.C. Penney Casualty Insurance Co. v. M.K., 52 Cal. 3d 1009 (1991)]

b. **Insured's duty of "cooperation":** [§712] An express or implied provision of every liability insurance contract is that the insured party will "cooperate" with the insurer, so that if the defendant acts collusively with the plaintiff, fails to testify when required, etc., the insurance carrier may be able to deny coverage as to any judgment against the defendant.

c. **Insurer's duty of "good faith" in settlement:** [§713] Every liability insurance policy has a maximum limit (*e.g.*, $25,000 for injuries to any one person), and should a judgment be returned that exceeds the limit, the defendant is personally liable for the excess. Hence, courts today recognize that an insurance company owes at least a *duty of good faith* to its insured (the defendant) to attempt to settle any claims against her within the policy limits, so as to avoid the risk of her being held personally responsible for satisfying part of the judgment. [Pavia v. State Farm Mutual Automobile Insurance Co., 82 N.Y.2d 445 (1993)]

    (1) **Stricter standard imposed by some courts:** [§714] Some courts have imposed a more stringent standard of liability on insurers than the "good faith" rule. Thus, for example, it has been held that the insurer has a duty to use *due care* to attempt to settle within policy limits *whenever there is a substantial likelihood* of a recovery exceeding those limits. *Unreasonable* failure to settle under these circumstances is at the insurer's risk of liability for the whole amount of any judgment against the defendant—whether or not "bad faith" is shown. [Comunale v. Traders & General Insurance Co., 50 Cal. 2d 654 (1958)]

    (2) **Effect of insurer's breach of duty:** [§715] If the insurance carrier is held liable for failure to settle within the policy limits, it may be held liable for the *full amount* of any judgment subsequently returned against the defendant (including the excess over policy limits). [Crisci v. Security Insurance Co., 66 Cal. 2d 425 (1967)]

(a) **Special damages also recoverable:** [§716]   Many states also permit the defendant to recover *any special damages* incurred as a result of the insurer's failure to settle—*e.g.*, the value of property taken in satisfaction of the excess judgment, or the defendant's mental suffering caused by the insurer's misconduct. [Crisci v. Security Insurance Co., *supra*]

(b) **Insured may assign claim against insurer:** [§717]   It is further recognized that the defendant's cause of action against her insurance company for failing to make a "good faith" effort to settle is *assignable*. Hence, where the plaintiff recovers a judgment in excess of the defendant's insurance limits, the defendant (to avoid personal liability for the excess) will usually assign to the plaintiff her cause of action against her insurance company. [Critz v. Farmers Insurance Group, 230 Cal. App. 2d 788 (1964)]

(3) **Compare—no duty to third persons:** [§718]   Most courts hold that the insurer's duties regarding settlement run only to the insured, and consequently no third person can sue—even where it was foreseeable that failure to settle would result in damages (*e.g.*, emotional distress) to such third person. [Moradi-Shalal v. Fireman's Fund Insurance Companies, 46 Cal. 3d 287 (1988)]

(4) **Compare—tort claims in "first party" insurance:** [§719]   Some states extend tort claims for "bad faith" to health, fire, accident, and life insurance, so-called first party insurance. [Gruenberg v. Aetna Insurance Co., 9 Cal. 3d 566 (1973)] Other states refuse to do so. [Lawton v. Great Southwest Fire Insurance Co., 392 A.2d 576 (N.H. 1978); Spencer v. Aetna Life & Casualty Insurance Co., 611 P.2d 149 (Kan. 1980)]

(a) **Arguments favoring tort claim:** States adopting the tort action rely on the uneven bargaining power of the parties, the value of delay to the insurer who can earn interest on the money that is owed, and the analogy of the third party insurance cases.

(b) **Argument against tort claims:** States rejecting the tort claim stress the purely contractual aspect of first party insurance and the existence of statutory and administrative penalties for failure to settle claims properly.

III. STRICT LIABILITY

chapter approach

In most fact situations the plaintiff claims that the defendant has intentionally (Chapter I) or negligently (Chapter II) caused her some harm. Occasionally, though, a defendant may be liable *without any fault* on his part. In other words, the defendant is strictly liable.

Unlike negligence, the problem in strict liability situations usually lies not in establishing the elements of the prima facie case, but in determining whether the facts involved fall into one of the recognized categories of cases in which courts are willing to impose strict liability. In spotting strict liability situations, especially look for the following facts:

(i) *Defendant's animals cause an injury*; or

(ii) *Defendant is involved in an abnormally dangerous activity* (*e.g.*, using explosives).

When you find a strict liability situation, be sure to consider the *limitations on strict liability* (foreseeability of plaintiff and foreseeability of hazard) and the possibility of a *defense* (assumption of risk).

A. IN GENERAL [§720]

The third broad basis for tort liability involves torts that are neither intentional nor the result of negligence. Rather, liability is imposed simply *because certain types of injuries happen*—even though no one is at fault. The justification for this policy of strict liability is based on the nature of the activity that caused the harm; if these certain activities cause harm, the view is that liability should rest on the party best able to avoid its recurrence—*i.e.*, the defendant.

Prima facie case (the same as for negligence, except as to duty):

> *Act or Omission by Defendant*
> *Duty to Avoid Harm*
> *Breach of Duty*
> *Actual Cause (Cause in Fact)*
> *Proximate Cause (Legal Cause)*
> *Damages*

B. ANIMALS

1. Domestic Animals

a. **Trespassing livestock:** [§721] The possessor of livestock trespassing on the land or chattels of another is strictly liable for the trespass itself and any harm done thereby. [Rest. 2d §504]

(1) **"Livestock":** [§722] "Livestock" is defined as any animal of domestic value that is relatively easy to control. This includes, for example, horses, cattle, pigs, and sheep, but *not* household pets.

b. **Domestic animals (including livestock) with known dangerous propensities:** [§723]   The possessor of a domestic animal with a known dangerous propensity (*e.g.,* a dog that bites) is strictly liable for all harm done *as the result of that dangerous propensity*. The rationale is that the social utility of keeping an animal known to have dangerous tendencies is outweighed by the magnitude of the risk involved. [Rest. 2d §509]

   (1) **Compare—normally dangerous domestic animals:** [§724]   If the domestic animal is of a class that normally has dangerous propensities (*e.g.,* a bull), the possessor is not *strictly liable* for injuries caused by that animal's normal dangerous propensity. Here, the rationale is that the social utility in keeping these somewhat dangerous animals outweighs their normal risk and thus possession should not be discouraged by strict liability. Note however that the possessor of such an animal may be liable for *negligence* if he does not use adequate care in keeping the animal.

   (2) **Limitation—harm must result from a known dangerous propensity:** [§725]   Where strict liability applies, the possessor is liable only for injuries *attributable* to the animal's known dangerous propensity (*e.g.,* knowledge that a horse is difficult to control may not be sufficient to impose strict liability when the horse bites someone). [Greeley v. Jameson, 164 N.E. 385 (Mass. 1929)]

c. **Domestic animals without known dangerous propensities:** [§726]   The general view is that the possessor of animals that have not in the past exhibited dangerous characteristics is *not* held to strict liability for their acts. It is therefore said that "every previously well-behaved dog is entitled to one free bite"—*i.e.,* only when the owner has reason to know the dog has vicious tendencies will strict liability apply. [Jividen v. Law, 461 S.E.2d 451 (W. Va. 1995)—"rambunctiousness and friskiness" of horse are insufficient to impose strict liability]

   (1) **Exception—dog bite statutes:** [§727]   However, statutes in several states reject the "one free bite" rule as to *dogs* (only), imposing strict liability on the owner for injuries suffered (excluding property damage) by any person bitten by the dog, even though the dog was *not* previously known to have dangerous characteristics. [*See, e.g.,* Cal. Civ. Code §3342] Some other states have reached the same result by case law.

      (a) **Note:** If the statute is not limited to "biting," it may apply even where no contact occurs. [Henry v. Brown, 495 A.2d 324 (Maine 1985)—statute applies where P fell while stepping back from charging dog]

2. **Wild Animals:** [§728]   The possessor of wild animals is strictly liable for any harm resulting from these animals' *normally dangerous* propensities. [Rest. 2d §507]

   a. **Knowledge of dangerous propensity:** [§729]   Scienter (knowledge of the dangerous propensity) is *not* necessary, provided the harm results from the *normal* propensities or characteristics of the animal.

(1) **Compare—damage resulting from trespass:** [§730]   The rule set forth above regarding "trespass by livestock" has been made applicable to wild animals so that, regardless of scienter, defendant would be strictly liable for any trespass by his wild animal.

b. **Exception—animals kept pursuant to public duty:** [§731]   Where wild animals are kept under a public duty (*e.g.,* in a zoo or under transport by common carrier), strict liability does *not* apply. Negligence must be shown—although the defendant would be held to a high amount of care. [Cowden v. Bear Country, Inc., 382 F. Supp. 1321 (D.S.D. 1974); Rest. 2d §517]

3. **Persons Protected:** [§732]   Strict liability clearly applies to injuries inflicted by an animal in public places. However, where the harm occurs on the defendant's premises, whether strict liability will be invoked depends on the *status* of the injured person:

a. **Invitees, licensees:** [§733]   Where a plaintiff enters private property with the express or limited consent of the land occupier (*e.g.,* as a guest or business visitor), strict liability clearly is applied. [McLane v. Northwest Gas Co., 467 P.2d 635 (Or. 1970)]

b. **Trespassers:** [§734]   On the other hand, most courts hold that strict liability does not extend to trespassers whose presence the owner had *no reason to know of or anticipate,* and thus, no recovery may be had for injuries inflicted by the animal. [Rest. 2d §511] (Of course, if the trespasser's presence was known, negligence liability would apply; *see supra,* §539.)

(1) **Limitation—vicious watchdogs:** [§735]   However, even though a trespasser's presence is *unknown,* a landowner may be liable for injuries by a *vicious watchdog*—unless adequate warnings of the dog's presence were posted. [Rest. 2d §516]

(a) **Rationale:** The landowner's privilege to use such dogs for protection of the property is similar to the privilege to use mechanical devices under the same circumstances (*supra,* §123)—*i.e.,* absent adequate warnings, the landowner is liable for the harm done, unless the intruder was *in fact* threatening death or serious bodily harm.

(2) **Limitation—foreseeable trespassers:** [§736]   Moreover, the no-liability rule also does not apply where the landowner had *reason to anticipate* trespassing upon the property (*e.g.,* where injured person is a CTULA, or child trespasser whose presence the owner had reason to foresee; *supra,* §§540, 547). In such cases, strict liability will be imposed unless *adequate warnings* of the animal's presence were given. [Rest. 2d §512]

C. ABNORMALLY DANGEROUS ACTIVITIES

1. **General Rule:** [§737]   One who maintains an abnormally dangerous condition or activity on his premises or engages in an activity that presents an unavoidable risk of harm to the person or property of others may be liable for the harm it causes

even though reasonable care to prevent such harm has been exercised. [Rest. 2d §519]

2. **"Abnormally Dangerous" Activities:** [§738] The problem in these cases is to determine what constitutes an "abnormally dangerous" activity or condition so as to give rise to strict liability.

   a. **Origin—*Rylands v. Fletcher*:** [§739] The landmark case of *Rylands v. Fletcher,* L.R. 3 H.L. 330 (1868), held that a person who brings something onto his land that involves a *"nonnatural* use" of the land and is *likely to cause substantial damage* if it escapes will be strictly liable if it in fact escapes and causes harm.

   b. **Application under First Restatement—"ultrahazardous activities":** [§740] Under the First Restatement, the key term was *"ultrahazardous."* An activity fit that description if it necessarily involved a risk of serious harm to the person, land, or chattels of others that could not be eliminated by the exercise of utmost care and was not a matter of common usage. [Rest. §520]

      (1) **Example—ultrahazardous:** Ultrahazardous activities include blasting, explosives manufacturing, drilling oil wells (in some states), fumigation [Old Island Fumigation, Inc. v. Barbee, 604 So. 2d 1246 (Fla. 1992)], and setting off public fireworks [Klein v. Pyrodyne Corp., 810 P.2d 917 (Wash. 1991)].

      (2) **Compare—dangerous:** Dangerous activities that are *not* ultrahazardous in nature—usually because they are commonly used—include use of fire, automobiles, firearms, and boilers. [Beck v. Bel Air, 134 Cal. App. 2d 834 (1955)]

   c. **Basis for liability under Second Restatement—"abnormally dangerous" activities:** [§741] The Second Restatement changed the critical term to "abnormally dangerous" activity because the drafters thought the prior term gave too little weight to the context in which the activity was being carried on. [Rest. 2d §519]

      (1) **Determinative factors:** [§742] Instead of defining when an activity is abnormally dangerous, the Second Restatement lists the following six factors to be considered and balanced:

         (i) Whether the *activity involves a high degree of risk* of harm;

         (ii) *The gravity* of that risk;

         (iii) Whether the *risk can be eliminated by the exercise of reasonable care*;

         (iv) Whether the *activity is a matter of common usage*;

         (v) Whether the *activity is appropriate to the place* where it is being carried on; and

         (vi) *The value* of the activity *to the community*.

[Rest. 2d §520; *and see* Lanagan v. Valicopters, Inc., 567 P.2d 218 (Wash. 1977)—applying this section to crop dusting; *but see* Indiana Harbor Belt Railroad v. American Cyanamid Co., 916 F.2d 1174 (7th Cir. 1990)—rejecting section in case against shipper of hazardous chemical that leaked from rail car]

(2) **Impact of new terminology?** [§743]   It is clear that the Second Restatement offers escapes from strict liability in its fifth and sixth factors that were not available under the First Restatement—appropriateness to location and value to the community. [New Meadows Holding Co. v. Washington Water Power Co., 687 P.2d 212 (Wash. 1984)—natural gas pipeline] This might affect such extreme cases as a dangerous mine that supports the economy of an entire town.

   (a) **But note:** Several courts have shown reluctance to adopt the Second Restatement's softening of strict liability. [Yukon Equipment v. Fireman's Fund Insurance Co., 585 P.2d 1206 (Alaska 1978)—per se rule of strict liability for explosion of stored explosives; Koos v. Roth, 652 P.2d 1255 (Or. 1982)—field burning warrants strict liability because society "has other ways to lighten the burdens of costly but unavoidable accidents on a valued industry than to let them fall haphazardly on the industry's neighbors"]

(3) **Application—airplane ground damage:** [§744]   Early cases deemed flying to be so dangerous that owners of aircraft were strictly liable for all harm caused by aircraft flight to persons and property on the ground.

   (a) **Modern cases split on this question:** [§745]   Some courts now hold that aviation has reached such a stage of safety and is of such common usage that the activity should be regulated by negligence principles. [Crosby v. Cox Aircraft Co., 746 P.2d 1198 (Wash. 1987)] However, other courts and the Second Restatement still adhere to the earlier view. [Rest. 2d §520A]

   (b) **Compare—unconventional aviation:** [§746]   But even those courts that no longer impose strict liability for conventional flying still impose strict liability for stunt flying, crop dusting, test flights, etc. [Loe v. Lenhardt, 362 P.2d 312 (Or. 1961)]

(4) **Application—common carriers:** [§747]   Although the Restatement and early cases refused to impose strict liability on a common carrier required to carry abnormally dangerous cargo [Rest. 2d §521], recent cases have imposed strict liability in such cases [National Steel Service Center, Inc. v. Gibbons, 319 N.W.2d 269 (Iowa 1982)].

(5) **Application—handguns:** [§748]   Appellate courts are virtually unanimous that hand guns do not come within the abnormally dangerous activity doctrine. [Burkett v. Freedom Arms, Inc., 704 P.2d 118 (Or. 1985)]

   (a) **Exception—"Saturday Night Specials":** [§749]   One court has held that cheap guns that have little accuracy or reliability have so little social utility that they may become the subject of strict liability. [Kelley v. R.G. Industries, Inc., 497 A.2d 1143 (Md. 1985)—strict liability for all in the chain of distribution of cheap, unreliable, inaccurate guns to all persons shot by criminals; *but note:* this case was sharply limited by statute]

3. **Compare—Products Liability Cases:** [§750]   As will be discussed *infra* (§§786 *et seq.*), strict liability has been extended to some claims against suppliers of defective products.

    a. **Showing of "defect" required:** [§751]   But note that the liability imposed on the manufacturer or supplier of defective products is different from that in cases of abnormally dangerous activities: It must appear that the product *was* defective. When dealing with damages arising from blasting cases, impounded water, etc., liability is imposed whether or not there was any defect.

D. EXTENT OF LIABILITY

1. **Scope of Duty Owed:** [§752]   Unlike negligence, the duty owed here is a duty to avoid harm from the animal or the activity or condition that is classified as "abnormally dangerous." Liability is therefore imposed for resulting injuries to person or property, regardless of whether anyone was at fault.

    a. **Duty owed only to foreseeable plaintiffs:** [§753]   The duty is owed only to *"foreseeable plaintiffs"—i.e.,* persons to whom a reasonable person would have foreseen a risk of harm in the circumstances. [Whitman Hotel Corp. v. Elliott & Watrous Engineering Co., 79 A.2d 591 (Conn. 1951)]

        (1) **Distinguish negligence cases:** [§754]   Although the courts are split over the "foreseeable plaintiff doctrine" in negligence cases (*supra*), the doctrine is the majority view in strict liability cases.

    b. **Duty extends only to foreseeable hazards:** [§755]   The harm that occurs must result from the kind of danger foreseeable from such abnormally dangerous activity. Thus, as indicated in the animal cases (*supra*), it must flow from the *"normally dangerous propensity" of the condition or thing involved*.

        (1) **Example:** Blasting operations conducted by D on his land frightened P's minks on adjoining property, causing them to kill their kittens. Although strict liability would extend to the hurling of rocks or debris from the blasting (foreseeable harm), it does not apply to the minks' killing their young, because such result is not ordinarily expected to occur from blasting operations. [Foster v. Preston Mill, 268 P.2d 645 (Wash. 1954)]

2. **Actual Cause:** [§756]   All courts use the same rules regarding actual cause as in negligence cases (*see supra,* §§327 *et seq.*).

3. **Proximate Cause**

    a. **Majority view:** [§757]   Virtually all courts apply the same rules of proximate causation in strict liability as they do in negligence. [Golden v. Amory, 109 N.E.2d 131 (Mass. 1952)—unforeseeable flood bars liability; *and see supra,* §§348 *et seq.*]

E. DEFENSES

1. **Contributory Negligence Traditionally No Defense:** [§758] The plaintiff's own lack of care is not a defense to strict liability, **unless** he knew of the danger and his contributory negligence was the very cause of the activity's miscarrying. For example, P, knowing he was following D's dynamite truck, negligently tried to pass it; a collision ensued, turning the truck over and causing it to explode. P cannot recover because his negligence was the very reason for the explosion. [Burke v. Fischer, 182 S.W.2d 638 (Ky. 1944)]

2. **Comparative Negligence:** [§759] Most courts in comparative negligence jurisdictions have reduced the plaintiff's recovery in strict liability cases where his injury was caused in part by his own carelessness. (*See* further discussion, *infra,* §874.)

3. **Assumption of Risk Is a Valid Defense:** [§760] Any *voluntary* encountering of a *known* risk may prevent the plaintiff's recovery.

   a. **Example:** P cannot recover for injuries sustained where, knowing the danger, she teases a leopard or voluntarily puts herself within its reach. [Lehnhard v. Robertson's Administratrix, 195 S.W. 441 (Ky. 1917)]

   b. **Determining "voluntariness":** [§761] Where the defendant's activity or condition is carried on in part for the *plaintiff's benefit* (*e.g.,* water or gas pipes maintained partially for his use), the plaintiff's consent to the risk (seepage, overflow, etc.) is usually *implied*.

      (1) **"Voluntary":** [§762] There is no "voluntary" assumption where the plaintiff attempts to run from his house to his car in the driveway, knowing the defendant's vicious hog is outside. *Rationale:* The plaintiff's remaining a prisoner inside his house would have meant surrendering his right to move freely on his own property—not a reasonable alternative. [Marshall v. Ranne, 511 S.W.2d 255 (Tex. 1974)]

IV. PRODUCTS LIABILITY

____chapter approach_____

Products liability questions basically come down to an issue of which theory of recovery is best for the plaintiff. When a defective product causes injury, the manufacturer of the product, as well as the distributor, wholesaler, and retailer who sold it, may be liable to the person injured on a number of distinct legal theories—some in tort and some deriving from contract. You will need to consider how well each theory fits your specific fact situation.

Tort liability may be predicated on any of the three previously considered bases for liability: intent, negligence, or strict liability. Also, there are the contract bases (breach of various warranties). Depending on the nature of the defendant's conduct, the same injury may be *actionable on several theories*. So do not stop writing your answer until you have considered all of the following bases of products liability:

1. Liability based on *intentional torts* (a battery).

2. Liability based on *negligence* (harm must be foreseeable).

3. Liability based on *strict liability* (*defective* product that *caused injury*).

4. Liability based on *breach of an express or implied warranty* (especially U.C.C. warranties of *fitness* for a particular purpose and *merchantability*).

Determining which bases for liability are involved in your exam question is vitally important since it affects such key issues as:

—*Scope of duty* owed;

—*Defenses* assertable (*e.g.,* contributory negligence is no defense to intentional torts);

—*Damages* recoverable (*e.g.,* punitive damages are not recoverable for negligence or for behavior without fault); and

—*Liability insurance coverage* (which may exclude some intentional torts).

A. IN GENERAL

1. **Introduction:** [§763]   The law of Products Liability focuses on the liability of a supplier of a product for *physical harm to person or property* caused by defects in the product. (If the product simply does not perform as well as expected, causing purely economic loss to the buyer, this is primarily a "sales" problem and is covered in detail in the Sales Summary.)

2. **Background:** [§764]   At early common law, a manufacturer or supplier of a chattel could be held liable for injuries sustained through its use only to those with whom he was in "privity of contract." If there was no "privity," there was no liability—either in tort or contract. Thus, an injured person who was not the purchaser

of the product could not recover, no matter how negligent the supplier's conduct. [*See, e.g.,* Winterbottom v. Wright, 10 M. & W. 109 (1842)—passenger who was injured when stagecoach collapsed had no cause of action against contractor who agreed with coach owner to keep it in repair, because "no privity of contract"]

a.   **Rejection of privity requirement:** Later, courts began to reject the strict "privity" requirement when dealing with specific types of chattels: first, with bailed goods (*see supra*, §§624-626), then with foodstuffs and *any* inherently dangerous chattel. Manufacturers and suppliers of such products were held to owe a tort duty of due care (*i.e.,* liability for negligence) respecting the condition of the chattel, even as to persons with whom they were not in "privity of contract" (*i.e.,* users, consumers, bystanders injured through another's use of the product, etc.).

b.   **Modern view:** As discussed below, the courts have now gone beyond negligence concepts and almost all impose some form of strict liability for any injury sustained through the use of defectively manufactured products. In a few jurisdictions, this result is reached through imposition of implied warranty liability (a contract action), but in most it is regarded as a tort concept. The scope of liability, measure of damages, available defenses, etc., will vary according to the theory on which liability is imposed.

B.   LIABILITY BASED ON INTENTIONAL ACTS

1.   **General Principle:** [§765]   A manufacturer or supplier who sells a chattel that he *knows* is defective or dangerous, without warning of the danger, may be held liable for *battery* to any person injured through use or consumption of the product. As long as he believed the injuries were "substantially certain" to result from the use of the chattel, the manufacturer or supplier will be held to have *intended* the consequences of his acts. [Huset v. J.I. Case, 120 F. 865 (8th Cir. 1903)]

2.   **Significance—Greater Recovery Potentially Available:** [§766]   While intent is difficult to establish, it may (if shown) justify a higher recovery; *i.e.,* the defendant may be liable for *punitive damages* in addition to damages for the plaintiff's physical injuries (*see supra*, §23). Also the injured party's contributory negligence would be no defense.

C.   LIABILITY BASED ON NEGLIGENCE [§767]

Few products liability cases involve intentional misconduct. The more typical problems concern the scope of liability to be imposed on a manufacturer or supplier for *unintentional* injuries caused by the use or consumption of its products.

1.   **Background—Gradual Abrogation of "Privity" Requirement:** [§768]   As already indicated, early decisions limited liability to cases in which there was "privity" between the supplier and the injured party, but this requirement was gradually eroded and standard negligence concepts applied.

2.   **Impact of *MacPherson v. Buick*—Liability Based on Foreseeability of Harm:** [§769]   Despite earlier inroads on the "privity" requirement, the real establishment of liability for simple negligence came with Judge Cardozo's landmark decision in *MacPherson v. Buick,* 217 N.Y. 382 (1916): If the reasonable person would *foresee* that the chattel would create a *risk of harm to human life or limb* if not

carefully made or supplied, the manufacturer or supplier of such chattel is under a duty of care in the manufacture or supply thereof—and this duty is owed to *all foreseeable users*.

3. **General Scope of Negligence Liability Today:** [§770]   The *MacPherson* rule has been adopted in all states and has been extended in several important respects:

   a. **Negligent design:** [§771]   First of all, the doctrine applies not only to negligence in manufacture but also to negligence in design—including failure to adequately test, install safety features, and the like. [Boeing Airplane Co. v. Brown, 291 F.2d 301 (9th Cir. 1961)] (*See* detailed discussion of design defects, *infra,* §§792 *et seq.*)

      (1) **Limitation—contractors following specifications:** [§772]   A contractor owes no duty to third persons to judge the plans, specifications, or instructions that he has contracted to follow, unless they are so obviously dangerous that no reasonable contractor would follow them. [Hunt v. Blasius, 384 N.E.2d 368 (Ill. 1978)]

   b. **Bystanders:** [§773]   Although *MacPherson* held the manufacturer or supplier liable only to foreseeable users, courts extended liability to *all persons foreseeably within the scope of use* of the defective product (*e.g.,* pedestrian injured by defective automobile). [Flies v. Fox Bros. Buick, 218 N.W. 855 (Wis. 1928)]

   c. **Property damages:** [§774]   Furthermore, courts extended the doctrine to *property* damage—even when there was no risk of personal injuries. [Dunn v. Ralston Purina Co., 272 S.W.2d 479 (Tenn. 1954)—manufacture of animal food that involved foreseeable risk of harm only to animals and to owner's business interests]

   d. **Real property:** [§775]   Most courts have extended the *MacPherson* rule to the design and construction of *real property*. [Wright v. Creative Corp., 498 P.2d 1179 (Colo. 1972)—home builder liable for negligence as to sliding glass door]

   e. **Liability of assembler of components manufactured by others:** [§776]   Most courts hold a supplier who markets a product under the supplier's name liable for negligence even though the supplier has only assembled components produced by others, and a negligently manufactured *component* has caused the injury.

      (1) **Example:** If Ajax Motors, a car manufacturer, assembles into its cars a steering control negligently manufactured by XYZ Co., and the defective wheel causes an accident, Ajax is liable for XYZ Co.'s negligence. [Rest. 2d §400]

      (2) **And note:** This rule applies even where the defect could *not* have been discovered by the defendant assembler in the exercise of due care. "One who puts out *as his own* product a chattel manufactured by another is subject to the same liability *as though he were in fact its manufacturer*." [Ford Motor Co. v. Mathis, 322 F.2d 267 (5th Cir. 1963)]

f. **Proving negligence—res ipsa loquitur:** [§777]   Where a manufacturing defect (*e.g.,* missing part) is involved, the injured party may invoke res ipsa loquitur simply by showing that the defect is of a kind that does not usually occur in the absence of negligence of the manufacturer or someone for whom the manufacturer is liable.

4. **Role of Dealer or "Middleman":** [§778]   There may be situations in which the manufacturer or supplier (D) and the dealer or "middleman" (X) will owe *concurrent duties* of care to the consumer or user (P).

a. **Where dealer has no reason to know of danger:** [§779]   A dealer or "middleman" owes *no duty to inspect or test* chattels manufactured by another before selling them, where she has no reason to know that the chattels may be dangerous in normal use. [Rest. 2d §402]

(1) **Example:** A retailer generally owes no duty to inspect or test *packaged* goods from a *reputable* manufacturer prior to their sale, in the absence of a reason to suspect that something is wrong (although she cannot blind herself to anything that becomes apparent while she is preparing the goods for sale). [Kirk v. Stineway, 187 N.E.2d 307 (Ill. 1963)]

b. **Where dealer has reason to know of danger:** [§780]   However, a dealer or "middleman" who has reason to know that the product may be dangerous in normal use owes a *duty to inspect and test* the goods, or at least to *warn* the purchaser of the potential danger. [6 A.L.R.3d 1; Rest. 2d §402]

(1) **Examples:** Dealer has at least a duty to warn when:

(a) *Goods are purchased from unreliable source of supply*—*e.g.,* dealer who buys unknown brand of hair dye from bankrupt company. [Outwater v. Miller, 3 App. Div. 2d 670 (1957)—duty to warn of uncertain quality]

(b) *Danger is not labeled by manufacturer*—*e.g.,* dealer who resells poisonous insecticide purchased in bulk from manufacturer.

(c) *Complaints are received from other customers* as to the very same goods. [Catlin v. Union Oil Co., 31 Cal. App. 597 (1916)]

(d) *Goods are those as to which purchaser normally relies on dealer inspection prior to purchase*, and nature of goods makes it likely that defects will lead to serious injury; *e.g.,* in purchasing an automobile, something more than a casual examination may be required. [Williams v. Steuart Motor Co., 494 F.2d 1074 (D.C. Cir. 1974)]

(2) **Effect of dealer's failure to inspect—manufacturer not excused:** [§781]   Note, however, that a dealer's negligence does *not* supersede the manufacturer's liability. The dealer's failure to inspect or test is regarded as a *foreseeable intervening force*, and hence does not affect the liability of the manufacturer. [Ellis v. Lindmark, 225 N.W. 395 (Minn. 1929)]

(3) **Compare—if dealer actually knows of danger:** [§782] On the other hand, if the dealer *actually knew* that the product was defective and dangerous, but nevertheless sold it to the purchaser without a warning, most courts hold that this *will* relieve the manufacturer of liability for unintended harm. The dealer's failure to warn under such circumstances is regarded as so culpable that it is treated as an *unforeseeable* intervening force—*i.e.*, a *superseding cause* of the ultimate injury which "neutralizes the risk" created by the manufacturer's original negligence. [Stultz v. Benson Lumber Co., 6 Cal. 2d 688 (1936)]

(a) **Caution—result differs from general rules of proximate cause:** [§783] In general negligence cases, *supra,* §§384 *et seq.*, it is often foreseeable that a third party might take criminal advantage of D's actions, *e.g.*, D's careless action renders P unconscious, after which T steals P's wallet. But in the products area, it would be extraordinary for a retailer who discovers a product defect to sell the product nonetheless.

5. **Damages:** [§784] In a negligence action, the plaintiff can recover for personal injury or property damage caused by the product. In most states, however, purely *economic* loss (*e.g.*, product does not work properly, needs repairs, etc.) is *not* recoverable in a negligence action; economic loss can only be recovered in an action for breach of warranty (*see* below).

a. **Note:** Even in an action initially brought as one for "negligence," the plaintiff may recover punitive damages upon showing recklessness (if the plaintiff has given appropriate notice of her intentions). The same is true even if the case is initially brought as one for "strict liability." [Fischer v. Johns-Manville Corp., 512 A.2d 466 (N.J. 1986)]

6. **Defenses:** [§785] As in any other negligence action, the injured party's *contributory negligence* or voluntary *assumption of the risk* can be asserted as a defense. Thus, if the plaintiff knowingly or recklessly exposes herself to the danger created by the product, she cannot recover for her injuries. Similarly, *comparative negligence* would reduce plaintiff's recovery where plaintiff is also at fault.

D. STRICT LIABILITY IN TORT [§786]

In recent years, most courts have entirely bypassed warranty and negligence concepts, and have held manufacturers and suppliers of *defective* products *strictly liable in tort to consumers and users for injures* caused by the defect. [Greenman v. Yuba Power Products, 59 Cal. 2d 57 (1963); Rest. 2d §402A] Almost all strict liability claims are based on common law principles; however, statutes may explicitly or implicitly create a strict liability cause of action. [Bencosme v. Kokoras, 507 N.E.2d 748 (Mass. 1987)—liability for failure to remove lead paint from premises despite defendant's lack of notice]

1. **Rationale for Strict Liability Action—Maximum Protection Demanded by Interest in Human Life and Safety:** [§787] "Liability without fault" is imposed here as a matter of public policy, due to the grave risk of harm in placing *defective* products in the "stream of commerce."

a. **Defendant better able to bear risk:** A defendant manufacturer is usually better able to distribute (or insure against) the risk of loss than is the innocent consumer; *i.e.,* the manufacturer can better estimate the risks and spread the cost over his operations or pass it on to the public in the form of higher prices. [69 Yale L.J. 1099]

b. **Negligence action may not be adequate remedy:** Negligence is often too difficult to prove in product cases to be an adequate remedy. [La Rossa v. Scientific Design Co., 402 F.2d 937 (3d Cir. 1968)]

c. **Incentive for safer products:** Moreover, imposing strict liability may increase the incentive for the manufacture and supply of safer products.

2. **Caution—Liability Not Absolute:** [§788]   Note that this doctrine requires the plaintiff to prove both a *defect* in the product that is *attributable* to the manufacturer or supplier, *and* that the *defect caused the injury*. Hence, although liability is strict, it is not absolute. [Kerr v. Corning Glass, 169 N.W.2d 587 (Minn. 1969)]

3. **Caution—Liability May Not Even Be "Nonfault":** [§789]   Although the courts and commentators generally speak of this area as one involving "strict" or "nonfault" liability, this almost certainly is not an accurate description of the state of the law. The type of "defect" involved may control whether the applicable law is that of strict liability or of negligence. It appears that the law of strict liability applies uniformly to "manufacturing" defects; but that "design" defect and "warning" defect cases are in fact decided as negligence cases, even though the courts rarely discuss the difference. This is discussed in the following sections.

   a. **Three kinds of defects:** [§790]   A product may be defective in manufacture, in design, or in the sufficiency of the warnings accompanying it.

      (1) **Manufacturing defects:** [§791]   In a manufacturing defect case, the product is *not in the condition that the manufacturer intended* at the time it left his control; *i.e.,* the product does not conform to the manufacturer's own production standards. Liability for this type of defect is indeed "strict."

         (a) **Example:** This covers the usual "assembly line" errors in production—cases in which negligence also would lie, bolstered by res ipsa loquitur. [Welge v. Planters Lifesavers Co., 17 F.3d 209 (7th Cir. 1994)—shattered glass peanut butter jar "must have contained a defect"]

         (b) **Example:** It also covers situations where there may be no negligence—*e.g.,* flaws or impurities in the product that were *not* the result of lack of due care.

      (2) **Design defects:** [§792]   In a design defect case, the product was in the condition intended by the manufacturer or supplier, but was *designed* in such a way that it *presented an undue risk* of harm in normal use. Although courts speak of strict liability in these cases, the identical result would almost always be reached by a negligence analysis, because that undue risk should have been discovered and prevented by due care. In the few cases in which this is not true, courts have *denied* strict liability. (*See infra,* §§840 *et seq.*)

(a) **Variety of defects:** [§793]   A product may be defective by posing an unreasonable risk to consumers [Matthews v. Lawnlite Co., 88 So. 2d 299 (Fla. 1956)—folding arm of metal rocking chair slices off occupant's fingers], or by not protecting against foreseeable risks, such as inadequate safeguards on an industrial machine.

  1) **Limitation:** The defendant will not be held liable, however, for manufacturing or selling a product that simply wears out with normal use. [Savage v. Jacobsen Manufacturing Co., 396 So. 2d 731 (Fla. 1981)—nonskid surface on tractor dismounting platform worn away]

  2) **Application—handguns:** A product, such as a handgun, that functions as intended and is dangerous in its ordinary use, has no defect and cannot give rise to liability based on defect. [Kelley v. R.G. Industries, Inc., *supra*, §749]

(b) **"Crashworthiness":** [§794]   A manufacturer can be held liable for failure to design its product so as to minimize foreseeable harm *caused by other parties or conditions*. For example, an auto manufacturer may be liable for not designing its cars to withstand at least some highway crashes caused by *negligent drivers* (including the buyer). [Larsen v. General Motors Corp., 391 F.2d 495 (8th Cir. 1968)]

  1) **Examples:** Manufacturers have been held liable for designing a gearshift lever that impaled the driver upon collision [Mickle v. Blackmon, 166 S.E.2d 178 (S.C. 1969)]; a fuel tank that caught fire following a "rear-end" collision [Nanda v. Ford Motor Co., 509 F.2d 213 (7th Cir. 1974)]; and a horn cap that came off the steering wheel, exposing sharp prongs that caused injuries greater than driver otherwise would have received from collision [Horn v. General Motors Corp., 17 Cal. 3d 359 (1976)].

  2) **Example:** Motorcycles may be defective for lack of crash bars to protect the driver's legs. [Camacho v. Honda Motor Co., 741 P.2d 1240 (Colo. 1987)]

(c) **Approaches to design defects:** [§795]   The elements of a design defect case depend on the standard used.

  1) **"Feasible alternative" test:** [§796]   Under the prevailing approach, called a "feasible alternative" test, the question for the jury is whether defendant could have removed the danger without serious adverse impact on the product's utility and price. [Phillips v. Kimwood Machine Co., 525 P.2d 1033 (Or. 1974); *and see* Dawson v. Chrysler Corp., 630 F.2d 950 (3d Cir. 1980), *cert. denied*, 450 U.S. 959 (1981)—calling it a "risk/utility analysis"]

    a) **Factors:** [§797]   Among the determinative factors are:

(i) *Usefulness* of the product;

(ii) *Type and purpose of the product* (functional utility of design);

(iii) *Style, attractiveness, and marketability* of product (psychological utility);

(iv) *Number and severity of injuries* actually resulting from current design (social cost);

(v) *Cost of design changes to alleviate problem* (safety cost—measured in both price and reduced utility of the product);

(vi) *User's anticipated awareness of inherent dangers* in product and their avoidability; and

(vii) *Feasibility of spreading the loss* by adjustments in the product's price.

[Dreisonstock v. Volkswagenwerk, A.G., 489 F.2d 1066 (4th Cir. 1974); Volkswagen of America v. Young, 321 A.2d 737 (Md. 1974); Dawson v. Chrysler Corp., *supra*]

b) **Note:** California has shifted to the *manufacturer* the burden of proving that the benefits of its design outweigh the risks of danger inherent in that design. [Barker v. Lull Engineering Co., 20 Cal. 3d 413 (1978)]

2) **"Consumer expectation" test:** [§798] Under an alternative approach, plaintiffs must prove that the product did not perform as safely as an ordinary consumer would have expected. [Toney v. Kawasaki Heavy Industries Ltd., 975 F.2d 162 (5th Cir. 1992)—claim barred since ordinary consumer would have realized danger of motorcycle without leg guards; *but compare* Camacho v. Honda Motor Co., *supra*, §794—claim for same danger was allowed under the "feasible alternative" test]

a) **Applicability to bystanders:** [§799] The consumer expectation test is generally not relevant when the victim was not the buyer or user. [Ewen v. McLean Trucking Co., 706 P.2d 929 (Or. 1985)—pedestrian struck by truck claimed to have poor visibility; *but see* Batts v. Tow-Motor Forklift Co., 978 F.2d 1386 (5th Cir. 1992)—since danger was obvious to ordinary buyer, product is not defective and no suit lies by bystander whether or not bystander knew or should have known of danger]

b) **Food cases:** [§800] The consumer expectation test is widely applied in food cases to test for defects. [Jackson v. Nestle-Beich, Inc., 589 N.E.2d 547 (Ill. 1992)—whether chocolate-covered pecan-caramel candy with hard pecan shell inside was defective depends on the reasonable expectation of buyers; *but see* Mexicali Rose v. Superior Court, 1 Cal. 4th 617 (1992)—if tooth broke on foreign substance (*e.g.,* glass) inside chicken enchilada P need not prove negligence, but if tooth broke on natural substance (*e.g.,* chicken bone) P must prove negligence]

3) **Combined approach:** [§801]   Some courts explicitly adopt a combined view under which recovery is permitted if the plaintiff establishes *either* (i) that the product failed to perform as safely as an ordinary consumer would expect when it is used in an intended or reasonably foreseeable manner; *or* (ii) that the product's design was defective under the feasibility analysis, above. [Welch v. Outboard Marine Corp., 481 F.2d 252 (5th Cir. 1973)]

   a) **Limitation:** Some courts permit the plaintiff to choose between the two approaches *only* when the "everyday experience of the product's users permits a conclusion that the product's design violated minimum safety assumptions." [Soule v. General Motors Corp., 8 Cal. 4th 548 (1994)—consumer expectation theory not available concerning to what extent a car's left front quadrant will collapse in a crash] In such a case, the plaintiff must pursue the "feasible alternative" theory.

(d) **Dangers not foreseeable at time of marketing (scientifically unknowable risks):** [§802]   Whatever test of defect is used, a critical question is whether to weigh the factors as of the time of manufacture or as of the time of injury or trial. In negligence cases, the proper time to use is that of manufacture and release of the product, because the courts are explicitly judging the defendant's behavior. In so-called strict liability cases, the courts are rarely explicit about the relevant time because "negligence" is said not to be the test. In fact, however, in cases in which some crucial new information has been discovered *after* the product's release, the courts generally insist on using the time of the product's release by the defendant.

   1) **Dominant approach:** The dominant view denies strict liability where the danger was something the manufacturer could not have guarded against "by the application of reasonably developed human skill or foresight." [Rest. 2d §402A, comment j; Owens-Illinois, Inc. v. Zenobia, 601 A.2d 633 (Md. 1992); Feldman v. Lederle Laboratories, 479 A.2d 374 (N.J. 1984)— retreating from Beshada v. Johns-Manville Products Corp., 447 A.2d 539 (N.J. 1992), which had held that D was liable for risks unknowable at time of D's actions; *but see* Simmons v. Monarch Machine Tool Co., 596 N.E.2d 318 (Mass. 1992); Johnson v. Raybestos-Manhattan, Inc., 740 P.2d 548 (Hawaii 1987)—following Beshada]

(e) **Discovery of danger:** [§803] Even if the state does not impose liability for unknowable dangers, when the scientifically unknowable risk becomes discoverable, the manufacturer or supplier no longer is shielded from liability.

1) *If the danger feasibly may be eliminated*, the manufacturer must do so before continuing to market the product or face liability for selling a defective product. (*See supra,* §796.)

2) *If the risk cannot be eliminated,* the product is **unavoidably unsafe**. The manufacturer must then provide a suitable warning or, if the danger outweighs the benefits from the product, discontinue distribution altogether. (*See infra,* §806.)

3) *A manufacturer is under a duty to take reasonable steps to warn earlier purchasers* of already marketed products about defects that only recently became discoverable. [Patton v. Hutchinson Wil-Rich Manufacturing Co., 861 P.2d 1299 (Kan. 1993)—duty imposed to use due care to warn about safety hazards discovered after sales; *but see* Romero v. International Harvester Co., 979 F. 2d 1444 (10th Cir. 1992)—no duty to notify buyers of earlier model that new safety devices have been developed to handle a long-known safety problem]

(3) **Inadequate warnings:** [§804] In addition to the actual product itself, defects may arise from packaging and inadequate instructions, warnings, labels, etc. Inadequate warnings may make a product defective when the dangers are not apparent to consumers and users. [Davis v. Wyeth Laboratories, 399 F.2d 121 (9th Cir. 1968)—failure to warn user that polio vaccine gave polio to a certain number of recipients; Benedi v. McNeil-P.P.C., Inc., 66 F.3d 1378 (4th Cir. 1995)—must warn against danger of even moderate consumption of alcoholic beverages while taking Tylenol; Emery v. Federated Foods, Inc., 863 P.2d 426 (Mont. 1993)—must warn against risk that young children may choke eating marshmallows]

(a) **Unexpected dangers:** [§805] The "danger" must be something that a reasonable user would have no reason to expect or anticipate in the product.

1) **Example:** The manufacturer of a flight of steps does not have a duty to warn of the dangers posed by use of the steps without handrails because those dangers are patently obvious. [Lorfano v. Dura Stone Steps, Inc., 569 A.2d 195 (Me. 1990)]

2) **Example:** A manufacturer of an above-ground swimming pool has no duty to warn of the danger of diving into the pool if it reasonably perceives that the potential danger is readily apparent or would be disclosed by casual inspection. [Glittenberg v. Doughboy Recreational Industries, 491 N.W.2d 208 (Mich. 1992)]

3) **Example:** The danger of an unlocked pilot seat during the takeoff of aircraft is sufficiently obvious that the defendant

manufacturer could not be held liable for failure to provide additional warning, especially where it had taken other safety precautions. [Argubright v. Beech Aircraft Corp., 868 F.2d 764 (5th Cir.), *cert. denied,* 493 U.S. 934 (1989)]

4) **Compare:** On the other hand, it may be reasonable to expect a martini olive to be pitted, so that strict liability might apply when a customer breaks her tooth while biting into that kind of olive.

5) **Caution:** If the danger is also unexpected by the defendant because it could not be anticipated, most courts will analyze it as a *negligence* question, as with design defects, *supra.* Just as most courts do not expect manufacturers to design a product with unknowable risks in mind, they do not expect them to warn about the unknowable. [Anderson v. Owens-Corning Fiberglas Corp., 53 Cal. 3d 987 (1991)—no duty to warn against unknowable risk]

(b) **Unavoidably unsafe products:** [§806]   Many useful products are unavoidably unsafe (*e.g.,* knives), but this does not render them "defective" because there is no safer way to make them. [Killeen v. Harmon Grain Products, Inc., 413 N.E.2d 767 (Mass. 1980)—cinnamon flavored toothpicks not unreasonably dangerous, even when used by a child]

1) **Relation to design defect:** It is clear that suppliers cannot avoid liability for a *design* defect by giving an adequate warning. In states that follow the feasible alternative approach, an adequate warning may suffice to avoid liability only if the product's design is not defective under that test. [Camacho v. Honda Motor Co., *supra,* §794]

a) **Compare:** Under the consumer expectation test, however, the obviousness of a danger may well make the product nondefective. In such a situation there would be no need to warn to avoid liability. [Sterling Drug v. Yarrow, 408 F.2d 978 (8th Cir. 1968)—duty to warn patient's doctor about side effect]

2) **Example:** Strict liability has been imposed for marketing short-burning dynamite fuses without suitable warning, the danger from such fuses being one that would *not* be apparent to or expected by the normal user. [Canifax v. Hercules Powder Co., 237 Cal. App. 2d 44 (1965)]

(c) **Testing the adequacy of warnings:** [§807]   A warning attached to an unreasonably dangerous product may be inadequate if, for example, it does not specify the risk the product presents, it is inconsistent with how the product is to be used, or it does not give the reason for the warning. [MacDonald v. Ortho Pharmaceutical Corp., 475 A.2d 65 (Mass. 1985)—warning on oral contraceptive must include mention of "stroke"]

1) **Limitation:** Although warnings usually must be written for the ordinary user [Laaperi v. Sears, Roebuck & Co., 787 F.2d 726 (1st Cir. 1986)], a supplier may take into account the nature of a special clientele [Mackowick v. Westinghouse Electric Corp., 575 A.2d 100 (Pa. 1990)—warning on electrical capacitor need not warn of dangers generally known to electricians].

2) **Caution:** Although it often seems virtually costless to add a marginal warning to a product [Moran v. Faberge, Inc., 332 A.2d 11 (Md. 1975)—duty to warn of danger of pouring cologne over candle], courts are increasingly recognizing that excessive warnings may reduce the impact of important warnings [Cotton v. Buckeye Gas Products Co., 840 F.2d 935 (D.C. Cir. 1988)—if every foreseeable danger needed a warning, the "list of foolish practices warned against would be so long it would fill a volume"].

(d) **Testing who must receive warning:** [§808]   Usually the warning must reach the person at risk from the danger. [McCullock v. H.B. Fuller Co., 981 F.2d 656 (2d Cir. 1992)—supplier of glue to book-binding plant must warn those workers who come in contact with the glue of its dangers; *but see* Mazur v. Merck & Co., 964 F.2d 1348 (3d Cir. 1992)—manufacturer met its duty to warn by imposing such a duty in its contract with the distributor]

1) **Learned intermediary exception:** [§809]   Most courts hold that in the case of pharmaceuticals, an adequate warning need reach only the prescribing physician. [Johnson v. American Cyanamid Corp., 718 P.2d 1318 (Kan. 1986); *but see* MacDonald v. Ortho Pharmaceutical Corp., *supra*—warning required by F.D.A. must reach patient] Some courts follow a similar rule as to the supplying of bulk products. [Adams v. Union Carbide, 737 F.2d 1453 (6th Cir.), *cert. denied,* 469 U.S. 1062 (1984); *but see* Hunnings v. Texaco Co., 29 F.3d 1480 (11th Cir. 1994)—bulk supplier must try to assure that warnings on bulk container are repeated as product is subdivided into smaller containers]

4. **Scope of Liability:** [§810]   The developing case law has broadened the application of strict tort liability as follows. (*See infra,* §§1099-1107, for statutory limitations on strict tort liability.)

a. **Parties liable—commercial suppliers:** [§811]   Any party who causes the product to "enter the stream of commerce" or "passes it on" in the stream of commerce—*i.e., all participants in the marketing* of the product—may be held strictly liable.

(1) **Application**

(a) **Sellers:** [§812]   The doctrine thus applies to *retailers and distributors,* as well as manufacturers. Each is "an integral part of the marketing enterprise," and therefore must share the business risk with the manufacturer. [Vandermark v. Ford Motor Co., 61 Cal. 2d 256 (1964)]

(b) **Lessors:** [§813] Likewise, the commercial *bailor or lessor* of a defective chattel may be held strictly liable for injuries caused by the defect. [Price v. Shell Oil Co., *supra*, §626]

    1) **Limitation—landlords:** [§814] Landlords are not treated as bailors or lessors of the furnishings or fixtures that come with a rental unit. [Peterson v. Superior Court, 10 Cal. 4th 1185 (1995)]

    2) **Limitation—financiers:** [§815] When a financier of a commercial deal becomes a "lessor" to protect a security interest, most courts refuse to apply strict liability. [Nath v. National Equipment Leasing Corp., 439 A.2d 633 (Pa. 1981)]

(c) **Assemblers of component parts:** [§816] As in negligence cases (*see supra*, §776), the manufacturer is responsible for the safety of all component parts. Hence, although the manufacturer only assembles those parts into a finished product, she can be held strictly liable for *defective components supplied by others*. The seller of a defective component part, of course, also may be liable.

    1) **Compare:** Although a manufacturer generally is not held liable for injuries caused by *replacement* parts made by others, if the replacement parts are necessitated by a defect originating in the defendant manufacturer's product design, the manufacturer may be held liable despite the fact that it did not make those parts. [Sage v. Fairchild-Swearingen Corp., 70 N.Y.2d 579 (1987)—manufacturer strictly liable for damages caused by replacement latch that it did not produce]

(d) **Contractors:** [§817] Although usually it is not negligent for a contractor to follow most specifications (*see supra*, §772), different considerations may apply in strict liability. Since the product is the issue, a contractor who provides a "defective" product may be liable. [Michalko v. Cooke Color & Chemical Corp., 451 A.2d 179 (N.J. 1982)—liability on contractor who rebuilt machine to specifications but without feasible safety devices and without warning about remaining nonobvious danger]

(e) **Successors in interest to manufacturers of defective products:** [§818] Normally, a company that has purchased the assets of a prior manufacturer, without expressly or impliedly assuming its liabilities, is not liable for injuries caused by defects in the predecessor's products. [Lemire v. Garrard Drugs, 291 N.W.2d 103 (Mich. 1980)—successor in interest to drugstore owner not liable for prior sale of defective drug] But most courts hold the new company strictly liable where: (i) the deal was a *merger or continuation* of the old corporation; (ii) the buying company *agreed to assume* the seller's liability; *or* (iii) the sale was a *fraudulent attempt* by the seller to escape liability. [Nissen Corp. v. Miller, 594 A.2d 564 (Md. 1991)]

1)   **Note:** A few courts go even further and hold the new company liable where it has *purchased the goodwill* and has *continued the product line* in question. In such cases, it is reaping the benefits of the prior manufacturer's activities, and courts may therefore hold the new company liable for defective products produced by that prior manufacturer. [Ray v. Alad Corp., 19 Cal. 3d 22 (1977)]

(f)   **Sellers of used products:** [§819]   Sellers of used products in some jurisdictions may be strictly liable for safety defects attributable to the design or manufacture if they conflict with the purchaser's reasonable expectations. In these cases an "as is" disclaimer does *not* shield the sellers from liability. [Turner v. International Harvester Co., 336 A.2d 62 (N.J. 1975)—used truck]

1)   **Compare:** Some courts bar strict liability against sellers of used products in the absence of representations of quality, because buyers of used products cannot reasonably expect the products to be free of defects. [Grimes v. Axtell Ford Lincoln-Mercury, 403 N.W.2d 781 (Iowa 1987)]

2)   **Note:** A separate question arises where the defect occurs not in the original design or manufacture but through modification, dilapidation, or misuse between the original and second sales. Strict liability is rarely imposed on the seller. [LaRosa v. Superior Court, 122 Cal. App. 3d 741 (1981)—used punch press sold 16 years after manufacture]

(g)   **Franchisors:** [§820]   Even though franchisors do not normally provide the bulk of the goods sold by franchisees, they still may be liable for product defects, particularly when they retain some control over franchisees' behavior. [Kosters v. Seven-Up Co., 595 F.2d 347 (6th Cir. 1979)]

(h)   **Trademark licensors:** [§821]   A trademark licensor that participates in the process of designing and marketing the defective product may be strictly liable even if the licensor did not manufacture the product. [Torres v. Goodyear Tire & Rubber Co., 786 P.2d 939 (Ariz. 1990)]

(i)   **Mass producers of homes:** [§822]   Strict liability does *not* extend to the occasional construction and sale of homes; it is limited to mass-produced homes (*see infra*, §833). [Oliver v. Superior Court, 211 Cal. App. 3d 86 (1989)]

(2)   **Compare—noncommercial suppliers:** [§823]   Strict liability applies only to persons *regularly engaged* in the *business* of manufacturing, selling, or leasing the product in question. Thus, persons who make only an *occasional* sale or bailment (*e.g.,* those who sell their own used car or

lend it to another) would *not* be liable on this theory. [Rest. 2d §402A, comment f; Stiles v. Batavia Atomic Horseshoes, Inc., 81 N.Y.2d 950 (1993)—no strict liability for sale of used punch press where D's normal business was making horseshoes and it did not regularly sell used products; *and see supra*, §785]

(a) **Endorsers of products:** [§824] Similarly, one who merely gives *commercial endorsement* to a product (*e.g.*, the "Good Housekeeping Seal of Approval") may be liable on a theory of *negligent misrepresentation* (*see infra*, §1412), but generally is *not* liable in warranty or strict liability in tort if the product proves defective. *Rationale:* The endorser has not put the defective product into the stream of commerce. [Hanberry v. Hearst Corp., 276 Cal. App. 2d 680 (1969)]

(b) **Publishers of advertising:** [§825] In the absence of a guaranty or warranty, a publisher is not strictly liable for defects in goods *advertised* in its publications. [Yuhas v. Mudge, 322 A.2d 824 (N.J. 1974)]

(c) **Auctioneers:** [§826] Auctioneers are generally not held to be sellers for purposes of strict liability. [Musser v. Vilsmeier Auction Co., 562 A.2d 279 (Pa. 1989)]

b. **Parties who may invoke liability**

(1) **Ultimate user or consumer:** [§827] The ultimate user or consumer, as well as the purchaser, clearly may invoke the doctrine. Thus family members, employees, guests, etc., of the purchaser are protected. [Alvarez v. Felker Manufacturing, 230 Cal. App. 2d 987 (1964); Rest. 2d §402A]

(a) **Note:** Passengers in a car, as well as the driver, are treated as "users."

(2) **Bystanders:** [§828] Virtually all states hold that *any person* injured by a defective product can invoke strict tort liability—*e.g.*, pedestrian hit by a car whose brakes have failed. [Codling v. Paglia, 32 N.Y.2d 330 (1973)]

(a) **Rationale:** Bystanders should be entitled to even greater protection than the purchaser or user of the product, because the purchaser or user at least had an opportunity to inspect for defects prior to injury. Furthermore, since the manufacturer's losses can be covered by insurance or passed on to the public in the form of increased costs, there is no economic reason for treating bystanders and purchasers differently. [Elmore v. American Motors Corp., 70 Cal. 2d 578 (1969)]

(3) **Rescuers:** [§829] There is some case authority allowing recovery by persons injured while attempting to aid another who was imperiled by a defective product. [Guarino v. Mine Safety Appliance, 25 N.Y.2d 460 (1969)]

(a) **Example—danger to property:** This rescue doctrine has been extended in some states to cover injury from nonreckless attempts to save personal property imperiled by a defect. [Caldwell v. Motor Co., 619 S.W.2d 534 (Tenn. 1981)—P suffered back injury while hurriedly removing load of building materials from truck after fire broke out in engine area]

(4) **Business firms:** [§830]   Courts are split over whether business entities may recover from each other for property damage on the basis of strict liability. In most cases, where the parties in a commercial setting are of equal bargaining strength and have negotiated, tort actions, whether for strict liability or for negligence, have been foreclosed when the claim is solely for lost profits or other economic loss. [Spring Motor Distributors, Inc. v. Ford Motor Co., 489 A.2d 660 (N.J. 1985)] A few courts go further, barring tort actions even when the claim is for damage to property as well as economic loss. [Hapka v. Paquin Farms, 458 N.W.2d 683 (Minn. 1990)—U.C.C. controls action for damage to commercial farmers' property from allegedly defective seeds]

c. **Liability extends only to "products":** [§831]   Strict tort liability applies only where the injuries or damages have resulted from a defective "product." However, the courts have taken an expansive view of what constitutes a "product":

(1) **Products in natural state:** [§832]   Although most products are manufactured or processed in some way, this is not essential; strict liability may apply to products in their natural state (*e.g.,* sales of unprocessed, poisonous mushrooms). [Rest. 2d §402A, comment e]

(2) **Real property as "product":** [§833]   As originally formulated by the courts, the doctrine of strict tort liability applied only to defective *goods*. However, courts have extended such liability to defects in the design or construction of mass-produced buildings (*i.e.,* tract homes). [Schipper v. Levitt, 207 A.2d 314 (N.J. 1965)—guest in home injured by boiler explosion; Del Mar Beach Club Owners Association v. Imperial Contracting Co., 123 Cal. App. 3d 898 (1981)—owners of planned development complex stated strict liability claim for design and construction of complex on unstable bluff]

(3) **"Products" vs. "services":** [§834]   Strict tort liability does not apply to the rendition of services any more than does warranty liability (*see infra,* §894). Thus, a passenger injured in an air crash cannot invoke strict liability if the cause of the crash was pilot error or improper repairs, but she can if the crash was due to a defect in the design or manufacture of the plane.

(a) **Application:** Courts refuse to apply strict liability where the product itself is not defective, and the injury is caused by the manner in which the product has been *installed, serviced, or used*. [Hoover v. Montgomery Ward, 528 P.2d 76 (Or. 1974)—tire dealer mounted nondefective tire on car; Hinojasa v. Automatic Elevator Co., 416 N.E.2d 45 (Ill. 1980)—nonmanufacturer-installer of elevator]

(b) **Professional conduct:** [§835]   Strict liability does not apply to a physician's diagnosis or treatment [Hoven v. Kelble, 256 N.W.2d

379 (Wis. 1977)] or to a pharmacist's sale of prescription drugs [Murphy v. E.R. Squibb & Sons, 40 Cal. 3d 672 (1985)].

(c) **Hybrid conduct:** [§836]   Where the defendant is providing services and a product, the courts look for the *dominant aspect*. [Newmark v. Gimbels, Inc., 258 A.2d 697 (N.J. 1969)—strict liability against beauty salon that applied defective hair solution to customer's head]

(d) **Electricity:** [§837]   Electric current flowing through high voltage transmission lines is not a product for this purpose. [Fuller v. Central Maine Power Co., 598 A.2d 457 (Me. 1991)]

(e) **Blood:** [§838]   Almost all states have passed statutes that bar courts from applying strict liability (or breach of warranty) in cases involving claimed defects (such as hepatitis virus or AIDS-related virus) in transfused blood. Plaintiffs in such cases must prove negligence. [Zichichi v. Middlesex Memorial Hospital, 528 A.2d 805 (Conn. 1987)]

1)   **Note:** Courts analyzing blood supply cases under common law principles have concluded that these products are unavoidably unsafe and, therefore, strict liability is inappropriate. [Miles Laboratories, Inc. v. Doe, 556 A.2d 1107 (Md. 1989)]

(4) **Product in stream of commerce:** [§839]   Remember that the "product" must have entered the stream of commerce to result in strict liability. Thus, where a plaintiff is injured by an experimental model of a machine that has been advertised but not yet sold, its manufacturer cannot be held strictly liable. [Woods v. Luertzing Corp., 400 A.2d 562 (N.J. 1979)]

d.   **Liability extends only to "defective" products:** [§840]   The area of greatest difficulty is what makes a product "defective" for purposes of imposing strict liability. This in turn depends on two separate issues: (i) the types of defect, and (ii) the standard used to determine the defect. The first of these two—manufacturing defects, design defects, and defects due to lack of adequate warning—were discussed *supra*, §§790 *et seq.* The following section considers the second issue, the standard to be applied.

(1) **Basic approaches**

(a) **Restatement approach—"defect" plus "unreasonable danger":** [§841]   The Restatement recognizes a product as "defective" only where it is *"unreasonably dangerous,"* meaning the defect that caused the plaintiff's injury must be something other than what a reasonable person would expect in normal use. [Rest. 2d §402A, comments g, i]

1)   **Latent vs. patent defects:** [§842]   This "consumer expectation" approach, literally applied, would insulate from liability any product that is patently dangerous.

a) **Modern view:** [§843]   However, as discussed *supra*, most courts no longer bar recovery simply because a defect was patent. [Nichols v. Union Underwear Co., 602 S.W.2d 429 (Ky. 1980)—consumer knowledge only one of several factors that determine unreasonableness; *but see* Curtis v. General Motors Corp., 649 F.2d 808 (10th Cir. 1981)—buyer of convertible vehicle cannot recover for rollover injuries even though available safety devices were not installed]

b) **Significance of modern view:** [§844]   Since most states follow either the "feasible alternative" test (*supra*, §796) or the combined approach (*supra*, §801), they have implicitly rejected the narrow Restatement view that allowed recovery only for latent dangers. Note however that some of these states may still decide to adopt the Restatement's requirement that any alleged danger be "unreasonably dangerous" before finding the product "defective."

(b) **Alternative approach—"defect" alone:** [§845]   The California courts have led a strong movement that rejects the Restatement terminology of "unreasonable danger" because of possible confusion with the concept of "unreasonable" as used in negligence cases. Under this view, an action lies for injuries from a defect that may *not* be unreasonably dangerous in terms of foreseeability.

1) **Example:** When the racks in the back of a bakery truck came loose in a crash, hurling the driver through the windshield, the driver need only prove that defective metal clamps caused the dislodging in order to establish the required defect; he need not show that it was foreseeable that such clamps posed a risk of personal injury. [Cronin v. JBE Olson, 8 Cal. 3d 121 (1972)]

2) **Note:** Many of the states that reject the Restatement's "unreasonably dangerous" approach *also* reject the Restatement's insistence on latent defects. These states follow the "defect alone" approach and *also* apply it to *both* patent and latent dangers. (It would also be possible for a state to accept the Restatement's requirement that the danger must be latent and yet reject the Restatement's requirement that the product be "unreasonably dangerous" before calling it defective.)

(2) **Misuse:** [§846]   Regardless of what kind of "defect" is claimed, it must have arisen during the *normal or foreseeable* use of the product. A manufacturer is not to be held liable for *all* possible harms caused by its product, but only for harms caused through its intended or foreseeable use. [Schemel v. General Motors Corp., 384 F.2d 802 (7th Cir. 1967)—no liability for car that went out of control at 115 m.p.h.; *but see* Ellsworth v. Sherne Lingerie, 495 A.2d 348 (Md. 1985)—wearing nightgown inside out is foreseeable use]

(a) **"Normal use":** [§847]   "Normal use" has a broader meaning than "intended use." A manufacturer must *foresee a certain amount of* *misuse or carelessness* by customers, and thus must warn them of any dangers that could be created thereby, or must build into its product appropriate safety devices. [Gardner v. Q.H.S. Inc. & J.M. Fields, 448 F.2d 238 (4th Cir. 1971)—strict liability imposed for failing to warn purchasers that hair rollers would explode if overheated; Reid v. Spadone Machine Co., 404 A.2d 1094 (N.H. 1979)—strict liability for design change on guillotine-like cutting machine that encouraged dangerous use by two workers, rather than safe use by one worker at a time]

(b) **And note:** Some products may involve *no* risk of harm when used as intended but a serious risk when used for other purposes (*e.g.,* laundry products may be safe when used for cleaning purposes, but may contain caustic chemicals that could be fatal if swallowed by children). To the extent such unintended uses are reasonably foreseeable, the product may be adjudged "defective" if adequate warnings are not given or if feasible safety measures are not taken (*e.g.,* use of child-proof top).

    1) **Compare:** In some cases, however, the misuse may be so extreme that the defendant need make no warnings or take other safety precautions against it. [Venezia v. Miller Brewing Co., 626 F.2d 188 (1st Cir. 1980)—eight-year-old child injured when he threw beer bottle against telephone pole and it shattered; no liability]

(3) **Abnormal reactions:** [§848] *Highly unusual* reactions to a product do *not* render it "defective." However, this refers only to the situation where a plaintiff's reaction is so bizarre or unexpected that it could not reasonably have been anticipated or guarded against. [Mountain v. Procter & Gamble Co., 312 F. Supp. 534 (E.D. Wis. 1970)—with over 200 million bottles of shampoo sold, only two confirmed allergic reactions before P's reaction]

(a) **Compare—not highly unusual reaction:** [§849] On the other hand, where the reaction is shared by any significant number of potential users—even a small percentage—the manufacturer must guard against the risk by changing the product, warning of the danger, or suggesting methods by which users can safely determine their own reactions (*e.g.,* patch tests). [Basko v. Sterling Drug, Inc., 416 F.2d 417 (2d Cir. 1969)]

(b) **Trend—duty to warn:** [§850] Indeed, the trend of authority is that if there is a *known* risk of harm to *any* number of potential users, no matter how small, the manufacturer owes a duty to warn—particularly if a self-administered test is available to the user that would disclose his sensitivity to the product. Under such circumstances, the manufacturer's failure to warn renders the product defective. [*See* Tiderman v. Fleetwood Homes, 684 P.2d 1302 (Wash. 1984)—appreciable number; Griggs v. Combe, Inc., 456 So. 2d 790 (Ala. 1984)—no liability where reaction unique]

e. **Proof required:** [§851]   The burden is on the plaintiff to prove (i) that the product *was in fact "defective"* when it left the defendant's control, and (ii) a *causal relationship* to plaintiff's injuries. Often, expert witnesses are required. [Friedman v. General Motors Corp., 331 N.E.2d 702 (Ohio 1975)]

(1) **Circumstantial evidence of "defect":** [§852]   Even though the plaintiff cannot prove a specific defect in the product, some courts permit recovery where an inference that the relatively new product *was* defective can be drawn from proof that it *functioned improperly in normal use.* [Greco v. Bucciconi Engineering, 407 F.2d 87 (3d Cir. 1969)]

(2) **Causation:** [§853]   The plaintiff must show that the injuries were caused *by* some defect in the product that *existed* at the time it was marketed by the defendant. [Moerer v. Ford Motor Co., 57 Cal. App. 3d 114 (1976)]

(a) **Defectiveness at time of marketing:** [§854]   The burden is on the plaintiff to establish that the product was defective at the time it left the defendant's hands; *i.e.,* strict liability will not be imposed upon the defendant if the defect is attributable to subsequent mishandling [Williams v. Ford Motor Co., 494 S.W.2d 678 (Mo. 1973)] or to a dangerous and unforeseeable alteration in the product after it was purchased [Seeborg v. General Motors Corp., 588 P.2d 1100 (Or. 1978)].

(b) **Cause in fact (actual cause):** [§855]   It is sufficient that the defect was a *substantial factor* in causing the injury. [Codling v. Paglia, 32 N.Y.2d 330 (1973)]

1) **Warning cases:** [§856]   In warning cases, the plaintiff must show that an adequate warning would have made a difference. [Odom v. G.D. Searle & Co., 979 F.2d 1001 (4th Cir. 1992)—alleged lack of adequate warning irrelevant where physician testified that he knew of danger of IUD and would still have used same product even if it had contained more extensive warning; Lussier v. Louisville Ladder Co., 938 F.2d 299 (1st Cir. 1991)—even though ladder may have lacked warnings against unsuitable uses and thus been a defective product, P used ladder in way he knew was unsuitable so that warning would not have mattered]

a) **Application—the "heeding presumption":** [§857]   In an effort to encourage suppliers to use adequate warnings, some courts have developed a "heeding presumption" under which it is presumed that if an adequate warning had accompanied the product, the buyer/user would have heeded it—and not been hurt. [Coffman v. Keene Corp., 628 A.2d 710 (N.J. 1993); Richter v. Limax International, Inc., 45 F.3d 1464 (10th Cir. 1995)—buyer need not persuade jury that she would have behaved differently if the missing warning had been present—causation was presumed; *but see* General Motors Corp. v. Saenz, 873 S.W.2d 353 (Texas 1993)—refusing to apply presumption in case where warning was given but was claimed to have been inadequate]

2) **Lack of safety features:** [§858]   A defendant manufacturer may be liable where it failed to provide safety features that decreased the severity of injuries from inevitable accidents—even where the product did not cause the accident. [Tafoya v. Sears, Roebuck & Co., 884 F.2d 1330 (10th Cir. 1989)—riding lawnmower lacked "deadman device" that would have lessened severity of plaintiff's injuries when mower tipped over]

(c) **Proximate cause—effect of intervening causes:** [§859]   If other causes are proved, their effect on causation is determined by the same proximate cause tests applicable in negligence cases (*see supra*, §§348 *et seq.*).

1) **Example:** The defect that caused a truck to stall on a highway (where P later ran into it) was not a proximate cause of the crash because the driver had abandoned the truck, and for three hours before the accident, cars had safely avoided it. [Peck v. Ford Motor Co., 603 F.2d 1240 (7th Cir. 1979)]

2) **Example:** The manufacturer of defective fire clothing is not liable for harm sustained by the sister of a burned firefighter who agreed to donate skin tissue for her brother's grafts. [Bobka v. Cook County Hospital, 422 N.E.2d 999 (Ill. 1981)]

3) **Application—injuries to third parties after supplier's adequate warning to purchaser:** [§860]   Under present case law, a supplier who has given *adequate* warning of a concealed danger to the original purchaser of the product may not be liable for injuries later suffered by third persons. The original purchaser's *failure to respond* to the warning may be treated as a *superseding cause* of the injury.

a) **Example—auto recall cases:** [§861]   Auto Manufacturer recalls all cars sold by it for replacement of potentially dangerous steering control. Purchaser receives recall notice but fails to return car for replacement of defective part. Later, Purchaser sells car to third party, without advising of recall. Purchaser's failure to return car or warn the new owner about the steering control terminates Manufacturer's liability (but *Purchaser* may be liable to new owner in a negligence case). [Ford Motor Co. v. Wagoner, 192 S.W.2d 840 (Tenn. 1946); *and see supra*, §782—retailer who knows about danger in a product]

b) **Example—prescription drugs:** [§862]   Similarly, the manufacturer of a new drug who has given *adequate* warning to prescribing physicians of the drug's potential hazards is not ordinarily strictly liable to a patient who suffers adverse reactions from the medication. The physician's failure to disclose such hazards to the patient is regarded as a superseding cause of the injury. (But the patient may have a valid claim against the physician for lack of informed consent; *see supra*, §§92-93.)

1/ **Exception—mass immunization:** [§863] Warning physicians may not be sufficient where the drug is the subject of mass immunization programs. Here, the manufacturer is required to warn the **ultimate recipients** or see to it that notice reaches such persons. *Rationale:* In these cases there is no physician to provide the patient with an individualized balancing of the risks; hence, consumers must be given sufficient information to balance the benefits and risks themselves. [Reyes v. Wyeth Laboratories, 498 F.2d 1264 (5th Cir. 1974)]

c) **Example—employer removes warnings from product:** [§864] Manufacturers may reasonably believe that an employer who has knowledge of dangers of products will pass those warnings on to its workers. Where the employer removes the warnings, its action will prevent the manufacturer's liability. [Whitehead v. Dycho Co., 775 S.W.2d 593 (Tenn. 1989)]

f. **Kinds of losses recoverable**

(1) **Personal injuries (or death):** [§865] Pain and suffering caused by injury from the defective product are recoverable, together with all damages consequential thereto—medical expenses, loss of income, etc. And if the injury results in death, a wrongful death action will lie.

(2) **Property damage:** [§866] Physical damage to other property is recoverable in almost all states. [J.R. Dudley Construction Co. v. Drott Manufacturing Co., 66 App. Div. 2d 368 (1979); Vaughn v. General Motors Corp., 466 N.E.2d 195 (Ill. 1984)]

(3) **Economic losses:** [§867] Most courts, however, do *not* allow recovery in tort for *purely economic losses* (*e.g.,* product does not perform well, and purchaser is deprived of profits she expected to make through its use or is forced to incur additional expenses to make it work, etc.). The purchaser's right to recover such losses is more of a "sales" problem than a "torts" problem, and she usually is limited to a contract action against the person who sold her the product (or, if there are warranties running from the manufacturer, against the manufacturer as well). [East River Steamship Corp. v. Transamerica Delaval Inc., 476 U.S. 858 (1986); Danforth v. Acorn Structures, Inc., 608 A.2d 1194 (Del. 1992)] This approach applies even where the defect created a serious risk of personal injury that did not come to pass. [Airport Rent-A-Car, Inc. v. Prevost, 660 So. 2d 628 (Fla. 1995); *but see* Washington Water Power Co. v. Graybar Electric Co., 774 P.2d 1199 (Wash. 1989)—adopting a minority rule that permits recovery of pure economics loss where a risk of personal injury had been created]

(a) **Minority view:** [§868]   A strong minority has extended strict tort liability for defective products to purely economic losses. [Chemtrol Adhesives, Inc. v. American Manufacturers Mutual Insurance Co., 537 N.E.2d 624 (Ohio 1989)—breach of warranty or strict liability claims can be maintained for purely economic loss; *and see* Alaskan Oil, Inc. v. Central Flying Service, 975 F.2d 553 (8th Cir. 1992)]

(b) **Misrepresentation:** [§869]   In any event, if the product has been *advertised* or represented to perform according to certain specifications, there may be a possibility of recovery in tort for *misrepresentation* (*see infra*, §§1428-1431).

(c) **Part of other action:** [§870]   Moreover, where the plaintiff suffers personal injury or property loss, all states permit economic loss to be recovered in tort with the other damages under strict liability.

5. Defenses to Strict Tort Liability

a. **Contributory negligence:** [§871]   Whether contributory negligence is a valid defense depends on how this term is used:

(1) **Failure to discover or guard against danger:** [§872]   Contributory negligence in the sense of *failing to exercise reasonable care to discover* the danger *or to guard against it* traditionally was *not a valid defense* to a strict liability claim in most states. [Rest. 2d §402A, comment n] Thus, where D leased an airplane without oil in it to P, who took off without checking the oil level, D could not allege contributory negligence as a defense when the plane crashed shortly after takeoff. [Rudisaile v. Hawk Aviation, Inc., 592 P.2d 175 (N.M. 1979)]

(2) **Unreasonable misuse:** [§873]   However, contributory negligence in the sense of *unreasonable misuse* of a defective product—in a manner or for a purpose for which no reasonable person would use it (*e.g.,* driving a passenger car at 150 m.p.h.)—traditionally *did bar* liability. [McDevitt v. Standard Oil, 391 F.2d 364 (5th Cir. 1968)]

(a) **And note:** As previously discussed, the better analysis is that a product will not be found "defective" if it did not stand up under the plaintiff's unforeseeable misuse. (Remember, however, that a certain amount of product misuse may be considered "normal"; *see supra*, §846.)

b. **Comparative fault:** [§874]   Most comparative negligence states reduce the plaintiff's recovery in strict liability cases by some amount to reflect the fact that the injury was caused in part by the plaintiff's own carelessness. This avoids the need to distinguish between "knowing" and "unknowing" contributory fault. [Daly v. General Motors Corp., 20 Cal. 3d 725 (1978); *but see* Simpson v. General Motors Corp., 483 N.E.2d 1 (Ill. 1985)—contra]

(1) **Comment:** There is a theoretical inconsistency in talking about "comparative negligence" here because the defendant seller may not have been negligent at all; *i.e.,* his liability may arise regardless of any fault on his part. Still, it is thought anomalous to allow the defense where the

claim is based on negligence and deny it where the claim is based on strict liability. Where contributory negligence is shown, these jurisdictions refuse to deprive the plaintiff of all recovery in strict liability. Therefore, courts recognizing comparative negligence in negligence cases apply a comparable notion here (sometimes called comparative "fault") that has the effect of reducing the plaintiff's recovery by an amount the jury deems appropriate. [Suter v. San Angelo Foundry & Machine Co., 406 A.2d 140 (N.J. 1979); Seay v. Chrysler Corp., 609 P.2d 1382 (Wash. 1980)]

(2) **Note:** Another approach is to compare the plaintiff's deviation from a reasonable standard and separately compare the deviation between the defendant's product and a good product—and then compare the two deviations. [*See* Sanford v. Chevrolet Division of General Motors, 642 P.2d 624 (Or. 1982)]

(3) **Crashworthiness:** [§875]   Where the plaintiff is hurt in a car accident that was totally his fault and then seeks to recover for enhanced injuries due to the lack of crashworthiness of the car's interior, most courts will reduce the plaintiff's recovery to reflect his fault. [Whitehead v. Toyota Motor Corp., 897 S.W.2d 684 (Tenn. 1995); *but see* Reed v. Chrysler Corp., 494 N.W.2d 224 (Iowa 1992)—contra]

c. **Assumption of the risk:** [§876]   One who *knows* of the danger or risk involved, and *unreasonably* continues to use the product, may be held to have assumed the risk. This is a *valid defense* to strict liability. [Sperling v. Hatch, 10 Cal. App. 3d 54 (1970)]

(1) **Application—warning of latent danger:** [§877]   Thus, even where the danger was not obvious, if the plaintiff has learned about it and still unreasonably continues to use the product, recovery may be barred. The analysis here may be similar to the analysis of actual cause *supra*, §§855-856.

(a) **"Adequately" warned:** [§878]   The crucial issue, of course, is the *adequacy* of the warning given. Courts tend to be demanding in judging this factor, holding the warning inadequate if it was either incomplete (as where the manufacturer disclosed some but not all risks) or was "watered down" by the manufacturer's own aggressive sales promotion, which had the effect of persuading users to disregard the warnings given. [Stevens v. Parke-Davis & Co., 9 Cal. 3d 51 (1973)]

(2) **Limitation—reasonable alternative required:** [§879]   There is no "voluntary" assumption of the risk where the plaintiff's continued use of the known defective product results from *economic duress*. [Messick v. General Motors Corp., 460 F.2d 485 (5th Cir. 1972)—traveling salesman (P) had asked D repeatedly to repair defective steering, and was "forced" to continue driving car because unable to replace it]

(3) **Limitation—voluntary and knowing assumption of risk required:** [§880]   The injured party must actually have known of the particular danger involved and freely decided to face it.

(a) **Example:** Where the injured party was run over and killed by a road grader, no assumption of risk defense lies. Deliberately confronting the machine would have been suicide, and the victim exhibited no such intention. [West v. Caterpillar Tractor Co., 547 F.2d 885 (5th Cir. 1977)]

(b) **And note:** The relevant knowledge and voluntary decision to face the risk is that of the *victim*, not that of the product's *buyer*. [Hammond v. International Harvester Co., 691 F.2d 646 (3d Cir. 1982)—manufacturer who removed safety device at request of knowledgeable buyer cannot argue that buyer's employee assumed the risk]

d. **Disclaimers:** [§881]   Contractual disclaimers of liability generally have been held *invalid as against public policy*—at least as to products liability claims involving personal injury arising out of *consumer* transactions. [Vandermark v. Ford Motor Co., *supra*, §812]

(1) **Compare:** Courts may uphold contractual disclaimers as between two business concerns with relatively equal bargaining positions. [Delta Airlines, Inc. v. McDonnell Douglas, 503 F.2d 239 (5th Cir. 1974)—upholding contract limiting liability for repair expenses due to defective nose gear]

e. **Statute of limitations:** [§882]   The personal injury (tort), rather than the contracts, statute of limitations applies to strict liability injury claims.

f. **Preemption:** [§883]   In a few situations, courts have concluded that federal legislation has impliedly preempted state tort law. [Cipollone v. Liggett Group, 505 U.S. 504 (1992)—federal statute preempted state tort claims in cigarette cases based on failure to warn in advertising and promotion and neutralization of warnings by advertising, but did not preempt claims based on fraud, testing and research, or express warranty; Freightliner Corp. v. Myrick, 115 S. Ct. 1483 (1995)—claim that tractor-trailer was defective because it lacked air brakes was not preempted by federal regulations]

E.   LIABILITY BASED ON BREACH OF WARRANTY [§884]

Rather than relying on negligence or strict liability as the basis for liability, courts may impose liability for breach of warranty in a *contract* action.

1. **Express Warranties:** [§885]   Whatever a seller represents to a purchaser about the product involved (by advertising or otherwise) may be an express warranty, *i.e.*, a part of the contract. And if the warranty is breached (the product is not as represented), causing damage or injury to the purchaser relying on the representation, that purchaser has a direct action against the seller *on the contract*.

2. **Implied Warranties:** [§886]   However, most warranty actions are based on *implied* warranties—the assurance (implied in law) from the seller to the buyer that the product purchased will do no harm in normal use.

a. **U.C.C. provisions:** [§887]   The Uniform Commercial Code ("U.C.C.") implies two pertinent warranties:

(1) **Fitness for particular purpose:** [§888]   Where the seller knows (or has reason to know) that the buyer is purchasing goods *for a particular purpose*, and is *relying on the seller's skill or judgment* in supplying appropriate goods, there is an implied warranty that the goods sold are in fact fit for *that* purpose. [U.C.C. §2-315]

(2) **Merchantability:** [§889]   Where goods are supplied by one who deals in goods of that kind, a warranty is implied that they are of at least "fair average" quality, *i.e.*, *generally fit for normal use*. [U.C.C. §2-314]

(3) **Compare—warranty and strict liability in tort:** [§890]   Warranties under the U.C.C. are judged from the consumer expectation perspective. It is thus possible that a product might be defective in tort because of the existence of feasible alternatives while at the same time not breaching either implied warranty. Similarly, a product might breach a warranty although it is not defective under tort analysis. [Denny v. Ford Motor Co., 87 N.Y.2d 248 (1995)—jury could consistently find that Ford Bronco II was not "defective" but had breached the warranty of fitness]

b. **Transactions covered:** [§891]   The U.C.C. itself applies only to *sales of goods* (*i.e.*, personal property).

(1) **Bailments:** [§892]   Most courts, however, have implied similar warranties ("by analogy") in connection with the *bailment* or *lease* of personal property. [48 A.L.R.3d 668]

(2) **Sale of real property:** [§893]   Some courts have held that a breach of warranty claim may exist in connection with the construction and sale of a new home. [Caceci v. DiCanio Construction Corp., 72 N.Y.2d 52 (1988)]

(3) **"Goods" vs. "services":** [§894]   But warranties will *not* be implied in contracts for *services*. Thus, a doctor does not "impliedly warrant" the safety or adequacy of the treatment furnished; a railroad does not warrant the fitness or safety of the transportation furnished; and a repair shop, in the absence of an express agreement, does not warrant the adequacy of its work. Any liability for injuries sustained as the result of improper services rendered must therefore be based on tort (or an explicit contract provision), not implied warranty. [Dennis v. Allison, 698 S.W.2d 94 (Tex. 1985)—no warranty in case of psychiatrist assaulting patient]

(a) **Borderline cases:** [§895]   Sometimes it is difficult to distinguish a "sale of goods" from "services rendered." This issue has frequently been encountered with regard to restaurants. Early cases concluded that no "sale of goods" was involved and hence no warranty implied. Virtually all courts now agree that even though a service is also provided, food served in restaurants is in fact "sold," so that the owner is subject to implied warranty liability. [Arnaud's Restaurant v. Cotter, 212 F.2d 883 (5th Cir. 1954)]

(b) **Blood:** [§896]   Almost all states have legislation barring warranty suits by persons who have received infected blood in a transfusion. [Zichichi v. Middlesex Memorial Hospital, *supra*, §838]

(4) **Defendants must be dealers:** [§897]   Liability for implied warranties generally is imposed only on those who "deal" regularly in the product. It generally does not apply to a person who sells his car or stereo system to a neighbor.

3.   **Effect of Breach of Warranty:** [§898]   Liability for breach of warranty is really a form of *strict liability*. If the product is defective, the warranty is breached and the manufacturer is automatically liable—whether or not due care was exercised in its manufacture, or the manufacturer was otherwise "at fault."

   a.   **Significance—tactical advantage to warranty action:** [§899]   For this reason, a plaintiff ordinarily will prefer to show breach of warranty (or strict liability in tort, *supra*) rather than attempt to establish negligence in manufacture, which requires proof of "breach of duty of due care."

4.   **Requirement of "Privity of Contract":** [§900]   The traditional problem with basing liability on breach of warranty is that it is a *contract* action, so that "privity of contract" between the injured party and the party sought to be held liable for such injuries normally must be shown.

   a.   **Former rule—implied warranties required pure privity:** [§901]   Since a seller's implied warranties ran only to the immediate buyer, a manufacturer's implied warranties normally would run only to its distributor or wholesaler. The ultimate *purchaser* or consumer of the goods had *no direct action against the manufacturer*, because there was no contract between them.

   (1)   **Result—multiplicity of suits:** [§902]   This led to a multiplicity of actions: injured purchaser sued retailer, who in turn sought indemnity from wholesaler, who in turn sought indemnity from manufacturer. Moreover, if the retailer was insolvent, the purchaser might have had no effective remedy, in which case the manufacturer escaped liability.

   (2)   **Compare—express warranties:** [§903]   But the result was different if the manufacturer made an *express* warranty to the public (*e.g.,* in advertising) upon which the ultimate purchaser *relied* in acquiring the product. Here, in the event of breach, the purchaser (but not other users or injured bystanders) was allowed a direct action against the manufacturer. [Hauter v. Zogarts, 14 Cal. 3d 104 (1975)]

   b.   **Modern law—modified interpretation of privity:** [§904]   The privity rules still apply to retailers, manufacturers, and other commercial sellers, but the rules have been relaxed considerably and no longer distinguish between implied and express warranties.

   (1)   **U.C.C. provisions:** [§905]   The U.C.C. offered three *alternative* versions for the states to adopt. [U.C.C. §2-318] Thus, depending on the state, privity extends to:

   (a)   *The family or guests of the immediate buyer* when personally injured; *or*

   (b)   *Any natural person who may reasonably be expected to use*, consume, or be affected by the goods and who suffers personal injury; *or*

(c) *Any person who may reasonably be expected to use*, consume, or be affected by the goods and who is injured.

(2) **Background:** [§906] These alternatives were not offered when the U.C.C. was first presented to the states, and therefore some states adopted no version of section 2-318 because the version initially offered was more restrictive than state law.

c. **Abandonment of "privity" requirement as to dangerous products:** [§907] Independent of the evolution under the U.C.C., courts struggling with warranty concepts have been chipping away at the old privity requirements in order to hold a manufacturer or supplier strictly liable to those hurt by use or consumption of its product.

(1) **Former view—exceptions regarding specific products:** [§908] The earliest cases involved foodstuffs, medicines, firearms, etc. Because of the great potential harm involved, courts held the manufacturer liable in warranty to the ultimate *user* of such products (whether or not such person was the actual purchaser).

(2) **Modern approach—"foreseeable scope of use" test:** [§909] Today, many courts have expanded this to encompass *any dangerous product*, and hold that implied warranties arising from the sale thereof extend not only to the purchaser or user of such products, but also to all persons within the *foreseeable scope of use*. [Henningsen v. Bloomfield Motors, Inc., 161 A.2d 69 (N.J. 1960)—auto manufacturer held liable in warranty for injuries caused by a defective steering wheel, not only to ultimate purchaser of the car but also to foreseeable users (*e.g.*, passengers in car)]

d. **Consumer protection statutes:** [§910] A few states have gone even further to abolish the requirement of "privity" between the manufacturer and purchaser of *all consumer goods* (whether or not generally thought of as dangerous). [Cal. Civ. Code §1790]

e. **Impact—"warranty" a device for justifying strict liability?** [§911] To the extent warranty liability is imposed on a manufacturer or supplier without privity, the latter is made an *insurer* of the safety and purity of its goods to the whole world. For this reason, there has been considerable disagreement among the courts as to the scope of warranty liability and the requirement of privity. In any event, the strict liability in tort action (*supra*) seems better suited to the imposition of such liability for certain situations than a warranty action. In a few states, the Uniform Commercial Code is held to preempt judicial application of strict liability tort actions. [*See, e.g.,* Cline v. Prowler Industries of Maryland, Inc., 418 A.2d 968 (Del. 1980)—strict liability tort would have destructive effect on sales remedies, and legislature can adopt strict liability]

f. **Causation:** [§912] Defendant is not liable where, because of an independent superseding event such as the plaintiff's assumption of risk, its breach is not the proximate cause of the damage.

(1) **Limited to latent dangers:** [§913]   The warranty approach is the source of the "consumer expectation" approach. This means that if the danger of the product is apparent to the ordinary buyer there will be no liability for breach of any warranty, either because there is no breach or because there is no causation. In effect, this means that plaintiffs in warranty cases are often limited to latent dangers.

(2) **Example:** Ps noticed sparks and smoke coming from their television set and called D for a service appointment. Before the repair, however, they turned on the set again and watched it for two hours, despite seeing more sparks and smoke. D was not liable for resulting fire. [Erdman v. Johnson Bros. Radio & Television Co., 271 A.2d 744 (Md. 1970)]

g.   **Damages:** [§914]   Damages for breach of warranty are substantially the same as in a successful strict liability tort action—*i.e.,* all damages proximately caused by the breach (including personal injury, pain and suffering). However, a few states bar damages for wrongful death (*see infra,* §§964-978) on a breach of warranty theory. [Geohagan v. General Motors Corp., 279 So. 2d 436 (Ala. 1973)]

5.   Defenses to Warranty Actions

a.   **Contributory negligence:** [§915]   Although the plaintiff's contributory negligence is not formally a defense to a claim for breach of warranty [Brown v. Chapman, 304 F.2d 149 (9th Cir. 1962)], most courts have developed an analogous defense to parallel the tort developments [West v. Caterpillar Tractor Co., *supra,* §880—comparative fault defense in warranty cases].

(1) **Compare—assumption of risk:** [§916]   If the plaintiff actually discovers a defect and unreasonably uses the product in such a condition, assumption of the risk *is* a complete defense in warranty actions. Some courts might analyze this as a lack of causation (*see supra,* §912).

b.   **Disclaimers:** [§917]   By appropriate language, a manufacturer or seller may limit or exclude warranties that would otherwise arise from the sale of goods. [U.C.C. §2-316]

(1) **Sufficient language:** [§918]   "No warranties, express or implied, are made as to the fitness or merchantability of this product beyond the description on the face hereof." If sufficiently conspicuous, such language may be sufficient to exclude all warranty liability to the purchaser of the product. (So also with a sale of something properly marked "as is.") [U.C.C. §2-316]

(2) **Consumer goods:** [§919]   However, some states now require much more specific language to disclaim warranties in the sale of consumer goods. [*See* Cal. Civ. Code §1792.4—requires such explicit warnings that few products could be sold on this basis]

(3) **Limitation—"unconscionability":** [§920]   If there has been no valid disclaimer, an attempt to limit consequential damages that may be recovered after a breach is deemed "prima facie unconscionable" as to

personal injuries arising out of the use of *consumer goods*. [U.C.C. §2-719(3)]

    (4) **Scope of disclaimers as effective defense—seller not insulated from liability:** [§921] Although the seller is able to successfully exclude warranties, disclaimers are binding only on the purchaser of the goods; they do not bar the claims of an injured third party who is *not* the purchaser. [Ferragamo v. Massachusetts Bay Transportation Authority, 481 N.E.2d 477 (Mass. 1985)]

  c. **Notice requirements:** [§922] Warranty actions may be barred if the injured purchaser fails to give the seller "timely notice of breach." [U.C.C. §2-607(3)(a)]

  d. **Statute of limitations:** [§923] The usual warranty limitations period is four years, running from the delivery of the goods. [U.C.C. §2-725]

V. NUISANCE

chapter approach

If you see a nuisance question on your exam, consider the following issues:

1. Is this a **public** or **private** nuisance (*i.e.,* whose interest is being invaded)? This issue affects a party's standing to sue.

2. Is this a **nuisance** situation or a **trespass to land**? The distinction between nuisance and trespass is very important. Nuisance protects the plaintiff against **interference with the use or enjoyment** of her land; trespass involves a **physical invasion** of plaintiff's land. Consider the facts carefully to make this determination. And don't forget that a particular fact situation could be **both** a nuisance and a trespass to land.

3. Is the harm **substantial and unreasonable**? In general, plaintiffs are accorded less protection against nuisance than against trespass. When someone has physically intruded onto your land either by entering it or by casting rocks on it, there are fewer defenses to such actions. But where the interference has involved something that is harder to keep contained, such as odor or noise, there must necessarily be less complete protection. This accounts for the introduction of questions of reasonableness, the nature of the neighborhood, etc. Therefore, although working carefully with all the facts you are given is important in all torts questions, it is particularly so in determining whether the facts amount to a nuisance.

A. IN GENERAL [§924]

Prima facie case: ***Act by Defendant***
Nontrespassory Invasion of Plaintiff's Interest
Intent, Negligence, or Strict Liability
Substantial and Unreasonable Harm
Causation

B. PRIVATE NUISANCE VS. PUBLIC NUISANCE

1. **Private Nuisance Defined:** [§925] A "private nuisance" is a nontrespassory invasion of the plaintiff's interest in the **use or enjoyment** of her property.

   a. **Compare—trespass:** Many types of conduct may be **both** a trespass and a nuisance; *e.g.,* blasting on the defendant's land may unreasonably interfere with the plaintiff's enjoyment of her land (and thus be a nuisance) and at the same time may throw rocks into the plaintiff's garden (and thus be a trespass). Similarly, the flooding of the plaintiff's land or seepage onto it may also constitute both a trespass and a nuisance.

   b. **Application:** Although D's act in casting microscopic, undetectable particulates from its smelters onto P's land may be a trespass [Bradley v. American Smelting & Refining, *supra*, §177], if the intrusion comes through noise waves, odor, or light, only nuisance will lie [Wilson v. Interlake Steel Co., 32 Cal. 3d 229 (1982)].

2. **Public Nuisance Defined:** [§926]   A "public nuisance" is an act by a defendant that obstructs or causes *inconvenience or damage to the public* in the exercise of *rights common to all*, or in the enjoyment or use of common property. For a public nuisance, criminal as well as civil sanctions may be imposed. [Armory Park Neighborhood Association v. Episcopal Community Services, 712 P.2d 914 (Ariz. 1985)]

    a. **Standing to sue:** [§927]   Generally, only the state acting through public officials can redress a public nuisance; a private individual therefore may maintain an action *only* if she suffers an injury *"peculiar in kind"*—*i.e.,* apart from that common to the public (*e.g.,* an obstruction on a public road is a public nuisance, but it is a private nuisance as to P if it also blocks her driveway). [Burgess v. M/V Tamano, 370 F. Supp. 247 (D. Me. 1973)]

    b. **Application—environmental damage:** [§928]   This distinction is of vital importance where a private citizen sues for environmental pollution. At present, most courts limit a private individual's recovery to those damages that she *personally* sustains, on the rationale that pollution is a public problem with which courts cannot deal effectively in litigation between private parties. [Boomer v. Atlantic Cement Co., 26 N.Y.2d 219 (1970)]

C.   PLAINTIFF'S INTEREST   [§929]

The defendant's act must have resulted in a nontrespassory invasion of the plaintiff's interest in the *use or enjoyment of land*.

1. **Possessory Interest in Land Required:** [§930]   The plaintiff's interest must be either *actual possession* or the *right to immediate possession*. Thus, for example, a lessee or adverse possessor can recover, whereas a lessor cannot. [Brink v. Moeschl Edwards, 133 S.W. 1147 (Ky. 1911)]

    a. **Who may sue:** [§931]   The plaintiff must be the one who has possession. Thus, an employee, a licensee, or even the spouse of the possessor does *not* have sufficient status to sue. [Page v. Niagara Chemical Division, 68 So. 2d 382 (Fla. 1953)]

2. **Expansion—Interference with Business Interest:** [§932]   Some courts have extended the tort of nuisance to interference with business interests, as well as use and enjoyment of land. For example, several cases have held that pollution of a lake or river is a private nuisance as to commercial fisheries operating thereon. [Hampton v. North Carolina Pulp, 27 S.E.2d 538 (N.C. 1943)]

D.   DEFENDANT'S CONDUCT

1. **Nature of Act:** [§933]   The defendant's act must be shown to have been (i) *intentional*, (ii) unintentional but *negligent, or* (iii) neither intentional nor negligent, but actionable under rules governing liability for abnormally dangerous conditions or activities (*strict liability*). [Rest. 2d §822; Copart Industries v. Commonwealth Edison Co., 41 N.Y.2d 564 (1977)]

    a. **Act is required:** [§934]   Some act is required because of the traditional view that a landowner has no duty to avoid harm to neighbors from natural conditions. [Lichtman v. Nadler, 74 App. Div. 2d 66 (1980)—no liability for mosquito infestation and unpleasant odors emanating from natural accumulation of water on D's land]

b. **Application:** [§935]   Of course, ***most nuisances are intentional*** because the plaintiff has usually complained to the defendant, and the defendant has ignored the complaints and continued his activities. [Smith v. Staso, 18 F.2d 736 (2d Cir. 1927)]

  (1) **Example—negligent nuisance:** Negligent nuisance is found in cases where the defendant has failed to exercise due care to abate a condition under his control (*e.g.,* a stench, or fires on his property that blow smoke onto plaintiff's land).

  (2) **Example—strict liability nuisance:** A nuisance may be predicated on ***strict liability*** even where the defendant has taken reasonable precautions to control the condition and is therefore not "at fault" (*e.g.,* storing explosives in a residential neighborhood, or noise and fumes from oil well drilling). [Cumberland Torpedo v. Gaines, 255 S.W. 1046 (Ky. 1923)]

    (a) **But note:** Strict liability applies only where the nuisance results from an abnormally dangerous activity or condition, or from an animal. (*See supra,* §§721 *et seq.*)

2. **Why Does It Matter?** [§936]   This distinction is of primary importance in determining what ***defenses*** are available. For example, contributory negligence is a good defense to a nuisance predicated on negligence but not to intentional nuisances. [McFarlane v. Niagara Falls, 247 N.Y. 340 (1928)]

E.   SUBSTANTIAL AND UNREASONABLE HARM TO PLAINTIFF [§937]

The nontrespassory invasion must result in ***substantial and unreasonable*** harm to the plaintiff's interest in the use and enjoyment of the land.

1. **"Substantial":** [§938]   This refers to the quantitative aspect of the interference: It must be something that a ***reasonable person*** would take offense at, rather than a de minimis annoyance to which only a grouchy neighbor or unduly sensitive person would object. [Dunlop v. Daigle, 444 A.2d 519 (N.H. 1982)—kennel for 38 dogs four feet from P's rental unit]

2. **"Unreasonable":** [§939]   When an intentional or negligent nuisance is alleged, the defendant's conduct must be unreasonable in the sense that, taking all the factors into consideration, the harm done by the interference ***outweighs*** justifications for the defendant's conduct. [Antonik v. Chamberlain, 78 N.E.2d 752 (Ohio 1947); *and see* Property Summary]

  a. **Factors to consider:** [§940]   Important factors in determining whether the conduct is unreasonable are:

    (i) The ***suitability*** of the invading use ***to the neighborhood*** where it takes place;

    (ii) The ***values*** of the respective properties;

        (iii) The *cost* to the defendant to eliminate the condition complained of; and

        (iv) The *social benefits* from allowing the condition to continue (employment of others, etc.).

        [Rest. 2d §828; *and see* Remedies Summary—doctrine of "balancing hardships" in deciding whether to enjoin a nuisance]

b. **Aesthetic considerations:** [§941] Most courts have held that aesthetic considerations may not ordinarily create a nuisance if the activity is being run without unreasonable noise, odors, etc. [Wernke v. Halas, 600 N.E.2d 117 (Ind. 1992)—tasteless yard decorations involving toilet seat and unattractive and vulgar graffiti not actionable; *and see* Akins v. Thomas Solvent Co., 487 N.W.2d 715 (Mich. 1992)—property owner cannot recover for lost value due to erroneous public fear that defendant's pollution will some day reach plaintiff's property]

    (1) **Exception:** Many states have concluded that funeral homes, no matter how carefully and tastefully run, may be nuisances if located in a residential district. [Travis v. Moore, 377 So. 2d 609 (Miss. 1979)—properly run funeral home that caused "depressed feelings" to residents in residential neighborhood was a nuisance; Mitchell v. Bearden, 503 S.W.2d 904 (Ark. 1974)]

c. **Prior occupation:** [§942] For some courts, a relevant question as to the reasonableness of a use is whether the use *preceded plaintiff's presence*. [McQuade v. Tucson Tiller Apartments, 543 P.2d 150 (Ariz. 1975)] This is especially true where the use offended no one until the plaintiff moved in. [Spur Industries v. Del E. Webb Development Co., 494 P.2d 700 (Ariz. 1972)]

    (1) **Compare—assumption of risk:** [§943] The plaintiff is not necessarily barred by assumption of risk simply because when she purchased the property she knew of some offensive use to which the defendant was then putting neighboring property; again, the defendant's conduct might not have become "unreasonable" until persons moved onto surrounding land.

d. **Effect of zoning:** [§944] Nor are zoning ordinances conclusive as to what is a "reasonable use" since activities permitted under zoning laws may still be unreasonable as to neighbors. [Armory Park Neighborhood Association v. Episcopal Community Services, *supra*, §926—center that provided care for indigent people could be held a nuisance despite its compliance with zoning provisions]

    (1) **Compare:** However, a *few* states (*e.g.,* California and New York) provide that a zoning ordinance is a *presumptive defense*; *i.e.,* if the use is permitted under local zoning ordinances, it is presumptively not a nuisance. (*See* Property Summary.)

3. **Minority Rule—Substantial Interference Enough:** [§945] A growing minority of states now hold that in cases of *intentional* nuisance, the plaintiff need only show a substantial interference with the use and enjoyment of the land; *i.e.,* the defendant may be liable even if his conduct is reasonable. [Jost v. Dairyland Power

Cooperative, 172 N.W.2d 647 (Wis. 1969)—very useful power plant provided much needed energy to area but also damaged crops on P's nearby land; even though benefits created by D outweighed harm, plant was held a nuisance]

a. **Compare—Restatement:** The Second Restatement provides that an intentional invasion is unreasonable "if the harm is substantial and greater than the other should reasonably be required to bear without compensation." [Rest. 2d §829A]

F. CAUSATION [§946]

If the case is one of intentional nuisance, causation is basically the same as for battery (*see supra*, §17); if the nuisance is predicated on negligence or strict liability, the rules of causation are based on negligence standards (*see supra*, §§327 *et seq.*).

G. REMEDIES

1. **Judicial Relief:** [§947] Compensatory *damages* may be awarded for the interference, and where the invasion is of a nonrecurring nature this usually suffices. However, most nuisances are continuing in nature, and the remedy sought in such cases is usually an *injunction* against future invasions together with damages for past invasions. [Valasek v. Baer, 401 N.W.2d 33 (Iowa 1987)—D enjoined from spreading hog manure on a section of his farmland close to P's home because of noxious odor] (For conditions governing injunctive relief, *see* Remedies Summary.)

   a. **Note:** When the nuisance is continuing but can be discontinued, the plaintiff may elect whether to sue once for all damages or sue periodically for past damages. [Baker v. Burbank-Glendale-Pasadena Airport Authority, 39 Cal. 3d 862 (1985)—D could stop airport nuisance at any time]

   b. **Punitive damages:** [§948] Punitive damages may be recovered where the defendant's conduct was willful and malicious. [Atlas Chemical Industries v. Anderson, 524 S.W.2d 681 (Tex. 1975)]

2. **"Self-Help":** [§949] The plaintiff may also be entitled to the "self-help" remedy of *abatement—i.e.,* entering the defendant's land to correct the nuisance. (*See* Property Summary.)

H. DEFENSES

1. **Contributory Negligence:** [§950] Depending on the type of nuisance involved, the defendant may reduce or escape liability by proving that the plaintiff was negligent. [Delaney v. Philbern Realty Corp., 280 N.Y. 461 (1939)]

   a. **Negligence:** [§951] Where a nuisance results from negligence, contributory negligence is an available defense. [Calder v. San Francisco, 50 Cal. App. 2d 837 (1942)] The jurisdiction's normal rules of comparative negligence (or contributory negligence) are used. [Nelson v. Hansen, 102 N.W.2d 251 (Wis. 1960)]

   b. **Intentional nuisance:** [§952] However, where the nuisance is intentionally committed, contributory negligence is *no defense*.

c. **Abnormally dangerous activity:** [§953]   Where the nuisance is based on an abnormally dangerous activity, *comparative* negligence is likely to apply (*see supra*, §759).

2. **Assumption of Risk:** [§954]   Whether a nuisance is intentional, negligent, or based on strict liability, assumption of risk *is* an available defense. [Jacko v. Bridgeport, 213 A.2d 452 (Conn. 1965)]

   a. **Consent:** [§955]   If the plaintiff has consented to the building of structures by the defendant, knowing that they will create a nuisance, the plaintiff cannot recover for damages caused by that construction. [Crawford v. Magnolia Petroleum Co., 62 S.W.2d 264 (Tex. 1933)]

   b. **"Coming to" the nuisance:** [§956]   However, the mere fact that an activity creating a nuisance existed before the plaintiff came within its scope is ordinarily *not* a defense.

      (1) **No knowledge of nuisance:** [§957]   If the plaintiff did not foresee the damage complained of, she is not precluded from seeking recovery for it. [Weston Paper Co. v. Pope, 57 N.E. 719 (Ind. 1900)]

      (2) **Knowledge of nuisance:** [§958]   Even when the plaintiff knew of the nuisance, the majority holds that the knowledge is generally no defense, and plaintiff may seek recovery. [Kellog v. Viola, 227 N.W.2d 55 (Wis. 1975)]

         (a) **Note:** These courts may still consider prior occupation as relevant to the reasonableness of the activity. (*See supra*, §942.)

         (b) **And note:** Even in the majority, if the plaintiff moved in solely to bring a lawsuit, recovery will be barred. [Rest. 2d §840D]

         (c) **Compare:** A minority of courts deny recovery altogether when a plaintiff comes to a nuisance with knowledge of it. [East St. John's Shingle Co. v. Portland, 246 P.2d 554 (Or. 1952)]

VI. MISCELLANEOUS FACTORS AFFECTING RIGHT TO SUE

chapter approach

The material in this chapter applies to *every tort action* considered in this Summary but is central to personal injury situations. It is rare that an exam question will build heavily on any part of this material, but on the other hand, it is quite common for these topics to be necessary to fill out your answer. Therefore, keep in mind the following:

1. Always check to see if anyone has died, because this will require you to address questions of *survival* and *wrongful death*.

2. If any of the parties are related, look for *new types of damage* (such as loss of consortium), and consider *intrafamily immunities* if one tries to sue the other.

3. If there is more than one person who has committed the tort, consider whether there may be *contribution* or *indemnity*.

A. SURVIVAL OF TORT ACTIONS

1. **Common Law—No "Survival":** [§959] The common law rule was, with few exceptions, that tort actions did not "survive," meaning that the death of *either* the tortfeasor *or* the person injured terminated any existing tort cause of action and prevented any recovery by or against the estate.

2. **Survival Statutes:** [§960] The common law rule has been changed to some extent by statute ("survival statutes") in almost every jurisdiction.

   a. **Personal injury and property damage:** [§961] These statutes allow survival of causes of action for personal injuries as well as property damage incurred up to the time of death.

   (1) **But note:** There is a split on whether recovery can be had for a *decedent's pain and suffering*. It is allowed in some states [DeLong v. County of Erie, 60 N.Y.2d 296 (1983)—$200,000 for 12 minutes of terror before death], but denied in others [Williamson v. Plant Insulation Co., 23 Cal. App. 4th 1406 (1994)—statute bars award for pain and suffering where plaintiff dies before final judgment].

   b. **Intangible personal interests:** [§962] Only a few states allow survival of actions for the invasion of intangible personal interests—*e.g.,* defamation, right of privacy, malicious prosecution, etc. [Canino v. New York News, Inc., 475 A.2d 528 (N.J. 1984)]

   c. **No punitive damages:** [§963] Even though a cause of action survives the death of the tortfeasor, it is generally recognized that the plaintiff *cannot* recover punitive damages against the estate of a deceased tortfeasor. [Hofer v. Lavender, 679 S.W.2d 470 (Tex. 1984)]

B. WRONGFUL DEATH

1. **Common Law—No Cause of Action:** [§964]   At common law, no action could be brought for wrongfully causing the death of a human being; *i.e.,* the person responsible for the death could be held criminally, but not civilly, responsible. Thus, apart from the law against murder, it was cheaper for defendant to kill plaintiff than to scratch him!

2. **Wrongful Death Statutes:** [§965]   This situation was remedied in England by the passage of Lord Campbell's Act in 1846, essentially a "true" wrongful death statute (*see* below). Today, every American jurisdiction has some type of statutory remedy for wrongful death.

   a. **Types of wrongful death statutes**

      (1) **"Survival" type:** [§966]   Some statutes authorize the survival of any action that the ***decedent himself*** might have maintained, and enlarge it to include the damages ***sustained by his estate*** by reason of his death ("survival type").

         (a) **Example:** Damages recoverable under this type of statute therefore include the decedent's pain and suffering and medical expenses, together with loss of future net earnings or savings.

      (2) **"True" type:** [§967]   Most jurisdictions have statutes that create a ***new cause of action*** for the benefit of particular ***surviving relatives*** (usually spouse, children, and parents), and permit recovery only of the ***pecuniary loss*** sustained by such relatives. [Cal. Civ. Proc. Code §377; *but see* Hopkins v. McBane, 427 N.W.2d 85 (N.D. 1988)—allowed recovery of damages for survivors' mental anguish]

         (a) **No recovery for decedent's damages:** [§968]   Under this type of statute, any claim that the victim would have had against the tortfeasor must be maintained in a ***separate survival action*** (by his estate), although the two actions are usually prosecuted concurrently and may ultimately benefit the same survivors. Thus, if the victim had incurred wage losses, medical expenses, etc., prior to his death, these are recoverable by his estate—as are pain and suffering in those states that permit survival of such claims (*see* above).

         (b) **Measure of damage—pecuniary loss:** [§969]   The measure of damages under the "true" type of wrongful death statute is the ***pecuniary loss*** suffered by the surviving relatives—*i.e.,* the loss of the value of the ***companionship, support, services, and contributions*** that they would have received from the victim had he not been killed. Even the value of lost inheritance is considered a pecuniary loss. [Schaeffer v. American Family Mutual Insurance Co., 531 N.W.2d 585 (Wis. 1995)] (Note that most states deny recovery for the survivors' grief or mental anguish caused by the wrongful death, although undoubtedly juries are influenced by this factor in evaluating the pecuniary loss. [Wardlow v. Keokuk, 190 N.W.2d 439 (Iowa 1971)])

1) **Computing pecuniary loss**

   a) **Wage earners:** [§970]   If the decedent was a wage earner, the damages to survivors are based on the estimated amount of *earnings* (less living expenses) over the remainder of the decedent's working expectancy and divided among the survivors.

   b) **Children:** [§971]   Where the victim was a child, the earnings are likely to be purely speculative—as are any "contributions" or support that the parent might have received. Even so, courts uniformly permit recovery, instructing the jury to fix an award based on the "pecuniary value" of the loss of the child's life, including contributions that might have continued after majority. [Mitchell v. Buchheit, 559 S.W.2d 528 (Mo. 1977)]

      1/ **Compare:** One way to calculate "pecuniary value" is to consider what the parents would otherwise have received in their expected later years from their (then) adult children, calculated in terms of what it would cost to obtain comparable care from nurses and comparable advice and counseling from advisers and therapists. [Green v. Bittner, 424 A.2d 210 (N.J. 1980)]

   c) **Non-wage earners:** [§972]   Where the victim was a spouse or parent with no earnings, courts generally permit recovery of an amount that would be required to *replace the services* performed in caring for the children and family. A non-wage earner's advice and companionship to the family are deemed lost "services," and hence substantial verdicts can be sustained as "pecuniary losses." Some courts do not require proof of the actual cost of replacing these services. [Wentling v. Medical Anesthesia Services, 701 P.2d 939 (Kan. 1985)—$786,166.64 to surviving husband and two children]

   d) **Retired persons:** [§973]   Again, there is a problem in computing damages because it is highly speculative what support or contributions the survivors could expect. But courts generally uphold reasonable awards on the theory that every life has *some* pecuniary value.

2) **Effect of remarriage:** [§974]   Where the decedent was married, most courts bar evidence that the surviving spouse has remarried (for fear of discouraging remarriage) or may remarry (on the rationale that it is too "speculative" whether remarriage will better the surviving spouse's position financially). The jury thus assesses evidence on the assumption that the survivor will remain a widow(er) for the rest of her (or his) life. [Groesbeck v. Napier, 275 N.W.2d 388 (Iowa 1979)]

(c) **No punitive damages:** [§975]   The general rule is that even in cases where punitive damages could have been awarded against the defendant had the victim survived (*i.e.,* where the defendant acted "maliciously," etc.), punitive damages are not awardable in a wrongful death action. Courts have held that such a distinction is constitutional. [Georgie Boy Manufacturing, Inc. v. Superior Court, 115 Cal. App. 3d 217 (1981)]

b. **Defenses assertable**

(1) **Victim's negligence, etc.:** [§976]   Under either type of wrongful death statute, defenses that could have been asserted against the decedent had she survived may be set up as defenses in the wrongful death action. Thus, the victim's *contributory negligence, assumption of the risk,* etc., will all be held to bar maintenance of a wrongful death action by her survivors. (In comparative negligence states, the victim's negligence may *reduce* the damages recoverable.) [Bevan v. Vassar Farms, Inc., 793 P.2d 711 (Idaho 1990)]

(2) **Victim's recovery inter vivos:** [§977]   Similarly, most courts hold that if the victim sued and *recovered* for the injury during her lifetime, such recovery *precludes* any action after death based on the same injury.

(3) **Beneficiary's negligence:** [§978]   In the majority of jurisdictions (*i.e.,* those having the "true" type of wrongful death statute), contributory negligence of the *sole* beneficiary in causing the accident that led to the victim's death is a bar to any recovery (or a basis for reducing recovery in a comparative negligence jurisdiction).

(a) **Note:** Where there are *several* beneficiaries under the statute, and only one was negligent, the damages recoverable are generally reduced proportionally (and the negligent beneficiary's recovery is reduced or barred). [Lucas v. Mississippi Housing Authority, 441 So. 2d 101 (Miss. 1983); *but see* Chang v. State Farm Mutual Automobile Insurance Co., 514 N.W.2d 399 (Wis. 1994)—where negligent beneficiary is sole defendant, no reduction is imposed; Teeter v. Missouri Highway & Transportation Commission, 891 S.W.2d 817 (Mo. 1993)—allowing full recovery and requiring defendant to bring a contribution action against the negligent beneficiary]

C. INJURIES TO MEMBERS OF THE FAMILY

1. **Loss of Consortium and Services**

a. **Common law**

(1) **Husband's right—services and consortium:** [§979]   The common law rule was that a husband had a right to the *services and consortium* (society and sexual relations) of his wife and was entitled to damages if deprived thereof. Thus, where a third person tortiously injured the wife, causing her illness or other bodily harm, the husband had his own ancillary cause of action against the tortfeasor for loss of his wife's services and consortium (together with the actual *expenses* he incurred for her care).

(2) **Parent's right—services only:** [§980]   *Either parent* (father or mother) having the custody and control of a minor child was deemed entitled to the child's *labor*, and could maintain an independent action against any third person who injured the child for loss of the child's earnings or services of economic value (together with any *expenses* incurred by the parent for the child's care). But *no* action was permitted for loss of the child's consortium (filial affection and society).

(3) **Compare—no wife's or child's right:** [§981]   A wife was *not* deemed to have any right to the services *or* consortium of her husband; nor was a child deemed to have any right to the support of the parent. The result was that although a wife or child was protected under wrongful death statutes in the event the tortfeasor *killed* the victim, they had *no* protection if the victim survived.

b.   **Modern law**

(1) **Either spouse can recover for loss of services and consortium:** [§982] Most states today have changed the common law rule so as to permit *either spouse* to recover for loss of the other's services and consortium, on the ground that both spouses have equal rights in the marital relationship. [*See, e.g.,* Rodriguez v. Bethlehem Steel Corp., 12 Cal. 3d 382 (1974)]

   (a) **What constitutes "loss of consortium":** [§983]   There must be a *complete* loss of the companionship and intercourse with the injured spouse for *some definite period* of time. Recovery is generally not permitted for injuries that merely put a "strain" on the marital relationship (*e.g.,* where injured spouse scarred or disfigured). [Park v. Standard Chem Way, 60 Cal. App. 3d 47 (1976)]

   1) **Spouses only:** [§984]   The relationship must be one of legal marriage. Thus, a long term live-in lover may not recover for injuries suffered by his or her partner, nor may a person recover for injuries suffered by his or her prospective spouse during their engagement. [Elden v. Sheldon, *supra*, §633; *but see* Dunphy v. Gregor, *supra*, §633—contra]

   a) **Note:** The deprived spouse has no cause of action for loss of consortium against the negligent injured spouse. [McIntosh v. Barr, 397 N.W.2d 516 (Iowa 1986)]

   2) **Compare—death of spouse:** [§985]   If a spouse has been killed, the only remedies available to the surviving spouse are the survival and wrongful death statutes. Almost all courts have refused to create common law loss of consortium actions in such cases. [Liff v. Schildkrout, 49 N.Y.2d 622 (1980); *but see* Gaudette v. Webb, 284 N.E.2d 222 (Mass. 1972)—recovery for wrongful death has common law origin]

   (b) **Minority view:** [§986]   Only Utah rejects consortium actions altogether. [Hackford v. Utah Power & Light Co., 740 P.2d 1281 (Utah 1987)]

(2) **Parent can recover for loss of child's services and consortium:** [§987] Most states permit the parent to recover for loss of the injured child's consortium. [United States v. Dempsey, 635 So. 2d 961 (Fla. 1994); Gallimore v. Children's Hospital Medical Center, 617 N.E.2d 1052 (Ohio 1993); *but see* Powell v. American Motors Co., 834 S.W.2d 184 (Mo. 1992)—contra; Wells v. Mount Sinai Medical Center, 515 N.W.2d 705 (Wis. 1994)—no action by parent for loss of companionship of adult child]

    (a) **Damages:** [§988] The older rule limited the recovery to economic losses, but later cases extend recovery to loss of the child's society and comfort. [Howard Frank, M.D., P.C. v. Superior Court, 722 P.2d 955 (Ariz. 1986)]

    (b) **Extent of harm:** [§989] For the parent to recover for loss of the child's consortium, the injury does *not* necessarily have to be the functional equivalent of death or be characterized as "catastrophic." [Pierce v. Casas Adobes Baptist Church, 782 P.2d 1162 (Ariz. 1989)— evidence of significant interference with child's capacity to interact with parents in a normally gratifying way may suffice]

    (c) **Limitation—minors:** [§990] Most states limit the action to injuries to minor children. A minority of states extend it to adult children. [Howard Frank, M.D., P.C. v. Superior Court, *supra*]

(3) **Child cannot recover for loss of parent's consortium:** [§991] Most states *deny* recovery when children sue for loss of the consortium of their injured parents. [Borer v. American Airlines, 19 Cal. 3d 441 (1979); *but see* Villareal v. Arizona, 774 P.2d 213 (Ariz. 1989)—small minority contra]

c. **Effect of victim's contributory negligence:** [§992] Most courts treat the spouse's or parent's claim for medical expenses and loss of consortium as "derivative" of the victim's claim. Thus, they hold that the victim's contributory negligence (or assumption of the risk or other valid defense) *bars* the spousal or parental claim as well (or, in comparative negligence states, reduces damages proportionately). [Blagg v. Illinois F.W.D. Truck & Equipment Co., 572 N.E.2d 920 (Ill. 1991)]

d. **Joinder requirement:** [§993] To minimize the possibility of double recovery, the spouse's or parent's claim for loss of consortium must be joined in the same action with the victim's claim for personal injury. Thus, no consortium recovery is allowed if the victim has settled or already recovered. [Schreiner v. Fruit, 519 P.2d 462 (Alaska 1974)]

2. Prenatal Injuries to Child

a. **Early view—no recovery:** [§994] Early cases denied a child any cause of action for injuries sustained prior to birth.

b. **Modern view—recovery allowed by virtually all courts:** [§995] The modern view allows recovery by a child after birth for any prenatal injuries, provided the child was shown to have been "viable" (capable of life apart from the mother) at the time of injury. [Williams v. Marion Rapid Transit, 87 N.E.2d 334 (Ohio 1949)]

(1) **Extension:** The modern trend is to allow a child to recover for prenatal injuries sustained at any time before birth—*even before the child was viable*. [Farley v. Sartin, 466 S.E.2d 522 (W. Va. 1995)]

(2) **But note:** Even courts that permit an action for prenatal injuries against third parties deny an action by the child against the mother. The reasoning is that it would be against public policy to turn mother and fetus into legal adversaries. [Stallman v. Youngquist, 531 N.E.2d 355 (Ill. 1988)—no action by infant for mother's negligent driving while pregnant]

c. **Wrongful death:** [§996]   There is a split as to whether an action can be maintained for the wrongful death of an unborn child (miscarriage or stillbirth). Many states allow the action if the child was viable (capable of life apart from the mother). [Volk v. Baldazo, 651 P.2d 11 (Idaho 1982)]

(1) **But note:** A number of states refuse to recognize a wrongful death action for miscarriage of a fetus or for a stillbirth, often on the basis that a fetus is not a "person" within the meaning of the wrongful death statute. [*See* Justus v. Atchison, 19 Cal. 3d 564 (1977)] However, these states generally allow the mother to recover for the physical and emotional injuries attending the stillbirth or miscarriage. [*See* Modaber v. Kelley, 348 S.E.2d 233 (Va. 1986)]

d. **"Wrongful birth":** [§997]   Likewise, there is a split of authority as to whether plaintiff parents can recover against a negligent defendant for the costs of raising and educating an unwanted child (*e.g.,* where physician D negligently performs a vasectomy, or D pharmacy negligently sells diet tablets in place of oral contraceptives). Generally, recovery is permitted by the mother for pain and suffering during pregnancy and delivery, for related medical expenses, and for loss of consortium during this time. [Miller v. Johnson, 343 S.E.2d 301 (Va. 1986); Wilson v. Kuenzi, 751 S.W.2d 741 (Mo.) (en banc), *cert. denied,* 488 U.S. 893 (1988)—no cause of action for wrongful birth, but listing 17 states recognizing such a cause of action; Goforth v. Porter Medical Associates, Inc., 755 P.2d 678 (Okla. 1988)]

(1) **Healthy children:** [§998]   The modern trend is to permit recovery for the costs of raising an unwanted healthy child [Zehr v. Haugen, 871 P.2d 1006 (Or. 1994)—negligently performed sterilization makes surgeon liable for costs of child's upbringing where goal of family was to avoid added financial stress], but not all courts agree [*see* O'Toole v. Greenberg, 64 N.Y.2d 427 (1985)—denying upbringing costs]. States that do permit the action usually *offset* benefits of the birth against the recoverable expenses. [Burke v. Rivo, 551 N.E.2d 1 (Mass. 1990); *but see* Marciniak v. Lundborg, 450 N.W.2d 243 (Wis. 1990)—emotional benefits of birth not set off against economic harm from birth]

(a) **Note:** If recovery is allowed, plaintiffs do *not* have a duty to limit their damages (under the doctrine of avoidable consequences in tort or mitigation in a breach of contract action) by aborting the child.

[Johnson v. University Hospital of Cleveland, 540 N.E.2d 1370 (Ohio 1989)]

(b) **Statutory limitation:** Some states have adopted legislation barring actions for the "wrongful birth" of healthy children. [Edmonds v. Western Pennsylvania Hospital Radiation Associates, 607 A.2d 1083 (Pa. 1992), *cert. denied,* 510 U.S. 814 (1993)—upholding such a statute against constitutional challenge]

(2) **Unhealthy children:** [§999] Courts are split on what recoveries are available to parents who, through medical malpractice, conceive and bear children with genetic defects.

(a) **Economic harm:** [§1000] Most courts permit recovery for the extraordinary medical and related expenses due to the nature of the child's condition, but not for the usual child-rearing expenses that would have occurred had the child been normal. [Schroeder v. Perkel, 432 A.2d 834 (N.J. 1981); Greco v. United States, 893 P.2d 345 (Nev. 1995)]

1) **Note:** The damages will include those for the child's adult life as well as childhood if the state requires parents to support disabled adult children. [Smith v. Cole, 531 A.2d 341 (N.H. 1986)]

(b) **Emotional distress:** [§1001] In many states, parents may recover for emotional distress caused by the birth of the unhealthy child. [Berman v. Allan, 404 A.2d 8 (N.J. 1979); Greco v. United States, *supra*]

(c) **No "wrongful life" suit by child:** [§1002] Almost all states bar a suit by the unhealthy child. [Walker v. Most, 790 P.2d 735 (Ariz. 1990)—no "legally recognizable" injury; *but see* Procanik v. Cillo, 478 A.2d 755 (N.J. 1984)—child can recover extraordinary expenses for specialized treatment likely to be needed as an adult, but not general damages for being born in an unhealthy condition]

3. **Intentional Interference with Family Relationships**

a. **Alienation of affections**

(1) **Early view—recovery:** [§1003] At common law, and still in many states, a husband could sue a third party who had intentionally alienated the affections of his wife. Since the wife was considered an "asset" of her husband, the wife was allowed no similar action.

(2) **Modern view—split over spousal claim**

(a) **Action abolished:** [§1004] Most states have abolished the action by either judicial or legislative action. [Russo v. Sutton, 422 S.E.2d 750 (S.C. 1992)—listing 40 states]

(b) **Action preserved:** [§1005] Where the action has been preserved, *either* spouse may bring it. [Kline v. Ansell, 414 A.2d 929 (Md. 1980)]

(3) **Modern view—parent-child claims rejected:** [§1006] When parents sue for alienation of a child's affections, or vice versa, the claim generally has been rejected because of fear of abuse and the potential impact on family relations. [Wheeler v. Luhman, 305 N.W.2d 426 (Iowa 1981)—child cannot recover for alienation of mother's affections; Bock v. Lindquist, 278 N.W.2d 326 (Minn. 1979)—father cannot recover for loss of 10-year-old child's affections]

    (a) **Application:** Suits by parents against religious groups for the alienation of the affection of their adult children have also been rejected. [Radecki v. Schackhardt, 361 N.E.2d 543 (Ohio 1976); Schuppin v. Unification Church, 435 F. Supp. 603 (D. Vt.), *aff'd without opinion,* 573 F.2d 1295 (2d Cir. 1977)]

    (b) **But note:** Some states recognize a cause of action against one who abducts or entices away a minor child. [Silcott v. Oglesby, 721 S.W.2d 290 (Tex. 1986)]

b. **Criminal conversation**

(1) **Early views:** [§1007] At early common law, a plaintiff could sue for damages for "criminal conversation" if he could prove that the defendant had had sexual relations with the plaintiff's wife. A few states did not require a showing of intercourse. In no state could the wife sue.

(2) **Modern view:** [§1008] Most states have *abolished* this action because of its potential for blackmail and doubt about its deterrent value. [Thomas v. Siddiqui, 869 S.W.2d 740 (Mo. 1994)]

c. **Intentional interference with custodial rights:** [§1009] In recent years, several states have recognized a cause of action for intentional interference with a parent-child custodial relationship, often arising in the context of a divorce or child-custody suit. [Rest. 2d §700; D&D Fuller CATV Construction, Inc. v. Pace, 780 P.2d 520 (Colo. 1989)—grandparents who aided father in kidnapping child from mother may be held liable; *but see* Larson v. Dunn, 460 N.W.2d 39 (Minn. 1990)—rejecting tort claim against spouse for felony refusal to return child because tort not in child's best interest]

d. **Compare—emotional distress claims:** [§1010] The courts are split over whether to permit an action for intentional infliction of emotional distress where the action closely resembles one for alienation of affections or criminal conversation that has been *barred* by the state. [Figueiredo-Torres v. Nickel, 584 A.2d 69 (Md. 1991)—despite abolition of actions for alienation of affections and criminal conversation, patient could sue psychologist for commencing romantic relationship with patient's wife while treating couple for marital problems; *but see* Koestler v. Pollard, 471 N.W.2d 7 (Wis. 1991)—state policy against actions for criminal conversation would be subverted if claim could be framed for emotional distress by alleging further facts]

D. TORT IMMUNITY

1. **Intrafamily Tort Immunity**

a. **Husband-wife**

(1) **Common law—absolute immunity between spouses:** [§1011] The common law regarded the husband and wife as a single legal entity, and accordingly provided that husband and wife could not sue each other for personal injury torts committed by one upon the other, whether before or during marriage. [Thompson v. Thompson, 218 U.S. 611 (1910)]

(2) **Abolition of immunity in most states:** [§1012] Virtually all jurisdictions today have *rejected* the doctrine of interspousal tort immunity entirely, rejecting the common law fiction of a single legal identity for husband and wife. Some have abolished the immunity only as to intentional torts, while others have abolished it as to *all* torts, intentional or negligent. [Price v. Price, 732 S.W.2d 316 (Tex. 1987); *but see* Alfree v. Alfree, 410 A.2d 161 (Del. 1979)—contra]

(3) **Where immunity not applicable:** [§1013] Even where interspousal immunity has been retained, it does not apply where:

(a) **Both spouses are deceased:** [§1014] If a husband and wife are both killed in a traffic accident caused by the husband's negligence, the wife's heirs are permitted to maintain suit against the husband's estate for the wrongful death of the wife. [First Union National Bank v. Hackney, 145 S.E.2d 352 (N.C. 1965)]

1) **Comment:** In such a case, the beneficiaries of the wife's estate are usually the same persons who are the beneficiaries of the husband's estate, but liability insurance motivates the suit.

(b) **Respondeat superior—third party liability:** [§1015] If the husband was acting in the course and scope of his employment for a third party (D) at the time he injured his wife, the fact that the husband is immune from suit for his wife's injuries does *not* shield the employer, D. Thus, the wife can sue employer D under respondeat superior; and D may have no right to indemnity from the husband. (*See* Agency and Partnership Summary.)

b. **Parent-child:** [§1016] Although no such immunity was recognized under the English common law, the early American decisions held that a child could not sue his parents (nor a parent her child) for *personal* torts. *Rationale:* This rule was to preserve family harmony and parental authority. [Hewlett v. George, 9 So. 885 (Miss. 1891)]

(1) **Limitation—no immunity for property torts:** [§1017] The immunity was recognized *only as to personal torts*. It never applied to bar causes of action by a child against a parent for damage to the child's property.

(2) **Modern trend rejects immunity:** [§1018] Because of the obvious unfairness in many cases, the clear trend of authority today is to *restrict or reject* the concept of parent-child immunity.

(a) **Restricted to negligence:** [§1019]   Most courts have confined any immunity to negligence cases, thus *allowing* a child to sue his parent, or vice versa, only for willful torts. [Schlessinger v. Schlessinger, 796 P.2d 1385 (Colo. 1990)]

(b) **Abolished:** [§1020]   A growing number of states have abolished parent-child immunity entirely—on the ground that *liability insurance* exists in most cases, so that there really is no "threat to family harmony." [Anderson v. Stream, 295 N.W.2d 595 (Minn. 1980)]

   1) **Limited duty:** [§1021]   Some states that have abolished the immunity nonetheless do not impose a full duty of due care in the parental situation. [Zikely v. Zikely, 98 App. Div. 2d 815 (1983), *affirmed on opinion below,* 62 N.Y.2d 907 (1984)—mother owes no duty of careful supervision over child who was scalded after being left unsupervised while tub was filling]

   2) **Full duty:** [§1022]   Other states have imposed a normal duty of due care on the parent with the fact of parentage being one of the factors going into the analysis. [Hartman by Hartman v. Hartman, 821 S.W.2d 852 (Mo. 1991)—test is what an ordinarily reasonable and prudent *parent* would have done in similar circumstances]

   3) **And note:** Parental immunity may not be a bar to recovery where there are allegations of negligence arising *apart* from any duty to supervise the child. [Cates v. Cates, 619 N.E.2d 715 (Ill. 1993)—father driving negligently]

c. **Other relationships:** [§1023]   Even where still recognized, the doctrine of intrafamily tort immunity does not extend to relationships other than husband-wife and parent-child. Thus, for example, brothers and sisters can sue each other on any type of claim [Midkiff v. Midkiff, 113 S.E.2d 875 (Va. 1960)], although some states bar suit by one child for harm caused by a sibling's negligent supervision [Smith v. Sapienza, 52 N.Y.2d 82 (1981)].

2. Governmental Tort Immunity (Sovereign Immunity)

a. **Traditional doctrine:** [§1024]   At common law, when a plaintiff attempted to sue the State for a personal wrong, the State was held to be immune from tort liability. [Russell v. Men of Devon, 100 Eng. Rep. 359 (1798)]

(1) **State and federal:** [§1025]   Following this doctrine, it is usually held that not only are state and federal governments immune from tort liability, but so also are various state and federal agencies (hospitals, schools, etc.).

(2) **Municipalities—no immunity for "proprietary" functions:** [§1026] A great deal of law has developed regarding the tort liability of municipal corporations. The law limits tort immunity to the *"governmental"* or "public" functions. A municipality's *"proprietary"* or "private" functions are *not* immune and may therefore result in tort liability.

(a) **"Governmental" vs. "proprietary" functions:** [§1027] The difficulty arises in attempting to determine which city functions are "governmental" and which are "proprietary":

1) **"Governmental" functions:** [§1028] "Governmental" functions are those functions that can be performed adequately *only* by the governments—*i.e.,* police, fire, courts, etc.

2) **"Proprietary" functions:** [§1029] "Proprietary" functions are those functions that the city performs, but which *could as well be provided by a private corporation* and particularly where the city derives revenue from the operation—water, gas, electricity, public halls, etc.

a) **Example:** The construction and maintenance of public streets, highways, sewers, or other public improvements are generally regarded as "proprietary" functions, but there is a minority view contra.

b. **Status of doctrine today:** [§1030] Many state courts have *abolished* the doctrine of sovereign immunity. [Molitor v. Kaneland Community Unit District No. 302, 163 N.E.2d 89 (Ill. 1959); Muskopf v. Corning Hospital District, 55 Cal. 2d 211 (1961)]

(1) **Legislative response:** [§1031] State legislatures have often responded to judicial abolition by reenacting some limited form of governmental immunity. [*See* Cal. Gov't Code §§945 *et seq.*]

(2) **Equal protection not violated:** [§1032] Sovereign immunity does not violate equal protection of the laws. [Martinez v. California, 444 U.S. 277 (1980)—statutory denial of state's liability for parole decision is valid]

(3) **Federal Tort Claims Act:** [§1033] The Federal Tort Claims Act ("FTCA") abolishes tort immunity (*i.e.,* permits the federal government to be held liable) for *"negligence* or other wrongful act or omission" by government employees, plus most *intentional* torts by *federal investigative or law enforcement* officers. However, immunity is *retained* for other intentional torts, and for strict liability and *"discretionary"* acts by government employees. [28 U.S.C. §§1346, 2671 *et seq.*]

(a) **Immunity for intentional tort of agent:** [§1034] Where a government employee commits a battery, but the suit claim is based on the negligence of the government in hiring the employee, some courts hold that the claim is based on battery and thus barred. [Johnson v. United States, 788 F.2d 845 (2d Cir.), *cert. denied,* 479 U.S. 914 (1986); *but see* Bennett v. United States, 803 F.2d 1502 (9th Cir. 1986)—contra]

(b) *Feres* **doctrine:** [§1035] Under a judicially created exception to the FTCA, members of the armed forces injured "in the course of activity incident to service" are *denied tort recoveries* against the government. [Feres v. United States, 340 U.S. 135 (1950)] The Supreme Court has expanded this restriction to injuries that occur outside the command structure [United States v. Stanley, 483 U.S. 669 (1987)—army officer given LSD without his knowledge during an experiment] and where the tort is committed by a federal civilian employee [United States v. Johnson, 481 U.S. 681 (1987)].

(c) **Government contractor defense:** [§1036] A government contractor may generally assert the federal government's immunity as a defense to a products liability claim where it can show that it followed reasonably precise government specifications, and that it warned the government about any patent errors in the design or use of the equipment. [Boyle v. United Technologies Corp., 487 U.S. 500 (1988)]

c. **Liability of governmental officers:** [§1037] In addition to the government's immunity, government officers in their private capacity may also be immune.

(1) **High-ranking officers:** [§1038] Judges, legislators, and high-ranking members of the executive branch (*e.g.,* cabinet members and department heads) are *completely immune* from tort liability for acts carried out *within the scope of their duties*, even if their conduct involves "malice" or "abuse of discretion." [Barr v. Matteo, *infra,* §1237—extending common law absolute privilege to acting director of a federal agency]

(2) **Lower-level officers**

(a) **Federal law:** [§1039] Lower-level administrative officers or employees are immune from claims of *negligence* under *federal* law; and some states also follow this position.

(b) **Some states—no immunity for "ministerial" functions:** [§1040] Other states retain the common law rule that granted immunity to lower-level governmental officers or employees only when performing "discretionary" (as opposed to "ministerial") functions.

1) **"Discretionary" functions:** [§1041] "Discretionary" functions are those in which the officer has some element of personal judgment or decisionmaking (*e.g.,* evaluating property for assessment purposes or designing or routing a highway). In carrying out these functions, the officer is granted immunity as long as she was acting *honestly and in good faith*. [*See* Ross v. Consumers Power Co., 363 N.W.2d 641 (Mich. 1984)]

2) **"Ministerial" functions:** [§1042] "Ministerial" functions are those in which the officer is left no choice of her own; she is carrying out orders of others or established duties of her office (*e.g.,* repairing roads, driving vehicles). Here, there is no tort immunity. If the officer negligently fails to perform her required duties properly, she can be held personally liable for any damages resulting therefrom—even if she was acting in good faith. [Gardels v. Murphy, 377 F. Supp. 1389 (N.D. Ill. 1974)—

White House "advancemen" liable for roughing up demonstrator]

(3) **Statutory changes:** [§1043]   Under the Civil Rights Act of 1871 [42 U.S.C. §1983], a person acting under color of *state law* who deprives anyone of a *federal* constitutional'right is subject to liability for damages.

(a) **Basis of liability:** [§1044]   It now appears that liability will lie only for intentional and malicious behavior or "deliberate indifference." [Estelle v. Gamble, 429 U.S. 97 (1976)—for a section 1983 action, failure to adequately treat prisoner's medical problems must be result of "deliberate indifference"; Wilson v. Seiter, 501 U.S. 294 (1991)]

(b) **Interests protected:** [§1045]   Although it is clear that interests in physical well-being and freedom from improper incarceration are protected under section 1983 [Imbler v. Pachtman, 424 U.S. 409 (1976)], beyond this the limits are not yet clear [Siegert v. Gilley, 500 U.S. 226 (1991)—interest in reputation not protected under Fourteenth Amendment as either "liberty" or "property"].

(c) **Defenses:** [§1046]   The statute is silent about defenses, and no general rules have emerged. Some officials have received absolute immunity from liability while others have been given only qualified immunity. [Briscoe v. LaHue, 460 U.S. 325 (1983)—police witness at trial has absolute immunity; Pierson v. Ray, 386 U.S. 547 (1967)—judge has absolute immunity against damage liability; Pulliam v. Allen, 466 U.S. 522 (1984)—judicial immunity no bar to award of attorney's fees; Scheuer v. Rhodes, 416 U.S. 232 (1974)—state governor has only qualified immunity, which requires reasonable behavior and good faith; Wood v. Strickland, 420 U.S. 308 (1975)—school official has only qualified immunity]

1) **Municipalities:** [§1047]   When municipalities are sued under section 1983 (usually for failure to establish official guidelines to guide staff behavior), they have *no immunities* at all and may not rely on the good faith of the officials involved. [Owen v. City of Independence, 445 U.S. 622 (1980)]

(d) **Compare—federal agents:** [§1048]   Although federal agents are not covered under section 1983 (since the statute applies only to persons acting under color of *state* law), analogous civil liability may still be imposed if their behavior violates federal constitutional rights. [Bivens v. Six Unknown Named Agents, 403 U.S. 388 (1971)—Fourth Amendment violation by FBI agents gives rise to damage action]

1) **Defenses:** [§1049]   The defenses are also analogous to those under section 1983. [Cleavinger v. Saxner, 474 U.S. 193 (1985)—members of federal prison disciplinary committee have qualified immunity; Hunter v. Bryant, 502 U.S. 224 (1992)—Secret Service agents have qualified immunity for arrest]

3. Charitable Immunity

a. **Common law doctrine:** [§1050] A separate ground of tort immunity was recognized at common law for nongovernmental, charitable organizations and enterprises. [Parks v. Northwestern, 75 N.E. 991 (Ill. 1905)]

   (1) **Rationale:** A rationale sometimes advanced for the doctrine of charitable immunity is that the funds upon which a charity operates are donated, and that subjecting such funds to the payment of tort claims would divert them from the purpose intended by the donor. [Feoffees of Heriot's Hospital v. Ross, 8 Eng. Rep. 1508 (1846)]

   (2) **Application:** Thus it was held for many years that private charities—hospitals, schools, community organizations (*e.g.,* Y.M.C.A.)—were not liable for torts committed by their agents or employees.

b. **Status today:** [§1051] Almost all states have repudiated the doctrine, with courts finding that any interest in protecting "a good Samaritan" is *outweighed* by the need to provide compensation to victims of the Samaritan's negligence. [Bing v. Thunig, 2 N.Y.2d 656 (1957); *but see* Moore v. Warren, 463 S.E.2d 459 (Va. 1995)—volunteer was immune from liability because driving for charitable organization at time of accident]

   (1) **Middle ground:** [§1052] Some states have legislation that makes charities liable in tort but only to a limited extent. [English v. New England Medical Center, Inc., 541 N.E.2d 329 (Mass. 1989), *cert. denied,* 493 U.S. 1056 (1990)—statute limiting size of judgments against charities to $20,000 is constitutional; *but see* Hanvey v. Oconee Memorial Hospital, 416 S.E.2d 623 (S.C. 1992)—statute limiting liability of charitable hospital to $100,000 violates state constitution's Equal Protection Clause]

E. RELEASE AND CONTRIBUTION AMONG JOINT TORTFEASORS

1. **Introduction:** [§1053] Various rules evolved at common law to cover "joint tortfeasors"—*i.e.,* persons who have either (i) acted *in concert* (by agreement) for the purpose of causing the plaintiff's injury; *or* (ii) acted entirely independently but whose acts have caused a single *indivisible injury* to plaintiff (*e.g.,* two negligent motorists who collide, causing a single injury to a pedestrian). Joint tortfeasors were traditionally *jointly and severally liable* for the harm they cause. (*See supra,* §329.)

   a. **Note:** Where there is an indivisible injury, simultaneous conduct may not be necessary to a finding of joint and several liability. [Ravo by Ravo v. Rogatnick, 70 N.Y.2d 533 (1987)—pediatrician whose negligent treatment of infant contributed to injury that infant suffered at birth due to negligence of obstetrician was jointly and severally liable for indivisible injury]

2. **Judgment and Satisfaction:** [§1054] An unsatisfied judgment against one of several joint tortfeasors does not bar the plaintiff's action against the others. [Verhoeks v. Gillivan, 221 N.W. 287 (Mich. 1928)] However, the *satisfaction* of a judgment against one tortfeasor extinguishes the cause of action and bars any later

suit for a greater or additional amount against any of the others. *Rationale:* Satisfaction of the court-ordered amount is the equivalent of payment of the damages sustained.

3. **Releases—Early Rule:** [§1055]   Some courts originally held that a claim or a judgment was extinguished if plaintiff released one of several joint tortfeasors—*i.e.,* "release of one operates to release all"—and this held true regardless of the sufficiency of compensation paid for the release. [Aljian v. Schlossberg, 73 A.2d 290 (N.J. 1950)]

   a. **Rejection of early rule:** [§1056]   A growing number of states have by statute *rejected* this rule entirely. [*See, e.g.,* Cal. Civ. Proc. Code §877—release does not discharge other tortfeasors, but reduces claims against them; Unif. Comp. Fault Act §6]

   b. **Avoidance of early rule:** [§1057]   Many courts have circumvented the doctrine that a release of one releases all joint tortfeasors by upholding a release with reservation of rights (*i.e.,* a provision in the release that it will not prejudice the plaintiff's rights against other tortfeasors) or by permitting a *covenant not to sue* (or a covenant not to execute on a judgment) in lieu of a release. [Cox v. Pearl Investment Co., 450 P.2d 60 (Colo. 1969)] Other courts have held that a release discharges only those parties it specifically names. [Alsup v. Firestone Tire & Rubber Co., 461 N.E.2d 361 (Ill. 1984)]

4. **Contribution**

   a. **Common law—no contribution:** [§1058]   The common law rule was that "no contribution is allowed between joint tortfeasors," meaning that if a judgment was recovered and satisfied against one tortfeasor, he had no right to recover from the others their pro rata share. *Rationale:* A "wrongdoer" should not invoke the aid of the courts to force other wrongdoers to help him shoulder the load.

   b. **Modern view—contribution allowed in negligence cases:** [§1059]   Today, virtually all states permit contribution among *negligent* (but not intentional) joint tortfeasors. Thus, contribution is *not* allowed where punitive damages are awarded. [Smith v. Lightning Bolt Productions, Inc., 861 F.2d 363 (2d Cir. 1988)—highly culpable defendant should not be allowed chance to escape payment of imposed penalty]

      (1) **But note:** Contribution operates only in systems that apply joint and several liability. Many states have abolished that rule or restricted its application. (*See infra,* §1118.)

   c. **Impact of comparative negligence:** [§1060]   Many states have retained the rule of joint and several liability among joint tortfeasors notwithstanding the adoption of comparative negligence. The purpose of comparative negligence is to protect negligent *plaintiffs* against the harshness of the "all or nothing" rule of contributory negligence, rather than to eliminate joint and several liability. [Ravo by Ravo v. Rogatnick, *supra,* §1053—each joint tortfeasor remains individually liable for all damages caused, but contribution allowed between them on *comparative* fault basis]

d. **Limitation:** [§1061]   Joint and several liability may be inconsistent with the rationale of market share liability (*see supra,* §338) if the goal is to match an individual defendant's *total* liability to its market share. Since a manufacturer with a small market share could be liable for damages of an insolvent manufacturer with a large market share, defendants are only *severally* liable for damages under most versions of market share liability theory. [Brown v. Superior Court, 44 Cal. 3d 1049 (1988)]

F. INDEMNITY

1. **Doctrine:** [§1062]   A defendant who is only *secondarily* liable for the plaintiff's injury, but is sued and forced to pay a judgment, is entitled to indemnification against the party who was *primarily* responsible for causing the injury. [Panasuk v. Seaton, 277 F. Supp. 979 (D. Mont. 1968)]

   a. **Rationale:** Indemnity is an *equitable* remedy granted to *prevent the unjust enrichment* that would occur if one whose liability was merely secondary could be forced to bear the debts of the real "wrongdoer."

   b. **Distinguish from contribution:** Contribution involves wrongdoers who are *jointly and severally* liable; it requires that each pay his *proportionate share*. Indemnity involves one who is *primarily* responsible for an injury; it shifts the *entire* loss to his shoulders from another who has been compelled to pay it because he was *secondarily* liable therefor.

2. **Application**

   a. **Vicarious liability cases:** [§1063]   The most common application of the doctrine is where the responsibility for the plaintiff's injury lies entirely with one defendant, but another has been held *vicariously* liable therefor. *Example:* Employee E is negligent in driving Employer R's truck, resulting in injuries to P; P sues and recovers judgment against R on the basis of respondeat superior (*see supra,* §497). R is entitled to indemnification against E—whether or not P sued E.

      (1) **Other examples:** Similarly, a defendant is entitled to indemnification where she has been held liable under "permissive use" statutes or the family purpose doctrine (*see supra,* §§491-492), or for negligent performance of work by an independent contractor.

   b. **Differing degrees of culpability:** [§1064]   In states with joint and several liability, indemnity is also available where the defendants are both directly liable to the plaintiff, but the *degree* of their culpability differs greatly. [Building Supply Co. v. McCabe, 77 A.2d 368 (Pa. 1951)]

      (1) **Example:** A retailer who is held *strictly liable* for injuries caused by a defective product she sells may obtain indemnity against the manufacturer whose *negligence* (usually shown by the defect itself) caused the product to malfunction.

      (2) **Example:** Similarly, where the plaintiff has been injured as a result of concurrent acts, one negligent and one intentional, the defendant who was only negligent may be entitled to indemnity against the defendant who committed the intentional tort.

(3) **And note:** In a few states, a defendant who was only *"passively"* negligent (*i.e.,* nonfeasance—such as failing to discover dangerous condition) may be entitled to indemnity from a defendant who was *"actively"* negligent (*i.e.,* misfeasance—such as creating a dangerous condition). [Rossmoor Sanitation, Inc. v. Pylon, Inc., 13 Cal. 3d 622 (1975)]

c. **Aggravation cases:** [§1065] Where an original negligent tortfeasor has been held liable under proximate cause principles for a physician's negligent aggravation (*see supra,* §373), the original tortfeasor is entitled to indemnity from the physician for the aggravation damages.

(1) **But note:** A minority view is contra. [Stuart v. Hertz Corp., 351 So. 2d 703 (Fla. 1977)]

VII. STATUTORY CHANGES IN PERSONAL INJURY LAW

chapter approach

In this century, pressure has repeatedly been brought to bear on state legislatures to change various aspects of traditional tort law. Motivations for change have varied from concerns about inadequate compensation or inefficiency in the system to concerns that damage awards had become excessive. Attempts at tort reform in response to these pressures highlight some of the basic policy problems in tort law. One example of the legislative response is comparative negligence (discussed _supra_, §§665 _et seq._), which was instituted by the state legislatures in most states. As with comparative negligence, the legislative response has sometimes been directed at the entire tort system; sometimes it has targeted specific kinds of tort claims.

A. CHANGES TARGETING SPECIFIC KINDS OF TORT CLAIMS

1. Workers' Compensation

a. **Motivation:** [§1066]   With the industrial revolution came a steadily increasing number of injuries and deaths among workers. Under traditional tort principles, many workers were completely barred from recovery by their own contributory negligence. In addition, two new tort principles emerged during this period: assumption of risk, which barred recovery by any worker who perceived the dangers of his employment, and the fellow-servant doctrine, which provided that the employer could not be held vicariously liable for the negligence of a plaintiff's co-worker. In combination, these three doctrines made recovery by injured workers virtually impossible.

b. **Response:** [§1067]   Early in the 20th century, the states removed from the tort system virtually all claims for personal injury by workers against their employers. The tort system was replaced with a comprehensive system of workers' compensation that now covers well over 80% of all workers, and is probably the most substantial statutory change in personal injury law to have occurred in the United States. (It is the subject of a separate course in many law schools.)

    (1) **Operation of workers' compensation system**

        (a) **Mandatory insurance:** [§1068]   In almost every state, private employers are required to acquire workers' compensation insurance to cover their employees.

        (b) **Scope of coverage:** [§1069]   The insurance extends to all claims for personal injury that arise out of and in the course of the worker's employment, **_without regard to fault_**.

        (c) **Processing of claims:** [§1070]   A worker who is not satisfied with the settlement offered by the insurance company may file an administrative claim. After the agency hearing, a dissatisfied party may appeal to an administrative board and then, in most states, to a state appellate court, but only on legal questions.

    (d) **Amounts recoverable:** [§1071] Most workers recover all their medical expenses and roughly two-thirds of their lost wages. Although traditional noneconomic damages, such as pain and suffering, are not available, all states provide lump sum payments for loss of bodily parts or functions.

(2) Impact of worker's compensation on tort recovery

    (a) **Exclusive remedy against employer:** [§1072] A worker whose claim falls within the workers' compensation system cannot sue the employer in tort. Claims by family members are generally also barred, even though workers' compensation may provide no benefits to an injured worker's family.

        1) **Application:** Even though the injury is covered, a particular harm suffered by the worker (such as loss of smell) may not be compensable under the statute. Generally, no tort remedy is available to the worker in this situation. [Fetterhoff v. Western Block Co., 49 App. Div. 2d 1001 (1975)—no tort remedy for worker's noncompensable loss of sexual function]

        2) **Exception—intentional tort:** [§1073] In some states a worker may escape coverage of the workers' compensation system by showing that the injury resulted from the employer's commission of an intentional tort that was not suffered in the course of the employment. [Magliulo v. Superior Court, 47 Cal. App. 3d 760 (1975)—allowing tort action to waitress who alleged that she was injured when her employer hit her in anger and threw her down; *but see* Livitsanos v. Superior Court, 2 Cal. 4th 744 (1992)—no tort remedy for emotional distress intentionally or negligently inflicted by employer if occurrence was within the "normal risks" of the employment relationship, even if the compensation system offered no remedy because no disability had been suffered]

    (b) **Claims against third parties allowed:** [§1074] In most states, workers can bring tort actions against third parties involved in the injury. For example, a worker can sue the manufacturer of a defective piece of equipment.

        1) **Effect of compensation:** [§1075] A worker who accepts compensation does not waive the right to sue a third party in tort.

        2) **Collateral sources rule:** [§1076] The collateral sources rule (*supra*, §434) generally **prevents** the third party from reducing its damages by bringing in evidence of the compensation payments made by the employer.

3) **Employer's right to reimbursement:** [§1077] The employer generally has a lien on the worker's tort recovery to cover the compensation payments it has made to the worker. In addition, if the worker fails to sue a third party, the employer can bring a tort action in the worker's name. [Boldman v. Mt. Hood Chemical Corp., 602 P.2d 1072 (Or. 1979)] In some states, the amount recoverable is reduced if the employer's negligence has contributed to the injury.

4) **Third party's right to reimbursement:** [§1078] If the employer was also at fault in the worker's injury, most states hold that the exclusivity of workers' compensation *bars* the third party from seeking contribution or indemnity from the employer. [1982 Duke L.J. 483]

2. "No-Fault" Auto Insurance

a. **Motivation:** [§1079] Because auto accidents are so numerous and include so many small claims, auto cases suffer particularly from many of the problems that critics identify with a fault-based system: delays in receiving payments from liability insurers, malapportionment of benefits by which small claims are treated very generously, inefficiency, high insurance premiums, and dishonesty.

b. **Response:** [§1080] Almost half the states have changed the handling of auto accident claims by adopting "no-fault" insurance plans.

(1) **Operation of "no-fault" plans:** [§1081] Although the plans adopted vary considerably, the following are the essential provisions:

(a) **Mandatory insurance:** [§1082] All car owners are required to obtain and keep in effect insurance to cover claims arising out of the operation of their cars.

(b) **Scope of coverage:** [§1083] The insurance extends to all claims of injury arising out of the use or operation of any motor vehicle, *without regard to fault*.

1) **Note:** This includes claims allowed under traditional tort concepts, as well as certain claims not currently allowed—*e.g.*, claims by drivers who hurt themselves solely through their own fault.

(c) **Claims handled on "first party" basis:** [§1084] Injured car occupants usually make claims against the policy covering the cars they were riding in, so that in the typical two-car crash, the occupants of each car claim against the insurance covering that car.

1) **Note:** Pedestrians injured by autos generally make claims against the insurance covering the cars that struck them. (Under a few plans, though, pedestrians who own cars make a claim against their own insurers.)

2) **Comment:** Since fault is immaterial, the claims procedure is relatively simple, and any disagreement between the policy holder and the insurance company as to the amount recoverable is subject to arbitration.

(d) **Damages recoverable:** [§1085] None of the statutes provides coverage for pain and suffering or disfigurement. Coverage is limited to economic losses (lost wages, medical bills, etc.). However, the plans vary considerably as to the maximum coverage, from $1,000 or $2,000 to as much as $50,000 and more.

(2) **Impact of "no-fault" plans**

(a) **Curtailment of tort litigation:** [§1086] The plans vary concerning the extent to which traditional negligence actions (with traditional "fault" principles) are still permitted.

1) **"Partial" abolition:** [§1087] All existing statutes allow tort actions in at least some situations.

a) **Application:** Under some plans, tort actions against other drivers can still be maintained for all but relatively minor cases. Thus, at one extreme, a plaintiff can sue for pain and suffering whenever medical expenses exceed $500.

b) **Compare:** Under other plans, specifically those (*e.g.*, in Michigan, New York) with generous first-party benefits, only cases of serious injury can be pursued in court—such as death, permanent injury or disfigurement, or inability to work for more than six consecutive months.

2) **"Add-on" statutes:** [§1088] Some states have simply added a no-fault system to the tort liability system already in place. Any auto victim who receives no-fault compensation can still sue in tort as before. The no-fault insurer has subrogation rights up to the amount it has paid to the victim under no-fault.

(b) **Elimination of double recovery by injured persons:** [§1089] Most plans prevent the injured party from obtaining a duplicate recovery for the same economic losses. This is usually accomplished by making no-fault insurance the primary source of benefits, or by providing for automatic subrogation for any payments made under any other insurance.

c. **Future of no-fault:** [§1090] The future of automobile no-fault insurance is somewhat uncertain. In recent years, some states have returned to the fault system.

3. **Medical Malpractice**

a. **Motivation:** [§1091] In the mid-1970s, physicians and surgeons were faced with rapidly escalating malpractice insurance rates.

b. **Response:** [§1092]   Virtually every state has since adopted legislation addressing the problem. However, statutory provisions vary.

    (1) **Shortened statute of limitations:** [§1093]   The most common change is to shorten the statute of limitations. Minors are often required to sue within eight or ten years of the infliction of injury, rather than being able to wait until they reach majority. [*But see* Kenyon v. Hammer, 688 P.2d 961 (Ariz. 1984)—statute violates state Equal Protection Clause]

    (2) **Limits on pain and suffering:** [§1094]   A few states have placed limits on the amount that can be recovered for pain and suffering. [Fein v. Permanente Medical Group, 38 Cal. 3d 137, *appeal dismissed*, 474 U.S. 892 (1985)—statute limiting pain and suffering recovery in malpractice cases to $250,000 is constitutional; *but see* Carson v. Maurer, 424 A.2d 825 (N.H. 1980)—cap on nonpecuniary damages violates equal protection under state constitution]

    (3) **Periodic payments:** [§1095]   Some states provide that if an award exceeds some minimum figure, the judge may or must require that it be paid periodically rather than in a single lump sum. If the victim dies before all payments are made, amounts still unpaid for pain and suffering and for expected future medical expenses need no longer be paid. [American Bank & Trust Co. v. Community Hospital, 36 Cal. 3d 359 (1984)]

    (4) **Legal fees:** [§1096]   Some states have set sliding scale limits on the size of contingent fees. The limits are lower than the rates generally prevailing. [Roe v. Lodi Medical Group, 37 Cal. 3d 920 (1985)—upholding limits; *but see* Carson v. Maurer, *supra*—limits violate equal protection]

    (5) **Collateral sources:** [§1097]   Some states have provided that if the plaintiff has received first party insurance benefits or other help in meeting the costs imposed by the defendant's malpractice, the trier may deduct these benefits from the award. [Barme v. Wood, 37 Cal. 3d 174 (1984)—upholding provision; *but see* Farley v. Engelken, 740 P.2d 1058 (Kan. 1987)—preferential treatment to health care providers violates equal protection]

    (6) **Malpractice panels:** [§1098]   A few states have created three-member panels, consisting of a physician, an attorney, and a judge, to conduct a pretrial liability review. If the panel reaches a unanimous decision on the merits of the malpractice claim after an informal hearing, that determination is admissible as evidence in any later trial. [Treyball v. Clark, 65 N.Y.2d 589 (1985)—statute does not violate party's right to jury trial nor deny due process; *but see* Bernier v. Burris, 497 N.E.2d 763 (Ill. 1986)—statute impermissibly requires judge to share decisionmaking authority with panel members]

4. **Products Liability**

a. **Motivation:** [§1099]   The common law development of products liability led groups of manufacturers and retailers to seek legislation to moderate the financial impact of the new rules.

b. **Response:** [§1100]   Despite calls for congressional action based on a need for national uniformity, Congress has so far refused to enact comprehensive statutory changes to govern products liability claims. About half of the states, most of them nonindustrial states, have adopted legislation drawing back in some respects from the common law rules of strict liability.

(1) **Statutes of repose:** [§1101]   The most common change has been the enactment of "statutes of repose," providing that no action may be brought on a defective product claim more than a certain number of years after the product's initial distribution. The period is usually 10 to 12 years. [Gibson v. West Virginia Department of Highways, 406 S.E.2d 440 (W. Va. 1991)—10-year statutory limitation constitutional; *but see* Berry v. Beech Aircraft Corp., 717 P.2d 670 (Utah 1985)—statute violates state constitution's guarantee of open courts]

(2) **State of the art:** [§1102]   Some states provide that a manufacturer's compliance with industry custom will bar recovery on a defective product theory.

(3) **Compliance with federal standards:** [§1103]   Some states provide that compliance with federal standards (*e.g.*, FDA regulations) may bar recovery, or may bar recovery of punitive damages.

(4) **Presumption of safety:** [§1104]   Some states provide that if the product has not caused harm for a certain number of years, the plaintiff must present "clear and convincing" proof of a claimed defect.

(5) **Manufacturer primarily liable:** [§1105]   Some statutes provide that a nonnegligent retailer or distributor may not be held liable, or may be held liable only if the manufacturer is insolvent. [Baker v. Promark Products West, Inc., 692 S.W.2d 844 (Tenn. 1985)]

(6) **Plaintiff's fault:** [§1106]   At least one state has provided that, notwithstanding comparative negligence in ordinary negligence cases, a plaintiff whose negligence contributes substantially to his injury is absolutely barred from recovery in a products liability case. [Reda Pump Co. v. Finck, 713 S.W.2d 818 (Ky. 1986)]

c. **Vaccines:** [§1107]   Vaccines pose a special problem because of their importance and the tremendous liability risk of producing them. In 1986, Congress enacted a modified no-fault compensation scheme for injuries resulting from certain childhood vaccines. The victims are first offered limited no-fault compensation. If they reject the no-fault award, they may sue in tort, but the federal statute reduces the situations in which defendants may be found liable. [42 U.S.C. §§300aa-10 *et seq.*]

5. Miscellaneous Statutory Changes to Personal Injury Law

a. **Duty to rescue:** [§1108]   A few states have passed statutes requiring a person to render reasonable assistance to one exposed to grave physical harm unless the effort would endanger the person or interfere with important duties that person owes to others. [12 Vt. Stat. Ann. §519]

b. **Dram shop liability:** [§1109]   A number of states have enacted restrictions on the liability of taverns and social hosts who serve alcohol to people who get drunk and injure third parties. [Cory v. Shierloh, 29 Cal. 3d 430 (1981)]

c. **Victims of violent crimes:** [§1110]   To meet the problems of insolvent defendants, most states have adopted legislation to provide aid to some victims of violent crimes.

    (1) **Common provisions:** [§1111]   Common features include requirements that the victim report the crime quickly and cooperate with the police. Crimes within the family are usually excluded.

    (2) **Financial hardship:** [§1112]   States are split over whether all victims are eligible, or only those who would suffer financial hardship if uncompensated. [Regan v. Crime Victims Compensation Board, 57 N.Y.2d 190 (1982)]

d. **International airplane crashes:** [§1113]   To meet problems of international legal conflicts, many nations, including the United States, have joined the Warsaw Convention, which provides the victims of any international air mishap with a strict liability recovery of a limited amount of damages. [Air France v. Saks, 470 U.S. 392 (1985); Eastern Airlines, Inc. v. Floyd, 499 U.S. 530 (1991)—no recovery for emotional distress unaccompanied by physical injury]

e. **Nuclear accidents:** [§1114]   Because of the inability of nuclear power plants to get adequate liability insurance, Congress enacted legislation to provide victims of nuclear accidents with limited no-fault compensation. Damages in excess of an individual firm's liability insurance are to be paid out of a fund to which all federal nuclear licensees must contribute. [Duke Power Co. v. Carolina Environmental Study Group, 438 U.S. 59 (1978)]

f. **Black lung compensation:** [§1115]   Because workers' compensation statutes often fail to compensate workers for occupational diseases, Congress has enacted legislation to provide no-fault compensatory payments to miners afflicted with black lung disease. [30 U.S.C. §3801]

B. CHANGES AFFECTING TORT CLAIMS GENERALLY

1. **Motivation:** [§1116]   In the mid-1980s, many perceived the entire tort system to be in a state of crisis. Damage awards were skyrocketing. Some defendants who were jointly and severally liable had to pay amounts that were grossly disproportionate to their degree of fault. Insurance premiums soared. For an increasing number of entities, liability insurance became completely unavailable.

2. **Response:** [§1117]   A large majority of the states have adopted legislation intended to deal with these problems. The most significant statutory provisions involve limitations on joint and several liability, on damages, and on the collateral sources rule.

    a. **Joint and several liability:** [§1118]   Some 40 states have enacted some form of limitation on joint and several liability. [*See* Coats v. Penrod Drilling Corp., 61 F.3d 1113 (5th Cir. 1995) (en banc)—summarizing state positions]

(1) **Abolition:** [§1119]   About 10 states have abolished joint and several liability entirely. Several more have abolished it for all *noneconomic damages*, and several more have done so for all cases in which the plaintiff is found to have been *comparatively negligent*.

(2) **Limitations based on defendant's degree of fault:** [§1120]   A number of states have decided that the fault percentages should control the abolition or restriction of joint and several liability.

    (a) **Application:** In cases in which the defendant's fault is less than the plaintiff's fault, or where the defendant's fault is less than a given percentage of the total fault, some states bar joint and several liability.

    (b) **Compare:** In a few states, the defendants are jointly and severally liable, but a defendant's liability cannot exceed his fault by more than a certain percentage (for example, a defendant who is 10% at fault may be jointly and severally liable for no more than 20% of the plaintiff's damages).

(3) **Exceptions based on nature of tort:** [§1121]   Some states that have enacted legislation curtailing joint and several liability provide that it will still be available in cases involving certain kinds of torts. For example, a state may provide that joint and several liability applies only if the defendants acted with a common plan, if they committed an intentional tort, or if the action involves defective products, toxic substances, or hazardous waste. [Smith v. Department of Insurance, 507 So. 2d 1080 (Fla. 1987)—upholding statute that abolishes joint and several liability with exceptions based on the defendant's relative fault, the nature of the tort, and the total amount of damages]

b. **Limitations on damages**

(1) **Noneconomic damages:** [§1122]   More than a quarter of the states have enacted restrictions on noneconomic damage awards. Usually these take the form of a cap on all noneconomic damages. [Murphy v. Edmonds, 601 A.2d 102 (Md. 1992)—$50,000 cap on noneconomic damages constitutional] In a few states, the cap may apply to all noneconomic damages except those for disfigurement or physical pain and suffering. [*But see* Smith v. Department of Insurance, *supra*—cap on noneconomic damages violates Florida Constitution's guarantee of access to courts]

(2) **Periodic payments:** [§1123]   A number of states have provided that if a plaintiff's award includes substantial future damages, the defendant may be permitted to make periodic payments for these future damages instead of paying a lump sum at the time of judgment. In about half of these states, periodic payments are required; in the remainder, they are at the discretion of the court. In some states, the requirement to make periodic payments ceases with the death of the plaintiff; in others, at least some payments survive the plaintiff. [22 Gonz. L. Rev. 155 (1986)]

(3) **Punitive damages:** [§1124]   Nearly half the states have enacted some form of restriction on punitive damages. [18 St. Mary's L.J. 1019 (1987)]

    (a) **Caps on damage awards:** [§1125]   Half of these states have enacted caps on punitive damage awards. These may take the form of a flat cap (*e.g.*, $150,000), a cap based on some multiple of the compensatory damages awarded, or some combination of the two.

    (b) **Heightened standard of proof:** [§1126]   A number of states have provided that the plaintiff must prove by clear and convincing evidence, or even beyond a reasonable doubt, that punitive damages are warranted. [*See* Linthicum v. Nationwide Life Insurance Co., 723 P.2d 675 (Ariz. 1986)]

    (c) **Procedural reforms:** [§1127]   Some states have called for bifurcated trials when punitive damages are sought. Others have prohibited plaintiffs from pleading punitive damages until after they have made a preliminary showing of the defendant's fault.

    (d) **Recipients:** [§1128]   Some states have required that a certain percentage of all punitive damage awards be paid to a state fund, usually either a general state fund or a victims' compensation fund. [Gordon v. State, 608 So. 2d 800 (Fla. 1992)—statute giving state 60% of all punitive damage awards is constitutional; *but see* Kirk v. Denver Publishing Co., 818 P.2d 262 (Colo. 1991)—statute giving state one-third of such awards is unconstitutional]

(4) **Miscellaneous damage provisions**

    (a) **Ad damnum clauses:** [§1129]   A handful of states have barred plaintiffs from stating in the complaint the amount of damages sought.

    (b) **Additur and remittitur:** [§1130]   A few states have increased the courts' power to modify the damage award or to order a new trial where damages awarded by the jury are either inadequate or excessive.

    (c) **Interest:** [§1131]   A handful of states have acted either to adjust the interest rate on damages or to allow plaintiffs to recover interest for the period preceding the judgment. [*See* Fleming v. Baptist General Convention, 742 P.2d 1087 (Okla. 1987)]

c. **Collateral sources rule:** [§1132]   More than a quarter of all the states have restricted the operation of the collateral sources rule (*see supra*, §434). [18 St. Mary's L.J. 883 (1987)]

(1) **Mandatory setoff:** [§1133]   Half of these states require that the amount reimbursed by a collateral source must be deducted from the plaintiff's damage award. [Ryan v. City of New York, 79 N.Y.2d 792 (1991)—statute applies only to reduce tort recovery to extent of collateral sources received for pre-verdict harm]

(2) **Discretionary setoff:** [§1134] In a few states, reduction of the plaintiff's award is at the discretion of the court or jury.

(3) **Evidentiary rules:** [§1135] A few states simply provide that evidence that the plaintiff was reimbursed will be admissible at trial.

(4) **Exceptions for certain kinds of sources:** [§1136] Generally, these statutes do not apply in cases in which the collateral source has a right of subrogation or where reimbursement was received from certain specified sources, such as life insurance.

d. **Miscellaneous general changes**

(1) **Regulation of attorneys' fees:** [§1137] A few states have set standards for the attorney's disclosure of the fee structure. Several others have provided that attorneys' fees must be based on the amount actually recovered by the plaintiff (rather than on the amount awarded), or have made fees subject to a judicial review for reasonableness. [18 St. Mary's L.J. 673 (1987)]

(2) **Sanctions for frivolous claims:** [§1138] Nearly half the states have enacted sanctions for frivolous claims. These generally provide that the attorney or the party asserting the frivolous claim must pay the costs and fees associated with defending it.

(3) **Alternative dispute resolution:** [§1139] A few states have required that claims below a certain minimum be submitted to arbitration.

VIII. DEFAMATION

___chapter approach___

The common law of defamation has always been confusing because it is such a mixture of political history, ecclesiastical law, and common law. It has always had a long prima facie case plus a long list of defenses and privileges. This alone made it hard to learn. But then the United States Supreme Court entered the field, complicating matters even more with its First Amendment rulings.

The key was that the common law operated on a principle of strict liability. The prima facie case did not include a requirement of fault. This meant that if a speaker hurt the reputation of the plaintiff by the recitation of some facts and those facts were not shown to be true, the speaker might be liable, despite a reasonable belief that the facts were true. The Supreme Court invalidated this rule of strict liability in most, but apparently not all, cases.

This means that your specific concerns in answering a defamation question include the following:

1. Note that historically the plaintiff did **not** have to prove that the statement was false. Rather, the **defendant** had to prove that it was true. (It was generally held that the plaintiff had to allege falsity, but this was a pro forma matter and did not ease the burden on the defendant.)

   But note: If the statement is made about a matter of **public concern**, constitutional limits require the **plaintiff to prove falsity**.

   And note: If the statement is made about a public figure, constitutional limitations require the plaintiff to **prove knowledge** that the defamatory statement was false **or reckless disregard** for its truth.

2. Note too the curious role played by damages in this tort. In some situations, the plaintiff must show a certain type of damages (special damages) **to recover any money at all**. At other times, that showing is not required. The type of damages suffered may control liability itself rather than simply measuring the extent of the recovery.

3. Remember that various common law **privileges** survive the constitutionalization of defamation law and may prevent liability under state law.

4. **Constitutional issues** are especially important in many defamation questions. In analyzing constitutional issues, be sure to focus on the **type of plaintiff**—whether the plaintiff is properly called "public" or "private"—and then on the nature of the defamatory statement.

5. Also remember to consider the related torts of **invasion of privacy** and **infliction of emotional distress**.

A. IN GENERAL [§1140]

Prima facie case at common law:

Publication to Third Person
Understood as Defamatory of Plaintiff
Allege Falsity
Causation
Damages
(*Falsity*—*see infra*, §§1195-1204)

1. **Common Law:** [§1141]   A prima facie case of defamation at common law required the **publication** to some **third person** of a statement that harmed the **reputation** of the **plaintiff**, thereby **causing** the plaintiff to suffer **damages**. Except for the defense of truth and for certain narrowly defined classes of **privileged communications**, defamation was generally a **strict liability** tort.

2. **Constitutional Considerations:** [§1142]   The Supreme Court has altered the common law framework in a series of cases holding that the **First Amendment** to the United States Constitution prohibits states from using strict liability because of the **chilling effect** such liability may have on **freedom of speech.**

3. **Importance of Common Law:** [§1143]   Despite the constitutional changes, the common law is still central to any analysis. Since the plaintiff's claim is based on state tort law, it must pass all state law tests before that state law need be judged against constitutional standards.

B. PUBLICATION TO A THIRD PARTY

1. **Language Uttered Only to Plaintiff Not Actionable:** [§1144]   The defamation must be "published" (*i.e.*, communicated) to someone **other than the plaintiff**. Statements uttered by the defendant directly to the plaintiff (in person, by phone, or by letter), and neither seen nor heard by anyone else, do not satisfy this requirement because there has been no harm to the plaintiff's **reputation**.

2. **Any Third Person Sufficient:** [§1145]   Publication to **any** third person may be a defamation, regardless of any relationship to the plaintiff or defendant.

   a. **Example:** Remarks made by a supervisor to his superiors that defame the plaintiff-employee are published for this purpose, although they may be protected by privilege (*see infra*, §1245). [Staples v. Bangor Hydro-Electric Co., 629 A.2d 601 (Me. 1993)] Similarly, remarks to one's **spouse** are published but are privileged (*see infra*, §1238).

   b. **Compare—dictation:** [§1146]   Courts split on whether **dictation** of a defamatory remark to one's **private secretary** for purposes of transcription is a sufficient "publication to third person." The better view finds that it is a publication. But some courts treat the private secretary as the alter ego of the employer, so that the dictation is deemed merely a process of putting thoughts onto paper and not a publication in itself. [Hanrahan v. Kelly, 305 A.2d 151 (Md. 1973)]

      (1) **Note:** Even in courts that treat dictation as a publication, there is a strong argument that such dictation should be **privileged**, because of the confidential relationship involved. [Ostrowe v. Lee, 256 N.Y. 36 (1931)]

3. **Manner of Publication:** [§1147]   Defamatory publications are not limited to statements that are printed and distributed. Since the gist of the tort is harm to reputation, **any action** by the defendant that causes the statement to be communicated to a third person is a "publication" of that statement.

   a. **Words, gestures, conduct:** [§1148]   Words are certainly the most common manner of publication, but they are not essential. Gestures or other conduct in public may suffice.

      (1) **Example:** Marching customer P handcuffed through a store to its security office was a pantomime that published a defamation. [K-Mart Corp. v. Washington, 866 P.2d 274 (Nev. 1993); Rest. 2d §568, comment d]

4. **Publication Must Have Been Intentional or Negligent:** [§1149]   To hold the defendant liable, the plaintiff must allege and prove that the defamation was **intentionally** communicated by the defendant to some third person **or** that the communication resulted from the defendant's failure to exercise due care—i.e., **negligence** (e.g., leaving the writing where it could foreseeably be read by third persons).

   a. **Application—mass media:** [§1150]   This element will always be satisfied with publications by the media since those publications are **intended** to reach third persons.

   b. **Application—communication with plaintiff overheard:** [§1151]   The issue of **negligence** in publication arises most frequently where the defendant has communicated directly to the plaintiff, but some third person has seen or overheard it (e.g., an accusation mailed by defendant to plaintiff, opened by plaintiff's spouse or secretary). In such cases, there is a negligent "publication to a third person" only if the defendant **had reason to foresee** that this would happen and a reasonable way to avoid it.

      (1) **Examples:** Mailing a defamatory letter to a blind person (foreseeable that she will ask another to read it to her) is publication, as is defamation printed on a postcard (foreseeable that mail carrier may read), or mailing a defamatory letter to P at her office, if D had reason to know that P's secretary usually opens her mail. [Barnes v. Clayton House Motel, 435 S.W.2d 616 (Tex. 1968)]

   c. **Application—plaintiff compelled to repeat defamation:** [§1152]   If the defendant makes a defamatory statement to the plaintiff and the defendant has reason to believe that the plaintiff may be forced to repeat the statement, a publication occurs at the time of the repetition. This may happen when the defendant is an employer terminating the plaintiff's employment if the plaintiff must then reveal to prospective employers defendant's explanation for discharging the plaintiff. [Churchey v. Adolph Coors Co., 759 P.2d 1336 (Colo. 1988)]

5. **Who Is a Publisher?** [§1153]   Three separate types of defendants may utter defamations. Each is subject to different analysis.

   a. **Original publishers:** [§1154]   Anyone who has any part in the original publication is treated as an original publisher and is therefore potentially liable for the defamation. For example, in the case of a defamation appearing in a newspaper, the reporter, editor, and publisher may all be held liable. [Davis v. Hearst, 160 Cal. 143 (1911)]

(1) **Distributors:** [§1155] Newspaper distributors and carriers might also be responsible for publication (*see* below).

(2) **Principles of respondeat superior apply:** [§1156] It need not be shown that a newspaper owner intended to publish the defamation or failed to exercise due care. All that need appear is that the elements be shown against someone for whom the owner is vicariously liable.

b. **Republishers:** [§1157] At common law, the republisher of a defamatory statement could be held liable equally with the original publisher. Thus, someone could be sued for accurately repeating someone else's defamatory statement. However, the common law rule is subject to certain exceptions for *privileged communications, infra.*

(1) **Rationale:** The last utterance may do more harm than the first.

(2) **Slander or libel:** [§1158] If the original defamation is libel (*see infra*, §1207), any republication—even an oral recitation of the writing—is libel. And putting an oral defamation (slander, *see infra*, §1208) into writing makes the repetition libel.

(3) **Basis for liability:** [§1159] Like original publishers, republishers—*unless privileged*—are held to the same rules of strict liability on every element of the prima facie case except the manner of publication, which must be intentional or negligent.

(a) **Failure to remove:** [§1160] Failing to remove a defamation posted on one's premises by someone else may also constitute a negligent republication thereof by the owner of the premises. [Hellar v. Bianco, 111 Cal. App. 2d 424 (1952)—tavernkeeper D obligated to use due care to remove defamatory statement about P's chastity that had been scrawled on the wall of the men's room; Tacket v. General Motors Corp., 836 F.2d 1042 (7th Cir. 1987)—D employer allowed defamation of P worker to remain on plant wall for seven months despite complaints]

(4) **Effect of republication on liability of original publisher:** [§1161] Where there is a republication of the defamation, the original defamer's liability is increased by whatever harm the repetition causes *if the republication was either*: (i) *intended* by the original defamer, or (ii) *reasonably foreseeable*. [Rest. 2d §576]

(5) **Legal duty to republish:** [§1162] One who has a legal duty to republish certain information has an *absolute privilege* to do so and may proceed even if the statement published would otherwise give rise to a defamation action, as in the case of an executor who is under a legal duty to probate a will even if it contains defamations.

c. **Disseminators:** [§1163] A disseminator is a type of republisher who circulates, sells, rents, or otherwise deals with the *physical embodiment* of defamatory matter (*i.e.*, libraries, dealers or distributors of books, newspapers, etc., that contain defamatory matter).

   (1) **Limited liability:** [§1164] Disseminators are *not* held to the same standards of liability as the original publisher and other republishers. Rather, a disseminator is held only to a *standard of due care*. Thus, a disseminator who has no knowledge of the defamation contained in the material being handled and has no reason to know thereof is not liable for defamation. [Rest. 2d §581]

   (2) **Compare—printers:** [§1165] Independent contract printers have *no duty to inspect* a publication for libelous content. [Maynard v. Port Publications, Inc., 297 N.W.2d 500 (Wis. 1980)]

   (3) **Compare—computer bulletin boards:** [§1166] The better view is that a computer bulletin board that permits subscribers to upload comments is functioning more like a newsstand or kiosk than as a newspaper. [Cubby, Inc. v. Compuserve, Inc., 776 F. Supp. 135 (S.D.N.Y. 1991); *compare* Stratton Oakmont Inc. v. Prodigy Services Inc., 23 Media L. Rep. 1794 (1995)—involving a service that held itself out as exercising editorial control over content of messages posted on its bulletin boards]

C. HARM TO REPUTATION

1. **Defamatory Meaning:** [§1167] To be actionable, a statement must have the potential to *injure the reputation* of the plaintiff. There are two aspects to this inquiry: (i) whether the *meaning* alleged by the plaintiff is defamatory, and, (ii) if so, whether the statement can be *interpreted* to carry that meaning.

   a. **Is the alleged meaning defamatory?** [§1168] To be defamatory, a statement must *tend to lower the plaintiff's* reputation in the estimation of the community where published *or* deter others from associating with the plaintiff. [Rest. 2d §559]

      (1) **Narrow view:** [§1169] Some states insist that the meaning expose the plaintiff to "hatred, contempt, or ridicule" in order to be actionable. This is narrower than "lowering" the plaintiff's reputation in the estimation of the community.

         (a) **Example:** Under the narrow standard, a charge that P is insane might *not* be considered defamatory. [*See* Grant v. Reader's Digest Association, 151 F.2d 733 (2d Cir. 1945)]

      (2) **Community standards control:** [§1170] Whichever standard of defamation is used, the question of whether a statement is defamatory generally depends on the attitudes and mores of the audience to whom it was communicated. To be actionable, a widely published statement must injure the plaintiff "in the eyes of a substantial and respectable minority" of the community. [Rest. 2d §559, comment e]

(3) **Defamatory effect:** [§1171] In determining whether a meaning is defamatory, the focus is on *how the words were reasonably understood* by the third persons to whom it was published, *not* on what the speaker meant.

    (a) **Rationale:** Unless someone understands the publication in a defamatory sense, the plaintiff's reputation is not harmed.

    (b) **Example—foreign language:** [§1172] Where the statement to a specific group of people is couched in a foreign language, the plaintiff must show that at least one group member understood the language. [Economopoulus v. A.G. Pollard Co., 105 N.E.2d 896 (Mass. 1914)]

    (c) **Who decides?** [§1173] Where the effect is clear, the question of whether the meaning is defamatory may be answered by the judge; where the effect of the meaning is unclear, a jury decides.

        1) **Example:** A statement that one committed a serious crime is defamatory on its face as a matter of law. [Lawrence v. Bauer Publishing & Printing Ltd., 446 A.2d 469 (N.J.), *cert. denied*, 439 U.S. 999 (1982)]

        2) **Example:** As a matter of law, a statement that one knows an imprisoned criminal and is interested in his well-being is not defamatory. [Romaine v. Kallinger, 537 A.2d 284 (N.J. 1988)]

        3) **Example:** A suggestion that a lawyer asked a client to sign an affidavit that the lawyer knew was false might be found defamatory by a jury. [Armstrong v. Simon & Schuster, 85 N.Y.2d 373 (1995)]

        4) **Example:** A statement that a Marine Corps lieutenant had asked his father, a United States Senator, to intervene to prevent him from being sent into combat may be defamatory to some but not to others. The jury must decide whether the statement is defamatory. [Robertson v. McCloskey, 666 F. Supp. 241 (D.D.C. 1987)]

(4) **"Libel-proof plaintiffs":** [§1174] At common law, some courts dismiss cases brought by persons whose reputations are so bad that a false statement could not hurt the reputation more than nominally. [Jackson v. Longcope, 476 N.E.2d 617 (Mass. 1985)—convicted murderer cannot sue over false report that he had also raped his victims]

    (a) **No constitutional basis:** [§1175] The libel-proof plaintiff doctrine is *not required by the First Amendment.* Thus, it is *solely a matter of state law*, and states are free to accept or reject it without constitutional constraint. [Masson v. New Yorker Magazine, Inc., 501 U.S. 496 (1991)]

b. **Can the words carry the suggested meaning?** [§1176] In determining the meaning attached to a statement, courts look at the *fair and natural meaning* the statement will be given by *reasonable persons of ordinary intelligence*. [Romaine v. Kallinger, *supra*]

(1) **Context important:** [§1177] Publications are generally read as a whole in light of the context in which the statement appears. [Romaine v. Kallinger, *supra*]

    (a) **Example:** Three sentences of a newspaper article about an arrest and assault did not say "alleged" although the other five did use that word. Viewed in its entirety, the publication could not reasonably be read as a charge by the newspaper that the plaintiff committed the assault. [Foley v. Lowell Sun Publishing Co., 533 N.E.2d 196 (Mass. 1989)]

    (b) **But note:** Although normally an article is to be read in its entirety for defamatory thrust, this may not apply where a particularly long article contains a defamatory implication near the beginning that is not explained away until much later in the article. [Kunst v. New York World Telegram Corp., 28 App. Div. 2d 662 (1967)]

    (c) **Format relevant:** [§1178] Typography and paragraphing may be crucial in determining a reasonable reader's reactions. [Vandenburg v. Newsweek, Inc., 507 F.2d 1024 (5th Cir. 1975)]

(2) **Defamation by implication and insinuation:** [§1179] The form of the language used by the defendant is not controlling, as long as third persons to whom it is published could *reasonably* interpret it in a sense defamatory to the plaintiff. [Rest. 2d §565, comment b; Davis v. Ross, 754 F.2d 80 (2d Cir. 1985); Aronson v. Wiersma, 65 N.Y.2d 592 (1985)]

    (a) **Example:** D newspaper reported that a man who had objected to YMCA policy had suffered a heart attack and died during a rally near a YMCA board meeting. The paper also reported that the man's family was upset because he was not treated quickly. The next paragraph stated that P, the president of the YMCA, was a doctor and was present at the meeting. The court held that a reasonable reader could draw a defamatory meaning from these two paragraphs. [Healey v. New England Newspapers, Inc., 555 A.2d 321 (R.I.), *cert. denied*, 493 U.S. 814 (1989)]

    (b) **Example:** Where D writes that P was one of "several women 'associated' with" a slain executive, the use of quotation marks around "associated" permits a defamatory interpretation. [Wildstein v. New York Post Corp., 40 Misc. 2d 586, *aff'd*, 24 App. Div. 2d 559 (1968)]

    (c) **Example:** Sometimes asking a question may be defamatory if it implies that the speaker is asserting underlying facts. [Chapin. v. Knight-Ridder, Inc., 993 F.2d 1087 (4th Cir. 1993)—not defamatory to ask, "Who will benefit more from [a project to send gifts to soldiers]—GIs or [plaintiff]?"]

(d) **Minority view—"possible innocent meaning rule":** [§1180] Illinois has taken the position that where the defamation appears only by implication or insinuation, it is not actionable if, in context, the statement is reasonably equivocal—*i.e.*, if it is possible to give the statement a reasonable innocent meaning. [Chapski v. Copley Press, 442 N.E.2d 195 (Ill. 1982)]

(3) **Incomplete defamation:** [§1181] If the defamatory meaning arises only when the words are combined with extrinsic facts not apparent on the face of the publication, the plaintiff must allege and prove the extrinsic facts (called the *"inducement"*), that these facts were known to some third person who heard the statement, and that the implication (*"innuendo"*) of the statement, when combined with those facts, is defamatory. [Whitby v. Associates Discount Corp., 207 N.E.2d 482 (Ill. 1965)]

(a) **Example:** Newspaper D published a notice that P's wife had just given birth to twin sons. The statement on its face certainly was not defamatory, but it became so when tied to the extrinsic fact—presumably known to some readers—that P and his wife had been married only one month, the innuendo being that P and his wife had been unchaste prior to marriage. [Morrison v. Ritchie & Co., 39 Scot. L. Rep. 432 (1902)]

2. **"Of and Concerning" the Plaintiff:** [§1182] For a statement to be actionable, some third person must have *reasonably interpreted* it to refer to the plaintiff.

a. **Defamed person unnamed—colloquium:** [§1183] A publication may clearly be defamatory of somebody, and yet on its face make no reference to the plaintiff (*e.g.*, "a certain well-known industrialist who lives on Queensbury Road is keeping company with prostitutes"). In such a case, the plaintiff must establish the *"colloquium"*—*i.e.*, that some persons to whom the statement was published *reasonably interpreted* it as applying to plaintiff.

(1) **Example:** A mother writes a letter to the editor attacking her child's teacher without naming the teacher. A jury might find that some readers knew that the speaker's only child was in third grade and that P was the only third grade teacher in that school. [Zelik v. Daily News Publishing Co., 431 A.2d 1046 (Pa. 1981)]

(2) **Fiction:** [§1184] Depending on resemblances, a jury may be permitted to find that statements in a novel are of and concerning a real plaintiff. [Bindrim v. Mitchell, 92 Cal. App. 3d 61, *cert. denied*, 444 U.S. 984 (1979)]

(3) **Compare—unintended but explicit use of plaintiff's name:** [§1185] On the other hand, where the plaintiff's name *is* used, he may maintain an action for defamation even though the defendant was really referring to another person by the same name—provided some persons to whom the defamation was published reasonably interpreted it as applying to the plaintiff.

(a) **Example:** D reports that "Artemus Jones," supposedly a fictitious person, was seen cavorting with a woman other than his wife. A real Artemus Jones satisfies this element if he can show that persons who read the article reasonably thought it referred to him. [Hulton v. Jones, 1910 A.C. 20 (1910)] The same result would follow if D was referring to a real Artemus Jones but some reasonable readers understood it to refer to a different Artemus Jones.

b. **Who may be defamed—in general:** [§1186]   Any living person, corporation, partnership, or other legally recognized entity may be the subject of a defamation and may bring an action therefor.

(1) **Compare—other groups:** [§1187]   Clubs, fraternities, and other unincorporated associations do not possess sufficient status as an entity to sue for defamation; however, individual members may sue if the matter clearly defames them (*see infra*). Some decisions, on the other hand, recognize the right of a labor union to sue *as an entity*—comparable to the rights accorded a corporation or partnership. [Daniels v. Sanitarium Association, 59 Cal. 2d 602 (1963)]

(2) **Deceased persons:** [§1188]   No action will lie for the defamation of one who is already dead. [Keys v. Interstate Circuit, 468 S.W.2d 485 (Tex. 1971)—no action by heirs of "Bonnie and Clyde"]

(a) **Compare—defamation of deceased reflecting upon living person:** [§1189]   Note, however, that certain defamations of a deceased person may also defame a living person, and hence may be actionable. Thus, if D states to someone that Z, a deceased woman, had no legitimate children, this might defame Z's living children. [Rest. 2d §564, comment e]

(b) **Compare—survival of action:** [§1190]   Most states following the usual tort rule, provide that when the plaintiff dies after being defamed but before suit or trial, the claim survives. A few states, however, hold that death before judgment destroys the defamation claim.

c. **Individual claims arising from group defamations:** [§1191]   No individual member of a class defamed may bring an action unless the group is so small that the statement may reasonably be interpreted as applying to each member. [Neiman-Marcus v. Lait, 13 F.R.D. 311 (1952)] Thus, the *size of the group* is the key factor in determining whether an action will lie.

(1) **Example:** The statement "all lawyers are shysters" cannot defame Attorney A unless other facts suggest that the recipients reasonably understood that A was being singled out (*e.g.*, the speaker pointed a finger at A while making the statement).

(a) **Compare:** If the statement was "the Election Board took bribes," the target group is smaller and, without more, the finger of defamation may point sufficiently at each individual member.

(2) **Minority view—"intensity of suspicion" test:** [§1192]   Some courts hold that the size of the group is not the sole consideration. Other factors, such as definition of the group's composition, degree of cohesiveness,

and prominence affect the intensity of suspicion that the defendant's statements cast on the group. [Brady v. Ottaway Newspapers, Inc., 84 App. Div. 2d 226 (1981)—fact question whether group of 53 police officers is too large a group to sue]

(3) **Reference to part of group:** [§1193]   If the group is small enough, a charge against "some" may be a charge against all. [Gross v. Cantor, 270 N.Y. 93 (1936)—group of 12; Neiman-Marcus v. Lait, *supra*—suit by 15 male salespersons over statement that "most" of 25 male salespersons on staff were "fairies"]

3. **Strict Liability:** [§1194]   Although the element of "publication" requires either an intentional or a negligent publication, the element of "harm to reputation" is based on *strict liability*. This means that at common law it is irrelevant whether the defendant anticipated or should have anticipated that some readers would understand an article as it is now claimed they did, or whether the defendant should reasonably have realized that a supposedly fictitious name was used by some real person. Constitutional law has restricted strict liability. (*See infra*, §1277.)

D. FALSE FACTS

1. **Falsity:** [§1195]   At common law, plaintiffs have to allege falsity but defendants bear the burden of proving that the statement was true. If the statement was true, any injury to reputation is not actionable.

    a. **Truth is complete defense:** [§1196]   The general view is that truth of the defamatory matter is a *complete* defense—even if the publication was made out of pure spite and even if the defendant did not believe the statement was true at the time it was made. [Craig v. Wright, 76 P.2d 248 (Okla. 1938)]

        (1) **Sting of the charge must be proven:** [§1197]   Defendant need not prove the literal truth of the charge, but must only establish its "sting." Thus, a claim that plaintiff robbed a bank of $50,000 may be shown to be true even if the amount taken was only $7,000. [Posadas v. City of Reno, 851 P.2d 438 (Nev. 1993)—charge of "lying under oath" not shown to be true by showing that P police officer lied to two other officers who questioned him while he was not under oath, since lying under oath is a crime and the latter was not]

        (2) **Constitutional rule as to public officials:** [§1198]   Even if a state were to assert that truth alone was not enough, this view cannot apply where a *public official* has been attacked in her public capacity. Freedom of speech requirements in such cases dictate that truth alone must be a sufficient defense. [Garrison v. Louisiana, 379 U.S. 64 (1964)]

2. **Plaintiff's Burden to Prove Falsity:** [§1199]   At least where the statement involves a *matter of public concern*, the First Amendment requires *all plaintiffs* to bear the burden of proving that the statement is false. [Philadelphia Newspapers, Inc. v. Hepps, 475 U.S. 767 (1986)]

    a. **Summary judgment:** [§1200]   Even though plaintiffs must prove the defamatory statement false, it may be that, as a practical matter, any defendant who seeks summary judgment on falsity grounds must demonstrate that the statement is true—in order to show that the plaintiff will be unable to prove it false at trial.

3. **Statement Cannot Be False Unless It Contains Assertions of Fact:** [§1201] Only facts can be true or false. Thus, the alleged defamation must contain explicit statements of fact or implied unstated facts that were *false*.

   a. **No automatic protection for "opinion":** [§1202] A statement generally characterized as an "opinion" may be defamatory if it can be *reasonably interpreted* by the recipients as being based on underlying defamatory facts. [Milkovich v. Lorain Journal Co., 497 U.S. 1 (1990)]

      (1) **Example:** An accusation that a high school wrestling coach committed perjury while testifying at a hearing in an attempt to get his team taken off probation was *"sufficiently factual* to be susceptible of being proved true or false." [Milkovich v. Lorain Journal Co., *supra*]

      (2) **Example:** Calling P a "racist" is not actionable because the word is used so casually today that it has lost its core meaning. [Stevens v. Tillman, 855 F.2d 394 (7th Cir. 1988), *cert. denied*, 489 U.S. 1065 (1989)]

      (3) **Note:** States may choose to protect this type of speech to a greater extent than required by the First Amendment. [Immuno A.G. v. Moor-Jankowski, 77 N.Y.2d 235, *cert. denied*, 500 U.S. 954 (1991)—New York state constitution allows consideration of the "tone and apparent purpose" of the communication in deciding whether D's statement is protected "opinion"]

   b. **Hyperbole in public debate:** [§1203] A broad statement made in the course of *public debate* will usually be characterized as "mere hyperbole" which is not actionable because reasonable people could not interpret it as being an assertion of fact.

      (1) **Rationale:** The audience expects a certain degree of name calling and overstatement in public debates and does not take broad statements literally. [Gregory v. McDonnell Douglas, 17 Cal. 3d 596 (1976)]

      (2) **Example:** A newspaper report of a "blackmail" charge hurled at city council meeting against a real estate developer for refusing to sell his land to the city unless it gave him a zoning variance on other property was not actionable. This could not reasonably be understood as charging the crime of blackmail. At most it was a claim that P was a hard bargainer—an accusation that was not defamatory. [Greenbelt Cooperative Publishing Co. v. Bresler, 398 U.S. 6 (1970)]

      (3) **Example:** The epithet "traitor" was not actionable when used in a union newspaper against an employee who refused to join the union. [Letter Carriers v. Austin, 418 U.S. 264 (1974)]

      (4) **Example:** Calling a woman "a bitch" at a public meeting is vituperation and abuse not meant to be taken seriously. [Ward v. Zelikovsky, 643 A.2d 972 (N.J. 1994)]

c. **Specificity of language:** [§1204]   The more specific the language used, the more likely it is to be reasonably interpreted as either a statement of fact or a statement based on underlying facts.

(1) **Example:** The accusation that a journalist has libeled others was held actionable, but not the charge that he ran an "openly fascist journal." [Buckley v. Littell, 539 F.2d 882 (2d Cir. 1976), *cert. denied*, 429 U.S. 1062 (1977)]

E.   CAUSATION [§1205]

The cause in fact and proximate cause requirements for defamation are the same as those for negligence (*see supra*, §§327-405). (Note, however, that recovery of special damages (below) is limited to *foreseeable* damages.)

F.   DAMAGES AND OTHER REMEDIES

1. **In General:** [§1206]   The scope of damages recoverable in a defamation action under common law rules depends on the *form* of the publication—whether it is libel or slander—and on the *motives* with which it was uttered. Recoverable damages are also constitutionally limited in several situations.

2. **"Libel" and "Slander" Distinguished**

   a. **"Libel" defined:** [§1207]   "Libel" is defamation usually appearing in some written or printed form, *i.e.*, reduced to some *permanent, physical embodiment* such as newspapers, letters, etc. Generally, representations to the *eye* are libel. Thus, words, pictures, signs, statues, films, and even certain conduct such as hanging the plaintiff in effigy may be libel. [Whitby v. Associates Discount Corp., *supra*, §1181]

   b. **"Slander" defined:** [§1208]   "Slander" is usually *oral* defamation, *i.e.*, representations to the *ear*. The principal characteristic is that the defamation is in less permanent and less physical form. Other examples include transitory gestures (*e.g.*, nod of head). [Rest. 2d §568, comment d]

   c. **Borderline cases—factors:** [§1209]   To decide whether a publication is libel or slander in difficult cases (*e.g.*, defamations contained on a phonograph record, or in a television or radio program), consider:

   (i) The *permanency* of the form of publication;

   (ii) The *extent of dissemination*; and

   (iii) Whether the publication was *deliberate or premeditated*.

   [Shor v. Billingsley, 4 Misc. 2d 857 (1956), *aff'd*, 4 App. Div. 2d 1017 (1957)—capacity for harm, including extent of dissemination, warrants treating extemporaneous remark on live television as libel]

   (1) **Broadcasting:** [§1210]   Under the newer view, all radio and television publications are considered libel, whether or not read from a manuscript. [First Independent Baptist Church v. Southerland, 373 So. 2d 647 (Ala. 1979); Rest. 2d §568A]

(a) **Note—statutory treatment:** Some states categorize media by statute. [*See, e.g.,* Cal. Civ. Code §46—defamations by radio or television are slander even if written scripts are used]

3. **Damages Rule for Slander:** [§1211] Defamation in the form of slander is not actionable without a showing of *special damages*, unless the slander is of a class that the law deems "*actionable per se.*"

   a. **"Special damages" defined:** [§1212] "Special damages" are those *actually suffered by plaintiff* and not presumed by law—*e.g.,* loss of employment or business, or failure of any firm expectancy (even a gratuity, such as a vacation paid for by friends).

      (1) **Recovery of general damages:** [§1213] A plaintiff who proves some amount of special damages may *also* recover general damages, even if they far exceed the proven special damages.

         (a) **"General damages" defined:** [§1214] General damages compensate for harm to the plaintiff's reputation. Their existence may be proven by such evidence as polls. But even if not provable, their existence may be presumed by the jury based on the likely effect of the defamation considering the number of people who learned of it, the nature of the charge, and the identity of the speaker and the plaintiff. Constitutional limits on the availability of general damages are discussed, *infra,* §§1286 *et seq.*

   b. **Slander per se—special damages not required:** [§1215] There are only four situations in which slanders are deemed "*actionable per se*"—*i.e.,* where a showing of special damages is *not* required before the plaintiff may recover general damages. (Of course, if the plaintiff has suffered any special damages, they are recoverable; but in these four cases she can recover general damages to her reputation regardless.) The four "slander per se" categories include charges that the plaintiff has committed a *serious crime*, has a *loathsome disease*, is *incompetent in her trade or profession*, or is *unchaste*.

      (1) **Crime:** [§1216] Where the defendant charges that the plaintiff has committed a *serious*, *morally reprehensible crime*, or has been incarcerated for such, the charge is slander per se.

         (a) **Note:** A specific offense need not be charged, as long as defendant clearly alleges that the plaintiff committed a fairly *serious* crime. Thus, the statement "you stole the money" has been held to be slander per se. [Hruby v. Kalina, 424 N.W.2d 130 (Neb. 1988); *but see* Liberman v. Gelstein, 80 N.Y.2d 429 (1992)—charge of bribing a police officer is sufficiently serious to be slander per se, but charge of the misdemeanor of harassment is not]

         (b) **But note:** Charging that plaintiff is a "crook" or a "thief" is generally not slander per se, absent some specific allegation of criminal misconduct. [Hruby v. Kalina, *supra*]

      (2) **Disease:** [§1217] Statements imputing to the plaintiff a *currently existing, loathsome, communicable disease* are slander per se. This is generally limited to venereal disease and leprosy; imputations of insanity,

tuberculosis, etc., do not qualify. [Rade v. Press Publishing Co., 37 Misc. 254 (1902)]

(3) **Ineptitude in trade or profession:** [§1218]   Statements imputing to the plaintiff *conduct, characteristics, or associations incompatible with the proper performance of the plaintiff's business, trade, office, or profession* are slander per se. These cases present the most frequent and difficult problems.

    (a) **Rationale:** The law is willing to presume actual damages in these cases because charges that a person is incompetent in, or unsuitable for, her trade or profession is likely to harm her livelihood.

    (b) **Defamation must be incompatible with business:** [§1219]   Whatever defamation is charged must actually be incompatible with the plaintiff's business or profession. Thus, the effect of a given charge may depend on the nature of the plaintiff's occupation.

        1) **Examples:** Calling a doctor a "butcher," a lawyer a "shyster," a teacher "immoral" or "insane," or a businessperson "uncreditworthy" may all be considered slanderous per se. [MacLeod v. Tribune Publishing Co., 52 Cal. 2d 536 (1959)]

        2) **Compare:** It is not actionable without a showing of special damages to charge that a physician has committed adultery, or that a gas company clerk has been consorting with prostitutes, because such imputations are not incompatible with their positions. [Lumby v. Allday, 148 Eng. Rep. 1434 (1831)]

(4) **Unchastity:** [§1220]   Statements imputing unchastity are slander per se. Traditionally this category of slander per se has been limited to charges leveled against *female* plaintiffs, but some states have extended the law to include males as well.

    (a) **Impotency:** [§1221]   In a few states, imputation of impotency to a man is also actionable per se. [Cal. Civ. Code. §46] The general view is contra.

    (b) **Homosexuality:** [§1222]   Even in a state that has legalized all private sexual conduct between consenting adults, a false imputation of the commission of a homosexual act may be slanderous per se. [Schomer v. Smidt, 113 Cal. App. 3d 828 (1980)]

4. **Damages Rule for Libel:** [§1223]   If the defamation is in the form of libel *and* is clear on its face, all jurisdictions *presume general damages* from the fact that it was published. The plaintiff *need not show special damages* to recover—although if she can show some, she can recover for these also. If clear on its face, the defamation need *not* fit within any of the slander per se categories.

    a. **Rationale:** Because of the permanency of form, possible extent of dissemination, and other features of libel, there is a greater likelihood of harm; thus, general damages may be presumed. [Rest. 2d §569]

    b. **Libel per quod:** [§1224] States disagree where the matter published is innocent on its face but becomes defamatory when linked up with certain extrinsic facts (*see supra*, §1181). Some follow the general libel rule and never require special damages. A second group presumes general damages only where the libel would have been actionable as one of the four types of "slander per se" (*see* above) if the words had been spoken. [Wegner v. Rodeo Cowboys Association, 417 F.2d 881 (10th Cir. 1969)]

5. **Punitive Damages:** [§1225] Most states allow punitive damages if the defamation can be shown to have been uttered with ***common law malice***, such as hatred, ill will, or spite.

    a. **Federal constitutional restrictions:** [§1226] The First Amendment ***prohibits*** the imposition of punitive damages for defamations involving ***matters of public concern*** where the falsity is attributable only to ***negligence***. [Gertz v. Robert Welch, Inc., 418 U.S. 323 (1974)] However, the Supreme Court has not ruled on whether the First Amendment provides any special protection against the imposition of punitive damages in libel cases. State courts have rejected this claim. [DiSalle v. P.G. Publishing Co., 544 A.2d 1345 (Pa. 1988), *cert. denied*, 492 U.S. 906 (1989)]

        (1) **But note:** The Supreme Court has held that where the defamation involves a confidential report to five subscribers about a private plaintiff, it does ***not*** involve a matter of public concern and punitive damages ***may*** be recovered even for negligent defamations. [Dun & Bradstreet, Inc. v. Greenmoss Builders, Inc., 472 U.S. 749 (1985)] To date, the case has not been applied against media defendants.

    b. **State constitutional restrictions:** [§1227] Some states disallow punitive damages under state constitutional law. [Wheeler v. Green, 593 P.2d 777 (Or. 1979)] Recall also the recent statutory limits on punitive damages generally, *supra*, §1124.

6. **Retraction:** [§1228] Several states have adopted "retraction statutes," the effect of which is to limit the damages recoverable against specified media that publish defamations. Typically, these statutes provide that the named defendant cannot be held liable for ***general damages*** resulting from a defamatory publication unless it has failed to fairly and promptly publish a retraction of the defamation after a formal demand by the injured party to do so. Special damages may still be recovered, however. [Cal. Civ. Code §48a]

7. **Injunctions:** [§1229] Courts traditionally have refused to enjoin defamatory speech. [Willing v. Mazzacone, 393 A.2d 1155 (Pa. 1978)]

G. DEFENSES

1. **Consent:** [§1230] Consent is a defense to defamation under the same rules that make it a defense to an intentional tort. [Live Oak Publishing Co. v. Cohagan, 234 Cal. App. 3d 1277 (1991); Cox v. Nasche, 70 F.3d 1030 (9th Cir. 1995)—release signed by job applicant protected former employer]

2. **Truth:** [§1231] As discussed previously, truth is a ***complete*** defense to a charge of defamation in most jurisdictions (*see supra*, §1196). Beyond that, most states,

either by constitutional mandate (*see supra*, §1199) or by common law, have imposed upon the plaintiff the burden of proving falsity in almost all cases.

3. **Common Law Absolute Privileges:** [§1232]   Absolute privilege is a *complete* defense to any defamation action; *i.e.*, it is not affected by a showing of malice, lying, abuse, or excessive publication, as in the case of conditional privileges (below). Absolute privilege exists in the following cases:

a. **Participation in the processes of government**

(1) **Legislative privilege:** [§1233]   All federal and state legislative members are absolutely privileged to utter defamations while on the floor of their legislatures or in committee sessions, etc. There is *no requirement of relevancy* to any matter at hand. [Rest. 2d §590] This protection is found in federal or state constitutional provisions. [Tenney v. Brandhove, 341 U.S. 367 (1951)]

(a) **Inferior legislative bodies:** The modern view is to accord inferior legislative bodies absolute privilege for statements made at meetings. [Rest. 2d §590; Sanchez v. Coxon, 854 P.2d 126 (Ariz. 1993)] Some states are contra (*see infra*, §1240).

(2) **Judicial privilege:** [§1234]   Any participant in a judicial proceeding is absolutely privileged to utter defamations in the course of the proceeding provided there is *some relevancy* (*i.e.*, a reasonable relationship) to the matter at hand. This includes the judge or any judicial officer, witnesses, attorneys, parties to the action, and jurors. [Irwin v. Ashurst, 74 P.2d 1127 (Or. 1938); Rest. 2d §587; *but see* Park Knoll Associates v. Schmidt, 59 N.Y.2d 205 (1983)—no absolute privilege for organizer advising tenants applying for rent refunds]

(a) **"Course of judicial proceeding":** [§1235]   The defamation need not occur at the trial itself; it may be in a pretrial hearing, deposition, etc. Judicial proceedings are generally deemed to start *when the complaint is filed*; hence defamations in the complaint or any document filed in conjunction therewith (*e.g.*, a lis pendens) are absolutely privileged. [Theran v. Rokoff, 602 N.E.2d 191 (Mass. 1992)]

1) **And note:** Some authority extends the privilege to communications preliminary to a *proposed* judicial proceeding (*e.g.*, demand letters by counsel prior to filing suit charging misconduct by opposing party, or; a complaint to a public official designed to prompt the investigation of plaintiff). [Lerette v. Dean Witter, 60 Cal. App. 3d 573 (1976); Rest. 2d §586, comment a; *but see* Green Acres Trust v. London, 688 P.2d 617 (Ariz. 1984)—denying any privilege for lawyers at press conferences announcing forthcoming filing of lawsuit]

(b) **Quasi-judicial proceedings:** [§1236]   Similarly, an absolute privilege applies in the case of quasi-judicial proceedings (*e.g.*, administrative hearings). [Miner v. Novotny, 498 A.2d 269 (Md. 1985)—citizen's brutality complaint against deputy sheriff]

(3) **Executive privilege:** [§1237]   Absolute privilege is also provided for high rank, *policymaking* executive officers (cabinet members, department heads, etc.) of state and federal governments when acting within the *scope of their discretionary duties*. However, as with judicial participants, there is a *requirement of relevancy* here. [Rest. 2d §591; Barr v. Matteo, 360 U.S. 564 (1959); Kilgore v. Younger, 30 Cal. 3d 770 (1982)]

   (a) **Note:** Some states extend this privilege to lower level executive officers. [City of Miami v. Wardlow, 403 So. 2d 414 (Fla. 1981); Williams v. Fischer, 581 N.E.2d 744 (Ill. 1991)]

   b. **Domestic privilege:** [§1238]   Either spouse is absolutely privileged to utter defamations of third persons to the other *spouse*. A few courts extend this absolute privilege to communications among the immediate family (parent-child, etc.), but most treat the latter as only conditionally privileged (*see* below). [Rest. 2d §592]

4. **Common Law Conditional or Qualified Privileges:** [§1239]   A "conditional" or "qualified" privilege exists when the potential speaker needs to be encouraged to speak—*i.e.*, needs protection from the strict liability that might otherwise inhibit the potential speaker from speaking. A qualified privilege, unlike an absolute privilege, can be lost through bad faith or abuse (*see infra*, §§1254 *et seq.*).

   a. **Recognized conditional privileges**

   (1) **Inferior legislative bodies and inferior executive and administrative officers:** [§1240]   Although, as noted above (*supra*, §1233), the modern view is that inferior legislative bodies and executive officials have absolute privilege for their statements within the scope of their offices, some states accord such statements only conditional privilege.

   (2) **Protection of private interests:** [§1241]   A defendant is conditionally privileged to defame another, if there is:

   (i) **Protectable interest:** [§1242]   The defendant must have a reasonable belief that some important interest in person or property is threatened; it can be *his own interest*, that of the *person to whom he publishes* the defamation, or that of some *third person*; and

   (ii) **Relevancy:** [§1243]   The defamation published must bear some *reasonable relevancy* to the interest sought to be protected; and

   (iii) **Purpose to protect:** [§1244]   The defendant must have published the defamation in the reasonable belief that the person to whom it was published was in a position to protect or assist in the lawful protection of that interest.

   (a) **Volunteering information where relationship or common interest exists:** [§1245]   Generally there must be some relationship between the publisher (the defendant) and the person to whom the information is published—either some family, business, or employment relationship, or a common interest in business affairs. If there is such a relationship, the defendant may be privileged to *volunteer* defamatory information. [Rest. 2d §595(2)]

1) **Examples:** This covers the situation where a brother tells his sister, "Don't marry X; he has venereal disease"; or an agent tells the principal, "Don't extend credit to X, she's a deadbeat"; or an employee tells his employer, "Don't believe anything that X has told you about me, he's a chronic liar." [Weenig v. Wood, 349 N.E.2d 235 (Ind. 1976)]

2) **But note:** Plaintiff's immediate supervisor at plaintiff's place of employment is not privileged to relate to a customer the reason for plaintiff's discharge (the alleged defamation) because no common relationship or interest exists between the supervisor and the customer. [Nelson v. Lapeyrouse Grain Corp., 534 So. 2d 1085 (Ala. 1988)]

(b) **Answering request for information where no relationship exists:** [§1246] If there is no such relationship or common interest, it usually must appear that the defamation was made in response to a *request* for information by the person to whom it was published, rather than volunteered by the defendant.

1) **Credit agencies:** [§1247] Frequently, a credit bureau asks a defendant for information regarding another person's credit. In this case, the defendant's response is privileged, but if the defendant had initiated the call to the credit bureau and volunteered the information, there would have been no privilege. [Stationers Corp. v. Dun & Bradstreet, 62 Cal. 2d 412 (1965)]

2) **Prospective employers:** [§1248] Some jurisdictions hold that former employers have a qualified privilege for responses (rather than volunteered statements) to the plaintiff's prospective employers where the prospective employers have a legitimate and obvious interest in the employee's qualifications. [Erickson v. Marsh & McLennan Co., 569 A.2d 793 (N.J. 1990); Coclin v. Lane Press, Inc., 210 App. Div. 2d 98 (1994)]

(c) **Self-defense:** [§1249] A person is privileged to respond to others' attacks on her whether or not any prior relationship exists. [Foretich v. Capital Cities/ABC, Inc., 37 F.3d 1541 (4th Cir. 1994)]

(3) **Protection of public interest:** [§1250] A person is conditionally privileged to defame another if he reasonably believes his utterances are necessary to protect a legitimate public interest, and that the person to whom the statement is made is empowered to protect that interest. Thus, D is conditionally privileged to run up to a police officer shouting, "There goes X—he just robbed the bank!"

(a) **But note—media defendants:** Mass media cannot claim the privilege of protecting the public interest for having published an article of general interest to the community—even though it warned the public against some asserted public problem. [Brown v. Kelly Broadcasting Co., 48 Cal. 3d 711 (1989)—consumer report broadcast about problems with licensed contractor was not privileged under common law]

b. **Conditional privilege may be lost through bad faith or abuse**

(1) **Lack of honest belief in truth of statements made:** [§1251] The general view is that the defendant must have an "actual, *honest*" belief in the truth of the defamatory matter. Hence, there is no privilege if the defendant knows that the statements are unfounded.

(a) **Belief need not be reasonable:** [§1252] Even totally unreasonable statements may be found to be privileged, but lack of reasonableness is *evidence* that the defendant did not honestly believe the truth of his statement. [Clark v. Molyneaux, 3 Q.B.D. 237 (1877)] *But note:* Some courts hold that a speaker who seeks to *protect the public interest* must have *reasonably* believed his statement. [Rest. 2d §598]

(b) **Credit reports—honest and reasonable belief:** [§1253] A minority view asserts that the defendant must have *both* an honest and a reasonable belief in the truth of assertions made in credit standing cases, or the privilege is lost. [Stationers Corp. v. Dun & Bradstreet, *supra*, §1247]

(2) **Malice in publication:** [§1254] The defendant's publication is privileged only when made at least in part in the public interest or in the protection of some lawful private interest. If it appears that the defendant was motivated *solely* by malice and an intent to injure the party defamed, whatever conditional privilege the defendant otherwise would have had is lost through abuse. [Mihlovan v. Grozavu, 72 N.Y.2d 506 (1988); Sanborn v. Chronicle Publishing Co., 18 Cal. 3d 406 (1976)]

(a) **Malice:** [§1255] The type of malice required here is the same as that required under state law for an award of punitive damages, *i.e.*, *hatred, spite, or ill will*.

1) **But note:** A few courts have interpreted malice here to require "knowing or reckless disregard" for the truth—a focus on the defendant's attitude toward falsity rather than on the defendant's feelings toward P. [Marchesi v. Franchino, 387 A.2d 1129 (Md. 1978)] A few other states have held that the plaintiff can show abuse of conditional privilege by showing *either* type of malice. [Liberman v. Gelstein, *supra*, §1216]

(3) **Excessive publication:** [§1256] Similarly, the defendant's publication must be no greater than necessary to carry out the purposes for which the privilege is recognized. [Coleman v. MacLennan, 98 P. 281 (Kan. 1908)]

(a) **Effect—defendant placed under "duty of care":** [§1257] For example, defendant will lose the privilege if he speaks so loudly in a public place that he is overheard by persons other than those to whom the defamation is privileged. [Kruse v. Rabe, 79 A. 316 (N.J. 1910)]

    (b) **Compare—incidental newspaper publication:** [§1258] Where the publication is by a newspaper and the defamation is of a local person, the probability that the newspaper will be sent to persons out of state is not enough by itself to constitute an excessive publication. [Coleman v. MacLennan, *supra*; *but see* Moyle v. Franz, 293 N.Y. 842 (1944)—excessive publication by religious magazine over story about an internal matter where magazine sent to readers who were not interested in matter]

5. **Fair Comment Privilege:** [§1259] Courts have long protected critics who comment on the efforts of others—whether writers, entertainers, athletes, restaurants, or politicians. [Cherry v. Des Moines Leader, 86 N.W. 323 (Iowa 1901)] The common law developed two views on this privilege.

    a. **Majority view:** Under the majority view, the critic was protected if the comment was on a matter of public interest, was based on true facts, and expressed an honestly believed opinion. [Post Publishing Co. v. Hallam, 59 Fed. 530 (6th Cir. 1893)]

    b. **Minority view:** Under the minority view, the privilege existed even if the facts were incorrectly stated, as long as the critic honestly believed the version of the facts on which the criticism was based. [Coleman v. MacLennan, *supra*] This view played an important role in the constitutional developments discussed *infra*.

6. **Record Libel Privilege:** [§1260] Reports of *judicial, legislative, or executive proceedings* (so-called record libel) are privileged if *fair and accurate*; *i.e.*, the reports must be either verbatim accounts or fair and impartial summaries of what happened. This privilege exists in all states either by statute or under the common law.

    a. **Nonofficial proceedings:** [§1261] Although the paradigm situation involves a public and official meeting [Rest. 2d §611], some courts have extended this privilege to reports of nongovernmental public meetings in which there is a *general interest*, such as political or medical conventions [Borg v. Boas, 231 F.2d 788 (9th Cir. 1956)—mass meeting to urge grand jury investigation].

    b. **Official but nonpublic document:** [§1262] Some courts have extended this privilege beyond meetings to government files or documents. [Medico v. Time, Inc., 643 F.2d 134 (3d Cir.), *cert. denied*, 464 U.S. 836 (1981)—summary of F.B.I. file]

    c. **Reports of foreign governments:** [§1263] At least one court has refused to extend the privilege to reports from foreign governments, because they are not as open or reliable as domestic government sources. [Lee v. The Dong-A-Ilbo, 849 F.2d 876 (4th Cir. 1988), *cert. denied*, 489 U.S. 1067 (1989)]

d. **How privilege is lost:** [§1264]   The record libel privilege is lost only when the defendant's report of what transpired is *inaccurate*; traditionally, false or garbled accounts are not protected. (But note the impact of recent constitutional developments—some inaccurate reports may now be privileged; *see infra*, §§1303 *et seq.*)

   (1) **Absolute privilege compared:** [§1265]   The privilege of record libel differs from absolute privilege in that the absolute privilege is available even to those who lie, whereas this privilege (at least in its common law form) is lost upon *inaccuracy*, far short of lying.

   (2) **Conditional privilege compared:** [§1266]   Unlike conditional privileges, which are lost if the publisher does not honestly believe the substance of his statement, the record libel privilege survives even if the reporter knows or strongly believes that one of the witnesses or officials who is being accurately quoted is in fact lying.

      (a) **Rationale:** The explanation for these differences is that the record libel privilege is intended to permit the public to learn what is happening in government activities; this requires accuracy of reporting, and the harm to victims from accurate quotations of even lying officials or witnesses is outweighed by the importance attached to allowing the public to know what government officials are doing and what is being said in trials and hearings.

7. **Federal Preemptive Privileges:** [§1267]   As discussed in connection with products liability (*see supra*, §883), all state laws must be consistent with federal law under the Supremacy Clause. Preemption principles apply to defamation as well.

   a. **Defamations in campaign speech broadcasts:** [§1268]   Radio and television stations are *not* liable for broadcast defamations contained in campaign speeches by candidates for public office. [Farmers Educational Cooperative v. WDAY, 360 U.S. 525 (1959)]

      (1) **Rationale:** Section 315 of the Federal Communications Act requires broadcasters to extend "equal opportunities" for all candidates for public office to use the station's facilities. This federal act *preempts state laws* that would impede its purposes—and state defamation laws would do so because stations fearful of being held liable for defamations in such broadcasts might refuse state and local candidates the right to use their facilities, in order to protect the stations from potential liability. (Stations can no longer bar federal candidates from such access.)

      (2) **Absolute immunity:** [§1269]   The immunity here is absolute; it *cannot be defeated* by claims that the radio or television station knew that the statements to be uttered were false.

   b. **Defamations in labor disputes:** [§1270]   Likewise, federal labor laws are held to *preempt* state defamation law insofar as defamatory statements published during labor disputes are concerned. Federal labor laws set the limits on "free speech" in labor disputes, and state defamation laws cannot be applied to narrow these limits. [Letter Carriers v. Austin, *supra*, §1203]

c. **Petitions to government officials:** [§1271] Private letters to government officials arguing against the appointment of the plaintiff to a government post are protected under the *New York Times* rule (*infra*). They are **not** absolutely privileged under the Petitions Clause of the First Amendment. [McDonald v. Smith, 472 U.S. 463 (1985); *but see* Miner v. Novotny, *supra*, §1236—common law absolute privilege for complainant against deputy sheriff in administrative proceeding]

8. **Defenses of Republishers:** [§1272] A republisher cannot automatically rely on any defense or privilege the original publisher may have. Each republisher must establish its own privilege.

a. **Exception—intermediary:** [§1273] However, certain intermediaries are protected by a special privilege: One whose **duty** is to dispatch messages (*e.g.*, a telegraph agent, perhaps a private secretary) is privileged to transmit a defamation, whether he believes it to be true or not. *Rationale:* Persons so employed have no authority or ability to check the accuracy of that which they are required to transmit. [Rest. 2d §612; *and see* Mason v. Western Union, 52 Cal. App. 3d 429 (1975)]

b. **Media reliance on usually reliable source:** [§1274] Because newspapers commonly must use information that is gathered by reporters outside of the publisher's control, most states have granted newspapers a *conditional privilege* to reprint wire service stories and syndicated features. [Layne v. Tribune Co., 146 So. 234 (Fla. 1933); *and see* Appleby v. Daily Hampshire Gazette, 478 N.E.2d 721 (Mass. 1985)]

c. **Media reports of statements made by other:** [§1275] Some courts have granted media a *constitutional privilege* called "neutral reportage" to permit media to cover a story in which some important persons or groups are accusing others of improprieties. [Edwards v. National Audubon Society, Inc., 556 F.2d 113, *cert. denied*, 434 U.S. 1002 (1977)—First Amendment prevents newspaper from being held liable for accurately *reporting* the false, libelous statements of a "responsible, prominent organization," since such statements are potentially *newsworthy* and thus important to readers; *but see* Hogan v. Herald Co., 58 N.Y.2d 630 (1982)—rejecting the privilege] The articles in these cases may be seen as extensions of the fair and accurate report privilege because there is nothing official or public about the proceedings being reported upon.

9. **SLAPP Suits:** [§1276] In response to concern that some libel actions are brought to silence critics on public issues—so-called SLAPP suits (Strategic Lawsuits Against Public Participation)—some states have adopted legislation to help defendants terminate such cases at an early stage of the litigation. The legislation provides for striking the pleading unless the court concludes that there is a "probability" that the plaintiff will prevail. [Cal. Code Civ. Proc. §425.16; Dixon v. Superior Court, 30 Cal. App. 4th 733 (1994)—applying statute to dismiss suit brought against professor who had been critical of surveyor's work in an environmental impact dispute]

H. CONSTITUTIONAL PRIVILEGES

1. **In General:** [§1277]   The state has a legitimate interest in protecting the reputation of each citizen. But the threat of a defamation action is inevitably a curb on the freedom of speech and press guaranteed by the First Amendment of the United States Constitution: "Whatever is added to the field of libel is taken from the field of public debate." [New York Times Co. v. Sullivan, 376 U.S. 254 (1964)] In certain instances, the interest in freedom of expression is held to *outweigh* the interest in protecting reputations, and in these cases, defamations may be *privileged as a matter of constitutional law* (superseding any state law to the contrary). We have already discussed some constitutional developments in such areas as the need for a statement capable of being proven false (*see supra*, §1201) and the burden of proving falsity (*see supra*, §1199). We turn now to the major constitutional development—the *rejection* of the common law rule of strict liability.

   a. **Status of plaintiff controls constitutional standard:** [§1278]   The crucial step in determining the constitutional protection available in defamation cases depends on the *status* of the plaintiff. [New York Times Co. v. Sullivan, *supra*; Gertz v. Robert Welch, Inc., *supra*, §1226]

      (1) **Types of plaintiffs:** [§1279]   For this constitutional analysis each plaintiff must be put into one of three categories: (i) public official, (ii) public figure, or (iii) private person.

      (2) **Caveat—status of defendant:** [§1280]   A few plurality Supreme Court opinions have suggested that the constitutional standards may also depend on the identity and status of the defendant speaker. [Philadelphia Newspapers, Inc. v. Hepps, *supra*, §1199] But this view has never commanded a majority in the Supreme Court and has been rejected by virtually all state courts and lower federal courts.

2. **Public Plaintiffs:** [§1281]   The Supreme Court has granted its highest level of protection for statements concerning "public officials" or "public figures." Although the standard of protection for each group is identical, it is useful to keep the two groups distinct because of the way in which persons are placed into one or the other of these two categories.

   a. **Public officials:** [§1282]   Those persons within the hierarchy of government who have (or appear to have) *substantial responsibility* over government affairs have the status of public plaintiffs in defamation actions. [Rosenblatt v. Baer, 383 U.S. 75 (1966)]

      (1) **Rationale:** It is important that members of the public be able to speak freely about—and criticize—the behavior of its public officials without running the risk of being held liable for every false defamatory statement. [New York Times Co. v. Sullivan, *supra*]

      (2) **"Public official" not yet defined:** [§1283]   The Supreme Court has not yet defined "public official." But it has said that the term does *not* encompass all public employees. [Hutchinson v. Proxmire, 443 U.S. 111, note 8 (1979); *and see* Kassel v. Gannett Co., 875 F.2d 935 (1st Cir. 1989)]

      (3) **Police:** [§1284]   Because police officers are highly visible to the public and have considerable authority to act with force, virtually all courts

have held even low ranking officers to be public officials. [Gray v. Udevitz, 656 F.2d 588 (10th Cir. 1981); Reed v. Northwestern Publishing Co., 530 N.E.2d 474 (Ill. 1988), *cert. denied*, 489 U.S. 1067 (1989)]

(4) **Compare—principals and teachers:** [§1285]   Courts are split over whether principals and teachers are public officials. [*Compare* Palmer v. Bennington School District, 615 A.2d 498 (Vt. 1992)—principals are public; *with* Ellerbee v. Mills, 422 S.E.2d 539 (Ga. 1992), *cert. denied*, 507 U.S. 1025 (1993)—contra; *compare* Richmond Newspapers, Inc. v. Lipscomb, 362 S.E.2d 32 (Va. 1987), *cert. denied*, 486 U.S. 1023 (1988)—teachers are public; *with* Kelley v. Bonney, 606 A.2d 693 (Conn. 1992)—contra]

b. **"Public figures":** [§1286]   A person ("P") who is not a "public official" nonetheless may be deemed a "public figure" on one of two grounds: (i) P has achieved *such pervasive fame or notoriety* that P becomes a public figure for *all* purposes and contexts (*e.g.*, celebrity sports figure); or (ii) more commonly, P *voluntarily* enters or is drawn into a particular public controversy, and thereby becomes a "public figure" for that *limited* range of issues. [Gertz v. Robert Welch, Inc., *supra*, §1278]

(1) **Rationale:** Although persons who are not in government do not have as direct a control over the lives and destinies of the public, there is much private power in this country that does exert great influence and that is not as easily scrutinized or removable by the electoral process. It is important that the public be able to comment freely on these persons as well. [Curtis Publishing Co. v. Butts, 388 U.S. 130 (1967) (opinion of Warren, C.J.)]

(2) **General public figures:** [§1287]   Plaintiffs who have been found to be general public figures include a famous journalist and political advocate [Buckley v. Littell, *supra*, §1204], and a well-known entertainer [Carson v. Allied News Co., 529 F.2d 206 (7th Cir. 1976); *and see* Waldbaum v. Fairchild Publications, Inc., 627 F.2d 1287 (D.C. Cir.), *cert. denied*, 449 U.S. 898 (1980)—a general public figure is a "well-known 'celebrity,' his name a 'household word.' The public recognizes his words and deeds . . . ."].

(3) **Limited purpose public figures:** [§1288]   Lower courts have tended to use three steps in identifying "limited purpose" public figures: (i) the court isolates the public controversy involved in the particular case; (ii) the court decides if the plaintiff has voluntarily assumed a central role in that controversy; and (iii) the court must find the alleged defamation germane to the plaintiff's participation in the controversy. [Waldbaum v. Fairchild Publications, Inc., *supra*—outspoken chief executive officer of corporation was limited purpose public figure for his report on reasons for P's dismissal; Foretich v. Capital Cities/ABC Inc., *supra*, §1249—couple did not become public figures by responding publicly and often to assertions that they had abused their granddaughter]

(a) **Application:** The Supreme Court has made it clear that not every person who seeks government aid or who draws attention by some voluntary behavior becomes a "public" plaintiff for libel purposes.

1) **Example:** A socially prominent woman does not become a "public figure" by seeking a divorce or by meeting with the press during the divorce trial. [Time, Inc. v. Firestone, 424 U.S. 448 (1976)]

2) **Example:** A scientist applying for a federal grant does not become a "public figure" by applying for the grant. [Hutchinson v. Proxmire, 443 U.S. 111 (1979)]

3) **Example:** A witness who refuses to testify before a grand jury does not thereby become a "public figure." [Wolston v. Reader's Digest Association, 443 U.S. 157 (1979)]

(b) **Involuntary public figures:** [§1289] In *Gertz*, the Court indicated that it might be possible for people to become public figures through no purposeful action of their own, but thought such instances "exceedingly rare."

1) **Example:** An air traffic controller who happened to be on duty during a newsworthy airplane crash may be a public figure. [Dameron v. Washington Magazine, Inc., 779 F.2d 736 (D.C. Cir. 1985), *cert. denied*, 476 U.S. 1141 (1986)]

c. **Constitutional standard in cases involving public plaintiffs:** [§1290] Plaintiffs who are either public officials or public figures for defamation purposes must prove that the false defamatory statement was published with what the Supreme Court has called *"actual malice"*—i.e., *knowledge of the falsity* of the defamatory statement or *reckless disregard for its truth*. [New York Times Co. v. Sullivan, *supra*, §1282]

(1) **Rationale:** The public interest in good faith debate regarding public persons outweighs the interest in protecting their reputations. But no public interest is served by a publication made with "knowing or reckless falsity," and hence there is no constitutional protection in such case. [Garrison v. Louisiana, *supra*, §1198]

(2) **What constitutes "knowing or reckless falsity":** [§1291] The plaintiff must show that the defendant was *subjectively aware* that the statement was false or was subjectively reckless as to its truth when making the statement. [New York Times Co. v. Sullivan, *supra*]

(a) **Motive to harm insufficient:** [§1292] It is *not* enough that the defendant be shown to have acted with spite, hatred, ill will, or intent to injure the plaintiff. Unless "knowing or reckless falsity" is established, there is not the requisite "malice" for constitutional purposes. [Rosenblatt v. Baer, *supra*, §1282]

1) **Example:** Newspaper reporter's statements that he wanted to "get" the plaintiff were insufficient to establish actual malice. [Margoles v. Hubbart, 760 P.2d 324 (Wash. 1988)]

2) **Compare—"malice" for punitive damages:** [§1293] Although the Supreme Court has talked in terms of "actual malice," this is really a term of art referring to the requirement of

deliberate falsity or reckless disregard for the ***truth*** of the information published. As such, it is quite different from the "malice" usually required under state tort law to support an award of ***punitive damages***—which requires a showing of hatred, spite, or ill will toward a plaintiff. [Cantrell v. Forest City Publishing Co., 419 U.S. 245 (1974)]

(b) **Negligence insufficient:** [§1294] "Reckless" conduct is ***not*** measured by a reasonable person standard or by whether a reasonable person would have investigated before publishing; *i.e.*, negligence is ***not*** enough. Rather, there must be a showing that the defendant ***in fact*** (subjectively) ***entertained serious doubts*** as to the truthfulness of the publication. [St. Amant v. Thompson, 390 U.S. 727 (1968)]

1) **Example:** If a scandal magazine completely fabricates a story about a celebrity, it necessarily entertained at least serious doubt as to the truth of the statements. [Carson v. Allied News Co., *supra*, §1287]

2) **Freelance authors:** [§1295] The rule of respondeat superior does not apply in the case of authors who are not employees but rather are hired for single assignments or who submit proposed pieces. In such cases, the plaintiff must prove that the defendant publisher either knew that the freelancer was a deliberate liar or disbelieved the contents of the completed piece but published it anyway. [Gertz v. Robert Welch, Inc., 680 F.2d 527 (7th Cir. 1982), *cert. denied*, 459 U.S. 1226 (1983)]

(3) **Proving "knowing or reckless falsity":** [§1296] Because the standard of liability is ***subjective***, it is difficult to meet.

(a) **Burden of proof:** [§1297] In this type of case, the plaintiff must prove "actual malice" with ***convincing clarity***; *i.e.*, a mere preponderance is insufficient. [New York Times Co. v. Sullivan, *supra*, §1291]

1) **Example:** Where the only evidence in support of a jury verdict for the plaintiff involves conflicting accounts of key conversations, a court may conclude that actual malice was not demonstrated with convincing clarity. [Long v. Arcell, 618 F.2d 1145 (5th Cir. 1980), *cert. denied*, 449 U.S. 1083 (1981)]

2) **Note:** Under the Federal Rules of Civil Procedure, federal courts, when considering motions for summary judgment in libel cases, must hold the plaintiff to the standard of convincing clarity if that is the standard the plaintiff must meet at trial. [Anderson v. Liberty Lobby, Inc., 477 U.S. 242 (1986)]

3) **And note:** Although the Supreme Court has required the plaintiff to prove falsity [Philadelphia Newspapers, Inc. v. Hepps, *supra*, §1280], whether the plaintiff must prove falsity with ***convincing clarity*** is an open question [Harte-Hanks Communications, Inc. v. Connaughton, 491 U.S. 657 (1989)].

(b) **Application** [§1298]

1) **Extremely questionable source:** A defendant may be found to have acted with actual malice where its source's credibility is seriously questioned by many other witnesses, where the defendant did not listen to taped conversations provided by the plaintiff to disprove defendant's projected story, where the defendant declined to interview a particular witness who could have verified the story, and where an earlier article by the defendant showed that it had already committed itself to attacking the plaintiff. [Harte-Hanks Communications, Inc., *supra*]

2) **Failure to investigate:** But failure to investigate alone does not amount to actual malice. [Sweeney v. Prisoners' Legal Services of New York, Inc., 84 N.Y.2d 786 (1995)]

3) **Publishing while knowing facts are incomplete:** A newspaper that publishes an Associated Press wire service story, even though the Associated Press announced that more would soon follow, did not publish with actual malice because there was no showing that the staff did not believe the first story. [Meisler v. Gannet Co., 12 F.3d 1026 (11th Cir. 1994)]

4) **Noting questionable varacity:** Where D newspaper carried an article defaming P based on a source that the article noted had been called a liar by others, and P sued for defamation, the article's attack on its own source was held to be a negation of actual malice rather than a showing of it. [McFarlane v. Esquire Magazine, 74 F.3d 1296 (D.C. Cir. 1996)]

(c) **Discovery:** [§1299] To prove the defendant's state of mind, the plaintiff may ask the defendant about it—even if the defendant is a reporter or editor. The First Amendment does not protect a journalist from discovery inquiries about his motives for reporting, belief in the accuracy of sources, the reason for pursuing some leads but not others, or the content of conversations among reporters and editors during the story's preparation. [Herbert v. Lando, 441 U.S. 153 (1979)]

(4) **Independent appellate review:** [§1300] Appellate courts, in determining whether the plaintiff has demonstrated convincing clarity, must undertake an independent review of the record, giving limited deference to trial court or jury findings. [Bose Corp. v. Consumers Union, 466 U.S. 485 (1984)] The Supreme Court has not yet decided whether independent appellate review must be applied to the jury's finding of falsity.

d. **Damages:** [§1301] Statements made with "knowing or reckless falsity" have no constitutional protection against defamation actions. So when a public person establishes the *New York Times* standard of liability against a media defendant, she may recover whatever damages are permitted under *state law* (*see supra*, §§1211 *et seq.*), subject as always to constitutional limitations on such items as punitive damages (*see supra*, §§23, 1226).

3. **Private Plaintiffs:** [§1302]   A plaintiff who is neither a public official nor a public figure is, for libel purposes, a private person. A lower constitutional standard applies in such cases because private persons are more vulnerable to injury from defamation since they lack the same opportunities for rebuttal as do public persons; and, unlike public persons, they did not voluntarily assume the risk of adverse comments. [Gertz v. Robert Welch, Inc., *supra*, §1286]

   a. **Constitutional limitation:** [§1303]   However, to protect the freedom of speech and press guaranteed by the First Amendment, liability without fault *cannot be imposed*, at least where a matter of public concern is involved. Where the statement published is such that substantial danger to the person's reputation would be *apparent* to a reasonably prudent editor or broadcaster, the plaintiff must prove that the publisher or broadcaster either *knew* that the defamatory words were false, *was reckless* as to truth, or *was negligent* as to their falsity. [Gertz v. Robert Welch, Inc., *supra*]

      (1) **Limited damages:** [§1304]   Under the *Gertz* approach, a plaintiff who proves no more than falsity due to negligence may recover only "actual injury" damages (*see infra*, §1212).

      (2) **Caveat—matters of private concern:** [§1305]   Defamation actions brought by a private plaintiff may not be subject to constitutional limitations *unless* a matter of public concern is involved. If the defamation involves a matter of purely private concern, a private plaintiff may recover presumed and punitive damages without proving actual malice (*see supra*, §§1223-1227). [Dun & Bradstreet, Inc. v. Greenmoss Builders, Inc., *supra*, §1226]

         (a) **"Public concern" defined:** [§1306]   In the *Dun & Bradstreet* case, the Court said that "public concern" was to be determined by looking at the "content, form, and context" of the defamatory statement.

            1) **Example:** D sent a confidential credit report to five subscribers that falsely stated that P had filed for bankruptcy. This statement was intended solely for the recipients, who were obligated not to reveal it to others. The content, form, and context of this statement indicated that it did not involve a matter of public concern. [Dun & Bradstreet, Inc. v. Greenmoss Builders, Inc., *supra*]

            2) **Note:** If the local newspaper had published the same report, the *context* would have been very different, and the report presumably would have been covered by the *Gertz* rule.

   b. **Applicable standard of liability:** [§1307]   The Supreme Court in *Gertz* left it to the states to determine their own respective standards for liability to private individuals (in public concern cases), as long as they do *not* apply strict liability.

      (1) **Majority view—negligence:** [§1308]   Almost all states have accepted the *Gertz* invitation and have set the standard for liability at the level of negligence. [Brown v. Kelly Broadcasting Co., *supra*, §1250]

(2) **Minority view—deliberate or reckless falsity:** [§1309] A few states have decided to adhere to the *New York Times* requirement (knowledge of falsity or reckless disregard for truth) in cases involving private plaintiffs in stories of general or public interest. [Sisler v. Gannett Co., 516 A.2d 1083 (N.J. 1986)]

(3) **New York view—grossly irresponsible manner:** [§1310] New York has decided that when a story's content is "arguably within the sphere of legitimate public concern," a private plaintiff must prove that the publisher acted in a "grossly irresponsible manner without due consideration for the standards of information gathering and dissemination ordinarily followed by responsible parties." [Gaeta v. New York News, Inc., 62 N.Y.2d 340 (1984)]

c. **Burden of proving falsity:** [§1311] A private plaintiff has the burden of proving falsity, at least where the speech is of public concern. The common law presumption of falsity has the potential to chill true speech on matters of public concern. [Philadelphia Newspapers, Inc. v. Hepps, *supra*, §1280]

d. **Damages:** [§1312] The First Amendment protects defendants in suits by private persons, if a matter of public concern is involved, by limiting the kinds of damages recoverable according to the degree of fault established by the plaintiff.

(1) **If defendant's falsity due to negligence, but not deliberate or reckless:** [§1313] Assuming the defendant was in fact negligent in ascertaining or reporting the truth of what it published—but had neither actual knowledge of the falsity nor reckless disregard for the truth—a private person *can* recover damages *limited to the "actual injury"* sustained. [Gertz v. Robert Welch, Inc., *supra*, §1303]

(a) **Rationale:** Allowing recovery for damages *not* based on "actual injury" would not further an important state interest and would invite juries to punish unpopular defendants, which may in turn cause undue self-censorship and restrictions on free debate. [Gertz v. Robert Welch, Inc., *supra*]

(b) **"Actual injury":** [§1314] The Supreme Court has not defined this term, but has stated that it is *not limited to out-of-pocket losses*. It may include impairment of reputation and standing in the community, personal humiliation, and mental anguish and suffering. The important point is that there must be *competent evidence* of "actual" injury (no presumed damages), although there need not be evidence that assigns an actual dollar value to the injury. [Time, Inc. v. Firestone, *supra*, §1288]

(2) **If defamation deliberate or reckless:** [§1315] It follows that a private plaintiff who cannot prove "actual injury" by the publication cannot recover *any* damages—*unless* she can show that the publication was made with knowledge of its falsity or with reckless disregard for the truth. In such a case, the plaintiff is entitled to whatever recovery is permitted under state law in such cases (*i.e.*, "*presumed*," and perhaps punitive damages). [Gertz v. Robert Welch, Inc., *supra*]

(a) **Note:** A private plaintiff who wishes to obtain presumed or punitive damages in a case involving a matter of public concern must meet *all* of the requirements set by the *New York Times* rule for public plaintiffs, including proof with convincing clarity and independent appellate review (*supra*, §§1297-1300).

I. RELATED TORTS [§1316]

For purposes of analysis, any problem that involves defamation may also involve an invasion of the right of *privacy* (*infra*) or the wrongful causing of *emotional distress* (*supra*). Therefore, consideration should always be given to establishing liability for those torts as well as defamation.

IX. WRONGFUL INVASION OF PRIVACY

chapter approach

Recognition of the right of privacy in tort law and in other areas of law has come fairly recently. As a result, the tort actions do not have the historical baggage and complexity that we saw in defamation cases. This means that the prima facie cases and defenses are shorter and more coherent. On the other hand, since privacy is frequently invaded by words, First Amendment defenses are often raised in privacy torts, just as in defamation.

The four separate categories of invasion of privacy that you have to remember are:

1. *An intrusion into plaintiff's private life*, usually done by the defendant secretly trying to learn something about the plaintiff;

2. *A public disclosure of private facts* about the plaintiff (this is perhaps the most famous privacy tort, derived from the famous Brandeis and Warren article in 4 Harv. L. Rev. 193);

3. *The use* by defendant of the *plaintiff's name or picture* for commercial purposes; and

4. *A publication placing the plaintiff in a "false light"* (basically a weaker form of defamation).

Each type of "invasion" is sufficiently different that it is dangerous to lump them together. It is better to think of them as four separate torts, learning the prima facie case of each as you would for any other tort. But note that, occasionally, two or more may be involved in the same case.

Also, although this area of law is generally developing by common law, a few states, led by New York, have a limited statutory right, especially on the "public disclosure" tort, which would foreclose a common law action on this tort.

A. INTRUSIONS INTO PLAINTIFF'S PRIVATE LIFE OR AFFAIRS

1. **Prima Facie Case:** [§1317]   To recover for this type of invasion of privacy, plaintiff must prove:

    Highly Offensive Intrusion by Defendant into Plaintiff's Private Life
    Intent or Negligence
    Causation

2. **Protected Area of Seclusion:** [§1318]   The law protects those areas of the plaintiff's life that the plaintiff can *reasonably expect* will not be intruded upon by one in the defendant's position. [Pearson v. Dodd, 410 F.2d 701 (D.C. Cir. 1969)]

    a. **Example:** Wiretapping P's home would be a clear invasion of privacy. [Hamberger v. Eastman, 206 A.2d 239 (N.H. 1964)] But if P had sought a disability pension or filed a personal injury complaint, an investigator's efforts to photograph P in public would not intrude on reasonable expectations of privacy. [Forster v. Manchester, 189 A.2d 147 (Pa. 1963); Jeffers v. Seattle, 597 P.2d 899 (Wash. 1979)]

b. **Compare—no right to privacy:** [§1319]   The *relationship* between the parties may convince some courts to deny recovery in what would otherwise give rise to an actionable invasion. Thus, even though urine testing clearly intrudes upon legitimate expectations of privacy, where that testing is ordered by an employer to find employment-related information—*i.e.*, whether employees are reporting to work with drugs in their system—it does not invade employees' privacy. [Baggs v. Eagle-Pilcher Industries Inc., 957 F.2d 268 (6th Cir. 1992)]

3. **Types of Intrusion:** [§1320]   *Any* behavior that intrudes on the plaintiff's solitude may be actionable.

a. **Intrusion onto plaintiff's property:** [§1321]   Invasions of privacy can occur when the defendant enters the plaintiff's property uninvited. Such intrusions can be tortious whether the defendant enters to obtain information (*e.g.*, an insurance investigator) or to convey information to the plaintiff.

(1) **Trespass:** [§1322]   Invasions of privacy that involve entry onto the plaintiff's property are also likely to be actionable trespasses.

(2) **But note:** Some trespasses may not amount to invasions of privacy. [McClain v. Boise Cascade Corp., 533 P.2d 343 (Or. 1975)—trespass on periphery of P's land did not show unreasonable surveillance]

b. **Nonphysical intrusions:** [§1323]   Nonproprietary impingements on the plaintiff's seclusion may also be tortious. [Nader v. General Motors Corp., 25 N.Y.2d 560 (1970)]

(1) **Example:** Owner of tanning salon secretly photographed patron while she was undressing and nude in tanning room. [Sabrina W. v. Willman, 540 N.W.2d 364 (Neb. 1995)]

(2) **Example:** D, from a hill some distance away, uses a high-powered telescope to look into P's upstairs bedroom, which cannot otherwise be observed.

(3) **Example:** Although P takes a risk that D will repeat P's statements, unauthorized recordings or films of the conversation intrude on P's right to control the range of his voice. [Ribas v. Clark, 38 Cal. 3d 355 (1985)]

(4) **Example:** D impedes P's movements on public streets. [Galella v. Onassis, 487 F.2d 986 (2d Cir. 1973)]

4. **Intrusion Must Be Highly Offensive:** [§1324]   For an intrusion into a plaintiff's solitude to be actionable, it must be *highly offensive* to a *reasonable person*. [Rest. 2d §652B]

a. **Example:** If D makes a few phone calls to try to collect a debt, P may be annoyed, but this would not be highly offensive to a reasonable person.

5. **Intent:** [§1325]   It is sufficient if the defendant *intended the intrusion* into the plaintiff's affairs although she did not intend it to offend the plaintiff. [Rest. 2d §652B]

    a. **Compare:** One court has held that a defendant who *negligently* permits a third party to intrude into the plaintiff's affairs is liable for that intrusion. [LeCrone v. Ohio Bell Telephone Co., 201 N.E.2d 533 (Ohio 1963)—phone company gave husband phone number of estranged wife]

    b. **And compare—respondeat superior:** A defendant whose employees were acting within the scope of their employment is liable for tort even though the employees' purpose had no relation to their duties. [Doe v. B.P.S. Guard Services, Inc., 945 F.2d 1422 (8th Cir. 1991)—department store security guards videotaping models while they changed clothes during fashion show]

    c. **And note:** The developing law of negligent infliction of emotional distress (*see supra*, §§627 *et seq.*) will apply here by analogy.

6. **No Publication Necessary:** [§1326]   Where the invasion of privacy consists of intrusion or eavesdropping (*e.g.*, by tapping phone wires) no publication is necessary, since the interest protected here is the plaintiff's "right to be let alone" rather than his interest in not having the information disseminated. [Rhodes v. Graham, 37 S.W.2d 46 (Ky. 1931)]

7. **Causation:** [§1327]   The defendant's conduct must have been the cause in fact and the proximate cause of the invasion of the plaintiff's interest in privacy and the ensuing damage.

8. **Defenses—Consent:** [§1328]   As with other torts, if the intrusion is authorized or permitted, there is no cause of action.

    a. **Conduct must not exceed scope of consent:** Consent is no defense, however, if the intrusions fall outside the plaintiff's actual or implied consent. [McDaniel v. Atlanta Coca-Cola Bottling Co., 2 S.E.2d 810 (Ga. 1939)—consent to investigators to investigate P's damage claim did not authorize investigators to install secret monitoring device in P's hospital room]

    b. **Note:** The issues involving consent in trespass cases, *supra*, §208, are also involved in intrusion cases. [Dietemann v. Time, Inc., 449 F.2d 245 (9th Cir. 1971)—consent to enter given to reporter posing as patient did not extend to making secret recordings or photographs]

9. **Damages:** [§1329]   Pure emotional distress and mental anguish *are* sufficient damages; thus, the plaintiff need not prove any special damages or pecuniary loss.

B. PUBLIC DISCLOSURE OF PRIVATE FACTS

1. **Prima Facie Case:** [§1330]   This action involves:

> *Highly Offensive Public Disclosure by Defendant of Private Facts about Plaintiff*
> *No Legitimate Public Interest*

Fault in Making the Disclosure
Causation

a. **Examples:** Motion picture discloses P's present identity and sordid details of her past life; P's doctor releases photos he has taken of P's anatomy or embarrassing information obtained in the course of treatment. [Melvin v. Reid, 112 Cal. App. 285 (1931); Horne v. Patton, 287 So. 2d 824 (Ala. 1974); *but see* Anderson v. Fisher Broadcasting Cos., 712 P.2d 803 (Or. 1986)—requiring some additional element, such as violating a duty of confidentiality, or wrongful acquisition of the information]

2. **What Are "Private Facts":** [§1331] The disclosed facts must involve the plaintiff's private life, *i.e.*, those aspects of her life that have not already received some publicity and that are not left open to public observation or inspection.

a. **Examples:** Publication of the names and photographs of mentally retarded children is a disclosure of private information where the parents have kept private the mental capacities of their children. [Deaton v. Delta Democratic Publishing Co., 326 So. 2d 471 (Miss. 1976)] So is the fact that P has a rare disease [Barber v. Time, Inc., 159 S.W.2d 291 (Mo. 1942)], and that P was involuntarily sterilized [Howard v. Des Moines Register & Tribune Co., 283 N.W.2d 289 (Iowa 1979)].

b. **Matters of public record:** [§1332] Facts that appear as a matter of public record do *not* fall in this category. Thus, a plaintiff cannot complain about a publication of her age if this appears in birth records, or about publication of a dishonorable discharge if this appears in public records of the plaintiff's military service. [Stryker v. Republic Pictures, 108 Cal. App. 2d 191 (1951); *and see infra*, §§1352-1353]

c. **Public occurrences:** [§1333] Facts that occur in public (*e.g.*, photos of the plaintiff taken in a public park or in a restaurant) are also outside this category. *Rationale:* Since anyone present would have observed the same thing, such facts are hardly "private."

(1) **Example:** Marching in a public gay parade will make it much more difficult to argue that P's homosexuality is a private fact. [Sipple v. Chronicle Publishing Co., 154 Cal. App. 3d 1040 (1984)]

(2) **But compare:** On the other hand, P's telling a group of friends and family that P had AIDS, with the understanding that it would be kept confidential, does not mean that the fact is no longer private. [Multimedia WMAZ, Inc. v. Kubach, 443 S.E.2d 491 (Ga. 1994)]

d. **Voluntary public figures:** [§1334] Persons who voluntarily come before the public eye, such as an actor or politician, have no right of privacy concerning reports of their public activities and appearances since these have not been kept private.

(1) **Example:** A town's public disclosure that its former bookkeeper had left the town's books in disarray did not reveal any protectable private matters, notwithstanding the claim that the town had agreed to keep such

matters private in exchange for the bookkeeper's resignation. [Loe v. Town of Thomaston, 600 A.2d 1090 (Me. 1991)]

(2) **Compare—involuntary public figure:** [§1335]   Those involuntarily before the public eye, such as those accused of crimes or involved in catastrophes, have not opened any of their lives to the public. If the facts disclosed did not occur before the public eye, reports may be considered to be of *private* matters. As discussed below, however, those disclosures are nonetheless privileged if they are newsworthy.

(a) **Example:** While P is on trial for tax evasion for one year, D obtains I.R.S. records and publicizes the fact that P has paid no taxes in 10 years. Since the I.R.S. records are not public, the report discloses private facts—but it may nonetheless be privileged (*see* below). Reports related to the trial are public facts even though P is involuntarily in the public eye.

3. **Publication Must Be "Highly Offensive":** [§1336]   Not every disclosure of plaintiff's private affairs is actionable. Everyone must expect some observation by others of their comings and goings. So to prevail, the plaintiff must establish that the disclosure was such as would be *highly offensive* to a *reasonable person*. [Sidis v. F-R Publishing Corp., 113 F.2d 806 (2d Cir. 1940)]

a. **Example:** Newspaper reports that P did the laundry yesterday or held a private party in her home are not highly offensive. [Rest. 2d §652D, comment c]

(1) **Compare:** A newspaper report that P is suffering from an embarrassing disease, had sex-change surgery, or is having an extramarital affair may well be highly offensive. [Diaz v. Oakland Tribune, Inc., 139 Cal. App. 3d 118 (1983)—sex-change surgery]

b. **Example:** There is no actionable invasion where a magazine publisher, credit card issuer, etc., sells *mailing lists* of its subscribers to others. [Shibley v. Time, Inc., 321 N.E.2d 791 (Ohio 1974)]

4. **Must Be a "Public" Disclosure:** [§1337]   The element of a "public" disclosure requires *more* than publication in the defamation sense. The disclosure must involve publicity—communication either to the *public at large* or to *enough individuals* that it is likely to reach the general public.

a. **Example:** A single letter from a collection agency to P's employer disclosing that P has not paid her bills and requesting assistance in collection of P's debt is not an invasion of privacy. [Timperly v. Chase Collection Service, 272 Cal. App. 2d 697 (1969)] But disclosing that fact in a newspaper ad, or in a notice posted in a public place, is sufficient publicity to be actionable. [Brents v. Morgan, 299 S.W. 967 (Ky. 1927)]

(1) **Compare:** Even without publicity, repeated letters or other unreasonable collection efforts may be actionable as intentional infliction of emotional distress (*see supra*, §§62 *et seq.*) or as an intrusion into private affairs.

b. **Example:** Improper disclosure of P's school transcript to a state commission is not a public disclosure. [Porter v. University of San Francisco, 64 Cal. App. 3d 825 (1976)]

(1) **But note:** A few courts hold that a letter to a big government agency may be a "public" disclosure. [Beaumont v. Brown, 257 N.W.2d 522 (Mich. 1977)]

5. **No Public Interest ("Newsworthiness"):** [§1338] If the defendant publicizes private facts about the plaintiff that are highly offensive, the plaintiff must show that the facts are not "newsworthy." [Diaz v. Oakland Tribune, Inc., *supra*]

    a. **What is "newsworthy":** [§1339] Courts have generally given the term a broad interpretation, holding it applicable to any matter as to which there is a *"legitimate public interest."*

        (1) **Example:** The publication of the plaintiff doctor's name and the report of her psychiatric and marital problems were newsworthy because they arguably related to the important public problem of medical malpractice. Additionally, the information added credibility to the story. [Gilbert v. Medical Economics Co., 665 F.2d 305 (10th Cir. 1981)]

        (2) **Example:** P had foiled an assassination attempt on President Ford. D, in reporting about P, stated that P was a homosexual. The court found the item was newsworthy because it attempted to dispel the myth that gays were "timid and weak" and to raise the issue of whether the President's belated thanks displayed any discriminatory attitudes toward homosexuals. [Sipple v. Chronicle Publishing Co., *supra*, §1333]

        (3) **Note:** If the published material involves a matter of legitimate public interest, the defendant will not be held liable, even if the material is in bad taste. [Neff v. Time, Inc. 406 F. Supp. 858 (W.D. Pa. 1976)—photo of football fan posing with trousers unzipped]

    b. **Application to voluntary public figures:** [§1340] Public interest in voluntary public figures often extends beyond their public appearances and activities. Disclosures of private facts concerning voluntary public figures are privileged where newsworthy.

        (1) **Example:** D discloses that a member of Congress has taken bribes or has committed adultery.

        (2) **Example:** D reports that P, a famous singer, is losing her voice because of excessive drinking.

        (3) **Matters not in legitimate public interest:** [§1341] Some aspects of a public figure's life may be so private or separate from her public life as to be beyond legitimate public interest. Publications of such private matters are *not privileged*.

            (a) **Example:** If a newspaper invites readers to reveal their "unique love relationships" and then reports an entry from P's ex-husband that identifies P by first name as having had several abortions, as being unable to have children, and as having engaged in spouse swapping, a jury could find that this information was not of legitimate public interest. [Winstead v. Sweeney, 517 N.W.2d 874 (Mich. 1994)]

(b) **Compare:** A book revealing that P had once been a heavy-drinking ne'er-do-well who neglected his children and could not keep a job, was unfaithful, and left his wife for another woman, was not actionable as a matter of law because the book was focused on the story of the woman P had left and was about the difficulties of urban migration. [Haynes v. Alfred A. Knopf, Inc., 8 F.3d 1222 (7th Cir. 1993)]

(c) **Note:** The distinction between disclosure of matters of legitimate public interest and impermissible prying into private lives may depend on community attitudes and is often a jury question. [Virgil v. Time, Inc., *infra*, §1350; Hawkins v. Multimedia, Inc., 344 S.E.2d 145 (S.C.), *cert. denied,* 479 U.S. 1012 (1986)—jury could find liability for story about teenage pregnancies that named P as a teenage father]

c. **Involuntary public figures:** [§1342]   Just as with voluntary public figures, publishers may disclose private facts concerning involuntary public figures **when they are newsworthy**, even though they go beyond the events that brought the plaintiff into the public eye.

(1) **Example:** Reports of P's past life and associations are privileged where P is on trial for murder. It does not matter if P is later acquitted.

(2) **Limitation:** Again, some aspects of P's life may be so private as to be beyond legitimate public interest. Although protection does not depend on whether P is voluntarily or involuntarily public, courts may take that fact into consideration.

d. **"Current" public interest:** [§1343]   The passage of time does not necessarily preclude a publication from being in the legitimate public interest. Thus, the life of one *formerly* in the public eye may be treated as "public property" and may be republished, although that individual is no longer in the public eye (*e.g.*, life history of former child prodigy; events from life of former prizefighter now retired; crimes committed in the past). [Sidis v. F-R Publishing Corp., *supra*, §1310]

(1) **But note:** The passage of time is likely to indicate a lack of newsworthiness more quickly in the cases of involuntary public figures than of voluntary ones.

6. **Fault:** [§1344]   Fault is an essential element of this tort because of its serious constitutional aspect. But the "fault" cannot be the same as in defamation (*supra*, §§1195 *et seq.*) because that was concerned with fault related to *falsity* and here the story is true. The fault element here instead is related to the action that gave rise to the highly offensive disclosure.

a. **Example:** A newspaper that runs a story about P's prior abortions, adultery, and sterility, where P is an ordinary private citizen may be found to have known that its revelations would be highly offensive and lack legitimate public interest. [Winstead v. Sweeney, *supra*]

b. **Note:** Although most revelations are intentional and are likely to be clear abuses of editorial discretion, a few actions may be based on negligence.

[Multimedia WMAZ, Inc. v. Kubach, *supra*, §1333—although D television station agreed to P's demand that his features be disguised by digitalization, a technician negligently failed to do so for seven seconds and P was identifiable]

7. **Causation:** [§1345]   As with intrusions, causation is an essential element of the public disclosure claim. (*See supra*, §1327.)

8. **Defenses**

   a. **Truth is no defense:** [§1346]   Since the gist of the tort is embarrassment about public awareness of private facts, truth is irrelevant. [Briscoe v. Reader's Digest Association, 4 Cal. 3d 529 (1971)]

   b. **Consent:** [§1347]   As with intrusions, consent is a complete defense for public disclosures.

      (1) **Information disclosed by plaintiff to defendant:** [§1348]   Normally, the fact that the plaintiff has voluntarily divulged facts about herself to the defendant bars any later claim against the defendant for repeating this information to others—even where the defendant promised to keep it "in the strictest confidence." A person's failure to keep things secret is not yet deemed a tort. [Wynne v. Orcutt, 17 Cal. App. 3d 1108 (1971)]

         (a) **Compare—breach of duty:** [§1349]   On the other hand, where the defendant was under a *legal duty not to disclose* the information without plaintiff's consent (*e.g.*, doctor-patient, attorney-client, etc.), the defendant's doing so may be actionable as an invasion of privacy. [Horne v. Patton, *supra*, §1330]

         (b) **Compare—consent to disclosure withdrawn:** [§1350]   A magazine cannot rely on consent to publish embarrassing private facts elicited from plaintiff during an interview, where plaintiff later changes his mind and, before publication, withdraws permission to print the story. [Virgil v. Time, Inc., 527 F.2d 1122 (9th Cir. 1975), *cert. denied*, 425 U.S. 998 (1976)]

   c. **Constitutional privilege:** [§1351]   To assure freedom of speech and press, a constitutional privilege for the media has been recognized in the public disclosure area.

      (1) **Matters of public record—absolute privilege:** [§1352]   Where the matters reported or published are taken from official court records and are accurately stated, the constitutional privilege is *absolute*. *Rationale:* The public interest in free reporting of such matters outweighs any interest in privacy on the part of those whose names appear in the records. [Cox Broadcasting Corp. v. Cohn, 420 U.S. 469 (1975)—broadcaster announcing name of deceased rape victim obtained from court records not liable for invasion of privacy of victim's family]

      (2) **Other matters—qualified privilege:** [§1353]   If the matter was *lawfully obtained from the government*, is truthful, and prohibition is not necessary to further a "state interest of the highest order," defendants are privileged to publish information. [The Florida Star v. B.J.F., 491 U.S.

524 (1989)—publication of rape victim's name that was obtained through inadvertent release by the police could not create civil (or criminal) liability]

9. **Damages:** [§1354]   The same rules apply to public disclosure as to intrusions. (*See supra*, §1329.) The damages here are more likely to be based on the humiliation arising from the public disclosure.

10. **Privacy Action Rejected:** [§1355]   A few states have rejected this type of privacy action where true facts are involved. These courts have expressed skepticism that the judiciary can develop adequate standards to determine what is highly offensive to a reasonable person and a fear that juries will second guess editorial judgments about truthful stories. [Anderson v. Fisher Broadcasting Cos., *supra*, §1330; Hall v. Post, 372 S.E.2d 711 (N.C. 1988)]

   a. **New York statute:** [§1356]   Under a New York statute [N.Y. Civ. Rts. Law §§50, 51], a true report about a person may be actionable only if published for "advertising purposes or for purposes of trade"—which have been limited to advertisers—with the result that media stories are virtually never actionable. [Finger v. Omni Publications International, Ltd., 77 N.Y.2d 138 (1990)]

C. APPROPRIATION OF PLAINTIFF'S NAME OR LIKENESS

1. **Prima Facie Case:** [§1357]   To recover for this type of invasion of privacy, the plaintiff must prove:

   Unauthorized Use by Defendant of Plaintiff's Name or Likeness for a Commercial Purpose
   Causation

2. **Unauthorized Use:** [§1358]   It is the ***unauthorized use*** of the plaintiff's name or likeness that is actionable. Therefore, it is no defense that the plaintiff is in fact a satisfied customer or user of the product involved. [Fairfield v. American Photocopy, 138 Cal. App. 2d 82 (1955)]

   a. **Note:** If the plaintiff is not a user of the product, and the advertisement hurts her reputation, it may also be defamation.

   b. **Consent:** [§1359]   A person who consents to the use of her likeness for a commercial purpose, and puts no limits on the nature of that use, cannot claim that her privacy has been invaded by the unforeseen manner in which her likeness was used. [Miller v. American Sports Co., 467 N.W.2d 653 (Neb. 1991)—model in bath towel pictured in hot tub brochure beneath the letters "S E X"]

   c. **Extension:** Some cases have extended protection beyond the "name or likeness" to other features associated with the plaintiff's identity. [Carson v. Here's Johnny Portable Toilets, Inc., 698 F.2d 831 (6th Cir. 1983)—product's name too close to words used to introduce television performer at each show; White v. Samsung Electronics America, Inc., 971 F.2d 1395 (9th Cir. 1992), *on petition for rehearing*, 989 F.2d 1512 (9th Cir. *en banc*), *cert. denied*, 113 S. Ct. 2443 (1993)—advertiser's robot too closely evoked image of woman who performed role on television quiz show]

3. **Right of Publicity vs. Right of Privacy:** [§1360]   Where the plaintiff is a *celebrity*, the use of her name clearly has commercial value so that she is entitled to damages not so much for invasion of privacy but rather for interference with her *right of publicity* (*i.e.*, her right to sell product endorsements to someone else). [Haelan Labs v. Topps Chewing Gum, Inc., 202 F.2d 806 (2d Cir.), *cert. denied*, 346 U.S. 816 (1953)]

   a. **Compare:** On the other hand, where the plaintiff is an unknown person, the unauthorized use of her name is more clearly an invasion of *privacy*; the plaintiff is entitled to compensation not for the commercial value of her name, but for interference with her "right to be let alone." [Fairfield v. American Photocopy, *supra*]

4. **Causation:** [§1361]   As with intrusion, causation is an essential element. (*See supra*, §1327.)

5. **Defense—Newsworthiness:** [§1362]   Where the plaintiff is a public figure or is a currently newsworthy figure, publication of the plaintiff's name or likeness is not actionable, as long as the use is not for the purposes of trade or advertising. [Montana v. San Jose Mercury News, Inc., 34 Cal. App. 4th 790 (1995)—constitutional right of newspaper to reprint action photos of recently retired football star since they report newsworthy items of public interest]

   a. **Compare:** A game manufacturer's use of a professional golfer's name in its product is actionable. [Palmer v. Schonhorn Enterprises, 232 A.2d 458 (N.J. 1967)]

   b. **No constitutional privilege for some noncommercial uses that destroy right of publicity:** [§1363]   There is no First Amendment privilege allowing media to film or broadcast an *entire* commercial entertainment or performance (*e.g.*, sports event) without the consent of the participant. It may be of public interest, but this does not give the media any privilege to impair the performer's right of publicity—*i.e.*, the right to get paid for this use of the performance. This is comparable to media publication of an entire copyrighted work without the owner's consent. [Zacchini v. Scripps-Howard Broadcasting Co., 433 U.S. 562 (1977)—unauthorized television news coverage of "human cannonball" act at county fair]

   c. **Newsworthiness privilege inapplicable to promotional materials depicting noncurrent events:** [§1364]   A promotional calendar distributed by a for-profit medical clinic where abortions were performed may not use an unaffiliated doctor's picture without her consent, even though the photograph was from a past newsworthy event or the calendar's theme (the history of women's rights) was of undisputed public interest. [Beverley v. Choices Women's Medical Center, Inc., 78 N.Y.2d 745 (1991)]

6. **Damages:** [§1365]   For celebrity plaintiffs, the damages for appropriations include the reasonable value of the use of the plaintiff's name or likeness. Thus, the defendant does not profit from the unauthorized use, and the plaintiff is compensated for any loss sustained by being unable to sell her name, features, or act to some other company. For private plaintiffs, emotional harm is likely to be the main element.

D. PUBLICITY PLACING PLAINTIFF IN A "FALSE LIGHT"

1. **Prima Facie Case:** [§1366]   This action involves:

   Publication by Defendant that Places Plaintiff in a False Light
   (Knowing or Reckless Falsity if "Newsworthy" Matter)
   Causation

   a. **Compare—appropriation of plaintiff's name or likeness:** [§1367]   This privacy action does not involve commercial appropriation; rather, the unauthorized use of the plaintiff's name or likeness is actionable if it places plaintiff in a false light in the public eye. [Cantrell v. Forest City Publishing Co., *supra*, §1293]

2. **Publication:** [§1368]   For the plaintiff to suffer damages from a "false light" publication, dissemination to a reasonable number of third persons is required. [Bernstein v. National Broadcasting Co., 129 F. Supp. 817 (D.D.C.), *aff'd*, 232 F.2d 369 (D.C. Cir. 1956)]

3. **Falsity Required:** [§1369]   The false light in which the plaintiff is placed must be ***highly offensive to a reasonable person***. [Rest. 2d §652E]

   a. **Example—false light by association:** D published photographs of P in *Hustler* magazine without her permission. The court found that the implication that P was associated with the magazine could be highly offensive to a reasonable person. [Douglass v. Hustler Magazine, Inc., 769 F.2d 1128 (7th Cir. 1985), *cert. denied*, 475 U.S. 1094 (1986)]

      (1) **But note:** Where the defendant magazine includes photographs of the plaintiff without her consent as a part of a book review, no association with the magazine is suggested. Thus, no false light privacy claim exists. [Faloona v. Hustler Magazine Inc., 799 F.2d 1000 (5th Cir. 1986), *cert. denied*, 479 U.S. 1088 (1987)]

   b. **Example:** Defendants reporter and camera crew conducted an "ambush interview" of P, with the film portraying P as unresponsive to charges of misconduct by P's company. The court found that the interview did not portray P in a false light since it was P's own conduct captured on film. [Machleder v. Diaz, 801 F.2d 46 (2d Cir. 1986), *cert. denied*, 479 U.S. 1088 (1987)]

4. **Compare—Defamation:** [§1370]   If the "false light" would affect the plaintiff's reputation in the community, an action for defamation may also lie. Most states will prevent the plaintiffs from escaping the restrictions of defamation law simply by calling the action one for privacy. This would apply to such matters as the need for special damages. [Fellows v. National Enquirer, Inc., 42 Cal. 3d 234 (1986)—applying state's libel retraction and special damages provisions to false light privacy action]

   a. **Note:** A handful of states do not recognize the false light privacy cause of action precisely because a defamation action so closely relates to the false light cause of action that it suffices to protect a plaintiff's reputation and other interests. [Cain v. Hearst Corp., 878 S.W.2d 577 (Tex. 1994)]

5. **Fault:** [§1371]   The First Amendment protects media (and other) defendants from liability for some "false light" publications.

   a. **Newsworthy matters:** [§1372]   Newsworthy statements by the media that put plaintiff in a false light are not actionable unless the "knowing or reckless falsity" standard is met (*i.e.*, publisher knew or was blind to the fact that publication would place the plaintiff in highly offensive false light in the public eye). [Time, Inc. v. Hill, 385 U.S. 374 (1967)]

      (1) **Example:** A letter sent by a private individual to the state governor, attorney general, and members of the media charging a state board president's husband with improperly thrusting himself into state affairs did not give rise to a false light claim in the absence of clear and convincing evidence of actual malice. [Dodson v. Dicker, 812 S.W.2d 97 (Ark. 1991)—plaintiff must prove that the writer entertained actual doubts about the accuracy of the charges]

      (2) **Compare—defamation:** [§1373]   Should constitutional protections in this privacy area develop by analogy to the *Gertz* case in defamation (*see supra*, §1226), the media would not be shielded from liability for false light publications of private matters if they were negligent in not recognizing that a private person was portrayed in a false light. The Court has left the question open. [Cantrell v. Forest City Publishing Co., *supra*]

6. **Causation:** [§1374]   As with intrusion, causation is an essential element. (*See supra*, §1327.)

7. **Damages:** [§1375]   Plaintiff may recover for damage to reputation, for any emotional distress suffered, and for pecuniary damages.

E.   CLAIMS INVOLVING PRIVACY OF THIRD PERSONS

1. **Publications Regarding Living Persons:** [§1376]   Most courts hold that a plaintiff **cannot** recover for an invasion of privacy based on publicity concerning another living person no matter how close their relationship. [Coverstone v. Davies, *supra*, §146—father denied recovery for invasion of his privacy based on newspaper publicity concerning arrest of son]

2. **Publications Concerning a Dead Person:** [§1377]   Nor can a cause of action ordinarily be maintained on account of publications regarding a person who is already dead.

   a. **Survivors' privacy claims:** [§1378]   Most courts hold that there is **no** "relational" right of privacy, so that a decedent's survivors (no matter how close) **cannot** complain of any invasion of **their** interests because of publicity concerning the decedent. [Metter v. Los Angeles Examiner, 35 Cal. App. 2d 304 (1939)—newspaper published photo of P's wife and lurid details of her suicide, causing P great anguish; no recovery allowed]

   b. **Decedent's claims:** [§1379]   And the **decedent's** right of privacy is a personal right that generally does not survive her death. Hence, no cause of action can be maintained on behalf of decedent by her estate or heirs for publications *after* her death. [*See, e.g.,* Maritote v. Desilu, 345 F.2d 418 (7th Cir. 1965)—suit by heirs of Al Capone]

(1) **Compare—publications during lifetime:** [§1380]   Where the invasion occurred *during* the decedent's lifetime (rather than after death), clearly the decedent could have sued. Whether her estate can sue, however, depends on the survival statute in effect (*see supra,* §960). If the statute is broad enough, an action can be maintained by the estate. [Estate of Berthiaume v. Pratt, 365 A.2d 792 (Me. 1976)—doctor took unauthorized pictures of dying cancer patient to show progression of illness; patient's estate allowed to sue for invasion of patient's privacy]

(2) **Celebrity's right of publicity:** [§1381]   Most courts hold that whatever right a celebrity has to exploit her name and likeness must be exercised during the person's life. If it is not, the heirs cannot inherit an exclusive right to that exploitation after death. [Lugosi v. Universal Pictures, 25 Cal. 3d 813 (1979); *but see* Martin Luther King Center For Social Change, Inc. v. American Heritage Products, Inc., 296 S.W.2d 697 (Ga. 1982)—contra]

(a) **Exploitation during life:** [§1382]   At least where the right of exploitation was exercised during the celebrity's lifetime and then assigned to the plaintiff, it has been held to survive. [Acme Circus Operating Co. v. Kuperstock, 711 F.2d 1538 (11th Cir. 1983)]

F.   IMPORTANT—RELATED TORTS

1. **Publication May Give Rise to Several Torts:** [§1383]   It should be emphasized again that the torts of *defamation, wrongful infliction of emotional distress,* and *wrongful invasion of privacy* frequently occur concurrently, and accordingly each should be considered whenever any one of them appears to be involved.

2. **Breach of Confidential Relationship:** [§1384]   If the parties have some preexisting relationship, courts may rely on that relationship instead of a privacy approach. [Humphers v. First Interstate Bank of Oregon, 696 P.2d 527 (Or. 1985)—physician who helped adopted person learn identity of her natural mother may have breached confidential relationship between physician and his former patient (the mother)]

3. **Limitation on Causes of Action Under Uniform Act:** [§1385]   Under the Uniform Single Publication Act, in effect in some states [*e.g.,* Cal. Civ. Code §3425.3], only a single cause of action is allowed for damages arising from any single publication—whether for defamation, invasion of privacy, or any other tort founded upon such publication. Recovery for one tort thus *bars any other claim* for damages *arising out of the same publication,* anywhere. (Any issue of a book or magazine, any radio or television broadcast, or any one exhibition of a movie is regarded as a "single publication"—no matter how many persons heard it, read it, etc.)

X. OTHER TORTS

chapter approach

The list of torts discussed up to now is by no means all-inclusive, although it probably covers the torts you studied in your law school class. A number of other torts, however, have also been recognized. (Some are discussed in other Summaries; *e.g.*, unfair competition and infringement of literary property are covered in the Remedies Summary.) Of the remaining recognized torts, the following are the most important for you to know:

1. *Misrepresentation* (based on intent, negligence, or strict liability);

2. *Injurious Falsehood* (interference with the prospect of a sale or other advantageous relationship affecting the plaintiff's property);

3. *Interference with Economic Relations* (interference with contract or prospective economic advantage); and

4. *Unjustifiable Litigation* (malicious prosecution, wrongful institution of a civil case, and abuse of process).

But also remember—there is *no fixed*, *rigid number of torts*; facts that do not fit any particular "classic tort" pattern may still be actionable. And many new tort actions have been created by statute, such as those authorizing damages for discrimination and civil rights violations.

A. MISREPRESENTATION

1. **Introduction:** [§1386] Misrepresentation—which protects the plaintiff's *economic* (not personal or physical) interests—may be predicated on any of the three bases of liability (intentional tort, negligence, or strict liability). However, with misrepresentation, there are substantial differences in the prima facie case and in the scope of liability, depending on which basis for liability is involved.

    a. **Example:** D physician gave an incorrect opinion to P's attorney, as a result of which, P did not try to sue a negligent surgeon within the statute of limitations. P's suit against D was for the economic loss caused by the dismissal of that earlier lawsuit—and was properly brought for the misrepresentation. The loss is equivalent to what would have been recoverable in the personal injury case. [Hart v. Browne, 103 Cal. App. 3d 947 (1980)]

2. **Intentional Misrepresentation ("Fraudulent Misrepresentation" or "Deceit"):** [§1387] Prima facie case:

    Misrepresentation by Defendant
    Scienter
    Intent to Induce Plaintiff's Reliance
    Causation—Actual Reliance

Justifiable Reliance
Damages

a. **Misrepresentation by defendant**

(1) **Affirmative misrepresentation:** [§1388]   Ordinarily, there must be a *false*, *material* representation of a past or present *fact*. However, in certain cases, false representations of opinion or law may also be actionable. (This is a question of justifiable reliance; *see* below.)

  (a) **"Material" misrepresentation:** [§1389]   "Material" covers any representation that would have influenced a reasonable person in the plaintiff's position in this type of business dealing, as well as any representation that defendant knew this specific plaintiff considered important.

  (b) **"Fact":** [§1390]   A misrepresentation of a *present state of mind or intention* is treated as a misrepresentation of fact (*e.g.*, promises to perform that the promisor *never intended* to perform). "A man's state of mind or intention is as much a fact as his state of digestion." [Channel Master Corp. v. Aluminum Ltd. Sales, Inc., 4 N.Y.2d 403 (1958); Lazar v. Superior Court, 12 Cal. 4th 631 (1996)]

    1) **Unauthorized promise:** A promise made by someone who knows he has no authority to make the promise is actionable as a misrepresentation. [Boivin v. Jones & Vining, Inc., 578 A.2d 187 (Me. 1990)—company held liable for fraud after employee, who was promised lifetime employment by vice president, was fired]

  (c) **"Representation":** [§1391]   The representation is usually by oral or written words, but it may be by conduct as well (*e.g.*, exhibiting a document, turning back the mileage indicator on a car offered for sale, etc.).

(2) **Fraudulent concealment:** [§1392]   Even though no affirmative representation is made by the defendant, the fraudulent concealment of facts will be a sufficient "misrepresentation," *except where*:

  (a) *The bill of sale or transaction is marked "as is"* (minority view is contra); or

  (b) *Plaintiff is charged with some knowledge or notice* of the facts concealed.

(3) **Failure to disclose:** [§1393]   On the other hand, the defendant is ordinarily *not* under any *duty to disclose* facts. Thus, failure to disclose (as distinguished from active concealment) all the defendant knows is not a "misrepresentation." [Rest. 2d §551]

  (a) **Exceptions:** [§1394]   In the following cases, the defendant's failure to disclose *will* support an action for intentional misrepresentation.

1) **Fiduciary relationship:** [§1395] Where the defendant and the plaintiff are in some special fiduciary relationship to each other (*e.g.*, trustee-beneficiary, guardian-ward), the defendant's failure to disclose will support an action for intentional misrepresentation.

2) **"Half-truths":** [§1396] A defendant who has made an incomplete or ambiguous statement or half-truth, knowingly misleading, comes under a duty to clarify the statement and disclose the truth. [Silva v. Stevens, 589 A.2d 852 (Vt. 1991)—discussion of leaks that had been fixed created duty to warn about other leaks that had not been fixed, even absent duty to speak in the first place]

3) **New information:** [§1397] A defendant has a duty to disclose when he has made a statement believing it to be true but later finds out that it is false, or where the statement was true when made but material facts have changed, and the defendant knows the plaintiff is relying on the first version.

4) **Reliance:** [§1398] Where the defendant has made a statement knowing it is false but not intending that anyone rely on it, and then finds out that the plaintiff is about to act on it, the defendant also has a duty to disclose.

5) **Sale of property:** [§1399] Several states (modern trend) recognize an additional exception: In cases involving the sale of property, where certain material facts are known to the seller and are both *unknown and not readily accessible to the buyer*, the seller is bound to disclose the facts to the buyer; the failure to do so constitutes misrepresentation actionable for damages or rescission. [Ollerman v. O'Rourke Co., 288 N.W.2d 95 (Wis. 1980); Johnson v. Davis, 480 So. 2d 625 (Fla. 1985)]

   a) **Examples:** Actionable misrepresentation includes the failure to disclose that: the land sold was filled; the building sold was infested by termites; the house sold had a badly leaking roof when it rained; improvements on the property sold violated local building, health, or zoning ordinances or regulations; or litigation was pending involving the business or property sold. [Strawn v. Canuso, 657 A.2d 420 (N.J. 1995)—duty on seller and broker to disclose existence of off-site closed landfill "not readily observable" by buyer]

b. **Scienter**

(1) **Defined:** [§1400] "Scienter" refers to the defendant's *knowledge* of the falsity of the representation made, or knowledge that he had an insufficient basis for determining the truth of the representation (*i.e.*, recklessness in making the statement). [Derry v. Peek, 14 A.C. 337 (1888); Rest. 2d §526]

(2) **Intent to deceive implied:** [§1401]   Negligence alone is not sufficient for scienter; *i.e.*, the defendant's honest belief in the truth of the representation, even if based on unreasonable grounds, will ***not*** support an action for intentional misrepresentation. But the enormity of the unreasonable behavior ***may*** allow a jury to ***infer lack of honest belief***, which would suffice for scienter.

(3) **Burden of proof:** [§1402]   Because it is relatively easy to claim fraud and often hard to disprove it, most courts demand that plaintiffs prove their claims of fraud by ***clear and convincing evidence***. [Greycas, Inc. v. Proud, 826 F.2d 1560 (7th Cir. 1987), *cert. denied*, 484 U.S. 1043 (1988); *but see* Liodas v. Sahadi, 19 Cal. 3d 278 (1977)—contra and retaining the preponderance standard]

c. **Intent to induce reliance of plaintiff:** [§1403]   The defendant must have intended to induce the reliance of the ***plaintiff, or a class of persons*** to which the plaintiff belongs, in a particular transaction. [Metric Investment, Inc. v. Patterson, 244 A.2d 311 (N.J. 1968)]

(1) **Exception—ongoing deception:** Where the misrepresentation is a "continuous deception" (*e.g.*, the mislabeling of a product by its manufacturer, or a misrepresentation contained in a negotiable instrument), it is not necessary that the reliance of a particular plaintiff (or reliance in a particular transaction) be intended. Anyone who acquires the product or instrument may sue.

d. **Causation:** [§1404]   It must be proven that the misrepresentation played a substantial part in inducing the plaintiff to act as she did—*i.e.*, ***actual*** reliance. The plaintiff's awareness of the falsity of the misrepresentation precludes reliance. [Van Ettinger v. Pappin, 588 P.2d 988 (Mont. 1978); Nader v. Allegheny Airlines, Inc., 626 F.2d 1031 (D.C. Cir. 1980)—P knew that airlines often "overbooked"]

e. **Justifiable reliance by plaintiff**

(1) **Plaintiff's reliance must be foreseeable:** [§1405]   For the plaintiff's reliance to be "justified" it must have been ***intended*** by the defendant ***or reasonably foreseeable***. Clearly, if the plaintiff ***knows*** that she was not the person whose reliance was intended by the defendant (as where the plaintiff was an agent of a third person and the defendant made the representation to the plaintiff only for purpose of transmission to that person, and intending only that person to rely thereon), the plaintiff cannot justifiably rely thereon.

(2) **Whether reliance is "justified" depends on type of representation:** [§1406]   Even assuming the plaintiff's reliance was intended or foreseeable, and that she did actually rely, the plaintiff's reliance on every type of representation made by the defendant may not be "justified."

(a) **Representations of fact:** [§1407]   The plaintiff's unconditional reliance on material misrepresentations of ***fact*** (including misrepresentations of present state of mind and intention) is ***always justified***, except where the facts are obviously false. [*See* Lockard v. Carson, 287 N.W.2d 871 (Iowa 1980)]

1) **No duty to investigate:** [§1408]   A plaintiff is under no duty to check the truth of the defendant's representations of fact, no matter how easy it would be to do so. If the plaintiff does investigate, however, she cannot rely on representations that are inconsistent with the facts she discovered or reasonably should have discovered during such investigation.

(b) **Representations of opinion:** [§1409]   A plaintiff is ordinarily *not* justified in relying on misrepresentations of *opinion, value, or quality unless* one of the following four exceptions applies:

1) *Defendant has a superior knowledge not available to plaintiff* (*e.g.*, D is a jeweler, art dealer, etc., seeking to make a sale). The difficult problem is to determine when a dealer's "puffing" or bragging about his wares turns from "loose sales talk" into an actionable misrepresentation (*i.e.*, statements that can reasonably be interpreted as assurances of specific facts). [Vulcan Metals v. Simmons, 248 F. 853 (2d Cir. 1918)]

2) *Defendant owes some fiduciary duty to plaintiff* (*e.g.*, trustee-beneficiary).

3) *Defendant and plaintiff are in some way affiliated or specially related*, so that defendant has *"secured the confidence"* of plaintiff (*e.g.*, P and D are members of a family or common fraternal or religious organization).

4) *Defendant offers plaintiff advice* on some transaction plaintiff was contemplating with a third person without disclosing that defendant has a financial interest in the deal (*e.g.*, bank president D recommends XYZ stock to customer P as a safe investment, without any reasonable grounds for believing this to be true and without disclosing that he has a financial interest in the sale of such stock). [Rest. 2d §543]

(c) **Representations of law:** [§1410]   A plaintiff's reliance on the defendant's representations of law is justified when the representation is in the nature of a *fact* (*e.g.*, "the Eighteenth Amendment was repealed yesterday"). However, if the representation constitutes an *opinion* (*e.g.*, "the city licensing ordinances do not affect your type of business"), reliance is justified only in the four situations discussed immediately above. [National Conversion Corp. v. Cedar Building Corp., 23 N.Y.2d 621 (1969)]

1) **But note:** There is no duty to disclose the existence of a regulation, because both parties have constructive knowledge of it. [Baskin v. Collins, 806 S.W.2d 3 (Ark. 1991)—no cause of action for nondisclosure of federal environmental regulations affecting gas station for sale]

f. **Damages:** [§1411]   Unlike most intentional torts, *proof of actual damages must be shown to obtain any recovery*. The measure of damages is discussed *infra*, §§1435-1440.

3. **Negligent Misrepresentation:** [§1412]   Prima facie case:

> *Misrepresentation by Defendant*
> *Negligence Toward Particular Group*
> *Cause in Fact—Actual Reliance*
> *Justifiable Reliance*
> *Proximate Cause*
> *Damages*

a. **Misrepresentation—made in business or professional capacity:** [§1413] The same type of misrepresentation may serve as a basis for an action in negligent misrepresentation as for an action in intentional misrepresentation, above. *Note:* The negligent representation must normally be made *by one in the business of supplying information for the guidance of others in business transactions* (accountants, lawyers, architects, surveyors, title abstractors, etc.). [Ritter v. Custom Chemicides, Inc., 912 S.W.2d 128 (Tenn. 1995)—extending liability beyond statements by "professionals" to cover instructions for growing tomatoes]

   (1) **Example:** P is induced to withdraw from participation in a benefit program in reliance upon negligent misrepresentation of insurance agent D. [Florenzano v. Olson, 387 N.W.2d 168 (Minn. 1986)]

   (2) **Compare—information volunteered under nonbusiness conditions:** [§1414]   Where the representation is volunteered in a nonprofessional or noncommercial setting (*e.g.*, "curbstone advice" offered by a lawyer to a neighbor), liability will result only if the statements are *not honestly made*.

   (3) **Compare—ordinary negligence:** [§1415]   When an attorney or other professional behaves carelessly, the resulting harm *need not* involve any reliance element. An attorney's failure to file suit before the statute of limitations expires, or the drafting of an invalid will that costs an intended legatee her inheritance, may cause harm without any negligent misrepresentation being made and relied on by the plaintiff. (*See infra*, §§1506-1507.)

b. **Negligence toward particular plaintiff:** [§1416]   If defendant provides information with the intent that the plaintiff rely on it in a business transaction or knows that such reliance is likely, the defendant is under a *duty to exercise reasonable care* to discover the truth or falsity of the representations made. [International Products Co. v. Erie Railroad, 244 N.Y. 331 (1927)] (Note how different this is from the scienter requirement in intentional misrepresentation, §1400, *supra*.)

   (1) **To whom duty owed:** [§1417]   A defendant owes a duty of care only to those persons to whom the representation was made or to those the defendant knew would rely upon it; *i.e.*, the *defendant must have contemplated the reliance of a particular plaintiff* or group of persons to which the plaintiff belongs.

(a) **Compare—deceit:** [§1418]   Where the action is for *intentional misrepresentation*, the defendant is liable to any person whose reliance was intended or *reasonably foreseeable* (*see supra*, §1405).

(b) **Privity of contract not required:** [§1419]   It is not essential that the plaintiff be in privity of contract with the defendant. Liability may be found where the defendant made a negligent representation to a third person (*e.g.*, client) *with knowledge* that the client intended to communicate the information to a *specific individual or group* for the purpose of inducing reliance thereon. *Example:* Public weigher issued certificate to a seller it knew would sell goods to a particular purchaser who would purchase in reliance on the certificate. [Glanzer v. Shepard, 233 N.Y. 236 (1922); *but see* Bronstein v. GZA GeoEnvironmental, Inc., 665 A.2d 369 (N.H. 1995)—announcing that report was for exclusive use of only one named person barred others from suing in reliance on information contained therein]

(2) **Professional liability:** [§1420]   Although professionals are always liable to clients for negligently prepared reports and documents (*e.g.*, financial statements), there is considerable disagreement as to how far liability may be extended to third parties.

(a) **Traditional view:** [§1421]   Under the traditional view, an accountant was *not liable to third parties* for negligently prepared statements unless the relationship between the accountant and the third party was essentially one of privity. [Ultramares Corp. v. Touche, Niven & Co., 255 N.Y. 170 (1931)—accountants negligently certified corporation's financial statements, knowing that corporation intended to use the statements in dealing with creditors generally, but not knowing the nature of the dealings or identity of particular persons who would be shown the statements]

1) **Rationale:** The reason behind this limitation is the *potential consequence* of imposing a duty of care to third persons—*i.e.*, the concern that the defendant's thoughtless slip in dealing with one person (client) might expose him to "liability in an indeterminate amount to an indeterminate class" of other persons. [Ultramares Corp. v. Touche, Niven & Co., *supra*]

(b) **Modern views:** [§1422]   Over the past decade, courts have become more willing to expand the scope of duty in *Ultramares*-type cases. Three different approaches have emerged:

1) **New York ("linkage") view:** [§1423]   Before an accountant (defendant) may be liable for negligence to a noncontractual party (plaintiff), defendant must be aware that a known party was intending to rely on the financial statement *and* some conduct must link defendant to plaintiff in a way that suggests the accountant's willingness to incur a duty to the creditor. [Security Pacific Business Credit, Inc. v. Peat Marwick Main & Co., 79 N.Y.2d 695 (1992)—a single unsolicited phone call to the accountant does not create the needed linkage]

2) **California ("specific foreseeability") view:** [§1424]   An accountant may be held liable if she knows that a specific third party plans to rely on the statement for a transaction whose nature and extent is known to the accountant. [Bily v. Arthur Young & Co., 3 Cal. 4th 370 (1992)—similar to Rest. 2d §552]

3) **New Jersey ("general foreseeability") view:** [§1425]   A very few states hold that an accountant may be liable if the third party (plaintiff) belongs to a class of people who could generally be foreseen to receive and rely on the statement. [Citizens State Bank v. T. Schmidt & Co., 335 N.W.2d 361 (Wis. 1983)]

(c) **Compare—liability based on statute:** [§1426]   Quite apart from common law negligence, liability to third persons may be based on a defendant's violation of *statutory* duties to provide accurate information. Such statutes create a duty to the general public; therefore it is not necessary to show the defendant's knowledge that a particular plaintiff would rely. For example, an accountant who negligently certifies a financial statement for a large corporate client may be held liable under S.E.C. Rule 10b-5 to any member of the public who purchases or sells the corporate shares in reliance thereon. (*See* Corporations Summary.)

c. **Cause in fact (actual reliance):** *See supra,* §§327 *et seq.*

d. **Justifiable reliance:** [§1427]   This is the same as in intentional misrepresentation (*see supra,* §§1405 *et seq.*), except that unreasonable failure to investigate may be *contributory negligence.*

e. **Proximate cause:** *See supra,* §§348 *et seq.*

f. **Damages:** *See* discussion below.

4. **Misrepresentation Predicated on Strict Liability ("Innocent Misrepresentation"):** [§1428]   A growing number of courts also impose damages for certain misrepresentations in connection with the *sale of land or chattels*—even where the falsity was neither known nor the result of negligence.

a. **Example:** D sells a tractor to P, representing that it is capable of performing certain functions, which in fact it is not. D is liable for the misrepresentations, even though D honestly and reasonably believed that the tractor could perform as represented. [Ford Motor Co. v. Lonon, 398 S.W.2d 240 (Tenn. 1966); Rest. 2d §552c; *but see* Shapiro v. Hu, 188 Cal. App. 3d 324 (1986)—rule of "caveat emptor" applies where property sold "as is" and P fails to allege fraudulent misrepresentation or concealment]

b. **Nature of liability:** [§1429]   The basis for liability here is very close to that for breach of express warranty (a contract theory); *i.e.,* having made a warranty as to the thing sold, the seller is bound thereby whether or not he had reason to know of its falsity.

(1) **Note:** Another analogy is unjust enrichment—in which the defendant gets something from the plaintiff without justification.

(2) **But note:** This is clearly *not* a contract action; hence, contractual defenses such as the *parol evidence rule* (which often excludes verbal warranties made in connection with a written contract of sale) do *not* apply.

c. **Prima facie case:** [§1430]   The prima facie case is the same as for negligent misrepresentation (*see supra*, §1412), except that there is *no requirement of fault at all*. All that need be shown is a *false representation made with the intent to induce the plaintiff's reliance* in a business transaction, and the plaintiff's *justifiable reliance* thereon to her *financial detriment* and to the defendant's gain.

(1) **Compare—products liability:** [§1431]   Recovery for misrepresentation is limited to pecuniary damages to the plaintiff's *business interests*. If physical harm has resulted from use or consumption of a product, consider the products liability rules (*see supra*, §§763 *et seq.*). [Rest. 2d §402B]

5. **Defenses**

a. **Contributory negligence:** [§1432]   Contributory negligence is a defense to *negligent* misrepresentation, but *not* to intentional misrepresentation or to misrepresentations pegged on strict liability. [FDIC v. W.R. Grace & Co., 877 F.2d 614 (7th Cir. 1989), *cert. denied*, 494 U.S. 1056 (1990)—contributory negligence not a defense to intentional fraud claim]

(1) **Note:** Most states apply comparative negligence. [Greycas, Inc. v. Proud, *supra*, §1402; *but see* Estate of Braswell v. People's Credit Union, 602 A.2d 510 (R.I. 1992)—contra]

b. **Assumption of risk:** [§1433]   Assumption of the risk is a defense to both *strict liability* misrepresentations and *negligent* misrepresentations.

c. **Exculpatory contracts:** [§1434]   In most states, exculpatory contracts that seek to exempt one from *fraud or intentional wrongdoing* (*e.g.*, "buyer hereby waives any misrepresentations," etc.) are *void*. [*See, e.g.*, Cal. Civ. Code §1668; Silva v. Stevens, *supra*, §1396—"as is" provision in contract does not bar actions for fraud or for negligent misrepresentation]

(1) **But note:** In a few states a contract that says the buyer is not relying on the seller's statement will bar a tort claim for fraud [Danann Realty Corp. v. Harris, 5 N.Y.2d 317 (1959)], but a general merger clause will not [Hobart v. Schuler, 55 N.Y.2d 1023 (1982)].

6. **Measure of Damages:** [§1435]   The courts are divided over the measure of damages to be awarded in misrepresentation cases, regardless of which basis for liability is involved:

a. **Benefit-of-bargain rule:** [§1436]   The majority of courts hold that the plaintiff is entitled to the benefit of the bargain: the *value* of the property as *contracted for* (*i.e.*, had the representation been true) less the value of the property as it actually was. [Hartwell Corp. v. Bumb, 345 F.2d 453 (9th Cir. 1965); Rungee v. Cox, 599 So. 2d 1151 (Ala. 1992)]

(1) **Note:** This is basically the same measure as applied in contract actions for breach of warranty. (*See* Contracts Summary.)

(2) **And note:** When the plaintiff is proceeding on an innocent misrepresentation theory, contract-based damages are *not* usually permitted because the action is thought of as one similar to restitution.

b. **Out-of-pocket loss rule:** [§1437]   A minority view limits the plaintiff's recovery to out-of-pocket loss (the *price paid* less the value of the property received) which is a more typical tort measure of compensatory damage.

(1) **Example:** D sells land to P for $10,000, falsely representing that the water well is adequate for irrigation purposes. Without adequate water, the land is worth no more than $7,000. With adequate water, it is realistically worth $25,000. Under the "benefit-of-bargain" rule, P recovers $18,000; whereas under the "out-of-pocket loss" rule, recovery is limited to $3,000.

c. **Middle ground positions:** [§1438]   A few courts will apply *either* rule, making it a question of *proof*: *i.e.*, if the value of the property as represented is proved to a *reasonable certainty*, the plaintiff gets the benefit of the bargain; otherwise, the plaintiff can recover only out-of-pocket loss. [Zeliff v. Sabatino, 104 A.2d 54 (N.J. 1954); Hinkle v. Rockville Motor Co., 278 A.2d 42 (Md. 1971)]

d. **Emotional distress:** [§1439]   Some states allow damages for emotional distress if it is a "natural and proximate" consequence of the misrepresentation. [Kilduff v. Adams, Inc., 593 A.2d 478 (Conn. 1991); *but see* Jourdain v. Dineen, 527 A.2d 1304 (Me. 1987)—contra]

e. **Punitive damages:** [§1440]   If the misrepresentation was intentional *and* made with "malice" (intent to harm), punitive damages may also be awarded.

(1) **Note:** In states that reject punitive damages, compensatory damages may be awarded "liberally" when the tortious act was "wanton, malicious, or oppressive." [Crowley v. Global Realty, 474 A.2d 1056 (N.H. 1984)]

B.   INJURIOUS FALSEHOOD

1. **Introduction:** [§1441]   "Injurious falsehood" covers the tort commonly known as "disparagement," "slander of title," and "trade libel." The gist of this tort is *interference with the prospect of sale* or some other advantageous relationship with respect to the plaintiff's *property*. The property involved may be real or personal, tangible or intangible (cases frequently involved the goodwill of plaintiff's business). But, as will be seen, the interest protected goes well beyond property. The prima facie case:

False Statement by Defendant
Publication to Others
Statement Disparaging Business, Property, Financial Interests, Etc. of Plaintiff
Intent

Causation
Special Damages

2. **False Statement:** [§1442]   First of all, the plaintiff must always prove that the defendant published the harmful statement and that the statement was in fact *false*.

3. **Publication to Third Persons:** [§1443]   As in defamation cases, the defendant must publish the statement to others. (*See supra*, §§1144 *et seq.*).

   a. **Form:** [§1444]   Note that the disparaging statements may be *oral or written*; *i.e.*, a "slander of title" may be in writing, and a "trade libel" may be oral.

4. **Statement Disparaging Plaintiff's Business, Property, Etc.:** [§1445]   A statement is "disparaging" if it is *reasonably likely to discourage others from dealing with the plaintiff* or otherwise interferes with the plaintiff's relations with others to the plaintiff's disadvantage. (The interest in noncommercial expectancies, such as anticipation of a legacy, is discussed *infra*, §1502.)

   a. **Statements denying plaintiff's ownership ("slander of title"):** [§1446]   A statement that casts reasonable doubt on the validity or extent of the plaintiff's title is clearly a disparagement. These are the cases commonly known as *"slanders of title."* [New England Oil & Pipe Co. v. Rogers, 7 P.2d 638 (Okla. 1932)]

      (1) **Examples:** These include recording a document falsely asserting an interest in P's property (thus denying that P has the entire ownership); or asserting that title to P's land is "clouded," or that anyone buying it is "buying a lawsuit." [Phillips v. Glazer, 94 Cal. App. 2d 673 (1949)]

   b. **Statements denying quality of plaintiff's property ("trade libel"):** [§1447]   Statements attacking the quality of the plaintiff's property (land, chattels, etc.), such that they would reasonably deter another from dealing with her, may be actionable as a disparagement.

      (1) **Examples:** Statements referring to P's merchandise as "seconds," "prison-made," or "defective" are disparaging statements of fact. [Rest. 2d §626]

   c. **Statements derogatory of plaintiff's business in general ("trade libel"):** [§1448]   Cases often involve statements that are derogatory of the plaintiff's business or the manner in which it is conducted, without necessarily reflecting on the title or quality of any particular property (*e.g.*, statements that service in the plaintiff's restaurant is "poor," that its customers are "ruffians," etc.).

      (1) **Example:** A common case is the false assertion that the sale of the plaintiff's product infringes some patent or copyright. Such cases (and those referred to in the preceding paragraph) are commonly referred to as *"trade libels."* [Dale System v. Time, Inc., 116 F. Supp. 527 (D. Conn. 1953)—claiming D's business is "unique" is not sufficient for action by D's competitor]

   d. **Statements interfering with nonbusiness relations:** [§1449]   Several courts have permitted actions for injurious statements that did not affect any commercial enterprise.

(1) **Example:** D may be liable for giving immigration officials false information about P's citizenship that results in efforts to deport P. [Raschid v. News Syndicate Co., 265 N.Y. 1 (1934)]

e. **Note—statement need not be defamatory:** [§1450] The defendant's statement need not be defamatory as long as it is false. For example, a false statement made to a potential customer that "P is dead (or out of business), so buy your goods from me" is not defamatory of P, but certainly is a trade libel—an "injurious falsehood."

(1) **Compare—defamatory statement:** On the other hand, if the statement imputes fraud or dishonesty to the company manufacturing the product ("Ajax soap is a hoax; it isn't as pure as advertised"), it may be defamatory of the manufacturer (because harmful to reputation) as well as a trade libel.

(2) **Comment:** Although it can be argued that nearly every imputation against a business or its product implies some personal inefficiency or incompetence on the part of the manufacturer or owner of the business, thus suggesting defamation in every case, the courts refuse to go this far; *i.e.*, defamation is found only where the imputation is of fraud or dishonesty, rather than mere ignorance or negligence. [Shaw Cleaners v. Des Moines Dress Club, 245 N.W. 231 (Iowa 1932)—dry cleaner not defamed by charge that garments only "half-cleaned"]

5. **Intent:** [§1451] The general view requires simply an *intent to disparage—i.e.*, to cast doubt on the plaintiff's property.

a. **Motive immaterial:** [§1452] It is not necessary to show that the defendant was motivated by malice or ill will toward the plaintiff, or was hoping to discourage some third person from dealing with the plaintiff. [Gudger v. Manton, 21 Cal. 2d 537 (1943); Rest. 2d §623A]

b. **Scienter:** [§1453] The modern view requires the plaintiff to show that the defendant knew that his statements were false, or that he did not have enough knowledge either way to make the statement. [Rest. 2d §623A(b)—D must "know" the statement is false or act in "reckless disregard of its truth or falsity"]

c. **Negligent falsity:** [§1454] Even though negligent falsity may not suffice here, note that such a statement may be actionable if it meets the negligent misrepresentation requirements (*see supra*, §1412).

6. **Causation and Damages:** [§1455] The usual requirement of actual and proximate causation exists. However, unlike defamation, where general damages are sometimes recoverable without a showing of pecuniary loss (*supra*, §§1215, 1223), here the plaintiff must always prove proximately caused *special damages*—actual, out-of-pocket, pecuniary damages.

a. **Slander of title:** [§1456] The usual damages in slander of title cases are *loss of profits* on a contemplated sale of property *and* costs of legal proceedings to remove the cloud on plaintiff's title.

b. **Trade libel:** [§1457] Typical damages in trade libel cases are *loss of profits* from specific sales to identifiable customers rather than a general decline in business resulting from the falsehood. [Waste Distillation Technology, Inc. v. Blasland & Bouck Engineers, P.C., 136 App. Div. 2d 633 (1988)—need special damages] Where this showing is impossible, courts may permit the plaintiff to recover on a showing of general decline in business. [Dale System v. Time, Inc., *supra*, §1448]

    (1) **Note:** In most states, *consequential damages* (*e.g.*, loss of business that forced plaintiff to close her doors or go into bankruptcy) are *not recoverable*. Nor are parasitic damages (*e.g.*, for mental distress). [Collier County Publishing Co. v. Chapman, 318 So. 2d 492 (Fla. 1975)—no damages for emotional distress]

7. Defenses

a. **Consent:** [§1458] Consent is a defense to injurious falsehood as with any intentional tort. (*See supra*, §80.)

b. **Truth:** [§1459] The falsity of the disparagement is an element of the prima facie case to be proved by the plaintiff. Hence, it is not necessary to consider truth as a defense, because unless the matter is shown to be false, the plaintiff has not proved a prima facie case. [Rest. 2d §634]

c. **Privilege:** [§1460] The *same privileges to defamation* are recognized as privileges to disparagement. [Rest. 2d §§635, 646A; *and see supra*, §§1232 *et seq.*]

    (1) **Judicial proceedings:** [§1461] The recording of a "lis pendens" (notice of lawsuit pending) in the county recorder's office, which may cloud title to real property, is treated as part of the judicial proceeding and hence is absolutely privileged. [Albertson v. Raboff, 46 Cal. 2d 375 (1956)]

        (a) **But note:** If this is done maliciously, an action for malicious proceedings may lie (*see infra*, §§1529-1534).

    (2) **Protection of private interests:** [§1462] A privilege of particular importance in disparagement cases is the *conditional* privilege to defame or disparage in protecting one's own interests or the interests of another.

        (a) **Privilege of competitors:** [§1463] Where the defendant and the plaintiff are competitors, the defendant is privileged to make general claims about *his own* product, even if false. However, the privilege does *not* extend to making specific false claims about the plaintiff's property or business.

            1) **Example:** D is privileged to claim that his product is "finer," of "higher quality" or performs "better than" P's—even if D does not honestly believe what he is saying. [Rest. 2d §649] This is similar to the "puffing" discussed *supra*, §1409.

            2) **Compare:** There is no privilege if D falsely states that P's goods are "seconds," or "prison-made," or contain impurities.

[National Refining Co. v. Benzo Gas Motor Fuel Co., 20 F.2d 763 (8th Cir. 1927)]

    (b) **Noncompetitors:** [§1464] Where the defendant and the plaintiff are *not* competitors, the defendant is generally protected if he honestly believes the truth of his statement and was speaking in any of the situations in which defamation would afford a privilege (*e.g.*, response to inquiry, protection of others, etc.).

        1) **Example:** Reports by a consumers' research organization commenting on new products on the market, or by doctors evaluating new drugs, are uniformly held to be privileged if made *in good faith*. [Rest. 2d §646A]

        2) **Constitutional protection:** [§1465] The constitutional privileges of libel law may apply here by analogy. [*See* Bose Corp. v. Consumers Union, *supra*, §1300]

C. INTERFERENCE WITH ECONOMIC RELATIONS

    1. **Introduction:** [§1466] Tort liability has also been imposed for *intentional* interference with the plaintiff's existing or prospective economic relationship with third persons, thereby protecting the plaintiff's interest in stabilizing his contract relations and expectations. Note that this is an area of still-emerging principles; most of the cases are of recent origin, reflecting development of social and economic policies in these areas. Recently, negligence principles have begun to emerge in specific situations. The two generally recognized facets of this theory of liability are: Interference with Contract and Interference with Prospective Advantage.

    2. **Interference with Contract:** [§1467] Prima facie case:

        Defendant's Interference with Existing Contract
        Intent
        Causation
        Special Damages

      a. **Nature of contract:** [§1468] This tort was first recognized in the master-servant relationship; *i.e.*, a third person who induced a servant to quit the master's employ might be held liable to the master in tort for loss of the servant's services. In the leading case of *Lumley v. Gye*, 118 Eng. Rep. 749 (1853), the doctrine was expanded to hold a defendant liable for inducing an opera star to breach her contract to sing at a particular opera house. Today, the tort can apply to *any* type of valid contract (except contracts to marry—as to which there generally is no tort liability for inducing breach). [Brown v. Glickstein, 107 N.E.2d 267 (Ill. 1952); Kenty v. Transamerica Premium Insurance Co., 650 N.E.2d 863 (Ohio 1995)—recognizing action against insurer]

        (1) **Illegal contracts:** [§1469] Contracts that are illegal or contrary to public policy do not qualify, since the law will not aid in upholding them. [Fairbanks, Morse & Co. v. Texas Electric Service, 63 F.2d 702 (5th Cir. 1933)—contract violative of antitrust laws]

(2) **Unenforceable contracts:** [§1470]   However, the original contract need *not* have been enforceable by the plaintiff (or against him). The gist of the tort is the interference with the existing *relationship*—not the contract.

    (a) **Application:** Thus, tort liability has been imposed even where the original contract was unenforceable because of the Statute of Frauds, lack of consideration, lack of mutuality, or even uncertainty as to its terms. [Childress v. Abeles, 84 S.E.2d 176 (N.C. 1954)]

    (b) **But note:** A few courts refuse to protect some of these contracts. [GuardLife Corp. v. S. Parker Hardware Manufacturing Corp., 50 N.Y.2d 183 (1980)—refusing to protect unenforceable exclusive dealership relation; Travel Masters, Inc. v. Star Tours, Inc., 827 S.W.2d 830 (Tex. 1991)—covenant not to compete cannot form the basis of a tortious interference with contract claim if covenant was unenforceable]

(3) **Contracts terminable at will:** [§1471]   Although some authorities refuse to impose tort liability for interfering with contracts that are terminable by either party at will, the general view is contrary. It is the *relationship* (rather than the particular contract) that is being interfered with, and the relationship might have continued *but for* the defendant's conduct. [Childress v. Abeles, *supra*; Sterner v. Marathon Oil Co., 767 S.W.2d 686 (Tex. 1989)]

    (a) **Note:** The possibility of termination does bear upon the issue of the *damages* sustained, as well as the issue of defendant's *privilege* to interfere (*see* below). [Scott v. Prudential Outfitting Co., 92 Misc. 195 (1915)]

b. **Defendant's interference:** [§1472]   The defendant must play some *active role* in causing the interference. For example, it is not enough that the defendant accepted an offer from the party with whom the plaintiff had been dealing, even where the defendant had knowledge of the plaintiff's relationship with that party. [Rest. 2d §766]

(1) **Breach not required:** [§1473]   Note that the defendant does not have to be shown to have induced a *breach* of the plaintiff's contract. All that must appear is that the defendant has prevented performance or made the performance more difficult and onerous.

    (a) **Examples:** D deliberately damages a highway that P is under contract to maintain and repair; D prevents X from performing his contract to supply P with goods, by calling a strike among X's workers; D threatens P's employees with bodily harm if they continue working for P. [*See* Snow v. West, 440 P.2d 864 (Or. 1968)]

(2) **Collective action:** [§1474]   A difficult case is the effect of *concerted action* by a number of individuals to do that which any one of them might be free to do alone (*e.g.*, refusal to deal, boycotts, etc.). This is the crux of the problem in collective refusals on the part of labor unions or

trade associations to deal with the plaintiff, resulting in strikes, etc. (*See* Labor Law Summary.)

(3) **Defendant not a party:** [§1475]   No action for interference with contract lies against a *party* to that contract. [Morrow v. L.A. Goldschmidt Associates, 492 N.E.2d 181 (Ill.1986)]

    (a) **But note:** A corporate officer acting for his own benefit may be liable for inducing the corporation to breach its contract with P. [Olympic Fish Products, Inc. v. Lloyd, 611 P.2d 737 (Wash. 1980)]

    (b) **Tortious breach of contract:** [§1476]   A few states permit one party to a contract to sue the other party in tort for a breach motivated by some interest other than the contract relationship, such as to help the defendant acquire a competitive benefit over the plaintiff in some other matter. [*See* Charles v. Onondaga Community College, 69 App. Div. 2d 144 (1979)]

        1) **And note:** Some states recognize a tort action for breach of implied covenant of good faith and fair dealing where there is a *special relationship* between the contracting parties, such as where an insurer unreasonably withholds payments from the insured [Gruenberg v. Aetna Insurance Co., 9 Cal. 3d 566 (1973)]; or where an employer unreasonably withholds monthly payments from an elderly employee [Wallis v. Superior Court, 160 Cal. App. 3d 1109 (1984)].

    (c) **Wrongful discharge:** [§1477]   The modern and majority view is that a tort action lies for discharging the plaintiff for an improper reason even though the hiring was at will. [Tameny v. Atlantic Richfield Co., 27 Cal. 3d 167 (1980)—firing P for refusal to participate in illegal price fixing scheme is actionable; McArn v. Allied Bruce-Terminix Co., 626 So. 2d 603 (Miss. 1993)—same; Mapco, Inc. v. Payne, 812 S.W.2d 483 (Ark. 1991)—employer liable for refusing to rehire employee after she filed for workers' compensation against employer; Hodges v. Gibson Products Co., 811 P.2d 151 (Utah 1991)—employer liable for wrongful discharge after firing employee on the basis of criminal accusation that employer knew was false; *but see* DeMarco v. Publix Super Markets, Inc., 384 So. 2d 1253 (Fla. 1980)—firing P because a relative filed a personal injury suit against D creates no tort]

c. **Intent:** [§1478]   It must be shown that the defendant acted with an awareness of the existing contract, and that she *intended to cause the interference* therewith that proximately resulted from her conduct.

    (1) **Negligent conduct insufficient:** [§1479]   The cases have refused to impose liability for mere *negligent* interference with contractual relationships. [Robins Dry Dock v. Flint, 275 U.S. 303 (1927)]

    (2) **Master-servant cases:** [§1480]   Although at common law, a master could recover for loss of the *services of his servant* where the servant

had been injured by the defendant's negligence, most courts have rejected such an action. [Hartridge v. State Farm Mutual Automobile Insurance Co., 271 N.W.2d 598 (Wis. 1978)—clinic has no action for loss *it* suffered when its employee was negligently injured]

d. **Causation and damages:** [§1481]   There is the usual requirement of actual and proximate causation and damages.

   (1) **Types of damages recoverable:** [§1482]   The modern view seems to allow recovery for all actual damages, consequential damages (unforeseen expenses), mental suffering, damage to reputation, and punitive damages in appropriate cases. [Duff v. Engleberg, 237 Cal. App. 2d 505 (1965)]

   (2) **Offset recovery for breach of contract:** [§1483]   The fact that the plaintiff may have an action against the party who breaches the contract does *not* bar the plaintiff's claim against the defendant for inducing the breach. The two are joint wrongdoers, and each may be liable for the loss (the defendant may be liable in tort, and the other in contract). However, any *recovery* against the breaching party must be offset against the damages recoverable from the defendant who induced the breach.

e. **Defenses—privilege:** [§1484]   The principal defense to this tort is one of privilege; *i.e.*, the defendant will not be liable if there was *proper justification* for the interference and only *reasonable methods* were employed. This requires proof that *both the ends and the means* were justifiable.

   (1) **Ends:** [§1485]   The privilege may arise from acts undertaken for a social good or to protect the defendant's own interests.

      (a) **Furtherance of nonpersonal interests:** [§1486]   Claims of privilege are generally upheld where the defendant was acting for a social good (*e.g.*, D attempts to exclude a diseased youngster from school that her child attends), or to protect a third person's interest (*e.g.*, attorney's sincere advice to client not to deal with plaintiff). [Terry v. Zachry, 272 S.W.2d 157 (Tex. 1954)]

         1) **Mixed motive does not defeat privilege:** [§1487]   The defendant's privilege is not defeated where part of the defendant's motive for interference with the plaintiff's contractual relations is personal ill-will, if the predominant motive is a legitimate safety concern. [Hatten v. Union Oil Co., 978 P.2d 1150 (Alaska 1989)]

      (b) **Furtherance of defendant's own financial interest:** [§1488]   Where the defendant is acting to further her own interests, any claim of privilege will turn on whether she is seeking to protect *existing* economic interests or merely a *prospective* advantage.

         1) **Protecting present interest:** [§1489]   Where the defendant has a present contract of her own with one of the parties, she is privileged to prevent the performance of another contract that

threatens hers. Thus, if D induces debtor X to pay off the bills owed to D, thereby rendering X unable to perform X's contract with P, D is *not* liable for inducing breach of the P-X contract. [Personal Preference Video, Inc. v. Home Box Office, Inc., 986 F.2d 110 (5th Cir. 1993)]

2) **Protecting prospective advantage:** [§1490] On the other hand, where the defendant has no existing relationship with either of the contracting parties and induces the breach solely to further her own business (*e.g.*, hiring away plaintiff's best employees, inducing his suppliers not to supply, etc.) the defendant's purpose is *not* protected, and generally no privilege is recognized.

a) **Exception—contracts terminable at will:** [§1491] The privilege to compete (and of employees to better themselves, etc.) takes precedence over the expectancy that an at-will contract will continue. Therefore, courts generally hold that one competitor *is* privileged to induce third persons (employees, suppliers, customers) to breach contracts that they had with a competitor where such contracts were terminable at will. [Diodes v. Franzen, 260 Cal. App. 2d 244 (1968)]

(2) **Means:** [§1492] Even if the interference is for a justifiable purpose, the defendant is never privileged to use unethical or wrongful means. Thus, violence, lies, bribery, or extortion will defeat the privilege.

(a) **Threats of "economic persuasion":** [§1493] Difficult cases involve threats of "economic persuasion"—*e.g.*, where D threatens that she will not deal with X unless X severs all dealings with P. Such cases are generally analyzed on their own facts; *i.e.*, the more unreasonable and coercive the threat is under the circumstances, the more likely that it will defeat the privilege.

(b) **Other torts:** [§1494] Where improper means are in fact used, always consider the possibility of other tort liability. For example, if D induces X to discontinue dealing with P because "P's business is run by organized crime," D may be liable for defamation and injurious falsehood, as well as wrongful interference with P's contractual relations.

(3) **Burden of proof:** [§1495] Although most courts have held that the defendant must establish a proper justification for the challenged behavior, [Sterner v. Marathon Oil Co., *supra*, §1471], most courts have also held that the plaintiff must allege and prove that the defendant's conduct was "wrongful" by showing more than only the interference itself. [Della Penna v. Toyota Motor Sales, U.S.A., Inc., 11 Cal. 4th 376 (1995)]

3. **Intentional Interference with Prospective Economic Advantage:** [§1496] By analogy to interference with existing contractual relations, tort liability has been imposed for intentional interference with *prospective* economic advantage—*i.e.*,

where there is no existing contract. [Buckaloo v. Johnson, 14 Cal. 3d 815 (1975)—prospective advantage between real estate broker and vendor or vendee of property] The right being protected is the right to *pursue* business without unjustifiable interference. [Printing Mart-Morristown v. Sharp Electronics Corp., 563 A.2d 31 (N.J. 1989)—tampering with bidding process so that plaintiff would not be awarded contract]

a. **Prima facie case:** [§1497]   The prima facie case is virtually the same as with interference with contract (*see supra*, §1467), except that *no existing contractual relationship* need be shown.

   (1) **Defendant's act:** [§1498]   The interfering act consists of (i) inducing a third party not to enter into a prospective relationship with the plaintiff; or (ii) preventing the plaintiff from acquiring the prospective relationship. [Rest. 2d §766B] States disagree about whether the plaintiff must show that the interference was "wrongful" in addition to showing the interference itself. The modern view requires such a showing. [Della Penna v. Toyota Motor Sales, U.S.A., Inc., *supra*]

   (2) **Defendant not a party:** [§1499]   As with interference with contract, the defendant need not be a party to the prospective economic relationship. An employee, acting to undermine the prospective relationship between his employer and the plaintiff, may be liable. [*See* Printing Mart-Morristown v. Sharp Electronics Corp., *supra*—deferring question]

b. **Privilege:** [§1500]   The chief difference between actions for interference with prospective advantage and interference with contract lies in recognition of *more extensive privileges* where the parties are competitors and there is no contract. (To the extent that courts insist that the plaintiff show an independent wrong as part of the prima facie case, *supra*, §1498, the role of privilege is reduced.)

   (1) **Example:** D is privileged to use any *bona fide competitive means* to solicit the customers for herself before they enter into a contract with P.

   (2) **Loss of privilege:** [§1501]   As before, to the extent that the defendant uses unlawful or tortious means, she loses the privilege—and may be liable for unfair competition (*see* Remedies Summary). [Tuttle v. Buck, 719 N.W. 946 (Minn. 1909)]

      (a) **But note:** A special rule protects perjurers whose lies under oath are intended to and do cause harm to the plaintiff. To encourage witnesses to testify and to do so fully, they are absolutely protected against suits from unhappy litigants. [Cooper v. Parker-Hughey, 894 P.2d 1096 (Okla. 1995)]

c. **Compare—interference with noncommercial expectancies (prospective gifts, etc.):** [§1502]   The modern trend is to allow recovery for wrongful interference with such expectancies—at least where there is a strong probability that they would have been realized.

   (1) **Example:** Tort recovery has been allowed where D, by use of fraud, *induces a testator to disinherit P*—if there is strong evidence that the testator otherwise would not have done so. [Bohannon v. Wachovia Bank, 188 S.E. 390 (N.C. 1936)] The falsehood may either attack P or enhance D.

(a) **And note:** Where D fraudulently causes X to convey property to D, and X has intended P to be a legatee of that property, P may sue D for wrongful interference with his intended legacy even if X is still alive. [Harmon v. Harmon, 404 A.2d 1020 (Me. 1979)]

(b) **But note:** Courts have refused to impose liability for interference in the context of sporting contests, such as horse racing. In addition to the difficulty of establishing a reasonable probability of winning, these sports are governed by other regulatory bodies, and allowance of claims would flood the courts with disgruntled losers. [Youst v. Longo, 43 Cal. 3d 64 (1987)—no recovery against jockey who caused plaintiff's horse to break stride during race]

4. **Negligent Interference with Prospective Economic Advantage:** [§1503] Prima facie case:

Duty of Due Care
Breach of Duty
Causation
Damages

a. **Duty:** [§1504] Duty is the crucial issue. Generally, the plaintiff's interest in protection from economic harm has been considered too remote for the imposition of a duty of due care. [Robins Dry Dock v. Flint, *supra*, §1479]

(1) **Compare—misrepresentation:** [§1505] Where the defendant's negligence has taken the form of misrepresentation upon which the plaintiff has relied, courts have imposed a duty on the defendants who are in the business of supplying information. (*See supra*, §1413.) Even there, however, the courts imposed limits based on the nature of the transaction and the foreseeability that the plaintiff would rely. (*See supra*, §§1414, 1416 *et seq.*)

(2) **Modern trend:** [§1506] Since the defendant's negligence may cause economic harm to the plaintiff even though the plaintiff has never met or relied on the defendant, some courts are imposing a duty of care where the defendant can *reasonably foresee* harm to the specific plaintiff. [Simpson v. Calivas, 650 A.2d 318 (N.H. 1994)—attorney cost P an inheritance by preparing T's will improperly]

(a) **Attorney liability:** [§1507] Most courts hold that attorneys may owe duties of due care to persons other than their clients in a negotiated deal. [Prudential Insurance Co. v. Dewey, Ballantine, Bushby, Palmer & Wood, 80 N.Y.2d 377 (1992); *but see* Goodman v. Kennedy, 18 Cal. 3d 335 (1976)—attorney must provide undiluted advice to client and should not incur any duties toward those with whom client is dealing, even though they are identified]

(3) **Limitation:** [§1508] As in the professional cases (*supra*, §1420), courts here are concerned about extending a general duty of care to a large undefined group of plaintiffs. The result is the denial of a duty of care unless the defendant knows that her conduct will affect a pinpointed

plaintiff. [Petition of Kinsman Transit Co. (No. 2), 388 F.2d 821 (2d Cir. 1968)—no liability after river accident to those who sustained solely economic burdens because damaged bridge made commercial activities more expensive; Phoenix Professional Hockey Club, Inc., 502 P.2d 164 (Ariz. 1972)—no liability on negligent driver who cost P money by running over P's hockey goalie; Milliken & Co. v. Consolidated Edison Co., 84 N.Y.2d 469 (1994)—tenant lacking direct contractual relation with utility could not sue for economic losses suffered due to utility's negligence; *but see* Union Oil Co. v. Oppen, 501 F.2d 558 (9th Cir. 1974)—commercial fishermen may recover for income loss caused by D's oil spill; People Express Airlines v. Consolidated Rail Corp., 495 A.2d 107 (N.J. 1985)—airline may recover for damage caused by evacuation of terminal due to D's negligence]

b. **Other elements:** [§1509]   Once duty is found, the other elements are analyzed as in regular negligence cases (*see* Chapter II). This may include the need for expert testimony to establish breach. [Mitchell v. Jackson, 627 A.2d 1014 (Me. 1993), *cert. denied*, 114 S. Ct. 903 (1994)—need expert where attorney refused to file complaint without having proof to support it]

D. UNJUSTIFIABLE LITIGATION

1. **Introduction:** [§1510]   Unjustifiable litigation includes several distinct torts involving the plaintiff's interest in freedom from unjustifiable legal proceedings.

2. **Malicious Prosecution:** [§1511]   The tort of malicious prosecution concerns the wrongful institution of *criminal proceedings* by one private citizen against another, resulting in damage. The prima facie case:

> *Instigation of Criminal Proceedings by Defendant*
> *Proceedings Terminated Showing Plaintiff Not Guilty*
> *Lack of Probable Cause*
> *Improper Purpose*

a. **Compare—false imprisonment:** [§1512]   Malicious prosecution must be distinguished from false imprisonment in several particulars. False imprisonment lies only where the *arrest* is "false"—in the sense that there was *no valid process* for the arrest (*i.e.*, no valid arrest warrant or no probable cause to arrest without a warrant). On the other hand, malicious prosecution lies where there has been a valid arrest but an *improper purpose in instigating* the criminal proceeding (*e.g.*, groundless charges by the defendant to the police, leading them to arrest the plaintiff). Furthermore, false imprisonment does not require any showing of malice or lack of probable cause to believe that the charges against the plaintiff are true; but these are essential elements of malicious prosecution.

b. **Instigation of proceedings by defendant:** [§1513]   Criminal proceedings are initiated by a charge made to the police or other public officials in such form as to cause the issuance of a warrant or indictment against the accused.

(1) **Procuring another to institute proceedings:** [§1514]   One who procures or is instrumental in causing a third person (police) to institute a prosecution is liable just as if he instituted it himself. [Rest. 2d §653]

(2) **Compare—merely providing information:** [§1515] But one who provides full and truthful incriminating information to a public officer and leaves the decision to that officer has not initiated the proceeding. [McHale v. W.S.B. Corp., 446 A.2d 815 (Conn. 1982)]

c. **Proceedings terminated favorably to plaintiff:** [§1516] A plaintiff must allege and prove that the criminal proceeding was terminated in a manner indicating his *innocence*.

(1) **Decisive termination:** [§1517] This generally requires some sort of a decisive termination—*e.g.*, acquittal after trial, dismissal of the case by a magistrate at the preliminary hearing for lack of evidence, quashing of an indictment, grand jury refusal to indict, etc.

(a) **Compare:** Conversely, a termination that is indecisive or consistent with guilt is not sufficient—*e.g.*, where the proceeding is dismissed on technical, procedural grounds or as an act of grace; or because of the impossibility of bringing the accused to trial; or a plea bargain. [Rest. 2d §660; Swick v. Liautaud, 662 N.E.2d 1238 (Ill. 1996)— since dismissal of criminal case on nolle prosequi is ambiguous, plaintiff must show favorable termination; Ward v. Silverberg, 85 N.Y.2d 993 (1995)—termination in criminal defendant's favor where charges dismissed "on consent" after colloquy between court and counsel]

d. **Lack of probable cause:** [§1518] The plaintiff must also show that the defendant instituted the proceedings without probable cause—*i.e.*, that the defendant had *no honest and reasonable belief* in the truth of the charge.

(1) **Objective standard:** [§1519] Attorneys are not liable for malicious prosecution if they pursued a claim that a reasonable attorney would have considered tenable. Courts use this standard to avoid the chilling effect on crime reporting or bringing a civil claim that would follow from the use of a subjective standard. [Sheldon Appel Co. v. Albert & Oliker, 47 Cal. 3d 863 (1989)]

(2) **Proof—cannot be inferred from improper purpose:** [§1520] Lack of probable cause must be proved *independently* from the improper purpose requirement (below), because even a person acting from improper motives may know of facts that give rise to a reasonable and honest belief of guilt.

(3) **Application:** [§1521] Because of its complex nature, the question of probable cause is usually decided by the court. [Rest. 2d 673(1)(c); Slade v. City of Phoenix, 541 P.2d 550 (Ariz. 1975); *but see* Hodges v. Gibson Products Co., *supra*, §1477—contra]

(a) **Effect of indictment or commitment by magistrate:** [§1522] The fact that the plaintiff was held to answer by the committing magistrate after a preliminary hearing, or was indicted by a grand jury, is *prima facie evidence* of probable cause. [Rest. 2d §663; Colon v.

City of New York, 60 N.Y.2d 78 (1983)—indictment creates presumption of probable cause rebuttable only by showing fraud, perjury, or suppression of evidence]

(b) **Effect of conviction:** [§1523]   And where the plaintiff was actually convicted without fraud, perjury, or other corruption, probable cause is *conclusively* established—even if the conviction was later overturned on appeal. *Rationale:* If a jury or trial judge was satisfied of guilt beyond a reasonable doubt, it can hardly be denied that the accuser had reasonable grounds in making the charges. [Hanson v. City of Snohomish, 852 P.2d 295 (Wash. 1993)]

1)   **But note:** A minority view treats the conviction as creating only a presumption of probable cause. [McRae v. Brant, 230 A.2d 753 (N.H. 1967)]

(c) **Effect of advice of counsel:** [§1524]   Reliance on advice of counsel will also *conclusively* establish probable cause, provided there was a *full* disclosure of the facts to the attorney and a resulting honest belief in the guilt of the injured party. [Rest. 2d §666; Kaarup v. St. Paul Fire & Marine Insurance, 485 N.W.2d 802 (S.D. 1992); Boshell v. Walker County Sheriff, 558 So. 2d 843 (Ala. 1992)]

e.   **Improper purpose:** [§1525]   It must appear that the defendant instituted the proceeding for some *improper purpose*, some motive other than bringing a guilty person to justice. This is sometimes called "malice."

(1)   **And note:** Although lack of probable cause cannot be inferred from improper purpose, improper purpose *may* be inferred from lack of probable cause. [Rest. 2d §669]

f.   **Causation and damages:** [§1526]   The plaintiff may recover all expenses incurred in defending against the criminal prosecution (*e.g.*, attorney's fees, investigative expenses, court costs, etc.). The plaintiff may also recover damages for mental suffering and embarrassment, harm to reputation, damage to business, etc., as well as punitive damages in appropriate cases.

g.   **Defenses**

(1)   **Plaintiff's guilt:** [§1527]   Notwithstanding the termination of criminal proceedings favorable to the plaintiff, the defendant may show as a defense that the plaintiff really *was* guilty of the crime. The acquittal in the criminal proceedings only establishes that the state could not prove the plaintiff's guilt "beyond a reasonable doubt," whereas in the civil tort proceedings, the standard of proof is only a preponderance of the evidence. [Shoemaker v. Selnes, 349 P.2d 473 (Or. 1960); Rest. 2d §657]

(2)   **Privilege:** [§1528]   Judges, prosecutors, and various other law enforcement officers are *absolutely privileged and immune* from charges of malicious prosecution.

3.   **Malicious Institution of Civil Proceedings:** [§1529]   Many states extend the concept of malicious prosecution to *civil proceedings* as well. The basic elements

are the same as those in actions based on malicious criminal proceedings, and the same types of damages may be recovered. [Dutt v. Kremp, 894 P.2d 354 (Nev. 1995)] A large minority rejects this action in order to encourage resort to the courts to settle disputes.

a. **Nature of proceedings:** [§1530]   The tort extends to any form of noncriminal proceedings—including administrative hearings, insanity or narcotics commitment proceedings, etc.

  (1) **Note:** An action may be maintained for malicious institution of civil proceedings where the damage complained of results solely from the recordation of a *lis pendens*—even though the notice itself would be absolutely *privileged* insofar as *slander of title* is concerned (*see supra*, §1461).

  (2) **Compare:** A small claims court proceeding, even if maliciously instituted, may *not* be the basis of a suit. Such proceedings are too inexpensive and informal to cause any real damage. [Pace v. Hillcrest Motor Co., 101 Cal. App. 3d 476 (1980)]

  (3) **And note:** Governmental units may not be plaintiffs in this type of case after successfully defending a false arrest claim. [City of Long Beach v. Bozek, 31 Cal. 3d 527 (1982)—absolute privilege to seek redress against government]

b. **Effect of prior verdict:** [§1531]   Unlike the criminal acquittal in malicious prosecution cases (*see* above), a verdict for the plaintiff in the prior civil proceedings *cannot* be questioned in a subsequent action for malicious institution of those proceedings; *i.e.*, all material issues decided in the first suit are *res judicata* between the parties.

c. **Application—countersuits by physicians following malpractice actions:** [§1532]   The most recent use of the malicious prosecution theory in civil cases has occurred in suits brought by physicians who have successfully defended malpractice actions. Virtually all such claims against patients and their attorneys have failed, some because the state rejects the action, others because lack of probable cause is much harder to prove in civil cases than in criminal cases. [Dutt v. Kremp, *supra*, §1529; Carroll v. Kalar, 545 P.2d 411 (Ariz. 1976)]

d. **Causation and damages:** [§1533]   The same causation rules apply as in the case of criminal prosecutions.

  (1) **Minority rule:** [§1534]   A minority of states hold that to recover when the unfounded case was a civil suit, the plaintiff must show special damages to person or property. Under this view, there is no claim when the plaintiff seeks to recover only attorney's fees. [Johnson v. Calado, 464 N.W.2d 647 (Wis. 1991)]

4. **Malicious Defense:** [§1535]   A few states have recognized that a defendant's behavior in raising totally unjustified defenses may cause plaintiffs the same sort of harm that is produced by unjustified complaints. These states have created an action that mirrors the action for malicious institution of civil proceedings (*supra*). [Aranson v. Schroeder, 671 A.2d 1023 (N.H. 1995)]

5. **Spoliation of Evidence:** [§1536]   Some parties, rather than raising unjustifiable legal arguments, have sought to affect legal outcomes by hiding or destroying adverse evidence. Courts confronted with this conduct have generally created a new action for such destruction. [Coleman v. Eddy Potash, Inc., 905 P.2d 185 (N.M. 1995)—claim that employer deliberately failed to preserve evidence crucial to plaintiff's action against a third party states claim for intentional spoliation by alleging (i) existence of a potential lawsuit; (ii) D's knowledge of it; (iii) destruction of mutilation or substantial alteration of evidence; (iv) D's intent to disrupt or defeat the lawsuit; (v) a casual connection between the act and the inability to prove the lawsuit; and (vi) damages]

   a. **Negligent spoliation:** [§1537]   Occasionally the loss of the evidence is alleged to have resulted from negligence. In such cases, courts generally require some special circumstance (contract, agreement, or statute) to create a duty on the defendant to take care to preserve the evidence. [Coleman v. Eddy Potash, Inc., *supra*—allegation that D "knew or should have reasonably anticipated that" future litigation would occur does not impose duty to take due care to preserve such evidence]

6. **Abuse of Process:** [§1538]   Abuse of process is a narrow tort committed by the misuse of process—civil or criminal—for some ulterior purpose. This means simply that defendant intentionally employed some court process (*e.g.*, attachment, execution, injunction, etc.) for a ***purpose other than that for which the process was designed***. [Rest. 2d §682]

   a. **Prima facie case:** [§1539]   The prima facie case is made simply by showing an ***intentional misuse*** of process and resulting ***damage*** to the plaintiff. [Yaklevich v. Kemp, Schaeffer & Rowe Co., 626 N.E.2d 115 (Ohio 1994)—recognizing action]

      (1) **No showing of lack of probable cause:** [§1540]   Unlike the previous torts, the plaintiff does *not* have to show that the defendant lacked probable cause.

      (2) **No showing of favorable result:** [§1541]   Nor does the plaintiff have to show that the proceedings were terminated in his favor.

      (3) **Counterclaim:** [§1542]   In fact, where A has abused process in connection with an action instituted by him against B, B may ***counterclaim in the same action*** for damages arising from the abuse. [White v. Wolfson, 68 Cal. 2d 336 (1968)]

   b. **Example:** Attachment on property exempt from execution, or on an excessive amount of P's property, for the purpose of driving P into bankruptcy or forcing him to settle or dismiss his claims against D, is actionable as abuse of process. [White v. Wolfson, *supra*]

      (1) **And note:** Husband is guilty of abusing process in causing the sheriff to levy attachment on Wife's car, where it appeared this was done to harass her and pressure her to settle a pending divorce action. [Spellens v. Spellens, 49 Cal. 2d 210 (1957)]

   c. **Who may sue:** [§1543]   The tort action may be maintained not merely by the other party to the abusive proceedings, but also by ***any third person whose***

property is injured thereby. Thus, for example, if D files suit against T, and to coerce payment causes an attachment to be levied against property owned by T's parents, D may be liable to the parents for abuse of process. [Templeton Feed & Grain v. Ralston Purina, 69 Cal. 2d 461 (1968)]

REVIEW QUESTIONS

INTENTIONAL TORTS TO PERSONS

1. Donna is shopping at the supermarket with her children, when someone yells "Fire!" In a blind panic to save her children, Donna pushes her cart through a crowd of shoppers to reach the exit, injuring Paula.

    a. Has Donna "acted" so as to have committed a battery upon Paula? _____

    b. Did Donna have the requisite "intent" for a battery upon Paula? _____

2. As part of his nightclub act, Waldo hypnotizes volunteers from the audience. Horace volunteers and is hypnotized. Waldo directs Horace to pour a glass of water on Betty, another member of the audience, and Horace does so.

    a. Has Horace committed a battery on Betty? _____

    b. Has Waldo committed a battery on Betty? _____

3. David is invited to a party at Peggy's apartment. During the course of events, David engages in the following activities:

    a. To liven up the party, David secretly puts LSD into the punchbowl. Greta, one of the other guests, becomes violently ill as a result of drinking the punch. Has David committed any tort upon Greta? _____

    b. Next, David asks Peggy to dance with him, and while holding her very close, he makes an indecent proposal, which causes Peggy to burst into tears. Has David committed any tort on Peggy? _____

    c. Then David wanders into the bedroom where he finds his pal, Zeke, fast asleep. To get Zeke to join the party, David roughly shakes him awake. Zeke is unhurt, but is angered at being awakened. Has David committed a battery upon Zeke? _____

    d. Later, as part of the horseplay between himself and Zeke, David takes a dart off the dartboard and throws it at the wall near where Zeke is standing, intending to startle Zeke. Unfortunately, Beth walks in front of Zeke and is struck by the dart. Has David committed a battery on Beth? _____

4. Prudence is walking home by herself, late at night, when the following events occur:

    a. Mildred, an elderly woman, observes Prudence walking in front of Mildred's house, and mistakes her for a prostitute. Mildred points a shotgun at Prudence, shouting, "Get off the streets, you hussy, or I'll fill you full of buckshot!" Has Mildred committed an assault on Prudence? _____

    b. As a joke, Prudence's younger brother, George, sneaks up behind her and sets off a firecracker, frightening her severely. Has George committed an assault on Prudence? _____

c.   Prudence turns to scold George and he responds by raising his fist as if to punch her. Prudence, however, is not frightened thereby because she knows that George is not strong enough to hurt her. Does George's raising his fist constitute an assault?   _____

d.   Later, Dominic approaches Prudence carrying what appears to be a knife, and demands that she submit to sexual intercourse with him immediately. Prudence is panicked thereby, although the "knife" in fact has a rubber blade, and Dominic is impotent. Has Dominic committed an assault on Prudence?   _____

5.   Tony was walking down the street when his enemy, Rocky, approached from behind and threw a knife at him, but missed. Tony's attention was diverted by traffic and he didn't know what had happened until Stranger yelled, "Watch out! That man is trying to kill you!" Tony whirled and saw Rocky being apprehended by a police officer, but nevertheless was shaken up by the realization that Rocky had made an attempt on his life.

    a.   Is Rocky liable to Tony for any tort?   _____

    b.   Is Stranger liable to Tony for any tort?   _____

6.   As a prank, Doug puts a stocking mask over his face and points a water pistol at his best friend, Pete, saying, "I'm going to let you have it!" Any reasonable person in Pete's position would have realized that Doug was only joking, but Pete is abnormally sensitive and thinks the gun is real and that Doug is going to kill him. Is Doug liable to Pete for an assault?   _____

7.   Bob stripped naked for a physical exam in his doctor's office. While he was being examined by the doctor, the nurse took Bob's clothes and locked them in a closet. The nurse refused to return them until Bob agreed to pay a disputed bill from the doctor. Can Bob recover against the nurse for false imprisonment?   _____

8.   Law Student fell asleep at the law library after a hard day's study. Janitor tried to awaken him, but finally gave up and locked the library for the night.

    a.   Assume Law Student slept through the night and was awakened only when Librarian opened the door the following morning. Is Janitor liable to Law Student for false imprisonment?   _____

    b.   Assume Law Student woke up during the night and found the door locked but decided to relax and go back to sleep, thinking one of his buddies had locked him in as a prank. However, he became angered when Librarian arrived and told him it was Janitor. Is Janitor liable to Law Student for false imprisonment?   _____

9.   As part of his initiation rites into Fraternity, Neal is blindfolded and taken on a long ride. Fraternity brothers abandon him in the desert, 20 miles away from any settlement or highway. Can Neal recover from Fraternity brothers for false imprisonment?   _____

10.   During a bank robbery, cashier Pete is locked in the bank vault by the robbers. After the robbery, the bank president, Dan, is angry that Pete did not put up a fight; therefore, to punish Pete, Dan leaves the vault locked for a few hours.

a. Can Pete recover from Dan for false imprisonment?   _____

b. Would it make any difference that Pete was unaware that he was being "punished" by Dan?   _____

11. In response to labor strife at the XYZ Manufacturing Co., union members Able and Baker place their autos across the driveway to the plant's only entrance, preventing those inside from driving their cars out, and preventing others from entering the plant.

    a. Can XYZ recover from Able and Baker for false imprisonment?   _____

    b. Can the workers in the plant who are unable to drive home recover from Able and Baker for false imprisonment?   _____

12. Virgil became suspicious that his neighbor, Ned, was engaged in selling narcotics. He reported his suspicions to the police, who arrested Ned. However, Ned was soon released because of lack of evidence. Can Ned recover from Virgil for false imprisonment?   _____

13. Dick rented a police uniform for a costume party. While driving to the party, he became enraged at the way Phil, another driver, was operating his car. Dick made sure Phil could see the police uniform and then yelled, "Pull over there," intending to give Phil a stern lecture on his driving. Phil, believing Dick to be a police officer, pulled his car to the curb.

    a. Is Dick subject to liability to Phil for false imprisonment?   _____

    b. Is it relevant that Phil's erratic driving constituted a crime for which even a private citizen would have had the **privilege to arrest** Phil?   _____

14. Charley received a traffic ticket and paid the fine. However, by error, her payment was not recorded, and therefore a warrant was issued for her arrest.

    a. Assume Sheriff called Charley on the telephone and told her about the warrant, and that she would have to come to court immediately, and Charley came. Could Charley later recover from Sheriff for false imprisonment?   _____

    b. Assume Sheriff went to Charley's house and told Charley that the only way she could avoid arrest would be to pay Sheriff the amount of the traffic fine again, plus $50 warrant costs, and Charley paid these. Could Charley later recover from Sheriff for false imprisonment?   _____

    c. Assume Sheriff went to Charley's house and showed Charley the warrant for her arrest, and Charley submitted to Sheriff's custody without telling Sheriff that she had already paid the traffic ticket. Could she later recover from Sheriff for false imprisonment?   _____

15. Emil is badly injured in an automobile collision. He is on the "critical list" at the hospital, and under strict orders from his doctor to remain quiet; all visitors are warned not to upset him. Harvey, an insurance adjuster representing the driver of the other car, barges into Emil's room, and after attempting to force a settlement,

accuses Emil of being a "phony, a faker, and a cheat!" Emil becomes angered and suffers a heart attack.

    a.   Is Harvey subject to liability to Emil for the intentional infliction of emotional distress? _____

    b.   Assume Emil had become angered and upset at Harvey but had *not* suffered the heart attack. Would this bar Emil's claim against Harvey for intentional infliction of emotional distress? _____

DEFENSES

16.   As passengers line up to board an Acme Airliner, they are informed that there has been a bomb threat and that everyone has to be searched. Phyllis is abnormally sensitive to being touched by anyone, but she is anxious to reach her destination and therefore says nothing while the airline personnel conduct a "patdown" over her clothing. Can she later sue the airline for battery? _____

17.   In the course of a free-swinging hockey match, Daniel strikes Pierre on the head with a hockey stick; and George, one of the fans, throws a beer bottle that hits Pierre on the back.

    a.   Is Daniel liable to Pierre for a battery? _____

    b.   Is George liable to Pierre for a battery? _____

18.   Barbara goes to her doctor, complaining of stomach pains. After routine tests, Doctor recommends exploratory surgery, and Barbara enters the hospital for the operation.

    a.   Assume that Doctor was called out of town on an emergency, and therefore arranged to have Specialist perform the operation without Barbara's knowledge. Assume further that the surgery was skillfully performed and was entirely successful. Would either Doctor or Specialist be subject to liability for a battery? _____

    b.   Assume that Doctor performed the operation carefully and properly, but that as a result of the surgery, the skin over Barbara's stomach was badly scarred, which interfered with her career as a swimsuit model. Could Barbara recover from Doctor for a battery? _____

    c.   Assume that during the course of surgery, Doctor discovered that the cause of Barbara's stomach pain was an ulcer which if not removed would grow progressively worse and could threaten her life. Doctor therefore removed the ulcerated portion of Barbara's stomach by careful surgical procedures. If Barbara had not expressly consented to the removal of any body organ, would Doctor be liable for a battery? _____

19.   During the course of a heated political discussion, Archie invites Bob outside to "settle the matter." Bob obliges, and a fist fight ensues, which is broken up only when both men are arrested for breach of the peace. Is either liable to the other for battery? _____

20. Myrna is cited for reckless driving by Police Officer. Police Officer offers to tear up the ticket if she will go to bed with him. Myrna reluctantly agrees because she has already had several tickets and this citation would cause her to lose her driver's license. If Police Officer goes back on his word and turns in Myrna's traffic citation, can she hold him liable for a battery?

21. After Harry and his wife, Betty, had an expensive dinner at Restaurant, Harry found that he had left his wallet at home. Restaurant Owner insisted that Betty remain at Restaurant while Harry went to get his wallet. During his absence, Owner threatened to have his bartender beat up Harry when he returned unless Betty submitted to certain sexual acts with Owner, which she did.

    a.   Is Restaurant Owner liable to Betty for false imprisonment?

    b.   Is Restaurant Owner liable to Betty for battery?

22. Archie throws a stone at Buford, striking him in the leg. Buford picks up the same stone and hurls it back, hitting Archie on the head. If Archie sues for battery, has Buford a valid claim of self-defense?

23. Charlie had threatened to kill Bob unless he stayed away from Charlie's wife, but Bob had not done so. As Bob was walking down the street, he saw Charlie approaching with his fist raised toward Bob. Which, if any, of the following statements is true?

    (A)   Bob would be privileged to shoot Charlie based on the threats Charlie had made on his life.

    (B)   Bob would be privileged to strike Charlie without waiting for Charlie to hit him first.

    (C)   Bob would be under a duty to retreat as an alternative to striking Charlie.

    (D)   Bob would not be privileged to use any force against Charlie, if in fact Charlie had only raised his fist as a joke.

24. Bruno is wearing brass knuckles which cannot be seen because they are concealed by a large glove. He raises his fist as if to strike Carl, who responds by stabbing Bruno with a knife. Can Carl successfully claim the privilege of self-defense?

25. Bob is showing off by juggling a hand grenade at a party at Tom's house. Suddenly, he draws his arm back as if he is going to throw the grenade at Tom. Which, if any, of the following statements is true?

    (A)   Tom is under a duty to retreat as an alternative to using deadly force against Bob.

    (B)   Tom is not entitled to use *any* force against Bob if he realizes that the safety pin is still in place so that the grenade could not explode.

    (C)   Tom would be entitled to shoot Bob, to prevent Bob's throwing the grenade, if he *honestly* believed that Bob was about to kill him, even though a reasonable person would have realized that Bob was only joking and that the "grenade" was a toy.

(D) If a reasonable person would have regarded Bob's threat as real, Tom would be privileged to use deadly force against Bob, even though his doing so might endanger others at the party.

26. Frank is walking down the street, carrying a long fishing pole in front of him. As he approaches Mildred, she becomes alarmed because the tip of the pole is whipping about and Frank is paying no attention. Which, if any, of the following statements is true?

(A) Mildred is under a duty to retreat as an alternative to using *any* force against Frank.

(B) Mildred would not be privileged to use *any* force against Frank if she realized that he was merely negligent and intended her no harm.

(C) If Mildred could not otherwise get out of the way, she would be privileged to draw a gun from her purse and yell at Frank, "Watch out where you're going, or I'll shoot you!"

27. In the midst of a barroom argument, Archie points a gun at Bruno and threatens to shoot. Bruno pulls out his own gun and fires at Archie, who ducks so that the bullet misses. The bullet travels out the window, across the street, and through a wall, hitting Clara. Assuming the risk to Clara was not foreseeable, can she recover from Bruno?

28. Mildred is visiting at the home of her favorite nephew, Phil. She enters the kitchen and finds Phil struggling with a stranger, Don. In fear for Phil's life, Mildred picks up a knife and plunges it into Don's back. Which, if any, of the following statements is true?

(A) If Phil had been the aggressor and hence not enticed to defend himself, Mildred was not privileged to use any force on his behalf.

(B) Mildred's conduct was not privileged if Phil's life was not actually in danger.

(C) Mildred's conduct was not privileged because she was not a member of Phil's immediate family or household.

29. Dude drives up to the gate across Farmer's driveway and asks for permission to enter and do a little hunting. Farmer responds by brandishing a shotgun at Dude, and cocking it as if to fire.

a. Was Farmer's conduct privileged?

b. Assume Dude ignores Farmer, and drives right through Farmer's gate. Although no warning is posted, the gate is electrically charged and Dude receives a severe shock. Is Farmer liable to Dude for a battery?

30. Knowing that Tom was going to Europe for the summer, Larry stole the key to Tom's apartment and moved in. The owner of the building discovered what

Larry had done, and demanded that Larry vacate, but he refused to do so. Is the owner privileged to use force to evict Larry? _____

31. Shifty rents a car from Apex Car Rentals, establishing credit by using a phony credit card. Shifty fails to return the car as agreed. One week later, Apex catches up with Shifty and demands return of the car. If Shifty refuses, is Apex privileged to use reasonable force against Shifty to take back the car? _____

32. Pierre loans a famous painting for exhibition at Don's Gallery. After the exhibition, Don takes the painting home and hangs it on his wall. Pierre finds out and demands return of the painting, but Don refuses. Is Pierre privileged to use reasonable force against Don to effect recapture of the painting? _____

33. Employer suspects that one of many employees is stealing merchandise from the store, but has no reason to suspect one employee over any other. After store hours, Employer locks all doors and refuses to allow the employees to leave until each submits to a personal search. Is Employer's conduct privileged? _____

34. Store Detective observes a customer, Maude, slip a small bottle of perfume into her purse and walk out the door.

   a. Assume Detective apprehends Maude on the street outside the store, and asks her to come back into the store to be questioned, but she refuses. Is Detective privileged to use force to detain Maude? _____

   b. Assume that the perfume bottle belonged to Maude all along and that Detective made a reasonable mistake in thinking that she was stealing from Store. Is Detective still privileged to use reasonable force to detain Maude? _____

   c. Assume further that Detective asked Maude to allow him to hold onto the bottle while the matter was being investigated, but she refused (the bottle in fact belonging to her). Is Detective privileged to use reasonable force to take the bottle from Maude? _____

35. The FBI posts a "wanted" bulletin for a certain person for murder. George reads the bulletin, and reasonably concludes from the description therein that his neighbor, Ned, is the wanted man. George thereupon arrests Ned without any warrant.

   a. Assume George is a private citizen (not a police officer). Was the arrest privileged if it turns out that Ned is *not* the wanted man? _____

   b. Assume George is a police officer. Was the arrest privileged if it turns out not only that Ned was *not* the wanted man, but also that *no felony* had actually been committed (*e.g.*, the "murder victim" was actually a suicide)? _____

36. The police are called to quell student riots at University. They arrest Bob, Carol, Ted, and Alice on charges of disorderly conduct, a misdemeanor. Although all four were present at the scene, only Bob was a participant in the rioting. Are the arrests all privileged? _____

37. Sheriff John has a warrant for the arrest of Tony on a charge of murder. He apprehends Tony's twin brother, Sam, thinking he is Tony. Sam resists arrest, and in order to subdue him, Sheriff John shoots Sam in the leg. Can Sam recover for battery? _____

INTENTIONAL TORTS TO PROPERTY

38. To clear some boulders out of her field, Farmer sets off dynamite charges. Unexpectedly, the explosion causes vibrations that extend to Neighbor's land, damaging a water well. Can Neighbor recover for trespass? _____

39. Rancher grants permission to Telephone Co. to erect and maintain telephone poles and wires across a portion of his land for a 10-year period. At the expiration of the 10 years, Rancher demands removal of the poles and wires, but Telephone Co. fails to comply.

    a.   Can Rancher recover from Telephone Co. for trespass? _____

    b.   Assume that Telephone Co. removed all of its poles, but later strung a telephone wire across one corner of his property from poles *outside* Rancher's land. Is this a trespass? _____

40. Jones has been dumping dirt on a corner of his property for years, to fill in a low spot. Without Jones's knowledge or consent, an adjoining landowner, Smith, throws a small amount of dirt on the same spot. Is Smith liable to Jones for trespass? _____

41. Able owns a parcel of land leased to Baker for 99 years. However, both Able and Baker reside elsewhere, and Charley has gone into adverse possession of the parcel. Dodge trespasses. To whom, if anyone, is Dodge subject to liability? _____

42. Bookworm carries home a rare book from Library, inadvertently forgetting to check it out at the library counter.

    a.   Is Bookworm subject to liability for trespass to chattels? _____

    b.   Is Bookworm subject to liability for conversion? _____

43. A rare book is in the display case at Library, under a "Do Not Touch" sign. Nevertheless, Bookworm reaches into the case to examine the book, accidentally tearing one page.

    a.   Is Bookworm subject to liability for trespass to chattels? _____

    b.   Is Bookworm subject to liability for conversion? _____

44. As a prank, Tom turns up the heat in Waldo's wine cellar, causing many bottles of wine to sour. Is Tom subject to liability either for trespass to chattels or conversion? _____

45. Angel buys a used car from Hood, believing Hood to be the owner. In fact, Hood stole the car.

a. Is Angel subject to liability for either trespass to chattels or conversion at the time he purchased the car? _____

b. If Owner later claims the car but Angel refuses to turn it over (honestly thinking he owns it), does his refusal constitute a conversion? _____

46. Being desperate for money, Sylvia pawns her fur coat at Benny's Pawnshop for a $500 loan. In which of the following cases could Sylvia recover against Benny for conversion of the coat? _____

(A) Before repaying the loan, Sylvia demanded return of her coat so that she could wear it to a party. Benny refused to give it back.

(B) A burglar broke into the pawnshop and stole Sylvia's coat.

(C) Benny forgot to put moth crystals in the closet where the coat was hanging, and it was destroyed by moths.

(D) Benny allowed his wife, Wilma, to wear the fur coat to a party one night; Sylvia was at the party and was very upset thereby.

(E) Same facts as in (D), except that someone spilled a drink on the fur, causing a stain that cannot be removed.

(F) At midnight, Sylvia telephoned Benny saying she wanted to repay the loan and for him to open up the store and give her back her coat. Benny told her to come in the next morning. Unfortunately, a fire occurred during the interim, destroying the coat.

47. Sucker purchases 100 shares of Goldray Uranium for $10 each through his stockbroker, Fastbuck. The shares are retained in Fastbuck's brokerage account. When the shares go up to $15 each, Fastbuck—without authority from Sucker—sells the shares and pockets the proceeds. Within a few weeks, the shares go up to $50 each, but then fraud is discovered and the company goes bankrupt so that the shares are now worthless. If Sucker sues Fastbuck for conversion, how much, if anything, will he recover? _____

PRIVILEGED INVASIONS OF PROPERTY

48. Because his own tractor is broken, Buford goes onto Clem's land and "borrows" Clem's tractor.

a. Assume Clem returns and sees his tractor sitting in Buford's field. Is Clem privileged to go onto Buford's land to reclaim his tractor without asking for Buford's permission? _____

b. Assume that Clem asks for his tractor back, but Buford refuses and attempts to bar Clem's entry. Thereupon, Clem shoves Buford aside and drives his tractor off the land, doing some damage to Buford's crops in the process. Is Clem liable to Buford either for battery or for damage to Buford's crops? _____

49. Wilbur's poodle ran away from home and entered Mary's yard. Mary fell in love with the dog and put a leash on it. When Wilbur came looking for his poodle, Mary refused to return it and locked the gate to her property.

   a. Is Wilbur privileged to break down Mary's gate if necessary to enter her land to reclaim his dog?   _____

   b. If he is privileged to break her gate, must he pay for the damage? _____

   c. Is Wilbur privileged to break and enter Mary's front door if Mary has taken the dog inside the house? _____

   d. Would it make any difference that the dog had run away several times previously, and Wilbur was negligent in not putting a leash on the dog? _____

50. Because of a gasoline shortage, Tom has hoarded almost 1,000 gallons of gasoline in his garage, located in a densely populated residential neighborhood. Neighbor, Ned, has unsuccessfully complained to Tom about the potential fire hazard, which is apparent because the containers in which the gasoline is stored are not airtight, and occasionally leak.

   While Tom and his family are away on vacation, a savage lightning storm develops. Ned knows there is no lightning rod on Tom's garage and fears that a bolt of lightning may ignite the gasoline. Therefore, he breaks into the garage and pours Tom's gasoline down the sewer.

   a. Was Ned's conduct privileged? _____

   b. Assuming it was privileged, would Ned have to pay Tom for the damage to his garage and the loss of the gasoline? _____

   c. Assume there was no lightning storm, but Ned simply decided to enter the garage and get rid of the gasoline in Tom's absence because Tom had ignored his requests to do so. Would Ned's conduct be privileged in such a case? _____

51. Wife is a diabetic, requiring insulin shots to survive. While on a vacation trip, Wife runs out of insulin and goes into a coma. Husband runs to the only drugstore in town to get insulin syringes, but Druggist refuses to sell him any because Husband did not bring a prescription. Husband thereupon goes behind the counter and forcibly takes the insulin from Druggist, after a violent struggle.

   a. If Druggist is injured thereby, is Husband subject to liability? _____

   b. Is Husband subject to liability to Druggist for damage to the drugstore counter caused in the struggle between Husband and Druggist? _____

   c. Is Husband subject to liability to Druggist for the value of the insulin taken? _____

NEGLIGENCE

52. Pete sues Don for negligence arising out of an intersection accident. Pete proves that Don did not slow down as he entered the intersection, notwithstanding a

yellow "Caution" sign. Which of the following evidence, if any, offered by Don in defense, ***conclusively proves*** (as a matter of law) that he was ***not*** negligent? — *C*

(A) Undisputed testimony by Don that he did not see the "Caution" sign at the intersection, because it was obstructed by a tree.

(B) Undisputed testimony by others in the community that it was customary to enter this particular intersection without stopping, even though there was a "Caution" sign.

(C) A city ordinance expressly provides that a driver is not required to stop or slow down at an intersection where the "Caution" sign is not fully visible.

53. Paula sues Donna for negligence arising out of an auto accident. Which of the following facts, if any, offered by Donna in defense, is ***relevant to show*** that she acted as a reasonable person under the circumstances and hence was not negligent? — *B*

(A) Donna's eyesight is so poor that she did not see Paula's car coming.

(B) Donna is mentally retarded, having the mentality of a 10-year-old.

(C) Donna had been drinking "Ripple" all morning and was slightly intoxicated so that she did not see Paula's car until too late to avoid the impact.

(D) Donna was not an experienced driver; she had just obtained a learner's permit, and had been driving for only a few weeks.

54. Martha is a 10-year-old child, but is unusually bright and very mature for her age.

a. Assume a neighbor asks Martha to babysit and a claim for negligence arises from her so doing. Is Martha's conduct to be judged according to ***her own*** superior intelligence (rather than the lesser abilities of the average 10-year-old child)? — *Yes*

b. Assume Martha drives the family car to the grocery store and is involved in an accident. Is her age a factor to be considered in determining whether she was negligent? — *N*

55. Dudley employs Attorney to represent him in a civil lawsuit. Which, if any, of the following statements is true in determining the standard of care owed by Attorney to Dudley? — _____

(A) It makes no difference that Attorney has just passed the bar exam and that Dudley is her first client.

(B) It makes no difference that Attorney advised Dudley that this was her first case.

(C) If Attorney was in fact a trial specialist, she would owe a higher standard of care than would a nonspecialist, regardless of whether Dudley was aware of Attorney's special skill.

56. While driving her car in heavy traffic, Gabby is distracted by a discussion she is having with her passenger, Peggy, and as a result strikes a truck being driven by Felix.

    a.   If Felix is injured, can he base a claim for negligence against Gabby *solely* on the basis that she wasn't watching where she was going? _____

    b.   Assume Felix's truck contained jet rocket fuel, and the collision set off an explosion, injuring Phillip, a pedestrian on the street. Is Gabby subject to liability for Phillip's injuries? _____

    c.   Assume that the same explosion knocked some bottles off a shelf in a medical laboratory nearby. The bottles shattered, and a worker, Wilma, was cut by the flying glass. Is Gabby subject to liability for Wilma's injury? _____

    d.   Assume that Gabby herself was injured and rendered unconscious in the collision, and her car set on fire. Assume further that a passerby, Sam, saw her predicament and rushed to her aid, but injured himself in so doing. Is Gabby subject to liability for Sam's injuries? _____

57. Alma buys a wrapped loaf of bread baked by Bakery. She takes it home, opens the sealed wrapper, eats a slice, and is injured by a piece of glass imbedded therein. Alma sues Bakery for negligence.

    a.   If Alma proves only the foregoing facts, has she made out a prima facie case of negligence? _____

    b.   If Bakery fails to put on any defense, is Alma entitled to a judgment against Bakery? _____

58. Should an inference of negligence by the defendant be drawn in any of the following cases?

    a.   Allen leaves his new Corvette parked on the side of a hill; 15 minutes later, the car rolls down the hill and crashes into Bob's house. _____

    b.   Trans-Global Flight 02, on which Charlie was a passenger, disappears and no trace is ever found. Charlie's heirs sue Trans-Global and produce the following known facts with regard to the flight: good flying weather at the time of flight; flat terrain from take-off to destination; and all luggage examined by electronic equipment for bombs or weapons. _____

    c.   Alpha's store premises are damaged by water escaping from a main under the street. The water main had been installed by Beta Co., but the City was in charge of inspecting and maintaining the pipes. Alpha sues both Beta and City. An expert testifies that the water mains could have broken *either* because they were improperly installed or improperly maintained; but he can't tell which. _____

    d.   While filling her car with gas at the Ajax self-service station, Dominica is killed by an explosion at the pump. The cause of the explosion is unknown. Dominica's heirs sue both Ajax and the manufacturer of the pump. _____

59. Amy is a passenger on a bus operated by Bus Co. The bus collides with a car driven by Chris, due to the negligence of both the bus driver and Chris. Amy is injured in the collision.

   a. Was Chris's negligence the "cause in fact" of Amy's injuries? Was the bus driver's? _____

   b. Assume that moments after the accident, the bus is struck again because of Denny's negligent driving. Within hours, Amy is paralyzed but it is impossible to determine whether the paralysis was caused by the first or second impact, or as the result of the combined impacts. Can Amy recover against Bus Co., Chris, or Denny? _____

60. City fails to properly maintain a sidewalk, causing irregularities in the pavement. Property Owner is under a duty to keep the walk in front of her property free of debris and ice. After a storm, Pedestrian slips and falls on the sidewalk on which ice has accumulated. It cannot be determined whether the fall was due to the sidewalk irregularities *or* to the ice. Can Pedestrian prove a prima facie case of negligence against *either* City or Property Owner? _____

61. Archie negligently operates his car so that it strikes a power line pole.

   a. Assume the pole falls on a car being driven by Bob, causing him severe personal injuries. Is Archie liable to Bob? _____

   b. Suppose that Bob has a heart condition and that the accident causes a severe attack resulting in Bob's death. A healthy person probably would not have died. Can Bob's heirs prevail in a wrongful death action? _____

   c. Assume that the impact with the pole cuts off power in a wide area and turns off all traffic signals and street lights. Several blocks away, two cars collide at an intersection because of the blackout. Is Archie liable for injuries and property damages sustained in this second collision? _____

62. While operating his lawnmower in a careless manner, Andy strikes and seriously injures Bill's dog. In a frenzy, the dog runs into the house and bites Bill. Is Andy liable to Bill? _____

63. Al negligently drives his car so as to endanger Bob, walking in a crosswalk. To escape being hit, Bob jumps out of the way, in the process knocking down Cindy, who suffers injuries. Is Al liable to Cindy? _____

64. Service station operator, Don, negligently fails to replace the cap on the gasoline tank on Paul's new car. Later, Paul's neighbor, Ned, notices that the gas cap is missing and throws a lighted match into Paul's gas tank. Is Don liable for the resulting destruction of Paul's car? _____

65. As Oscar is walking across the highway at night, he is struck and rendered unconscious by a car negligently driven by Felix. Felix hurriedly drives away, leaving Oscar lying helpless in the middle of the road.

   a. Assume that Oscar is run over by another car, driven by Phoebe; and that had Phoebe been paying attention to where she was going she could have avoided hitting Oscar. Is Felix liable for the additional injuries suffered by Oscar as the result of being run over by Phoebe's car?

b. Assume that another motorist, Max, sees Oscar unconscious in the road, realizes that Oscar is helpless, and proceeds to "mug" him, stealing Oscar's wallet and gold watch. Is Felix liable to Oscar for the loss of the wallet and watch?

c. Assume that while Oscar is still unconscious in the middle of the road a storm develops, and Oscar is struck by a bolt of lightning. Is Felix liable for the additional injuries suffered by Oscar as the result of being struck by lightning?

66. Contractor excavates a deep pit next to a public sidewalk, and fails to place barriers or warning lamps around it. Pedestrian falls into the pit, and cuts his head. His cries of help are heard by Neighbor, who could have summoned help, but it was late at night and Neighbor chose not to "get involved." As a result, Pedestrian bleeds to death.

a. Is Contractor liable for Pedestrian's death?

b. Is Neighbor liable for Pedestrian's death?

67. Doug negligently causes an auto accident in which the other driver, Pam, sustains a small cut on her arm. Pam neglects to obtain medical treatment for the cut, and as a result, infection sets in and the wound becomes gangrenous, necessitating amputation of her arm. Is Doug subject to liability for the loss of Pam's arm?

68. Doug negligently causes an auto accident in which the other driver, Pat, sustains personal injuries. The cost of hospital and medical treatment for Pat's injuries is $2,500, all of which is covered by Pat's group insurance. Is Pat entitled to recover against Doug for the medical and hospital bills, even though these bills were in fact paid by Pat's insurance?

NEGLIGENCE—SPECIAL DUTY QUESTIONS

69. In response to a gasoline shortage, a statute is enacted prohibiting auto travel on Sundays except for emergencies. Notwithstanding, Driver drives his car on Sunday to play golf. On the way back, he strikes Pedestrian, causing severe injuries. Can Pedestrian recover based solely on a showing that Driver violated the statute banning Sunday driving?

70. A statute makes it a crime to drive a vehicle after dusk unless both front and rear lights are lit. At night, Pedestrian is struck and injured by a car driven by Driver with its lights out.

a. Would Pedestrian establish a prima facie case of negligence against Driver merely by showing that Driver had violated the statute?

b. Would Driver be permitted to introduce evidence that even though her lights were out, she was driving carefully and maintaining a proper lookout on the road ahead?

c.   Would Driver be permitted to introduce evidence that her lights had failed just prior to impact with Pedestrian and that she had no opportunity to pull over to the side of the road? _____

71. Rich is driving his new Rolls Royce when he strikes Barbara, knocking her to the ground and causing her serious injuries.

a.   If the accident was not Rich's fault (*e.g.*, Barbara was negligent in stepping in front of his car), is Rich under any duty at common law to stop and render aid to Barbara? _____

b.   Assume Rich stopped his car and agreed to drive Barbara home. However, as he approached her house, the road was unpaved, and Rich refused to drive his new Rolls Royce further. Therefore, Barbara was forced to walk the remaining mile in the rain, aggravating her original injuries. Is Rich liable at common law to Barbara for the aggravation of her injuries? _____

72. Acme Airlines Flight 02 is hijacked in mid-air by a person who demands that the flight be diverted to Cuba, which is within the plane's cruising range. The pilot attempts to disarm the hijacker, but a gunfight ensues in which Hijacker shoots Passenger. Is Acme subject to liability to Passenger on a negligence theory? _____

73. Because his leg is in a cast, Willard cannot drive his car. He therefore asks Ben to drive him to the doctor in Willard's car. En route, Willard notices that Ben is driving recklessly, but Willard says nothing.

a.   Assume that immediately thereafter, Ben negligently collides with a car driven by Chris. In the absence of statute, is Willard liable for Chris's injury? _____

b.   Assume that the collision occurred after Ben had dropped Willard off at the doctor's office. In the absence of statute, would Willard be liable for Chris's injury? _____

74. Archie, a truck driver for Widget Co., is driving back to the factory after making his last delivery of the day. On the way, he negligently causes a collision with a car driven by Stella, injuring her.

a.   Can Stella recover damages from Widget Co., even though Widget Co. was not negligent in hiring or supervising Archie? _____

b.   If Archie and Stella got into an argument as to whose fault the accident was, and Archie punched Stella in the nose, could Stella recover against Widget Co. for injury to her nose? _____

c.   Assume that Widget Co. was **not** otherwise liable for Archie's punching Stella in the nose. Could Stella recover against Widget by showing that when they employed Archie, he had a police record for committing batteries and Widget was aware of this record? _____

75. Trans-Global Airlines engages Aero Repair Co. to overhaul the engine in one of Trans-Global's planes. The job is done negligently by Aero. As a result, the plane crashes, injuring Passenger. Passenger sues Trans-Global.

a.   Assume that Trans-Global was **not** negligent in selecting Aero Repair to do the work. Is Trans-Global liable for Aero's negligence? _____

b.   Assume that Trans-Global **is** otherwise liable for Aero's negligence. Can it defend by showing that, under the repair contract, Aero assumed liability for injuries to others caused by its negligence? _____

76.   Mother employs Babysitter to care for Junior, age eight. Mother fails to advise Babysitter that Junior is proficient in karate. Babysitter engages in horseplay with Junior and is felled by a karate chop. Is Mother subject to liability for Babysitter's injuries? _____

77.   In a state with a typical "Dram Shop Act," Waldo gets drunk at Tavern. Shortly thereafter, he drives his car into a telephone pole, fracturing his neck. Can Waldo recover against Tavern for his injuries? _____

78.   Harry and Georgia form a car pool to drive to work, the understanding being that each will take his or her car on alternate days. Harry is driving on his day and negligently causes a collision with a car driven by Phil.

a.   If Georgia is injured in the accident, can Georgia recover against Harry under a typical "guest statute"? _____

b.   If **Phil** is injured in the accident can he recover from **Georgia** on a "joint enterprise" theory? _____

79.   Is the following jury instruction a correct statement of the law? "Every occupier of land owes to persons coming onto his land a duty to exercise reasonable care with respect to any condition or activity on his land which involves a foreseeable risk of harm." _____

80.   Pedestrian is walking on a city sidewalk adjoining Owner's property.

a.   Assume that Pedestrian is struck by a branch falling from a native tree located on Owner's property. If Owner has never inspected the tree to make sure it is safe, is Owner subject to liability for any injuries resulting to Pedestrian? _____

b.   If Pedestrian is struck on the head by a baseball hit in a game being played on Owner's land, is Owner subject to liability therefor? _____

81.   Thief was attempting to burglarize (at night) Rich's home in Bellaire, when he fell into Rich's partially completed swimming pool and was severely injured. If Rich had failed to erect any fence or post any warning or lights around the pool, is he subject to liability for Thief's injuries? _____

82.   Philpott owns a large sandy lot adjacent to a public beach. He knows that beach users often park their cars on his lot, notwithstanding a large "No Trespassing" sign. To discourage this use, Philpott strews broken bottles in the sand where they park. One of the beach users, Beachbum, cuts his foot on the broken glass.

a.   Is Philpott subject to liability therefor? _____

b.   Would Philpott be subject to liability if the broken glass had been carelessly strewn **by other beach users** (rather than by Philpott), and Philpott had taken no action to clean it up?   _____

83.   Cement Co. maintains large piles of sand on its premises for use in making concrete. The sand is impure and often contains sharp pebbles and bits of glass. Over the weekend, the premises are unattended, although a fence and "no trespassing" signs have been erected. A group of 10-year-olds climb through the fence one weekend and are cut while playing in the sandpiles. Is Cement Co. subject to liability for their injuries?   _____

84.   Tamura raises goldfish in a small pond on his property, which is located next door to a nursery school for preschool age children. Tamura knows that sometimes children from the nursery school trespass onto his property to look at his fish, but he does nothing to prevent this because he enjoys having the children come onto his property. One day, in his absence, a three-year-old child from the nursery school trespasses, falls into the pond, hits her head and is rendered unconscious and drowns in the water. Is Tamura liable for the child's death even though he never realized there was any risk of harm to the children?   _____

85.   Seymour, a door-to-door salesman, suffers a broken leg when he trips on a broken stair of Owner's front porch. Owner was not at home at the time, but he knew that the stair needed repair and that the danger was not readily visible. Is Owner liable for Seymour's injuries?   _____

86.   Benny operates a gasoline service station. One of his customers inadvertently spilled a lot of water in the men's room, making the entrance very slippery. However, no one complained to Benny about the condition until several hours later, when Larry slipped and fell, hurting his back. Larry was not a customer of the service station, but rather, a 12-year-old child on his way home from school. Is Benny subject to liability for Larry's injuries?   _____

87.   While Benny was servicing a car on the lube rack, some oil leaked onto the ground, making the surrounding area quite slippery. Before noticing the oil, Benny was called to the pumps to attend to a customer. While Benny was not looking, Larry, a 12-year-old on his way home from school, walked into the lube area, slipped, and fell. Is Benny subject to liability for Larry's injuries?   _____

88.   Rich and his friend, Bob, went hunting on Rich's rural estate. Tom was trespassing across one of the fields. Neither Rich nor Bob saw Tom because they were engrossed in conversation.

a.   If Rich negligently fired his gun without keeping a proper lookout and thereby wounded Tom, would Rich be subject to liability to Tom?   _____

b.   If Bob negligently fired his gun without keeping a proper lookout and thereby wounded Tom, would Bob be subject to liability to Tom?   _____

89.   Larry is the owner of a house which he leases to Tricia. Larry knows, but forgets to mention to Tricia, that the faucet on the bathtub does not work properly. When Tricia goes to turn it on the first time, it comes off in her hand, and she is scalded by hot water.

a. Is Larry subject to liability for Tricia's injuries? _____

b. Suppose it was Tricia's fiance, Bob, who was injured by the defective hot water faucet. Would Larry be subject to liability for Bob's injuries? _____

90. Leonard is the owner of an apartment house. Is he subject to liability for the following injuries?

a. Tenant #1 is injured by an electric shock from a light switch which Leonard had negligently repaired. _____

b. Tenant #2 is injured by an electric shock from a light switch which Leonard had failed to repair, notwithstanding a lease obligation and request from the tenant to do so. _____

c. Visitor to Tenant #2 is injured by an electric shock from the same light switch referred to in "b." _____

d. Tenant #3 is injured when she falls in the apartment house elevator, as the result of a broken floor tile which caught the heel of her shoe; the broken floor tile had been reported to Leonard, but he had forgotten to fix it. _____

e. Visitor to Tenant #3 is injured when he falls in the elevator as the result of the same broken floor tile. _____

91. Edith is seated on a curbside bench waiting for a bus, when a car negligently driven by Archie roars past her at high speed.

a. Assume that Archie's car splatters mud and debris from the gutter all over Edith's dress, causing her extreme embarrassment and anguish. Is Archie subject to liability for negligent infliction of emotional distress to Edith? _____

b. Assume that Archie's car appeared to be careening out of control toward Edith herself, but swerved away at the last moment, and Edith fainted out of fright, but otherwise sustained no injury. Is Archie subject to liability for negligently causing emotional distress to Edith? _____

92. Mother is preparing lunch in her kitchen while her five-year-old daughter, Child, is playing outdoors. Mother hears the screeching of brakes and runs outside; she sees Child lying in the gutter—having been struck by a car negligently operated by Drunk. Mother's emotional distress at this sight results in her suffering a heart attack. Is Mother entitled to recover against Drunk for the heart attack? _____

DEFENSES TO NEGLIGENCE

93. Don drove his car into an intersection without stopping at a posted stop sign. He broadsided a car being driven by Paula, causing her severe injuries.

a. Assume that Paula was at fault in failing to keep a proper lookout on the road ahead of her, so that she was unable to avoid the impact. Assume further, however, that Paula's carelessness was slight as compared to Don's. Is Don excused from liability because of Paula's relatively slight negligence? _____

b. Assume that Paula was not at all negligent in causing the accident, but thereafter carelessly failed to obtain medical attention for her injuries, causing aggravation thereof. Is Don excused from liability because of Paula's careless failure to obtain medical aid? _____

94. Able rushes into the street to rescue a child in the direct path of Baker's negligently driven car. Able failed to see another car coming from a different direction, negligently driven by Charlie, and is struck and injured thereby.

a. Is Charlie excused from liability because of Able's failure to look both ways before dashing into the street? _____

b. Is Baker subject to liability for Able's injuries? _____

c. Assume that the child was Able's son, and that the *child was negligent* in wandering into the street, so that in some jurisdictions the child could not have recovered against either Baker or Charlie. Is this a valid defense to Able's cause of action against either defendant? _____

95. In a *contributory negligence* state, Pedestrian entered the crosswalk at an intersection while reading a newspaper. He didn't realize that he was walking against the traffic signal and into the path of oncoming traffic.

a. Brenda was driving down the street at an excessive speed. She would have been able to avoid Pedestrian, but for the fact that she glanced away from the road while lighting a cigarette. As a result, her car hit Pedestrian and knocked him unconscious. Assume that had Pedestrian looked up he would have seen Brenda's car coming and would have been able to get out of the way until just before the impact. Is Brenda subject to liability to Pedestrian? _____

b. Same facts as in previous paragraph, except assume that Brenda was traveling so fast, and the street was so narrow, that even if Pedestrian had looked up he would *not* have been able to get out of the way in time. Under those circumstances would Brenda be subject to liability to Pedestrian? _____

96. In a *comparative negligence* jurisdiction, Plaintiff proves that he sustained $8,000 damages, while Defendant proves that she sustained $2,000 damages, as the result of an accident in which both were equally at fault. How much is Plaintiff entitled to recover against Defendant? _____

(A) $8,000

(B) 8/10 of $8,000 (*i.e.*, $6,400)

(C) $4,000

(D) Zero

97. Harry and Georgia have a car pool for riding to work, the agreement being that Georgia will reimburse Harry for half the expenses incurred in driving, parking,

etc. On the way to work one day, a collision occurs between Harry's car and another car driven by Phil in which both drivers were negligent. Georgia is the only one injured.

 a. If Georgia sues Phil, will she be barred from recovery because Harry was contributorily negligent in causing the collision? ————

 b. Assume that, instead of a car pool, Harry was in fact Georgia's chauffeur. In such a case, would Georgia be barred from recovering against Phil because of Harry's negligence? ————

98. Louise is a passenger on a bus operated by Bus Co. The driver of the bus operates it at an excessive speed, causing it to go off the road and crash. Louise is seriously injured in the crash and sues Bus Co. Which of the following, if any, constitutes an assumption of the risk? ————

 (A) The ticket that Louise purchased expressly provided that Bus Co. would not be liable for personal injuries to passengers regardless of cause; and a large sign at the bus station provided the same.

 (B) Louise was aware when she got on the bus that the driver had been drinking.

 (C) Louise sat right behind the bus driver, saw that he was speeding, and laughingly encouraged him to go "faster, faster!"

99. Interstate Oil Company fails to maintain properly its oil pipelines; as a result, one of the lines ruptures and spreads crude oil over a busy highway. The highway becomes so slippery as to be impassable. Harry is driving to work, sees the condition of the highway, and knows that the only available detour will cause him to be one-half hour late to work. Rather than risk his job, he decides to drive carefully through the oil spill. However, his car goes out of control and crashes, and he is injured. Has Harry assumed the risk? ————

STRICT LIABILITY

100. Buckeroo operates a riding stable at a summer resort. One of the horses has a habit of breaking into a gallop on his own, but most riders are able to handle this. Buckeroo rents this horse to Tenderfoot, after warning him that the horse was likely to gallop. Tenderfoot is thrown when the horse breaks into a gallop.

 a. Is Buckeroo subject to liability for Tenderfoot's injuries in the absence of a showing of negligence? ————

 b. Is Buckeroo subject to liability on a negligence theory? ————

101. Buckeroo operates a riding stable at a summer resort. He rents a very gentle riding horse to Tenderfoot, but the horse throws and injures Tenderfoot because it is "spooked" by a rattlesnake. The snake is actually a pet kept in a cage in Buckeroo's office as a visitor's attraction. The snake had escaped from the cage, but was incapable of harming anyone as it had been defanged. Is Buckeroo subject to liability for Tenderfoot's injuries in the absence of any showing of negligence? ————

102. Priscilla keeps a Doberman Pinscher as a watchdog. It has never attacked anyone, but Priscilla knows that Dobermans as a breed are characteristically ferocious toward strangers.

   a.   One night, George, the next door neighbor, comes home drunk and tries to crawl in the window of Priscilla's house, thinking it is his own. George is attacked and severely bitten by the Doberman. Is Priscilla subject to liability therefor in the absence of any showing of negligence? _____

   b.   The following morning, the Doberman playfully trips the mail carrier on the front porch, causing her severe injuries. Is Priscilla subject to liability in the absence of any showing of negligence? _____

   c.   That afternoon, while the Doberman is sitting on the front porch, a bill collector comes to knock on the door. The Doberman growls menacingly, but the bill collector ignores him and keeps coming. Finally, the Doberman attacks and severely injures the bill collector. Is Priscilla subject to liability in the absence of any showing of negligence on her part? _____

103. Which, if any, of the following activities should be regarded as "abnormally dangerous" for purposes of imposing strict liability for harms caused thereby? _____

   (A) Firing a shotgun at birds to prevent them from roosting in a residential neighborhood.

   (B) Fumigating a house with cyanide gas to kill termites.

   (C) Storing a large quantity of "cherry bombs" (firecrackers containing gunpowder) in a garage in a residential neighborhood.

104. Contractor is blasting rock at a remote desert quarry. Unexpectedly, the vibrations trigger an underground avalanche, resulting in a shifting of subsurface formations miles away, which knocks out Farmer's water well. Assuming no negligence, is Contractor liable for the damage to Farmer's well? _____

PRODUCTS LIABILITY

105. Duro Drugs markets a new eye medicine after having been warned by its laboratory staff that there is a strong likelihood of an adverse side effect (potential blindness) to users. Pamela purchases and uses the drug and suffers blindness as a result thereof.

   a.   Can Pamela recover for a battery? _____

   b.   Assuming Pamela could otherwise recover for a battery, could Duro defend on the ground that Pamela was contributorily negligent in failing to read the label on the medicine that warned of possible adverse side effects? _____

106. Retailer sells a shotgun to Sport. The shotgun has a "hair trigged" (not common for this type gun), but Retailer neglects to warn Sport about this. While Sport is using the shotgun, it discharges prematurely due to the "hair trigger," resulting in injuries to Child.

a. Is Retailer liable to Child for negligence? _____

b. Is Retailer liable to Child under strict liability? _____

107. Dealer sells and installs in Archie's house a water heater manufactured by Biltrite Water Heater Co. Shortly after installation, the water heater explodes. Archie sues Biltrite for *negligence*. Which of the following would be a valid defense? _____

(A) The water heater exploded because of poor design, rather than as a result of carelessness in the manufacturing process.

(B) The cause of the explosion was a defective valve manufactured by another company (and merely assembled by Biltrite into its heater).

(C) Biltrite had warned all of its dealers that the particular model was potentially dangerous. Dealer was negligent in selling and installing the water heater in Archie's house after having received such warning.

(D) The damage done by the explosion was only property damage (ruined floors, etc.), and not personal injuries.

108. Dealer purchases a closeout on dynamite caps from a company that is going out of business. Dealer has had no previous knowledge or dealings with that company or its products. Dealer sells some of the dynamite caps to Contractor. The caps prove defective in use, causing injury to Bystander.

a. If Dealer had no prior knowledge that the caps were defective, is Dealer liable in *negligence* for Bystander's injuries? _____

b. If Dealer had warned Contractor that the dynamite caps were a "closeout" and could not be guaranteed in any way, would Dealer be liable in *negligence* for Bystander's injuries? _____

109. Art purchases a new mattress from Ben's Furniture Store. The mattress had been manufactured by Sleeptite Co., a reputable concern. When Art gets the mattress home, he flops down on it. Unfortunately, one of the inner springs had broken inside the mattress and a sharp wire pierces Art's back.

a. Assume Art sues Ben for negligence. Is Art entitled to recover if he can show that Ben made absolutely no inspection of the mattress; and that if he had, the dangerous wire would have been disclosed and Art's injury prevented? _____

b. Assume Art sues Ben on a warranty theory. Is Art entitled to recover even if he cannot show that Ben had any reason to know that the mattress was dangerous? _____

c. Assume Art sues *Sleeptite* on a warranty theory. Can Art recover? _____

110. Art purchases a new Duro power lawnmower from Ben's Hardware Store, choosing the Duro because of its nationwide advertising as "engineered for safety." While using the lawnmower, Art is struck in the eye by a small pebble

kicked up by the Duro and which passed through a gap in the safety guard surrounding the blades.

a. Can Art recover from Duro on a negligence theory? _____

b. Can Art recover from Duro on a warranty theory? _____

c. Assume another small pebble struck **Bystander** in the eye. Can Bystander recover from Duro on a negligence theory? _____

111. Art purchases a new Duro power lawnmower from Ben's Hardware Store. The tag on the lawnmower recites that it is sold "without any warranty express or implied," and Art read this when he bought the Duro. If Art's child, Son, is struck in the eye by a pebble which passed through a gap in the safety guard on the mower, can Son recover against Ben's on a warranty theory? _____

112. A manufactures and packs a can of barbecued beans, which he sells to wholesaler, B. B in turn sells the beans to jobber, C, who resells to retail grocer, D. Minnie buys the can of beans, takes it home and consumes the contents, and in so doing breaks her tooth on a small pebble which was of the same size, shape and color as the beans in the can. Assume that no reasonable inspection could have revealed the pebble, and further that the beans were sold with an **effective** disclaimer against all warranty liability.

a. Minnie sues A, B, C, and D. Is she entitled to recover against any of them on any theory? _____

b. Assume that it was Minnie's friend, Pearl, who ate the beans and broke her tooth. Can Pearl recover **against Minnie** on any theory? _____

c. Could Pearl recover from A, B, C, or D on any theory? _____

113. Father purchases a bicycle manufactured by Whizzo Co. as a birthday present for Son. Unbeknownst to anyone, the bicycle has defective handbrakes, which cause Son to lose control of the bicycle and injure Pedestrian who is crossing the street.

a. If Pedestrian is unable to prove any negligence on the part of Whizzo, can Pedestrian recover from Whizzo for his injuries? _____

b. Assume that Samaritan attempted to go to the aid of the injured Pedestrian, but was struck by a passing car, negligently driven by Bankrupt. Can Samaritan recover against Whizzo for his injuries? _____

114. Loveless Products markets a new face cream which Thelma purchases and uses as per instructions. However, it causes serious inflammation and discoloration of her facial skin. Without further evidence, can Thelma recover from Loveless on a strict products liability theory? _____

115. Loveless Products markets a new hair dye which is safe when used on the scalp, but contains certain chemicals which could cause burns to the eyes. The label on the dye states that it is intended solely for use on the scalp, but no specific warning is made about the hazard to the eyes. Betty purchases the dye, uses it on her

eyebrows and a drop gets into her eye, causing severe injury. Can Betty recover from Loveless on a strict liability theory? _____

116. National Refrigerator Co. ships its appliances in heavy cardboard cartons. These cartons are normally thrown away when the appliances are sold. However, Employer keeps some of the cartons in his warehouse and uses them to store bedding materials which he also sells. Employee is injured while climbing on one of these cartons when it collapses. Can Employee recover against National Refrigerator Co. on a strict liability theory? _____

117. No-Pest manufactures a garden insecticide packaged in a push-button spray can that is produced by Container Co. George buys a can of the spray to use on his roses, and is injured when, on pushing the spray button, the insecticide sprays back into his face and eyes due to a defect in the spray mechanism. Can George recover on a strict products liability theory against **both** No-Pest and Container Co.? _____

118. Bob was injured while driving his new sports car manufactured by Kamikaze Motors, Inc. In which of the following cases could Bob recover against Kamikaze on either a negligence or strict products liability theory? _____

    (A) Bob's injuries were caused when the steering in his Kamikaze failed as he was driving straight down the highway at 110 m.p.h.

    (B) Bob's injuries were caused by his Kamikaze rolling over when he slammed on the brakes at 55 m.p.h. to avoid a freeway crash ahead of him.

    (C) Bob's injuries were caused by the lack of any side braces or supports to shield him from the impact when his car was broadsided by another car.

119. Presto Glue Co. manufactures a pleasant-smelling liquid glue used in industrial plants. Archie has been employed for over 20 years at an industrial plant at which such glue is used. A government-sponsored research study discloses that prolonged inhalation of fumes from the type of glue manufactured by Presto can cause brain damage. Archie sues Presto for damage to his brain, claiming such inhalation. Can he recover on a strict liability theory? _____

120. Bob was injured when his new Kamikaze sports car crashed into a highway barrier. Bob testified that he was traveling at the legal speed limit, he attempted to turn the steering wheel while rounding a curve and heard something crack, and thereafter the wheels would not turn and the car went out of control and crashed.

    a. Without any further evidence, could Bob recover against Kamikaze on a negligence theory? _____

    b. Without any further evidence, could Bob recover against Kamikaze on a strict products liability theory? _____

    c. Assume that Bob had purchased the Kamikaze as a used car, and that it had about 50,000 miles on it at the time of purchase. Would this alter your answer to either "a." or "b." above? _____

121. Bob is injured when the brakes fail on his new Kamikaze sports car, causing it to crash. Which of the following is a valid defense to a strict liability claim by Bob against Kamikaze?

  (A) Kamikaze had warned all dealers of a potential hazard in the braking system, and had asked that all cars sold be checked for this hazard, but the dealer who sold the car to Bob neglected to do so.

  (B) Kamikaze had notified Bob a week before the accident that there was a potential hazard in the braking system, but Bob failed to bring his car in for inspection and repair.

  (C) Bob had attempted to repair the brakes himself, but performed the job incorrectly and thereby increased the risk of failure.

122. Pete purchases a new truck from Motorco. The truck's suspension system is defectively designed so that when fully loaded the weight shifts and the truck rolls over. Pete escapes injury, but the truck and load are seriously damaged.

  a. Can Pete recover from Motorco for the damage to his truck and load on a theory of strict liability?

  b. Can Pete recover, on a strict liability theory, damages based on the fact that even after repair, Pete cannot operate the truck fully loaded, and therefore it is not worth what he paid for it?

NUISANCE

123. Ajax Chemical Co. discharges certain chemical residues into a stream adjoining its manufacturing plant. These residues render the water unfit for human consumption but do not prevent its use for agricultural or other industrial purposes.

  a. Donald, who is active in the ecology movement, sues Ajax for damages to all residents of the state on a nuisance theory. Can Donald recover?

  b. Frances, who owns land downstream from Ajax, sues Ajax for damages to the water supply on a nuisance theory. Can Frances recover?

124. Archie installs an air conditioning unit on the roof of his house. When the unit is turned on, it emits a very loud motor noise. The noise is particularly bothersome to Archie's neighbor, Tom, whose lot is located on a hillside immediately above Archie's lot; the noise makes it difficult for Tom and his family to sleep, to enjoy normal conversation, etc.

  a. Does the maintenance of the air conditioning unit on top of Archie's roof constitute a sufficient interference with Tom's enjoyment of his property to constitute an actionable nuisance?

  b. If Archie had no reason to know or foresee the annoyance to Tom, and did not intend to cause such annoyance, will a nuisance action lie?

  c. Assume Tom asked Archie to modify the air conditioning unit so as to reduce the noise output, and Archie refused. If Archie continues to run the air conditioner, is it legally possible for a court to award *punitive* damages to Tom? _____

    d.   Suppose Archie proved that he had installed and used the air conditioner on his roof long before Tom moved into the neighborhood, and that Tom should have been aware of the noise problem when he bought his house. Is this a valid defense to Tom's nuisance action? _____

    e.   Assuming an actionable nuisance exists, can Tom recover *both* damages and an injunction requiring Archie to modify the air conditioner so as to abate the noise? _____

LIMITATIONS ON RIGHT TO SUE

125. P is seriously injured in an auto accident as a result of D's negligence. P files suit for property damage, loss of earnings, medical expenses, and pain and suffering.

    a.   Assume P dies prior to trial. Can the executor of his estate recover for any of the damages sued for by P? _____

    b.   If P's executor recovers a judgment in the action filed by P, does this affect the right of P's wife and children to sue for wrongful death? _____

    c.   Assume P's wife and children are permitted to maintain a wrongful death action. Is it a valid defense to such an action that P was contributorily negligent in the action that caused his death? _____

    d.   Is it a valid defense to the wrongful death action brought by P's wife and children, that *P's wife* was negligent in the accident that caused P's death? _____

126. P is seriously injured in an auto accident as a result of D's negligence. P ultimately recovers from the accident, however.

    a.   Can *P's wife* recover against D for the loss of P's services and company during the time he was incapacitated by his injuries? _____

    b.   Can *P's children* recover against D for the loss of P's services and company during the time he was incapacitated by his injuries? _____

127. Husband is seriously injured in an auto accident as a result of Wife's negligent operation of the family car. Assume no guest statute is in effect.

    a.   Can Husband recover against Wife for his injuries? _____

    b.   Assume that the parties' child, Son, was also injured in the same accident. Can Son recover for his injury against his mother? _____

    c.   Assume Husband's father, Grandpa, was injured in the same accident. Can Grandpa recover for his injuries against his son's wife? _____

128. In responding to an emergency call, Police Officer drives her police car negligently and strikes Pedestrian.

a. Is Police Officer subject to liability for Pedestrian's injuries? _____

b. Is City (which employs Police Officer) subject to liability for Pedestrian's injuries? _____

129. Tom and Jerry are both negligent in operating their cars, causing a collision which results in a piece of debris striking and injuring pedestrian, Pat.

a. Assume Pat sues and obtains a judgment against Tom. Can Pat thereafter file a separate action against Jerry to recover more money for the same injury? _____

b. Assume Pat entered into a settlement with Tom for $100. Would this bar Pat from thereafter recovering more money from Jerry? _____

c. Assume Pat obtained a judgment against Tom for $1,000, and Tom paid this judgment. Could *Tom* thereafter recover $500 from Jerry (half the judgment paid to Pat)? _____

d. Assume Pat obtained a judgment against Tom for $1,000, which Tom paid. Assume further that Tom had been working for Employer at the time of the accident. Is Tom entitled to *indemnity* against Employer for the amount of the judgment? _____

DEFAMATION

130. Could a defamation action be successfully based on any of the following published statements?

a. "P's father [now deceased] was a convicted murderer." _____

b. "Police officers in the 54th Precinct have been taking payoffs from local vice lords for years." (P is an officer in the Precinct.) _____

c. "P has been having a torrid love affair with Tom." (P is married to Fred.) _____

d. "P has been spending an awful lot of time with Tom." (P is married to Fred.) _____

131. Secretary Amy has told many of her friends, "All of my jobs were fun except for one where the boss was a pervert." Most of her friends don't know to whom she is referring, but a few interpret this to apply to Waldo, the only employer to ever fire Amy. Actually, Amy was referring to a different person. Is Amy liable to Waldo for defamation? _____

132. The *Daily Tribune* publishes a report that "Engelbert Q. Schultz was arrested last night in a narcotics raid." Actually, there are two men by that name. Is the *Tribune* subject to liability for defamation to the Engelbert Q. Schultz who was not arrested if his friends read the report and think it referred to him? _____

133. In the course of a live television broadcast of a football game, the cameras pan over the huge crowd. A picture is transmitted showing several members of the crowd carrying a large banner reading, "No wonder we lose . . . Coach Jones spends all his time chasing college girls!"

a. Assuming Coach Jones is not a public personage, is the television station subject to liability to Coach Jones for defamation? _____

b. Assume that the television station was subject to liability for defamation based on the picture shown. Would Coach Jones be entitled to recover without proof of actual damage? _____

134. After losing a jury trial, Lawyer goes back to his office and dictates to his secretary a letter to Judge, in which he calls Judge "an incompetent boob" and "unfit to sit on the bench."

a. Is Lawyer subject to defamation based on his dictation of the remarks to his secretary? _____

b. If Judge then angrily shows Lawyer's letter to Clerk, is Lawyer subject to liability to Judge for defamation? _____

135. After losing a jury trial, Lawyer asks to speak to Judge in chambers. Lawyer tells Judge that he is a "prejudiced boob" and "unfit to sit on the bench." Judge had been expecting some sort of outburst from Lawyer, and therefore had left open his intercom line, and Lawyer's remarks were overheard by Clerk.

a. Is Lawyer subject to liability for defamation because Clerk overheard Lawyer's remarks to Judge? _____

b. Assume Lawyer is otherwise subject to liability for defamation. Were his remarks privileged? _____

c. Assume Lawyer is otherwise subject to liability for defamation. Is Judge entitled to recover without proof of any damage? _____

136. Which, if any, of the following oral statements would be actionable without proof of any actual damages suffered by the person defamed—assuming D deliberately lied? _____

(A) "P is a dirty crook!"

(B) "P [a man] chases everything in skirts!"

(C) "P [a woman] sleeps with every man in town!"

(D) "Father Mulcahy [a clergyman] was seen in the company of prostitutes."

(E) "Dentist Smith was seen in the company of prostitutes."

(F) "P is being investigated for the murder of his wife."

137. Which, if any, of the statements listed in the preceding paragraph would be actionable without proof of any actual damages, if they were published in writing? _____

138. The *Daily Tribune* prints in its "Letters to the Editor" column a letter from Teller accusing Banker of misusing Bank funds. This letter is widely read, and Banker is summarily dismissed by Bank. Because there is a "retraction statute" in effect, Banker demands and receives a retraction from the *Daily Tribune*.

a. Does the published retraction affect Banker's right to recover loss of income in a defamation suit against the *Tribune*? _____

b. Does the published retraction affect Banker's right to recover general damages from Teller? _____

139. Eager, a reporter for the *Daily Tribune*, writes a story accusing Warden of inhumane treatment of prisoners in a local jail. The story is published in the Tribune, having a total circulation of 10,000 readers. However, the following week, *Newsbeat Magazine*, having a nationwide circulation, repeats the story, carefully stating its source. The entire story is untrue, and both the newspaper and magazine were negligent in publishing it. (Assume Warden is not a "public official.")

a. Is the owner of the *Daily Tribune* subject to liability even if she reasonably believed Eager's story was accurate when she published it? _____

b. Is *Newsbeat Magazine* subject to liability even though it carefully ascribed the story to the *Daily Tribune*? _____

c. Assuming *Newsbeat Magazine* is subject to liability, are the news dealers and distributors who handle the magazine also subject to such liability? _____

140. Snitch and Sterling are young executives at Acme Manufacturing, competing for promotion. To prevent Sterling from getting ahead of her, Snitch tells Acme's president that Sterling uses narcotics. This is in fact *true*, although Snitch was merely making an educated guess about it when she informed the president; and she did so with the intent of injuring Sterling's business career. Can Sterling recover against Snitch for defamation? _____

141. Partner Alan sues Partner Bob for dissolution of their partnership. Alan sets forth in his complaint as grounds for dissolution irreconcilable business differences with Bob, and that Bob was a member of the Mafia. This latter statement is untrue. Is Alan subject to liability for defamation? _____

142. During the recess of a jury trial, Judge remarks to Clerk, "Plaintiff's attorney is absolutely incompetent—he is either drunk, or stupid, or both!" Is Judge subject to liability for defamation? _____

143. A Senate Investigating Committee is looking into cost overruns on a highway construction project. An auditor for one of the contractors is subpoenaed as a witness and volunteers testimony that his boss, Contractor, is a "card-carrying communist."

a. Is Auditor subject to liability for defamation? _____

b. Senator interjects, "Yes, we know that Contractor is a communist, but that is irrelevant to the issue here." Is Senator subject to liability for defamation? _____

c. That evening, the *Daily Tribune* carries a report of the committee proceedings, which includes the statement that "The only interesting thing that happened all day was the accusation by Auditor that Contractor was a 'card-carrying communist'." Assume the *Daily Tribune* had reason to doubt the accuracy of Auditor's charge. Is the *Daily Tribune* subject to liability for defamation?

    d.   The following day, several reporters asked the Attorney General if he had seen the reports that Contractor was a "card-carrying communist." He replied: "Yes, I have. This is hardly new information, however. I've known Contractor was a 'commie' for many years." Is Attorney General subject to liability for defamation?

144. Stalwart and Sterling are young executives competing for a promotion at Acme Insurance Co. The president of Acme interviews each of them in turn. In the course of the interview, Stalwart says, "I just want to make sure you have all the facts on Sterling. Are you aware that he smokes marijuana regularly?" This is in fact untrue, although Stalwart reasonably believed what he said was true. Is Stalwart subject to liability for defamation?

145. Stalwart and Sterling are young executives competing for a promotion at Acme Insurance Co. Although neither is requested to obtain letters of recommendation, Stalwart thinks it would be a good idea to do so. Therefore, he asks one of his friends, Pompous, to write a letter to Acme's president, recommending Stalwart for the promotion. In the course of the letter, Pompous writes, "In any case, make sure you don't give the job to that no-good, potsmoking Sterling." Pompous reasonably believed what he wrote about Sterling was true, but it was not. Is Pompous subject to liability for defamation?

146. Coward Hosell, the famous sports broadcaster, states on the air that the reason that Quarterback has "slowed down so much" this season is that he is "spending all his energy chasing dames." Quarterback is happily married and is not a woman-chaser. Assume Hosell had ***no information*** one way or the other on Quarterback's sex life when he made the statement. Is Hosell subject to liability for defamation?

147. In a heated election campaign for City Clerk, Candidate charges Incumbent with having committed statutory rape many years ago. This is in fact untrue, but Candidate honestly believed what he said, having received inaccurate information from one of his staff. Is Candidate subject to liability for defamation?

148. In the midst of an energy crisis, the *Daily Tribune* publishes an editorial containing the following statement: "It is perfectly obvious that the federal energy administrator, Jones, has been conspiring with the president of our local private power company, Smith, to drive up the cost of electricity to the public." This is in fact untrue, and the editor was negligent in making these charges.

    a.   Is the *Daily Tribune* subject to liability to Jones (the federal energy administrator)?

    b.   Is the *Daily Tribune* subject to liability to Smith (the president of local private corporation)?

149. *Newsbeat Magazine* publishes a feature article on Senator Claghorn. The article falsely states that Claghorn is a "compulsive gambler."

    a.   Does this statement fall within the scope of constitutional privilege?

b. Assume *Newsbeat* based its article on a sworn statement given by Claghorn's ex-secretary, but *Newsbeat* did nothing to verify the statement because it was on a vendetta to "get" Claghorn and wanted to publish the information as soon as possible. Is this sufficient "malice" to defeat any claim of privilege?

INVASION OF PRIVACY

150. The *Daily Tribune* prints a story captioned, "The Mini-Skirt Survives!", accompanied by a photo showing local women wearing minis on the streets. One of the photos is of Phoebe, and it is rather unflattering of her. Phoebe gave no permission to the *Daily Tribune* to take or publish her photograph. Can she recover for an invasion of her privacy?

151. In an effort to discourage local screening of sex films, Police Chief stations a police photographer next to the box office of a movie theatre showing such films, with instructions to take the picture of every person entering the theatre. Eager purchases a ticket and has his picture taken by the police photographer. Without any further use or publication of Eager's photo, is Police Chief subject to liability for invasion of Eager's privacy?

152. The *San Francisco Daily News* publishes a series of articles dealing with the psychology of those who commit suicide by jumping off the Golden Gate Bridge. As a "typical" suicide, they focus on Jumper, who leapt to his death 10 years ago. The story sets forth details of Jumper's life, including the fact that he was despondent because his wife, Portia, had left him for another man. Accompanying the article is a picture of Jumper's corpse after it was retrieved from the water.

a. Is the *Daily News* subject to liability to Jumper's estate for an invasion of his right to privacy?

b. Is the *Daily News* subject to liability to Jumper's heirs (children) for the embarrassment and anguish of seeing the picture of Jumper's corpse in the newspaper?

c. Is the *Daily News* subject to liability to Portia for publication of the facts of her life (*i.e.*, that she left Jumper for another man)?

d. Assume that the *Daily News* inadvertently got the facts wrong, and that Portia had been a faithful wife all along. Would its error preclude the *Daily News* from claiming that its publication was privileged as "newsworthy"?

153. Smirnup Vodka markets a new canned cocktail called "The Businessman's Pickup." To publicize their product, they hire a sexy female model to stand in a doorway on a public street, and then, with a concealed camera, they capture the glances from men passing by. One of these photos shows a portly businessman named Pompous ogling the model; he was totally unaware that his picture was being taken. This photo is used by Smirnup in its national advertising campaign.

a. If Pompous sues for an invasion of privacy, is it a valid defense that Smirnup merely publicized what had occurred on a public street?

b. If Pompous is otherwise entitled to recover for an invasion of privacy, must he prove some special damages as a result of the publicity? _____

154. Actress Amy is very sensitive about her age, and has been passing herself off for years as "39 or so." Rona Rumor, the Hollywood columnist, publishes the following item: "Thought you'd like to know . . . the Hall of Records showed me Amy's birth certificate . . . the poor girl is only 62 this year. Amazing!"

a. Is Rona Rumor subject to liability for invasion of privacy as to Amy? _____

b. Assume Rona Rumor's column went on to state that Amy has had three face lifts in the past few years from Dr. Patchum, plus silicone injections in her buttocks. Would such disclosures be actionable invasions of Amy's privacy? _____

MISREPRESENTATION

155. Pamela purchases an expensive home in Belleaire from Dudley. Prior to signing, Pamela asks Dudley if the house is free of termites. Is there an actionable misrepresentation in any of the following responses by Dudley?

a. Dudley replied that he had recently obtained a termite report showing no visible infestation. In fact, no such report had been obtained; and, unbeknownst to Dudley, the house is full of termites. _____

b. Dudley replied that there were no termites, because he had never seen any, but afterwards, just to check, he crawled under the house and found a large infestation. He decided not to tell Pamela about this, because she hadn't asked him to crawl under the house and report back to her. _____

c. Dudley made no reply to Pamela's inquiry, but knew that there was extensive infestation of termites. _____

d. Dudley's only reply to Pamela's inquiry was that the house was being sold "as is," while all along Dudley knew there was extensive infestation of termites. _____

156. Pamela purchases an expensive home in Belleaire. Prior to signing, Pamela asks Dudley if the house is free of termite infestation, and he replies that it is. It turns out, however, that the house is termite-infested. Is Dudley subject to liability for misrepresentation in any of the following cases?

a. Dudley honestly believed that there were no termites when he said so, having made a careful inspection of the premises himself recently, and having seen none. _____

b. Dudley made his statement in reliance on a report by a reputable pest control company which had conducted a recent inspection of the premises, and reported to him no infestation. _____

c. Dudley had never seen any termites, but on the other hand, he had never made an inspection of the premises to check for termite infestation. _____

d. Dudley was not the seller of the house, but rather a licensed pest control inspector whom Pamela had hired to inspect the property, and he simply did a poor job, overlooking the infestation. _____

157. Flako Enterprises, Inc., applies to Bank for a loan, and submits a financial statement certified by Accountant. The statement contains several material misrepresentations, known by Flako to be false.

a. Assume Bank turns down the loan application, but Bank's lending officer reads the financial statement and decides to invest personally in Flako stock. If he later discovers the financial statements were false, can he sue Flako for fraud? _____

b. Assume Bank granted the loan on the basis of the financial statements submitted, without doing any independent checking of Flako's credit. If Bank later discovered that the financial statements were false, could Flako defend a fraud suit on the ground that Bank was imprudent in relying exclusively on the statements submitted? _____

c. Assume Bank granted the loan on the basis of the financial statements certified by Accountant. If Flako subsequently went bankrupt, and the falsity of the financial statements was then discovered, could Bank recover from Accountant the amount of its loss? _____

d. Assume that Bank had made an independent credit check on Flako, and realized that financial statements submitted were not accurate. Would this bar Bank's misrepresentation action against Flako and Accountant? _____

158. As part of the negotiations leading up to the sale of an apartment house, Seller made the following representations to Buyer, each of which was false. Which of these representations would subject Seller to liability for misrepresentation if relied upon by Buyer? _____

(A) "This property is worth at least $150,000, but I'll sell it to you for $120,000."

(B) "I have not previously offered this property for sale."

(C) "Nothing in the City Building Code prevents you from splitting the larger apartments into smaller ones, if you want to, thereby increasing the rents."

159. While playing golf at the country club, Swinger tells his friend, Duffer, that he is considering making a loan to a company called Flako Enterprises, and asks Duffer if he knows the company. Duffer replies that he does, and that he considers it "a fine company with great business prospects." Actually, Flako Enterprises is on the verge of bankruptcy, and Duffer knows this because he is its major stockholder (a fact he does not disclose to Swinger).

a. If Swinger makes the loan in reliance on Duffer's assurances, and Flako later goes bankrupt, can Swinger recover from Duffer for misrepresentation? _____

b.   Assume that Flako did *not* go bankrupt, and actually repaid the loan when due. Could Swinger sue Duffer for fraud on the theory that Duffer had deceived him into making a loan which Swinger otherwise would not have made?   _____

160. Fastbuck advertises lots for sale in Golden Years Subdivision, which consists of undeveloped desert acreage. Eager visits the subdivision, and asks what improvements are planned. Fastbuck tells Eager all about planned swimming pools, shopping centers, etc., and relying thereon Eager buys one of the lots for $5,000. The swimming pools, shopping centers, etc., are never built.

a.   Assume that Fastbuck never had the funds to build the promised swimming pools, etc., and never had *any reasonable prospects* of being able to do so. Can Eager recover damages for misrepresentation?   _____

b.   Assume that Eager is entitled to recover damages for misrepresentation. Assume further that the lot he purchased for $5,000 would have been worth $10,000 if the promised improvements had been completed, but that, as is, the lot is not worth more than $2,000. What is the proper measure of recovery to which Eager is entitled?   _____

OTHER TORTS

161. Pioneer Aviation Co. and Aerospace Industries, Inc. are competing to obtain a government contract. Pioneer's sales manager tells the government procurement officer, "Be careful about accepting any bids from Aerospace . . . they're in real hot water with their creditors . . . they could be in bankruptcy any day now." If Aerospace files a tort action against Pioneer based on the foregoing statement, which of the following statements, if any, is true?   _____

(A)   No cause of action for disparagement lies because Pioneer's sales manager was only expressing her opinion.

(B)   If the statements made are actionable as disparagement, the burden is on Pioneer to prove as a defense that the sales manager's statements were true.

(C)   No action for disparagement lies unless malice toward the defendant is established.

(D)   If the statements made are otherwise actionable as disparagement, Aerospace can recover against Pioneer even if Aerospace ends up with the government contract.

162. Sly opens a hamburger stand across the street from a stand operated by Fry. Sly tells people in the neighborhood, "Be careful about eating at Fry's; his so-called '100% beefburgers' are actually horsemeat!" Sly's statements are untrue. Can Fry recover against Sly *in the absence of special damages*?   _____

163. Wiley filed an action against Bright, claiming an interest in certain land to which Bright held title. Concurrently with filing the lawsuit, Wiley recorded a lis pendens, which put all persons on notice of the action, and effectively clouded

Bright's title. Bright eventually won the lawsuit. If Wiley filed the suit without a good faith belief in its merits, can Bright recover for a *slander of title* based on the filing of the lis pendens?

164. Vera is the national sales manager for Loveless Cosmetics, and is employed at a salary of $5,000 per month. Regal, a competitor of Loveless, offers to double Vera's salary if she will come to work for them; she accepts. Which if any of the following statements is true?

   (A) An action for inducing breach of contract cannot be maintained because Vera's employment was terminable by her at will.

   (B) The fact that Vera's contract was terminable at will is relevant to the measure of damages, if Loveless is entitled to recover.

   (C) Regal was privileged to induce Vera to terminate her contract with Loveless.

165. National Motors is negotiating with Sparko Batteries for the purchase of one million auto batteries. Sparko purchases its battery cases exclusively from Case. National Motors tells Sparko if it wants to do business with National, it will have to purchase all battery cases from another supplier. Can Case recover against National Motors for interference with its contractual relationship with Sparko?

166. Employer finds her cash drawer rifled and accuses Employee of having taken the money. Employee denies it. Employer thereupon calls the police and has Employee arrested on a theft charge. However, the charges against Employee are subsequently dismissed for insufficient evidence. Employee thereupon files an action against Employer for malicious prosecution. Which of the following statements, if any, are true?

   (A) The action will not lie because Employee was not acquitted of the criminal charges against him.

   (B) The burden is on Employee to prove that Employer instituted the action against him for some purpose other than bringing a guilty person to justice.

   (C) The burden is on Employee to prove that Employer had no honest or reasonable belief in Employee's guilt when she called police.

   (D) Employer may prove as a defense that Employee actually took the money from the cash drawer.

   (E) If Employee is entitled to recover, he may recover damages to his reputation in addition to the actual costs incurred in defending against the criminal charge.

ANSWERS TO REVIEW QUESTIONS

1.a. YES Any volitional act suffices. Donna may have acted in panic, but she was in command of her senses, and hence her act was "volitional." [§§2, 4]

b. YES All that is required is that Donna believed the consequences (harmful touching of one of the shoppers) were substantially certain to occur. No hatred or ill will need be shown. [§§6-9]

2.a. NO For two reasons: Since Horace was under hypnosis, there was no *"voluntary"* act; and there was *no intent* to inflict such a touching. [§§3-6]

b. YES Although there was no direct touching, Waldo *set in motion the forces* which caused the touching (Horace and the water). He will be deemed to have intended that which was *substantially certain* to happen. [§17]

3.a. YES He committed a battery. David intended to cause a "harmful touching" (intoxication) of everyone at the party. This act was a substantial factor in bringing about the result which occurred (Greta's illness), and hence causation is established. Again, even without any direct "touching" of Greta, David set in motion the force which caused the touching, and that is sufficient. [§17]

b. PROBABLY NOT No battery because the touching (by dancing) was consented to. [§82] No assault because words by themselves are usually not sufficient to create apprehension of *immediate* harmful or offensive touching. [§26] And probably no liability for infliction of emotional distress because David did not intend to inflict such on Peggy (although arguably David was "reckless" in this regard). [§67]

c. DEPENDS On whether a *reasonable person* in Zeke's position would have been offended by the shaking. (The fact that Zeke was offended is not conclusive, unless David knew that Zeke was particularly sensitive about being shaken.) Because they were "pals," there may be some latitude in what a reasonable person would regard as "offensive." [§§13-16]

d. YES Under the *transfer of intent* doctrine, David is liable for a battery even though he intended only an assault (to frighten Zeke), and even though the person struck was not the person he intended to frighten. Even though David and Zeke were "pals," and therefore it's arguable that there was some sort of consent to horseplay between them, Zeke's "consent" would not apply to Beth's cause of action. [§10]

4.a. YES If Prudence heard it and was placed in apprehension of an immediate harmful touching thereby. The fact that the threat was *conditional* ("get off the streets or else") is immaterial, because the command was not one which Mildred was privileged to make. [§§30-38]

b. YES It is immaterial that George was only "joking" or that he had no intent to actually harm his sister. He intended to place her in apprehension of an imminent contact and that is sufficient. [§29] (*Note:* Intrafamily tort immunity does *not* apply to claims between brothers and sisters.) [§1023]

c. YES It is sufficient that she be in apprehension of a *touching.* She need not be frightened. [§37]

d. **YES**		*Apparent* ability is all that is required for the tort of assault. (The rule is contra under many criminal statutes.) [§38]

5.a. **PROBABLY NOT**   No battery because no actual touching. [§11] No assault because Tony was *unaware* of Rocky's attempt at the time thereof; and by the time he turned, Rocky was under arrest so no apprehension of further danger. [§§30-31] (And probably no liability for intentional infliction of emotional distress, because this was not what Rocky was intending—although again, arguably, Rocky was "reckless" in this regard.) [§§67-69]

(*Compare:* Rocky could be *criminally* prosecuted in many states for an attempted battery.)

b. **NO**   While Stranger intentionally placed Tony in apprehension of harm from Rocky, his doing so was probably *privileged.* [§83]

6. **YES**   If Doug was intending to put Pete in apprehension, and such apprehension actually resulted from Doug's acts, it makes no difference that a "reasonable" person would not have been apprehensive. *The test is subjective.* [§37]

7. **YES**   There was as much a confinement as if Bob had been locked in the office. A plaintiff is not required to escape by means that would offend a reasonable sense of personal dignity. No damages need be shown. [§§47, 55, 60]

8.a. **NO**   There must be *knowledge* of the confinement *at the time* thereof. [§48]

b. **YES**   It is *not* necessary that a person know by whom he was confined, as long as he realized he *was* confined during the confinement. Janitor is liable even though he had no intent to harm Law Student; it is sufficient that he took action (locking up) that he knew would result in confinement. [§§44-45, 48]

9. **PROBABLY NOT**   He cannot recover on the basis of being driven in the car because he apparently consented to this (as part of frat initiation). Whether he can recover based on his being abandoned in the desert depends on whether this was a "confinement." If "reasonable" means of escape are available, there is no confinement; and it would seem that for a young man to walk the 20 miles is not an unreasonable means of escape. (Of course, the result would be contra if Neal was disabled *and* Fraternity brothers *knew* it.) [§§47, 55]

10.a. **YES**   Failure to release a person when under a *legal duty* to come to his aid (employer-employee) constitutes a sufficient "act" of confinement. [§56]

b. **NO**   As long as Pete was conscious that he was being confined by someone (the robbers), it is not necessary that he know by whom else (Dan). [§§45, 48]

11.a. **NO**   The obstruction of a private driveway is *not* a "confinement." [§§46-47] (*Compare:* XYZ may recover on a theory of private nuisance.) [§§924 *et seq.*]

b. **NO**   False imprisonment relates to confinement of one's person, not one's car. (Result could be contra, however, if the plant was so remotely situated that auto transportation is the only way out, in which event depriving the workers of auto transportation might "confine" them personally.) [§§45-47]

12.	**NO**	Since Virgil took no part in the decision to make an arrest or in the actual arrest, he is not liable for false imprisonment. [§58] (*Compare:* He might be liable for **malicious prosecution** however, *if* Ned can show that Virgil acted without probable cause.) [§§1483 *et seq.*]
13.a.	**YES**	Dick was asserting legal authority, and Phil submitted thereto. [§57]
b.	**NO**	Because Dick was not intending to take Phil before any court; he was intending only to "lecture" him. Hence, not a proper exercise of citizen's privilege of arrest. [§145]
14.a.	**NO**	Because a submission to authority must be in the **presence** of the person asserting the authority (not over the telephone). [Rest. 2d §41, comment f] [§57]
b.	**NO**	Because **no submission** to Sheriff's custody. Compliance with Sheriff's demands—even if illegal—is not a submission to arrest. Hence, no false imprisonment. [§57]
c.	**NO**	But not because she did not tell Sheriff about paying the traffic ticket. Rather, because Sheriff is **privileged** in taking a person into custody under any warrant that is **fair on its face**—even though it may have been issued in error. [§§147-148]
15.a.	**PROBABLY**	The intent or recklessness required for the intentional tort can be inferred where defendant knows that plaintiff is particularly susceptible to emotional distress (the fact that Harvey had been warned ["all visitors"] not to upset Emil is certainly evidentiary). If intent is found, then his conduct could be viewed as so extreme and outrageous that liability **would** be imposed. [§§67-69]
		Note: **Words alone** may constitute sufficient "outrageous conduct" for imposition of liability for intentional infliction of emotional distress. [§63]
b.	**SPLIT**	The older view requires demonstrable **physical** injuries; mere shock or anger is not enough. [§71] But the modern trend is contra—*i.e.,* where defendant **intends** to cause severe emotional distress in plaintiff, the outrageous nature of D's conduct is deemed a more reliable indication of damage than physical injury. [§72]
16.	**NO**	By failing to object, she has manifested her apparent consent to being searched. The fact that she was "anxious to reach her destination" does **not** constitute "duress" so as to vitiate the consent given. [§§82, 88]
17.a.	**PROBABLY NOT**	There is implied consent to all physical contacts that are a **normal** part of the sport, and being hit with a hockey stick is probably not abnormal for the game. [§82]
b.	**PROBABLY**	Pierre's consent would extend only to touchings by those with whom contact was foreseeable (*i.e.,* other players). Unless violence from the fans is found to be a customary part of the sport, Pierre's consent would not extend to George's acts. [§85]
18.a.	**YES**	Specialist would be. Barbara's consent to a touching by Doctor is not effective as to anyone else, no matter how skillful, and even though the operation was successful. [§85]

b. **POSSIBLY**   The issue would be whether Barbara's consent was sufficiently *"informed."* If Doctor failed to advise her as to size and location of possible scars, her consent would not be effective (particularly if Doctor was aware of Barbara's modeling career). She might have chosen to forgo the operation rather than suffer the scars. [§§92-93]

c. **NO**   First of all, this is an unusual situation because except in emergencies, doctors generally insist on an express consent (including right to remove diseased organs) before they operate. Even without this, however, most courts would probably hold that the consent given here (to determine *cause* of stomach pains) would be broad enough to justify removal of whatever was causing the pain. Alternately, a court might find *"implied consent"* based on the fact that the removal was ultimately necessary to protect her life. [§§83-85]

19. **YES (most courts)**   Most courts hold that where **breach of the peace** is involved, public interest requires that participants be held liable civilly, as well as criminally; and hence, their "consent" is not effective to prevent tort liability. Some courts hold a plaintiff's consent effective in any case, thus barring later claims based on the fight. [§§95-97]

20. **NO**   The "fraud" goes to a **collateral matter** (disposition of the traffic ticket) rather than to the act (sexual intercourse) to which she consented. And, threat of loss of one's driver's license does not constitute "duress" so as to vitiate the consent given. [§§86-88]

21.a. **PROBABLY NOT**   There was no actual force, and Owner's "insisting" that Betty remain probably did not constitute duress, because there was no threat of **unlawful** conduct. [§§50-53, 88]

b. **YES**   Threats of harm to a spouse (Harry) *are* sufficient duress to negate her consent to the sexual acts. [§88]

22. **NO**   When Buford acted, there apparently was **no further threat** from Archie; *i.e.,* Buford acted in retaliation, not in self-defense. (Of course, result might be contra if Buford could show that Archie was about to throw another stone.) [§§100, 111]

23. **(B)**   (A) is false because there is no privilege to use deadly force in self-defense where the only present threat is of nondeadly force. [§104]

(B) is true so long as a reasonable person (objective test) would believe he was in danger of imminent battery. [§100]

(C) is false because there is *no* duty to retreat before using *nondeadly* force. [§102]

(D) is false because Bob is entitled to rely on the *apparent* threat, regardless of Charlie's actual intentions. [§100]

24. **NO**   If the only apparent threat of harm is **nonserious** (fist), Carl would be privileged to use only **nonserious** force. It makes no difference that serious bodily harm (brass knuckles) was in fact being threatened, because Carl was ignorant of the danger. [§§104, 116]

25. **(D)**   (A) is false because even in jurisdictions which recognize the duty to retreat, it does not apply where the actor (Tom) is in his own home. [§§105-108]

(B) is false because even though the grenade might not kill Tom, it still would be a battery (harmful or offensive touching), and Tom would be entitled to use nondeadly force to prevent same. [§100]

(C) is false because the privilege of self-defense is conditioned on a ***reasonable*** belief (objective standard). [§116]

(D) is true insofar as Tom's liability ***to Bob***. But, of course, the fact that Tom's acts are privileged as to Bob would not insulate him from liability (for negligence, if not battery) to anyone else foreseeably injured thereby. [§§114-116]

26. **(A) AND (C)**   (A) is true. Since Frank's conduct appears to be negligent, rather than intentional, there is a duty to retreat. [§102]

(B) is false. There is a privilege to use reasonable force to prevent even a negligent touching. [§100]

(C) is true. A person is entitled to ***threaten*** more force than he would be privileged to inflict [§109]

27. **NO**   Because his act was neither intentional nor negligent as to her (risk unforeseeable), and was otherwise reasonable conduct in self-defense. [§115]

28. **(A) AND (B)**   (A) is true (under majority view, at least) because Mildred must "stand in the shoes" of Phil, and hence would not be privileged unless Phil was ***actually*** privileged. (The minority view is that Mildred would be privileged to defend Phil if it ***reasonably appeared*** that he was privileged to defend himself.) [§§119-121]

(B) is true (under majority view) because Mildred was privileged to use only the means of defense which Phil was actually privileged to use. [§119-121]

(C) is false because under modern law, any third person may be defended. [§118]

29.a. **NO**   While deadly force ***may*** be ***threatened*** to prevent a trespass upon his land, no force or threat is privileged unless it is ***reasonably necessary*** to prevent the intrusion, and a ***demand*** to leave has been ignored. The latter conditions have not been met here. [§122]

b. **YES**   A landowner is not privileged to use mechanical devices to prevent a trespass, unless the use thereof is reasonable under the circumstances; and ***adequate warning*** of any hidden danger is an essential element of "reasonableness." [§123]

30. **NO**   Most courts today hold there is ***no*** privilege to use force to recover possession of land, regardless of how possession was lost. A few courts allow the land occupier to use force if he was "tortiously dispossessed" (but that would not apply here, because ***Tom***, not Larry, was the land occupier who was dispossessed). [§§126-129]

31.	**DEPENDS**	On when Apex discovered the fraud (the credit card being phony). No force is privileged unless Apex acted *promptly* on discovering that it had been tortiously dispossessed. (*Compare:* But Apex would still be entitled to *reclaim the car it-self,* if this could be done *without* using any force on Shifty.) [§§130-133]
32.	**NO**	Because Pierre loaned the painting to Don originally; hence, no tortious dispossession. (Arguably contra if Don was intending all along to take the painting.) [§135]
33.	**PROBABLY NOT**	A privilege to detain for investigation is recognized where the actor has reasonable grounds to suspect *the person detained.* It is doubtful that courts would extend this to allow search of a group of people. [§§137-142]
34.a.	**YES**	Reasonable force is permitted under so-called "shopkeeper's privilege." Some courts would deny privilege where (as here) customer was apprehended *outside* of store; but better view is contra because until then, she could always claim she intended to pay. [§§137-142]
b.	**YES**	Privilege to detain for investigation applies where actor had *reasonable grounds* to suspect tortious dispossession. [§139]
c.	**NO**	Unlike the privilege to detain for investigation (above), there is *no* privilege to use force *to retake possession* of a chattel unless the actor is *in fact* entitled to such possession (reasonable belief is not enough). [§131]
35.a.	**YES**	A private citizen is privileged to arrest for a felony which has *in fact* been committed, if he has *reasonable grounds* to believe the person arrested committed it. [§144]
b.	**YES**	A police officer (unlike a private citizen) is privileged to arrest on the basis of reasonable belief that a felony has been committed. [§144]
36.	**NO (most courts)**	Most courts hold *no* police privilege to arrest those who are innocent of a misdemeanor charge, no matter how reasonable the police mistake. A minority is contra, extending the privilege to cover such mistakes. [§145]
37.	**YES (most courts)**	There is no privilege of arrest under a warrant, unless the person arrested is the person named therein. (A few states extend privilege to cover reasonable mistakes, as here.) *Note:* In some states, it is a *crime to resist arrest by a police of-ficer*—regardless of the validity of the arrest—in which case since Sam's conduct was illegal, Sheriff John would be privileged to use force to overcome. [§157]
38.	**NO**	Trespass is usually limited to *physical* intrusions. Nonphysical intrusions such as vibrations are usually treated as nuisance rather than trespass. [§164]
39.a.	**YES**	Although the initial entry was consented to, the intentional failure to remove the poles within a reasonable period after the expiration of the license constitutes a trespass. [§164]
b.	**YES**	An intrusion into the space immediately above land is treated the same as an intrusion on the surface. [§§171-174]

40. **YES** Unless consented to, any intentional intrusion onto Jones's land is a trespass. No damages need be shown. (And no privilege here because entry not "necessary" to protect landowner's interests.) [§164]

41. **CHARLEY** The person in *actual* possession is the only one who can sue (even if her right to possession could be terminated by another). [§§166-168]

42.a. **YES** The only intent required is to deal with the chattel as he did; no intent to steal or dispossess Library is required. And the taking without Library's consent *was* a dispossession. [§§180-182]

 b. **YES** A dispossession is actionable either as trespass to chattels or conversion. [§§182, 191]

43.a. **YES** Any *intermeddling* with chattels of another is actionable as trespass. [§183]

 b. **NO** Tearing one page would probably not amount to a destruction of the book; and a mere intermeddling is not a conversion. [§§192-193]

44. **YES** Tom is liable for *conversion*. He intentionally did an act which caused a *material alteration* (if not outright destruction) of the chattel. No intent to injure or direct touching is required. (No trespass to chattels, however, because *no physical contact* with the wine.) [§193]

45.a. **YES** Angel is liable for *either* trespass or conversion. Again, the only intent required is to deal with the chattel as he did; honest mistake of fact as to ownership is immaterial. [§§180, 189, 195]

 b. **YES** Such refusal is a separate act of conversion (again, no matter how bona fide Angel's belief that he was entitled to possession). *Compare:* A *qualified* refusal (*e.g.,* to give Angel time to investigate Owner's claim) would *not* be actionable. [§§198, 199]

46. **ONLY (E)** (A) is not conversion, because by pawning the coat she gave up right to possession until loan is repaid. [§200]

(B) is not conversion by Benny, because no intent by Benny to cause loss; a bailee is not an insurer. [§189]

(C) is not conversion for same reason; but Benny might be liable for *negligence.* [§189]

(D) is not a conversion (in most courts) because—even though no right to use the coat was given—the single unauthorized use caused no harm to the chattel (regardless of Sylvia's feelings) and hence was not a "material" breach of bailment contract. [§194]

(E) *is* a conversion because if any *harm* comes to the chattel during the unauthorized use, it constitutes a conversion, *regardless whose fault* it is. [§194]

(F) is *not* a conversion because a bailee's obligation to return is based on a *reasonable* demand (and opening up at midnight would seem unreasonable). And destruction by fire is not a conversion because no intent by Benny (again, consider negligence). [§§189, 198]

| 47. | **SPLIT** | Fastbuck's selling his client's stock without authority was the act of conversion. Some courts limit recovery to value of stock at that time ($15 per share), the amount he pocketed. Others permit recovery of *highest value* ($50 per share) between date of conversion and time of trial particularly where, as here, Fastbuck was apparently intending to swindle his client. [§205] |

48.a. **NO**
Even though he has been tortiously dispossessed, the chattel owner must ordinarily make demand for permission to enter, unless such demand would be futile, etc. Nothing here indicates demand would be futile; hence demand is prerequisite to right to enter. [§§210-212]

b. **NO**
Since the chattel is on Buford's land through Buford's (landowner's) own fault, Clem's privilege is *complete*—he is not liable for damage to property in the *reasonable* exercise of privilege. And he is permitted to use *reasonable force* against Buford as long as he is in "fresh pursuit" of his tractor. [§§213-215]

49.a. **YES**
Provided Wilbur was *not negligent* in allowing the dog to escape or come onto Mary's land. [§§216-217]

b. **YES**
Because the privilege is *incomplete*—the dog got onto the land without the fault of Wilbur *or* Mary. [§218]

c. **NO**
The privilege does not extend to breaking into dwellings. [§219]

d. **YES**
If Wilbur *was at fault* in the dog's coming onto Mary's land, then he would have no *privilege* to enter. If he wanted the dog back, he would have to sue for it (replevin, etc.). [§216]

50.a. **PROBABLY**
On either of two theories: If it *reasonably appeared* that disposal of the gasoline down the sewer was necessary to prevent an "imminent public disaster" (residential neighborhood), the trespass to land and conversion of the gasoline would be privileged as a *public necessity*. [§225] Alternatively, if the only apparent threat was to Ned and immediate neighbors, such conduct might be privileged as a *private necessity*. [§§231-233]

b. **NO**
If privilege was based on a public necessity, the privilege is *complete*. [§§225-226] If based on private necessity, it is normally *incomplete* (meaning Tom would have to pay for damage), except where, as here, the dangerous condition was caused by the tortious conduct (negligence) of the landowner. In such cases, the privilege is complete. [§§231-235]

c. **DEPENDS**
If the storage of gasoline in a residential neighborhood posed an *unreasonable* interference (threat) to Ned's use and enjoyment of his own land, he would be privileged to enter and *abate a private nuisance*. This also would be a *complete* privilege (although pouring the gasoline down the drain probably would *not* be privileged; only its removal to a safe place). [§§236-240]

51.a. **NO**
If it reasonably appeared that Wife's life was endangered, Husband was privileged to take the insulin (private necessity—to save Wife's life), and Druggist's resistance was *not* privileged. Therefore, Husband was *privileged to use reasonable force to overcome* Druggist's (nonprivileged) resistance. [§235]

b. NO Husband's privilege to overcome Druggist's nonprivileged interference is a *complete* privilege. [Rest. 2d §197, comment k] [§235]

c. YES Husband's privilege to take the insulin was *incomplete* because Husband was acting to protect his own interests or those of a third person (here, Wife). [§234]

52. NONE While all of the evidence offered is *admissible* on the issue of negligence, none of it by itself disproves negligence as a matter of law. The legal standard is the amount of care that a *reasonable* person would have exercised under the circumstances. [§247]

(A) is not conclusive because a reasonable person might have seen the "Caution" sign even though Don did not. [§249]

(B) is not conclusive because a reasonable person might have exercised a higher degree of care than was "customary" in the community. [§§252-254]

(C) is not conclusive because a reasonable person might still have slowed down or stopped even though not required by statute to do so. [§255]

53. NONE None of the evidence would affect the duty of care owed by Donna under the circumstances.

(A) A person's physical disability normally is relevant in determining the standard of care owed; *but not* where he knowingly engages in any activity (driving a car) that a reasonable person with such disability would not have attempted. [§§262-263]

(B) A person's mental deficiency is disregarded in determining the standard of care owed. [§265]

(C) The standard of care owed is the reasonable person standard; her intoxication is not relevant in this regard. [§264]

(D) Learners or beginners in any activity involving a known risk to others (driving car) are held to the same standards as experienced persons. [§281]

54.a. YES The standard of care required of children is that of a reasonable person of *like age, intelligence, and experience.* However, if a child has superior intelligence, etc., she is to be judged according to *her own* (not the "average") intelligence. [§§259-261, 267]

b. NO The restricted standard of care afforded to children (above) generally does *not* apply where the child engages in adult activities (driving a car). [§261]

55. ALL (A) A professional is held to certain minimum standards even though not personally possessing the skills required. [§§267-269]

(B) A warning of lack of skill does *not* change the standard of care required. [*See* Rest. 2d §301] [§268]

(C) A person possessing *superior* competence in any field is required to perform accordingly. [§267]

56.a. **YES**	Inattentiveness by the driver of an automobile in heavy traffic may be enough in itself to violate the reasonable person standard. [§§247-249]
b. **YES**	Under the "Cardozo view," Gabby owed a duty of due care to all persons within the *"zone of danger"* (*i.e.*, foreseeable plaintiffs); and pedestrians on the sidewalk would fall in this category, even though the *manner* of the injury was not foreseeable. [§284] Under the "Andrews view," Gabby's duty was owed to all persons injured as a *proximate result* of her acts—regardless of the foreseeability of the risk of harm. [§283]
c. **SPLIT**	*Not* under the "Cardozo view," because Wilma was not a foreseeable plaintiff. But, under the "Andrews view," Gabby might be held liable because Wilma's injuries were the direct and proximate result of Gabby's negligent act. [§§283-284]
d. **YES**	Under either the "Andrews" or "Cardozo" views, the duty of care extends to *rescuers*. If a rescue attempt is foolhardy under the circumstances, the defendant may not be liable for the resulting injuries. [§§286, 289]
57.a. **YES**	The doctrine of res ipsa loquitur permits a plaintiff to prove the negligent act (*i.e.*, breach of duty) through circumstantial evidence, and thereby raises an inference or presumption that the defendant was at fault. To bring the doctrine into play, the plaintiff must establish *three factors:* (1) that the event would not occur in the absence of someone's negligence; (2) that the source of the negligence is within the scope of a duty owed by defendant to plaintiff (*i.e.*, the injury to P is one which D owed a duty to guard against); and (3) that neither plaintiff nor any third person contributed to the injury sustained. All three elements appear here: Glass would not normally be found in a loaf of bread but for someone's negligence since the package was sealed when A purchased the bread; B, the Bakery, is the indicated source of such negligence; and since the package was sealed, neither A nor any third person contributed to the injury. [§§310-321]
b. **SPLIT**	Most courts treat res ipsa as raising only an *inference* of negligence which the trier of fact may accept or reject. [§324] However, a few courts treat it as a *rebuttable presumption* which shifts the burden of proof to the defendant. If the defendant fails to rebut the presumption by a preponderance of the evidence, the trier of fact is then bound by the presumption of negligence. In other states, res ipsa is a presumption that can be dispelled by *any* counterevidence. [§§325-326]
58.a. **YES**	Where the period of time is relatively short (here, only 15 minutes), and no other explanation appears for the car rolling downhill, the driver's negligence in parking the car can be inferred from the mere happening of the accident. (*Note:* A few courts are contra on this, holding that the lapse of any appreciable period of time suggests at least the possibility of other causes—*e.g.*, third persons tinkering with the car—which is enough to take the case out of res ipsa.) [§§310-321]
b. **YES**	Since aviation has become a common mode of transportation, courts will probably infer negligence by the airline on a res ipsa theory where other possible causes have been eliminated. [§312]

c. **YES (most courts)** Even though Alpha is unable to establish *which* of the two defendants working on the same enterprise was negligent, res ipsa has been extended to situations where all of the defendants owed a duty to the plaintiff. [§320]

d. **NO** No inference of negligence by a defendant can be drawn until the plaintiff's own conduct is eliminated as a responsible cause. Here, the fact that Dominica was at the gas pump filling her car precludes the inference that the accident was *necessarily* the fault of Ajax or the pump manufacturer (*i.e.*, it is possible that Dominica was lighting a cigarette, etc.). However, if there is *other evidence* to eliminate Dominica's conduct as a cause of the explosion, the inference of negligence could be drawn. [§321]

59.a. **YES (both)** Where an injury was caused by the *concurrent* negligent acts of two or more defendants, *both* are liable to the plaintiff—*i.e.*, if the accident would not have occurred "but for" the negligent acts of *both* Bus Co. and Chris, Amy can recover from both. [§329]

b. **YES** If each of the negligent acts was a *"substantial factor"* in causing the injury, each defendant is equally liable to the plaintiff—unless any one of the *defendants can prove* that the ultimate injuries were the result of the other defendant's negligence (*i.e.*, the burden of proof is shifted to the defendants). [§332]

60. **YES** Since either City *or* Property Owner caused Pedestrian's injuries, he would not be able to establish "but for" cause against either of them. In recognition of this problem, courts generally shift the burden to each defendant to prove that the injuries sustained by Pedestrian were *not* caused by negligence of that defendant. [§§334-343]

61.a. **YES** Archie's negligence is the direct cause of Bob's injuries, and the injures are of the type reasonably foreseeable. Hence Archie's conduct is the actual and proximate cause of Bob's injuries. [§§353, 360-362]

b. **YES** Although Bob's death might not be foreseeable (especially from a heart attack) Archie's negligent conduct aggravated a preexisting condition and he is therefore liable for the ultimate injuries. The victim's abnormal sensitivities do *not* limit the tortfeasor's liability. "A tortfeasor takes his victim as he finds him." [§370]

c. **PROBABLY NOT** Although it can be shown that the injuries sustained were a direct result of Archie's negligence, some courts limit the extent of liability on the theory that they were *too remote and unforeseeable.* Note that under the "Cardozo view," these plaintiffs would not be in the "zone of danger"; hence one would not get past the "duty" element of plaintiff's prima facie case. Under the "Andrews view," however, there *is* a duty owed to the plaintiffs which *may* be limited because of the unforeseeability of the injuries (*i.e.*, no proximate cause). [§§366-369]

62. **PROBABLY** The dog's actions constitute an intervening force between the defendant's act and the plaintiff's injury. However, if the intervening act is a *normal response* to the defendant's act, it will be deemed a *dependent intervening force*—meaning it will ordinarily not break the chain of causation. Here, it is arguable

that the dog's actions *were* a normal response to Andy's acts (pain causing the dog to act in frenzy), and hence he would be liable for the resultant injuries. [§§372-378]

63. **YES**   Attempts to escape threatened harm are usually deemed normal responses even if the escape injures others. Thus, Al's liability to Cindy would not be cut off by Bob's act. (*Abnormal* escape attempts, however, are treated as superseding causes.) [§376]

64. **NO**   Even though the defendant's (Don's) negligence created the opportunity for the third person (Ned) to act, the third person's intentionally tortious or criminal conduct is generally held to be a *superseding cause* of the harm (an unforeseeable, independent intervening force). (*Compare:* Result could be contra if Don *had reason to foresee* that Ned might avail himself of the opportunity to set Paul's car on fire.) [§§388-389]

65.a. **YES**   Ordinarily, the negligent acts of a third person are held foreseeable intervening forces, and hence *not* superseding causes. By placing Oscar in a position where another's negligence could aggravate his injuries, Felix becomes liable therefor. [§373]

b. **NO**   Again, the intentional or criminal acts of a third person are usually held to be unforeseeable intervening forces—hence, superseding causes. (Arguably contra if it was in a high-crime area, where such acts could be foreseen; in which event, Felix could be held liable for leaving Oscar in a helpless condition in such an area.) [§389]

c. **NO**   Injuries sustained as a result of storms (acts of God) are treated as superseding causes where they cause a *result different* than that threatened by D's original negligence. Here, being struck by lightning would probably be regarded as a different result than being struck by a negligently driven car. (Again, arguably contra, if the lightning storm was raging *at the time* of the original impact; in such event, the injuries to Oscar might be held foreseeable.) [§386]

66.a. **YES**   Generally, the inaction of a third party (even one under a duty to act) does not affect causation. It is *not* so extraordinary or unforeseeable as to constitute a superseding cause. [§391]

b. **NO**   Negligence *cannot* be based on nonfeasance (failure to act) unless there was an *affirmative duty to act*; and there is no duty to go to the aid of another in this case. [§§246, 455]

67. **NO**   The doctrine of avoidable consequences excuses Doug from liability for those consequences which Pam *could have avoided* in the exercise of due care. (Doug would still be liable for the cut, however.) [§§426-428]

68. **YES**   Doug's liability is not reduced by the fact that Pat was covered by insurance ("collateral sources rule"). Note, however, that Pat's insurance company may be entitled to *subrogation* as to such recovery. [§§434-436]

69. **NO**   Violation of a statute establishes duty and breach only where (1) the statute was enacted for the *purpose* of preventing the type of harm suffered by plaintiff;

and (2) plaintiff is a **member of the class** sought to be protected by the statute. Neither of these conditions appears here; the statute was enacted for the apparent purpose of conserving gasoline, not protecting pedestrians against highway injuries. [§§440-444]

70.a. **NO**

Violation of a criminal statute (which was enacted for the purpose of preventing this type of injury, and providing plaintiff is a member of the class sought to be protected) establishes only the **duty** and **breach** elements of the prima facie case. It is still up to the plaintiff to prove the other requisite elements (causation and damages). [§454]

b. **NO (most states)**

Showing such violation establishes a **conclusive presumption**—meaning that it cannot be rebutted by evidence that Driver was acting carefully. (Some states are contra on this.) [§§447-453]

c. **YES (most states)**

Even when the conclusive presumption applies, most courts recognize "exceptions" (or "excused violations" in Restatement terminology) to cover cases where the violation is in fact excused or justified. [§§451-453]

71.a. **NO**

Not at common law, if the accident was not his fault. (Many states are contra by statute, imposing a duty to aid any person injured by the driver's car, regardless of fault.) [§§455-460]

b. **YES**

If Rich's forcing her to walk home in the rain put her in **worse position** than if he had not acted at all. Even though Rich was under no duty to aid her originally (*see* above), once having undertaken to do so, he owed a duty to act with reasonable care. [§462]

72. **PROBABLY**

A common carrier owes the duty to choose the course of action **least likely** to expose its passengers to a risk of harm. (Landing in Cuba would probably be less likely a risk than shooting it out in mid-air.) [§§477-478]

73.a. **YES**

The bailor of a car owes a **duty to control** erratic driving of his car by another, where such occurs **in his presence**. The risk of harm to third persons is clearly foreseeable. [§§485-486]

b. **PROBABLY**

On a "negligent entrustment" theory; *i.e.*, knowing that Ben had been driving carelessly, Willard was probably negligent in allowing Ben to drive the car. [§487]

74.a. **YES**

Under the doctrine of respondeat superior, Widget Co. is liable for torts committed by Archie within the scope of his employment (driving truck) regardless of any showing of negligence on the part of the employer, Widget Co. [§§497-500]

b. **NO**

Batteries and intentional torts by an employee are usually considered outside the scope of employment where the employment does not otherwise involve employee using physical force on others. [§498]

c. **POSSIBLY**

On the theory that the employer failed to exercise reasonable care in hiring, and thereby exposed persons coming into contact with such employee to a foreseeable risk of harm. [§496]

75.a.	**YES**	Ordinarily, the negligence of an independent contractor is not imputed to the person who employs him. But the result is different where—as here—the work contracted out involves a ***high risk of harm to members of the public*** if not carefully performed. In such cases, the employer cannot shield himself from liability by engaging an independent contractor to do the job. [*See* Rest. 2d §425] [§509]
b.	**NO**	Such an agreement (indemnification) merely fixes rights as between the contracting parties (Trans-Global and Aero). It does not affect the rights of third parties (Passenger) and hence, is not a defense to suit by Passenger. [§510]
76.	**POSSIBLY**	Ordinarily, a parent is not liable for a child's torts (negligent or intentional). But if the parent knows or has reason to know that the child is ***likely to inflict harm*** to others, recovery may be allowed because of the parent's own negligence. Here, knowledge that the child is "proficient in karate" is not enough by itself to create liability; there would also have to be a showing that Mother knew that Junior was likely to ***use*** his karate on unsuspecting adults. [§§515-517]
77.	**NO**	Under typical "dram shop acts," only third parties (and ***not*** the intoxicated patron) can recover. [§521]
78.a.	**YES**	Most courts treat car pools involving the sharing of expenses as rides for ***consideration***, thus giving riders "passenger" status. [§482]
b.	**NO**	Because a business purpose or joint ***control*** is required to establish the joint enterprise theory. Mere sharing of expenses is not enough. [§§512-514]
79.	**NO (most states)**	The "reasonable person" standard does ***not*** apply in most cases. Rather, a land occupier's duty to persons coming onto his land is ***limited*** to specific standards of care which in many cases may be ***less*** than what a "reasonable person" would have done. (Some modern courts are contra, however, and would apply the "reasonable person" standard in every case.) [§531]
80.a.	**YES**	A landowner generally owes no duty of care regarding natural conditions on his land. But an exception is recognized as to native trees in urban areas—the owner has a duty of reasonable care including inspection. [§§534-535]
b.	**DEPENDS**	On whether a risk of harm to passersby was ***foreseeable***. The ***reasonable person*** standard applies where a person outside the land is injured by activities on the land. [§536]
81.	**NO**	A land occupier owes ***no duty*** to ***unknown*** adult trespassers. (*Compare:* If Rich had ***seen*** Thief enter his land, he would have owed a duty to warn of dangerous conditions that Thief would be ***unlikely to discover***; and the pool excavation at night probably would qualify.) [§§538-539]
82.a.	**YES**	If a land occupier knows that there are constant trespassers upon a limited area ("CTULAs"), he owes a duty to warn them of any artificial condition created by him involving a risk of death or ***serious bodily harm*** and which is not apparent to them. (Broken glass in sand would apparently pose such a risk.) [§§540-546]

b. **NO (most courts)**	Land occupier's liability here is limited to conditions *for which he is responsible*. Foreseeability of harm to trespassers is not the test. [Rest. 2d §335, comment d] [§§543-546]
83. **DEPENDS**	On whether Cement Co. knew or had *reason to know* that children were likely to trespass, notwithstanding the fence and signs. If it did, then Cement Co. is probably liable because the sharp pebbles and bits of glass are not the *kind of risk* children would expect in a pile of sand. [§§547-555]
84. **PROBABLY**	Whether Tamura personally foresaw any risk to the children is not the test. The test is whether a "reasonable person" would realize that the pond posed any risk of harm to such young children; and whether the child who trespassed was old enough to appreciate the risk; and whether the risk to the children outweighed the burden of eliminating the danger (by fences, gates, etc.). [§§550-555]
85. **YES**	Door-to-door salespeople are usually treated as licensees (coming onto the land with the "implied" permission of the land occupier). As such, land occupier owes a duty to make safe any *known* dangerous condition on his property. [§§562-567] (*Compare:* Result would be different if Owner had posted a large "No Solicitors" sign. In such a case, door-to-door salespeople would be regarded as *trespassers*, to whom *no duty* owed.) [§562]
86. **YES**	Even though Larry was not a customer, the premises were apparently open for public admission, and hence Larry would be treated as an *invitee*. A land occupier owes to invitees a duty to use due care to *inspect and discover* dangerous conditions on his premises and to *make them safe*. Since the accident occurred "several hours later," Benny apparently had time to discover the condition and remedy it. [§§568-570, 576]
87. **NO**	The service area in a gasoline station would probably be regarded as an area into which the public is *not* invited. Hence, Larry would not be regarded as an invitee; at most, he was a licensee. As such, Benny owed a duty to warn or make safe any *known* dangerous conditions (and here, the spilled oil was not yet known). [§§564-570]
88.a. **NO**	Because a land occupier owes no duty to adult trespassers of whose presence he is not actually aware. [§538]
b. **YES (most courts)**	Because a licensee on another's land is *not entitled to* the land occupier's restricted scope of liability. Rather, he owes the same standard of care to others (*i.e.,* trespasser Tom) as if they were both in some neutral place, and here the facts stipulate that Bob was negligent. [§§588-590]
89.a. **YES**	A landlord owes a duty to his tenant to remedy or warn of dangerous conditions known by the landlord at time tenant takes possession. [§§600-601]
b. **SPLIT**	The older view is that landlord's duty is limited to those with whom he is in "privity"; no privity exists with guests of tenant and hence, no liability. However, the Restatement Second and modern trend are contra, holding landlord owes same duty to tenant's guest as to tenant. [§§610-614]

90.a.	**YES**	Where a landlord undertakes repairs (whether obligated by lease or not), he owes a duty of care. [§603]
b.	**YES**	Failure to repair *when under a duty* to repair (here, by lease) is a basis for negligence liability as well as breach of contract. [§§605-608]
c.	**SPLIT**	*See* answer to "89.b.," above. [§§610-614]
d.	**YES**	A landlord is treated as the *land occupier* of common areas (elevators, stairways, etc.). As to those areas he is liable *both* to tenants and their visitors (no "privity" necessary). [§616]
e.	**YES**	For reasons stated in answer to "d.," above. [§616]
91.a.	**NO (most courts)**	Most courts would deny recovery where the emotional distress is attributable solely to property damage, and plaintiff suffers no demonstrable physical injuries. [§§638-641]
b.	**PROBABLY NOT**	Where the defendant's conduct is negligent, most courts would deny recovery in the absence of *actual physical injuries*. (However, shock to the nervous system would be a sufficient allegation of "physical" injury.) [§639]

Note: If Archie was acting intentionally, most courts would be willing to impose liability in a case of this type (*i.e.,* by finding Archie's conduct to be "extreme and outrageous"). [§72]

| 92. | **NO (most courts)** | Where the defendant's conduct is only negligent, most courts retain the requirement that the plaintiff (Mother) must have been subjected to *actual impact or threat* thereof. [§§628-630] Some jurisdictions have relaxed this requirement where, as here, plaintiff is a close family member of one imperiled by the defendant's conduct, and suffers *contemporaneous* emotional distress (and resulting physical injury) from observing such peril. In such jurisdictions, Mother might recover even though she did not actually observe the accident, but came upon the scene immediately thereafter. [§§631-635] |

Note: Even in such jurisdictions, however, Mother might be denied recovery if Child had been contributorily negligent (*e.g.,* playing in street), as Mother's cause of action is viewed as *derivative* in nature. [§637]

93.a.	**NO (most states)**	Most states reject the notion that contributory negligence is a complete defense. Most states have adopted *comparative negligence* laws, which allow the plaintiff to recover even though she was at fault. [§§655, 665]
b.	**NO**	He remains liable for her original injuries. Under doctrine of *avoidable consequences*, however, Don is not liable for the aggravation thereof caused by Paula's carelessness. [§644]
94.a.	**PROBABLY NOT**	In a comparative negligence jurisdiction, a person's own negligence does not bar recovery. [§665] Even in a contributory negligence jurisdiction, the standard of care owed by plaintiff for his own protection is that which a reasonable person would exercise under the circumstances—*including emergencies*. If a reasonable person would have dashed into the street to save the child, Able's doing so is *not* contributory negligence. [§§646-647]

b. **YES**		On theory that "danger invites rescue," and that negligent acts of others are *foreseeable* intervening forces. [§§286, 390]
c. **SPLIT**		One person's contributory negligence is *not imputed* to another who reasonably comes to his or her rescue (regardless of the relationship between them). [§659] On the other hand, the availability of comparative negligence has led some courts to permit imputation of negligence. [§682]
95.a. **NO**		Pedestrian placed himself in a position of *inattentive peril* (he would have been able to get out of the way had he looked up). In such cases, Pedestrian is barred by his contributory negligence unless defendant had *actual knowledge* of plaintiff's peril. Brenda did not, and hence last clear chance doctrine does *not* apply. [§658]
b. **YES (most courts)**		Here, Pedestrian would be in a position of *helpless peril* (could not escape even by exercise of due care). In such cases, most courts hold defendant *liable* if he had actual knowledge of plaintiff's peril or should have had such knowledge. (Minority view still requires actual knowledge, however.) [§§656-657]
96. **SPLIT**		Many comparative negligence jurisdictions *deny any recovery*—(D)—where the plaintiff was *equally (or more)* at fault than the defendant. Others are contra (allowing plaintiff to recover even if he was more at fault than the defendant), and would permit a recovery based on the *degree* of his fault; in this case (C)—one-half of damages proved. [§§666-670]
97.a. **NO**		The car pool did not create a "joint enterprise" (no mutuality of control). Hence, no basis for imputing Harry's negligence—or contributory negligence—to Georgia. [§§512-514, 659]
b. **YES**		On theory of *respondeat superior*, Harry's negligence—or contributory negligence—would be imputed to his employer (Georgia). [§660]
98. **NONE**		(A) does not constitute an assumption of the risk because such clauses in public transportation contracts (ticket) *violate public policy*. Thus, no effective assumption of risk by contract. [§§688-692]
		(B) does not constitute an assumption of the risk because there is no assumption of risk by conduct unless it is shown that plaintiff was aware and voluntarily assumed the *particular risk* that caused her injury. Here, the fact that Louise knew that the driver had been drinking does not establish that she knew he would drive at an excessive speed. Also, on public policy grounds, companies furnishing public services are generally not allowed to claim that a member of the public assumed the risk in seeking to use those services. [Rest. 2d §396C, comment j] [§§694-698]
		(C) is probably *not an assumption of the risk*, because no showing that Louise was aware of the particular risk (*i.e.*, that driver's going "faster, faster" would result in the bus going off the road). [§§694-698]
99. **PROBABLY**		The issue is whether his assumption was a "voluntary" one. This boils down to whether he had *any reasonable alternative* to driving through, which means *balancing the harm threatened* by the delay (potential loss of job, etc.) versus

the *harm to which he exposed himself.* Unless it is absolutely clear that being a half-hour late would forfeit his job (that the employer would not accept any excuses, etc.), it would seem that taking the detour was a more reasonable alternative, and hence that in driving through the oil spill he assumed the risk. [§699]

100.a. **NO**

The horse's propensity to gallop would probably *not* be regarded as "abnormally dangerous" because most riders were able to handle it. Hence, no basis for strict liability. [§§723-725]

b. **POSSIBLY**

Merely warning Tenderfoot of the horse's propensity to gallop may not have been enough to discharge a bailor's duty of care with respect to condition of bailed chattel. He owes a duty to exercise reasonable care to ascertain *whether the chattel was likely to cause harm to bailee*; here, this would probably include *duty to ascertain whether Tenderfoot was capable* of handling the horse in the first place. [§626]

101. **YES**

Even though defanged, the rattlesnake was a wild animal with a dangerous propensity—that of *instilling fear* in other animals (or even humans) if it escaped. Accordingly, Buckeroo is strictly liable for any harm caused thereby, even though the snake escaped without any fault on Buckeroo's part. As to causation, the horse's rearing and throwing Tenderfoot must be regarded as a foreseeable intervening force (normal reaction), and hence not affecting the chain of causation. [§§728-730]

102.a. **YES**

Although a land occupier ordinarily owes *no duty to unknown trespassers* (even innocent ones), strict liability may be imposed for injuries inflicted by a *vicious* watchdog. Thus, if Priscilla's Doberman is regarded as a domestic animal with a *known* dangerous propensity she would be liable—even though the dog had never previously bitten anyone. (*Distinguish:* Not every dog would be so regarded; the breed here might be distinguished by its reputation.) [§§723-725, 734-736]

Alternative analysis: If the Doberman's reputation is *not* enough to constitute a "known dangerous propensity," Priscilla would not be strictly liable, because in most courts "every previously well-behaved dog is entitled to one free bite." [§726]

b. **NO**

Business visitors (mail carriers) *can* invoke strict liability. However, the injury here was *not* the result of the animal's "dangerous propensity" (biting, etc.). Consequently, no strict liability would attach. Negligence is ruled out by the facts. [§§723-725]

c. **YES**

A bill collector is normally treated as a licensee, and hence *can* invoke strict liability. The possessor of an animal *with a known* dangerous propensity (either by its reputation or the fact it had bitten George) is strictly liable for harm done thereby, even where (as here) the plaintiff may have been guilty of conduct which might be regarded as *contributory negligence.* (*Compare:* However, if the bill collector had deliberately provoked the animal, *knowing* the danger, a court might find assumption of the risk, which *is* a valid defense to strict liability as well as to negligence.) [§§723-725, 733, 760]

| 103. | **(B), (C)** | Whether an activity is "abnormally dangerous" is a legal conclusion based on the following factors: Whether the activity is one of "common usage" in the community; the *value* of the activity to the community; the *appropriateness* of the activity to its location; the *degree of risk* involved in the activity; the *gravity* of the risk of harm; and the extent to which the risk could have been *avoided or guarded against*. [§742] |

(A) Firing a weapon—even in a city—is generally regarded as a matter of common usage. Hence, no liability in the absence of negligence. [§742]

(B) is probably "abnormally dangerous," because fumigating with cyanide involves risks that cannot be effectively guarded against, and is not a matter of common usage in most communities. [§742]

(C) is "abnormally dangerous" because it is neither a common nor an appropriate use of the property, and of no apparent value to the community (same activity in desert might be treated differently). [§742]

| 104. | **NO (most courts)** | The blasting would be regarded as an abnormally dangerous activity. However, most courts follow the "foreseeable plaintiff" test for proximate cause (unlike negligence); and therefore hold *no* strict liability where the particular harm that occurred was not reasonably foreseeable. (Minority view is contra, on the basis that strict liability extends to all harm *directly* caused by the abnormally dangerous activity.) [§752] |

| 105.a. | **POSSIBLY** | Battery requires showing of *intent to inflict* harmful touching. If Duro was *"substantially certain"* that users would suffer adverse side effects it will be deemed to have *intended* those results. If it simply didn't believe the lab reports, etc. (even if a reasonable person would have), or thought the risk was exaggerated, there is not sufficient intent for battery. [§765] |

| b. | **NO** | Contributory negligence is *no defense* to battery. [§655] |

| 106.a. | **YES** | Retailer has a duty to warn about the dangerous characteristics of his goods. This duty is owed not only to the purchaser, but to all persons within the foreseeable *scope of use* of the goods (*i.e.,* no privity is required). So Child, a bystander and foreseeable victim, may recover for Retailer's negligent failure to warn of the "hair trigger" or make it safe. [§§768-769, 780] |

| b. | **YES (most jurisdictions)** | The "hair trigger" made the gun defective and unreasonably dangerous. Virtually all states hold that any person injured by a defective product can invoke strict tort liability. [§§786, 828] |

| 107. | **NONE** | (A) No defense because a *design* may be as negligent as lack of care in manufacturing. [§771] |

(B) No defense because its duty of care extends to all components; some courts say that by assembling another company's components into its product, the other company's carelessness is *imputed* to Biltrite. [§776]

(C) No defense because negligence of third parties (Dealer) is deemed a foreseeable intervening force, not affecting chain of causation. [§781]

(D) No defense because negligence liability extends to property damage as well as personal injuries (as long as risk of harm to property was foreseeable). [§774]

108.a. **PROBABLY**   A highly dangerous product (dynamite caps) purchased from an unknown supplier should be regarded as inherently dangerous—meaning Dealer is under duty of care to inspect, or at least to warn purchaser that product comes from an uncertain source of supply. [§780]

   b. **PROBABLY NOT**   Dealer's duty to warn has apparently been discharged; therefore Dealer is not liable in negligence. Contractor now would owe a duty to test or inspect; and failing to do so, his negligence would be regarded as the superseding cause of injury to Bystander. [§§778-782]

109.a. **NO**   A mattress cannot be regarded as an inherently dangerous product, and therefore the dealer generally owes no duty to inspect or test same prior to sale (at least where dealing in goods of reputable manufacturer). [§779]

   b. **YES**   Regardless of whether or not a product is tested, and regardless of whether the dealer's not testing it was negligence, every seller *impliedly* warrants the fitness of the product sold for its normally intended use. [§889]

   c. **YES**   In all but a very few states, privity requirements have been relaxed so that a manufacturer's implied warranty extends beyond its immediate purchaser (usually a distributor or retailer) at least as far as the consumer. [§§900-905]

110.a. **PROBABLY**   The failure of the safety guard to screen out pebbles should be regarded as a design defect, and the manufacturer's duty extends to defect in design as well as in the manufacturing process. [§771]

   b. **YES**   The nationwide advertising should be regarded as an *express warranty* by the manufacturer which runs to all potential customers. The language is specific enough so as not to be mere "puffing" by the manufacturer. [§§885, 903]

   c. **YES**   The manufacturer's duty of care extended to all persons within *foreseeable scope of use* of product. [§773]

111. **YES**   The manufacturer's and retailer's implied warranties extend *at least* to members of the consumer's family. (In most jurisdictions they extend to anyone foreseeably injured by the product.) Even if the warranty disclaimer is valid—and disclaimer requirements for consumer goods are especially strict—it does not apply to nonpurchasers. [§§905, 921]

112.a. **YES (modern courts)**   She is entitled to recover against *all* of them on a *strict liability* theory. All persons who participate in *marketing* of a defective and unreasonably dangerous product are liable for injuries caused thereby—without any showing of negligence or privity (warranty); and regardless of warranty disclaimers. [§§786-788, 810-822]

   b. **NO**   No liability in negligence because Minnie had no reason to know of danger. And no warranty or strict liability because Minnie was a host, *not a commercial supplier* of the beans. [§§823-824]

c. YES Pearl can recover from all of them on an implied warranty theory. As a guest of the purchaser, she is in sufficient privity with defendants to benefit from the implied warranty of merchantability, and the disclaimer does not apply to her. [§905] Alternatively, Pearl could recover on a *strict liability* theory. The ultimate user or consumer of a product can invoke strict liability, as well as the actual purchaser. [§827]

113.a. YES All persons within the foreseeable scope of use of an unreasonably dangerous and defective product can invoke strict liability for injuries caused by the defect. *Rationale:* The purchaser (Father) or user (Son) could certainly recover if they were the ones injured; and bystanders have even less opportunity to inspect the product for defects. [§828] *Note:* Most states permit bystanders to recover under the manufacturer's implied warranty as well. [§§907-911]

b. UNCLEAR A *few* courts have extended the "danger invites rescue" rationale of negligence cases to products liability cases so that anyone going to the aid of someone imperiled by a defective product can invoke the same liability as the person imperiled. But the law is still unsettled. [§829]

114. NO She would also have to prove that the product was "defective"—meaning that it would be harmful in normal use to a *reasonable number* of persons (*i.e.,* injury to Thelma not enough in itself to prove product "defective"). Stated differently, Thelma must prove that her adverse reaction was *not* a "one in a million" situation. [§§840-850]

115. PROBABLY Even though Betty's use on her eyebrows may not have been the intended use of the product, it probably would be held foreseeable. And the doctrine of strict liability extends both to normal (intended) *and foreseeable* uses of the product. [§846]

116. NO Strict products liability applies to a product's packaging as well as to the product itself. But it doesn't apply where the injury results from an *unintended or unforeseeable use*. Here, the cartons were clearly not intended to be used for supporting a person's weight after being emptied, and it is doubtful that such a use would be held foreseeable. [§846]

117. YES Strict liability is imposed against *all* persons placing the defective product in the stream of commerce, regardless of which person is actually responsible for the defect. Thus, dangers inherent in the packaging of a product are attributable to the manufacturer even though the defective packaging (container) was obtained from another. [§811]

118. ALL THREE (A) Since Kamikaze built the car to go 110 m.p.h., it was foreseeable that someone would drive it that fast; Kamikaze cannot claim that doing so was an unforeseeable use. Since a defect apparently caused the car to go out of control, Kamikaze will be strictly liable. However, it can defend on a theory of comparative fault or, in some jurisdictions, contributory negligence, [§§805, 846, 871-876]

Kamikaze may also be liable for negligence depending upon what caused the steering failure, and Bob's negligence might be relevant. [§§770, 785]

(B) The car's failure under emergency conditions (foreseeable in normal use) would be regarded as a design defect; *i.e.,* the manufacturer was under a duty to anticipate (hence, negligence liability as well). [§§792-797]

(C) It is foreseeable that an automobile will be involved in a highway accident, and Kamikaze will be strictly liable for not providing the protection to the car's occupants which consumers could reasonably expect. (This does not mean, of course, that Kamikaze must build a crash-proof car since no consumer could expect total protection in the event of a serious accident.) [§§794, 841]

119.	**PROBABLY NOT**	Most courts to date limit strict products liability to cases in which the danger involved was *reasonably foreseeable* at the time the product was manufactured. Hence unless Presto has reason to know of the danger *prior to the government research study,* most courts would not impose strict liability. (*But note:* Continuing to market the glue *after* the government study would be basis for strict liability or negligence, unless *adequate warnings given.*) [§§802-803]
120.a.	**YES**	By invoking *res ipsa loquitur*: Steering mechanism on new car not likely to fail in absence of negligence; Kamikaze is indicated source of that negligence; and Bob's testimony indicates that he did not cause or contribute to causation of failure. (Of course, res ipsa raises at most a presumption of negligence, and Kamikaze would be free to rebut by evidence showing that it had exercised due care in manufacture.) [§§310-326, 777]
b.	**YES (most courts)**	The same factors which create res ipsa in a negligence case, create at least an *inference* of "defectiveness" for strict products liability purposes. (Again, this is *not* conclusive; Kamikaze is free to introduce evidence showing that the mechanism was not defective or that it failed for some other reason.) [§§777, 852]
c.	**YES**	Where other causes for failure are apparent (wear and tear, etc.), no inference of negligence or defectiveness can be drawn from the mere fact that the mechanism failed in use (*i.e.,* after 50,000 miles usage, reasonable persons can conceive other causes as being responsible). [§§853-858]
121.	**(B) and (C)**	(A) is not a defense because a third person's (dealer's) foreseeable negligence does not cut off liability in negligence or strict liability cases. [§781]
		(B) is a valid defense, because receiving such warning and failing to respond, Bob may be deemed to have assumed the risk. [§§876-878]
		(C) is a defense (or more accurately, it negates proximate cause) because any "substantial" change in the condition of the car terminates the manufacturer's liability; and here, Bob's repair work increased the risk of failure. [§§851-854]
122.a.	**YES**	Physical damage to the product itself or other property, caused by a defect in the product, is recoverable under a strict products liability theory (as well as personal injuries). [§866]
b.	**NO (most courts)**	Economic losses alone are compensable in a "sales" or contract action, but not in tort. [§867]

123.a. **NO (most states)** Most courts do not permit a private individual to maintain an action for a public nuisance, unless it is shown that the nuisance has caused him some injury peculiar in kind. (Such actions must be prosecuted by the state, not a private citizen.) [§927]

b. **YES** Adjoining riparian owners would have sustained damage to the extent the water supply was diminished in quality (fact that certain uses—drinking—could no longer be made of the water). Frances might even be permitted to maintain a class action on behalf of all downstream riparian owners. [§§926-927]

124.a. **PROBABLY** To constitute a nuisance, the interference with plaintiff's use of his land must be "substantial" and "unreasonable." Running an air conditioning system is not necessarily an unreasonable use by Archie of his land, but it may become such because of the disproportionate interference with Tom's use of his land. The controlling issue is likely to be whether Archie can abate the noise without unreasonable expense, as compared to the harm to Tom's use of his land if the noise continues unabated. [§§937-940]

b. **YES** Nuisance liability arises from the harm done—not the actor's state of mind; *i.e.*, a nuisance can be predicated on either intent, negligence, or strict liability. [§933]

c. **YES** The actor's refusal to abate a nuisance, after request to do so, makes his continued interference with his neighbor's property an *intentional* tort. Hence, if sufficient "malice" (intent to injure) can be inferred from the continued operation of the air conditioner, it is legally possible for the court to award punitive damages to Tom. [§§933, 935, 948]

d. **NO** The fact that the condition existed in advance is *not* enough *by itself* to show that it was reasonable. [§942]

e. **YES** Tom can recover damages for the interference to date, and an injunction to prevent future interference. Damages alone would not be an effective remedy because it would require Tom to sue again in the future; an injunction alone would not compensate for past interference. [§947]

125.a. **YES** A decedent's estate can be substituted as plaintiff and recover for all of the damages claimed by P, *except* that some states do not permit recovery for decedent's *pain and suffering*. [§§960-961]

b. **NO (most states)** Most states by statute recognize a *new cause of action* in the decedent's relatives for his wrongful death. The damages recoverable are distinct from those recoverable by the decedent's estate (above). Rather, the heirs are entitled to recover for their loss of *support and companionship* by decedent's death. [§§967-969]

c. **YES** Any defense that could have been asserted against the decedent, had he brought an action during his lifetime, can be set up as a defense against an action for wrongful death filed by his heirs. [§976]

d. **PARTIALLY** Most courts will reduce the amount of any wrongful death award by the negligent beneficiary's *share* thereof (or degree of fault in a comparative negligence jurisdiction). To this extent, therefore, it is a valid defense. [§978]

126.a. **YES (modern law)**   The common law rule is that a wife has *no action* for loss of husband's consortium. But most modern states are contra, giving wives the same rights as husbands to recover against third persons causing injury to their spouse. [§§982-984]

b. **NO**   At least where D's conduct was merely negligent, no cause of action is recognized in favor of a child for loss of a parent's consortium. [§991]

127.a. **YES (most courts)**   Intrafamily tort immunity was the rule at common law, but it has been rejected in virtually all jurisdictions today. The common law rule was based on the notion that it was essential to preserve "domestic tranquility," but modern courts recognize the reality that most of these cases are covered by insurance, so that there is no danger of marital disruption. [§§1011-1012]

b. **SPLIT**   More courts retain parent-child immunity than husband-wife immunity. Again, a modern trend is to reject it entirely. [§§1016-1020]

c. **YES**   Intrafamily tort immunity never extended beyond the immediate family relationships. [§1023]

128.a. **YES**   Most courts hold that employees or agents of government are personally liable for the torts they commit, while performing "ministerial" (required) duties. [§§1040-1042]

b. **NO (most courts)**   Governmental tort immunity has been retained in most jurisdictions. Where a municipality is involved, it is limited to "governmental" (as opposed to "proprietary") functions. Police functions are clearly classified as "governmental" because they can be performed adequately only by the government. Hence, the City is immune from suit. (Modern trend, however, is to limit or abrogate governmental tort immunity.) [§§1026-1029]

129.a. **DEPENDS**   On whether the judgment against Tom was *satisfied* (paid) or not. If it was, then Pat cannot sue again on the same cause of action. [§1054]

b. **NO (most courts)**   A few courts hold that the *release* of one tortfeasor releases them all. But most courts today are contra, although the amount received from one (here, $100) *reduces* the claims against the others. [§§1055-1057]

c. **YES (most courts)**   Common law rule was that there is *no contribution* between joint tortfeasors. But today, virtually all states permit contribution, at least where only negligent conduct is involved. [§§1058-1059]

d. **NO**   Indemnity is available only in favor of a party who has been held *vicariously* liable for the acts of another. It does *not* apply where, as here, the party *primarily* liable (Tom) is the one who has had to pay the judgment. There's no reason to allow Tom to shift any portion of his loss to Employer. [§1062]

130.a. **POSSIBLY**   No action can be brought on behalf of the father, because defamation actions cannot be brought on behalf of one already dead (their reputations are not protectible). However, *if* the statement would cause a substantial minority of the community *to defer from association with P* (as the child of a murderer), it could be regarded as defamatory of P. [§§1188-1189]

b. DEPENDS   On whether the statement can reasonably be interpreted as applying to any particular police officer in the precinct. If the group is small enough that a reasonable person would regard it as applying to *each* police officer in the unit, then any of them could sue; contrariwise, if it is a large enough group, none of them can claim to have been individually defamed. [§§1191-1193]

c. YES   While the statement that P has been having a "torrid love affair" is probably not defamatory on its face, it becomes defamatory (capable of lowering P's reputation in the community) when coupled with other facts not apparent on the face of the publication—here, that P was a married woman, and hence apparently guilty of adultery. (So-called defamation per quod cases.) [§1179]

d. YES   It is enough that the statement is *capable* of defamatory interpretation by a reasonable person; defamation can be committed *by insinuation and implication* as well as outright statements. (One or two courts cling to the so-called possible innocent meaning rule.) [§§1179-1180]

131. DEPENDS   All that is required is that *some* third person *reasonably* interpret it as applying to the plaintiff, Waldo. Hence, if the few who interpreted the statement as applying to Waldo did so *reasonably,* Amy is liable, even though in fact she had someone else in mind (and even though most of her friends did not know about whom she was speaking). The burden of proving this "colloquium" is on Waldo. [§§1183-1185]

132. YES   All that is required is that some third person reasonably interpret it as applying to the plaintiff—even though the reference was unintended, and the *Tribune* report really was referring to another person by the same name. [§1185] (But it will have to be shown that the *Tribune* was *negligent* in not knowing there were several persons in the community by the same name. News media cannot be held liable unless published defamations were at least negligent.) [§1303]

133.a. NO   It is essential that a defamation be *intentionally or negligently* published (this is the one element where strict liability does *not* apply). [§1149] Moreover, where news media are involved, *all* elements of the prima facie case must be based on *at least negligence* (no strict liability). [§§1307-1308]

b. NO   A private person's recovery for a defamation by the news media is limited to damages for actual injury unless more than negligence is shown. [§§1312-1314]

134.a. SPLIT   Some courts hold that there is no "publication to a third person" here—treating the dictation to the secretary as merely a step in the process of communication to the intended recipient. Others are contra, treating the secretary as any third person (and certainly this is the case where the secretary is not a private secretary). [§§1145-1146]

b. NO   Not unless Judge's showing the letter to Clerk was intended by Lawyer or reasonably foreseeable. Again, no publication *by Lawyer.* [§1149]

135.a. PROBABLY NOT   Again, there is no liability for defamation unless the publication to a third person was intended or negligent. Unless Lawyer had reason to foresee that someone else could hear, *defamatory remarks uttered in private are not actionable.* [§1149]

b. **NO**	Participants in "judicial proceedings" are absolutely privileged to utter defamations related to the matter at hand. But it must occur at some stage of the proceeding itself; conversations in corridors or chambers are not within the scope of the privilege. [§§1234-1235]
c. **YES**	Calling a judge a "prejudiced boob" certainly imputes conduct incompatible with his office, and thus is "actionable per se" (without proof of actual damages). [§§1218-1219]

136. **(C) and (D)** (A) is not actionable per se because it does not sufficiently charge P with a "serious offense." [§1216]

Neither is (B) because, traditionally, imputation of unchastity to a *man* is not actionable per se in most courts. The rule is the opposite as to women; *see* (C). [§§1220-1222]

(D) *is* actionable per se because it imputes to P a characteristic (consorting) that is incompatible with his profession, the priesthood. But the result is contra where the profession does not demand the same moral standards; *e.g.,* the dentist, *see* (E). [§1219]

(F) is not actionable per se because it does not charge P with the *commission* of the crime; it only indicates that he is under suspicion. [§1216]

137. **ALL** Any defamation in written form (libel) is actionable without proof of special damage. (Possible exception as to libel per quod cases.) [§§1223-1224]

138.a. **NO** In states having retraction statutes, an adequate retraction cuts off only the right to recover *general* damages; it does not affect the right to recover actual (special) damages. (And in states not having such statutes, a retraction has no effect on liability.) [§1228]

But remember: In an action against news media, *negligence* must be proved; *i.e.,* it would have to be shown that the *Tribune* was at least negligent in publishing a letter containing such charges. [§1307]

b. **NO** In states having retraction statutes, an adequate retraction limits the action only *against the newspaper* and its employees, not any other defendants. [§1228]

139.a. **YES** On a respondeat superior theory. The employer is liable for the intentional or negligent acts of employees (Eager) committed within the course and scope of employment. [§§1154-1156]

b. **YES** Every republication of a defamation (unless privileged) is treated as a *new publication*. A republisher *cannot* limit liability by stating its source. The republication may well do more harm than the original (here, it was nationwide). [§§1157-1162]

c. **NO** One who merely distributes or sells (rather than publishes) is treated as a *"disseminator,"* and is held only to a standard of due care. In the absence of knowledge or reason to know that the story was false, there would be no liability. [§§1163-1165]

140.	**NO (most states)**	Truth is an absolute defense in most states—even where, as here, the defamatory remark was published maliciously and without certainty that the matter was true. [§§1196-1198, 1231]
141.	**PROBABLY NOT**	Statements published in the course of a judicial proceeding (complaint filed) are absolutely privileged, as long as they bear a "reasonable relationship" to the matter at hand. Here, a partner's underworld (Mafia) connections, if true, would reflect adversely on the partnership and hence it would seem sufficiently related to be absolutely privileged. [§§1234-1235]
142.	**PROBABLY**	Statements uttered during recess are not protected under the judicial proceedings privilege; that privilege extends only to utterances during the course of the proceedings themselves. [§§1234-1235]
143.a.	**YES**	Statements made by a *witness* in legislative hearings are protected to the same extent as in judicial proceedings (above)—*i.e.,* there is a requirement of reasonable relevancy. Here, Contractor's political beliefs or activities would seem unrelated to whether he has overcharged on the highway project. [§§1234-1235]
b.	**NO**	Defamations uttered by a *legislative member* are absolutely privileged—there is *no requirement of relevancy* to the matter at hand. [§1233]
c.	**NO**	Having reason to doubt the accuracy of the charge, the *Tribune* could *not* escape liability on the theory that publication was nonnegligent. However, it could rely on the so-called *privilege of "record libel"*—*i.e.,* the right to publish *"full and fair"* reports of proceedings in which there is a public interest. [§§1260-1266]
d.	**DEPENDS**	On whether the defamation was somehow related to the discharge of Attorney General's official duties. Top-grade cabinet officers are absolutely privileged to utter defamations, but there is a *requirement of relevancy* here. (Arguably, keeping track of "commies" is part of the Attorney General's official duties, and if so, this would be privileged.) [§1237]
144.	**NO**	Defamations uttered in an effort to advance one's own interests (or the interests of any third persons) are conditionally privileged if uttered in the reasonable belief that they are true, and relevant to a matter involving the person to whom uttered. *No request* for the information need be made where a sufficient *relationship* exists between the person uttering the defamation and the person to whom made (here, employer-employee). [§§1241-1248]
145.	**YES**	Because there was *no relationship* between Pompous and Acme's president. In the absence of such a relationship, defamations are conditionally privileged only where there was a prior *request* for the information by the person to whom the defamation was published. Here, no such request was made by Acme's president. [§1246]
146.	**NO**	Quarterback is probably a "public figure" so that Hosell's statements are constitutionally privileged as long as no actual malice (knowing or reckless falsity) is shown. Malice is *not* established merely by proof that Hosell didn't know what he was talking about; it would have to be shown that he in fact entertained serious doubts as to the truth of what he said. [§§1286-1294]

147. **NO**   The statement was constitutionally privileged. Charges of *criminal* conduct involving a candidate for *any* elected office (even a minor city post) are *never considered irrelevant* to the candidate's fitness for office, no matter how remote in time or place. Absent some showing of "malice" (reckless disregard for truth, or intentional falsehood), the constitutional privilege applies. [§1290]

148.a. **NO**   Constitutional privilege protects defamatory remarks about *public officials* respecting matters of public concern. [§§1278-1281]

     The privilege applies unless "malice" is shown (intentional falsehood, or *reckless disregard* for the truth). But simple inaccuracy or even negligence in ascertaining the facts is *not* enough to establish "malice." [§§1290-1294]

     b. **UNCLEAR**   If Smith is *not* a "public figure"—either because he is not a celebrity or because he has not voluntarily injected himself into the limelight—he will win in most states. Accordingly, the statements regarding him would *not* be protected by constitutional privilege; and, since the *Tribune* was *negligent* in making such charges, it would be liable for defamation. But if Smith turns out to be a public figure, he will lose. [§§1278-1315]

149.a. **YES**   Senator is a public official and his illegal gambling probably would be relevant to his official conduct. [§1282]

     b. **NO**   Constitutional privilege is defeated only by a showing that the defendant either *knew* that the statement was false, or published it with such *reckless disregard* for the truth that he must have subjectively entertained serious doubts as to its truth. Negligence or unprofessionalism is not enough to establish "malice." [§§1291-1294]

150. **NO**   Normally, unauthorized publication of a photograph taken *in public* is not actionable; it does nothing more than expose what anyone then present would have been free to see. [§1333] (*Compare:* The result is different where *commercial advantage* is taken.) [§1360]

151. **PROBABLY**   Normally, merely *taking* another's picture is not actionable; some publication thereof is required. But this is not always essential. Certain intrusions into one's privacy are so "unreasonable" that the intrusion itself is actionable. Here, the interference is for a *constitutionally impermissible purpose* (to inhibit sex films not necessarily "obscene"), and to impair Eager's right to attend anonymously. Since no legitimate purpose is served thereby, it would probably be deemed an "unreasonable" intrusion. [§§1317-1330]

152.a. **NO**   The right of privacy is strictly a personal right. It does *not* survive; and hence no cause of action can be maintained by a decedent's estate or heirs. [§1379]

     b. **NO**   Most courts have held that a decedent's survivors, no matter how close, cannot complain of any invasion of their interests because of the publicity concerning a decedent. [§1378]

     c. **PROBABLY NOT**   The issue here is *newsworthiness.* If there is a "legitimate" public interest in the details of the life of one who committed suicide 10 years ago, then it would seem that the reasons for his killing himself are also within the public interest. Mere passage of time does not by itself negate newsworthiness. [§§1331-1334, 1338-1343]

d. NO   The newsworthiness privilege is lost only where the defendant published with knowledge of falsity or *reckless disregard* for the truth. Inadvertent errors do not defeat the privilege. [§§1371-1373]

153.a. NO   The defendant is not entitled to take *commercial advantage* of plaintiff's appearance. His unauthorized use of plaintiff's picture is actionable—whether based on plaintiff's appearance in public or otherwise. [§§1358-1360]

b. NO   No pecuniary loss or other special damage need be shown. Mere embarrassment or anguish are sufficient damages. And where, as here, commercial advantage is taken, the value of the use made by defendant is evidentiary of the damages to be awarded. [§§1329, 1365]

154.a. NO   There is *no* right of action where the facts disclosed are already *public* facts (here, birth records). There is no invasion of privacy in such a case. [§1332]

b. YES   These are clearly *not* public facts. The issue here is whether the disclosure was privileged as "newsworthy." A few cases hold that *anything* affecting a celebrity is newsworthy. But the better view is that such intimate details of a celebrity's life are *not* "fair game." Hence, Rona can be held liable for their disclosure, even though true. [§§1334, 1338-1341]

155.a. YES   A false statement of a *material* fact is an actionable misrepresentation. A termite clearance report is a "material" fact because Dudley knew Pamela considered it important, and it is the kind of factor upon which reasonable persons customarily rely in buying houses. *Note:* It is not required that Dudley have knowledge that the house was termite-ridden; it is sufficient that he made a false statement of fact (termite report). (*Compare:* If there were *no termites*, the false statement might not be deemed "material.") [§§1388-1399]

b. YES   Having made a statement which he believed to be true, and knowing Pamela was relying thereon, Dudley came under a duty to disclose facts *later acquired* that made his earlier statement untrue. [§1397]

c. SPLIT   Traditionally, there is *no duty to disclose* facts in a sale transaction unless there is a special relationship between the parties, or the defendant has made a prior statement which requires correction (as in "b." above). However, several states now require disclosure of facts known to the seller and both unknown and *not readily accessible* to the buyer. In these states, Dudley's failure to disclose would be actionable. [§1399]

d. NO   If the parties agree that the property is being sold "as is," or the plaintiff is charged with notice that facts are being withheld, the seller is not liable for failing to disclose. [§1392]

156.a. NO   No scienter or intent to deceive where defendant honestly and reasonably believes his statement was true. [§§1400-1401]

b. NO   Again, no scienter or intent to deceive where defendant honestly believed statement to be true. It makes no difference that his belief was based on reports from third persons, as long as belief was honestly entertained. (*Compare:* Result could be contra if Dudley had *reason to doubt* the accuracy of the inspection report; in such a case, his doubts might color whether he **honestly** believed the premises were termite free when he so stated to Pamela.) [§§1400-1401]

c. **PROBABLY**   Knowledge by a defendant that he did not know one way or the other as to the truth of the matter, is sufficient to establish scienter. Hence, if Dudley **knew** he didn't know whether there were any termites, and he said there were none, he is subject to liability. [§1400]

d. **PROBABLY**   On a theory of **negligent misrepresentation** by a person in the business of supplying information for the guidance of others in a business transaction. In such cases, many courts recognize a duty of care in gathering and reporting the facts, and impose liability for innocent, but negligent, misrepresentations. [§§1413-1426]

157.a. **NO**   Most courts deny recovery to a plaintiff who was not a member of the class of persons whom the defendant intended to influence. Here Flako's financial statement was submitted to induce Bank's reliance in making a loan, rather than to entice the lending officer to purchase Flako stock. [§1405]

b. **NO**   Reliance on a false statement of **fact** is always justified; the plaintiff is not required (insofar as the defendant is concerned) to check the accuracy of the statement before relying thereon. [§1407] Moreover, even if Bank's conduct constituted contributory negligence, this is no defense to a fraud suit. (But it may be a defense to negligent misrepresentation; *see* below.) [§1432]

c. **POSSIBLY**   On a theory of **negligent** misrepresentation, if it was shown that Accountant was negligent in not discovering the falsity of the statements it certified. Most courts, however, have limited liability by requiring that the reliance of a **particular** plaintiff must have been intended or foreseen. Hence, it would have to be shown that Accountant knew or contemplated that Flako was going to use the statements to obtain a loan from Bank. [§§1413-1425] (*Note:* Bank's failure to make any independent check of Flako's credit might be regarded as **contributory negligence**, which would be a valid defense by Accountant to Bank's claim against him for negligent misrepresentation.) [§1432]

d. **YES**   Because **justifiable** reliance is an essential element in either suit, and Bank cannot justifiably rely on a statement which it knows to be false. (Of course, this would not bar enforcement of the loan itself.) [§1404]

158. **NONE**   (A) is a mere representation of value or quality and the buyer's reliance thereon is not deemed justified (in the absence of some special relationship, etc.). [§1409]

(B) Reliance is justified only on **material** misrepresentations of fact. It is a question of whether a reasonable person's investment decision would have been affected by the misrepresentation. This seems doubtful here because, whether or not offered for the first time, the investment decision would seem to be based on price and terms. [§1381]

(C) is an apparent misrepresentation of **law,** and reliance thereon by the plaintiff is not justified, absent special circumstances which do not appear here. [§1410]

159.a. **PROBABLY**   Since Duffer knew the condition of the company, he was apparently intending to deceive Swinger—hence, sufficient *scienter*. The real issue is whether Swinger can show *justifiable reliance* on Duffer's assurances that Flako had "great business prospects." Normally, reliance on representations of opinion or value is *not justified*. But a different rule applies where, as here, there is a special relationship between the parties, and one of the parties *conceals his interest* in the transaction about which he is offering apparently disinterested advice. (Duffer's interest as a stockholder stood to be wiped out in bankruptcy if the loan was not obtained.) [§§1405-1409]

b. **NO**   Because unless *damages* are proved, no action lies for misrepresentation (unlike the rule as to other intentional torts). [§1411]

160.a. **NOT NECES-SARILY**   Broken promises by themselves are not bases for fraud claims. However, if the promises were made *without the intent to perform* them, they will be treated as misrepresentations of the promisor's state of mind. The "reasonableness" of the promisor's prospect of being able to perform is evidentiary of his state of mind but is *not conclusive* (*i.e.,* a good faith intent to perform may exist notwithstanding lack of reasonable prospects). [§§1390, 1400-1401]

b. **SPLIT**   Most courts award the defrauded plaintiff the benefit of his bargain—the difference between the value of that which he was promised ($10,000) and that which he received ($2,000); here, $8,000. [§1436] *Note:* The minority rule awards only out-of-pocket loss—difference between the value paid ($5,000) and the value received ($2,000); here $3,000. [§1437]

161. **NONE**   (A) is untrue because *dishonest* expressions of opinion are as actionable as false statements of fact in a disparagement action. [§1441]

(B) is untrue because the burden is on the *plaintiff* in a disparagement action to prove the falsity of the facts or opinion expressed. [§1442]

(C) is untrue because the only intent required is the intent to disparage (and a dishonest expression of facts or opinion would suffice). [§§1451-1453]

(D) is untrue because the action cannot be maintained in the absence of special damages (out-of-pocket losses); and if Aerospace obtained the contract it probably could not show any such damages. [§1455]

162. **YES**   On a theory of *defamation*, rather than disparagement. Not every trade libel is defamatory of the product manufacturer. However, where the disparaging statement also impairs the *reputation* of the manufacturer, either action will lie. Here, Sly's statement in effect accuses Fry of *fraud* (passing off horsemeat as beef). Such an imputation is *defamatory per se*—actionable even without proof of special damage. [§§1448, 1450]

163. **NO**   The same privileges are recognized in disparagement actions as in defamation actions. One of these is an *absolute* privilege for statements filed as part of a judicial proceeding. And, a lis pendens is generally so regarded. [§1461] *Compare:* If Bright can prove that Wiley filed the lis pendens for an *ulterior purpose* (unrelated to the lawsuit), he may be able to recover for *abuse of civil process* (below). [§1540]

164. **(B) and (C)**   (A) is not true because the tort lies for interference with the *relationship* that exists—*i.e.*, it might have continued but for the interference. [§1471]

(B) is true; the possibility that Vera may have terminated anyhow must be taken into consideration in assessing damages. [§1471]

(C) is true. A defendant is privileged to interfere with an existing contract even though he was acting for his own selfish interests, where the contract is terminable at will. The privilege to compete takes precedence over a mere expectancy that such a contract will continue. [§1491]

165. **DEPENDS**   On National's motives. Where the interference is *justified*, there can be no recovery. Thus, no recovery if National has acted to protect its own interests (*e.g.*, in obtaining quality products, or in directing business to what it considers a more reliable supplier). On the other hand, if National was acting for an improper purpose (*e.g.*, solely to harm Case) the conduct would be actionable. [§§1484-1491]

166. **ALL except (A)**   (A) is false; it is only required that the proceedings be "terminated favorably" as to the plaintiff; and a dismissal for insufficient evidence is so regarded. [§§1516-1517]

(B) and (C) are both true. The plaintiff in a malicious prosecution must prove *both* that there was *no probable cause* for the criminal charge, and that it was filed for an improper purpose. [§§1518-1525]

(D) is true. The dismissal (or even an actual acquittal) in the criminal proceedings only means that the prosecution was unable to prove Employee guilty "beyond a reasonable doubt." But a *lesser standard of proof*—a mere "preponderance" of the evidence—suffices in civil cases; and thus Employer may defend on the ground that Employee was in fact guilty all along. [§1527]

(E) is true. A successful plaintiff is entitled to recover all damages proximately caused by the institution of the criminal charge. [§1526]

SAMPLE EXAM QUESTION I

Adam, a retired merchant, was driving his car in a careful manner when suddenly it swerved to the left across the center line and crashed into Brenda's parked car. Brenda had parked in the wrong direction on the left-hand side of the street in violation of a local ordinance. Just prior to the accident, Adam had taken his car for repairs to Smith's Garage. The car swerved because Smith had negligently assembled the steering apparatus after working on the car. As a result of the collision, both cars were badly damaged, Adam received a severe blow on the head, and a bottle of liquor that Adam had purchased fell from the seat and broke.

While extricating himself from his car, Adam felt and acted distinctly groggy because of the blow to his head. Brenda, drawn from her house by the noise, smelled the odor of whiskey occasioned by the broken liquor bottle, noted Adam's groggy behavior, and assumed Adam was intoxicated. In the presence of a group of persons who had gathered, she said, "I'll take this drunk to the police station." Then, despite Adam's protestations, she grabbed Adam by the arm and forcibly compelled him to go to the police station a block away. There Adam was examined by a physician and pronounced sober. He was released approximately a half hour after the accident had occurred.

Adam was greatly humiliated both by Brenda's reference to him as a drunkard and by his being compelled to go to the police station at Brenda's insistence, but he suffered no special damages on that account.

What are the rights of the various parties? Discuss.

SAMPLE EXAM QUESTION II

Tom, Bill, and Harry were riding in Tom's convertible bound for a football game. Tom was driving, Bill agreed to pay for the gasoline, and Harry purchased all three tickets as his contribution to the excursion. Due to the joint negligence of Tom and one Smith, who was driving his sedan, an accident occurred. As a result of the collision, the two cars were damaged and both Bill and Harry were injured.

After the accident, Tom and Smith became engaged in a heated argument as to who was responsible for the collision. Finally, Smith challenged Tom to a fight, Tom accepted the challenge, and both men removed their coats and proceeded to fight. They stopped only after Smith had knocked out two of Tom's front teeth. At that point, a reporter for the *Evening Chronicle* arrived at the scene and snapped a picture showing Tom bleeding at the mouth and holding a tooth in his hand. Realizing he had been photographed in this embarrassing position, Tom turned to the reporter and said, "I don't want you to publish that picture." Nonetheless, the picture was published in the *Evening Chronicle* along with an appropriate news item.

In due course, Tom had Dr. Todd, a reputable dentist, perform the necessary dental work and sent the dentist's bill to Smith, demanding payment. Smith replied by letter saying, "I won't pay this bill, and besides, I'm surprised that you would go to such a quack dentist as Dr. Todd." Smith, when writing Tom, had in good faith confused Dr. Todd with Dr. Dott, the latter being a truly disreputable dentist.

What are the rights and liabilities of the various parties? Discuss.

SAMPLE EXAM QUESTION III

D was the owner of a three-story brick building abutting the sidewalk. The first floor was rented to a chiropodist who used it for an office and sometimes spent the night there. The second floor was used by D himself as a storage space for his fine art collection. The third floor was occupied by T and his family as a dwelling. D employed W, a window cleaner, to clean the windows in the building, giving him a belt attached to a stout rope with instructions to wear the belt around his waist and to tie the other end of the rope to the radiators under the second and third floor windows while he was cleaning them. W neglected to do this, choosing instead to stand on the eight-inch ledge below the windows, holding on to an awning hook with one hand while he washed the windows with the other. While standing in this position outside the second floor window, W was startled when a lighted cigarette fell on his bald head from the apartment on the third floor, where T and his wife were entertaining guests at a cocktail party. Losing his hold on the awning hook and thereafter his balance, W fell to the sidewalk below and was severely injured. While the ambulance was taking W to the hospital, D telephoned Mrs. W, who—to his knowledge—was seriously afflicted with heart trouble, to tell her that her husband had fallen from the second floor and had been badly hurt. Mrs. W fell over in a faint, struck her head against a doorknob, and died a month later from the head injury. A state statute required owners of "multiple-dwelling" buildings to provide "approved" safety devices for window cleaners. The rope device provided by D had not been approved. The devices that had been approved could not be used on D's building because it lacked the proper hooks in the wall; it would not have been as effective in preventing falls as the rope and belt that D had supplied.

Discuss the rights of the parties. Assume that W is not covered by workers' compensation laws.

SAMPLE EXAM QUESTION IV

Nerv was an extremely nervous person. He discussed his problems with his friend Phil, a licensed pharmacist who owned and operated a drugstore. Phil recommended "Dreamy," a new tranquilizer manufactured by Drugco that did not require a prescription. Dreamy had been extensively tested by Drugco and four months previously had been approved for sale to the public without prescription by the Federal Food and Drug Administration ("FDA"). Nerv purchased a bottle of Dreamy and began taking it in accordance with the instructions. The label on the bottle stated, "Normal dosage two pills every 12 hours—safe for adult use—not habit-forming."

The day after the purchase, Nerv took two Dreamy pills upon arising, had breakfast, and then got in his car and headed for the golf course. While driving on a public street, Nerv suddenly became dizzy and lost control of his car. The car swerved onto the sidewalk, hit Ima, seriously injuring her, and then ran into a pole, seriously injuring Nerv.

Subsequent analysis revealed that Nerv's dizziness was caused by an allergic reaction to Dreamy, but that only five persons out of 10,000 would have such a reaction. None of this had been discovered during the extensive premarketing tests which led to approval by the FDA. It was also learned that during the four months since Dreamy was first marketed, two other persons had reactions similar to those of Nerv, and Drugco had been so informed. As a result, Drugco had conducted further tests and had ordered new labels that would contain the following message: "CAUTION—Dizziness may result from normal dosage."

What are the rights of Ima against Nerv and Drugco? Discuss.

What are the rights of Nerv against Phil and Drugco? Discuss.

SAMPLE EXAM QUESTION V

Mower Company ("M") manufactures a 12-horsepower cub tractor with a riding seat and a rotary cutter. The cutter is advertised as capable of cutting through brush with stalks up to one inch in diameter. Park ("P") purchased one of M's tractors from Retail Company ("R") on the condition that it could be returned anytime during the first week if it was not performing properly. The entire price of $1,200 was paid at the time of delivery. Before delivery, R inspected and serviced the vehicle.

During the first week, P noted that the cutter would not cut through brush of slightly less than one inch. When he used it over very rough terrain, he thought he noticed an increasing vibration and that the cutter was cutting closer on one side than on the other. Since he was enjoying its use, however, he made no attempt to return it to R. At the end of the first month, the vibration increased considerably, but then the first snow came and the tractor was put in the barn for the winter.

The following spring, P got the tractor out to demonstrate it to a neighbor, Smith ("S"), who was interested in the purchase of one. S, an amateur mechanic of considerable ability, offered to fix the vibration by a simple adjustment of the nut that held the rotary cutter. S adjusted the nut. Subsequently, each took turns driving the cutter over very rough, stony, and brushy ground. The vibration continued but was not as great as before. While S was riding the tractor, the rotary cutter came off, broke through its housing, and severed the left foot of P. The evidence showed a crack on the nut that held the cutter.

P sued M and R for damages due to the tractor's failure to cut one-inch brush, for the damages to the equipment, and for his physical injuries.

What result? Discuss. Include in your discussion all possible theories of liability and defenses available to M and R.

SAMPLE EXAM QUESTION VI

The four-story law school building of University, a private institution, had a defective elevator which frequently stopped between floors. The elevator had an alarm button which, if pressed, would ring a bell in the hallway and thus alert persons in the building to the fact that the elevator had stopped between floors, with passengers inside it. The defective condition did not create any danger that the elevator might fall or otherwise physically injure any passenger.

Elco, an elevator maintenance company, had a contract with University to inspect, service, and maintain the elevator.

One night, Prof, a law teacher, and his secretary, Prim, had been working late in Prof's office on the fourth floor of the building on an overdue manuscript. They entered the elevator to leave at about 11:20 p.m. The official closing hour for the building was 11 p.m., but there were exit doors from the building which could be opened from the inside. Both Prof and Prim knew that the elevator frequently stopped between floors.

The elevator stopped between the second and third floors. Prof pressed the alarm button, and the bell could be heard ringing in the hallway. Smith, a law student, was the only other person still in the building. He heard the alarm bell and realized that someone was trapped in the elevator. He thought this was very funny, and he deliberately did not call the campus maintenance staff.

Prof and Prim were not discovered and released until 8 a.m. the next day.

Prof suffered from high blood pressure. This condition and his fright at being confined in the elevator caused him to sustain a heart attack after two hours in the elevator.

Prim suffered severe nervous shock due to being confined in the elevator and her fear that Prof was dying. She was subsequently embarrassed and humiliated by remarks of students who suggested that perhaps some amorous activity in the elevator might have caused Prof's heart attack.

What rights do Prof and Prim each have against Smith, Elco, and University? Discuss.

SAMPLE EXAM QUESTION VII

Alana, while in a variety store owned by Bernard, noticed a sign on the wall reading "FREE—PLEASE TAKE ONE," below which was a box of transistor radios. Alana put one of the radios in her pocket and walked out of the store. Bernard rushed out of the store after Alana shouting, "Come back here with that radio, you thief!" The street was crowded, and Alana, humiliated by the accusation, eluded Bernard and ran home.

Later that day, Carla, a customer who resembled Alana, went into the restroom of Bernard's store. Bernard, thinking Carla was Alana, locked the restroom door and called the police. There was an open window in the restroom. Carla mounted a chair, planning to climb out the window. As she put her weight on the back of the chair, the chair tipped. Carla fell to the floor and broke her leg.

Alana learned later that the "FREE—PLEASE TAKE ONE" sign referred to advertising bulletins that were usually beneath the sign and not to the transistor radios. She offered to return the radio. Bernard refused to accept it.

Discuss the rights of Alana and Bernard against each other and the rights of Carla against Bernard.

SAMPLE EXAM QUESTION VIII

Twenty years ago Resco erected a building in what was then an unsettled area. Resco conducts experimental work in connection with cattle virus diseases in that building. The area surrounding the Resco property has now become a thriving cattle and dairy district.

Cattle ranchers in the area tried to induce Zoe, a cattle auctioneer, to establish a local market. Zoe was reluctant to do so because of his fear that a virus might escape from Resco's property and infect cattle.

Some of the ranchers called on Prex, the president of Resco. They told Prex of their desire to establish a market in the area and asked him to make a statement that would dispel Zoe's fears.

Prex called a conference and, without having made any investigation and without naming Zoe, stated that there was "no danger at all" of any virus escaping from the Resco premises, and that only a "driveling idiot" could conclude otherwise. This statement was printed in the

News, a local newspaper, and received wide attention. As a result, Zoe was frequently referred to in the community as a "driveling idiot." This caused him considerable embarrassment.

In the belief that Prex's statement concerning the safety of the Resco operation was correct and to escape further embarrassment, Zoe established a market in the area for the auction of cattle. Shortly thereafter, without negligence on the part of Resco, a virus escaped from Resco's premises and infected cattle in the area.

To stop the spread of the infection, public authorities ordered the slaughter of all infected or exposed cattle, and Zoe had to abandon his market with consequent financial loss to him.

What are Zoe's rights against Resco? Prex? the *News?* Discuss all issues.

SAMPLE EXAM QUESTION IX

Transit operates buses in a city. One morning Driver, a Transit driver, awoke with a bad cold. He consulted the yellow pages of the telephone directory and called Dr. Ard, a physician listed under the category, "Physicians & Surgeons—M.D.—Eye, Ear, Nose & Throat." Driver told Dr. Ard that he had a bad cold and was scheduled to report for work at noon that day. Dr. Ard listened to Driver describe his symptoms, said he could not give Driver an appointment, and told him to buy a bottle of "Pyrib" at a drugstore and to use its contents as directed on the label. Pyrib is a cold remedy antihistamine prepared and marketed by Drugco. Driver obtained the Pyrib from a drugstore, took the first dosage called for on the label, and reported for work at noon.

At 1:30 p.m. that day, while driving his bus, Driver felt drowsy. However, he continued driving and shortly thereafter fell asleep. The bus jumped a curb and hit a pole. Pat, a paying passenger on the bus, was injured.

Pyrib is known to cause drowsiness and sleep in about 20% of the persons who take it. Dr. Ard did not warn Driver that the medication prescribed might cause drowsiness and sleep, and the label on the bottle did not contain any such warning.

Discuss Pat's rights against Drugco, Transit, and Dr. Ard.

SAMPLE EXAM QUESTION X

Twenty years ago, P worked in the research department of Bomm-Bay, a private armaments manufacturer doing substantial business with the government. At that time, P and his colleagues were testing a newly developed strain of bacteria for use in germ warfare. From tests on animals, they found the agent to be effective, and it has since been incorporated into weapons sold to the government. The strain of bacteria has never been used in combat and has never been tested on humans. However, because of inadequate safety mechanisms at Bomm-Bay's laboratories, P was accidentally exposed to the bacteria.

The exposure was very brief and P did not suffer immediate harm, but his health has gradually deteriorated. It recently became so poor that he checked into a hospital. Doctors quickly traced his maladies to the bacteria, but cannot cure him.

R, a reporter for the *Yellow Journal,* learned of P's condition and entered P's hospital room wearing a white coat and stethoscope. P, thinking R was a doctor, disclosed that his mental capacities were impaired, that a lung and a kidney were no longer functioning, that he wore a wig because all his hair had fallen out, and that he was now impotent.

The next day R published a story attacking the use of inhumane weapons by the government and the lack of safety precautions used by local arms manufacturers such as Bomm-Bay. The story included P's name, an account of his accident 20 years ago, and a description of the symptoms P had disclosed to R. In addition, the story falsely stated that P's son, born a year after the accident, was mentally retarded, and that P experienced temporary seizures during which he became uncontrollably violent, once even beating his wife and child. R had no reason to think these false statements were true, and included them because he felt entitled to a certain poetic license as to assertions that cast no personal blame on P.

Discuss P's rights against the *Yellow Journal.*

ANSWER TO SAMPLE EXAM QUESTION I

Brenda v. Smith

Brenda will bring a negligence action against Smith for the damage to her car. Smith, as an automobile repairer undertaking to service a car, owes a general duty of care—and this is particularly true when the work affects parts of the car that could cause injury if not properly repaired, such as the steering apparatus in this case. Breach of duty is given in the facts by use of the word "negligently." Actual causation is present because but for Smith's negligent reassembly there would not have been a steering difficulty and Adam's car would not have crashed into Brenda's. Proximate cause is established by the fact that a foreseeable result (crash) occurred in a quite foreseeable manner (car swerving from faulty steering apparatus). And because both cars were "badly damaged," the prima facie case of negligence is complete.

Smith might allege that Brenda was contributorily negligent in parking her car in violation of an ordinance. However, this argument will fail because the ordinance undoubtedly is meant to protect against danger to oncoming traffic created by drivers who pull across the street to a parking space facing the wrong direction and then pull out again and try to merge with the proper flow of traffic. But here Brenda's car was already parked, and it posed no danger to oncoming traffic. Hence, it cannot be said that the purpose of the ordinance was to avoid the kind of harm that in fact occurred, and the violation of the ordinance is therefore irrelevant. (Note that even if Brenda's car had been properly parked in the space in question, it would still have been hit by Adam's car.)

Since the facts do not raise any other possible defense, it appears that Brenda will prevail in a negligence action against Smith.

(Smith cannot be held strictly liable here because he did not distribute a product, but simply rendered a service.)

Brenda v. Adam

Brenda will not meet with equal success in a negligence action against Adam for the damage to her car. The problem here is that although Adam—as a driver on the road and as owner of a car—owed a duty of due care to those who might foreseeably be hurt by his carelessness, there is no evidence that Adam breached that duty. In other words, there is no reason to believe that Adam knew that the car was defective before the episode occurred, and hence no indication that he acted unreasonably.

Adam v. Brenda

Property damage and personal injury: Brenda cannot be held liable to Adam for property damage and personal injury arising out of the crash itself, because there is no showing of any negligence on her part with respect to the occurrence of the accident. Her only misbehavior prior to the crash was parking in the wrong direction but, as discussed above, violation of the parking ordinance cannot be used to establish liability for this type of accident.

On the other hand, Adam has several possible bases for recovery against Brenda for harm suffered after the crash. First, by grabbing hold of Adam's arm (a "touching"), Brenda committed a battery. Second, an action for assault may lie—arguably Brenda's behavior led Adam reasonably to believe that if he were to try to break away or refuse to accompany Brenda to the station, he would be subject to further physical violence. Finally, a prima facie case is made out for false imprisonment, by the fact that Brenda restrained Adam through fear of force.

The crucial issue is whether there is a valid defense or privilege to the three intentional torts. Brenda will argue that she was arresting someone she reasonably believed to be guilty of drunk driving, so that her conduct was privileged. However, the general common law regarding arrests by private citizens without a warrant (even if drunk driving is considered a felony) is that despite the citizen's reasonable belief that a crime has been committed, the privilege is lost if in fact no crime was committed. Since the facts indicate that Adam did not commit a crime, Brenda's reasonable belief to the contrary will not protect her from liability for the intentional torts.

Therefore, Adam can recover at least nominal damages for all three torts, as well as compensatory damages for the half-hour detention.

Defamation: Arguably, Adam was slandered when Brenda referred to him as a "drunk." There was an intentional publication of words that would tend to damage Adam's reputation in the community. However, since we are told that he suffered no special damages, he can only recover upon a showing that Brenda's statement was "slander per se." It seems doubtful that the accusation of committing the crime of drunk driving or of being a public drunkard comes within one of the four categories of "slander per se." Even as a crime, such behavior probably lacks sufficient moral turpitude to support a slander per se recovery; and since Adam is retired, it is quite unlikely that the statement can be regarded as imputing conduct incompatible with his profession for purposes of a slander per se recovery. Being that the other two categories for recovery, a loathsome disease and unchastity of a woman, are not even arguably on point, an action for defamation will most probably fail.

Emotional distress: A claim for intentional infliction of emotional distress is also unlikely to succeed because it would be difficult to characterize Brenda's conduct as "extreme" or "outrageous." Brenda had reason to believe that drunk driving occurred, and there is no basis for inferring that she was acting for any other motive or in any way committing a practical joke.

Adam v. Smith

Smith will be liable to Adam for property damage (car and liquor bottle) as well as for personal injury occasioned by his negligence. Adam's case in this regard is at least as strong as Brenda's case against Smith (above), and there are no apparent defenses against Adam.

A further question, however, is whether Smith is liable for the harm and humiliation that Adam suffered after the crash because of Brenda's behavior. Certainly Smith's negligence was an actual cause of what transpired, but it is unlikely to be considered a proximate cause. The foreseeable result of Smith's negligence involved personal injury but not the likelihood that the person injured would have a broken liquor bottle in the car and be mistakenly assumed to be drunk by someone else who would take the law into her own hands. In that sense, Brenda became an unforeseeable intervening force for which Smith is not responsible. (Some courts, however, might allow recovery because of the proximity in time and space between the crash and the subsequent harm—an Andrews analysis.)

Adam would also have an action for breach of the repair contract, Smith's negligence being the breach. But again, the damages would not extend beyond those suffered in the accident because recovery in contract is limited to foreseeable damages.

ANSWER TO SAMPLE EXAM QUESTION II

Bill and Harry v. Smith

Smith, as a driver, owed a general duty of care to those in and around the road who might foreseeably be injured by his carelessness. Bill and Harry, as passengers in another car, were within the zone of foreseeability and hence were owed that duty of care. The facts stipulate that Smith violated that duty by acting negligently. And because Smith's negligence was the actual and proximate cause of the harm Bill and Harry suffered (their injury being a foreseeable result), the prima facie case is complete.

Moreover, there are no apparent defenses. The fact that Tom was also negligent would be a defense only if negligence could be imputed to Bill and Harry on a joint enterprise theory. However, in this case the parties were not engaged in a joint enterprise: Although sharing expenses may remove Bill and Harry from "guest" status (below), it alone does not give them joint enterprise status. A joint enterprise also requires an equal right to control its operation, and here the facts do not indicate that the three had common control of the vehicle. The car was Tom's, he was driving, and he was apparently in control of how to drive, the route to take, etc.

Bill and Harry v. Tom

Bill and Harry have an action against Tom because of his negligent driving. At common law, a driver owes others in the car a duty of due care while driving. This duty has been breached, and that breach is the actual and proximate cause of the harm. Furthermore, no defenses are evident from the facts.

However, should the state have a guest statute, the problem is more difficult. If Bill and Harry are considered "guests," these statutes require proof that Tom's driving was "reckless" or, in some states, "grossly negligent," rather than simply negligent. But here the facts do not support such a showing (it is only stated that Tom was "negligent"). Nonetheless, Bill and Harry have two possible avenues of escape from this situation. First, they can argue that the guest statute is unconstitutional because it violates the Equal Protection Clause. Several state courts have adopted this position. Additionally, they can argue that they are "passengers," not "guests"—on the theory that there was an agreement to share expenses. Generally, for the rider to be characterized as a "passenger," there must be some payment that serves as a motivating influence for the driver's furnishing the ride. It is quite likely that Bill's buying the gas and Harry's purchasing the tickets would qualify (although states have split on whether buying gas is enough to negate "guest" status). Given these facts, Bill and Harry most probably will not be deemed "guests," and thus will succeed in their common law actions.

Smith v. Tom

The likelihood of Smith succeeding in a suit against Tom for the damage to his car will depend on whether the jurisdiction has adopted comparative negligence. If not, then his own negligence completely bars any action against Tom. On the other hand, if comparative negligence principles do apply, then the outcome depends on what type of comparative negligence is followed ("pure" or "partial") and the degree to which Smith and Tom were each at fault.

Tom also apparently assaulted and battered Smith during the fight and would be liable for nominal damages but for the fact that these actions are barred in some states by reason of Smith's consent to the fight (discussed further below).

Tom v. Smith

So far as damage to Tom's car is concerned, the analysis here is identical to the one discussed above in Smith's action against Tom (*i.e.,* the issue turns on applicability of comparative negligence).

Tom will also sue for battery to recover damages sustained in the fight. The prima facie case is made out because Smith intentionally hit Tom and it may be assumed that it was meant to be a harmful touching. Additionally, there may be a cause of action for assault, since Tom was undoubtedly apprehensive (and properly so) of Smith's efforts to hit him during the fight.

The obvious defense to the above two actions would be consent. By accepting Smith's challenge, Tom consented to a fight, and it appears that Smith did nothing to go beyond the consent or otherwise vitiate it. Tom, however, will argue that the consent was invalid—on the theory that one cannot effectively consent to a breach of the peace. The courts are split on this question. In some states such consent is invalid (as a deterrence to fighting), and Tom would be permitted to recover for the harm to his teeth and related injuries. In states following the Restatement, however, it is irrelevant that a criminal act and breach of the peace were involved, so that Tom's consent would effectively preclude his right to recover.

Tom v. *Evening Chronicle*

A common law action for invasion of privacy lies for the mass circulation of private facts. The problem here, however, is that even though the picture of Tom was unauthorized, the event occurred in public in full view of all those who happened to be around. Moreover, one who undertakes to fight in public may not subsequently complain about the embarrassment that ensues simply because a photographer happened to come upon the scene. The point is not necessarily that the photograph was newsworthy—which is a defense—but rather that because there was no publication of private facts that would offend a reasonable person, there was no prima facie case for invasion of privacy in the first place. (Note that in the unlikely event that a prima facie case could be made out, consent would not be available as a defense because it was explicitly withdrawn by Tom before any publication occurred.)

Dr. Todd v. Smith

Smith's letter to Tom is an intentional publication of a libel concerning Dr. Todd, and the libel is apparent on its face because it holds him up to ridicule and contempt as an incompetent dentist. Where a defamatory publication takes the form of libel and is clear on its face, no state requires a showing of special damages. Hence, the prima facie case is complete.

The issue then is whether there is an applicable defense. Since the statement is not true, the only apparent defense under state law would be one of qualified privilege. But is this an occasion that calls for a conditional privilege? There seemingly is no common interest between Smith and Tom that would justify Smith's statement. On the other hand, Smith probably is concerned with his own financial interests should he be held liable to Tom—it may well be that Smith is afraid that Tom's going to an incompetent dentist will subject him to excessive dental bills. Had there been remaining dental work to be done, this theory might support a finding of a conditional privilege and Smith's "good faith" would protect him. Unfortunately for Smith, however, it appears that all necessary dental work has been completed so that there is nothing to be gained by Smith's telling Tom after the fact what he believes about Dr. Todd. Thus, there do not appear to be any state privileges on point.

It is highly doubtful whether the *Gertz* privilege would apply in this suit by a private citizen against another private citizen over a private communication. If it were to apply, Dr. Todd would have to prove negligence on the part of Smith to recover actual injury damages. Although Smith was writing in good faith, the facts do not seem to support the notion that he was acting reasonably in making such a clear mistake between Todd and Dott. If this is so, Smith was indeed negligent and *Gertz* would not stand in the way of Dr. Todd's recovery of actual injury damages, but Smith's good faith belief in the truth of what he wrote would prevent Todd's recovery of general damages.

ANSWER TO SAMPLE EXAM QUESTION III

W v. D

One who employs another to perform tasks owes a duty of due care to provide reasonably safe working conditions. Here, W would claim that D breached that duty by failing to supply the approved safety mechanism required by statute. Arguably D's brick building was not a "multiple dwelling" within the meaning of the statute—because only one floor was regularly used as a dwelling unit. If this is so, it cannot be said that D breached his duty by reason of a statutory violation. However, assuming the building is a "multiple dwelling" (perhaps because adaptable to such purposes), the result favors W. The purpose of the statute undoubtedly is to prevent accidents of the sort that occurred here—*i.e.*, something causing the window cleaner to lose his balance and fall—and W, being a window cleaner, is clearly within the class of persons to be protected. Therefore, D's failure to furnish the requisite safety device will be considered "negligence per se" in most states, as long as his violation is unexcused. Here the infraction does not appear to be excusable: There is no indication that D could not have refit his building to allow for use of the approved devices; indeed, he should have delayed the window washing until the necessary accommodations could have been made. It follows then that D's statutory violation sufficiently establishes breach for a negligence action.

Actual cause presents two problems for W. First, even though D violated the statute without excuse, he nevertheless gave W a safety mechanism that would have been more effective than an "approved" device. In other words, W was not put in a more dangerous position because of the statutory infraction. (Note that this factor could also be analyzed under the breach discussion, arguing that D's violation was not contemplated by the statute because the statute was only meant to preclude use of safety devices that were more dangerous than the approved ones.) The second problem relates to W's failure to use the device that D gave him—*i.e.*, even if D had provided the approved device, would W have used it? This is unclear from the facts; hence, the actual cause issue cannot clearly be resolved.

On the issue of proximate cause, D may argue that the cigarette falling on W's head was an unforeseeable intervening force that should terminate his liability. However, this contention is weak at best, because the statutory purpose is to protect the window cleaner from losing his balance no matter what the reason. It is therefore irrelevant that in this case the fall was occasioned by an unusual event. Moreover, there is clearly a foreseeable result—loss of balance and subsequent fall. Thus, there most probably is a sufficient showing of proximate cause. (Perhaps the result would be different had the intervening force amounted to a malicious tort or crime, but the facts do not indicate that such was the case.)

Assuming W can overcome the actual cause problem, his injury completes the prima facie case. However, D appears to have a good defense. W should have realized that any number of factors could have caused him to lose his balance. Such being the case, his failure to use any safety device casts serious doubt on the reasonableness of his behavior. If it was unreasonable, in a contributory negligence state, W's conduct will completely bar his recovery; and in a comparative negligence jurisdiction, W's recovery will at least be reduced (if not barred altogether)—the result turning on the type of comparative negligence adopted and the degree to which W and D were each at fault.

(In some cases a statute is perceived to have been enacted for the benefit of a group unable to protect itself, and the failure of a member of that group to behave reasonably has been totally disregarded. This most often applies to children and to workers on dangerous jobs who are told to undertake a hazardous task with the risk of being fired if they refuse. However, this is not the case here because W was given safety equipment to use but nonetheless failed to use it—apparently unreasonably.)

W v. T, *et al.*

W will claim that T behaved negligently, either by tossing a lighted cigarette out the window or by allowing his guest to do so. The major problem, however, is proving who in fact dropped the cigarette (all we know is that T and his wife were having a cocktail party—from the facts given, anyone could have been responsible). Assuming W can gather proof that T or his wife was at fault, a prima facie case will not be difficult to establish. Persons in apartments abutting public sidewalks must exercise due care so as not to endanger persons outside. T might contend that under the Cardozo view W was owed no duty because he was not a foreseeable plaintiff, being a window washer (possibly unexpected) and not a passerby on the sidewalk below. However, T is unlikely to succeed with this argument—even Cardozo would agree that it would be ludicrous to restrict the class of foreseeable plaintiffs to those passing on the sidewalk. A window washer part way down is even more clearly in the zone of danger than are others on the street below. Hence, the better conclusion would be that W was owed a duty of due care. Moreover, there is no problem with causation: But for the incident, W would not have lost his balance and been hurt—hence, actual cause. Assuming W is a foreseeable plaintiff, his injury was a foreseeable direct result of the cigarette hitting his head. Thus, proximate cause is present.

Liability would therefore seem to follow except for the fact that T can rely on the same defense analysis as discussed in the suit against D—*i.e.*, contributory negligence or comparative negligence may well bar (or at least reduce) W's recovery.

Going back to the issue raised earlier, if W cannot show that T or his wife was at fault, the likelihood of his making out a prima facie case greatly diminishes. An effort to hold T vicariously liable for the misbehavior of whomever dropped the cigarette is unlikely to succeed because the relationship of host and guest does not give rise to imputed liability. Nor can there be primary negligence unless the host has some reason to know that one of his guests is creating unreasonable risks toward others. Absent such a showing, W will have to identify the particular individual who dropped the cigarette; however, this is virtually impossible from the facts given. W might try to rely on a res ipsa claim against everyone in the apartment, invoking *Ybarra v. Spangard* principles. However, the likelihood of his succeeding is dubious—the cocktail party seems to be entirely different from *Ybarra*, where it was known that each defendant had some contact with the plaintiff.

Mrs. W v. D

A duty is owed to exercise due care so as not to subject others to a foreseeable risk of physical injury, through physical impact or threat thereof, that might foreseeably result in emotional distress and consequent physical injury. The problem here is that although D's conduct (phone conversation) was directed at Mrs. W, there was no "threat of physical impact." Hence, these facts are far removed from the typical case. Nonetheless, arguably D's knowledge of Mrs. W's heart trouble may well have subjected him to a duty not to impose an unreasonable emotional burden on her. If such is the case, the outcome turns on whether he in fact acted unreasonably in making the phone call, taking into consideration the frantic state of events. Would a reasonable person under similar circumstances have found a more gentle way to handle the situation? This is debatable. Should it be decided that D was negligent, he will be liable to Mrs. W's estate for her injury and for expenses attending her subsequent death. Additionally, a wrongful death action may lie; although, should W be a beneficiary in such an action, recovery would be barred or reduced because of his own negligence that occasioned D's call in the first place.

ANSWER TO SAMPLE EXAM QUESTION IV

Ima v. Nerv

Ima's claim against Nerv will be based on a negligence theory. Nerv owes a duty to those in and around the road to exercise due care while driving and while preparing himself to drive. The problem here, however, is that there is no clear breach of that duty—*i.e.,* the facts do not indicate that Nerv could have anticipated his allergic reaction. Arguably Nerv was negligent in driving after taking a tranquilizer whose strength and effect he had not previously determined, but seeing that the label raised no suspicion of side effects, and given the reality that persons often take medication before driving unless warned otherwise, this theory is not strongly supported by the facts.

Actual causation is present because, but for Nerv's having taken the drug, he would not have sustained the allergic reaction and would not have hurt Ima. On the other hand, proximate cause raises a problem because although the foreseeable risks undoubtedly included drowsiness, Nerv should have had time to pull over to the side of the road. But here he "suddenly" became dizzy and lost control of the car. Even though attributable to his taking the pills, the suddenness of the reaction arguably was not the risk reasonably to be anticipated. Hence, many courts would hold this to be an unforeseeable result, precluding a finding of proximate cause. Others, however, might hold that losing control of the car was the foreseeable risk involved and that it did in fact occur—although through unexpected dizziness rather than predictable drowsiness. Damages are given and there are no apparent defenses so that if the problems of breach and proximate cause can be overcome, Nerv will be liable to Ima.

Ima v. Drugco

Ima may pursue several theories against Drugco. First, strict liability in tort is possible, but Ima faces the problem that she is a "bystander." Almost all states allow any person injured by a defective product to invoke strict liability, on the theory that bystanders are in need of even greater protection than users or consumers. Assuming the court follows the modern trend, the case turns on whether the product was "defective." Here we are dealing with a claim of design defect since the entire batch can potentially cause allergic reactions. The question, however, is whether a product that is perfectly safe for 9,995 persons out of 10,000 is defectively designed because of the danger to the others. Given the fact that extensive premarketing tests had not disclosed the danger, most courts would probably treat the side effect as a scientifically unknowable risk, thus precluding a finding of design defect.

Should Ima attempt an action for breach of implied warranty of merchantability, she would run into the dilemma that she was not in privity with Drugco, the manufacturer. The Uniform

Commercial Code offers several alternatives to the traditional strict privity requirement. States adopting the narrowest provision would not allow recovery, but those following the broader provisions might well find for Ima as a person reasonably to be expected to be affected by the product. Arguably Dreamy is not fit for normal use and hence, unmerchantable.

Another possible theory is breach of express warranty—because the label states that the drug is "safe for adult use." However, Ima faces the same privity problem as she does in the implied warranty action.

A strict liability action for innocent misrepresentation would be futile because there was no reliance by Ima on the label's representation.

Turning to negligence theories, it is clear that under the expanded interpretation of *MacPherson v. Buick*, Drugco owes a duty of due care to anyone who might be adversely affected by its products. The negligence here is apparently not in the failure to discover the allergic danger, because we are told that extensive testing—including testing by the FDA—did not reveal the defect. And it is unlikely that the testing was performed unreasonably. Rather, the negligence may be in the failure to respond faster once Drugco learned that others were having adverse reactions. Although further tests had been conducted and new labels ordered, perhaps the reasonable course of behavior would have been to inform all pharmacists immediately that potential problems were being reported and studied. If this had been done, a jury might well find that Phil would not have recommended the potentially dangerous tranquilizer to his friend Nerv. Causation would be present since an earlier warning of sudden dizziness might very well have avoided the harm that occurred here.

Nerv v. Phil

There appears to be serious doubt regarding the propriety of a strict liability in tort action against pharmacists. Even though technically there may have been a "sale," courts are rejecting this theory of liability: Sometimes the justification is that pharmacists are only providing a "service," but the better rationale is one of policy to provide pharmacists with the same protection afforded doctors and dentists by limiting the extent to which they may be subject to potential no-fault liability. Hence, even assuming the drug was "defective," a strict liability suit against Phil would probably fail.

On the other hand, arguably there should be liability for breach of implied warranty of fitness for a particular purpose, since having discussed his problems with Phil, Nerv probably relied on Phil's judgment as a licensed pharmacist to supply appropriate medication. In that sense, Phil is no different from any retailer who selects a product in response to a customer's requirements—if the product does not work properly, it is at the risk of the one who selected it.

A negligence action probably would not be successful because there is no showing that Phil behaved unreasonably. Although he chose Dreamy, he had no reason to know that there was any problem, and the product had been adequately tested and certified for sale by the FDA.

Nerv v. Drugco

Nerv may have several actions against Drugco. In a strict liability in tort action, he will have to show that the product was "defective" (*e.g.*, under the Restatement approach, that the drug was "unreasonably dangerous"). However, as noted earlier, most courts would probably treat the problem as a scientifically unknowable risk and thus find no "defect" for strict liability purposes.

Breach of implied warranty of merchantability is available here if Nerv can surmount the privity problem—being that he bought the product from Phil. Again, states differ on this.

An express warranty theory would also be available, assuming Nerv had read the label "safe for adult use" before he bought the drug (or at least before he used it). The fact that it was Nerv's idiosyncrasy that made the product unsafe for him is irrelevant because the label gave no reason to believe that allergic reactions might follow; hence, Nerv had no reason to doubt the safety of the drug.

Drugco may also be liable on a strict tort liability theory for innocent misrepresentation. [Rest. 2d §402B] Actual and justifiable reliance on the label's representation can probably be shown.

Finally, Nerv has a negligence action against Drugco similar to that discussed above in "Ima v. Drugco"—*i.e.,* unreasonable delay in alerting the public of the drug's potential dangers. Had there been a timely warning, it is likely that Nerv would have taken appropriate precautions, thereby avoiding the result in this case. Thus, causation is present, and since there are no apparent defenses, liability should follow.

ANSWER TO SAMPLE EXAM QUESTION V

Personal Injury Claims by P v. M

Negligence: M as a supplier of chattels owes a duty of due care in the manufacturing and designing of its cub tractors. This duty extends to buyers, users of the product, and "bystanders"—a category P may fit into in this case because, at the time, he was watching S using the tractor. The apparent cause of the accident was a crack in the nut that held the rotary cutter (though this must be proven). From what we know at this point, if the evidence should suggest that this type of crack (assuming cause can be shown) is one that more often than not is attributable to negligence in the selection of metal for the nut or in the manufacturing of the nut, then P may be able to establish breach of duty by the use of res ipsa loquitur. If the defect is in fact visible and should have been found through the inspection process before leaving M's plant, then that would be another approach that P may take to showing breach of duty. If the evidence supports the notion that this defect could as plausibly have occurred after the product left M's control and that M was in no way responsible for what subsequently happened (R's inspection or S's adjustment), then P would be unable to use res ipsa loquitur and would have to show some specific negligence that occurred while the product was under M's control.

A final negligence theory might be that M negligently failed to design a housing sufficiently strong to prevent the escape of a detached cutter. More facts are needed here.

If P can meet the negligence showing, then on the question of proximate cause, P may lose if it is shown that R did in fact discover the defects but marketed the product anyway in callous disregard of the rights of consumers or that S did something unexpected in his efforts to tighten what appeared to be a loose nut.

No apparent defenses can be asserted against P. It is true that he knew the product was not cutting evenly and not cutting one-inch branches, but there is no reason to think that he had unreasonably failed to perceive a danger to his physical security from the way the tractor had been performing. Assumption of the risk is absent here because P seems not to have been aware of any particular danger from the machine. Even in comparative negligence jurisdictions, it is difficult to see what conduct on P's part a jury might consider in reducing the recovery against M.

Strict liability: If P should sue M on a strict products liability theory, P would have to establish that the cutter was defective when it left M's control and that the defect was the cause of the accident. If the cracked nut existed at the time the product left M's control, then the defective nature of the product and the unreasonable danger created for users and bystanders are quite clear. The bystander's case is somewhat more difficult here, but P might get around that if the state is one of almost all that has extended strict liability to bystanders or if P can establish that he was a user who was only temporarily out of control of the product. If the product cannot be shown to have had the defect at the time it left M's control, then a strict liability case will fail for lack of the showing of the marketing of a defective product.

On proximate cause, M might again try to argue that S's repair was an unforeseeable misuse of the product. But the facts indicate that all he did was tighten a loose nut—and there is no showing that he was aware of the danger but nonetheless failed to warn P. (The same may be said of any claim that R found the defect but failed to notify customers.) Nor can M defend on the ground that P put the product to an abnormal use by riding it over rough terrain. It was marketed for the clearing of brush and its use, even if not exactly what the manufacturer expected, was certainly within the range of foreseeable uses.

So far as defenses are concerned, there appears to be no contributory negligence. But if the court should rule that a jury could find some contributory negligence on P's part, a growing number of states will allow that to reduce his recovery against M on a strict liability theory.

Warranty: It is not clear who advertised that the product would cut one-inch brush. But in any event, this seems not proximately related to the claim for personal injury (*see* below). But the implied warranties under the Uniform Commercial Code would be available in P's action against M for breach of the implied warranty of merchantability unless the most restrictive privity version of section 2-318 (limited to family members and "guests") is enforced. But even then some courts have expanded upon that statute to allow warranty recoveries for personal injury beyond its terms. If M argues that the one-week return provision was a permissible limitation on remedy for breach of warranty, then P may respond that section 2-719(3) declares that limitations of warranties against personal injury are prima facie unconscionable. Another answer may well be that this limitation was offered only by R and cannot help M.

The notice requirement of section 2-607(3) is very generously construed in personal injury cases and is unlikely to provide a defense.

If there are defenses, the trend is to use comparative fault here.

P v. R

Negligence: P's negligence action here must be based on the fact that R created the defect while it was in R's control or that R negligently failed to find the defect that was previously there as a result of defective manufacture. The first claim seems unlikely from the facts. The second possibility, failure to discover, will depend on whether the crack was visible and whether the inspection and service that R did in this case, if done reasonably, should have disclosed the problem of the nut. The proximate cause problem of S and the defenses would be the same as in P's case against M.

Strict liability: The claim here would be easier since the presence of the defect at the time it left R's hands is apparently clear from the facts and nothing that S did in tightening the nut was likely to have created the defect. Thus we have R marketing a defective product, and traditional products liability law will apply since this product was certainly unreasonably and unexpectedly dangerous to the buyer. Again the defense questions would be the same.

Warranty action against R: Here there are no privity problems and the implied warranty of merchantability existed and was breached by this product. If any defenses are available, they would be a form of contributory negligence—as to which some states now use comparative fault and will reduce P's warranty recovery. The one-week return privilege cannot serve to bar P's action for personal injuries because of section 2-719(3) (discussed earlier).

Action for damage to the tractor

P's action against both M and R for damage to the tractor would be analyzed the same way as a personal injury action as far as the negligence claim is concerned. Under a strict liability theory, however, some states have not allowed an action in the absence of privity for harm to the product itself, which is what happened in this case. The jurisdictions are split. The claim for product loss in warranty would likely be analyzed the same as the personal injury action above. If the jurisdiction allows M to be liable for breach of warranty under section 2-318, then that liability should extend to both the personal injury and the product. So far as defenses are concerned, however, P may not have the advantage of section 2-719(3) since that applies only to personal injury claims and not to property damage claims. Nonetheless, the one-week return situation seemed to apply only to a customer who was dissatisfied because the product would not perform properly. It seemed not to contemplate a limitation on an action involving destruction of property.

Failure to cut one-inch thick brush

This is purely economic loss, and most courts would not recognize a negligence action for failure of a product to perform its function leading only to economic disappointment. The same seems to be true in strict liability, although here again the states are split. The best way to pursue this claim is an action for breach of express warranty. This warranty does not require privity; therefore an action should be available against both M and R. The only possible defense is the one-week provision, and the question would then be whether that condition written into the contract serves to exclude all other remedies for failure to cut the one-inch brush.

Even so, P cannot recover damages for both the destroyed tractor and for its failure to cut the brush in this case, since recovery of the $1,200 for loss of the tractor would cover P's loss from the failure to cut.

ANSWER TO SAMPLE EXAM QUESTION VI

Prof & Prim v. Smith

Smith was not an employee of University and bore no special relationship to Prof or Prim. He did not cause the plaintiffs' predicament and so was under no obligation to attempt a rescue or to call for help. Since no duty existed, none was breached, and no negligence action lies. Other theories of liability do not apply.

Prof & Prim v. Elco

By not repairing a well-known defect in the elevator, Elco breached its contract with University. Even if plaintiffs are able to sue as third-party beneficiaries, damages for breach of contract are limited to those reasonably contemplated by the parties when the contract was made. Since the facts state that no danger of falling or physical injury existed, the harm in this case was probably beyond the parties' contemplation when the contract was signed.

Since it does not appear that Elco sold or installed the elevator, negligence is the only available tort theory. In some states, if Elco never began to perform its contract, its conduct would be called nonfeasance, and no tort action would lie. Even though the elevator often stopped between floors and needed a maintenance worker to start it again, this restarting did not go to the defect and may not be misfeasance.

If Elco committed misfeasance by trying to fix the defect, all states would find liability a close question. The physical harm suffered by plaintiffs was foreseeable; Elco's failure to do the repairs properly would be unreasonable. Prof's harm may be foreseeable in tort even though not recoverable in contract. His damages would be medical expenses and economic losses incurred as a result of the heart attack plus pain and suffering. Prim suffered "severe nervous shock" from her confinement and fear. Some states would call this purely emotional harm and bar recovery. In addition, her chances of getting damages for her embarrassment are small. Elco could not reasonably have foreseen this type of harm coming from its misfeasance.

Elco may claim that plaintiffs were contributorily negligent in using the elevator after the building was closed, knowing of the defect. Even though it had an alarm bell, the likelihood that it would not be heard should have been considered. In comparative negligence states, there would be no complete bar in any event.

A second defense is assumption of the risk. Both plaintiffs were aware that the elevator often stopped between floors and should have foreseen the possibility of delayed rescue late at night. Unless Prof did not know of his high blood pressure, he may have voluntarily assumed the risk of a heart attack. The assumption of risk defense is less strong against Prim since she may not have known of the danger to Prof.

Prof & Prim v. University

If University was negligent in hiring Elco, then University may be liable for its own negligence. However, nothing in the facts suggests that Elco was not an appropriate company to hire for elevator maintenance.

In any case, University may be liable for Elco's negligence since the duties assumed by Elco were nondelegable. Maintaining elevators in the law school was part of University's duty to provide a safe place to work for employees. It might also go toward keeping public premises safe for visitors, but it is not clear that the law school was open to the public.

Damages and defenses are the same as discussed above. However, workers' compensation may bar suit against University.

ANSWER TO SAMPLE EXAM QUESTION VII

Bernard v. Alana

Although Alana acted innocently, she intentionally took a radio from Bernard's store, and Bernard has an action against her for conversion of a chattel. That Alana thought the radio was free is no defense. However, she may contend that Bernard's actions induced her to think it was free, that a reasonable person would think so as well, and that by placing the sign and radio as he did, Bernard is estopped from claiming conversion. If that fails, Bernard's remedies are to recover the radio or its market value, and any damages from the dispossession. Because Alana acquired the radio in good faith and offered to return it, she has mitigated damages and will not be liable for harm done by the conversion after Bernard refused the offer. Bernard may try to get Alana to indemnify him for any liability to Carla, but because Carla's injuries were the result of intervening acts that were unforeseeable by Alana, she is not the proximate cause of Carla's harm. Indemnification should not lie.

Alana v. Bernard

Publicly accusing Alana of being a thief was a defamation by Bernard. The statement was made intentionally, in the presence of many people, and would tend to lower the reputation of Alana in their eyes. The defamation was a slander which Alana will argue is actionable per se. Bernard's statement accused Alana of a serious crime, but the weight of authority is that calling one a "thief" does not impute sufficient moral reprehensibility to constitute slander actionable per se. Since the statement is not under any other category of slander per se, Alana cannot recover for general harm to her reputation, unless she can prove special damages. None is apparent from the facts of the case.

In a state that does not demand special damages for a statement calling plaintiff a "thief," Bernard will be unable to defend his actions on grounds of truth because Alana was not in fact or law a thief, because she lacked criminal intent. A stronger claim would be that Bernard enjoyed a conditional privilege to defame Alana to protect his own property. Bernard saw a radio of his being taken and may have meant simply "that's mine!" The "publication" may have been unreasonably excessive given the circumstances, which include the fact that Alana was walking away and not running. Otherwise, honest belief will sustain the privilege. If Bernard did not realize the ambiguity of his sign, a jury might well find he honestly believed a theft had occurred.

Carla v. Bernard

By locking her in a restroom, Bernard falsely imprisoned Carla. The act was intentional and temporarily succeeded in confining Carla to a specific area, since Carla knew of the imprisonment and was not aware of a means of escape beforehand. Even if the possibility of climbing through the window was immediately apparent, it was not so simple and safe an escape as to negate the confinement. Not only did Carla have to stand on a chair to get to the window, she had to step on its back, and she was under no duty to take the risk of such a maneuver.

Bernard may not claim that he was attempting to recover a chattel wrongfully withheld because he was not in "fresh pursuit" after the theft, did not demand return of the radio before resorting to confinement, and used the force of confinement on the wrong person. Nor can Bernard argue that the confinement was pursuant to a citizen's arrest. First of all, Bernard never actually made an arrest. He didn't even tell Carla that she was being held. Calling the police does not constitute an arrest. In addition, Bernard did not enjoy the privilege to arrest for a misdemeanor since he was not in fresh pursuit and since he had the wrong person. At common law, the privilege is not given to a citizen who mistakenly arrests the wrong person.

Bernard's most credible defense is the "shopkeeper's privilege," accepted in most jurisdictions. Here, a reasonable mistake is forgiven. Since Bernard had seen a customer resembling

Carla take a radio, he could reasonably suspect that Carla was the thief and temporarily detain her to investigate. However, the method of detention was probably unreasonable. Few shopkeepers lock suspected shoplifters in restrooms. Furthermore, Bernard did not inform Carla of his suspicions, ask for an explanation, or even mention that the confinement was intentional.

Carla may recover nominal damages for false imprisonment. In addition, she can get damages for her broken leg, since injuries suffered in a reasonable attempt to escape false imprisonment are recoverable. Even if Carla were deemed negligent for trying to escape as she did, such negligence would not be a defense to an intentional tort.

ANSWER TO SAMPLE EXAM QUESTION VIII

Zoe v. Resco

In this case it appears that Prex was acting in the scope of his employment to further Resco's relations with the community and that his actions will be chargeable to Resco.

Defamation: Prex intentionally published to third persons a statement that hurt Zoe's reputation in the community. This was not simply name-calling in a fit of anger. In this situation, the words used conveyed the idea that anyone who believed that Resco's operation created a danger of escaping virus was an ignorant person whose intellectual abilities were far below normal. This would be enough to lower Zoe's reputation in the eyes of a substantial segment of the community. The fact that Zoe was not named is irrelevant. He can readily prove that hearers and readers understood that he was being referred to by Prex. Finally, Prex's assertion was one of fact because he had access to secret information that apparently induced him to condemn the intellect of disbelievers.

The next critical question is whether Zoe must show special damages. Since the damage occurred through the publication in the *News,* Zoe will argue that Prex committed libel even though he only spoke the words. Resco and Prex will argue a slander theory. If slander is the conclusion, this may not be slander per se because it does not suggest that Zoe is incompetent in his trade or profession—unless cattle auctioneers are expected to be familiar with the risks of experimental research involving cattle virus. If this is part of the knowledge demanded of auctioneers, then Zoe has an action for slander per se.

If the claim is considered libel—a more likely result given Prex's effort to obtain widespread dissemination through the press—it is not a libel clear on its face. In some states such libel never requires special damages. In others, special damages are always required. In other states, special damages are required unless the words, if spoken, would have been slander per se. That will depend on the slander analysis above. If special damages are required, the financial loss Zoe suffered will not suffice because it was not the result of public reaction to the defamation.

As to defenses, Resco may argue it has the qualified privilege to speak to protect its reputation as a safe activity in the community. But even if such a privilege were accorded, it would be lost if Prex did not have an actual, honest belief in the truth of the defamatory matter.

Since Zoe has not voluntarily thrust himself into this controversy, he will be a private person under the *Gertz* case. However, a majority of the Supreme Court Justices would apply *Gertz* to nonmedia defendants if the defamation regarded a matter of public concern. In this case, a matter of public concern is definitely involved (*i.e.,* safety of cattle virus research in a cattle and dairy district). *Gertz* probably applies; Zoe may recover actual injury damages—which may include the financial loss here and proven emotional distress and embarrassment—upon proof of negligence. That should be easy here given the lack of any investigation before speaking. If Zoe wants general damages, he must prove deliberate falsity or reckless disregard for truth under the *New York Times* test. In a few states, private plaintiffs must prove this to recover any damages at all.

To the extent damages are attributable to the republication of the statement by the *News*, Resco will be responsible since the republication was both intended and foreseeable.

Intentional infliction of emotional distress: Can calling Zoe a "driveling idiot" (without any basis in fact) be considered extreme and outrageous behavior? On the one hand, Prex was trying to embarrass Zoe into taking action—and succeeded. The language itself seems to fit more comfortably into the nonactionable insult category. Yet this was a premeditated effort to humiliate Zoe, which might warrant liability—even though Prex was trying to achieve something for himself in the process, not simply playing the practical joker. Zoe's "considerable embarrassment" appears serious enough to be actionable. (There is no requirement of physical injury.)

False light privacy: Some states permit actions when D has placed P in a false, but not necessarily defamatory, light in the eyes of the community. If an actionable defamation exists, this action adds little. But if no defamation was found because of lack of an actionable defamation or special damages, this action might help Zoe. He was falsely portrayed in the community as an ignorant person. Although a constitutional privilege might exist, Prex has forfeited it by being recklessly responsible for the falsity by speaking without having made any investigation. A jury could find that he knew he did not know the truth of the statements he was making.

Misrepresentation: Resco, through Prex, falsely stated that "no danger at all" existed from the plant. This statement was made recklessly, with knowledge that Prex did not know the truth, and with intent to induce Zoe to take certain steps in reliance. Even though the reliance was not to benefit Resco directly, that is not required with fraud. Zoe actually relied (though motivated in part by other reasons), and this appeared justifiable since nothing signalled that the statement was obviously false. Resco's argument that the statement was only one of opinion will be rejected because the words were spoken by one claiming to have special knowledge about secret experimental work. Zoe's economic losses were caused by his reliance—whether the cattle died from the virus or were killed to prevent its spread. The latter was a foreseeable result of the reckless statement.

Strict liability for abnormally dangerous activity: Resco's operation seems to qualify as an activity that should give rise to strict liability because of its dangerous and uncontrollable nature. (Even among the courts that also ask whether the activity can only be conducted in this community, the answer is negative and strict liability would be imposed.) Zoe's damages were actually and proximately caused by the miscarriage of the activity, since the destruction of the cattle was a foreseeable result of the escape of the virus.

The major problem with this claim is that the type of loss suffered—financial—is not the personal injury or property damage claim usually brought in these cases. As with the law of defective products, the reasons that motivated the development of strict liability for these losses may not extend to pure economic loss. On the other hand, some courts might conclude that a dangerous activity should be liable for all types of losses caused by its dangerous features, particularly when, as in this case, some victims sustained serious property damage.

If the action can be established, Zoe would not be barred by his own conduct. He did not assume the risk because he did not know about the danger. Since his behavior seems entirely reasonable in the situation, he was not negligent in any way.

Nuisance: This action is brought for interference with use and enjoyment of one's land. It may be based on strict liability if the manner of interference is one that results from an abnormally dangerous activity—as in this case. The problem with nuisance here is that Zoe's loss was not caused by any inability to use his land. The land was usable—it was his business that was hurt by the lack of cattle in the area. Whether or not the virus invaded his land, his loss was peculiarly the result of the harm to others in the community rather than a possessor of land.

Zoe v. Prex

Prex is personally liable for the torts discussed in the foregoing discussion—except for strict liability for abnormally dangerous activity and nuisance, as to which Resco alone bears any liability.

Zoe v. the *News*

Defamation: The prima facie case against the *News* will be the same as that against Resco and Prex—except that now we clearly are dealing with libel. The privilege situation is quite different. The *News* may assert the state common law privilege of record libel. Although most courts limit this to accurate reports of governmental proceedings, some states do extend it to accurate reports of general open meetings—and they might be persuaded to extend it another step to any openly made statement about a matter of public concern. Such an extension might be based in part on reliance on the recently developed constitutional privilege of "neutral reportage" that protects press reports of both sides of an ongoing dispute of public concern—in that case the effect of pesticides on birds. That privilege does not easily cover this case because here we are not dealing with an ongoing controversy or with two sides to a debate—or even with a public person such as was involved in the pesticide case.

In any event, the *News* has the *Gertz* privilege for reasons already discussed. Zoe must prove falsity due to negligence. If the *News* did not know and had no reason to know that the statements were aimed at Zoe before it published the story, then the *News* can defend on the ground that it cannot be liable because the statement did not show that damage to reputation was likely to result. Even if the *News* knew about the goal of the statement, it may have had no reason to doubt what Prex was saying—and thus was not negligent for printing the story without further investigation. On the other hand, the known self-interest of Prex might have alerted the *News* to the need for further research before printing the story. If Zoe proves negligence, he may recover actual injury damages.

The only constitutional privilege that avoids concern with negligent falsity would be an expansion of the neutral reportage approach—in which it is irrelevant whether the *News* believed that Prex was speaking accurately.

Intentional infliction of emotional distress: The *News* cannot be shown to have engaged in extreme and outrageous conduct by reporting Prex's statement. A showing of negligence would be insufficient for liability.

False light privacy: Even if a prima facie case can be established, Zoe will have to show that the *News* was reckless in making its error in its report of a story of public interest. At most, negligence seems likely.

Misrepresentation: Whether Zoe alleges intentional or negligent misrepresentation, this should fail. The *News* reported the representation of another, and presumably credited Prex's appraisal of the danger of a virus infection to Prex. The only representation of the *News* was that it reported accurately what was said. Zoe, therefore, did not rely on any representation of the *News*.

Even if the *News* claimed on its own that no danger existed, Zoe will not likely recover. The *News* did not intend to deceive anyone, had no knowledge that a danger existed, and did not mean for Zoe to rely on its statement, so it committed no intentional misrepresentation. The *News* may have been negligent in not investigating the claim, but probably did not intend that Zoe should rely on it in a business transaction, so it should not be liable for a negligent misrepresentation.

ANSWER TO SAMPLE EXAM QUESTION IX

Pat v. Drugco

Strict liability: Pat's most promising action against Drugco is for strict liability. Although Pat is not in privity with Drugco, virtually all states have abandoned privity requirements in strict liability actions and permit even injured bystanders to recover.

Pat may allege that failure to warn users that Pyrib often induces drowsiness made the drug unreasonably dangerous. For purposes of strict liability, a product may be defective not only in manufacture and design, but also in the warnings or instructions needed to make it safe. Pyrib was defective because, in the absence of a warning of the drug's side effects, a consumer could reasonably expect his alertness to remain unaffected. A specific caution against driving was also called for, since Drugco should have foreseen the special dangers posed to drivers who may fall asleep.

Pat should be able to show that the lack of warnings caused her injuries since Driver, if warned, either would not have taken Pyrib or would have stayed home. Driver's conduct was foreseeable, so even if it was negligent, the defective product remains a proximate cause. Dr. Ard's failure to warn Driver, even if negligent, does not supersede Drugco's liability.

Drugco has no defenses to a strict liability action, and Pat may recover for all her damages.

Negligence: Since Pyrib is known to have the side effect, Pat should be able to make out a negligence action by the same showing as above. The only differences are that Pat must show that the danger created by the inadequate label was one that Drugco should reasonably have anticipated, and that the label could easily have been made adequate.

Pat v. Transit

Pat's action against Transit is for negligence. Transit is a common carrier, so it owes Pat, a passenger, a *high* standard of care. Pat can argue that Transit breached its duty in several ways: (1) that it failed to observe Driver's condition; (2) that it failed to warn its bus drivers not to drive after taking medication; and (3) that it failed to provide a doctor to treat its drivers without endangering passengers. "But for" each of these failures, the accident apparently would not have occurred, so each failure could have been an actual cause of Pat's injuries. The crash was foreseeable as a result of each failure, so if any of the three was an actual cause it was also a proximate cause. Should the jury find that Transit breached its duty of care, and that the breach caused the accident, Pat may recover for all of her damages. Transit has no defenses.

Pat may also hold Transit liable for any negligence of Driver. Especially in light of the high duty of care owed to passengers, Driver appears to have been negligent in continuing to drive after he began feeling drowsy. Stopping and getting a replacement, or calling in to the office for advice, would have prevented the accident; thus, Driver's negligence was an actual and proximate cause of Pat's injuries. His negligence may be *imputed* to Transit under the doctrine of respondeat superior. Again, Transit has no defenses, but it may seek *indemnity* from Driver.

Pat v. Dr. Ard

In treating his patients, Dr. Ard owes a duty of care to third persons who will be affected by that treatment—at least to Pat since she was a foreseeable plaintiff. Whether he breached that duty is a jury question, and will largely depend on whether he knew that Driver was a bus driver or that Pyrib did not come with a warning of its side effects. If Dr. Ard knew either of these facts, he was probably negligent in not warning Driver that Pyrib might make him drowsy. Moreover, since most people drive, Dr. Ard may be negligent for failing to warn about potential drowsiness even if he thought the Pyrib label mentioned the risk. Pat can show that the failure to warn was an actual and proximate cause of her injuries. (Driver's own negligence, if any, would not exonerate Dr. Ard since it was foreseeable.) Dr. Ard has no defenses, and Pat may recover for all her damages.

ANSWER TO SAMPLE EXAM QUESTION X

Under agency rules and the doctrine of respondeat superior, the *Yellow Journal* is liable for the torts committed by R since the reporter was acting within the scope of his employment.

Defamation

R's false statements could be found by a jury to lower P's reputation in the community. Even though the statements do not charge P with acts that reflect badly on his character or integrity, the law holds that defamation may be found in statements that lead others to think less well of P, such as charges that P was of illegitimate birth or is insane. The charges in this case are of the same sort—suffering a seizure and hurting others during the seizure. Fathering a retarded child might be read to suggest that P was suffering from some genetic problem that might lead others to shun or avoid him. If the jury finds the statements actionable, there is no question about their falsity (although P has the burden of proof on this issue). (P has no cause of action for defamations of his son.)

Since this story involves a matter of public concern, P must prove more than the fact that he was defamed. The standard of liability P must establish depends on whether he is a public person. Since P was never a government employee, he cannot be a public official. Although the public may be interested in the work he did for Bomm-Bay and in the accident he had there, P has never voluntarily brought himself to the public's attention or injected himself into a public controversy; thus, he is not a public figure for defamation purposes.

As a private plaintiff, P is constitutionally required to prove only that R and the *Yellow Journal* were negligent in not recognizing the falsity of their statements. Since R invented the defamatory portions of his story, negligence can be easily proven. P may therefore recover for any "actual injury" which he can prove to the jury. His damages may include harm to his reputation, humiliation, or other emotional distress, and any monetary injuries he suffered. But since the action is for defamation, he may recover only for those injuries caused by the defamatory portions of the story—above and beyond the embarrassment and ostracism occasioned by the true revelations.

Besides negligence, P should be able to show that R published the story with knowing or reckless falsity. Although R did not *know* the defamatory statements were false, he did not honestly believe they were true. This amounts to recklessness. Statements published with knowing or reckless falsity receive no constitutional protection; thus, P's damages, if he can meet this standard of liability, will not be limited to "actual injuries." He may recover any damages the state law permits, including presumed and punitive damages.

Privacy

Public disclosure of private facts: A number of the facts included in the article were intimate details of P's life, and he should have no trouble establishing a prima facie case that they were wrongfully disclosed. P's impotence, loss of hair, and other impairments are private facts—even though some persons may already know about each. A jury could conclude that a reasonable person would find public disclosure of such facts—particularly facts involving medical or sexual details—highly offensive. The fact of the accident itself may be a private fact since it took place in a private area, but disclosure would not normally be highly offensive and so is not actionable.

The *Yellow Journal* will point out in its defense that P voluntarily disclosed all the intimate details being sued on. (The false statements in the article, though they concern private matters, are not actionable as disclosures of private facts. P may recover damages caused by them in a defamation or a "false light" action.) Normally, voluntary disclosure bars any action, even when the defendant has misrepresented his identity or promised confidentiality. An individual assumes some risk that a person he confides in is not who he seems. In this case, however, P reasonably believed that his statements were made under the legally binding doctor-patient privilege. Had R actually been a doctor, R's disclosure would have been actionable. Since R intentionally caused and knew of P's misapprehension, the consent defense fails.

The *Yellow Journal* will also contend that its story is privileged because it is newsworthy. Under privacy rules, an accident involving a bacteria warfare agent is of legitimate public interest, even when it has not been discovered for 20 years. Although P in no way acted intentionally to attract public attention, his involvement in the accident makes him a public figure (for *privacy* action purposes) because of its newsworthiness. Similarly the disabilities that P has developed are of public concern. P is apparently the only human ever to be exposed to the bacteria, and the public is understandably interested in discovering the effects of a powerful weapon in its government's arsenal.

The problem is that P's identity does not involve the same level of public interest. The disclosure of newsworthy information would not have been any less effective if the *Yellow Journal* had protected P's anonymity. Normally the disclosure of a name is not actionable. Although many personal and embarrassing details of P's life were published, most courts would probably deny a privacy action on the ground that use of names adds credibility and impact to the story and should be a matter for editorial judgment alone.

If the newsworthiness defense is rejected, the *Yellow Journal* would try to extend the limited constitutional holding in *Cox Broadcasting v. Cohn* from public records to matters of public interest. This question was explicitly left open in *Cox.*

If P establishes liability, he may recover for any emotional distress or other damages incurred because of the public disclosures.

False light privacy: The false disclosures about P, especially concerning his temperament, placed him in a "false light." The statements were not simply minor inaccuracies but were so central as to make their disclosure highly offensive to a reasonable person. The "false light" statements were disseminated to a large number of third persons, so P can make out a prima facie case.

Again, the newsworthiness defense is the *Yellow Journal's* best chance for success. The statements that turned out to be false nonetheless involve newsworthy information since they purport to describe effects of the bacteria. However, P may defeat the defense by showing that the disclosures were made with knowing or reckless falsity because the First Amendment affords no protection to such statements in tort cases. As discussed above, P should be able to meet this standard since R did not believe the statements to be true.

P may recover whatever damages the state law permits.

Wrongful intrusion privacy: An intentional, highly offensive intrusion into an individual's privacy is actionable. In this case, R did not enter onto P's own property, but he did gain access to an area in which P had a reasonable expectation of privacy. The nature of the intrusion, with R falsely representing himself to be a doctor, would be highly offensive to a reasonable person. The intrusion would be no less serious than if R had bugged P's room and listened in on the private conversations between P and his doctors.

The only relevant defense here is consent, but as discussed above, it is likely to fail since R knew that P was mistakenly relying on R's deceptive appearance.

Although publication is not required to recover for a wrongful intrusion, some courts allow P to recover damages suffered from the newspaper article as consequential damages of R's tortious intrusion. P may therefore recover for any physical or emotional injury from the initial intrusion as well as for any monetary damages incurred. Courts disagree over whether damages from the publication of the article are recoverable when the facts were tortiously obtained. Because of the sensitive First Amendment aspects, it seems preferable to require P to show an actionable publication before being allowed to recover such damages.

TABLE OF CITATIONS
TO RESTATEMENT (SECOND) OF TORTS

Section	Text Reference	Section	Text Reference
2	§2	121	§144
13	§§17, 18	131	§152
13(a)	§6	136	§156
18	§11	146	§158
19	§§14, 16	147	§158
22	§31	157	§166
24	§37	158	§164
25	§33	159(2)	§174
26	§32	162	§176
27	§§15, 37, 38	163	§177
29(2)	§35	195	§227
30	§36	196	§225
31	§§26, 27	197	§232
36	§47	198	§§211, 218, 221
38	§55	200	§216
39	§50	201	§§239, 240
40	§52	204	§155
40A	§§51, 53	214(1)	§242
41	§57	214(2)	§243
42	§48	217	§181
45	§56	229	§195
46	§§63, 64, 72	237	§198
60	§97	244	§189
62	§83	260	§223
63	§99	263	§232
65	§§103, 107	281(b)	§284
65(2)	§108	283	§247
70(2)	§109	283B	§265
71	§112	283C	§262
72	§113	288B	§448
73	§114	288C	§256
76	§121	289(b)	§267
77	§122	291	§305
81	§125	295A	§252
84	§123	296	§249
85	§124	299	§281
88	§129	299A	§§268, 269
89	§127	321	§459
91	§127	324	§463
101	§130	330	§562
102	§130	332	§568
103	§130	333	§539
104	§130	335	§545
105	§130	336	§539
106	§130	337	§539
119	§144	339	§§547, 555, 560
120A	§137	342	§565

TABLE OF CASES

Gray v. Udevitz - §1284

Greco v. Bucciconi Engineering - §852

Greco v. United States - §§1000, 1001

Greeley v. Jameson - §725

Green v. Bittner - §971

Green Acres Trust v. London - §1235

Green Valley School, Inc. v. Cowles Florida Broadcasting, Inc. - §231

Greenbelt Cooperative Publishing Co. v. Bresler - §1203

Greenman v. Yuba Power Products - §786

Green-Wheeler Shoe Co. v. Chicago Rock Island & Pacific Railway - §395

Gregory v. McDonnell Douglas - §1203

Greycas, Inc. v. Proud - §§1402, 1432

Griffin v. Hustis - §376

Griggs v. Combe, Inc. - §850

Grimes v. Axtell Ford Lincoln-Mercury - §819

Grimsby v. Samson - §73

Groesbeck v. Napier - §974

Gross v. Cantor - §1193

Gruenberg v. Aetna Life Insurance Co. - §§719, 1476

GuardLife Corp. v. S. Parker Hardware Manufacturing Corp. - §1470

Guarino v. Mine Safety Appliance - §829

Gudger v. Manton - §1452

H. R. Moch Co. v. Rensselaer Water Co. - §476

Hackett v. Perron - §505

Hackford v. Utah Power & Light Co. - §986

Haelan Labs v. Topps Chewing Gum, Inc. - §1360

Haft v. Lone Palm Hotel - §347

Hale v. Allstate Insurance Co. - §486

Haley v. Pan American World Airways, Inc. - §420

Hall v. Duke - §562

Hall v. Dumitru - §428

Hall v. May Department Stores - §79

Hall v. Post - §1355

Hamberger v. Eastman - §1318

Hamman v. County of Maricopa - §294

Hammond v. County of Madera - §176

Hammond v. International Harvester Co. - §880

Hampton v. North Carolina Pulp - §932

Hanberry v. Hearst Corp. - §824

Hanke v. Global Van Lines - §§63, 68

Hanrahan v. Kelly - §1146

Hanson v. City of Snohomish - §1523

Hanvey v. Oconee Memorial Hospital - §1052

Hapka v. Paquin Farms - §830

Hardy v. Dahl - §443

Harmon v. Harmon - §1502

Harper v. Herman - §465

Harrell v. Travelers Indemnity Co. - §711

Harris v. Jones - §74

Hart v. Browne - §1386

Hart v. Geysel - §97

Harte-Hanks Communications, Inc. v. Connaughton - §§1297, 1298

Hartke v. McKelway - §276

Hartley v. Floyd - §471

Hartman by Hartman v. Hartman - §1022

Hartridge v. State Farm Mutual Automobile Insurance Co. - §1480

Hartwell Corp. v. Bumb - §1436

Hastie v. Handeland - §379

Hatten v. Union Oil Co. - §1487

Hauter v. Zogarts - §903

Hawkins v. Multimedia, Inc. - §1341

Haynes v. Alfred A. Knopf, Inc. - §1341

Head v. Phillips - §274

Healy v. New England Newspapers, Inc. - §1179

Heath v. Swift Wings, Inc. - §268

Heil Valley Ranch, Inc. v. Simkin - §689

Heimer v. Privratsky - §273

Helfend v. Southern California Rapid Transit - §434

Hellar v. Bianco - §1160

Helms v. Harris - §115

Henningsen v. Bloomfield Motors, Inc. - §909

Henry v. Brown - §727

Herbert v. Lando - §1299

Hewlett v. George - §1016

Higgins v. Mason - §480

Hildebrand v. Minyard - §695

Hill v. Edmonds - §329

Hill v. Glenwood - §262

Hill v. Thompson - §318

Hills v. Lyons - §625

Hines v. Garrett - §380

Hinkle v. Rockville Motor Corp. - §1438

Hinojasa v. Automatic Elevator Co. - §834

Hobart v. Schuler - §1434

Hodges v. Gibson Products Co. - §§1477, 1521

Hofer v. Lavender - §963

Hogan v. Herald Co. - §1275

Hogle v. Franklin Manufacturing Co. - §495

Holland v. Baltimore & Ohio Railroad - §557

Hollerud v. Malamis - §94

Holzheimer v. Johannesen - §573

Hoover v. Montgomery Ward - §834

Hopkins v. McBane - §967

Horn v. General Motors Corp. - §794
Horne v. Patton - §§1330, 1349
House v. Thornton - §623
Hoven v. Kelble - §835
Hoven v. Rice Memorial Hospital - §320
Howard v. Des Moines Register & Tribune Co. - §1331
Howard Frank, M.D., P.C. v. Superior Court - §§988, 990
Howe v. Stubbs - §577
Hruby v. Kalina - §1216
Hudson v. Craft - §98
Hull v. L. & A. Montagnard Social Club, Inc. - §311
Hulton v. Jones - §1185
Humphers v. First Interstate Bank of Oregon - §1384
Hunnings v. Texaco Co. - §809
Hunt v. Blasius - §772
Hunter v. Bryant - §1049
Huset v. J. I. Case - §765
Hustler Magazine v. Falwell - §77
Hutchinson v. Proxmire - §§1283, 1288
Hymowitz v. Eli Lilly & Co. - §336

Imbler v. Pachtman - §1045
Immuno A. G. v. Moor-Jankowski - §1202
In re—see name of party
Indiana Harbor Belt Railroad v. American Cyanamid Co. - §742
Indianapolis Street Railway v. Dawson - §564
International Products Co. v. Erie Railroad - §1416
Irwin v. Ashurst - §1234

J. v. Victory Tabernacle Baptist Church - §496
J. C. Penney Casualty Insurance Co. v. M.K. - §711
J. R. Dudley Construction Co. v. Drott Manufacturing Co. - §866
Jacko v. Bridgeport - §954
Jackson v. Longcope - §1174
Jackson v. Nestle-Beich, Inc. - §800
Jacobson v. Leventhal - §604
Jeffers v. Seattle - §§300, 1318
Jensen v. Chicago & Western Indiana Railroad - §205
Jividen v. Law - §726
Johnson v. American Cyanamid Corp. - §§809, 834
Johnson v. Bathey - §548
Johnson v. Calado - §1534

Johnson v. Davis - §1399
Johnson v. Kosmos Portland Cement Co. - §383
Johnson v. Manhattan & Bronx Surface Transit Operating Authority - §412
Johnson v. Raybestos-Manhattan, Inc. - §802
Johnson v. Rogers - §425
Johnson v. Ruark Obstetrics & Gynecology Associates - §641
Johnson v. State - §640
Johnson v. United States - §1034
Johnson v. University Hospital of Cleveland - §998
Jones v. Hansen - §585
Jones v. Robbins - §292
Jones & Laughlin Steel Corp. v. Pfeifer - §416
Jordan, City of v. Rome - §467
Josephson v. Meyers - §256
Jost v. Dairyland Power Cooperative - §945
Jourdain v. Dineen - §1439
Judson v. Giant Powder Co. - §322
Juiditta v. Bethlehem Steel Corp. - §419
Justus v. Atchison - §996

K.A.C. v. Benson - §629
K-Mart Corp. v. Washington - §1148
Kaarup v. St. Paul Fire & Marine Insurance - §1524
Kahlenberg v. Goldstein - §487
Kassel v. Gannett Co. - §1283
Katko v. Briney - §124
Kearns v. Smith - §599
Kelley v. Bonney - §1285
Kelley v. R. G. Industries, Inc. - §§749, 793
Kellog v. Viola - §958
Kelly v. Gwinnell - §529
Kelly v. Henry Muhs Co. - §444
Kelly, Estate of v. Falin - §684
Kelly, Estate of v. Moguls, Inc. - §684
Kelman v. Wilen - §168
Kennedy v. Povidence Hockey Club - §695
Kenty v. Transamerica Premium Insurance Co. - §1468
Kenyon v. Hammer - §1093
Kerr v. Corning Glass - §788
Keys v. Interstate Circuit - §1188
Kilduff v. Adams, Inc. - §1439
Kilgore v. Younger - §1237
Killeen v. Harmon Grain Products, Inc. - §806
Kindt v. Kaufman - §526
King v. Lennen - §558
Kingsland v. Erie County Agricultural Society - §392

McCutcheon v. United Homes Corp. - §692

McDaniel v. Atlanta Coca-Cola Bottling Co. - §1329

McDevitt v. Standard Oil - §873

McDonald v. Smith - §1271

McDougald v. Garber - §§421, 422

McFarlane v. Esquire Magazine - §1298

McFarlane v. Niagara Falls - §936

McGuire v. Almy - §5

McHale v. W.S.B. Corp. - §1515

McIntosh v. Barr - §984

McKenzie v. Cheetam - §611

McKiddy v. Des Moines Electric Co. - §547

McLane v. Northwest Gas Co. - §733

McLaughlin v. Mine Safety Appliances Co. - §384

McQuade v. Tuscon Tiller Apartments - §941

McRae v. Brandt - §1523

Machleder v. Diaz - §1369

Mackowick v. Westinghouse Electric Corp. - §807

Maddox v. City of New York - §695

Magliulo v. Superior Court - §1073

Malloy v. Commonwealth Highland Theatres, Inc. - §323

Maloney v. Rath - §505

Maltman v. Sauer - §290

Malvicini v. Stratfield Motor Hotel, Inc. - §318

Mapco, Inc. v. Payne - §1477

Marchesi v. Franchino - §1255

Marciniak v. Lundborg - §998

Marek v. Professional Health Services - §507

Margoles v. Hubbart - §1292

Maritote v. Desilu - §1379

Marshall v. Ranne - §762

Marshall & Michel Grain Co. v. Kansas City, Ft. Scott & Memphis Railroad - §197

Martin v. Abbott Laboratories - §340

Martin v. Herzog - §448

Martin v. Houck - §§43, 57

Martin Luther King Center for Social Change, Inc. v. American Heritage Products, Inc. - §1381

Martinez v. California - §1032

Martinez v. Lazaroff - §393

Mason v. Western Union - §1273

Masson v. New Yorker Magazine, Inc. - §1175

Matamco Oil Co. v. Arctic Mechanical, Inc. - §443

Matthews v. Lawnlite Co. - §783

Mauro v. Raymark Industries, Inc. - §345

Maynard v. Port Publications, Inc. - §1165

Mazur v. Merck & Co. - §808

Medico v. Time, Inc. - §1262

Meirs v. Koch - §584

Meisler v. Gannett Co. - §1298

Meistrich v. Casino Arena - §702

Melville v. Southward - §272

Melvin v. Reed - §1330

Meritor Savings Bank v. Vinson - §66

Merrill v. Central Maine Power Co. - §555

Merritt v. Nickelson - §532

Messick v. General Motors Corp. - §879

Metric Investment, Inc. v. Patterson - §1403

Metter v. Los Angeles Examiner - §1378

Metz v. United Technologies Corp. - §416

Meyers v. Delaney - §534

Mexicali Rose v. Superior Court - §800

Miami, City of v. Wardlow - §1237

Michalko v. Cooke Color & Chemical Corp. - §817

Mickle v. Blackmon - §794

Micromanolis v. The Woods School, Inc. - §538

Midkiff v. Midkiff - §1023

Mieske v. Bartell Drug Co. - §424

Mihlovan v. Grozavu - §1254

Miles Laboratories, Inc. v. Doe - §838

Milkovich v. Lorain Journal Co. - §1202

Miller v. American Sports Co. - §1359

Miller v. Arnal Corp. - §463

Miller v. Johnson - §997

Miller v. Rhode Island Hospital - §83

Milliken & Co. v. Consolidated Edison Co. - §1508

Miner v. Novotny - §§1236, 1271

Misiulis v. Milbrand Maintenance Corp. - §506

Mist v. Westin Hotels, Inc. - §682

Mitchell v. Bearden - §941

Mitchell v. Buchheit - §971

Mitchell v. Churches - §487

Mitchell v. Jackson - §1509

Modaber v. Kelley - §996

Moerer v. Ford Motor Co. - §853

Mohr v. Williams - §85

Molitor v. Kaneland Community Unit District No. 302 - §1030

Molko v. Holy Spirit Association for the Unification of World Christianity - §78

Montana v. San Jose Mercury News, Inc. - §1362

Moore v. Hart - §653

Moore v. Regents of the University of California - §275

Moore v. Warren - §1051

Moradi-Shalal v. Fireman's Fund Insurance Companies - §718

proof of falsity, §1442
protection of defendant's interests, §§1462-1465
publication, §§1443-1444
scienter, §1453
slander of title, §§1446, 1456
special damages required, §1455
trade libel, §§1447-1448, 1457
truth as defense to, §1459

INSANITY
See Incompetents

INSULTS
See also Emotional distress, intentional infliction of
carriers, §65
liability for, §64
public utilities, §65

INSURANCE
See Liability insurance, effect of

INTENT
abuse of process, §1541
assault, §29
battery, §§6-10
consequences substantially certain to follow, §7
conversion, §189
emotional distress, §§67-69
false imprisonment, §44
injurious falsehood, §§1451-1452
interference, §§1478-1480
malice distinguished, §9
misrepresentation, §§1400-1403
motive immaterial to, §9
nuisance, §§933-936
privacy, invasion of, §1325
products liability, §§765-766
punitive damages based on, §9
test of, §§7, 29
transferred, §§10, 29, 69
trespass to chattels, §180
trespass to land, §161

INTENTIONAL TORTS
See Assault, Battery; Conversion; Emotional distress, intentional infliction of; False imprisonment; Trespass to chattels; Trespass to land

INTERFERENCE WITH CONTRACT
breach not required, §1473
burden of proof, §1495
causation, §§1481-1483
collective action, §1474
damages, §§1481-1483
defendant's interest, protection of, §§1484-1491
employer and employee, §1480
illegal contracts, §1469
illegal means, §§1492-1494
intent to interfere, §§1472, 1478-1480
nature of contract, §1468
negligent interference, §1479
prima facie case, §1467
privilege, §§1484-1494
public interest, action in, §§1486-1487
terminable at will, §§1471, 1491
unenforceable contracts, §1470

INTERFERENCE WITH ECONOMIC RELATIONS
in general, §1466
labor unions, §1474

INTERFERENCE WITH FAMILY RELATIONSHIPS
alienation of affections, §§1003-1006
common law, §1003
parent-child claims, §1006
criminal conversation, §§1007-1010

INTERFERENCE WITH PROSPECTIVE ADVANTAGE
in general, §§1466, 1475, 1496
intentional interference, §§1496-1502
prima facie case, §1497
negligent interference, §§1503-1509
prima facie case, §1503
noncommercial expectancies, §1502
privilege, §§1500-1501

INTERVENING FORCES
See Proximate cause

INTOXICATION
as negligence, §§264, 425
Dram Shop acts, §§519-523, 1109
liability of social host, §§527-529
liability of tavernkeeper
as to land occupier, §530
as to purchaser, §§518-526
to third parties, §§518-524
standard of conduct for voluntary, §264

INVASION OF PRIVACY
See Privacy, invasion of

INVITEES
area of invitation, §575
business visitors, §§572-574
change of status, §575
chattels supplied to, §579
defined, §§568-571
duty required toward, §§576-579
duty to inspect, §§576-577
liability of occupier, §§576-579, 585-587
liability of third person to, §§588-590
protection against third person, §578
public entrants, §§580-584
public invitees, §§569-571
strict liability to, §733

J

JOINT ENTERPRISE
automobile trips, §514
common purpose, §513
contributory negligence, imputed, §661
extension beyond business purposes, §514
mutual right of control, §513
vicarious liability, §512

JOINT TORTS
concurrent liability, §§329-330
contribution, §1058
comparative negligence, impact, of, §1060
indemnity distinguished, §1062
negligence cases, §1059

Notes

Notes

Notes

Notes

gilbert
LAW SUMMARIES

Conflict of Laws
By Dean Herma Hill Kay, U.C. Berkeley
Domicile; Jurisdiction (including Notice and Opportunity to be Heard, Minimum Contacts, Types of Jurisdiction); Choice of Law (including Vested Rights Approach, Most Significant Relationship Approach, Governmental Interest Analysis); Choice of Law in Specific Substantive Areas; Traditional Defenses Against Application of Foreign Law; Constitutional Limitations and Overriding Federal Law (including Due Process Clause, Full Faith and Credit Clause, Conflict Between State and Federal Law); Recognition and Enforcement of Foreign Judgments.
ISBN: 0-15-900424-1   Pages: 273 $20.95

Constitutional Law
By Professor Jesse H. Choper, U.C. Berkeley
Powers of Federal Government (including Judicial Power, Powers of Congress, Presidential Power, Foreign Affairs Power); Intergovernmental Immunities, Separation of Powers; Regulation of Foreign Commerce; Regulation of Interstate Commerce; Taxation of Interstate and Foreign Commerce; Due Process, Equal Protection; "State Action" Requirements; Freedoms of Speech, Press, and Association; Freedom of Religion.
ISBN: 0-15-900375-X   Pages: 355 $21.95

Contracts
By Professor Melvin A. Eisenberg, U.C. Berkeley
Consideration (including Promissory Estoppel, Moral or Past Consideration); Mutual Assent; Defenses (including Mistake, Fraud, Duress, Unconscionability, Statute of Frauds, Illegality); Third-Party Beneficiaries; Assignment of Rights and Delegation of Duties; Conditions; Substantial Performance; Material vs. Minor Breach; Anticipatory Breach; Impossibility; Discharge; Remedies (including Damages, Specific Performance, Liquidated Damages).
ISBN: 0-15-900014-9   Pages: 326 $21.95

Corporations
By Professor Jesse H. Choper, U.C. Berkeley, and Professor Melvin A. Eisenberg, U.C. Berkeley
Formalities; "De Jure" vs. "De Facto"; Promoters; Corporate Powers; Ultra Vires Transactions; Powers, Duties, and Liabilities of Officers and Directors; Allocation of Power Between Directors and Shareholders; Conflicts of Interest in Corporate Transactions; Close Corporations; Insider Trading; Rule 10b-5 and Section 16(b); Shareholders' Voting Rights; Shareholders' Right to Inspect Records; Shareholders' Suits; Capitalization (including Classes of Shares, Preemptive Rights, Consideration for Shares); Dividends; Redemption of Shares; Fundamental Changes in Corporate Structure; Applicable Conflict of Laws Principles.
ISBN: 0-15-900342-3   Pages: 319 $21.95

Criminal Law
By Professor George E. Dix, University of Texas
Elements of Crimes (including Actus Reus, Mens Rea, Causation); Vicarious Liability; Complicity in Crime; Criminal Liability of Corporations; Defenses (including Insanity, Diminished Capacity, Intoxication, Ignorance, Self-Defense); Inchoate Crimes; Homicide; Other Crimes Against the Person; Crimes Against Habitation (including Burglary, Arson); Crimes Against Property; Offenses Against Government; Offenses Against Administration of Justice.
ISBN: 0-15-900217-6   Pages: 317 $20.95

Criminal Procedure
By Professor Paul Marcus, College of William and Mary, and Professor Charles H. Whitebread, U.S.C.
Exclusionary Rule; Arrests and Other Detentions; Search and Seizure; Privilege Against Self-Incrimination; Confessions; Preliminary Hearing; Bail; Indictment; Speedy Trial; Competency to Stand Trial; Government's Obligation to Disclose Information; Right to Jury Trial; Right to Counsel; Right to Confront Witnesses; Burden of Proof; Insanity; Entrapment; Guilty Pleas; Sentencing; Death Penalty; Ex Post Facto Issues; Appeal; Habeas Corpus; Juvenile Offenders; Prisoners' Rights; Double Jeopardy.
ISBN: 0-15-900449-7   Pages: 271 $20.95

Estate and Gift Tax
By Professor John H. McCord, University of Illinois
Gross Estate; Allowable Deductions Under Estate Tax (including Expenses, Indebtedness, and Taxes, Deductions for Losses, Charitable Deduction, Marital Deduction); Taxable Gifts; Deductions; Valuation; Computation of Tax; Returns and Payment of Tax; Tax on Generation-Skipping Transfers.
ISBN: 0-15-900425-X   Pages: 327 $20.95

Evidence
By Professor Jon R. Waltz, Northwestern University, and Roger C. Park, University of Minnesota
Direct Evidence; Circumstantial Evidence; Rulings on Admissibility; Relevancy; Materiality; Character Evidence; Hearsay and the Hearsay Exceptions; Privileges; Competency to Testify; Opinion Evidence and Expert Witnesses; Direct Examination; Cross-Examination; Impeachment; Real, Demonstrative, and Scientific Evidence; Judicial Notice; Burdens of Proof; Parol Evidence Rule.
ISBN: 0-15-900385-7   Pages: 387 $22.95

Federal Courts
By Professor William A. Fletcher, U.C. Berkeley
Article III Courts; "Case or Controversy" Require-ment; Justiciability; Advisory Opinions; Political Questions; Ripeness; Mootness; Standing; Congressional Power Over Federal Court Juris-diction; Supreme Court Jurisdiction; District Court Subject Matter Jurisdiction (including Federal Question Jurisdiction, Diversity Jurisdiction); Pendent and Ancillary Jurisdiction; Removal Jurisdiction; Venue; Forum Non Conveniens; Law Applied in the Federal Courts (including Erie Doctrine); Federal Law in the State Courts; Abstention; Habeas Corpus for State Prisoners; Federal Injunctions Against State Court Proceedings; Eleventh Amendment.
ISBN: 0-15-900232-X   Pages: 313 $21.95

Future Interests & Perpetuities
By Professor Jesse Dukeminier, U.C.L.A.
Reversions; Possibilities of Reverter; Rights of Entry; Remainders; Executory Interest; Rules Restricting Remainders and Executory Interest; Rights of Owners of Future Interests; Construc-tion of Instruments; Powers of Appointment; Rule Against Perpetuities (including Reforms of the Rule).
ISBN: 0-15-900218-4   Pages: 185 $19.95

Income Tax I - Individual
By Professor Michael R. Asimow, U.C.L.A.
Gross Income; Exclusions; Income Splitting by Gifts, Personal Service Income, Income Earned by Children, Income of Husbands and Wives, Below-Market Interest on Loans, Taxation of Trusts; Business and Investment Deductions; Personal Deductions; Tax Rates; Credits; Computation of Basis, Gain, or Loss; Realization; Nonrecognition of Gain or Loss; Capital Gains and Losses; Alter-native Minimum Tax; Tax Accounting Problems.
ISBN: 0-15-900421-7   Pages: 312 $21.95

Income Tax II - Partnerships, Corporations, Trusts
By Professor Michael R. Asimow, U.C.L.A.
Taxation of Partnerships (including Current Part-nership Income, Contributions of Property to Partnership, Sale of Partnership Interest, Distributions, Liquidations); Corporate Taxation (including Corporate Distributions, Sales of Stock and Assets, Reorganizations); S Corporations; Federal Income Taxation of Trusts.
ISBN: 0-15-900384-9   Pages: 238 $19.95

Labor Law
By Professor James C. Oldham, Georgetown Univer-sity, and Robert J. Gelhaus
Statutory Foundations of Present Labor Law (including National Labor Relations Act, Taft-Hartley, Norris-LaGuardia Act, Landrum-Griffin Act); Organizing Campaigns, Selection of the Bargaining Representative; Collective Bargaining (including Negotiating the Agreement, Lockouts, Administering the Agreement, Arbitration); Strikes, Boycotts, and Picketing; Concerted Activity Protected Under the NLRA; Civil Rights Legislation; Grievance; Federal Regulation of Compulsory Union Membership Arrangements; State Regulation of Compulsory Membership Agreements; "Right to Work" Laws; Discipline of Union Members; Election of Union Officers; Corruption.
ISBN: 0-15-900340-7   Pages: 260 $19.95

Legal Ethics
By Professor Thomas D. Morgan, George Washington University
Regulating Admission to Practice Law; Prevent-ing Unauthorized Practice of Law; Contract Between Client and Lawyer (including Lawyer's Duties Regarding Accepting Employment, Spheres of Authority of Lawyer and Client, Obligation of Client to Lawyer, Terminating the Lawyer-Client Relationship); Attorney-Client Privilege; Professional Duty of Confidentiality; Conflicts of Interest; Obligations to Third Persons and the Legal System (including Counseling Illegal or Fraudulent Conduct, Threats of Criminal Prosecution); Special Obligations in Litigation (including Limitations on Advancing Money to Client, Duty to Reject Certain Actions, Lawyer as Witness); Solicitation and Advertising; Specialization; Disciplinary Process; Malpractice; Special Responsibilities of Judges.
ISBN: 0-15-900026-2   Pages: 258 $20.95

Legal Research, Writing and Analysis
By Professor Peter J. Honigsberg, University of San Francisco
Court Systems; Precedent; Case Reporting System (including Regional and State Reporters, Headnotes and the West Key Number System, Citations and Case Finding); Statutes, Constitutions, and Legislative History; Secondary Sources (including Treatises, Law Reviews, Digests, Restatements); Administrative Agencies (including Regulations, Looseleaf Services); Shepard's Citations; Computers in Legal Research; Reading and Understanding a Case (including Briefing a Case); Using Legal Sourcebooks; Basic Guidelines for Legal Writing; Organizing Your Research; Writing a Memorandum of Law; Writing a Brief; Writing an Opinion or Client Letter.
ISBN: 0-15-900436-5   Pages: 187 $17.95

Multistate Bar Examination
By Professor Richard J. Conviser, Chicago Kent
Structure of the Exam; Governing Law; Effective Use of Time; Scoring of the Exam; Jurisdictions Using the Exam; Subject Matter Outlines; Practice Tests, Answers, and Subject Matter Keys; Glossary of Legal Terms and Definitions; State Bar Examination Directory; Listing of Reference Materials for Multistate Subjects.
ISBN: 0-15-900246-X   Pages: 776 $24.95

Personal Property
Gilbert Staff
Acquisitions; Ownership Through Possession (including Wild Animals, Abandoned Chattels); Finders of Lost Property; Bailments; Possessory Liens; Pledges, Trover; Gift; Accession; Confusion (Commingling); Fixtures; Crops (Emblements); Adverse Possession; Prescriptive Rights (Acquiring Ownership of Easements or Profits by Adverse Use).
ISBN: 0-15-900360-1   Pages: 140 $14.95

Professional Responsibility
(see Legal Ethics)

Legalines

Legalines gives you authoritative, detailed briefs of every major case in your casebook. You get a clear explanation of the facts, the issues, the court's holding and reasoning, and any significant concurrences or dissents. Even more importantly, you get an authoritative explanation of the significance of each case, and how it relates to other cases in your casebook. And with Legalines' detailed table of contents and table of cases, you can quickly find any case or concept you're looking for. But your professor expects you to know more than just the cases. That's why Legalines gives you more than just case briefs. You get summaries of the black letter law, as well. That's crucial, because some of the most important information in your casebooks isn't in the cases at all … it's the black letter principles you're expected to glean from those cases. Legalines is the only series that gives you both case briefs and black letter review. With Legalines, you get everything you need to know—whether it's in a case or not!

Call To Order: 1-800-787-8717 or Order On-Line at http://www.gilbertlaw.com

on the Internet!

Employment Guides

A collection of best selling titles that help you identify and reach your career goals.

Guerrilla Tactics for Getting the Legal Job of Your Dreams
Kimm Alayne Walton, J.D.

Whether you're looking for a summer clerkship or your first permanent job after school, this revolutionary book is the key to getting the job of your dreams!

Guerrilla Tactics for Getting the Legal Job of Your Dreams leads you step-by-step through everything you need to do to nail down that perfect job! You'll learn hundreds of simple-to-use strategies that will get you exactly where you want to go. You'll Learn:

- The seven magic opening words in cover letters that ensure you'll get a response.
- The secret to successful interviews every time.
- Killer answers to the toughest interview questions they'll ever ask you.
- Plus Much More!

Guerrilla Tactics features the best strategies from the country's most innovative law school career advisors. The strategies in *Guerrilla Tactics* are so powerful that it even comes with a guarantee: Follow the advice in the book, and within one year of graduation you'll have the job of your dreams … or your money back!

Pick up a copy of *Guerrilla Tactics* today … you'll be on your way to the job of your dreams!

ISBN: 0-15-900317-2 $24.95

Proceed With Caution: A Diary Of The First Year At One Of America's Largest, Most Prestigious Law Firms
William R. Keates

Prestige. Famous clients. High-profile cases. Not to mention a starting salary approaching six figures.

In *Proceed With Caution*, the author takes you behind the scenes, to show you what it's really like to be a junior associate at a huge law firm. After graduating from an Ivy League law school, he took a job as an associate with one of New York's blue-chip law firms.

He also did something not many people do. He kept a diary, where he spelled out his day-to-day life at the firm in graphic detail.

Proceed With Caution excerpts the diary, from his first day at the firm to the day he quit. From the splashy benefits, to the nitty-gritty on the work junior associates do, to the grind of long and unpredictable hours, to the stress that eventually made him leave the firm — he tells story after story that will make you feel as though you're living the life of a new associate.

Whether you're considering a career with a large firm, or you're just curious about what life at the top firms is all about — *Proceed With Caution* is a must read!

ISBN: 0-15-900181-1 $17.95

The Official Guide To Legal Specialties
National Association for Law Placement

With *The Official Guide To Legal Specialties* you'll get a behind the scenes glimpse at dozens of legal specialties. Not just lists of what to expect, real life stories from top practitioners in each field. You'll learn exactly what it's like to be in some of America's most desirable professions. You'll get expert advice on what it takes to get a job in each field. How much you'll earn and what the day-to-day life is really like, the challenges you'll face, and the benefits you'll enjoy. With *The Official Guide To Legal Specialties* you'll have a wealth of information at your fingertips!

Includes the following specialties:

Banking	Intellectual Property
Communications	International
Corporate	Labor/Employment
Criminal	Litigation
Entertainment	Public Interest
Environmental	Securities
Government Practice	Sports
Health Care	Tax
Immigration	Trusts & Estates

ISBN: 0-15-900391-1 $19.95

Beyond L.A. Law: Inspiring Stories of People Who've Done Fascinating Things With A Law Degree
National Association for Law Placement

Anyone who watches television knows that being a lawyer means working your way up through a law firm — right?

Wrong!

Beyond L.A. Law gives you a fascinating glimpse into the lives of people who've broken the "lawyer" mold. They come from a variety of backgrounds — some had prior careers, others went straight through college and law school, and yet others have overcome poverty and physical handicaps. They got their degrees from all different kinds of law schools, all over the country. But they have one thing in common: they've all pursued their own, unique vision.

As you read their stories, you'll see how they beat the odds to succeed. You'll learn career tips and strategies that work, from people who've put them to the test. And you'll find fascinating insights that you can apply to your own dream, whether it's a career in law or anything else!

From Representing Baseball In Australia. To International Finance. To Children's Advocacy. To Directing a Nonprofit Organization. To Entrepreneur.

If You Think Getting A Law Degree Means Joining A Traditional Law Firm — Think Again!

ISBN: 0-15-900182-X $17.95

America's Greatest Places To Work With A Law Degree
Kimm Alayne Walton, J.D.

"Where do your happiest graduates work?" That's the question that author Kimm Alayne Walton asked of law school administrators around the country. Their responses revealed the hundreds of wonderful employers profiled in *America's Greatest Places To Work With A Law Degree.*

In this remarkable book, you'll get to know an incredible variety of great places to work, including:

- Glamorous sports and entertainment employers — the jobs that sound as though they would be great, and they are!
- The 250 best law firms to work for between 20 and 600 attorneys.
- Companies where law school graduates love to work and not just as in-house counsel.
- Wonderful public interest employers – the "white knight" jobs that are so incredibly satisfying.
- Court-related positions, where lawyers entertain fascinating issues, tremendous variety, and an enjoyable lifestyle.
- Outstanding government jobs, at the federal, state, and local level.

Beyond learning about incredible employers, you'll discover:

- The ten traits that define a wonderful place to work … the sometimes surprising qualities that outstanding employers share.
- How to handle law school debt, when your dream job pays less than you think you need to make.
- How to find — and get! — great jobs at firms with fewer than 20 attorneys.

And no matter where you work, you'll learn expert tips for making the most of your job. You'll learn the specific strategies that distinguish people headed for the top … how to position yourself for the most interesting, high-profile work … how to handle difficult personalities … how to negotiate for more money … and what to do now to help you get your next great job!

ISBN: 0-15-900180-3 $24.95

Call To Order: 1-800-787-8717 or Order On-Line at http://www.gilbertlaw.com